READINGS
IN THE
PHILOSOPHY
OF MAN

William L. Kelly, S.J., Ph.D.
Associate Professor
of Philosophy and Psychology
Georgetown University

Andrew Tallon, Ph.D.
Assistant Professor
of Philosophy
Marquette University

READINGS IN THE PHILOSOPHY OF MAN

Second Edition

McGraw-Hill Book Company
New York
St. Louis
San Francisco
Düsseldorf
Johannesburg
Kuala Lumpur
London
Mexico
Montreal
New Delhi
Panama
Rio de Janeiro
Singapore
Sydney
Toronto

FOR MARYBETH

This book was set in News Gothic by Brown Bros. Lino-
typers, Inc., and printed and bound by The Maple Press
Company. The designer was J. E. O'Connor. The editors were
Samuel B. Bossard and Joseph F. Murphy. Sally Ellyson
supervised production.

READINGS IN THE PHILOSOPHY OF MAN

Copyright © 1967, 1972 by McGraw-Hill, Inc. All rights reserved.
Printed in the United States of America. No part of this publication may be reproduced, stored in a retrieval system, or transmitted, in any form or by any means, electronic, mechanical,
photocopying, recording, or otherwise, without prior written per-
·ssion of the publisher.

ary of Congress Catalog Card Number 74-38581

31415 MAMM 9876

CONTENTS

PREFACE

This book is intended for college students beginning to acquaint themselves with the philosophy of man. It has been composed with practical rather than scholarly considerations in mind. Hence, documentation, comprehensiveness, and depth of explanatory matter have been sacrificed with a view to the student's needs. The biographical and thematic essays as well as the bibliographic sections are intended for the undergraduate student rather than for the scholar. Few libraries contain all the authors in this collection; fewer have the same philosophers in English translation; still fewer have these writings in such numbers as to render them available to students in large classes who must meet reading assignments within a specific time. We hope, hereby, to render the professor and the student of a course in the philosophy of man a positive service. By an initial division of labor, choosing the selections and writing the introductions for Plato to Nietzsche became the work of Father Kelly, and Berdyaev to Nédoncelle that of Dr. Tallon. As in any work of collaboration, however, the final product must be a joint effort, and both editors bear full responsibility for the entire book. However, because translations were printed verbatim, in accordance with the terms of publishers' permission agreements, the editors disclaim responsibility for those inconsistencies and solecisms that appear in some of the readings.

The plan of the book is simple. For each philosopher, a brief biography has been sketched, and there is a general introduction to the main contributions of that philosopher to the Western philosophy of man. It is obvious how inadequate such thematic introductions are. Their inadequacy makes them all the more difficult to compose, but we feel that they will help orient the beginning student of philsophy and invite his continued efforts in the scholarly works which his professor may recommend.

The editors are indebted to the following authors on whom they relied in general for thematic and biographical materials: *The History of Philosophy*, Émile Bréhier; *A Short History of Philosophy*, François Joseph Thonnard; *History of Modern European Philosophy: The Existentialists*, James Collins; *Contemporary European Philosophy*, Innocentius M. Bochenski; *The Phenomenological Movement, A Historical Introduction*, Herbert Spiegelberg; *A History of Philosophy*, Frederick Charles Copleston; *The History of Philosophy*, Johannes Hirschberger.

We also acknowledge with gratitude the services of Catita Stolbach, Nancy Moorhead, Ellen Sullivan, Judy Wells, Patricia Kirby and Barbara Neal in the preparation of the materials for publication. Special gratitude goes to Susan Walsh for her editorial and research assistance. We are also deeply grateful to Rev. Stephen X. Winters, S.J. for his helpful suggestions concerning the text.

For the second edition the introductions, selections, and bibliographies were reviewed, and corrections, deletions, and additions were made. The Jaspers selection was replaced by another. Chapters on Hegel, Ricoeur, and Nédoncelle are new.

It is, of course, always gratifying to be asked to prepare a new edition, confident in the knowledge that a need is being met. The editors hope that this second edition will prove as helpful to professors and students as has the first.

William L. Kelly
Andrew Tallon

1

PLATO
427–347 B.C.

Introduction

Born of Athenian nobility, Plato was destined to enter public life and thereby to influence the political and cultural heritage of Greece. He witnessed the dictatorship of the Thirty around 404 B.C. and the rule of the Democrates shortly thereafter. Plato was disturbed by abuses in government. Moreover, he was convinced that justice could exist in a state only if the proponents of a genuine philosophy assumed power or the ones in power accepted a genuine philosophy. Thus, he devoted himself to the search for truth which would at the same time afford an equitable way of life for the individual as well as provide for the common good. He polemicized against the Sophists and rhetoricians who but "flattered and said what men wished to hear." The task of the philosopher was to know man. This attitude he inherited from his master, Socrates, who was condemned to death by the politicians because of his teachings.

Plato went into exile, returned for the Corinthian War, and traveled to Egypt and Cyrene. On a visit to Sicily he incurred the displeasure of the tyrant Dionysius the Elder, who placed him on the slave market. He was quickly saved by Anniceris, a follower of Socrates. In 387 B.C. he founded his famous Academy in Athens in the vicinity of Heros Academos. This was the first European university. Philosophy, mathematics, astronomy, and perhaps zoology and botany were taught. The Academy was interested not only in theoretical learning but in the formation of young men for participation in public life. Plato's Academy was often involved in the politics of Athens. One of Plato's renowned pupils was Aristotle.

The dialogue, now so popular in certain academic circles, provided Plato's philosophy with a method which allowed a degree of freedom and a literary excellence found in few philosophers. Through symbolism and even dramatic presentation Plato treated problems meaningful to the world he lived in.

Thematically, Plato's thoughts were concerned with dialectics, physics, and ethics. The *dialectical* effort was mostly concerned with the origin, existence, world of, and theory of ideas. Questions dealing with the nature of knowledge, truth, the good, and beauty are interwoven in masterful style reflecting brilliance and intuitive deftness, particularly in the dialogues: *Phaedrus, Phaedo, Symposium* among others. The world of phenomena is treated in Plato's *physics*. This world is the world of sense, change, being, and nonbeing. The famed doctrine of *participation* and *imitation* he treats in the *Parmenides*. Limitation and multiplication of being, the metaphysics of matter, and related questions are treated in the *Timaeus*. He also writes of the origin of the universe and of the world soul in the *Timaeus*. His anthropology treats of the preexistence (*Timaeus*) of the human tripart soul (*Phaedo*), the theory of reminiscence (*Meno*), and immortality (*Phaedo* and *Phaedrus*). Plato's *ethics* are concerned with moral and political themes. It would seem that the heart of Plato's philosophy is the *good* and the *beautiful*. The pursuit of the highest good is happiness (*Symposium*) for which virtue is essential. It should be the object of the state to maintain morality through the guidance of philosophy (*Republic*).

The following selections from the *Symposium* and *Phaedrus* exemplify several significant characteristics in Plato's philosophy of man: love, beauty, and immortality.

LOVE, BEAUTY *

And now I will take my leave of you, and rehearse the tale of love which I heard once upon a time from Diotima of Mantineia, who was a wise woman in this and many other branches of knowledge. She was the same who deferred the plague of Athens ten years by a sacrifice, and was my instructress in the art of love. For, like Agathon, she spoke first of the being and nature of love, and then of his works. And I said to her in nearly the same words which he used to me, that love was a mighty god, and likewise fair; and she proved to me as I proved to him that, in my way of speaking about him, love was neither fair nor good. "What do you mean, Diotima," I said, "is love then evil and foul?" "Hush," she cried; "is that to be deemed foul which is not fair?" "Certainly," I said. "And is that which is not wise, ignorant? do you not see that there is a mean between wisdom and ignorance?" "And what is this?" I said. "Right opinion," she replied; "which, as you know, being incapable of giving a reason, is not knowledge (for how could knowledge be devoid of reason? nor again, ignorance, for neither can ignorance attain the truth), but is clearly something which is a mean between ignorance and wisdom." "Quite true," I replied. "Do not then insist," she said, "that what is not fair is of necessity foul, or what is not good evil; or infer that because love is not fair and good he is therefore foul and evil; for he is in a mean between them." "Well," I said, "love is surely admitted by all to be a great god." "By those who know or by those who don't know?" "By all." "And how, Socrates," she said with a smile, "can love be acknowledged to be a great god by those who say that he is not a god at all?" "And who are they?" I said. "You and I are two of them," she replied. "How can that be?" I said. "That is very intelligible," she replied; "as you yourself would acknowledge that the gods are happy and fair—of course

you would—would you dare to say that any god was not?" "Certainly not," I replied. "And you mean by the happy, those who are the possessors of things good or fair?" "Yes." "And you admitted that love, because he was in want, desires those good and fair things of which he is in want?" "Yes, I admitted that." "But how can he be a god who has no share in the good or the fair?" "That is not to be supposed." "Then you see that you also deny the deity of love."

"What then is love?" I asked; "Is he mortal?" "No." "What then?" "As in the former instance, he is neither mortal nor immortal, but in a mean between them." "What is he then, Diotima?" "He is a great spirit ($\delta\alpha\acute{\iota}\mu\omega\nu$), and like all that is spiritual he is intermediate between the divine and the mortal." "And what is the nature of this spiritual power?" I said. "This is the power," she said, "which interprets and conveys to the gods the prayers and sacrifices of men, and to men the commands and rewards of the gods; and this power spans the chasm which divides them, and in this all is bound together, and through this the arts of the prophet and the priest, their sacrifices and mysteries and charms, and all prophecy and incantation, find their way. For God mingles not with man; and through this power all the intercourse and speech of God with man, whether awake or asleep, is carried on. The wisdom which understands this is spiritual; all other wisdom, such as that of arts or handicrafts, is mean and vulgar. Now these spirits or intermediate powers are many and divine, and one of them is love." "And who," I said, "was his father, and who his mother?" "The tale," she said, "will take time; nevertheless I will tell you. On the birthday of Aphrodite there was a feast of the gods, at which the god Poros or Plenty, who is the son of Metis or Discretion, was one of the guests. When the feast was over, Penia or Poverty, as the manner was, came about the doors to beg. Now Plenty, who was the worse for nectar (there was no wine in those days), came into the

* From Plato, "The Symposium," in *The Works of Plato*, B. Jowett, translator. The Dial Press, Inc., New York, 1936.

garden of Zeus and fell into a heavy sleep; and Poverty considering her own straitened circumstances, plotted to have him for a husband, and accordingly she lay down at his side and conceived Love, who partly because he is naturally a lover of the beautiful, and because Aphrodite is herself beautiful, and also because he was born on Aphrodite's birthday is her follower and attendant. And as his parentage is, so also are his fortunes. In the first place he is always poor, and anything but tender and fair, as the many imagine him; and he is hard-featured and squalid, and has no shoes, nor a house to dwell in; on the bare earth exposed he lies under the open heaven, in the streets, or at the doors of houses, taking his rest; and like his mother he is always in distress. Like his father too, whom he also partly resembles, he is always plotting against the fair and good; he is bold, enterprising, strong, a hunter of men, always at some intrigue or other, keen in the pursuit of wisdom, and never wanting resources; a philosopher at all times, terrible as an enchanter, sorcerer, sophist; for as he is neither mortal nor immortal, he is alive and flourishing at one moment when he is in plenty, and dead at another moment, and again alive by reason of his father's nature. But that which is always flowing in is always flowing out, and so he is never in want and never in wealth, and he is also in a mean between ignorance and knowledge. The truth of the matter is just this: No god is a philosopher or seeker after wisdom, for he is wise already; nor does any one else who is wise seek after wisdom. Neither do the ignorant seek after wisdom. For herein is the evil of ignorance, that he who is neither good nor wise is nevertheless satisfied: he feels no want, and has therefore no desire." "But who then, Diotima," I said, "are the lovers of wisdom, if they are neither the wise nor the foolish?" "A child may answer that question," she replied; "they are those who, like love, are in a mean between the two. For wisdom is a most beautiful thing, and love is of the beautiful; and therefore love is also a philosopher or lover of wisdom, and being a lover of wisdom is in a

mean between the wise and the ignorant. And this again is a quality which Love inherits from his parents; for his father is wealthy and wise, and his mother poor and foolish. Such, my dear Socrates, is the nature of the spirit Love. The error in your conception of him was very natural, and as I imagine from what you say, has arisen out of a confusion of love and the beloved—this made you think that love was all beautiful. For the beloved is the truly beautiful, delicate, and perfect and blessed; but the principle of love is of another nature, and is such as I have described."

I said: "O thou stranger woman, thou sayest well, and now, assuming love to be such as you say, what is the use of him?" "That, Socrates," she replied, "I will proceed to unfold: of his nature and birth I have already spoken; and you acknowledge that love is of the beautiful. But some one will say: Of the beautiful in what, Socrates and Diotima—or rather let me put the question more clearly, and ask: When a man loves the beautiful, what does he love?" I answered her, "That the beautiful may be his." "Still," she said, "the answer suggests a further question, which is this: What is given by the possession of beauty?" "That," I replied, "is a question to which I have no answer ready." "Then," she said, "let me put the word 'good' in the place of the beautiful, and repeat the question: What does he who loves the good desire?" "The possession of the good," I said. "And what does he gain who possesses the good?" "Happiness," I replied; "there is no difficulty in answering that." "Yes," she said, "the happy are made happy by the acquisition of good things. Nor is there any need to ask why a man desires happiness; the answer is already final." "That is true," I said. "And is this wish and this desire common to all? and do all men always desire their own good, or only some men?—what think you?" "All men," I replied; "the desire is common to all." "But all men, Socrates," she rejoined, "are not said to love, but only some of them; and you say that all men are always loving the same things." "I myself wonder," I said, "why that is." "There is nothing to wonder at," she replied; "the reason is that one part of love is separated off and receives the name of the whole, but the other parts have other names." "Give an example," I said. She answered me as follows: "There is poetry, which, as you know, is complex and manifold. And all creation or passage of non-being into being is poetry or making, and the processes of all art are creative; and the masters of arts are all poets." "Very true." "Still," she said, "you know that they are not called poets, but have other names; the generic term 'poetry' is confined to that specific art which is separated off from the rest of poetry, and is concerned with music and metre; and this is what is called poetry, and they who possess this kind of poetry are called poets." "Very true," I said. "And the same holds of love. For you may say generally that all desire of good and happiness is due to the great and subtle power of love; but those who, having their affections set upon him, are yet diverted into the paths of money-making or gymnastic philosophy, are not called lovers —the name of the genus is reserved for those whose devotion takes one form only— they alone are said to love, or to be lovers." "In that," I said, "I am of opinion that you are right." "Yes," she said, "and you hear people say that lovers are seeking for the half of themselves; but I say that they are seeking neither for the half, nor for the whole, unless the half or the whole be also a good. And they will cut off their own hands and feet and cast them away, if they are evil; for they love them not because they are their own, but because they are good, and dislike them not because they are another's, but because they are evil. There is nothing which men love but the good. Do you think that there is?" "Indeed," I answered, "I should say not." "Then," she said, "the conclusion of the whole matter is, that men love the good." "Yes," I said. "To which may be added that they love the possession of the good?" "Yes, that may be added." "And not only the possession, but the everlasting possession of the good?" "That may be added too." "Then, love," she said, "may be described generally as the love of the everlast-

ing possession of the good?" "That is most true," I said.

"Then if this be the nature of love, can you tell me further," she said, "what is the manner of the pursuit? what are they doing who show all this eagerness and heat which is called love? Answer me that." "Nay, Diotima," I said, "if I had known I should not have wondered at your wisdom, or have come to you to learn." "Well," she said, "I will teach you;—love is only birth in beauty, whether of body or soul." "The oracle requires an explanation," I said; "I don't understand you." "I will make my meaning clearer," she replied. "I mean to say, that all men are bringing to the birth in their bodies and in their souls. There is a certain age at which human nature is desirous of procreation; and this procreation must be in beauty and not in deformity: and this is the mystery of man and woman, which is a divine thing, for conception and generation are a principle of immortality in the mortal creature. And in the inharmonical they can never be. But the deformed is always inharmonical with the divine, and the beautiful harmonious. Beauty, then, is the destiny or goddess of parturition who presides at birth, and therefore when approaching beauty the conceiving power is propitious, and diffuse, and benign, and begets and bears fruit: on the appearance of foulness she frowns and contracts in pain, and is averted and morose, and shrinks up, and not without a pang refrains from conception. And this is the reason why, when the hour of conception arrives, and the teeming nature is full, there is such a flutter and ecstasy about beauty whose approach is the alleviation of pain. For love, Socrates, is not, as you imagine, the love of the beautiful only." "What then?" "The love of generation and birth in beauty." "Yes," I said. "Yes, indeed," she replied. "But why of birth?" I said. "Because to the mortal, birth is a sort of eternity and immortality," she replied; "and as has been already admitted, all men will necessarily desire immortality together with good, if love is of the everlasting possession of the good."

And this she taught me at various times

when she spoke of love. And on another occasion she said to me, "What is the reason, Socrates, of this love, and the attendant desire? See you not how all animals, birds as well as beasts, in their desire of procreation, are in agony when they take the infection of love;—this begins with the desire of union, to which is added the care of offspring, on behalf of whom the weakest are ready to battle against the strongest even to the uttermost, and to die for them, and will let themselves be tormented with hunger or suffer anything in order to maintain their offspring. Man may be supposed to do this from reason; but why should animals have these passionate feelings? Can you tell me why?" Again I replied, that I did not know. She said to me: "And do you expect ever to become a master in the art of love, if you do not know this?" "But that," I said, "Diotima, is the reason why I come to you, because, as I have told you already, I am aware that I want a teacher; and I wish that you would explain to me this and the other mysteries of love." "Marvel not at this," she said, "if you believe that love is of the immortal, as we have already admitted; for here again, and on the same principle too, the mortal nature is seeking as far as is possible to be everlasting and immortal: and this is only to be attained by generation, because the new is always left in the place of the old. For even in the same individual there is succession and not absolute unity: a man is called the same; but yet in the short interval which elapses between youth and age, and in which every animal is said to have life and identity, he is undergoing a perpetual process of loss and reparation—hair, flesh, bones, blood, and the whole body are always changing. And this is true not only of the body, but also of the soul, whose habits, tempers, opinions, desires, pleasures, pains, fears, never remain the same in any one of us, but are always coming and going. And what is yet more surprising is, that this is also true of knowledge; and not only does knowledge in general come and go, so that in this respect we are never the same; but particular knowledge also experiences a like change. For what is implied in the word "recollection," but the departure of knowledge, which is ever being forgotten and is renewed and preserved by recollection, appearing to be the same although in reality new, according to that law of succession by which all mortal things are preserved, not by absolute sameness of existence, but by substitution, the old worn-out mortality leaving another new and similar one behind—unlike the immortal in this, which is always the same and not another? And in this way, Socrates, the mortal body, or mortal anything, partakes of immortality; but the immortal in another way. Marvel not then at the love which all men have of their offspring; for that universal love and interest is for the sake of immortality."

When I heard this, I was astonished, and said: "Is this really true, O thou wise Diotima?" And she answered with all the authority of a sophist: "Of that, Socrates, you may be assured;—think only of the ambition of men, and you will marvel at their senselessness, unless you consider how they are stirred by the love of an immortality of fame. They are ready to run risks greater far than they would have run for their children, and to spend money and undergo any amount of toil, and even to die for the sake of leaving behind them a name which shall be eternal. Do you imagine that Alcestis would have died on behalf of Admetus, or Achilles after Patroclus, or your own Codrus in order to preserve the kingdom for his sons, if they had not imagined that the memory of their virtues, which is still retained among us, would be immortal? Nay," she said, "for I am persuaded that all men do all things for the sake of the glorious fame of immortal virtue, and the better they are the more they desire this; for they are ravished with the desire of the immortal.

"Men whose bodies only are creative, betake themselves to women and beget children—this is the character of their love; their offspring, as they hope, will preserve their memory and give them the blessedness and immortality which they desire in the future. But creative souls—for there are men who are more creative in their souls than in their bodies—conceive that which is proper for the soul to conceive or retain. And what are these conceptions?—wisdom and virtue in general. And such creators are all poets and other artists who may be said to have invention. But the greatest and fairest sort of wisdom by far is that which is concerned with the ordering of states and families, and which is called temperance and justice. And he who in youth has the seed of these implanted in him and is himself inspired, when he comes to maturity desires to beget and generate. And he wanders about seeking beauty that he may beget offspring—for in deformity he will beget nothing—and embraces the beautiful rather than the deformed; and when he finds a fair and noble and well-nurtured soul, and there is union of the two in one person, he gladly embraces him, and to such an one he is full of fair speech about virtue and the nature and pursuits of a good man; and he tries to educate him; and at the touch and presence of the beautiful he brings forth the beautiful which he conceived long before, and the beautiful is ever present with him and in his memory even when absent, and in company they tend that which he brings forth, and they are bound together by a far nearer tie and have a closer friendship than those who beget mortal children, for the children who are their common offspring are fairer and more immortal. Who, when he thinks of Homer and Hesiod and other great poets, would not rather have their children than any ordinary human ones? Who would not emulate them in the creation of children such as theirs, which have preserved their memory and given them everlasting glory? Or who would not have such children as Lycurgus left behind to be the saviors, not only of Lacedaemon, but of Hellas, as one may say? There is Solon, too, who is the revered father of Athenian laws; and many others there are in many other places, both among Hellenes and barbarians. All of them have done many noble works, and have been the parents of virtue of every kind, and many temples have been raised in honor of their children, which were never raised in honor of the mortal children of any one.

"These are the lesser mysteries of love, into which even you, Socrates, may enter; to the greater and more hidden ones which are the crown of these, and to which, if you pursue them in a right spirit, they will lead, I know not whether you will be able to attain. But I will do my utmost to inform you, and do you follow if you can. For he who would proceed rightly in this matter should begin in youth to turn to beautiful forms; and first, if his instructor guide him rightly, he should learn to love one such form only—out of that he should create fair thoughts; and soon he would himself perceive that the beauty of one form is truly related to the beauty of another; and then if beauty in general is his pursuit, how foolish would he be not to recognize that the beauty in every form is one and the same! And when he perceives this he will abate his violent love of the one, which he will despise and deem a small thing, and will become a lover of all beautiful forms; this will lead him on to consider that the beauty of the mind is more honorable than the beauty of the outward form. So that if a virtuous soul have but a little comeliness, he will be content to love and tend him, and will search out and bring to the birth thoughts which may improve the young, until his beloved is compelled to contemplate and see the beauty of institutions and laws, and understand that all is of one kindred, and that personal beauty is only a trifle; and after laws and institutions he will lead him on to the sciences, that he may see their beauty, being not like a servant in love with the beauty of one youth or man or institution, himself a slave mean and calculating, but looking at the abundance of beauty and drawing toward the sea of beauty, and creating and beholding many fair and noble thoughts and notions in boundless love of wisdom; until at length he grows and waxes strong, and at last the vision is revealed to him of a single science, which is the science of beauty everywhere. To this I will proceed; please to give me your very best attention.

"For he who has been instructed thus far in the things of love, and who has learned to see the beautiful in due order and succession, when he comes toward the end will suddenly perceive a nature of wondrous beauty—and this, Socrates, is that final cause of all our former toils, which in the first place is everlasting—not growing and decaying, or waxing and waning; in the next place not fair in one point of view and foul in another, or at one time or in one relation or at one place fair, at another time or in another relation or at another place foul, as if fair to some and foul to others, or in the likeness of a face or hands or any other part of the bodily frame, or in any form of speech or knowledge, nor existing in any other being; as for example, an animal, whether in earth or heaven, but beauty only, absolute, separate, simple, and everlasting, which without diminution and without increase, or any change, is imparted to the ever-growing and perishing beauties of all other things. He who under the influence of true love rising upward from these begins to see that beauty, is not far from the end. And the true order of going or being led by another to the things of love, is to use the beauties of earth as steps along which he mounts upwards for the sake of that other beauty, going from one to two, and from two to all fair forms, and from fair forms to fair actions, and from fair actions to fair notions, until from fair notions he arrives at the notion of absolute beauty, and at last knows what the essence of beauty is. This, my dear Socrates," said the stranger of Mantineia, "is that life above all others which man should live, in the contemplation of beauty absolute; a beauty which if you once beheld, you would see not to be after the measure of gold, and garments, and fair boys and youths, which when you now behold you are in fond amazement, and you and many a one are content to live seeing only and conversing with them without meat or drink, if that were possible—you only want to be with them and to look at them. But what if man had eyes to see the true beauty—the divine beauty, I mean, pure and clear and unalloyed, not clogged with the pollutions of mortality, and all the colors and vanities of human life—thither looking, and holding converse with the true beauty divine and simple, and bringing into being and educating true creations of virtue and not idols only? Do you not see that in that communion only, beholding beauty with the eye of the mind, he will be enabled to bring forth, not images of beauty, but realities; for he has hold not of an image but of a reality, and bringing forth and educating true virtue to become the friend of God and be immortal, if mortal man may. Would that be an ignoble life?". . .

IMMORTALITY *

The soul is immortal, for that is immortal which is ever in motion; but that which moves and is moved by another, in ceasing to move ceases also to live. Therefore, only that which is self-moving, never failing of self, never ceases to move, and is the fountain and beginning of motion to all that moves besides. Now, the beginning is unbegotten, for that which is begotten has a be-

* From Plato, "The Phaedrus," in *The Works of Plato*, B. Jowett, translator. The Dial Press, Inc., New York, 1936.

ginning; but the beginning has no beginning, for if a beginning were begotten of something, that would have no beginning. But that, which is unbegotten must also be indestructible; for if beginning were destroyed, there could be no beginning out of anything, nor anything out of a beginning; and all things must have a beginning. And therefore the self-moving is the beginning of motion; and this can neither be destroyed nor begotten, for in that case the whole heavens and all generation would collapse and stand still, and never again have motion or birth. But if the self-moving is immortal, he who affirms that self-motion is the very idea and essence of the soul will not be put to confusion. For the body which is moved from without is soulless; but that which is moved from within has a soul, and this is involved in the nature of the soul. But if the soul be truly affirmed to be the self-moving, then must she also be without beginning, and immortal. Enough of the soul's immortality. . . .

Bibliography

Texts

The works of Plato are published, under the editorship of J. Burnet, in the *Oxford Classical Texts*. A translation, in five volumes, is that by B. Jowett, 3d ed. London: Oxford University Press, 1892.

Studies

Stewart, J. A. *The Myths of Plato.* London: Oxford University Press, 1905.

―――. *Plato's Doctrine of Ideas.* Oxford: Clarendon Press, 1909.

Taylor, A. E. *Plato, the Man and His Work.* London: Methuen & Co., Ltd., 1926.

―――. *A Commentary on Plato's Timaeus.* Oxford: Clarendon Press, 1928.

―――. "Plato" in the *Encyclopaedia Britannica*, 14th ed.

―――. *Platonism and Its Inflence.* Boston: Marshall Jones Co., 1924.

2

Introduction

Born in Stagira in Macedonia, Aristotle was the son of the physician to the Macedonian king Amyntas. At eighteen, Aristotle entered Plato's Academy and remained till the death of his master, twenty years later. Though Aristotle later came to differ with Plato's philosophical position, his reverence for Plato remained unchanged.

At Plato's death, Aristotle departed for Assos in Troas, where he and some others from the Academy founded a daughter school. Aristotle stayed there only three years and went in 342 B.C. to the court of Philip of Macedonia, where he tutored the thirteen-year-old Alexander. When Alexander assumed governing responsibility, Aristotle went to Athens where he founded his Lyceum in the vicinity of the temple of Apollo. The scholars of this school were called the "Peripatetics" because they walked about (peripatein) as they discussed their matter. Not only was Aristotle a biologist and philosopher, he was also an effective academic organizer. He instituted courses in philosophy, history of philosophy, natural sciences, medicine, history, archeology, politics, and philology.

With the death of Alexander (323 B.C.) the anti-Macedonian party came into power. Aristotle chose exile lest the Athenians be forced to "sin against philosophy," as they had in the death of Socrates. He died the following year in Euboea. His prolific writings cover three phases: the Platonic period of the Academy, the transitional, and the phase at the Lyceum, which was devoted mostly to logic, metaphysics, natural sciences, ethics, politics, and philosophy.

The philosophy of Aristotle follows a division similar to that seen in Plato, namely, logic, metaphysics, and ethics. In his writings on logic, Aristotle treats with systematic precision topics such as concepts, judgments, and syllogisms. He discusses their functions and the principles which regulate their use. The five modes of predication called "predicables" (genus, species, specific differences, property, and accident) and nine accidents are discussed in the Categories. On Interpretation, Prior Analytics, Posterior Analytics, and the Topics, usually combined in Byzantine times under the title Organon. Aristotle's treatise of the origin of knowledge differs from Plato's in that idea is in the world and grasped through a process of abstraction by the intellect from sensory perception data (On the Soul).

The general metaphysics of Aristotle posits a world of substances composed of matter and form (hylomorphism) related as potency and act, principles of determinability and actuality. Change, movement, causality, teleology, and individuality are interpreted by means of these principles of being. Aristotle's special metaphysics deals with the soul, world, and God. The human soul (On the Soul) Aristotle treats as the life principle: as rational, the soul distinguishes man from all other living animals. The questions of human free will and immortality are also discussed.

In his Physics world themes such as time, space, and eternity of the world are investigated. The question of God is taken up in Aristotle's reflections on movement, where he proposes a proof for God's existence, a God that is real, thinking spirit and blessed life. It is not thereby established that Aristotle conceives the First Cause as a person.

Aristotle's Ethics (Nicomachean Ethics) treats of the character and principles of morality and their relation to human nature. The nature and function of the state Aristotle analyzes in his Politics. The following passage from On the Soul is about the unity and definition of the soul, the distinction between the parts of the soul, and the relation of the human soul to the body.

SOUL AS SUBSTANTIAL FORM *

Let the foregoing suffice as our account of the views concerning the soul which have been handed on by our predecessors; let us now dismiss them and make as it were a completely fresh start, endeavouring to give a precise answer to the question, What is soul? i.e. to formulate the most general possible definition of it.

We are in the habit of recognizing, as one determinate kind of what is, substance, and that in several senses, (a) in the sense of matter or that which in itself is not "a this," and (b) in the sense of form or essence, which is that precisely in virtue of which a thing is called "a this," and thirdly (c) in the sense of that which is compounded of both (a) and (b). Now matter is potentiality, form actuality; of the latter there are two grades related to one another as e.g. knowledge to the exercise of knowledge.

Among substances are by general consent reckoned bodies and especially natural bodies; for they are the principles of all other bodies. Of natural bodies some have life in them, others not; by life we mean self-nutrition and growth (with its correlative decay). It follows that every natural body which has life in it is a substance in the sense of a composite.

But since it is also a *body* of such and such a kind, viz. having life, the *body* cannot be soul; the body is the subject or matter, not what is attributed to it. Hence the soul must be a substance in the sense of the form of a natural body having life potentially within it. But substance is actuality, and thus soul is the actuality of a body as above characterized. Now the word actuality has two senses corresponding respectively to the possession of knowledge and the actual exercise of knowledge. It is obvious that the soul is actuality in the first sense, viz. that of knowledge as possessed,

for both sleeping and waking presuppose the existence of soul, and of these waking corresponds to actual knowing, sleeping to knowledge possessed but not employed, and, in the history of the individual, knowledge comes before its employment or exercise.

That is why the soul is the first grade of actuality of a natural body having life potentially in it. The body so described is a body which is organized. The parts of plants in spite of their extreme simplicity are "organs"; e.g. the leaf serves to shelter the pericarp, the pericarp to shelter the fruit, while the roots of plants are analogous to the mouth of animals, both serving for the absorption of food. If, then, we have to give a general formula applicable to all kinds of soul, we must describe it as the first grade of actuality of a natural organized body. That is why we can wholly dismiss as unnecessary the question whether the soul and the body are one: it is as meaningless as to ask whether the wax and the shape given to it by the stamp are one, or generally the matter of a thing and that of which it is the matter. Unity has many senses (as many as "is" has), but the most proper and fundamental sense of both is the relation of an actuality to that of which it is the actuality.

We have now given an answer to the question, What is soul?—an answer which applies to it in its full extent. It is substance in the sense which corresponds to the definitive formula of a thing's essence. That means that it is "the essential whatness" of a body of the character just assigned. Suppose that what is literally an "organ," like an axe, were a *natural* body, its "essential whatness," would have been its essence, and so its soul; if this disappeared from it, it would have ceased to be an axe, except in name. As it is, it is just an axe; it wants the character which is required to make its whatness or formulable essence a soul; for that, it would have had to be a *natural* body of a particular kind, viz. one having in *itself* the power of setting itself in movement and arresting it-

* From Aristotle, "On the Soul," in *The Basic Works of Aristotle*, the Oxford translation of Aristotle, reprinted by permission of the Clarendon Press, Oxford.

self. Next, apply this doctrine in the case of the "parts" of the living body. Suppose that the eye were an animal—sight would have been its soul, for sight is the substance or essence of the eye which corresponds to the formula, the eye being merely the matter of seeing; when seeing is removed the eye is no longer an eye, except in name—it is no more a real eye than the eye of a statue or of a painted figure. We must now extend our consideration from the "parts" to the whole living body; for what the departmental sense is to the bodily part which is its organ, that the whole faculty of sense is to the whole sensitive body as such.

We must not understand by that which is "potentially capable of living" what has lost the soul it had, but only what still retains it; but seeds and fruits are bodies which possess the qualification. Consequently, while walking is actuality in a sense corresponding to the cutting and the seeing; the soul is actuality in the sense corresponding to the power of sight and the power in the tool; the body corresponds to what exists in potentiality; as the pupil *plus* the power of sight constitutes the eye, so the soul *plus* the body constitutes the animal.

From this it indubitably follows that the soul is inseparable from its body, or at any rate that certain parts of it are (if it has parts)—for the actuality of some of them is nothing but the actualities of their bodily parts. Yet some may be separable because they are not the actualities of any body at all. Further, we have no light on the problem whether the soul may not be the actuality of its body in the sense in which the sailor is the actuality of the ship.

This must suffice as our sketch or outline determination of the nature of soul. . . .

FUNCTIONS OF THE SOUL

We resume our inquiry from a fresh starting-point by calling attention to the fact that what has soul in it differs from what has not in that the former displays life. Now this word has more than one sense, and provided any one alone of these is found in a thing we say that thing is living. Living, that is, may mean thinking or perception or local movement and rest, or movement in the sense of nutrition, decay and growth. Hence we think of plants also as living, for they are observed to possess in themselves an originative power through which they increase or decrease in all spatial directions; they grow up *and* down, and everything that grows increases its bulk alike in both directions or indeed in all, and continues to live so long as it can absorb nutriment.

This power of self-nutrition can be isolated from the other powers mentioned, but not they from it—in mortal beings at least. The fact is obvious in plants; for it is the only psychic power they possess.

This is the originative power the possession of which leads us to speak of things as *living* at all, but it is the possession of sensation that leads us for the first time to speak of living things as animals; for even those beings which possess no power of local movement but do possess the power of sensation we call animals and not merely living things.

The primary form of sense is touch, which belongs to all animals. Just as the power of self-nutrition can be isolated from touch and sensation generally, so touch can be isolated from all other forms of sense. (By the power of self-nutrition we mean that departmental power of the soul which is common to plants and animals: all animals whatsoever are observed to have the sense of touch.) What the explanation of these two facts is, we must discuss later. At present we must confine ourselves to saying that soul is the source of these phenomena and is characterized by them, viz. by the powers of self-nutrition, sensation, thinking, and motivity.

Is each of these a soul or a part of a soul?

And if a part, a part in what sense? A part merely distinguishable by definition or a part distinct in local situation as well? In the case of certain of these powers, the answers to these questions are easy, in the case of others we are puzzled what to say. Just as in the case of plants which when divided are observed to continue to live though removed to a distance from one another (thus showing that in *their* case the soul of each individual plant before division was actually one, potentially many), so we notice a similar result in other varieties of soul, i.e. in insects which have been cut in two; each of the segments possesses both sensation and local movement; and if sensation, necessarily also imagination and appetition; for, where there is sensation, there is also pleasure and pain, and, where these, necessarily also desire.

We have no evidence as yet about mind or the power to think; it seems to be a widely different kind of soul, differing as what is eternal from what is perishable; it alone is capable of existence in isolation from all other psychic powers. All the other parts of soul, it is evident from what we have said, are, in spite of certain statements to the contrary, incapable of separate existence though, of course, distinguishable by definition. If opining is distinct from perceiving, to be capable of opining and to be capable of perceiving must be distinct, and so with all the other forms of living above enumerated. Further, some animals possess all these parts of soul, some certain of them only, others one only (this is what enables us to classify animals); the cause must be considered later. A similar arrangement is found also within the field of the senses; some classes of animals have all the senses, some only certain of them, others only one, the most indispensable, touch.

Since the expression "that whereby we live and perceive" has two meanings, just like the expression "that whereby we know" —that may mean either (*a*) knowledge or (*b*) the soul, for we can speak of knowing *by* or *with* either, and similarly that whereby we are in health may be either (*a*) health or (*b*)

the body or some part of the body; and since of the two terms thus contrasted knowledge or health is the name of a form, essence, or ratio, or if we so express it an actuality of a recipient matter—knowledge of what is capable of knowing, health of what is capable of being made healthy (for the operation of that which is capable of originating change terminates and has its seat in what is changed or altered); further, since it is the soul by or with which primarily we live, perceive, and think:—it follows that the soul must be a ratio or formulable essence, not a matter or subject. For, as we said, the word substance has three meanings—form, matter, and the complex of both—and of these three what is called matter, is potentiality, what is called form actuality. Since then the complex here is the living thing, the body cannot be the actuality of the soul; it is the soul which is the actuality of a certain kind of body. Hence the rightness of the view that the soul cannot be without a body, while it cannot *be* a body; it is not a body but something relative to a body. That is why it is *in* a body, and a body of a definite kind. It was a mistake, therefore, to do as former thinkers did, merely to fit it into a body without adding a definite specification of the kind or character of that body. Reflection confirms the observed fact; the actuality of any given thing can only be realized in what is already potentially that thing, i.e. in a matter of its own appropriate to it. From all this it follows that soul is an actuality or formulable essence of something that possesses a potentiality of being besouled. . . .

It is now evident that a single definition can be given of soul only in the same sense as one can be given of figure. For, as in that case there is no figure distinguishable and apart from triangle, &c., so here there is no soul apart from the forms of soul just enumerated. . . . The cases of figure and soul are exactly parallel; for the particulars subsumed under the common name in both cases—figures and living beings—constitute a series, each successive term of which potentially contains its predecessor, e.g. the square the triangle, the sensory power the self-nutritive. Hence we must ask in the case of each order of living things, What is its soul, i.e. What is the soul of plant, animal, man? Why the terms are related in this serial way must form the subject of later examination. But the facts are that the power of perception is never found apart from the power of self-nutrition, while—in plants—the latter is found isolated from the former. Again, no sense is found apart from that of touch, while touch *is* found by itself; many animals have neither sight, hearing, nor smell. Again, among living things that possess sense some have the power of locomotion, some not. Lastly, certain living beings —a small minority—possess calculation and thought, for (among mortal beings) those which possess calculation have all the other powers above mentioned, while the converse does not hold—indeed some live by imagination alone, while others have not even imagination. The mind that knows with immediate intuition presents a different problem.

It is evident that the way to give the most adequate definition of soul is to seek in the case of *each* of its forms for the most appropriate definition.

It is necessary for the student of these forms of soul first to find a definition of each, expressive of what it is, and then to investigate its derivative properties, &c. But if we are to express what each is, viz. what the thinking power is, or the perceptive, or the nutritive, we must go farther back and first give an account of thinking or perceiving, for in the order of investigation the question of what an agent does precedes the question, what enables it to do what it does. If this is correct, we must on the same ground go yet another step farther back and have some clear view of the objects of each; thus we must *start* with these objects, e.g. with food, with what is perceptible, or with what is intelligible.

Nutrition and Reproduction

It follows that first of all we must treat of nutrition and reproduction, for the nutritive soul is found along with all the others and is the most primitive and widely distributed power of soul, being indeed that one in virtue of which all are said to have life. The acts in which it manifests itself are reproduction and the use of food—reproduction, I say, because for any living thing that has reached its normal development and which is unmutilated, and whose mode of generation is not spontaneous, the most natural act is the production of another like itself, an animal producing an animal, a plant a plant, in order that, as far as its nature allows, it may partake in the eternal and divine. That is the goal towards which all things strive, that for the sake of which they do whatsoever their nature renders possible. The phrase "for the sake of which" is ambiguous; it may mean either (a) the end to achieve which, or (b) the being in whose interest, the act is done. Since then no living thing is able to partake in what is eternal and divine by uninterrupted continuance (for nothing perishable can for ever remain one and the same), it tries to achieve that end in the only way possible to it, and success is possible in varying degrees; so it remains not indeed as the self-same individual but continues its existence in something *like* itself—not numerically but specifically one.

The soul is the cause or source of the living body. The terms cause and source have many senses. But the soul is the cause of its body alike in all three senses which we explicitly recognize. It is (a) the source or origin of movement, it is (b) the end, it is (c) the essence of the whole living body.

That it is the last, is clear; for in everything the essence is identical with the ground of its being, and here, in the case of living things, their being is to live, and of their being and their living the soul in them is the cause or source. Further, the actuality of whatever is potential is identical with its formulable essence.

It is manifest that the soul is also the final cause of its body. For Nature, like mind, always does whatever it does for the sake of something, which something is its end. To that something corresponds in the case of animals the soul and in this it follows the order of nature; all natural bodies are organs of the soul. This is true of those that enter into the constitution of plants as well as of those which enter into that of animals. This shows that that for the sake of which they are is soul. We must here recall the two senses of "that for the sake of which," viz. (a) the end to achieve which, and (b) the being in whose interest, anything is or is done.

We must maintain, further, that the soul is also the cause of the living body as the original source of local movement. The power of locomotion is not found, however, in all living things. But change of quality and change of quantity are also due to the soul. Sensation is held to be a qualitative alteration, and nothing except what has soul in it is capable of sensation. The same holds of the quantitative changes which constitute growth and decay; nothing grows or decays naturally except what feeds itself, and nothing feeds itself except what has a share of soul in it. . . . .

Sensation, Perception, Thinking

Each sense then is relative to its particular group of sensible qualities: it is found in a sense-organ as such and discriminates the differences which exist within that group; e.g. sight discriminates white and black, taste sweet and bitter, and so in all cases. Since we also discriminate white from sweet, and indeed each sensible quality from every other, with what do we perceive that they are different? It must be by sense; for what is before us is sensible objects. (Hence it is also obvious that the flesh cannot be the ultimate sense-organ; if it were, the discriminating power could not do its work without immediate contact with the object.)

Therefore (1) discrimination between white and sweet cannot be effected by two agencies which remain separate; both the qualities discriminated must be present to something that is one and single. On any other supposition even if I perceived sweet

and you perceived white, the difference between them would be apparent. What says that two things are different must be one; for sweet is different from white. Therefore what asserts this difference must be self-identical and as what asserts, so also what thinks or perceives. That it is not possible by means of two agencies which remain separate to discriminate two objects which are separate is therefore obvious; and that (2) it is not possible to do this in separate moments of time may be seen if we look at it as follows. For as what asserts the difference between the good and the bad is one and the same, so also the time at which it asserts the one to be different and the other to be different is not accidental to the assertion (as it is for instance when I now assert a difference but do not assert that there is now a difference); it asserts thus— both now and that the objects are different now; the objects therefore must be present at one and the same moment. Both the discriminating power and the time of its exercise must be one and undivided.

But, it may be objected, it is impossible that what is self-identical should be moved at one and the same time with contrary movements in so far as it is undivided, and in an undivided moment of time. For if what is sweet be the quality perceived, it moves the sense or thought in this determinate way, while what is bitter moves it in a contrary way, and what is white in a different way. Is it the case then that what discriminates, though both numerically one and indivisible, is at the same time divided in its being? In one sense, it is what is divided that perceives two separate objects at once, but in another sense it does so *qua* undivided; for it is divisible in its being, but spatially and numerically undivided.

But is not this impossible? For while it is true that what is self-identical and undivided may be both contraries at once *potentially*, it cannot be self-identical in its being—it must lose its unity by being put into activity. It is not possible to be at once white and black, and therefore it must also be impossible for a thing to be affected at one and the same moment by the forms of both, assuming it to be the case that sensation and thinking are properly so described.

The answer is that just as what is called a "point" is, as being at once one and two, properly said to be divisible, so here, that which discriminates is *qua* undivided one, and active in a single moment of time, while so far forth as it is divisible it twice over uses the same dot at one and the same time. So far forth then as it takes the limit as two, it discriminates two separate objects with what in a sense is divided: while so far as it takes it as one, it does so with what is one and occupies in its activity a single moment of time.

About the principle in virtue of which we say that animals are percipient, let this discussion suffice.

There are two distinctive peculiarities by reference to which we characterize the soul —(1) local movement and (2) thinking, discriminating, and perceiving. Thinking, both speculative and practical, is regarded as akin to a form of perceiving; for in the one as well as the other the soul discriminates and is cognizant of something which *is*. Indeed the ancients go so far as to identify thinking and perceiving; e.g. Empedocles says "For 'tis in respect of what is present that man's wit is increased," and again "whence it befalls them from time to time to think diverse thoughts," and Homer's phrase "For suchlike is man's mind" means the same. They all look upon thinking as a bodily process like perceiving, and hold that like is *known* as well as *perceived* by like, as I explained at the beginning of our discussion. Yet they ought at the same time to have accounted for error also; for it is more intimately connected with animal existence and the soul continues longer in the state of error than in that of truth. They cannot escape the dilemma: either (1) whatever seems is true (and there are some who accept this) or (2) error is contact with the unlike; for that is the opposite of the knowing of like by like.

But it is a received principle that error as well as knowledge in respect to contraries is one and the same.

That perceiving and practical thinking are not identical is therefore obvious; for the former is universal in the animal world, the latter is found in only a small division of it. Further, speculative thinking is also distinct from perceiving—I mean that in which we find rightness and wrongness—rightness in prudence, knowledge, true opinion, wrongness in their opposites; for perception of the special objects of sense is always free from error, and is found in all animals, while it is possible to think falsely as well as truly, and thought is found only where there is discourse of reason as well as sensibility. For imagination is different from either perceiving or discursive thinking, though it is not found without sensation, or judgement without it. That this activity is not the same kind of thinking as judgement is obvious. For imagining lies within our own power whenever we wish (e.g. we can call up a picture, as in the practice of mnemonics by the use of mental images), but in forming opinions we are not free: we cannot escape the alternative of falsehood or truth. Further, when we think something to be fearful or threatening, emotion is immediately produced, and so too with what is encouraging; but when we merely imagine we remain as unaffected as persons who are looking at a painting of some dreadful or encouraging scene. Again within the field of judgement itself we find varieties—knowledge, opinion, prudence, and their opposites; of the differences between these I must speak elsewhere.

Thinking is different from perceiving and is held to be in part imagination, in part judgement: we must therefore first mark off the sphere of imagination and then speak of judgement. If then imagination is that in virtue of which an image arises for us, excluding metaphorical uses of the term, is it a single faculty or disposition relative to images, in virtue of which we discriminate and are either in error or not? The faculties in virtue of which we do this are sense, opinion, science, intelligence.

That imagination is not sense is clear from the following considerations: (1) Sense is either a faculty or an activity, e.g. sight or seeing: imagination takes place in the absence of both, as e.g. in dreams. (2) Again, sense is always present, imagination not. If actual imagination and actual sensation were the same, imagination would be found in all the brutes: this is held not to be the case; e.g. it is not found in ants or bees or grubs. (3) Again, sensations are always true, imaginations are for the most part false. (4) Once more, even in ordinary speech, we do not, when sense functions precisely with regard to its object, say that we imagine it to be a man, but rather when there is some failure of accuracy in its exercise. And (5), as we were saying before, visions appear to us even when our eyes are shut. Neither is imagination *any* of the things that are never in error: e.g. knowledge or intelligence; for imagination may be false.

It remains therefore to see if it is opinion, for opinion may be either true or false.

But opinion involves belief (for without belief in what we opine we cannot have an opinion), and in the brutes though we often find imagination we never find belief. Further, every opinion is accompanied by belief, belief by conviction, and conviction by discourse of reason: while there are some of the brutes in which we find imagination, without discourse of reason. It is clear then that imagination cannot, again, be (1) opinion *plus* sensation, or (2) opinion mediated by sensation, or (3) a blend of opinion and sensation; this is impossible both for these reasons and because the content of the supposed opinion cannot be different from that of the sensation (I mean that imagination must be the blending of the perception of white with the opinion that it is white: it could scarcely be a blend of the opinion that it is good with the perception that it is white): to imagine is therefore (on this view) identical with the thinking of exactly the same as what one in the strictest sense perceives. But what we imagine is sometimes false though our contemporaneous judgement about it is true; e.g. we imagine the sun to be a foot in diameter though we are convinced that it is larger than the inhabited part of the earth, and the following dilemma presents itself. Either (*a*) while the fact has not changed and the observer has neither forgotten nor lost belief in the true opinion which he had, that opinion has disappeared, or (*b*) if he retains it then his opinion is at once true and false. A true opinion, however, becomes false only when the fact alters without being noticed.

Imagination is therefore neither any one of the states enumerated, nor compounded out of them.

But since when one thing has been set in motion another thing may be moved by it, and imagination is held to be a movement and to be impossible without sensation, i.e. to occur in beings that are percipient and to have for its content what can be perceived, and since movement may be produced by actual sensation and that movement is necessarily similar in character to the sensation itself, this movement must be (1) necessarily (*a*) incapable of existing apart from sensation, (*b*) incapable of existing except when we perceive, (2) such that in virtue of its possession that in which it is found may present various phenomena both active and passive, and (3) such that it may be either true or false.

The reason of the last characteristic is as follows. Perception (1) of the special objects of sense is never in error or admits the least possible amount of falsehood. (2) That of the concomitance of the objects concomitant with the sensible qualities comes next: in this case certainly we may be deceived; for while the perception that there is white before us cannot be false, the perception that what is white is this or that may be false. (3) Third comes the perception of the universal attributes which accompany the concomitant objects to which the special sensibles attach (I mean e.g. of movement and magnitude); it is in respect of these that the greatest amount of sense-illusion is possible.

The motion which is due to the activity of sense in these three modes of its exercise will differ from the activity of sense; (1) the first kind of derived motion is free from error while the sensation is present; (2) and (3) the others may be erroneous whether it is present or absent, especially when the object of perception is far off. If then imagination presents no other features than those enumerated and is what we have described, then imagination must be a movement resulting from an actual exercise of a power of sense.

As sight is the most highly developed sense, the name *phantasia* (imagination) has been formed from *phaos* (light) because it is not possible to see without light.

And because imaginations remain in the organs of sense and resemble sensations, animals in their actions are largely guided by them, some (i.e. the brutes) because of the non-existence in them of mind, others (i.e. men) because of the temporary eclipse in them of mind by feeling or disease or sleep.

About imagination, what it is and why it exists, let so much suffice.

Turning now to the part of the soul with which the soul knows and thinks (whether this is separable from the others in definition only, or spatially as well) we have to inquire (1) what differentiates this part, and (2) how thinking can take place.

If thinking is like perceiving, it must be either a process in which the soul is acted upon by what is capable of being thought, or a process different from but analogous to that. The thinking part of the soul must therefore be, while impassible, capable of receiving the form of an object; that is, must be potentially identical in character with its object without being the object. Mind must be related to what is thinkable, as sense is to what is sensible.

Therefore, since everything is a possible object of thought, mind in order, as Anaxagoras says, to dominate, that is, to know, must be pure from all admixture; for the co-presence of what is alien to its nature is a hindrance and a block: it follows that it too, like the sensitive part, can have no nature of its own, other than that of having a cer-

tain capacity. Thus that in the soul which is called mind (by mind I mean that whereby the soul thinks and judges) is, before it thinks, not actually any real thing. For this reason it cannot reasonably be regarded as blended with the body: if so, it would acquire some quality, e.g. warmth or cold, or even have an organ like the sensitive faculty: as it is, it has none. It was a good idea to call the soul "the place of forms," though (1) this description holds only of the intellective soul, and (2) even this is the forms only potentially, not actually.

Observation of the sense-organs and their employment reveals a distinction between the impassibility of the sensitive and that of the intellective faculty. After strong stimulation of a sense we are less able to exercise it than before, as e.g. in the case of a loud sound we cannot hear easily immediately after, or in the case of a bright colour or a powerful odour we cannot see or smell, but in the case of mind, thought about an object that is highly intelligible renders it more and not less able afterwards to think objects that are less intelligible: the reason is that while the faculty of sensation is dependent upon the body, mind is separable from it.

Once the mind has become each set of its possible objects, as a man of science has, when this phrase is used of one who is actually a man of science (this happens when he is now able to exercise the power on his own initiative), its condition is still one of potentiality, but in a different sense from the potentiality which preceded the acquisition of knowledge by learning or discovery: the mind too is then able to think *itself*.

Since we can distinguish between a spatial magnitude and what it is to be such, and between water and what it is to be water, and so in many other cases (though not in all; for in certain cases the thing and its form are identical), flesh and what it is to be flesh are discriminated either by different faculties, or by the same faculty in two different states: for flesh necessarily involves matter and is like what is snub-nosed, a *this* in a *this*. Now it is by means of the sensitive faculty that we discriminate the hot and the cold, i.e. the factors which combined in a certain ratio constitute flesh: the essential character of flesh is apprehended by something different either wholly separate from the sensitive faculty or related to it as a bent line to the same line when it has been straightened out.

Again in the case of abstract objects what is straight is analogous to what is snub-nosed; for it necessarily implies a continuum as its matter: its constitutive essence is different, if we may distinguish between straightness and what is straight: let us take it to be two-ness. It must be apprehended, therefore, by a different power or by the same power in a different state. To sum up, in so far as the realities it knows are capable of being separated from their matter, so it is also with the powers of mind.

The problem might be suggested: if thinking is a passive affection, then if mind is simple and impassible and has nothing in common with anything else, as Anaxagoras says, how can it come to think at all? For interaction between two factors is held to require a precedent community of nature between the factors. Again it might be asked, is mind a possible object of thought to itself? For if mind is thinkable *per se* and what is thinkable is in kind one and the same, then either (*a*) mind will belong to everything, or (*b*) mind will contain some element common to it with all other realities which makes them all thinkable.

(1) Have not we already disposed of the difficulty about interaction involving a common element, when we said that mind is in a sense potentially whatever is thinkable, though actually it is nothing until it has thought? What it thinks must be in it just as characters may be said to be on a writing-tablet on which as yet nothing actually stands written: this is exactly what happens with mind.

(2) Mind is itself thinkable in exactly the same way as its objects are. For (*a*) in the case of objects which involve no matter, what thinks and what is thought are identical; for speculative knowledge and its object are identical. (Why mind is not always

thinking we must consider later.) (*b*) In the case of those which contain matter each of the objects of thought is only potentially present. It follows that while *they* will not have mind in them (for mind is a potentiality of them only in so far as they are capable of being disengaged from matter) mind may yet be thinkable.

Since in every class of things, as in nature as a whole, we find two factors involved, (1) a matter which is potentially all the particulars included in the class, (2) a cause which is productive in the sense that it makes them all (the latter standing to the former, as e.g. an art to its material), these distinct elements must likewise be found within the soul.

And in fact mind as we have described it is what it is by virtue of becoming all things, while there is another which is what it is by virtue of making all things: this is a sort of positive state like light; for in a sense light makes potential colours into actual colours.

Mind in this sense of it is separable, impassible, unmixed, since it is in its essential nature activity (for always the active is superior to the passive factor, the originating force to the matter which it forms).

Actual knowledge is identical with its object: in the individual, potential knowledge is in time prior to actual knowledge, but in the universe as a whole it is not prior even in time. Mind is not at one time knowing and at another not. When mind is set free from its present conditions it appears as just what it is and nothing more: this alone is immortal and eternal (we do not, however, remember its former activity because, while mind in this sense is impassible, mind as passive is destructible), and without it nothing thinks.

The thinking then of the simple objects of thought is found in those cases where falsehood is impossible: where the alternative of true or false applies, there we always find a putting together of objects of thought in a quasi-unity. As Empedocles said that "where heads of many a creature sprouted without necks" they afterwards by Love's power were combined, so here too objects of thought which were given separate are combined, e.g. "incommensurate" and "diagonal": if the combination be of objects past or future the combination of thought includes in its content the date. For falsehood always involves a synthesis; for even if you assert that what is white is not white you have included not-white in a synthesis. It is possible also to call all these cases division as well as combination. However that may be, there is not only the true or false assertion that Cleon is white but also the true or false assertion that he *was* or *will be* white. In each and every case that which unifies is mind.

Since the word "simple" has two senses, i.e. may mean either (a) "not capable of being divided" or (b) "not actually divided," there is nothing to prevent mind from knowing what is undivided, e.g. when it apprehends a length (which is actually undivided) and that in an undivided time; for the time is divided or undivided in the same manner as the line. It is not possible, then, to tell what part of the line it was apprehending in each half of the time: the object has no actual parts until it has been divided: if in thought you think each half separately, then by the same act you divide the time also, the half-lines becoming as it were new wholes of length. But if you think it as a whole consisting of these two possible parts, then also you think it in a time which corresponds to both parts together. (But what is not quantitatively but qualitatively simple is thought in a simple time and by a simple act of the soul.)

But that which mind thinks and the time in which it thinks are in this case divisible only incidentally and not as such. For in them too there is something indivisible (though, it may be, not isolable) which gives unity to the time and the whole of length; and this is found equally in every continuum whether temporal or spatial.

Points and similar instances of things that divide, themselves being indivisible, are realized in consciousness in the same manner as privations.

A similar account may be given of all other cases, e.g. how evil or black is cognized; they are cognized, in a sense, by means of their contraries. That which cognizes must have an element of potentiality in its being, and one of the contraries must be in it. But if there is anything that has no contrary, then it knows itself and is actually and possesses independent existence.

Assertion is the saying of something concerning something, e.g. affirmation, and is in every case either true or false: this is not always the case with mind: the thinking of the definition in the sense of the constitutive essence is never in error nor is it the assertion of something concerning something, but, just as while the seeing of the special object of sight can never be in error, the belief that the white object seen is a man may be mistaken, so too in the case of objects which are without matter.

Actual knowledge is identical with its object: potential knowledge in the individual is in time prior to actual knowledge but in the universe it has no priority even in time; for all things that come into being arise from what actually is. In the case of sense clearly the sensitive faculty already was potentially what the object makes it to be actually; the faculty is not affected or altered. This must therefore be a different kind from movement; for movement is, as we saw, an activity of what is imperfect, activity in the unqualified sense, i.e. that of what has been perfected, is different from movement.

To perceive then is like bare asserting or knowing; but when the object is pleasant or painful, the soul makes a quasi-affirmation or negation, and pursues or avoids the object. To feel pleasure or pain is to act with the sensitive mean towards what is good or bad as such. Both avoidance and appetite when actual are identical with this: the faculty of appetite and avoidance are not different, either from one another or from the faculty of sense-perception; but their being *is* different.

To the thinking soul images serve as if they were contents of perception (and when it asserts or denies them to be good or bad it avoids or pursues them). That is why the soul never thinks without an image. The process is like that in which the air modifies the pupil in this or that way and the pupil transmits the modification to some third thing (and similarly in hearing), while the ultimate point of arrival is one, a single mean, with different manners of being.

With what part of itself the soul discriminates sweet from hot I have explained before and must now describe again as follows: That with which it does so is a sort of unity, but in the way just mentioned, i.e. as a connecting term. And the two faculties it connects, being one by analogy and numerically, are each to each as the qualities discerned are to one another (for what difference does it make whether we raise the problem of discrimination between disparates or between contraries, e.g. white and black?). Let then C be to D as A is to B: it follows *alternando* that $C:A::D:B$. If then C and D belong to one subject, the case will be the same with them as with A and B; A and B form a single identity with different modes of being; so too will the former pair. The same reasoning holds if A be sweet and B white.

The faculty of thinking then thinks the forms in the images, and as in the former case what is to be pursued or avoided is marked out for it, so where there is no sensation and it is engaged upon the images it is moved to pursuit or avoidance. E.g. perceiving by sense that the beacon is fire, it recognizes in virtue of the general faculty of sense that it signifies an enemy, because it sees it moving; but sometimes by means of the images or thoughts which are within the soul, just as if it were seeing, it calculates and deliberates what is to come by reference to what is present; and when it makes a pronouncement, as in the case of sensation it pronounces the object to be pleasant or painful, in this case it avoids or pursues; and so generally in cases of action.

That too which involves no action, i.e. that which is true or false, is in the same province with what is good or bad: yet they differ in this, that the one set imply and the other do not a reference to a particular person.

The so-called abstract objects the mind thinks just as, if one had thought of the snub-nosed not as snub-nosed but as hollow, one would have thought of an actuality without the flesh in which it is embodied: it is thus that the mind when it is thinking the objects of Mathematics thinks as separate, elements which do not exist separate. In every case the mind which is actively thinking is the objects which it thinks. Whether it is possible for it while not existing separate from spatial conditions to think anything that is separate, or not, we must consider later.

Let us now summarize our results about soul, and repeat that the soul is in a way all existing things; for existing things are either sensible or thinkable, and knowledge is in a way what is knowable, and sensation is in a way what is sensible: in *what* way we must inquire.

Knowledge and sensation are divided to correspond with the realities, potential knowledge and sensation answering to potentialities, actual knowledge and sensation to actualities. Within the soul the faculties of knowledge and sensation are *potentially* these objects, the one what is knowable, the other what is sensible. They must be either the things themselves or their forms. The former alternative is of course impossible: it is not the stone which is present in the soul but its form.

It follows that the soul is analogous to the hand; for as the hand is a tool of tools, so the mind is the form of forms and sense the form of sensible things.

Since according to common agreement there is nothing outside and separate in existence from sensible spatial magnitudes, the objects of thought are in the sensible forms, viz. both the abstract objects and all the states and affections of sensible things. Hence (1) no one can learn or understand anything in the absence of sense, and (2) when the mind is actively aware of anything it is necessarily aware of it along with an image; for images are like sensuous contents except in that they contain no matter.

Imagination is different from assertion and denial; for what is true or false involves a synthesis of concepts. In what will the primary concepts differ from images? Must we not say that neither these nor even our other concepts are images, though they necessarily involve them?

The soul of animals is characterized by two faculties, (a) the faculty of discrimination which is the work of thought and sense, and (b) the faculty of originating local movement. Sense and mind we have now sufficiently examined. Let us next consider what it is in the soul which originates movement. Is it a single part of the soul separate either spatially or in definition? Or is it the soul as a whole? If it is a part, is that part different from those usually distinguished or already mentioned by us, or is it one of them? The problem at once presents itself, in what sense we are to speak of parts of the soul, or how many we should distinguish. For in a sense there is an infinity of parts: it is not enough to distinguish, with some thinkers, the calculative, the passionate, and the desiderative, or with others the rational and the irrational; for if we take the dividing lines followed by these thinkers we shall find parts far more distinctly separated from one another than these, namely those we have just mentioned: (1) the nutritive, which belongs both to plants and to all animals, and (2) the sensitive, which cannot easily be classed as either irrational or rational; further (3) the imaginative, which is, in its being, different from all, while it is very hard to say with which of the others it is the same or not the same, supposing we determine to posit *separate* parts in the soul; and lastly (4) the appetitive, which would seem to be distinct both in definition and in power from all hitherto enumerated.

It is absurd to break up the last-mentioned faculty: as these thinkers do, for wish is found in the calculative part and desire and passion in the irrational; and if the soul is tripartite appetite will be found in all three parts. Turning our attention to the present object of discussion, let us ask what that is which originates local movement of the animal.

The movement of growth and decay, being found in all living things, must be attributed to the faculty of reproduction and nutrition, which is common to all: inspiration and expiration, sleep and waking, we must consider later: these too present much difficulty: at present we must consider local movement, asking what it is that originates forward movement in the animal.

That it is not the nutritive faculty is obvious; for this kind of movement is always for an end and is accompanied either by imagination or by appetite; for no animal moves except by compulsion unless it has an impulse towards or away from an object. Further, if it were the nutritive faculty, even plants would have been capable of originating such movement and would have possessed the organs necessary to carry it out. Similarly it cannot be the sensitive faculty either; for there are many animals which have sensibility but remain fast and immovable throughout their lives.

If then Nature never makes anything without a purpose and never leaves out what is necessary (except in the case of mutilated or imperfect growths; and that here we have neither mutilation nor imperfection may be argued from the facts that such animals (a) can reproduce their species and (b) rise to completeness of nature and decay to an end), it follows that, had they been capable of originating forward movement, they would have possessed the organs necessary for that purpose. Further, neither can the calculative faculty or what is called "mind" be the cause of such movement; for mind as speculative never thinks what is practicable, it never says anything about an object to be avoided or pursued, while this movement is always in something which is avoiding or pursuing an object. No, not even when it is aware of such an object does it at once enjoin pursuit or avoidance of it; e.g. the mind often thinks of something terrifying or pleasant without enjoining the emotion of fear. It is the heart that is moved (or in the case of a pleasant object some other part). Further, even when the mind does command and thought bids us pursue or avoid something, sometimes no movement is produced; we act in accordance with desire, as in the case of moral weakness. And, generally, we observe that the possessor of medical knowledge is not necessarily healing, which shows that something else is required to produce action in accordance with knowledge; the knowledge alone is not the cause. Lastly, appetite too is incompetent to account fully for movement; for those who successfully resist temptation have appetite and desire and yet follow mind and refuse to enact that for which they have appetite.

These two at all events appear to be sources of movement: appetite and mind (if one may venture to regard imagination as a kind of thinking; for many men follow their imaginations contrary to knowledge, and in all animals other than man there is no thinking or calculation but only imagination).

Both of these then are capable of originating local movement, mind and appetite: (1) mind, that is, which calculates means to an end, i.e. mind practical (it differs from mind speculative in the character of its end); while (2) appetite is in every form of it relative to an end: for that which is the object of appetite is the stimulant of mind practical; and that which is last in the process of thinking is the beginning of the action. It follows that there is a justification for regarding these two as the sources of movement, i.e. appetite and practical thought; for the object of appetite starts a movement and as a result of that thought gives rise to movement, the object of appetite being to it a source of stimulation. So too when imagination originates movement, it necessarily involves appetite.

That which moves therefore is a single faculty and the faculty of appetite; for if there had been two sources of movement —mind and appetite—they would have produced movement in virtue of some common character. As it is, mind is never found producing movement without appetite (for wish is a form of appetite; and when movement is produced according to calculation it is also according to wish), but appetite can originate movement contrary to calculation, for desire is a form of appetite. Now mind is always right, but appetite and imagination may be either right or wrong. That is why, though in any case it is the object of appetite which originates movement, this object may be either the real or the apparent good. To produce movement the object must be more than this: it must be good that can be brought into being by action; and only what can be otherwise than as it is can thus be brought into being. That then such a power in the soul as has been described, i.e. that called appetite, originates movement is clear. Those who distinguish parts in the soul, if they distinguish and divide in accordance with differences of power, find themselves with a very large number of parts, a nutritive, a sensitive, an intellective, a deliberative, and now an appetitive part; for these are more different from one another than the faculties of desire and passion.

Since appetites run counter to one another, which happens when a principle of reason and a desire are contrary and is possible only in beings with a sense of time (for while mind bids us hold back because of what is future, desire is influenced by what is just at hand: a pleasant object which is just at hand presents itself as both pleasant and good, without condition in either case, because of want of foresight into what is farther away in time), it follows that while that which originates movement must be specifically one, viz. the faculty of appetite as such (or rather farthest back of all the object of that faculty; for it is it that itself remaining unmoved originates the movement by being apprehended in thought or imagination), the things that originate movement are numerically many.

All movement involves three factors, (1) that which originates the movement, (2) that by means of which it originates it, and (3) that which is moved. The expression "that which originates the movement" is ambiguous: it may mean either (*a*) something which itself is unmoved or (*b*) that which at once moves and is moved. Here that which moves without itself being moved is the realizable good, that which at once moves and is moved is the faculty of appetite (for that which is influenced by appetite so far as it is actually so influenced is set in movement, and appetite in the sense of actual appetite *is* a kind of movement), while that which is in motion is the animal. The instrument which appetite employs to produce movement is no longer psychical but bodily: hence the examination of it falls within the province of the functions common to body and soul. To state the matter summarily at present, that which is the instrument in the production of movement is to be found where a beginning and an end coincide as e.g. in a ball and socket joint; for there the convex and the concave sides are respectively an end and a beginning (that is why while the one remains at rest, the other is moved): they are separate in definition but not separable spatially. For everything is moved by pushing and pulling. Hence just as in the case of a wheel, so here there must be a point which remains at rest, and from that point the movement must originate.

To sum up, then, and repeat what I have said, inasmuch as an animal is capable of appetite it is capable of self-movement; it is not capable of appetite without possessing imagination; and all imagination is either (1) calculative or (2) sensitive. In the latter all animals, and not only man, partake.

Bibliography

Texts

The Oxford translation of the works of Aristotle is published in eleven volumes under the editorship of J. A. Smith and W. D. Ross.

The Basic Works of Aristotle. Edited by Richard McKeon. New York: Random House, Inc., 1941.

Studies

Ross, Sir W. C. *Aristotle,* 2d ed. London: Methuen & Co., Ltd., 1930.

————. *Aristotle's Metaphysica,* 2 vols. Oxford: Clarendon Press, 1924.

————. *Aristotle's Physics.* Oxford: Clarendon Press, 1936.

Taylor, A. E. *Aristotle.* New York: Thomas Nelson & Sons, 1943.

3

Introduction

Born in Tagaste in North Africa of a pagan nobleman and of a Christian mother, Aurelius Augustine pursued a worldly student life in Carthage, till his studies in rhetoric brought him in touch with a book of Cicero's entitled *Hortensius*. This work turned his mind to philosophy and to a search for truth which brought him to a new view of life. He gave up Manichaeism and fell into the ambivalence of scepticism.

In Rome Augustine lectured on rhetoric. When he went to Milan, he became acquainted with Plato's works and learned of the world of the spirit. Through the discourses of Ambrose he came into contact with Christianity. In 386 he began a year of retirement during which he thought through the whole new world of ideas which he had recently encountered. He then wrote his *Confessions,* underwent a radical conversion, and allowed himself to be baptized a Christian by Ambrose in 387. A year later Augustine returned to Tagaste and began writing on Manichaeism. He was ordained a priest in 391 and made coadjutor bishop of Hippo in 395.

His writings in philosophy and theology are one of the most fruitful testimonies to the spirit of man in Western philosophy. He was, in the opinion of experts, not only the acme of his own patristic times but perhaps of all Christian philosophy.

Augustine was a prolific writer in both theology and philosophy. His works (exclusive of letters) amount to ninety-three and are divided into 232 books. He wrote on dogmatic, apologetic, and exegetical topics in theology. In philosophy his most important works are *On the Beautiful and the Becoming, On the Happy Life, On the Immortality of the Soul, On the Quantity of the Soul,* and *On Free Choice.*

The philosophy of Augustine is primarily concerned with the existence and attributes of God, the question of creation, the qualities of the human soul and its relation to the body, moral goodness and its relation to happiness, and social order and the philosophy of the world's history. In many of his expositions Augustine followed Plato and Aristotle, though always from a Christian viewpoint. His philosophy is *theocentric.* In God are contained the *rationes aeternae* or exemplars, patterns of created natures. To know God is to know His creation. Human ideas come into being through the intellect's ability to abstract from sensations. And the knowledge of God illuminates the human mind in its knowing which is both natural intellect and faith.

The doctrine of the *rationes seminales* of Augustine holds that brute matter is endowed with a germ or seed force whereby it develops into a determined species. All such species are inseminated from the beginning in matter. Hence, a doctrine of transformation or of evolution in the sense that one species develops into another cannot be predicated of Augustine's position.

The Christian doctrine of the hereditary transmission of original sin perplexed Augustine so much that some historians claim Augustine preferred the doctrine of *traducianism* to *creationism.* Creationism holds that God infuses each individual soul directly, whereas traducianism explains the origin of the human soul as a derivation from the souls of the parents, somewhat as one candle is ignited from another without diminishing the flame of the original candle. Augustine admitted he was perplexed over the origin of the human soul. His traducianist theory has been attacked by many as incompatible with the simplicity and immateriality of the soul for which he argued. Aristotelian Christian philosophers have called Augustine's views on the union of soul and body Platonic and unacceptable in terms of the unity of the human composite. Certainly the outstanding Christian philosopher of patristic times, Augustine may be the outstanding Christian philosopher of all times. In the following passages from the *Confessions* the humane qualities of his person as well as the mind of the philosopher become apparent as he treats of his existential encounter with his own human nature in dialogue with God, its source.

THE ORIGIN OF EVIL AND FREEDOM *

But I also, as yet, although I said and was firmly persuaded, that Thou our Lord, the true God, who madest not only our souls but our bodies, and not our souls and bodies alone, but all creatures and all things, wert uncontaminable and inconvertible, and in no part mutable; yet understood I not readily and clearly what was the cause of evil. And yet, whatever it was, I perceived that it must be so sought out as not to constrain me by it to believe that the immutable God was mutable, lest I myself should become the thing that I was seeking out. I sought, therefore, for it free from care, certain of the untruthfulness of what these asserted, whom I shunned with my whole heart; for I perceived that through seeking after the origin of evil, they were filled with malice, in that they liked better to think that Thy Substance did suffer evil than that their own did commit it.

And I directed my attention to discern what I now heard, that free will was the cause of our doing evil, and Thy righteous judgment of our suffering it. But I was unable clearly to discern it. So, then, trying to draw the eye of my mind from that pit, I was plunged again therein, and trying often, was as often plunged back again. But this raised me towards Thy light, that I knew as well that I had a will as that I had life: when, therefore, I was willing or unwilling to do anything, I was most certain that it was none

but myself that was willing and unwilling; and immediately I perceived that there was the cause of my sin. But what I did against my will I saw that I suffered rather than did, and that I judged not to be my fault, but my punishment; whereby, believing Thee to be most just, I quickly confessed myself to be not unjustly punished. But again I said: "Who made me? Was it not my God, who is not only good, but goodness itself? Whence came I then to will to do evil, and to be unwilling to do good, that there might be cause for my just punishment? Who was it that put this in me, and implanted in me the root of bitterness, seeing I was altogether made by my most sweet God? If the devil were the author, whence is that devil? And if he also, by his own perverse will, of a good angel became a devil, whence also was the evil will in him whereby he became a devil, seeing that the angel was made altogether good by that most good Creator? By these reflections was I again cast down and stifled; yet not plunged into that hell of error (where no man confesseth unto Thee), to think that Thou dost suffer evil, rather than that man doth it. . . .

And what is this? I asked the earth; and it answered, "I am not He"; and whatsoever are therein made the same confession. I asked the sea and the deeps, and the creeping things that lived, and they replied, "We are not thy God, seek higher than we." I asked the breezy air, and the universal air with its inhabitants answered, "Anaximenes was deceived, I am not God." I asked the heavens, the sun, moon, and stars: "Neither," say

*From Saint Augustine, "The Confessions," in *Basic Writings of Saint Augustine*. Edited by Whitney J. Oates. Copyright 1948 by Random House, Inc., New York. Reprinted by permission of Random House, Inc., New York, and T. & T. Clark, Edinburgh, Scotland.

they, "are we the God whom thou seekest." And I answered unto all these things which stand about the door of my flesh, "Ye have told me concerning my God, that ye are not He; tell me something about Him." And with a loud voice they exclaimed, "He made us." My questioning was my observing of them; and their beauty was their reply. And I directed my thoughts to myself, and said, "Who art thou?" And I answered, "A man." And lo, in me there appear both body and soul, the one without, the other within. By which of these should I seek my God, whom I had sought through the body from earth to heaven, as far as I was able to send messengers—the beams of mine eyes? But the better part is that which is inner; for to it, as both president and judge, did all my corporeal messengers render the answers of heaven and earth and all things therein, who said, "We are not God, but He made us." These things my inner man knew by the ministry of the outer; I, the inner man, knew all this—I, the soul, through the senses of my body. I asked the vast bulk of the earth of my God, and it answered me, "I am not He, but He made me."

Is not this beauty visible to all whose senses are unimpaired? Why then doth it not speak the same things unto all? Animals, the very small and the great, see it, but they are unable to question it, because their senses are not endowed with reason to enable them to judge on what they report. But men can question it, so that the invisible things of Him . . . are clearly seen, being understood by the things that are made; but by loving them, they are brought into subjection to them; and subjects are not able to judge. Neither do the creatures reply to such as question them, unless they can judge; nor will they alter their voice (that is, their beauty), if so be one man only sees, another both sees and questions, so as to appear one way to this man, and another to that; but appearing the same way to both, it is mute to this, it speaks to that—nay, rather it speaks to all; but they only understand it who compare that voice received from without with the truth within. For the truth declareth unto me, "Neither heaven, nor earth, nor any body is thy God." This, their nature declareth unto him that beholdeth them. "They are a mass; a mass is less in part than in the whole." Now, O my soul, thou art my better part, unto thee I speak; for thou animatest the mass of thy body, giving it life, which no body furnishes to a body; but thy God is even unto thee the Life of life.

What then is that I love when I love my God? Who is He that is above the head of my soul? By my soul itself will I mount up unto Him. I will soar beyond that power of mine whereby I cling to the body, and fill the whole structure of it with life. Not by that power do I find my God; for then the horse and the mule, which have no understanding, might find Him, since it is the same power by which their bodies also live. But there is another power, not that only by which I quicken, but that also by which I endow with sense my flesh, which the Lord hath made for me; bidding the eye not to hear, and the ear not to see; but that, for me to see by, and this, for me to hear by; and to each of the other senses its own proper seat and office, which being different, I, the single mind, do through them govern. I will soar also beyond this power of mine; for this the horse and mule possess, for they too discern through the body.

MEMORY

I will soar, then, beyond this power of my nature also, ascending by degrees unto Him who made me. And I enter the fields and roomy chambers of memory, where are the treasures of countless images, imported into it from all manner of things by the senses. There is treasured up whatsoever likewise we think, either by enlarging or diminishing, or by varying in any way whatever those things which the sense hath arrived at; and whatever else hath been entrusted to it and stored up, which oblivion hath not yet engulfed and buried. When I am in this storehouse, I demand that what I wish should be brought forth, and some things immediately appear; others require to be longer sought after, and are dragged, as it were, out of some hidden receptacle; others, again, hurry forth in crowds, and while another thing is sought and inquired for, they leap into view, as if to say, "Is it not we, perchance?" These I drive away with the hand of my heart from before the face of my remembrance, until what I wish be discovered making its appearance out of its secret cell. Other things suggest themselves without effort, and in continuous order, just as they are called for—those in front giving place to those that follow, and in giving place are treasured up again to be forthcoming when I wish it. All of which takes place when I repeat a thing from memory.

All these things, each of which entered by its own avenue, are distinctly and under general heads there laid up: as, for example, light, and all colors and forms of bodies, by the eyes; sounds of all kinds by the ears; all smells by the passage of the nostrils; all flavors by that of the mouth; and by the sensation of the whole body is brought in what is hard or soft, hot or cold, smooth or rough, heavy or light, whether external or internal to the body. All these does that great receptacle of memory, with its many and indescribable departments, receive, to be recalled and brought forth when required; each, entering by its own door, is laid up in it. And yet the things themselves do not enter it, but only the images of the things perceived are there ready at hand for thought to recall. And who can tell how these images are formed, notwithstanding that it is evident by which of the senses each has been fetched in and treasured up? For even while I live in darkness and silence, I can bring out colors in memory if I wish, and discern between black and white, and what others I wish; nor yet do sounds break in and disturb what is drawn in by mine eyes, and which I am considering, seeing that they also are there, and are concealed—laid up, as it were, apart. For these too I can summon if I please, and immediately they appear. And though my tongue be at rest, and my throat silent, yet can I sing as much as I will; and those images of colors, which notwithstanding are there, do not interpose themselves and interrupt when another treasure is under consideration which flowed in through the ears. So the remaining things carried in and heaped up by the other senses, I recall at my pleasure. And I discern the scent of lilies from that of violets while smelling nothing; and I prefer honey to grape-syrup, a smooth thing to a rough, though then I neither taste nor handle, but only remember.

These things I do within, in that vast chamber of my memory. For there are nigh me heaven, earth, sea, and whatever I can think upon in them, besides those which I have forgotten. There also do I meet with myself, and recall myself—what, when, or where I did a thing, and how I was affected when I did it. There are all which I remember, either by personal experience or on the faith of others. Out of the same supply do I myself with the past construct now this, now that likeness of things, which either I have experienced, or, from having experienced, have believed; and thence again future actions, events, and hopes, and upon all these again do I meditate as if they were present. "I will do this or that," I say to myself in that vast womb of my mind, filled with the images of things so many and so great, "and this or that shall follow upon it." "Oh that this or that might come to pass!" "God avert this or that!" Thus I speak to myself; and when I speak, the images of all I speak about are present, out of the same treasury of memory; nor could I say anything at all about them were the images absent.

Great is this power of memory, exceeding great, O my God—an inner chamber large and boundless! Who has plumbed its depths? Yet it is a power of mine, and appertains unto my nature; nor do I myself grasp all that I am. Therefore is the mind too narrow to contain itself. And where should that be which it does not contain of itself? Is it outside and not in itself? How is it, then, that it does not grasp itself? A great admiration rises upon me; astonishment seizes me. And men go forth to wonder at the heights of mountains, the huge waves of the sea, the broad flow of the rivers, the extent of the ocean, and the courses of the stars, and omit to wonder at themselves; nor do they marvel that when I spoke of all these things, I was not looking on them with my eyes, and yet could not speak of them unless those mountains, and waves, and rivers, and stars which I saw, and that ocean which I believe in, I saw inwardly in my memory, and with the same vast spaces between as when I saw them abroad. But I did not by seeing appropriate them when I looked on them with my eyes; nor are the things themselves with me, but their images. And I knew by what corporeal sense each made impression on me.

And yet are not these all that the illimitable capacity of my memory retains. Here also is all that is apprehended of the liberal sciences, and not yet forgotten—removed as it were into an inner place, which is not a place; nor are they the images which are retained, but the things themselves. For what is literature, what skill in disputation, whatsoever I know of all the many kinds of questions there are, is so in my memory, that I have not taken in the image and left the thing without, or that it should have sounded and passed away like a voice imprinted on the ear by that trace, whereby it might be recorded, as though it sounded when it no longer did so; or as an odor while it passes away, and vanishes into wind, affects the sense of smell, whence it conveys the image of itself into the memory, which we realize in recollecting; or like food, which assuredly in the belly has now no taste, and yet has a kind of taste in the memory, or like anything that is by touching felt by the body, and which even when removed from us is imagined by the memory. For these things themselves are not put into it, but the images of them only are caught up, with a marvellous quickness, and laid up, as it were, in most

wonderful cabinets, and wonderfully brought forth when we remember.

But truly when I hear that there are three kinds of questions, "Whether a thing is—what it is—of what kind it is?" I do indeed hold fast the images of the sounds of which these words are composed, and I know that those sounds passed through the air with a noise, and now are not. But the things themselves which are signified by these sounds I never arrived at by any sense of the body, nor ever perceived them otherwise than by my mind; and in my memory have I laid up not their images, but themselves, which, how they entered into me, let them tell if they are able. For I examine all the gates of my flesh, but find not by which of them they entered. For the eyes say, "If they were colored, we announced them." The ears say, "If they sounded, we gave notice of them." The nostrils say, "If they smell, they passed in by us." The sense of taste says, "If they have no flavor, ask not me." The touch says, "If it have not body, I handled it not, and if I never handled it, I gave no notice of it." Whence and how did these things enter into my memory? I know not how. For when I learned them, I gave not credit to the heart of another man, but perceived them in my own; and I approved them as true, and committed them to it, laying them up, as it were, whence I might fetch them when I willed. There, then, they were, even before I learned them, but were not in my memory. Where were they, then, or wherefore, when they were spoken, did I acknowledge them, and say, "So it is, it is true," unless as being already in the memory, though so put back and concealed, as it were, in more secret caverns, that had they not been drawn forth by the advice of another I would not, perchance, have been able to conceive of them?

Wherefore we find that to learn these things, whose images we drink not in by our senses, but perceive within as they are by themselves, without images, is nothing else but by meditation as it were to concentrate, and by observing to take care that those notions which the memory did before contain scattered and confused, be laid up at hand, as it were, in that same memory, where before they lay concealed, scattered and neglected, and so the more easily present themselves to the mind well accustomed to observe them. And how many things of this sort does my memory retain which have been found out already, and, as I said, are, as it were, laid up ready to hand, which we are said to have learned and to have known; which, should we for small intervals of time cease to recall, they are again so submerged and slide back, as it were, into the more remote chambers, that they must be evolved thence again as if new (for other sphere they have none), and must be marshalled [co-genda] again that they may become known; that is to say, they must be collected [col-ligenda], as it were, from their dispersion; whence we have the word *cogitare*. For *cogo* [*I collect*] and *cogito* [*I re-collect*] have the same relation to each other as *ago* and *agito*, *facio* and *factito*. But the mind has appropriated to itself this word [cogitation], so that not that which is collected anywhere, but what is collected, that is marshalled, in the mind, is properly said to be cogitated.

The memory contains also the reasons and innumerable laws of numbers and dimensions, none of which has any sense of the body impressed, seeing they have neither color, nor sound, nor taste, nor smell, nor sense of touch. I have heard the sound of the words by which these things are signified when they are discussed; but the sounds are one thing, the things another. For the sounds are one thing in Greek, another in Latin; but the things themselves are neither Greek, nor Latin, nor any other language. I have seen the lines of the craftsmen, even the finest, like a spider's web; but these are of another kind, they are not the images of those which the eye of my flesh showed me; he knows them who, without any idea whatsoever of a body, perceives them within himself. I have also observed the numbers of the things with which we number all the senses of the body; but those by which we number are of another kind, nor are they the images of these, and therefore they certainly exist. Let him who sees not these things

mock me for saying them; and I will pity him, while he mocks me.

All these things I retain in my memory, and how I learnt them I retain. I retain also many things which I have heard most falsely objected against them, which though they be false, yet is it not false that I have remembered them; and I remember, too, that I have distinguished between those truths and these falsehoods uttered against them; and I now see that it is one thing to distinguish these things, another to remember that I often distinguished them, when I often reflected upon them. I both remember, then, that I have often understood these things, and what I now distinguish and comprehend I store away in my memory, that hereafter I may remember that I understood it now. Therefore also I remember that I have remembered; so that if afterwards I shall call to mind that I have been able to remember these things, it will be through the power of memory that I shall call it to mind.

This same memory contains also the affections of my mind; not in the manner in which the mind itself contains them when it suffers them, but very differently according to a power peculiar to memory. For without being joyous, I remember myself to have had joy; and without being sad, I call to mind my past sadness; and that of which I was once afraid, I remember without fear; and without desire recall a former desire. Again, on the contrary, I at times remember when joyous my past sadness, and when sad my joy. Which is not to be wondered at as regards the body; for the mind is one thing, the body another. If I, therefore, when happy, recall some past bodily pain, it is not so strange a thing. But now, as this very memory itself is mind (for when we give orders to have a thing kept in memory, we say, "See that you bear this in mind;" and when we forget a thing, we say, "It did not enter my mind," and, "It slipped from my mind," thus calling the memory itself mind), as this is so, how comes it to pass that when being joyful I remember my past sorrow, the mind has joy, the memory sorrow—the mind, from the joy that is in it, is joyful, yet the memory, from the sadness that is in it, is not sad? Does not the memory perchance belong to the mind? Who will say so? The memory doubtless is, so to say, the belly of the mind, and joy and sadness like sweet and bitter food, which, when entrusted to the memory, are, as it were, passed into the belly, where they can be reposited, but cannot taste. It is ridiculous to imagine these to be alike; and yet they are not utterly unlike.

But behold, out of my memory I educe it, when I affirm that there be four perturbations of the mind—desire, joy, fear, sorrow; and whatsoever I shall be able to dispute on these, by dividing each into its peculiar species, and by defining it, there I find what I may say, and thence I educe it; yet I am not disturbed by any of these perturbations when by remembering them I call them to mind; and before I recollected and reviewed them, they were there; wherefore by remembrance could they be brought thence. Perchance, then, even as meat is in ruminating brought up out of the belly, so by calling to mind are these educed from the memory. Why, then, does not the disputant, thus recollecting, perceive in the mouth of his meditation the sweetness of joy or the bitterness of sorrow? Is the comparison unlike in this because not like in all points? For who would willingly discourse on these subjects, if, as often as we name sorrow or fear, we should be compelled to be sorrowful or fearful? And yet we could never speak of them, did we not find in our memory not merely the sounds of the names according to the images imprinted on it by the senses of the body, but the notions of the things themselves, which we never received by any door of the flesh, but which the mind itself, recognising by the experience of its own passions, entrusted to the memory, or else which the memory itself retained without their being entrusted to it.

But whether by images or no, who can well affirm? For I name a stone, I name the sun, and the things themselves are not present to my senses, but their images are near to my memory. I name some pain of the body, yet it is not present when there is no pain; yet if its image were not in my memory, I should be ignorant what to say concerning it, nor in arguing be able to distinguish it from pleasure. I name bodily health when sound in body; the thing itself is indeed present with me, but unless its image also were in my memory, I could by no means call to mind what the sound of this name signified. Nor would sick people know, when health was named, what was said, unless the same image were retained by the power of memory, although the thing itself were absent from the body. I name numbers whereby we enumerate; and not their images, but they themselves are in my memory. I name the image of the sun, and this, too, is in my memory. For I do not recall the image of that image, but itself, for the image itself is present when I remember it. I name memory, and I know what I name. But where do I know it, except in the memory itself? Is it also present to itself by its image, and not by itself?

When I name forgetfulness, and know, too, what I name, whence should I know it if I did not remember it? I do not say the sound of the name, but the thing which it signifies; which, had I forgotten, I could not know what that sound signified. When, therefore, I remember memory, then is memory present with itself, through itself. But when I remember forgetfulness, there are present both memory and forgetfulness—memory, whereby I remember, forgetfulness, which I remember. But what is forgetfulness but the privation of memory? How, then, is that present for me to remember, since when it is so, I cannot remember? But if what we remember we retain in memory, yet, unless we remembered forgetfulness, we could never at the hearing of the name know the thing meant by it, then is forgetfulness retained by memory. Present, therefore, it is, lest we should forget it; and being so, we do forget. Is it to be inferred from this that forgetfulness when we remember it, is not present to the memory through itself, but through its image; because, were forgetfulness present through itself, it would not lead us to remember, but to forget? Who will now investigate this? Who shall understand how it is?

Bibliography

Texts

Confessions. Frank J. Sheed. London: Sheed & Ward Ltd., 1943.

Studies

Bardy, G. *Saint Augustine*, 6th ed. Paris: Desclée de Brouwer, 1946.

Bourke, Vernon J. *Augustine's Quest of Wisdom.* Milwaukee: The Bruce Publishing Company, 1945.

4

Introduction

Born of noble parentage at Roccasecca, Thomas Aquinas went to the monastery at Monte Cassino at the age of five. At fourteen, he went to Naples to take the quadrivium, where he became acquainted with Greek philosophy. At the age of twenty he entered the Dominican order. One year later he went to Paris, where he studied from 1248 till 1252. During this period he also studied in Cologne under Albert the Great. In 1256 he became a master at the University of Paris. After three years of teaching, he returned to Italy and lectured at the court of Pope Urban IV in Orvieto and thereafter at the court of Pope Clement IV in Viterbo. At this time Thomas became acquainted with another Dominican, Wilhelm von Moerbeke, who provided him with various Greek philosophical works (among them the works of Aristotle) translated into Latin. Thomas returned to Paris in 1269 and remained there till 1272. This was the high point of his academic career, a time marked by opposition from the secular clergy, which strongly felt that academic chairs should not be held by members of religious orders. He also fought the radical Aristotelianism of Siger of Brabant and Boethius of Dacien, as well as the opposition of the Franciscan school, particularly that of John Peckham. Latin Averroism, condemned by the Church, was confused with Thomas's Aristotelianism. Thereby Thomas was in discredit even with his own order. But he maintained his position with dignity and objectivity. Called by Pope Gregory X to the Council of Lyon, Thomas died on the way at Fossanuova. He is a master of clarity and synthesis in the scholastic tradition.

Thomas, like Augustine, distinguished himself by his theological writings as well as by his philosophical works. Many of his greatest philosophical contributions are found in works dedicated primarily to speculation on theological problems. He is the author of monumental synthetic works besides numerous lesser treatises; the following are the most worthy of recognition: *Commentaries* on the works of Aristotle, e.g., on the *Metaphysics,* on the *Soul,* on the *Sensible,* on the *Sensed,* on *Reminiscence; Commentaries on the Sentences of Peter Lombard; Summa Theologica; Summa Contra Gentiles; On Essence and Existence; Disputed Questions* (e.g., *On Truth* —two volumes, *On Potency, On Evil,* and *On the Soul*).

Some of the doctrines of Thomas were condemned between 1277 and 1286 by the Universities of Oxford and Paris and by members of the hierarchy, such as Archbishop Robert Kilwarby of Canterbury and his successor, Archbishop John Peckham, and were vigorously opposed by fellow Dominicans like Roland of Crimona, famous Franciscans like Peter Olivi, and renowned secular clergymen like Henry of Ghent. However, his teachings managed to survive and be recognized by many as meriting unique eminence in systematic scholasticism at its best.

Thomas owed some of his unpopularity to the fact that he opposed traditional doctrines, such as plurality of forms, the *rationes seminales,* and special divine illumination in the formation of spiritual ideas. In his voluminous and profound systematic works, Thomas remained basically Aristotelian, though he extended Aristotle on many points and clarified many issues which had been somewhat confused by the influence of certain Arabian commentaries and interpretative translations of Aristotle's works.

Thomas was most likely the first to present a clear, developed methodological distinction between the disciplines of theology and philosophy, based on the nature of their material and formal objects.

Thomas followed the moderate realism of Aristotle on the question of universals and further developed the theory of abstraction. The intelligibility of essences was "grasped" from sensory input by the agent intellect of each individual. Thereby Thomas explained the origin of ideas and at the same time rejected the Averroistic position of the one universal agent intellect which was assumed to operate on the sensory knowledge of each human individual in the production of ideas. Thomas further postulated three degrees of abstraction: physical (ideas plus sensory image), mathematical (quantity simply as intelligible), and metaphysical (ideas and principles predicable of all beings). Closely related to his theory of knowledge are his metaphysical contributions, e.g., the analogy of proportionality, the real distinction between the essence and existence of created things, and further developments in Aristotle's doctrines of act and potency and of matter and form. Thomas rejected the *rationes seminales* of Augustine and explained the multiplication of species with a theory largely based on Aristotle's concept of substantial form and limiting matter. The problem of the diversity of individuals within the same species he explained with an analysis of the quantification of matter.

On the human soul Thomas wrote much. Mainly, he held the soul to be the sole substantial principle of the fully formed body in its vegetative and sentient life. The same soul is also the principle of human, rational life. It is spiritual, simple, immortal, and wholly present to every part of the body it informs. The soul has faculties or proximate powers of operation: the locomotive, vegetative-nutritive, sensitive (cognitive and appetitive), and rational (intellect and will). The rational soul does not preexist the body but is created. Thus Thomas rejected traducianism (generationism) and held that the human soul is created when the human embryo has passed through various preparatory phases which dispose it for information by the rational soul. On the origin of life Thomas held that life comes only from living beings, though he maintained that some inferior forms of life, such as maggots, may have generated spontaneously, for example, from rotting matter. Thomas extended and harmonized Aristotle's *Ethics* with the doctrines of Christian revelation. His doctrine of *physical premotion* evoked centuries of debate on the question of how God moves man as the prime mover without destroying man's free will.

The following passages exemplify some of his thoughts on the philosophy of abstraction in human knowledge.

INTELLECTUAL KNOWLEDGE DERIVED FROM SENSIBLE THINGS (Q. 84, Art. 6) *

We proceed thus to the Sixth Article:—

Objection 1. It would seem that intellectual knowledge is not derived from sensible things. For Augustine says that *we cannot expect to acquire the pure truth from the senses of the body.* This he proves in two ways. First, because, *whatever the bodily*

* From Thomas Aquinas, "The Summa Theologica," in *Introduction to St. Thomas Aquinas.* Edited by Anton C. Pegis. Copyright 1948 by Random House, Inc., New York, reprinted by their permission. Reprinted also by permission of Burns & Oates Ltd., London.

senses reach is continually being changed: and what is never the same cannot be perceived. Secondly, because, *whatever we perceive by the body, even when not present to the senses, may be present in their images, as when we are asleep or angry; yet we cannot discern by the senses whether what we perceive be the sensible things themselves, or their deceptive images. Now nothing can be perceived which cannot be distinguished from its counterfeit.* And so he concludes that we cannot expect to learn the truth from the senses. But intellectual knowledge apprehends the truth. Therefore intellectual knowledge cannot be conveyed by the senses.

Obj. 2. Further, Augustine says: *We must not think that the body can make any impression on the spirit, as though the spirit were to subject itself like matter to the body's action; for that which acts is in every way more excellent than that which it acts on.* Whence he concludes that *the body does not cause its image in the spirit, but the spirit itself causes it in itself.* Therefore intellectual knowledge is not derived from sensible things.

Obj. 3. Further, an effect does not surpass the power of its cause. But intellectual knowledge extends beyond sensible things, for we understand some things which cannot be perceived by the senses. Therefore intellectual knowledge is not derived from sensible things.

On the contrary, The Philosopher proves that the origin of knowledge is from the senses.

I answer that, On this point the philosophers held three opinions. For Democritus held that *all knowledge is caused by images issuing from the bodies we think of and entering into our souls,* as Augustine says in his letter to Dioscorus. And Aristotle says that Democritus held that knowledge is caused by a *discharge of images.* And the reason for this opinion was that both Democritus and the other early philosophers did not distinguish between intellect and sense, as Aristotle relates. Consequently, since the sense is immuted by the sensible, they thought that all our knowledge is caused merely by an immutation from sensible things. This immutation Democritus held to be caused by a discharge of images.

Plato, on the other hand, held that the intellect differs from sense, and that it is an immaterial power not making use of a corporeal organ for its action. And since the incorporeal cannot be affected by the corporeal, he held that intellectual knowledge is not brought about by sensible things immuting the intellect, but by the participation in separate intelligible forms by the intellect, as we have said above. Moreover he held that sense is a power operating through itself. Consequently not even the sense itself, since it is a spiritual power, is affected by sensible things; but the sensible organs are affected by the sensible, with the result that the soul is in a way roused to form within itself the species of the sensible. Augustine seems to touch on this opinion where he says that the *body feels not, but the soul through the body, which it makes use of as a kind of messenger, for reproducing within itself what is announced from without.* Thus according to Plato, neither does intellectual knowledge proceed from sensible knowledge, nor does sensible knowledge itself come entirely from sensible things; but these rouse the sensible soul to sensation, and the senses likewise rouse the intellect to the act of understanding.

Aristotle chose a middle course. For with Plato he agreed that intellect and sense are different. But he held that the sense has not its proper operation without the cooperation of the body; so that *to sense is not an act of the soul alone,* but of the *composite.* And he held the same in regard to all the operations of the sensitive part. Since, therefore, it is not incongruous that the sensible things which are outside the soul should produce some effect in the *composite,* Aristotle agreed with Democritus in this, that the operations of the sensitive part are caused by the impression of the sensible on the sense; not indeed by a discharge, as Democritus said, but by some kind of operation. Democritus, it must be remembered, maintained that every action is by way of a discharge of atoms, as we gather from *De Gener.* i. But Aristotle held that the intellect has an operation in which the body does not share. Now nothing corporeal can make an impression on the incorporeal. And therefore, in order to cause the intellectual operation, according to Aristotle, the impression caused by sensible bodies does not suffice, but something more noble is required, *for the agent is more noble than the patient,* as he says. Not, be it observed, in the sense that the intellectual operation is effected in us by the mere impression of some superior beings, as Plato held; but that the higher and more noble agent which he calls the agent intellect, of which we have spoken above, causes the phantasms received from the senses to be actually intelligible, by a process of abstraction.

According to this opinion, then, on the part of the phantasms, intellectual knowledge is caused by the senses. But since the phantasms cannot of themselves immute the possible intellect, but require to be made actually intelligible by the agent intellect, it cannot be said that sensible knowledge is the total and perfect cause of intellectual knowledge, but rather is in a way the matter of the cause.

Reply Obj. 1.   These words of Augustine mean that truth is not entirely from the senses. For the light of the agent intellect is needed, through which we know the truth of changeable things unchangeably, and discern things themselves from their likeness.

Reply Obj. 2.   In this passage Augustine speaks not of intellectual but of imaginary knowledge. And since, according to the opinion of Plato, the imagination has an operation which belongs to the soul only, Augustine, in order to show that corporeal images are impressed on the imagination, not by bodies but by the soul, uses the same argument as Aristotle does in proving that the agent intellect must be separate, namely, because *the agent is more noble than the patient.* And without doubt, according to the above opinion, in the imagination there must needs be not only a passive but also an active power. But if we hold, according to the opinion of Aristotle, that the action of the imaginative power is an action of the *composite,* there is no difficulty; because the sensible body is more noble than the organ of the animal, in so far as it is compared to it as a being in act to a being in potentiality; even as the object actually colored is com-

pared to the pupil which is potentially colored. Now, although the first immutation of the imagination is through the agency of the sensible, since *the phantasm is a movement produced in accordance with sensation,* nevertheless, it may be said that there is in man an operation which by division and composition forms images of various things, even of things not perceived by the senses. And Augustine's words may be taken in this sense.

Reply Obj. 3.   Sensitive knowledge is not the entire cause of intellectual knowledge. And therefore it is not strange that intellectual knowledge should extend beyond sensitive knowledge.

Intelligible Species and the Phantasm (Q. 84, Art. 7)

We proceed thus to the Seventh Article:—

Objection 1.   It would seem that the intellect can understand actually through the intelligible species of which it is possessed, without turning to the phantasms. For the intellect is made actual by the intelligible species by which it is informed. But if the intellect is in act, it understands. Therefore the intelligible species suffices for the intellect to understand actually, without turning to the phantasms.

Obj. 2.   Further, the imagination is more dependent on the senses than the intellect on the imagination. But the imagination can actually imagine in the absence of the sensible. Therefore much more can the intellect understand without turning to the phantasms.

Obj. 3.   There are no phantasms of incorporeal things, for the imagination does not transcend time and space. If, therefore, our intellect cannot understand anything actually without turning to the phantasms, it follows that it cannot understand anything incorporeal. Which is clearly false, for we understand truth, and God, and the angels.

On the contrary, The Philosopher says

that *the soul understands nothing without a phantasm.*

I answer that, In the state of the present life, in which the soul is united to a corruptible body, it is impossible for our intellect to understand anything actually, except by turning to phantasms. And of this there are two indications. First of all because the intellect, being a power that does not make use of a corporeal organ, would in no way be hindered in its act through the lesion of a corporeal organ, if there were not required for its act the act of some power that does make use of a corporeal organ. Now sense, imagination and the other powers belonging to the sensitive part make use of a corporeal organ. Therefore it is clear that for the intellect to understand actually, not only when it acquires new knowledge, but also when it uses knowledge already acquired, there is need for the act of the imagination and of the other powers. For when the act of the imagination is hindered by a lesion of the corporeal organ, for instance, in a case of frenzy, or when the act of the memory is hindered, as in the case of lethargy, we see that a man is hindered from understanding actually even those things of which he had a previous knowledge. Secondly, anyone can experience this of himself, that when he tries to understand something, he forms certain phantasms to serve him by way of examples, in which as it were he examines what he is desirous of understanding. For this reason it is that when we wish to help someone to understand something, we lay examples before him, from which he can form phantasms for the purpose of understanding.

Now the reason for this is that the power of knowledge is proportioned to the thing known. Therefore the proper object of the angelic intellect, which is entirely separate from a body, is an intelligible substance separate from a body. Whereas the proper object of the human intellect, which is united to a body, is the quiddity or nature existing in corporeal matter; and it is through these natures of visible things that it rises to a certain knowledge of things invisible. Now it belongs to such a nature to exist in some individual, and this cannot be apart from corporeal matter; for instance, it belongs to the nature of a stone to be in an individual stone, and to the nature of a horse to be in an individual horse, and so forth. Therefore the nature of a stone or any material thing cannot be known completely and truly, except in as much as it is known as existing in the individual. Now we apprehend the individual through the sense and the imagination. And, therefore, for the intellect to understand actually its proper object, it must of necessity turn to the phantasms in order to perceive the universal nature existing in the individual. But if the proper object of our intellect were a separate form, or if, as the Platonists say, the natures of sensible things subsisted apart from the individual, there would be no need for the intellect to turn to the phantasms whenever it understands.

Reply Obj. 1.   The species preserved in the possible intellect exist there habitually when it does not understand them actually, as we have said above. Therefore for us to understand actually, the fact that the species are preserved does not suffice; we need further to make use of them in a manner befitting the things of which they are the species, which things are natures existing in individuals.

Reply Obj. 2.   Even the phantasm is the likeness of an individual thing; and so the imagination does not need any further likeness of the individual, whereas the intellect does.

Reply Obj. 3.   Incorporeal beings, of which there are no phantasms, are known to us by comparison with sensible bodies of which there are phantasms. Thus we understand truth by considering a thing in which we see the truth; and God, as Dionysius says, we know as cause, by way of excess and by way of remotion. Other incorporeal substances we know, in the state of the present life, only by way of remotion or by some comparison to corporeal things. Hence, when we understand something about these beings, we need to turn to the phantasms of bodies, although there are no phantasms of these beings themselves. . . .

Material Things Understood by Abstraction (Q. 85, Art. 1)

We proceed thus to the First Article:—

Objection 1. It would seem that our intellect does not understand corporeal and material things by abstraction from the phantasms. For the intellect is false if it understands a thing otherwise than as it is. Now the forms of material things do not exist in abstraction from the particular things represented by the phantasms. Therefore, if we understand material things by the abstraction of species from phantasms, there will be error in the intellect.

Obj. 2. Further, material things are those natural things which include matter in their definition. But nothing can be understood apart from that which enters into its definition. Therefore material things cannot be understood apart from matter. Now matter is the principle of individuation. Therefore material things cannot be understood by the abstraction of the universal from the particular; and this is to abstract intelligible species from the phantasm.

Obj. 3. Further, the Philosopher says that the phantasm is to the intellectual soul what color is to the sight. But seeing is not caused by abstraction of species from color, but by color impressing itself on the sight. Therefore neither does the act of understanding take place by the abstraction of something from the phantasms, but by the phantasms impressing themselves on the intellect.

Obj. 4. Further, the Philosopher says that there are two things in the intellectual soul—the possible intellect and the agent intellect. But it does not belong to the possible intellect to abstract the intelligible species from the phantasm, but to receive them already abstracted. Neither does it seem to be the function of the agent intellect, which is related to phantasms as light is to colors; since light does not abstract anything from colors, but rather acts on them. Therefore in no way do we understand by abstraction from phantasms.

Obj. 5. Further, the Philosopher says that *the intellect understands the species in the phantasms,* and not, therefore, by abstraction.

On the contrary, The Philosopher says that *things are intelligible in proportion as they are separable from matter.* Therefore material things must needs be understood according as they are abstracted from matter and from material images, namely, phantasms.

I answer that, As stated above, the object of knowledge is proportionate to the power of knowledge. Now there are three grades of the cognitive powers. For one cognitive power, namely, the sense, is the act of a corporeal organ. And therefore the object of every sensitive power is a form as existing in corporeal matter; and since such matter is the principle of individuation, therefore every power of the sensitive part can have knowledge only of particulars. There is another grade of cognitive power which is neither the act of a corporeal organ, nor in any way connected with corporeal matter. Such is the angelic intellect, the object of whose cognitive power is therefore a form existing apart from matter; for though angels know material things, yet they do not know them save in something immaterial, namely, either in themselves or in God. But the human intellect holds a middle place; for it is not the act of an organ, and yet it is a power of the soul, which is the form of the body, as is clear from what we have said above. And therefore it is proper to it to know a form existing individually in corporeal matter, but not as existing in this individual matter. But to know what is in individual matter, yet not as existing in such matter, is to abstract the form from individual matter which is represented by the phantasms. Therefore we must needs say that our intellect understands material things by abstracting from phantasms; and that through material things thus considered we acquire some knowledge of immaterial things, just as, on the contrary, angels know material things through the immaterial.

But Plato, considering only the immateriality of the human intellect, and not that it is somehow united to the body, held that the objects of the intellect are separate Ideas, and that we understand, not by abstraction, but rather by participating in abstractions, as was stated above.

Reply Obj. 1. Abstraction may occur in two ways. First, by way of composition and division, and thus we may understand that one thing does not exist in some other, or that it is separate from it. Secondly, by way of a simple and absolute consideration; and thus we understand one thing without considering another. Thus, for the intellect to abstract one from another things which are not really abstract from one another, does, in the first mode of abstraction, imply falsehood. But, in the second mode of abstraction, for the intellect to abstract things which are not really abstract from one another, does not involve falsehood, as clearly appears in the case of the senses. For if we said that color is not in a colored body, or that it is separate from it, there would be error in what we thought or said. But if we consider color and its properties, without reference to the apple which is colored, or if we express in word what we thus understand, there is no error in such an opinion or assertion; for an apple is not essential to color, and therefore color can be understood independently of the apple. In the same way, the things which belong to the species of a material thing, such as a stone, or a man, or a horse, can be thought without the individual principles which do not belong to the notion of the species. That is what we mean by abstracting the universal from the particular, or the intelligible species from the phantasm; in other words, this is to consider the nature of the species apart from

its individual principles represented by the phantasms. If, therefore, the intellect is said to be false when it understands a thing otherwise than as it is, that is so, if the word *otherwise* refers to the thing understood; for the intellect is false when it understands a thing to be otherwise than as it is. Hence, the intellect would be false if it abstracted the species of a stone from its matter in such a way as to think that the species did not exist in matter, as Plato held. But it is not so, if the word *otherwise* be taken as referring to the one who understands. For it is quite true that the mode of understanding, in one who understands, is not the same as the mode of a thing in being; since the thing understood is immaterially in the one who understands, according to the mode of the intellect, and not materially, according to the mode of a material thing.

Reply Obj. 2. Some have thought that the species of a natural thing is a form only, and that matter is not part of the species. If that were so, matter would not enter into the definition of natural things. Therefore we must disagree and say that matter is twofold, common and *signate,* or individual: common, such as flesh and bone; individual, such as this flesh and these bones. The intellect therefore abstracts the species of a natural thing from the individual sensible matter, but not from the common sensible matter. For example, it abstracts the species of *man* from *this flesh and these bones,* which do not belong to the species as such, but to the individual, and need not be considered in the species. But the species of man cannot be abstracted by the intellect from *flesh and bones.*

Mathematical species, however, can be abstracted by the intellect not only from individual sensible matter, but also from common sensible matter. But they cannot be abstracted from common intelligible matter, but only from individual intelligible matter. For sensible matter is corporeal matter as subject to sensible qualities, such as being cold or hot, hard or soft, and the like; while intelligible matter is substance as subject to quantity. Now it is manifest that quantity is in substance before sensible qualities are. Hence quantities, such as number, dimension, and figures, which are the terminations of quantity, can be considered apart from sensible qualities, and this is to abstract them from sensible matter. But they cannot be considered without understanding the substance which is subject to the quantity, for that would be to abstract them from common intelligible matter. Yet they can be considered apart from this or that substance, and this is to abstract them from individual intelligible matter.

But some things can be abstracted even from common intelligible matter, such as *being, unity, potency, act,* and the like, all of which can exist without matter, as can be verified in the case of immaterial substances. And because Plato failed to consider the twofold kind of abstraction, as above explained, he held that all those things which we have stated to be abstracted by the intellect, are abstract in reality.

Reply Obj. 3. Colors, as being in individual corporeal matter, have the same mode of being as the power of sight; and therefore they can impress their own image on the eye. But phantasms, since they are images of individuals, and exist in corporeal organs, have not the same mode of being as the human intellect, as is clear from what we have said, and therefore they have not the power of themselves to make an impression on the possible intellect. But through the power of the agent intellect, there results in the possible intellect a certain likeness produced by the turning of the agent intellect toward the phantasms. This likeness represents what is in the phantasms, but includes only the nature of the species. It is thus that the intelligible species is said to be abstracted from the phantasm; not that the identical form which previously was in the phantasm is subsequently in the possible intellect, as a body transferred from one place to another.

Reply Obj. 4. Not only does the agent intellect illumine phantasms, it does more;

by its power intelligible species are abstracted from phantasms. It illumines phantasms because, just as the sensitive part acquires a great power by its conjunction with the intellectual part, so through the power of the agent intellect phantasms are made more fit for the abstraction of intelligible intentions from them. Now the agent intellect abstracts intelligible species from phantasms inasmuch as by its power we are able to take into our consideration the natures of species without individual conditions. It is in accord with their likenesses that the possible intellect is informed.

Reply Obj. 5. Our intellect both abstracts the intelligible species *from* phantasms, inasmuch as it considers the natures of things universally, and yet understands these natures *in* the phantasms, since it cannot understand the things, of which it abstracts the species, without turning to phantasms, as we have said above.

Whether the Intelligible Species Abstracted from Phantasms Are Related to Our Intellect as That Which Is Understood? (Q. 85, Art. 2)

We proceed thus to the Second Article:—

Objection 1. It would seem that the intelligible species abstracted from phantasms are related to our intellect as that which is understood. For the understood in act is in the one who understands: since the understood in act is the intellect itself in act. But nothing of what is understood is in the actually understanding intellect save the abstracted intelligible species. Therefore this species is what is actually understood.

Obj. 2. Further, what is actually understood must be in something; or else it would be nothing. But it is not in something outside the soul; for, since what is outside the soul is material, nothing therein can be actually understood. Therefore what is actually understood is in the intellect. Consequently it can be nothing else than the aforesaid intelligible species.

Obj. 3. Further, the Philosopher says that *words are signs of the passions in the soul.* But words signify the things understood, for we express by word what we understand. Therefore these passions of the soul, viz., the intelligible species, are what is actually understood.

On the contrary, The intelligible species is to the intellect what the sensible species is to the sense. But the sensible species is not *what* is perceived, but rather that *by which* the sense perceives. Therefore the intelligible species is not what is actually understood, but that by which the intellect understands.

I answer that, Some have asserted that our intellectual powers know only the impressions made on them; as, for example, that sense is cognizant only of the impression made on its own organ. According to this theory, the intellect understands only its own impressions, namely, the intelligible species which it has received.

This is, however, manifestly false for two reasons. First, because the things we understand are also the objects of science. Therefore, if what we understand is merely the intelligible species in the soul, it would follow that every science would be concerned, not with things outside the soul, but only with the intelligible species within the soul; just as, according to the teaching of the Platonists, all the sciences are about Ideas, which they held to be that which is actually understood. Secondly, it is untrue, because it would lead to the opinion of the ancients who maintained that *whatever seems, is true,* and that consequently contradictories are true simultaneously. For if a power knows only its own impressions, it can judge only of them. Now a thing *seems* according to the impression made on the cognitive power. Consequently the cognitive power will always judge of its own impression as such; and so every judgment will be true. For instance, if taste perceived only its own impression, when anyone with a healthy taste perceives

that honey is sweet, he would judge truly, and if anyone with a corrupt taste perceives that honey is bitter, this would be equally true; for each would judge according to the impression on his taste. Thus every opinion, in fact, every sort of apprehension, would be equally true.

Therefore it must be said that the intelligible species is related to the intellect as that by which it understands. Which is proved thus. Now action is twofold, as it is said in *Metaph.* ix: one which remains in the agent (for instance, to see and to understand), and another which passes into an external object (for instance, to heat and to cut). Each of these actions proceeds in virtue of some form. And just as the form from which proceeds an act tending to something external is the likeness of the object of the action, as heat in the heater is a likeness of the thing heated, so the form from which proceeds an action remaining in the agent is a likeness of the object. Hence that by which the sight sees is the likeness of the visible thing; and the likeness of the thing understood, that is, the intelligible species, is the form by which the intellect understands. But since the intellect reflects upon itself, by such reflection it understands both its own act of understanding, and the species by which it understands. Thus the intelligible species is secondarily that which is understood; but that which is primarily understood is the thing, of which the species is the likeness.

This also appears from the opinion of the ancient philosophers, who said that *like is known by like.* For they said that the soul knows the earth outside itself by the earth within itself; and so of the rest. If, therefore, we take the species of the earth instead of the earth, in accord with Aristotle who says *that a stone is not in the soul, but only the likeness of the stone,* it follows that by means of its intelligible species the soul knows the things which are outside it.

Reply Obj. 1. The thing understood is in the knower by its own likeness. It is in this sense that we say that the thing actually understood is the intellect in act, because the likeness of the thing understood is the form of the intellect, just as the likeness of a sensible thing is the form of the sense in act. Hence it does not follow that the abstracted intelligible species is what is actually understood; but rather that it is the likeness thereof.

Reply Obj. 2.   In these words *the thing actually understood* there is a double meaning:—the thing which is understood, and the fact that it is understood. In like manner, the words *abstract universal* mean two things, the nature of a thing and its abstraction or universality. Therefore the nature itself which suffers the act of being understood, or the act of being abstracted, or the intention of universality, exists only in individuals; but that it is understood, abstracted or considered as universal is in the intellect. We see something similar to this in the senses. For the sight sees the color of the apple apart from its smell. If therefore it be asked where is the color which is seen apart from the smell, it is quite clear that the color which is seen is only in the apple; but that it be perceived apart from the smell, this is owing to the sight, inasmuch as sight receives the likeness of color and not of smell. In like manner, the humanity which is understood exists only in this or that man; but that humanity be apprehended without the conditions of individuality, that is, that it be abstracted and consequently considered as universal, befalls humanity inasmuch as it is perceived by the intellect, in which there is a likeness of the specific nature, but not of the individual principles.

Reply Obj. 3.   There are two operations in the sensitive part. One is limited to immutation, and thus the operation of the senses takes place when the senses are impressed by the sensible. The other is formation, inasmuch as the imagination forms for itself an image of an absent thing, or even of something never seen. Both of these operations are found in the intellect. For in the first place there is the passion of the possible intellect as informed by the intelligible species; and then the possible intellect, as thus informed, then forms a definition, or a division, or a composition, which is expressed by language. And so, the notion signified by a *term* is a definition; and a *proposition* signifies the intellect's division or composition. Words do not therefore signify the intelligible species themselves; but that which the intellect forms for itself for the purpose of judging of external things.

Bibliography

Texts

The English Dominican Fathers have published translations of the *Summa Theologica*, the *Summa Contra Gentiles*, and the *Quaestiones Disputatae*. 22 vols. London: Burns, Oates, & Washbourne, Ltd., 1912–1936.

Basic Writings of St. Thomas Aquinas. Edited by A. Pegis. 2 vols. New York: Random House, 1945.

Studies

Maritain, J. *St. Thomas Aquinas.* London: Sheed & Ward Ltd., 1946 (reprint).

Sertillanges, A. D. *Foundations of Thomistic Philosophy.* Translated by Godfrey Anstruther. London: Sands and Co., 1931.

———. *S. Thomas d'Aquin,* 4th ed. 2 vols. Paris: F. Alcan, 1925.

5

RENÉ DESCARTES
1596–1650

Introduction

Born in La Haye in Touraine, France, René Descartes was educated at the Jesuit school at La Flèche. He studied in Paris from 1613 till 1617 and achieved the licentiate in law. For a while he gave up academic pursuits and did military service in armies fighting in Holland and Bavaria. It was at his winter quarters in Neuburg on the Danube that Descartes had the illuminating experience which was to be a milestone of philosophical history—his *"Cogito ergo sum"* (I think, therefore I am). Having made a pilgrimage to Loretto and returned to a studious life in Paris, he enjoyed the close fellowship of Mersenne and of Cardinal Berulle, founder of the Oratorians of Jesus, whose highly theocentric form of piety influenced Descartes's philosophy of substance and causality. The full effect of this influence apparently found fuller expression in the metaphysics of occasionalism which quickly followed upon the rationalistic metaphysics of Descartes. He spent the most productive years of his life in Holland (1628 to 1649), where he could not be spared the hostile feelings of those who opposed the positions he held. In 1649 at the invitation of Christine, Queen of Sweden, he went to Stockholm, where he died on February 11, 1650.

Descartes is called "the father of modern Western philosophy." His effort to bring a method and exactitude to philosophy reflects his mathematical endowments. The *clear and distinct idea* as criterion of truth, the *methodical doubt* as the point of departure for his philosophy, the *"Cogito ergo sum"* as the first "given," . . . are Cartesian contributions to the method of philosophy which still exercise vital influence in philosophical thought. His concepts of *substance, God, soul,* and *body* begot whole schools and directions of philosophy such as one finds in occasionalism and psychophysical parallelism. His theory of *innate ideas* is echoed in the apriorism of Kant, and the shadows of his incisive spirit overcast every bridge which attempts to join modern with ancient Western philosophical thought. Descartes's main works are *Rules for the Direction of the Mind* (*ca.* 1629), *Discourses on Method* (1637), *Principles of Philosophy* (1644), and *Meditations on the First Philosophy* (1641). The following selections from his *Discourse on Method* exemplify some of Descartes's basic philosophical concepts and were chosen particularly for their bearing upon method in philosophy.

METHODICAL DOUBT AND THE THINKING SUBJECT *

I do not know that I ought to tell you of the first meditations there made by me, for they are so metaphysical and so unusual that they may perhaps not be acceptable to everyone. And yet at the same time, in order that one may judge whether the foundations which I have laid are sufficiently secure, I find myself constrained in some measure to refer to them. For a long time I had remarked that it is sometimes requisite in common life to follow opinions which one knows to be most uncertain, exactly as though they were indisputable, as has been said above. But because in this case I wished to give myself entirely to the search after Truth,

* From Descartes, "Discourse on Method," in *The Philosophical Works of Descartes*, E. S. Haldane and G. R. T. Ross, translators. 2 vols, 1912; corrected 1934. By permission of Cambridge University Press, New York.

I thought that it was necessary for me to take an apparently opposite course, and to reject as absolutely false everything as to which I could imagine the least ground of doubt, in order to see if afterwards there remained anything in my belief that was entirely certain. Thus, because our senses sometimes deceive us, I wished to suppose that nothing is just as they cause us to imagine it to be; and because there are men who deceive themselves in their reasoning and fall into paralogisms, even concerning the simplest matters of geometry, and judging that I was as subject to error as was any other, I rejected as false all the reasons formerly accepted by me as demonstrations. And since all the same thoughts and conceptions which we have while awake may also come to us in sleep, without any of them being at that time true, I resolved to assume that everything that ever entered into my mind was no more true than the illusions of my dreams. But immediately afterwards I noticed that whilst I thus wished to think all things false, it was absolutely essential that the "I" who thought this should be somewhat, and remarking that this truth *"I think, therefore I am"* was so certain and so assured that all the most extravagant suppositions brought forward by the sceptics were incapable of shaking it, I came to the conclusion that I could receive it without scruple as the first principle of the Philosophy for which I was seeking.

And then, examining attentively that which I was, I saw that I should conceive that I had no body, and that there was no world nor place where I might be; but yet that I could not for all that conceive that I was not. On the contrary, I saw from the very fact that I thought of doubting the truth of other things, it very evidently and certainly followed that I was; on the other hand if I had only ceased from thinking, even if all the rest of what I had ever imagined had really existed, I should have no reason for thinking that I had existed. From that I knew that I was a substance the whole essence or nature of which is to think, and that for its existence there is no need of any place, nor does it depend on any material thing; so that this "me," that is to say, the soul by which I am what I am, is entirely distinct from body, and is even more easy to know than is the latter; and even if body were not, the soul would not cease to be what it is.

CRITERION OF TRUTH

After this I considered generally what in a proposition is requisite in order to be true and certain; for since I had just discovered one which I knew to be such, I thought that I ought also to know in what this certainty consisted. And having remarked that there was nothing at all in the statement *"I think, therefore I am"* which assures me of having thereby made a true assertion, excepting that I see very clearly that to think it is necessary to be, I came to the conclusion that I might assume, as a general rule, that the things which we conceive very clearly and distinctly are all true—remembering, however, that there is some difficulty in ascertaining which are those that we distinctly conceive.

GOD

Following upon this, and reflecting on the fact that I doubted, and that consequently my existence was not quite perfect (for I saw clearly that it was a greater perfection to know than to doubt), I resolved to inquire whence I had learnt to think of anything more perfect than I myself was; and I recognised very clearly that this conception must proceed from some nature which was really more perfect. As to the thoughts which I had of many other things outside of me, like the heavens, the earth, light, heat, and a thousand others, I had not so much difficulty in knowing whence they came, because, remarking nothing in them which seemed to render them superior to me, I could believe that, if they were true, they were dependencies upon my nature, in so far as it possessed some perfection; and if they were not true, that I held them from nought, that is to say, that they were in me because I had something lacking in my nature. But this could not apply to the idea of a Being more perfect than my own, for to hold it from nought would be manifestly impossible; and because it is no less contradictory to say of the more perfect that it is what results from and depends on the less perfect, than to say that there is something which proceeds from nothing, it was equally impossible that I should hold it from myself. In this way it could but follow that it had been placed in me by a Nature which was really more perfect than mine could be, and which even had within itself all the perfections of which I could form any idea—that is to say, to put it in a word, which was God. To which I added that since I knew some perfections which I did not possess, I was not the only being in existence (I shall here use freely, if you will allow, the terms of the School); but that there was necessarily some other more perfect Being on which I depended, or from which I acquired all that I had. For if I had existed alone and independent of any others, so that I should have had from myself all that perfection of being in which I participated to however small an extent, I should have been able for the same reason to have had all the remainder which I knew that I lacked; and thus I myself should have been infinite, eternal, immutable, omniscient, all-powerful, and, finally, I should have all the perfection which I could discern in God. For, in pursuance of the reasonings which I have just carried on, in order to know the nature of God as far as my nature is capable of knowing it, I had only to consider in reference to all these things of which I found some idea in myself, whether it was a perfection to possess them or not. And I was assured that none of those which indicated some imperfection were in Him, but that all else was present; and I saw that doubt, inconstancy, sadness, and such things, could not be in Him considering that I myself should have been glad to be without them. In addition to this, I had ideas of many things which are sensible and corporeal, for, although I might suppose that I was dreaming, and that all that I saw or imagined was false, I could not at the same time deny that the ideas were really in my thoughts. But because I had already recognized very clearly in myself that the nature of the intelligence is distinct from that of the body, and observing that all composition gives evidence of dependency, and that dependency is manifestly an imperfection, I came to the conclusion that it could not be a perfection in God to be composed of these two natures, and that consequently He was not so composed. I judged, however, that if there were any bodies in the world, or even any intelligences or other natures which were not wholly perfect, their existence must depend on His power in such a way that they could not subsist without Him for a single moment.

After that I desired to seek for other truths, and having put before myself the object of the geometricians, which I conceived to be a continuous body, or a space indefinitely extended in length, breadth, height or depth, which was divisible into various parts, and which might have various figures and sizes, and might be moved or transposed in all sorts of ways (for all this the geometricians suppose to be in the object of their contemplation), I went through some of their simplest demonstrations, and having noticed that this great certainty which everyone attributes to these demonstrations is founded solely on the fact that they are conceived of with clearness, in accordance with the rule which I have just laid down, I also noticed that there was nothing at all in them to assure me of the existence of their object.

For, to take an example, I saw very well that if we suppose a triangle to be given, the three angles must certainly be equal to two right angles; but for all that I saw no reason to be assured that there was any such triangle in existence, while on the contrary, on reverting to the examination of the idea which I had of a Perfect Being, I found that in this case existence was implied in it in the same manner in which the equality of its three angles to two right angles is implied in the idea of a triangle; or in the idea of a sphere, that all the points on its surface are equidistant from its centre, or even more evidently still. Consequently it is at least as certain that God, who is a Being so perfect, is, or exists, as any demonstration of geometry can possibly be.

What causes many, however, to persuade themselves that there is difficulty in knowing this truth, and even in knowing the nature of their soul, is the fact that they never raise their minds above the things of sense, or that they are so accustomed to consider nothing excepting by imagining it, which is a mode of thought specially adapted to material objects, that all that is not capable of being imagined appears to them not to be intelligible at all. This is manifest enough from the fact that even the philosophers in the Schools hold it as a maxim that there is nothing in the understanding which has not first of all been in the senses, in which there is certainly no doubt that the ideas of God and of the soul have never been. And it seems to me that those who desire to make use of their imagination in order to understand these ideas, act in the same way as if, to hear sounds or smell odours, they should wish to make use of their eyes: excepting that there is indeed this difference, that the sense of sight does not give us less assurance of the truth of its objects, than do those of scent or of hearing, while neither our imagination nor our senses can ever assure us of anything, if our understanding does not intervene.

If there are finally any persons who are not sufficiently persuaded of the existence of God and of their soul by the reasons which I have brought forward, I wish that they should know that all other things of which they perhaps think themselves more assured (such as possessing a body, and that there are stars and an earth and so on) are less certain. For, although we have a moral assurance of these things which is such that it seems that it would be extravagant in us to doubt them, at the same time no one, unless he is devoid of reason, can deny, when a metaphysical certainty is in question, that there is sufficient cause for our not having complete assurance, by observing the fact that when asleep we may similarly imagine that we have another body, and that we see other stars and another earth, without there being anything of the kind. For how do we know that the thoughts that come in dreams are more false than those that we have when we are awake, seeing that often enough the former are not less lively and vivid than the latter? And though the wisest minds may study the matter as much as they will, I do not believe that they will be able to give any sufficient reason for removing this doubt, unless they presuppose the existence of God. For to begin with, that which I have just taken as a rule, that is to say, that all the things that we very clearly and very distinctly conceive of are true, is certain only because God is or exists, and that He is a Perfect Being, and that all that is in us issues from Him. From this it follows that our ideas or notions, which to the extent of their being clear or distinct are ideas of real things issuing from God, cannot but to that extent be true. So that though we often enough have ideas which have an element of falsity, this can only be the case in regard to those which have in them somewhat that is confused or obscure, because in so far as they have this character they participate in negation—that is, they exist in us as confused only because we are not quite perfect. And it is evident that there is no less repugnance in the idea that error or imperfection, inasmuch as it is imperfection, proceeds from God, than there is in the idea of truth or perfection proceeding from nought. But if we did not know that all that is in us of reality and truth proceeds from a perfect and infinite Being, however clear and distinct were our ideas, we should not have any reason to assure ourselves that they had the perfection of being true.

But after the knowledge of God and of the soul has thus rendered us certain of this rule, it is very easy to understand that the dreams which we imagine in our sleep should not make us in any way doubt the truth of the thoughts which we have when awake. For even if in sleep we had some very distinct idea such as a geometrician might have who discovered some new demonstration, the fact of being asleep would not militate against its truth. And as to the most ordinary error in our dreams, which consists in their representing to us various objects in the same way as do our external senses, it does not matter that this should give us occasion to suspect the truth of such ideas, because we may be likewise often enough deceived in them without our sleeping at all, just as when those who have the jaundice see everything as yellow, or when stars or other bodies which are very remote appear much smaller than they really are. For, finally, whether we are awake or asleep, we should never allow ourselves to be persuaded excepting by the evidence of our Reason. And it must be remarked that I speak of our Reason and not of our imagination nor of our senses; just as though we see the sun very clearly, we should not for that reason judge that it is of the size of which it appears to be; likewise we could quite well distinctly imagine the head of a lion on the body of a goat, without necessarily concluding that a chimera exists. For Reason does not insist that whatever we see or imagine thus is a truth, but it tells us clearly that all our ideas or notions must have some foundation of truth. For otherwise it could not be possible that God, who is all perfection and truth, should have placed them within us. And because our reasonings are never so evident nor so complete during sleep as during wakefulness, although sometimes our imaginations are then just as lively and acute, or even more so, Reason tells us that since our thoughts cannot possibly be all true, because we are not altogether perfect, that which they have of truth must infallibly be met with in our waking experience rather than in that of our dreams. . . .

BODY

I had explained all these matters in some detail in the Treatise which I formerly intended to publish. And afterwards I had shown there, what must be the fabric of the nerves and muscles of the human body in order that the animal spirits therein contained should have the power to move the members, just as the heads of animals, a little while after decapitation, are still observed to move and bite the earth, notwithstanding that they are no longer animate; what changes are necessary in the brain to cause wakefulness, sleep and dreams; how light, sounds, smells, tastes, heat and all other qualities pertaining to external objects are able to imprint on it various ideas by the intervention of the senses; how hunger, thirst and other internal affections can also convey their impressions upon it; what should be regarded as the "common sense" by which these ideas are received, and what is meant by the memory which retains them, by the fancy which can change them in diverse ways and out of them constitute new ideas, and which, by the same means, distributing the animal spirits through the muscles, can cause the members of such a body to move in as many diverse ways, and in a manner as suitable to the objects which present themselves to its senses and to its internal passions, as can happen in our own case apart from the direction of our free will. And this will not seem strange to those, who, knowing how many different *automata* or moving machines can be made by the industry of man, without employing in so doing more than a very few parts in comparison with the great multitude of bones, muscles, nerves, arteries, veins, or other parts that are found in the body of each animal. From this aspect the body is regarded as a machine which, having been made by the hands of God, is incomparably better arranged, and possesses in itself movements which are much more admirable, than any of those which can be invented by man. Here I specially stopped to show that if there had been such machines, possessing the organs and outward form of a monkey or some other animal without reason, we should not have had any means of ascertaining that they were not of the same nature as those animals. On the other hand, if there were machines which bore a resemblance to our body and imitated our actions as far as it was morally possible to do so, we should always have two very certain tests by which to recognise that, for all that, they were not real men. The first is, that they could never use speech or other signs as we do when placing our thoughts on record for the bene-

fit of others. For we can easily understand a machine's being constituted so that it can utter words, and even emit some responses to action on it of a corporeal kind, which brings about a change in its organs; for instance, if it is touched in a particular part it may ask what we wish to say to it; if in another part it may exclaim that it is being hurt, and so on. But it never happens that it arranges its speech in various ways, in order to reply appropriately to everything that may be said in its presence, as even the lowest type of man can do. And the second difference is, that although machines can perform certain things as well as or perhaps better than any of us can do, they infallibly fall short in others, by the which means we may discover that they did not act from knowledge, but only from the disposition of their organs. For while reason is a universal instrument which can serve for all contingencies, these organs have need of some special adaptation for every particular action. From this it follows that it is morally impossible that there should be sufficient diversity in any machine to allow it to act in all the events of life in the same way as our reason causes us to act.

MEN AND BRUTE ANIMALS

By these two methods we may also recognise the difference that exists between men and brutes. For it is a very remarkable fact that there are none so depraved and stupid, without even excepting idiots, that they cannot arrange different words together, forming of them a statement by which they make known their thoughts; while, on the other hand, there is no other animal, however perfect and fortunately circumstanced it may be, which can do the same. It is not the want of organs that brings this to pass, for it is evident that magpies and parrots are able to utter words just like ourselves, and yet they cannot speak as we do, that is, so as to give

evidence that they think of what they say. On the other hand, men who, being born deaf and dumb, are in the same degree, or even more than the brutes, destitute of the organs which serve the others for talking, are in the habit of themselves inventing certain signs by which they make themselves understood by those who, being usually in their company, have leisure to learn their language. And this does not merely show that the brutes have less reason than men, but that they have none at all, since it is clear that very little is required in order to be able to talk. And when we notice the inequality that exists between animals of the same species, as well as between men, and observe that some are more capable of receiving instruction than others, it is not credible that a monkey or a parrot, selected as the most perfect of its species, should not in these matters equal the stupidest child to be found, or at least a child whose mind is clouded, unless in the case of the brute the soul were of an entirely different nature from ours. And we ought not to confound speech with natural movements which betray passions and may be imitated by machines as well as be manifested by animals; nor must we think, as did some of the ancients, that brutes talk, although we do not understand their language. For if this were true, since they have many organs which are allied to our own, they could communicate their thoughts to us just as easily as to those of their own race. It is also a very remarkable fact that although there are many animals which exhibit more dexterity than we do in some of their actions, we at the same time observe that they do not manifest any dexterity at all in many others. Hence the fact that they do better than we do, does not prove that they are endowed with mind, for in this case they would have more reason than any of us, and would surpass us in all other things. It rather shows that they have no reason at all, and that it is nature which acts in them according to the disposition of their organs, just as a clock, which is only composed of wheels and weights is able to tell the hours and measure the time more correctly than we can do with all our wisdom.

RATIONAL SOUL

I had described after this the rational soul and shown that it could not be in any way derived from the power of matter, like the other things of which I had spoken, but that it must be expressly created. I showed, too, that it is not sufficient that it should be lodged in the human body like a pilot in his ship, unless perhaps for the moving of its members, but that it is necessary that it should also be joined and united more closely to the body in order to have sensations and appetites similar to our own, and thus to form a true man. In conclusion, I have here enlarged a little on the subject of the soul, because it is one of the greatest importance. For next to the error of those who deny God, which I think I have already sufficiently refuted, there is none which is more effectual in leading feeble spirits from the straight path of virtue, than to imagine that the soul of the brute is of the same nature as our own, and that in consequence, after this life we have nothing to fear or to hope for, any more than the flies and ants. As a matter of fact, when one comes to know how greatly they differ, we understand much better the reasons which go to prove that our soul is in its nature entirely independent of body, and in consequence that it is not liable to die with it. And then, inasmuch as we observe no other causes capable of destroying it, we are naturally inclined to judge that it is immortal.

Bibliography

Texts

The Philosophical Works of Descartes. Translated by E. S. Haldane and G. R. T. Ross. 2 vols. Cambridge University Press, 1911–1912 (corrected edition 1934; reprinted New York: Dover Publications, Inc., 1955).

Descartes' Philosophical Writings. Selected and translated by N. K. Smith. New York: St. Martin's Press, Inc., 1953.

Studies

Maritain, J. *The Dream of Descartes.* Translated by M. L. Andison. New York: Philosophical Library, Inc., 1944.

Smith, N. K. *Studies in the Cartesian Philosophy.* London: Macmillan & Co., Ltd., 1902.

6

JOHN LOCKE
1632–1704

Introduction

John Locke, the English philosopher, was born at Wrington, Somersetshire. His father was an attorney. In 1652 he went to Christ Church, Oxford, where he disliked the scholastic philosophy taught there. He became a tutor at Exeter House through friendship with Lord Ashley. With Ashley's fall, Locke was driven from English political circles and went to France (1675–1679), where he met men of science and letters, particularly François Bernier, the expositor of Gassendi, whom Locke studied carefully. Locke was also impressed by the Cartesianism and scientific approach to philosophy which he encountered on the Continent. Returning to London, amid much political intrigue, he found himself held suspect at court. Locke's position on toleration in the state and on religious freedom in the church forced him to leave England once more. This time he went to Holland. Just as Descartes, Spinoza, and Bayle had come to the home of Erasmus and Grotius, so too, Locke found refuge there. With the seizure of the throne by William of Orange, whom he had met in Holland, Locke returned to England in 1689. His famous *Essay Concerning Human Understanding* appeared the following year. Somewhat disappointed with the course of public affairs because the revolution fell short of his ideal of toleration and civil liberty, Locke went in the spring of 1691 to the Oates Manor in Essex, county seat of Sir Francis Masham, whose wife was the daughter of Ralph Cudworth, his friend. Till his death he continued to write on the polemic topics of civil liberty, and on education, currency, and theology.

Like other notable philosophers of the seventeenth century, Locke was concerned with the question of the nature and value of human knowledge. In the tradition of Francis Bacon and Hobbes, Locke developed a theory of human knowledge rooted in empiricism. He denied innate ideas and made little distinction between sensation and intellection. "Idea" is any object of knowledge, be it phantasm, notion, sensation, or reflection. Simple ideas from the senses represent sense qualities of things, namely, those qualities which are formally objective and always found in bodies, such as color and sound. These qualities are only causally objective and are called "secondary qualities." Compound ideas are the product of the mind's power to combine simple ideas and are classified under modes, substances, and relations. "Substance," a postulate of the mind, is a substrate supporting sense qualities, which is wholly unknown and unknowable. Hence essences are beyond the mind's grasp. Hence nominalism. Certitude is subjectively found in the agreement or disagreement of ideas in terms of identity of relation or coexistence. The existence of God can be demonstrated, but the knowledge of God and of the human soul is no more certain than the "uncertainly known" unknowable corporeal substance. Morality is based on opinion, divine and human law, not on any intrinsic principles of things or human acts related to them. The following passages exemplify part of Locke's theory on the association of ideas.

COMPLEX IDEAS OF SUBSTANCES, SPIRITUAL AND CORPOREAL *

The mind being, as I have declared, furnished with a great number of the simple ideas,

* From John Locke, *An Essay Concerning Human Understanding*. Edited by A. C. Fraser. 1894. By permission of the Clarendon Press, Oxford.

conveyed in by the senses as they are found in exterior things, or by reflection on its own operations, takes notice also that a certain number of these simple ideas go constantly together; which being presumed to belong to one thing, and words being suited to common apprehensions, and made use of for quick dispatch, are called, so united in one subject, by one name; which, by inadvertency, we are apt afterward to talk of and consider as one simple idea, which indeed is a complication of many ideas together: because, as I have said, not imagining how these simple ideas *can* subsist by themselves, we accustom ourselves to suppose some *substratum* wherein they do subsist, and from which they do result, which therefore we call *substance*.

So that if any one will examine himself concerning his notion of pure substance in general, he will find he has no other idea of it at all, but only a supposition of he knows not what *support* of such qualities which are capable of producing simple ideas in us; which qualities are commonly called accidents. If any one should be asked, what is the subject wherein colour or weight inheres, he would have nothing to say, but the solid extended parts; and if he were demanded, what is it that solidity and extension adhere in, he would not be in a much better case than the Indian before mentioned who, saying that the world was supported by a great elephant, was asked what the elephant rested on; to which his answer was—a great tortoise: but being again pressed to know what gave support to the broad-backed tortoise, replied—*something, he knew not what*. And thus here, as in all other cases where we use words without having clear and distinct ideas, we talk like children: who, being questioned what such a thing is, which they know not, readily give this satisfactory answer, that it is *something*: which in truth signifies no more, when so used, either by children or men, but that they know not what; and that the thing they pretend to know, and talk of, is what they have no distinct idea of at all, and so are perfectly ignorant of it, and in the dark. The idea then we have, to which we give the *general* name substance, being nothing but the supposed, but unknown, support of those qualities we find existing, which we imagine

cannot subsist *sine re substante*, without something to support them, we call that support *substantia;* which, according to the true import of the word, is, in plain English, standing under or upholding.

Particular Sorts of Substances

An obscure and relative idea of *substance in general* being thus made we come to have the ideas of *particular sorts of substances,* by collecting *such* combinations of simple ideas as are, by experience and observation of men's senses, taken notice of to exist together; and are therefore supposed to flow from the particular internal constitution, or unknown essence of that substance. Thus we come to have the ideas of a man, horse, gold, water, &c.; of which substances, whether any one has any other *clear* idea, further than of certain simple ideas co-existent together, I appeal to every one's own experience. It is the ordinary qualities observable in iron, or a diamond, put together, that make the true complex idea of those substances, which a smith or a jeweller commonly knows better than a philosopher; who, whatever *substantial forms* he may talk of, has no other idea of those substances, than what is framed by a collection of those simple ideas which are to be found in them: only we must take notice, that our complex ideas of substances, besides all those simple ideas they are made up of, have always the confused idea of something to which they belong, and in which they subsist: and therefore when we speak of any sort of substance, we say it is a thing having such or such qualities; as body is a thing that is extended, figured, and capable of motion; spirit, a thing capable of thinking; and so hardness, friability, and power to draw iron, we say, are qualities to be found in a loadstone. These, and the like fashions of speaking, intimate that the substance is supposed always *something besides* the extension, figure, solidity, motion, thinking, or other observable ideas, though we know not what it is.

Hence, when we talk or think of any particular sort of corporeal substances, as horse, stone, &c., though the idea we have of either of them be but the complication or collection of those several simple ideas of sensible qualities, which we used to find united in the thing called horse or stone; yet, *because we cannot conceive how they should subsist alone, nor one in another*, we suppose them existing in and supported by some common subject; which support we denote by the name substance, though it be certain we have no clear or distinct idea of that thing we suppose a support.

Spiritual and Corporeal Substance

The same thing happens concerning the operations of the mind, viz. thinking, reasoning, fearing, &c., which we concluding not to subsist of themselves, nor apprehending how they can belong to body, or be produced by it, we are apt to think these the actions of some other *substance*, which we call *spirit;* whereby yet it is evident that, having no other idea or notion of matter, but something wherein those many sensible qualities which affect our senses do subsist; by supposing a substance wherein thinking, knowing, doubting, and a power of moving, &c., do subsist, we have as clear a notion of the substance of spirit, as we have of body; the one being supposed to be (without knowing what it is) the *substratum* to those simple ideas we have from without; and the other supposed (with a like ignorance of what it is) to be the *substratum* to those operations we experiment in ourselves within. It is plain then, that the idea of *corporeal substance* in matter is as remote from our conceptions and apprehensions, as that of *spiritual substance*, or spirit: and therefore, from our not having any notion of the substance of spirit, we can no more conclude its non-existence, than we can, for the same reason, deny the existence of body; it being as rational to affirm there is no body, because we have no clear and distinct idea of the substance of matter, as to say there is no spirit, because we have no clear and distinct idea of the substance of a spirit.

Ideas of Particular Substances

Whatever therefore be the secret abstract nature of substance in general, all the ideas we have of particular distinct sorts of substances are nothing but several combinations of simple ideas, co-existing in such, though unknown, cause of their union, as makes the whole subsist of itself. It is by such combinations of simple ideas, and nothing else, that we represent particular sorts of substances to ourselves; such are the ideas we have of their several species in our minds; and such only do we, by their specific names, signify to others, v.g. man, horse, sun, water, iron: upon hearing which words, every one who understands the language, frames in his mind a combination of those several simple ideas which he has usually observed, or fancied to exist together under that denomination; all which he supposes to rest in and be, as it were, adherent to that unknown common subject, which inheres not in anything else. Though, in the meantime, it be manifest, and every one, upon inquiry into his own thoughts, will find, that he has no other idea of any substance, v.g. let it be gold, horse, iron, man, vitriol, bread, but what he has barely of those sensible qualities, which he supposes to inhere; with a supposition of such a *substratum* as gives, as it were, a support to those qualities or simple ideas, which he has observed to exist united together. Thus, the idea of the sun,— what is it but an aggregate of those several simple ideas, bright, hot, roundish, having a constant regular motion, at a certain distance from us, and perhaps some other: as he who thinks and discourses of the sun has been more or less accurate in observing those sensible qualities, ideas, or properties, which are in that thing which he calls the sun.

For he has the perfectest idea of any of

the particular sorts of substances, who has gathered, and put together, most of those simple ideas which do exist in it; among which are to be reckoned its active power, and passive capacities, which, though not simple ideas, yet in this respect, for brevity's sake, may conveniently enough be reckoned amongst them. Thus, the power of drawing iron is one of the ideas of the complex one of that substance we call a loadstone; and a power to be so drawn is a part of the complex one we call iron: which powers pass for inherent qualities in those subjects. Because every substance, being as apt, by the powers we observe in it, to change some sensible qualities in other subjects, as it is to produce in us those simple ideas which we receive immediately from it, does, by those new sensible qualities introduced into other subjects, discover to us those powers which do thereby mediately affect our senses, as regularly as its sensible qualities do it immediately: v.g. we immediately by our senses perceive in fire its heat and colour; which are, if rightly considered, nothing but powers in it to produce those ideas in *us:* we also by our senses perceive the colour and brittleness of charcoal, whereby we come by the knowledge of another power in fire, which it has to change the colour and consistency of *wood.* By the former, fire immediately, by the latter, it mediately discovers to us these several powers; which therefore we look upon to be a part of the qualities of fire, and so make them a part of the complex idea of it. For all those powers that we take cognizance of terminating only in the alteration of some sensible qualities in those subjects on which they operate, and so making them exhibit to us new sensible ideas, therefore it is that I have reckoned these powers amongst the simple ideas which make the complex ones of the sorts of substances; though these powers considered in themselves, are truly complex ideas. And in this looser sense I crave leave to be understood, when I name any of these *potentialities* among the simple ideas which we recollect in our minds when we think of *particular substances.* For the

powers that are severally in them are necessary to be considered, if we will have true distinct notions of the several sorts of substances.

Nor are we to wonder that powers make a great part of our complex ideas of substances; since their secondary qualities are those which in most of them serve principally to distinguish substances one from another, and commonly make a considerable part of the complex idea of the several sorts of them. For, our senses failing us in the discovery of the bulk, texture, and figure of the minute parts of bodies, on which their real constitutions and differences depend, we are fain to make use of their secondary qualities as the characteristical notes and marks whereby to frame ideas of them in our minds, and distinguish them one from another: all which secondary qualities, as has been shown, are nothing but bare powers. For the colour and taste of opium are, as well as its soporific or anodyne virtues, mere powers, depending on its primary qualities, whereby it is fitted to produce different operations on different parts of our bodies.

The ideas that make our complex ones of corporeal substances, are of these three sorts. First, the ideas of the primary qualities of things, which are discovered by our senses, and are in them even when we perceive them not; such are the bulk, figure, number, situation, and motion of the parts of bodies; which are really in them, whether we take notice of them or not. Secondly, the sensible secondary qualities, which, depending on these, are nothing but the powers those substances have to produce several ideas in us by our senses; which ideas are not in the things themselves, otherwise than as anything is in its cause. Thirdly, the aptness we consider in any substance, to give or receive such alterations of primary qualities, as that the substance so altered should produce in us different ideas from what it did before; these are called active and passive powers: all which powers, as far as we have any notice or notion of them, terminate only in sensible simple ideas. For whatever alteration a loadstone has the power to make in the minute particles of iron, we should have no notion of any power it had at all to operate on iron, did not its sensible motion discover it: and I doubt not, but there are a thousand changes, that bodies we daily handle have a power to cause in one another, which we never suspect, because they never appear in sensible effects.

Powers therefore justly make a great part of our complex ideas of substances. He that will examine his complex idea of gold, will find several of its ideas that make it up to be only powers; as the power of being melted, but of not spending itself in the fire; of being dissolved in *aqua regia*, are ideas as necessary to make up our complex idea of gold, as its colour and weight: which, if duly considered, are also nothing but different powers. For, to speak truly, yellowness is not actually in gold, but is a power in gold to produce that idea in us by our eyes, when placed in a due light: and the heat, which we cannot leave out of our ideas of the sun, is no more really in the sun, than the white colour it introduces into wax. These are both equally powers in the sun, operating, by the motion and figure of its sensible parts, so on a man, as to make him have the idea of heat; and so on wax, as to make it capable to produce in a man the idea of white.

Had we senses acute enough to discern the minute particles of bodies, and the real constitution on which their sensible qualities depend, I doubt not but they would produce quite different ideas in us: and that which is now the yellow colour of gold, would then disappear, and instead of it we should see an admirable texture of parts, of a certain size and figure. This microscopes plainly discover to us; for what to our naked eyes produces a certain colour, is, by thus augmenting the acuteness of our senses, discovered to be quite a different thing; and the

thus altering, as it were, the proportion of the bulk of the minute parts of a coloured object to our usual sight, produces different ideas from what it did before. Thus, sand or pounded glass, which is opaque, and white to the naked eye, is pellucid in a microscope; and a hair seen in this way, loses its former colour, and is, in a great measure, pellucid, with a mixture of some bright sparkling colours, such as appear from the refraction of diamonds, and other pellucid bodies. Blood, to the naked eye, appears all red; but by a good microsocope, wherein its lesser parts appear, shows only some few globules of red, swimming in a pellucid liquor, and how these red globules would appear, if glasses could be found that could yet magnify them a thousand or ten thousand times more, is uncertain.

Bibliography

Texts

The Philosophical Works of John Locke (On the Conduct of the Understanding, An Essay Concerning Human Understanding, The Controversy with Stillingfleet, An Examination of Malebranche's Opinion, Elements of Natural Philosophy, and Some Thoughts Concerning Reading). Edited by J. A. St. John, 2 vols. London: G. Bell & Sons, Ltd., 1854, 1908.

Second Treatise of Civil Government and Letter on Toleration. Edited by J. W. Gough. Oxford: Basil Blackwell & Mott, Ltd., 1948.

Studies

Gibson, J. *Locke's Theory of Knowledge and Its Historical Relations.* London: Cambridge University Press, 1917.

Gough, J. W. *John Locke's Political Philosophy.* Fair Lawn, N. J.: Oxford University Press, 1950.

7

GEORGE BERKELEY
1685–1753

Introduction

George Berkeley was born near Dysert Castle, Thomastown, Ireland. He attended Trinity College in Dublin (1700), where the doctrines of Descartes and Newton were in vogue and the *Essay* of Locke was much discussed. In physics and metaphysics it was a time of reaction to scholasticism. In 1671 Berkeley's *Common Place Book* stated a theory of knowledge which he was to work out more specifically in his *Essay Towards a New Theory of Vision* (1709) and in *A Treatise Concerning the Principles of Human Knowledge*, Part I (1710).

In the *Analyst* (1734) he attacked higher mathematics as leading to freethinking; in the *Querist* (three parts, 1735, 1736, 1737) he wrote on practical social reform. In 1744 he published *Siris* in which he discussed the efficacy of tar water for smallpox.

Berkeley had a full and varied career. He lectured and served as tutor and chaplain to various personages, visited the Continent, and was liked universally. It was his good fortune to inherit half the property of Miss Vanborough, a woman he was supposed to have met but once at dinner. Berkeley's imagination was clearly displayed when he visited Bermuda with the intent of opening a college which would be open to Americans as well as British subjects. The endeavor was unsuccessful. He returned to England and in 1743 was raised to the bishopric of the Established Church at Cloyne. In 1752 he went with his family to Oxford in the interest of his son George, who was studying there. He died suddenly on January 14, 1753.

In the eighteenth century there were some serious efforts to correct materialistic implications of British empiricism and sensism. Whereas spirit had been reduced to matter by philosophers like Hobbes, matter now was reduced to spirit by authors like Berkeley. As Locke denied objectivity to secondary sensory qualities, Berkeley denied the existence of primary sense qualities in his process of dematerializing reality. Hence, Berkeley admitted no material substrate of things. Mind and mind-dependent phenomena alone exist. *To be* is *to be perceived*— *"esse est percipi."* Human minds and God, the uncreated cause of the ideas perceived by sense, are the only noumenal realities. Hence, there are no secondary causes, and in reality the laws of nature are the laws of the Eternal Spirit. Berkeley's theological concern about the threat of materialism led him to a philosophical immaterialism which limited human knowledge to ideas only. The following passage indicates his opposition to Locke's theory of abstraction and the beginning of his rejection of both the popular and philosophical conceptions of matter.

SENSIBLE QUALITIES *

It is evident to any one who takes a survey of the *objects of human knowledge*, that they are either *ideas* actually imprinted on the senses; or else such as are perceived by attending to the passions and operations of the mind; or lastly, *ideas* formed by help of memory and imagination—either compounding, dividing, or barely representing those originally perceived in the aforesaid ways. By sight I have the ideas of light and colours,

* From George Berkeley, "The Principles of Human Knowledge," in *The Works of George Berkeley.* Edited by A. C. Fraser. 1901. By permission of the Clarendon Press, Oxford.

with their several degrees and variations. By touch I perceive hard and soft, heat and cold, motion and resistance; and of all these more and less either as to quantity or degree. Smelling furnishes me with odours; the palate with tastes; and hearing conveys sounds to the mind in all their variety of tone and composition.

And as several of these are observed to accompany each other, they come to be marked by one name, and so to be reputed as one *thing*. Thus, for example, a certain colour, taste, smell, figure and consistence having been observed to go together, are accounted one distinct thing, signified by the name apple; other collections of ideas constitute a stone, a tree, a book, and the like sensible things; which as they are pleasing or disagreeable excite the passions of love, hatred, joy, grief, and so forth.

But, besides all that endless variety of ideas or objects of knowledge, there is likewise Something which knows or perceives them; and exercises divers operations, as willing, imagining, remembering, about them. This perceiving, active being is what I call *mind, spirit, soul,* or *myself.* By which words I do not denote any one of my ideas, but a thing entirely distinct from them, wherein they exist, or, which is the same thing, whereby they are perceived; for the existence of an idea consists in being perceived.

ESSE IS PERCIPI

That neither our thoughts, nor passions, nor ideas formed by the imagination, exist without the mind is what everybody will allow. And to me it seems no less evident that the various sensations or ideas imprinted on the Sense, however blended or combined together (that is, whatever objects they compose), cannot exist otherwise than in a mind perceiving them. I think an intuitive knowledge may be obtained of this, by any one that shall attend to what is meant by the term *exist* when applied to sensible things. The table I write on I say exists; that is, I see and feel it: and if I were out of my study I should say it existed; meaning thereby that if I was in my study I might perceive it, or that some other spirit actually does perceive it. There was an odour, that is, it was smelt; there was a sound, that is, it was heard; a colour or figure, and it was perceived by sight or touch. This is all that I can understand by these and the like expressions. For as to what is said of the *ab-* *solute* existence of unthinking things, without any relation to their being perceived, that is to me perfectly unintelligible. Their *esse* is *percipi;* nor is it possible they should have any existence out of the minds or thinking things which perceive them.

It is indeed an opinion strangely prevailing amongst men, that houses, mountains, rivers, and in a word all sensible objects, have an existence, natural or real distinct from their being perceived by the understanding. But, with how great an assurance and acquiescence soever this Principle may be entertained in the world, yet whoever shall find in his heart to call it in question may, if I mistake not, perceive it to involve a manifest contradiction. For, what are the forementioned objects but the things we perceive by sense? and what do we perceive besides our own ideas or sensations? and is it not plainly repugnant that any one of these, or any combination of them, should exist unperceived?

ABSTRACTION

If we thoroughly examine this tenet it will, perhaps, be found at bottom to depend on the doctrine of *abstract ideas.* For can there be a nicer strain of abstraction than to distinguish the existence of sensible objects from their being perceived, so as to conceive them existing unperceived? Light and colours, heat and cold, extension and figures—in a word the things we see and feel—what are they but so many sensations, notions, ideas, or impressions on the sense? and is it possible to separate, even in thought, any of these from perception? For my part, I might as easily divide a thing from itself. I may, indeed, divide in my thoughts, or conceive apart from each other, those things which perhaps I never perceived by sense so divided. Thus, I imagine the trunk of a human body without the limbs, or conceive the smell of a rose without thinking on the rose itself. So far, I will not deny, I can abstract; if that may properly be called *abstraction* which extends only to the conceiving separately such objects as it is possible may really exist or be actually perceived asunder. But my conceiving or imagining power does not extend beyond the possibility of real existence or perception. Hence, as it is impossible for me to see or feel anything without an actual sensation of that thing, so is it impossible for me to conceive in my thoughts any sensible thing or object distinct from the sensation or perception of it. In truth, the object and the sensation are the same thing, and cannot therefore be abstracted from each other.

NON-EXISTENCE OF MATERIAL ENTITIES

Some truths there are so near and obvious to the mind that a man need only open his eyes to see them. Such I take this important one to be, viz. that all the choir of heaven and furniture of the earth, in a word all those bodies which compose the mighty frame of the world, have not any subsistence without a mind; that their *being* is to be perceived or known; that consequently so long as they are not actually perceived by me, or do not exist in my mind, or that of any other created spirit, they must either have no existence at all, or else subsist in the mind of some Eternal Spirit: it being perfectly unintelligible, and involving all the absurdity of abstraction, to attribute to any single part of them an existence independent of a spirit. (To be convinced of which, the reader need only reflect, and try to separate in his own thoughts the *being* of a sensible thing from its *being perceived*.)

From what has been said it is evident there is not any other Substance than *Spirit*, or that which perceives. But, for the fuller proof of this point, let it be considered the sensible qualities are colour, figure, motion, smell, taste, and such like, that is, the ideas perceived by sense. Now, for an idea to exist in an unperceiving thing is a manifest contradiction; for to have an idea is all one as to perceive: that therefore wherein colour, figure, and the like qualities exist must perceive them. Hence it is clear there can be no unthinking substance or *substratum* of those ideas.

But, say you, though the ideas themselves do not exist without the mind, yet there may be things like them, wherof they are copies or resemblances; which things exist without the mind, in an unthinking substance. I answer, an idea can be like nothing but an idea; a colour or figure can be like nothing but another colour or figure. If we look but never so little into our thoughts, we shall find it impossible for us to conceive a likeness except only between our ideas. Again, I ask whether those supposed *originals*, or external things, of which our ideas are the pictures or representations, be themselves perceivable or no? If they are, then *they* are ideas, and we have gained our point: but if you say they are not, I appeal to any one whether it be sense to assert a colour is like something which is invisible; hard or soft, like something which is intangible; and so of the rest.

PRIMARY AND SECONDARY QUALITIES

Some there are who make a distinction betwixt *primary* and *secondary* qualities. By the former they mean extension, figure, motion, rest, solidity or impenetrability, and number; by the latter they denote all other sensible qualities, as colours, sounds, tastes, and so forth. The ideas we have of these last they acknowledge not to be the resemblances of anything existing without the mind, or unperceived; but they will have our ideas of the *primary qualities* to be patterns or images of things which exist without the mind, in an unthinking substance which they call Matter. By Matter, therefore, we are to understand an inert, senseless substance, in which extension, figure, and motion do actually subsist. But it is evident, from what we have already shewn, that extension, figure, and motion are only ideas existing in the mind, and that an idea can be like nothing but another idea; and that consequently neither they nor their archetypes can exist in an unperceiving substance. Hence, it is plain that the very notion of what is called *Matter* or *corporeal substance*, involves a contradiction in it. (Insomuch that I should not think it necessary to spend more time in exposing its absurdity. But, because the tenet of the existence of Matter seems to have taken so deep a root in the minds of philosophers, and draws after it so many ill consequences, I choose rather to be thought prolix and tedious than omit anything that might conduce to the full discovery and extirpation of that prejudice.)

They who assert that figure, motion, and the rest of the primary or original qualities do exist without the mind, in unthinking substances, do at the same time acknowledge that colours, sounds, heat, cold, and suchlike secondary qualities, do not; which they tell us are sensations, existing in the mind alone, that depend on and are occasioned by the different size, texture, and motion of the minute particles of matter. This they take for an undoubted truth, which they can demonstrate beyond all exception. Now, if it be certain that those *original* qualities are inseparably united with the other sensible qualities, and not, even in thought, capable of being abstracted from them, it plainly follows that *they* exist only in the mind. But I desire any one to reflect, and try whether he can, by any abstraction of thought, conceive the extension and motion of a body without all other sensible qualities. For my own part, I see evidently that it is not in my power to frame an idea of a body extended and moving, but I must withal give it some colour or other sensible quality, which is acknowledged to exist only in the mind. In short extension, figure, and motion, abstracted from all other qualities, are inconceivable. Where therefore the other sensible qualities are, there must these be also, to wit, in the mind and nowhere else.

Again, *great* and *small*, *swift* and *slow*, are allowed to exist nowhere without the mind; being entirely relative, and changing as the frame or position of the organs of sense varies. The extension therefore which exists without the mind is neither great nor small, the motion neither swift nor slow; that is, they are nothing at all. But, say you, they are extension in general, and motion in general. Thus we see how much the tenet of extended moveable substances existing without the mind depends on that strange doctrine of *abstract ideas*. And here I cannot but remark how nearly the vague and indeterminate description of Matter, or corporeal substance, which the modern philosophers are run into by their own principles, resembles that antiquated and so much ridiculed notion of *materia prima*, to be met with in Aristotle and his followers. Without extension solidity cannot be conceived: since therefore it has been shewn that extension exists not in an unthinking substance, the same must also be true of solidity.

That *number* is entirely the creature of the mind, even though the other qualities be allowed to exist without, will be evident to whoever considers that the same thing bears a different denomination of number as the mind views it with different respects. Thus, the same extension is one, or three, or thirty-six, according as the mind considers it with reference to a yard, a foot, or an inch. Number is so visibly relative, and dependent on men's understanding, that it is strange to think how any one should give it an absolute existence without the mind. We say one book, one page, one line, &c.; all these are equally units, though some contain several of the others. And in each instance, it is plain, the unit relates to some particular combination of ideas *arbitrarily* put together by the mind.

Unity I know some will have to be a simple or uncompounded idea, accompanying all other ideas into the mind. That I have any such idea answering the word *unity* I do not find; and if I had, methinks I could not miss finding it; on the contrary, it should be the most familiar to my understanding, since it is said to accompany all other ideas, and to be perceived by all the ways of sensation and reflection. To say no more, it is an *abstract idea*.

I shall farther add, that, after the same manner as modern philosophers prove certain sensible qualities to have no existence in Matter, or without the mind, the same thing may be likewise proved of all other sensible qualities whatsoever. Thus, for instance, it is said that heat and cold are affections only of the mind, and not at all patterns of real beings, existing in the corporeal substances which excite them; for

that the same body which appears cold to one hand seems warm to another. Now, why may we not as well argue that figure and extension are not patterns or resemblances of qualities existing in Matter; because to the same eye at different stations, or eyes of a different texture at the same station, they appear various, and cannot therefore be the images of anything settled and determinate without the mind? Again, it is proved that sweetness is not really in the sapid thing; because the thing remaining unaltered the sweetness is changed into bitter, as in case of a fever or otherwise vitiated palate. Is it not as reasonable to say that motion is not without the mind; since if the succession of ideas in the mind become swifter, the motion, it is acknowledged, shall appear slower, without any alteration in any external object?

In short, let any one consider those arguments which are thought manifestly to prove that colours and tastes exist only in the mind, and he shall find they may with equal force be brought to prove the same thing of extension, figure, and motion. Though it must be confessed this method of arguing does not so much prove that there is no extension or colour in an outward object, as that we do not know by sense which is the true extension or colour of the object. But the arguments foregoing plainly shew it to be impossible that any colour or extension at all, or other sensible quality whatsoever, should exist in an unthinking subject without the mind, or in truth that there should be any such thing as an outward object.

MATERIAL SUBSTANCE

But let us examine a little the received opinion. It is said extension is a *mode* or *accident* of Matter, and that Matter is the *substratum* that supports it. Now I desire that you would explain to me what is meant by

Matter's *supporting* extension. Say you, I have no idea of Matter; and therefore cannot explain it. I answer, though you have no positive, yet, if you have any meaning at all, you must at least have a relative idea of

Matter; though you know not what it is, yet you must be supposed to know what relation it bears to accidents, and what is meant by its supporting them. It is evident *support* cannot here be taken in its usual or literal sense, as when we say that pillars support a building. In what sense therefore must it be taken? (For my part, I am not able to discover any sense at all that can be applicable to it.)

If we inquire into what the most accurate philosophers declare themselves to mean by *material substance*, we shall find them acknowledge they have no other meaning annexed to those sounds but the idea of Being in general, together with the relative notion of its supporting accidents. The general idea of Being appeareth to me the most abstract and incomprehensible of all other; and as for its supporting accidents, this, as we have just now observed, cannot be understood in the common sense of those words: it must therefore be taken in some other sense, but what that is they do not explain. So that when I consider the two parts or branches which make the signification of the words *material substance*, I am convinced there is no distinct meaning annexed to them. But why should we trouble ourselves any farther, in discussing this material *substratum* or support of figure and motion and other sensible qualities? Does it not suppose they have an existence without the mind? And is not this a direct repugnancy, and altogether inconceivable?

But, though it were possible that solid, figured, moveable substances may exist without the mind, corresponding to the ideas we have of bodies, yet how is it possible for us to know this? Either we must know it by Sense or by Reason. As for our senses, by them we have the knowledge only of our sensations, ideas, or those things that are immediately perceived by sense, call them what you will: but they do not inform us that things exist without the mind, or unperceived, like to those which are perceived. This the materialists themselves acknowledge.—It remains therefore that if we have any knowledge at all of external things, it must be by reason inferring their existence from what is immediately perceived by sense. But (I do not see) what reason can induce us to believe the existence of bodies without the mind, from what we perceive, since the very patrons of Matter themselves do not pretend there is any necessary connexion betwixt them and our ideas? I say it is granted on all hands (and what happens in dreams, frensies, and the like, puts it beyond dispute) that it is possible we might be affected with all the ideas we have now, though no bodies existed without resembling them. Hence it is evident the supposition of external bodies is not necessary for the producing our ideas; since it is granted they are produced sometimes and might possibly be produced always, in the same order we see them in at present, without their concurrence.

But, though we might possibly have all our sensations without them, yet perhaps it may be thought easier to conceive and explain the manner of their production, by supposing external bodies in their likeness rather than otherwise; and so it might be at least probable there are such things as bodies that excite their ideas in our minds. But neither can this be said. For, though we give the materialists their external bodies, they by their own confession are never the nearer knowing how our ideas are produced; since they own themselves unable to comprehend in what manner body can act upon spirit, or how it is possible it should imprint any idea in the mind. Hence it is evident the production of ideas or sensations in our minds, can be no reason why we should suppose Matter or corporeal substances; since that is acknowledged to remain equally inexplicable with or without this supposition. If therefore it were possible for bodies to exist without the mind, yet to hold they do so must needs be a very precarious opinion; since it is to suppose, without any reason at all, that God has created innumerable beings that are entirely useless, and serve to no manner of purpose.

In short, if there were external bodies, it is

impossible we should ever come to know it; and if there were not, we might have the very same reasons to think there were that we have now. Suppose—what no one can deny possible—an intelligence, without the help of external bodies, to be affected with the same train of sensations or ideas that you are, imprinted in the same order and with like vividness in his mind. I ask whether that intelligence hath not all the reason to believe the existence of Corporeal Substances, represented by his ideas, and exciting them in his mind, that you can possibly have for believing the same thing? Of this there can be no question. Which one consideration were enough to make any reasonable person suspect the strength of whatever arguments he may think himself to have, for the existence of bodies without the mind.

Were it necessary to add any farther proof against the existence of Matter, after what has been said, I could instance several of those errors and difficulties (not to mention impieties) which have sprung from that tenet. It has occasioned numberless controversies and disputes in philosophy, and not a few of far greater moment in religion. But I shall not enter into the detail of them in this place, as well because I think arguments *a posteriori* are unnecessary for confirming what has been, if I mistake not, sufficiently demonstrated *a priori*, as because I shall hereafter find occasion to speak somewhat of them.

Bibliography

Texts

The Works of George Berkeley, Bishop of Cloyne. Edited by A. A. Luce and T. E. Jessop. 9 vols. New York: Thomas Nelson & Sons, 1948 (critical edition).

Berkeley: Philosophical Writings. Selected and edited by T. E. Jessop. New York: Thomas Nelson & Sons, 1952.

Studies

Broad, C. D. *Berkeley's Argument about Material Substance.* London: British Academy, 1942.

Hedenius, I. *Sensationalism and Theology in Berkeley's Philosophy.* Oxford: Uppsala, Almqvit & Wiksells, 1936.

8

Introduction

David Hume was born in Edinburgh. In 1723 he entered the University of Edinburgh and, like other English philosophers before him, visited France. In 1739 the first two volumes of his *Treatise of Human Nature* appeared. In 1740 his *Of Morals* was published. Hume described its reception as follows: "It fell dead born from the press, without reaching such distinction as even to excite a murmur among the zealots." Hume then began publishing his *Essays,* which dealt with politics and political economy. Having failed to obtain the chair of moral philosophy at Edinburgh, he served as tutor to the Marquis of Annandale and secretary to General St. Clair, whom he accompanied to France, Vienna, and Turin. Perhaps his most famous work, the *Philosophical Essays* (afterward entitled *An Inquiry Concerning Human Understanding*) appeared in 1748. His *Political Discourses* was published in 1751. His *History of England* appeared in five volumes between 1754 and 1762. The first two volumes were well received. In the later volumes Hume became obsessed with the idea that there was a conspiracy to destroy everything Scottish. His hatred of everything English, of society in London, of Whig principles, among other things, marred his objectivity. As a consequence he no longer enjoyed the popularity that the first two volumes had won him. Hume constructed a house which served as a center for cultivated and literary society. It was in this society that Hume's kindness to literary aspirants and to those who differed from his views won him universal respect and affection. He died in 1776, one year after completing his autobiography, *My Own Life.*

Unlike the empiricists who attempted to resolve the problem of reconciling spirit and matter by reducing spirit to matter, and the idealists, who attempted to reduce matter to mind, Hume simply denied the existence of spirit and matter. All valid knowledge is limited to experienced mental phenomena. Mind is the psychic content, the state of consciousness, the bundle of perceptions which are called *impressions* if they are the more lively sensations, and feelings or *ideas* (thoughts) if they are faint images of impressions. Hume held that it is not substances or qualities that man perceives but his own subjective states, i.e., the impressions which enter by the senses. Mind is constituted by successive perceptions, and hence the substantiality of the ego is delusion. The bundle of perceptions is bound together by certain relations of resemblance, contrast and contiguity. The idea of causation is derived from the habitual psychological perception of events preceding or following another in space and time. The necessity of causality is thus not in things but only in the mind, as an experienced union of phenomena. The following passage exemplifies some of Hume's thoughts on causation.

KNOWLEDGE OF CAUSATION *

Let us therefore cast our eye on any two objects, which we call cause and effect, and

* From David Hume, *A Treatise of Human Nature.* Copyright 1951, by permission from the Clarendon Press, Oxford.

turn them on all sides, in order to find that impression, which produces an idea of such prodigious consequence. At first sight I perceive, that I must not search for it in any of the particular *qualities* of the objects; since, which-ever of these qualities pitch on, find some object, that is not possest of it, and yet falls under the denomination of cause or effect. And indeed there is nothing existent, either externally or internally, which is not to be consider'd either as a cause or an effect; tho' 'tis plain there is no one quality, which universally belongs to all beings, and gives them a title to that denomination.

Contiguity

The idea, then, of causation must be deriv'd from some *relation* among objects; and that relation we must now endeavour to discover. I find in the first place, that whatever objects are consider'd as causes or effects, are *contiguous;* and that nothing can operate in a time or place, which is ever so little remov'd from those of its existence. Tho' distant objects may sometimes seem productive of each other, they are commonly found upon examination to be link'd by a chain of causes, which are contiguous among themselves, and to the distant objects; and when in any particular instance we cannot discover this connexion, we still presume it to exist. We may therefore consider the relation of CONTIGUITY as essential to that of causation; at least may suppose it such, according to the general opinion, till we can find a more proper occasion to clear up this matter, by examining what objects are or are not susceptible of juxtaposition and conjunction.

Priority in Time of Cause

The second relation I shall observe as essential to causes and effects, is not so universally acknowledg'd, but is liable to some controversy. 'Tis that of PRIORITY of time in the cause before the effect. Some pretend that 'tis not absolutely necessary a cause shou'd precede its effect; but that any object or action, in the very first moment of its existence, may exert its productive quality, and give rise to another object or action, perfectly co-temporary with itself. But beside that experience in most instances seems to contradict this opinion, we may establish the relation of priority by a kind of inference or reasoning. 'Tis an establish'd maxim both in natural and moral philosophy, that an object, which exists for any time in its full perfection without producing another, is not its sole cause; but is assisted by some other principle, which pushes it from its state of inactivity, and makes it exert that energy, of which it was secretly possest. Now if any cause may be perfectly co-temporary with its effect, 'tis certain, according to this maxim, that they must all of them be so; since any one of them, which retards its operation for a single moment, exerts not itself at that very individual time, in which it might have operated; and therefore is no proper cause. The consequence of this wou'd be no less than the destruction of that succession of causes, which we observe in the world; and indeed, the utter annihilation of time. For if one cause were co-temporary with its effect, and this effect with *its* effect, and so on, 'tis plain there wou'd be no such thing as succession, and all objects must be co-existent.

If this argument appear satisfactory, 'tis well. If not, I beg the reader to allow me the same liberty, which I have us'd in the preceding case, of supposing it such. For he shall find, that the affair is of no great importance.

Having thus discover'd or suppos'd the two relations of *contiguity* and *succession* to be essential to causes and effects, I find I am stopt short, and can proceed no farther in considering any single instance of cause and effect. Motion in one body is regarded upon impulse as the cause of motion in another. When we consider these objects with the utmost attention, we find only that the one body approaches the other; and that the motion of it precedes that of the other, but without any sensible interval. 'Tis in vain to rack ourselves with *farther* thought and reflexion upon this subject. We can go no *farther* in considering this particular instance.

Shou'd any one leave this instance, and

pretend to define a cause, by saying it is something productive of another, 'tis evident he wou'd say nothing. For what does he mean by *production*? Can he give any definition of it, that will not be the same with that of causation? If he can; I desire it may be produc'd. If he cannot; he here runs in a circle, and gives a synonimous term instead of a definition.

Shall we then rest contented with these two relations of contiguity and succession, as affording a compleat idea of causation? By no means. An object may be contiguous and prior to another, without being consider'd as its cause. There is a NECESSARY CONNEXION to be taken into consideration; and that relation is of much greater importance, than any of the other two above-mention'd.

Necessary Connexion

Here again I turn the object on all sides, in order to discover the nature of this necessary connexion, and find the impression, or impressions, from which its idea may be deriv'd. When I cast my eye on the *known qualities* of objects, I immediately discover that the relation of cause and effect depends not in the least on *them*. When I consider their *relations*, I can find none but those of contiguity and succession; which I have already regarded as imperfect and unsatisfactory. Shall the despair of success make me assert, that I am here possest of an idea, which is not preceded by any similar impression? This wou'd be too strong a proof of levity and inconstancy; since the contrary principle has been already so firmly establish'd, as to admit of no farther doubt; at least, till we have more fully examin'd the present difficulty.

We must, therefore, proceed like those, who being in search of any thing that lies conceal'd from them, and not finding it in the place they expected, beat about all the neighbouring fields, without any certain view or design, in hopes their good fortune will at last guide them to what they search for. 'Tis necessary for us to leave the direct survey of this question concerning the nature of that *necessary connexion*, which enters into our idea of cause and effect; and endeavour to find some other questions, the examination of which will perhaps afford a hint, that may serve to clear up the present difficulty. Of these questions there occur two, which I shall proceed to examine, *viz.*

First, For what reason we pronounce it *necessary*, that every thing whose existence has a beginning, shou'd also have a cause?

Secondly, Why we conclude, that such particular causes must *necessarily* have such particular effects; and what is the nature of that *inference* we draw from the one to the other, and of the *belief* we repose in it?

I shall only observe before I proceed any farther, that tho' the ideas of cause and effect be deriv'd from the impressions of reflexion as well as from those of sensation, yet for brevity's sake, I commonly mention only the latter as the origin of these ideas; tho' I desire that whatever I say of them may also extend to the former. Passions are connected with their objects and with one another; no less than external bodies are connected together. The same relation, then, of cause and effect, which belongs to one, must be common to all of them.

To begin with the first question concerning the necessity of a cause: 'Tis a general maxim in philosophy, that *whatever begins to exist, must have a cause of existence.* This is commonly taken for granted in all reasonings, without any proof given or demanded. 'Tis suppos'd to be founded on intuition, and to be one of those maxims, which tho' they may be deny'd with the lips, 'tis impossible for men in their hearts really to doubt of. But if we examine this maxim by the idea of knowledge above-explain'd, we shall discover in it no mark of any such intuitive certainty; but on the contrary shall find, that 'tis of a nature quite foreign to that species of conviction.

All certainty arises from the comparison

of ideas, and from the discovery of such re-lations as are unalterable, so long as the ideas continue the same. These relations are *resemblance, proportions in quantity and number, degrees of any quality, and con-trariety;* none of which are imply'd in this proposition, *Whatever has a beginning has also a cause of existence.* That proposition therefore is not intuitively certain. At least any one, who wou'd assert it to be intuitively certain, must deny these to be the only in-fallible relations, and must find some other relation of that kind to be imply'd in it; which it will then be time enough to examine.

But here is an argument, which proves at once, that the foregoing proposition is nei-ther intuitively nor demonstrably certain. We can never demonstrate the necessity of a cause to every new existence, or new modi-fication of existence, without shewing at the same time the impossibility there is, that any thing can ever begin to exist without some productive principle; and where the latter proposition cannot be prov'd, we must despair of ever being able to prove the former. Now that the latter proposition is utterly incapable of a demonstrative proof, we may satisfy ourselves by considering, that as all distinct ideas are separable from each other, and as the ideas of cause and effect are evidently distinct, 'twill be easy for us to conceive any object to be non-existent this moment, and existent the next, without conjoining to it the distinct idea of a cause or productive principle. The separation, therefore, of the idea of a cause from that of a beginning of existence, is plainly possible for the imagination; and consequently the actual separation of these objects is so far possible, that it implies no contradiction nor absurdity; and is therefore incapable of being refuted by any reasoning from mere ideas; without which 'tis impossible to dem-onstrate the necessity of a cause.

Accordingly we shall find upon examina-tion, that every demonstration, which has been produc'd for the necessity of a cause, is fallacious and sophistical. All the points of time and place, say some philosophers, in which we can suppose any object to begin to exist, are in themselves equal; and unless there be some cause, which is peculiar to one time and to one place, and which by that means determines and fixes the existence, it must remain in eternal suspence; and the object can never begin to be, for want of something to fix its beginning. But I ask; Is there any more difficulty in supposing the time and place to be fix'd without a cause, than to suppose the existence to be deter-min'd in that manner? The first question that occurs on this subject is always, *whether* the object shall exist or not: The next, *when* and *where* it shall begin to exist. If the re-moval of a cause be intuitively absurd in the one case, it must be so in the other: And if that absurdity be not clear without a proof in the one case, it will equally require one in the other. The absurdity, then, of the one supposition can never be a proof of that of the other; since they are both upon the same footing, and must stand or fall by the same reasoning.

The second argument, which I find us'd on this head, labours under an equal difficulty. Every thing, 'tis said, must have a cause; for if any thing wanted a cause, *it* wou'd pro-duce *itself;* that is, exist before it existed; which is impossible. But this reasoning is plainly unconclusive; because it supposes, that in our denial of a cause we still grant what we expressly deny, *viz.* that there must be a cause; which therefore is taken to be the object itself; and *that*, no doubt, is an evident contradiction. But to say that any thing is produc'd, or to express myself more properly, comes into existence, without a cause, is not to affirm, that 'tis itself its own cause; but on the contrary in excluding all external causes, excludes *a fortiori* the thing itself which is created. An object, that exists absolutely without any cause, certainly is not its own cause; and when you assert, that the one follows from the other, you sup-pose the very point in question, and take it for granted, that 'tis utterly impossible any thing can ever begin to exist without a cause, but that upon the exclusion of one productive principle, we must still have re-course to another.

'Tis exactly the same case with the third argument, which has been employ'd to demonstrate the necessity of a cause. Whatever is produc'd without any cause, is produc'd by *nothing;* or in other words, has nothing for its cause. But nothing can never be a cause, no more than it can be something, or equal to two right angles. By the same intuition, that we perceive nothing not to be equal to two right angles, or not to be something, we perceive, that it can never be a cause; and consequently must perceive, that every object has a real cause of its existence.

I believe it will not be necessary to employ many words in shewing the weakness of this argument, after what I have said of the foregoing. They are all of them founded on the same fallacy, and are deriv'd from the same turn of thought. 'Tis sufficient only to observe, that when we exclude all causes we really do exclude them, and neither suppose nothing nor the object itself to be the causes of the existence; and consequently can draw no argument from the absurdity of these suppositions to prove the absurdity of that exclusion. If every thing must have a cause, it follows, that upon the exclusion of other causes we must accept of the object itself or of nothing as causes. But 'tis the very point in question, whether every thing must have a cause or not; and therefore, according to all just reasoning, it ought never to be taken for granted.

They are still more frivolous, who say, that every effect must have a cause, because 'tis imply'd in the very idea of effect. Every effect necessarily pre-supposes a cause; effect being a relative term, of which cause is the correlative. But this does not prove, that every being must be preceded by a cause; no more than it follows, because every husband must have a wife, that therefore every man must be marry'd. The true state of the question is, whether every object, which begins to exist, must owe its existence to a cause; and this I assert neither to be intuitively nor demonstratively certain, and hope to have prov'd it sufficiently by the foregoing arguments.

Since it is not from knowledge or any scientific reasoning, that we derive the opinion of the necessity of a cause to every new production, that opinion must necessarily arise from observation and experience. The next question, then, shou'd naturally be, *how experience gives rise to such a principle?* But as I find it will be more convenient to sink this question in the following, *Why we conclude, that such particular causes must necessarily have such particular effects, and why we form an inference from one to another?* we shall make that the subject of our future enquiry. 'Twill, perhaps, be found in the end, that the same answer will serve for both questions.

Reasonings Concerning Cause and Effect

Tho' the mind in its reasonings from causes or effects carries its view beyond those objects, which it sees or remembers, it must never lose sight of them entirely, nor reason merely upon its own ideas, without some mixture of impressions, or at least of ideas of the memory, which are equivalent to impressions. When we infer effects from causes, we must establish the existence of these causes; which we have only two ways of doing, either by an immediate perception of our memory or senses, or by an inference from other causes; which causes again we must ascertain in the same manner, either by a present impression, or by an inference from *their* causes, and so on, till we arrive at some object, which we see or remember. 'Tis impossible for us to carry on our inferences *in infinitum;* and the only thing, that can stop them, is an impression of the memory or senses, beyond which there is no room for doubt or enquiry.

To give an instance of this, we may chuse any point of history, and consider for what reason we either believe or reject it. Thus we believe that CÆSAR was kill'd in the senate-house on the *ides* of *March;* and that because this fact is establish'd on the unanimous testimony of historians, who agree to assign this precise time and place to that event. Here are certain characters and letters present either to our memory or senses; which characters we likewise remember to have been us'd as the signs of certain ideas; and these ideas were either in the minds of such as were immediately present at that action, and receiv'd the ideas directly from its existence; or they were deriv'd from the testimony of others, and that again from another testimony, by a visible gradation, 'till we arrive at those who were eye-witnesses and spectators of the event. 'Tis obvious all this chain of argument or connexion of causes and effects, is at first founded on those characters or letters, which are seen or remember'd, and that without the authority either of the memory or senses our whole reasoning wou'd be chimerical and without foundation. Every link of the chain wou'd in that case hang upon another; but there wou'd not be any thing fix'd to one end of it, capable of sustaining the whole; and consequently there wou'd be no belief nor evidence. And this actually is the case with all *hypothetical* arguments, or reasonings upon a supposition; there being in them, neither any present impression, nor belief of a real existence.

I need not observe, that 'tis no just objection to the present doctrine, that we can reason upon our past conclusions or principles, without having recourse to those impressions, from which they first arose. For even supposing these impressions shou'd be entirely effac'd from the memory, the conviction they produc'd may still remain; and 'tis equally true, that all reasonings concerning causes and effects are originally deriv'd from some impression; in the same manner, as the assurance of a demonstration proceeds always from a comparison of ideas, tho' it may continue after the comparison is forgot.

Impressions of the Senses and Memory

In this kind of reasoning, then, from causation, we employ materials, which are of a mix'd and heterogeneous nature, and which, however connected, are yet essentially different from each other. All our arguments concerning causes and effects consist both of an impression of the memory or senses, and of the idea of that existence, which produces the object of the impression, or is produc'd by it. Here therefore we have three things to explain, *viz. First,* The original impression. *Secondly,* The transition to the idea of the connected cause or effect. *Thirdly,* The nature and qualities of that idea.

As to those *impressions,* which arise from the *senses,* their ultimate cause is, in my opinion, perfectly inexplicable by human reason, and 'twill always be impossible to decide with certainty, whether they arise immediately from the object, or are produc'd by the creative power of the mind, or are deriv'd from the author of our being. Nor is such a question any way material to our present purpose. We may draw inferences from the coherence of our perceptions, whether they be true or false; whether they represent nature justly, or be mere illusions of the senses.

When we search for the characteristic, which distinguishes the *memory* from the imagination, we must immediately perceive, that it cannot lie in the simple ideas it presents to us; since both these faculties borrow their simple ideas from the impressions, and can never go beyond these original perceptions. These faculties are as little distinguish'd from each other by the arrangement of their complex ideas. For tho' it be a peculiar property of the memory to preserve the original order and position of its ideas, while the imagination transposes and changes them, as it pleases; yet this difference is not sufficient to distinguish them in their operation, or make us know the one from the other; it being impossible to recall the past impressions, in order to compare them with our present ideas, and see whether their arrangement be exactly similar. Since therefore the memory is known, neither by the order of its *complex* ideas, nor the nature of its *simple* ones; it follows, that the difference betwixt it and the imagination lies in its superior force and vivacity. A man may indulge his fancy in feigning any past scene of adventures; nor wou'd there be any possibility of distinguishing this from a remembrance of a like kind, were not the ideas of the imagination fainter and more obscure.

Bibliography

Texts

The Philosophical Works of David Hume. Edited by T. H. Green and T. H. Grosse, 4 vols. London: Longmans, Green & Co., Ltd., 1874–1875.

A Treatise of Human Nature. Edited by L. A. Selby-Bigge. Fair Lawn, N. J.: Oxford University Press, 1951. (Reprint of 1888 edition.)

Studies

Laird, J. *Hume's Philosophy of Human Nature.* London: Methuen & Co., Ltd., 1932.

Smith, N. K. *The Philosophy of David Hume.* New York: St. Martin's Press, Inc., 1941.

9

IMMANUEL KANT
1724–1804

Introduction

Born in Königsberg, Immanuel Kant, grandson of a Scotch emigrant, was raised in the strict and pietistic Lutheran faith of his father, a saddler. In 1740, he entered the university in his home town and in 1755 completed his doctorate work. As a *Privatdozent* he lectured fifteen years and received a poor salary. Kant's lectures were well attended, and he had the reputation of possessing a brilliant, humorous, and excellent presentation. When he was forty-five years old, Kant received the position of Ordinary Professor of logic and metaphysics at the University of Königsberg. He was also invited to the universities of Erlangen and Jena, but Kant seldom left his home town and only for short distances. Though he was the first in Germany to lecture on physical geography, it is unlikely that he ever saw the sea. Kant never married but devoted himself unsparingly to his academic profession. Though he had lectured in the beginning of his career on physics, he later turned largely to philosophy. His inaugural lecture as professor was his *De mundi sensibilis et inteligibilis forma et principiis* (1770). Eleven years later there appeared his famous *Kritik der reinen Vernunft* (*Critique of Pure Reason*) (1781), which rapidly became the basis for philosophical courses and lectures held throughout Germany. Students soon came from all quarters to hear the famous professor. By 1792, Kant was in collision with the government because of his religious doctrines, particularly his moral rationalism, which could not be reconciled with Lutheranism. When the first part of Kant's *Die Religion innerhalb der Grenzen der blossen Vernunft* (*Religion within the Limits of Pure Reason*) appeared in Berlin, the publication of the full work was forbidden. In 1793 he published the full work in Königsberg. The government then exacted a promise that he would not continue to write on religion till the death of the King, Frederick William II. Kant complied, but he was depressed and in 1794 withdrew from society. The following year he gave up all his lectures but one on logic and metaphysics. After forty-two years of teaching, he finished his *Die Metaphysik der Ethik* and his *Anthropologie* (1798). In 1797 the king died, and in 1798 he published *Streit der Fakultaten* (*Strife of the Faculties*) to reassert his right to discourse on religious topics.

In his *Critique of Pure Reason*, Kant is concerned with the speculative consideration of what must be the conditions prerequisite for the knowledge prior to and independent of experience. In his *Critique of Practical Reason*, he discusses what ought to be the consequence of felt duty, a given of moral experience. For Kant all certain conceptual knowledge must contain a sensory element (*Anschauung*) and an element of thought (*Denken*). In a section of the *Critique of Pure Reason*, the "Transcendental Aesthetic," Kant treats of the a priori conditions of space and time. These pure forms are the basis for scientific universality and the sensory conditions for all valid knowledge. In the section "Transcendental Analytic," intellect is understood as containing the a priori forms of pure understanding (judgment) called the categories. There are twelve such categories expressed in judgments of quantity, quality, relation, and modality. These categories are imposed on the data of intuition to produce valid scientific knowledge. They are *synthetic a priori* judgments: synthetic because the predicate is not found by an analysis of the subject, and a priori since they are independent of empirical and intuitional content. Reason as treated in the section "Transcendental Dialectic," is regulated by three formal elements (ideas or notions): God, soul, and world. These ideas regulate the speculations of reason and are a priori conditions for its noncontradictory functioning. These ideas as such are not representative of reality, since they lack the sensory element required for all valid knowledge. Hence, only sensible phenomena are known and no reality is known with certainty in its noumenal (essential) character. Kant did not deny the existence of God, the soul, or the world. He said man did not know them with certainty. In the *Critique of Practical Reason*, Kant argues differently. The overwhelm-

ing and undeniable moral experience of duty (ought), the inner authority, whose command is unconditional and imperative, Kant called the "categorical imperative." As a result of the necessity of this moral urgency, practical reason discovers the existence of God, the lawgiver. The supremacy of moral law and moral experience over speculative considerations may be seen in the following passage. The last part of the reading is a selection from Kant's theory of the limits of human knowledge viewed speculatively.

DIFFERENCE BETWEEN PURE AND EMPIRICAL KNOWLEDGE *

That all our knowledge begins with experience there can be no doubt. For how is it possible that the faculty of cognition should be awakened into exercise otherwise than by means of objects which affect our senses, and partly of themselves produce representations, partly rouse our powers of understanding into activity, to compare, to connect, or to separate these, and so to convert the raw material of our sensuous impressions into a knowledge of objects, which is called experience? In respect of time, therefore, no knowledge of ours is antecedent to experience, but begins with it.

But, though all our knowledge begins with experience, it by no means follows that all arises out of experience. For, on the contrary, it is quite possible that our empirical knowledge is a compound of that which we receive through impressions, and that which the faculty of cognition supplies from itself (sensuous impressions giving merely the *occasion*), an addition which we cannot distinguish from the original element given by sense, till long practice has made us attentive to, and skilful in separating it. It is, therefore, a question which requires close

* From Immanuel Kant, *Critique of Pure Reason*, J. M. D. Meiklejohn, translator. Everyman's Library. Reprinted by permission of E. P. Dutton & Co., Inc., New York, and J. M. Dent and Sons Ltd., London, 1934.

investigation, and is not to be answered at first sight—whether there exists a knowledge altogether independent of experience, and even of all sensuous impressions? Knowledge of this kind is called *à priori*, in contradistinction to empirical knowledge, which has its sources *à posteriori*, that is, in experience.

But the expression, "*à priori*," is not as yet definite enough adequately to indicate the whole meaning of the question above stated. For, in speaking of knowledge which has its sources in experience, we are wont to say, that this or that may be known *à priori*, because we do not derive this knowledge immediately from experience, but from a general rule, which, however, we have itself borrowed from experience. Thus, if a man undermined his house, we say, "he might know *à priori* that it would have fallen"; that is, he needed not to have waited for the experience that it did actually fall. But still, *à priori*, he could not know even this much. For, that bodies are heavy, and, consequently, that they fall when their supports are taken away, must have been known to him previously, by means of experience.

By the term "knowledge *à priori*," therefore, we shall in the sequel understand, not such as is independent of this or that kind of experience, but such as is absolutely so of *all* experience. Opposed to this is empirical knowledge, or that which is possible only *à posteriori*, that is, through experience. Knowledge *à priori* is either pure or impure. Pure knowledge *à priori* is that with which no empirical element is mixed up. For example, the proposition, "Every change has a cause," is a proposition *à priori*, but impure, because change is a conception which can only be derived from experience.

À *PRIORI* COGNITIONS OF THE HUMAN INTELLECT

The question now is as to a *criterion*, by which we may securely distinguish a pure from an empirical cognition. Experience no doubt teaches us that this or that object is constituted in such and such a manner, but not that it could not possibly exist otherwise. Now, in the first place, if we have a proposition which contains the idea of necessity in its very conception, it is a judgment *à priori;* if, moreover, it is not derived from any other proposition, unless from one equally involving the idea of necessity, it is absolutely *à priori*. Secondly, an empirical judgment never exhibits strict and absolute, but only assumed and comparative universality (by induction); therefore, the most we can say is—so far as we have hitherto observed, there is no exception to this or that rule. If, on the other hand, a judgment carries with it strict and absolute universality, that is, admits of no possible exception, it is not derived from experience, but is valid absolutely *à priori*.

Empirical universality is, therefore, only an arbitrary extension of validity, from that which may be predicated of a proposition valid in most cases, to that which is asserted of a proposition which holds good in all; as, for example, in the affirmation, "all bodies are heavy." When, on the contrary, strict universality characterizes a judgment, it necessarily indicates another peculiar source of knowledge, namely, a faculty of cognition *à priori*. Necessity and strict universality, therefore, are infallible tests for distinguishing pure from empirical knowledge, and are inseparably connected with each other. But as in the use of these criteria the empirical limitation is sometimes more easily detected than the contingency of the judgment, or the unlimited universality which we attach to a judgment is often a more convincing proof than its necessity, it may be advisable to use the criteria separately, each being by itself infallible.

Now, that in the sphere of human cognition, we have judgments which are necessary, and in the strictest sense universal, consequently pure *à priori*, it will be an easy matter to show. If we desire an example from the sciences, we need only take any proposition in mathematics. If we cast our eyes upon the commonest operations of the understanding, the proposition, "every change must have a cause," will amply serve our purpose. In the latter case, indeed, the conception of a cause so plainly involves the conception of a necessity of connection with an effect, and of a strict universality of the law, that the very notion of a cause would entirely disappear, were we to derive it, like Hume, from a frequent association of what happens with that which precedes, and the habit thence originating of connecting representations—the necessity inherent in the judgment being therefore merely subjective. Besides, without seeking for such examples of principles existing *à priori* in cognition, we might easily show that such principles are the indispensable basis of the possibility of experience itself, and consequently prove their existence *à priori*. For whence could our experience itself acquire certainty, if all the rules on which it depends were themselves empirical, and consequently fortuitous? No one, therefore, can admit the validity of the use of such rules as first principles. But, for the present, we may content ourselves with having established the fact, that we do possess and exercise a faculty of pure *à priori* cognition; and, secondly, with having pointed out the proper tests of such cognition, namely, universality and necessity.

Not only in judgments, however, but even in conceptions, is an *à priori* origin manifest. For example, if we take away by degrees from our conceptions of a body all that can be referred to mere sensuous experience— color, hardness or softness, weight, even impenetrability the body will then vanish, but the space which it occupied still remains, and this it is utterly impossible to annihilate in thought. Again, if we take away, in like manner, from our empirical conception of any object, corporeal or incorporeal, all properties which mere experience has taught us to connect with it, still we cannot think away those through which we cogitate it as substance, or adhering to substance, although our conception of substance is more determined than that of an object. Compelled, therefore, by that necessity with which the conception of substance forces itself upon us, we must confess that it has its seat in our faculty of cognition *à priori*.

POSSIBILITY, PRINCIPLES, AND EXTENT OF HUMAN KNOWLEDGE À *PRIORI*

Of far more importance than all that has been above said, is the consideration that certain of our cognitions rise completely above the sphere of all possible experience, and by means of conceptions, to which there exists in the whole extent of experience no corresponding object, seem to extend the range of our judgments beyond its bounds. And just in this transcendental or supersensible sphere, where experience affords us neither instruction nor guidance, lie the investigations of *Reason*, which, on account of their importance, we consider far preferable to, and as having a far more elevated aim than, all that the understanding can achieve within the sphere of sensuous phenomena. So high a value do we set upon these investigations, that even at the risk of error, we persist in following them out, and permit neither doubt nor disregard nor indifference to restrain us from the pursuit. These unavoidable problems of mere pure reason are God, Freedom (of will) and Immortality. The science which, with all its preliminaries, has for its especial object the solution of these problems is named metaphysics—a science which is at the very outset dogmatical, that is, it confidently takes upon itself the execution of this task without any previous investigation of the ability or inability of reason for such an understanding.

Now the safe ground of experience being thus abandoned, it seems nevertheless natural that we should hesitate to erect a building with the cognitions we possess, without knowing whence they come, and on the strength of principles, the origin of which is undiscovered. Instead of thus trying to build without a foundation, it is rather to be expected that we should long ago have put the question, how the understanding can arrive at these *à priori* cognitions, and what is the extent, validity, and worth which they may possess? We say, this is natural enough, meaning by the word natural that which is consistent with a just and reasonable way of thinking; but if we understand by the term, that which usually happens, nothing indeed could be more natural and more comprehensible than that this investigation should be left long unattempted. For one part of our pure knowledge, the science of mathematics, has been long firmly established, and thus leads us to form flattering expectations with regard to others, though these may be of quite a different nature. Besides, when we get beyond the bounds of experience, we are of course safe from opposition in that quarter; and the charm of widening the range of our knowledge is so great, that unless we are brought to a standstill by some evident contradiction, we hurry on undoubtingly in our course. This, however, may be avoided, if we are sufficiently cautious in the construction of our fictions, which are not the less fictions on that account.

Mathematical science affords us a brilliant example, how far, independently of all experience, we may carry our *à priori* knowledge. It is true that the mathematician occupies himself with objects and cognitions only in so far as they can be represented by means of intuition. But this circumstance is easily overlooked, because the said intuition can itself be given *à priori*, and therefore is hardly to be distinguished from a mere pure conception. Deceived by such a proof of the power of reason, we can perceive no limits to the extension of our knowledge. The light dove cleaving in free flight the thin air, whose resistance it feels, might imagine that her movements would be far more free and rapid in airless space. Just in the same way did Plato, abandoning the world of sense because of the narrow limits it sets to the understanding, venture upon the wings of ideas beyond it, into the void space of pure intellect. He did not reflect that he made no real progress by all his efforts; for he met with no resistance which might serve him for a support, as it were, whereon to rest, and on which he might apply his powers, in order to let the intellect acquire momentum for its progress. It is, indeed, the common fate of human reason in speculation, to finish the imposing edifice of thought as rapidly as possible, and then for the first time to begin to examine whether the foundation is a solid one or no. Arrived at this point, all sorts of excuses are sought after, in order to console us for its want of stability, or rather indeed, to enable us to dispense altogether with so late and dangerous an investigation. But what frees us during the process of building from all apprehension or suspicion, and flatters us into the belief of its solidity, is this. A great part, perhaps the greatest part, of the business of our reason consists in the analyzation of the conceptions which we already possess of objects. By this means we gain a multitude of cognitions, which, although really nothing more than elucidations or explanations of that which (though in a confused manner) was already thought in our conceptions, are, at least in respect of their form, prized as new introspections; while, so far as regards their matter or content, we have really made no addition to our conceptions, but only disinvolved them. But as this process does furnish real *à priori* knowledge, which has a sure progress and useful results, reason, deceived by this, slips in, without being itself aware of it, assertions of a quite different kind; in which, to given conceptions it adds others, *à priori* indeed, but entirely foreign to them, without our knowing how it arrives at these, and, indeed, without such a question ever suggesting itself. I shall therefore at once proceed to examine the difference between these two modes of knowledge.

ANALYTICAL AND SYNTHETICAL JUDGMENTS

In all judgments wherein the relation of a subject to the predicate is cogitated (I mention affirmative judgments only here; the application to negative will be very easy), this relation is possible in two different ways. Either the predicate B belongs to the subject A, as somewhat which is contained (though covertly) in the conception A; or the predicate B lies completely out of the conception A, although it stands in connection with it. In the first instance, I term the judgment analytical, in the second, synthetical. Analytical judgments (affirmative) are therefore those in which the connection of the predicate with the subject is cogitated through identity; those in which this connection is cogitated without identity, are called synthetical judgments. The former may be called *explicative*, the latter *augmentative* [1] judgments; because the former add in the predicate nothing to the conception of the subject, but only analyze it into its constituent conceptions, which were thought already in the subject, although in a confused manner; the latter add to our conceptions of the subject a predicate which was not contained in it, and which no analysis could ever have discovered therein. For example, when I say, "all bodies are extended," this is an analytical judgment. For I need not go beyond the conception of *body* in order to find extension connected with it, but merely analyze the conception, that is, become conscious of the manifold properties which I think in that conception, in order to discover this predicate in it: it is therefore an analytical judgment. On the other hand, when I say, "all bodies are heavy," the predicate is something totally different from that which I think in the mere conception of a body. By the addition of such a predicate, therefore, it becomes a synthetical judgment.

Judgments of experience, as such, are always synthetical. For it would be absurd to think of grounding an analytical judgment on experience, because in forming such a judgment, I need not go out of the sphere of my conceptions, and therefore recourse to the testimony of experience is quite unnecessary. That "bodies are extended" is not an empirical judgment, but a proposition which stands firm *à priori*. For before addressing myself to experience, I already have in my conception all the requisite conditions for the judgment, and I have only to extract the predicate from the conception, according to the principle of contradiction, and thereby at the same time become conscious of the necessity of the judgment, a necessity which I could never learn from experience. On the other hand, though at first I do not

at all include the predicate of weight in my conception of body in general, that conception still indicates an object of experience, a part of the totality of experience, to which I can still add other parts; and this I do when I recognize by observation that bodies are heavy. I can cognize beforehand by analysis the conception of body through the characteristics of extension, impenetrability, shape, etc., all which are cogitated in this conception. But now I extend my knowledge, and looking back on experience from which I had derived this conception of body, I find weight at all times connected with the above characteristics, and therefore I synthetically add to my conceptions this as a predicate, and say, "All bodies are heavy." Thus it is experience upon which rests the possibility of the synthesis of the predicate of weight with the conception of body, because both conceptions, although the one is not contained in the other, still belong to one another (only contingently, however), as parts of a whole, namely, of experience, which is itself a synthesis of intuitions.

But to synthetical judgments *à priori*, such aid is entirely wanting. If I go out of and beyond the conception A, in order to recognize another B as connected with it, what foundation have I to rest on, whereby to render the synthesis possible? I have here no longer the advantage of looking out in the sphere of experience for what I want. Let us take, for example, the proposition, "Everything that happens has a cause." In the conception of *something that happens*, I indeed think of an existence which a certain time antecedes, and from this I can derive analytical judgments. But the conception of a cause lies quite out of the above conception, and indicates something entirely different from "that which happens," and is consequently not contained in that conception. How then am I able to assert concerning the general conception—"that which happens"—something entirely different from that conception, and to recognize the conception of cause although not contained in it, yet as belonging to it, and even necessarily? What is here the unknown = X, upon

[1] That is, judgments which really add to, and do not merely analyze or explain the conceptions which make up the sum of our knowledge.

which the understanding rests when it believes it has found, out of the conception A a foreign predicate B, which it nevertheless considers to be connected with it? It cannot be experience, because the principle adduced annexes the two representations, cause and effect, to the representation existence, not only with universality, which experience cannot give, but also with the expression of necessity, therefore completely *à priori* and from pure conceptions. Upon such synthetical, that is augmentative propositions depends the whole aim of our speculative knowledge *à priori;* for although analytical judgments are indeed highly important and necessary, they are so only to arrive at that clearness of conceptions which is requisite for a sure and extended synthesis, and this alone is a real acquisition.

Mathematical judgments are always synthetical. Hitherto this fact, though incontestably true and very important in its consequences, seems to have escaped the analysts of the human mind, nay, to be in complete opposition to all their conjectures. For as it was found that mathematical conclusions all proceed according to the principle of contradiction (which the nature of every apodictic certainty requires), people became persuaded that the fundamental principles of the science also were recognized and admitted in the same way. But the notion is fallacious; for although a synthetical proposition can certainly be discerned by means of the principle of contradiction, this is possible only when another synthetical proposition precedes, from which the latter is deduced, but never of itself.

Before all, be it observed, that proper mathematical propositions are always judgments *à priori,* and not empirical, because they carry along with them the conception of necessity, which cannot be given by experience. If this be demurred to, it matters not; I shall then limit my assertion to *pure* mathematics, the very conception of which implies that it consists of knowledge altogether non-empirical and *à priori.*

We might, indeed, at first suppose that the proposition $7 + 5 = 12$, is a merely analytical proposition, following (according to the principle of contradiction), from the conception of the sum of seven and five. But if we regard it more narrowly, we find that our conception of the sum of seven and five contains nothing more than the uniting of both sums into one, whereby it cannot at all be cogitated what this single number is which embraces both. The conception of twelve is by no means obtained by merely cogitating the union of seven and five; and we may analyze our conception of such a possible sum as long as we will, still we shall never discover in it the notion of twelve. We must go beyond these conceptions, and have recourse to an intuition which corresponds to one of the two—our five fingers, for example, or like Segner in his "Arithmetic," five points, and so by degrees, add the units contained in the five given in the intuition, to the conception of seven. For I first take the number 7, and, for the conception of 5 calling in the aid of the fingers of my hand as objects of intuition, I add the units, which I before took together to make up the number 5, gradually now by means of the material image my hand, to the number 7, and by this process, I at length see the number 12 arise. That 7 should be added to 5, I have certainly cogitated in my conception of a sum $= 7 + 5$, but not that this sum was equal to 12. Arithmetical propositions are therefore always synthetical, of which we may become more clearly convinced by trying large numbers. For it will thus become quite evident, that, turn and twist our conceptions as we may, it is impossible, without having recourse to intuition, to arrive at the sum total or product by means of the mere analysis of our conceptions. Just as little is any principle of pure geometry analytical. "A straight line between two points is the shortest," is a synthetical proposition. For my conception of *straight,* contains no notion of *quantity,* but is merely *qualitative.* The conception of the *shortest* is therefore wholly an addition, and by no analysis can it be extracted from our conception of a straight line. Intuition must therefore here lend its aid, by means of which and thus only, our synthesis is possible.

Some few principles preposited by geometricians are, indeed, really analytical, and depend on the principle of contradiction. They serve, however, like identical propositions, as links in the chain of method, not as principles—for example, $a = a$, the whole is equal to itself, or $(a + b) > a$, the whole is greater than its part. And yet even these principles themselves, though they derive their validity from pure conceptions, are only admitted in mathematics because they can be presented in intuition. What causes us here commonly to believe that the predicate of such apodictic judgments is already contained in our conception, and that the judgment is therefore analytical, is merely the equivocal nature of the expression. We must join in thought a certain predicate to a given conception, and this necessity cleaves already to the conception. But the question is, not what we must join in thought to the given conception, but what we really think therein, though only obscurely, and then it becomes manifest, that the predicate pertains to these conceptions, necessarily indeed, yet not as thought in the conception itself, but by virtue of an intuition, which must be added to the conception.

The science of Natural Philosophy (Physics) contains in itself synthetical judgments *à priori,* as principles. I shall adduce two propositions. For instance, the proposition, "In all changes of the material world, the quantity of matter remains unchanged"; or,

that, "in all communication of motion, action and reaction must always be equal." In both of these, not only is the necessity, and therefore their origin, *à priori* clear, but also that they are synthetical propositions. For in the conception of matter, I do not cogitate its permanency, but merely its presence in space, which it fills. I therefore really go out of and beyond the conception of matter, in order to think on to it something *à priori,* which I did not think in it. The proposition is therefore not analytical, but synthetical, and nevertheless conceived *à priori;* and so it is with regard to the other propositions of the pure part of natural philosophy.

As to Metaphysics, even if we look upon it merely as an attempted science, yet, from the nature of human reason, an indispensable one, we find that it must contain synthetical propositions *à priori.* It is not merely the duty of metaphysics to dissect, and thereby analytically to illustrate, the conceptions which we form *à priori* of things; but we seek to widen the range of our *à priori* knowledge. For this purpose, we must avail ourselves of such principles as add something to the original conception—something not identical with, nor contained in it, and by means of synthetical judgments *à priori,* leave far behind us the limits of experience; for example, in the proposition, "the world must have a beginning," and such like. Thus metaphysics, according to the proper aim of the science, consists merely of synthetical propositions *à priori.*

THE UNIVERSAL PROBLEM OF PURE REASON

It is extremely advantageous to be able to bring a number of investigations under the formula of a single problem. For in this manner, we not only facilitate our own labor, inasmuch as we define it clearly to ourselves, but also render it more easy for others to decide whether we have done justice to our undertaking. The proper problem

of pure reason, then, is contained in the question, "How are synthetical judgments *à priori* possible?"

That metaphysical science has hitherto remained in so vacillating a state of uncertainty and contradiction is only to be attributed to the fact that this great problem, and perhaps even the difference between analytical and synthetical judgments, did not sooner suggest itself to philosophers. Upon the solution of this problem, or upon sufficient proof of the impossibility of synthetical knowledge *à priori*, depends the existence or downfall of the science of metaphysics. Among philosophers David Hume came the nearest of all to this problem; yet it never acquired in his mind sufficient precision, nor did he regard the question in its universality. On the contrary, he stopped short at the synthetical proposition of the connection of an effect with its cause (*principium causalitatis*), insisting that such proposition *à priori* was impossible. According to his conclusions, then, all that we term metaphysical science is a mere delusion, arising from the fancied insight of reason into that which is in truth borrowed from experience, and to which habit has given the appearance of necessity. Against this assertion, destructive to all pure philosophy, he would have been guarded, had he had our problem before his eyes in its universality. For he would then have perceived that, according to his own argument, there likewise could not be any pure mathematical science, which assuredly cannot exist without synthetical propositions *à priori*—an absurdity from which his good understanding must have saved him.

In the solution of the above problem is at the same time comprehended the possibility of the use of pure reason in the foundation and construction of all sciences which contain theoretical knowledge *à priori* of objects, that is to say, the answer to the following questions:

How is pure mathematical science possible?

How is pure natural science possible?

Respecting these sciences, as they do certainly exist, it may with propriety be asked, *how* they are possible?—for that they must be possible, is shown by the fact of their really existing.[2] But as to metaphysics,

the miserable progress it has hitherto made, and the fact that of no one system yet brought forward, as far as regard its true aim, can it be said that this science really exists leaves anyone at liberty to doubt with reason the very possibility of its existence.

Yet, in a certain sense, this kind of knowledge must unquestionably be looked upon as *given;* in other words, metaphysics must be considered as really existing, if not as a science, nevertheless as a natural disposition of the human mind (*metaphysica naturalis*). For human reason, without any instigations imputable to the mere vanity of great knowledge, unceasingly progresses, urged on by its own feeling of need, towards such questions as cannot be answered by any empirical application of reason, or principles derived therefrom; and so there has ever really existed in every man some system of metaphysics. It will always exist, so soon as reason awakes to the exercise of its power of speculation. And now the question arises —How is metaphysics, as a natural disposition, possible? In other words, how, from the nature of universal human reason, do those questions arise which pure reason proposes to itself, and which it is impelled by its own feeling of need to answer as well as it can?

But as in all the attempts hitherto made to answer the questions which reason is prompted by its very nature to propose to itself, for example, whether the world had a beginning, or has existed from eternity, it has always met with unavoidable contradictions, we must not rest satisfied with the mere natural disposition of the mind to metaphysics, that is, with the existence of the faculty of pure reason, whence, indeed, some sort of metaphysical system always arises; but it must be possible to arrive at certainty in regard to the question whether

---

[2] As to the existence of pure natural science, or physics, perhaps many may still express doubts. But we have only to look at the different propositions which are commonly treated of at the com- mencement of proper (empirical) physical science —those, for example, relating to the permanence of the same quantity of matter, the *vis inertiae*, the equality of action and reaction, etc.—to be soon convinced that they form a science of pure physics (*physica pura*, or *rationalis*), which well deserves to be separately exposed as a special science, in its whole extent, whether that be great or confined.

we know or do not know the things of which metaphysics treats. We must be able to arrive at a decision on the subjects of its questions, or on the ability or inability of reason to form any judgment respecting them; and therefore either to extend with confidence the bounds of our pure reason, or to set strictly defined and safe limits to its action. This last question, which arises out of the above universal problem, would properly run thus: How is metaphysics possible as a science?

Thus, the critique of reason leads at last, naturally and necessarily, to science; and, on the other hand, the dogmatical use of reason without criticism leads to groundless assertions, against which others equally specious can always be set, thus ending unavoidably in scepticism.

Besides, this science cannot be of great and formidable prolixity, because it has not to do with objects of reason, the variety of which is inexhaustible, but merely with reason herself and her problems; problems which arise out of her own bosom, and are not proposed to her by the nature of outward things, but by her own nature. And when once reason has previously become able completely to understand her own power in regard to objects which she meets with in experience, it will be easy to determine securely the extent and limits of her attempted application to objects beyond the confines of experience.

We may and must, therefore, regard the attempts hitherto made to establish metaphysical science dogmatically as non-existent. For what of analysis, that is, mere dissection of conceptions, is contained in one or other, is not the aim of, but only a preparation for metaphysics proper, which has for its object the extension, by means of synthesis, of our à priori knowledge. And for this purpose, mere analysis is of course useless, because it only shows what is contained in these conceptions, but not how we arrive, à priori, at them; and this it is her duty to show, in order to be able afterwards to determine their valid use in regard to all objects of experience, to all knowledge in

general. But little self-denial, indeed, is needed to give up these pretensions, seeing that the undeniable and, in the dogmatic mode of procedure, inevitable contradictions of Reason with herself have long since ruined the reputation of every system of metaphysics that has appeared up to this time. It will require more firmness to remain undeterred by difficulty from within, and opposition from without, from endeavoring, by a method quite opposed to all those hitherto followed, to further the growth and fruitfulness of a science indispensable to human reason—a science from which every branch it has borne may be cut away, but whose roots remain indestructible.

From all that has been said, there results the idea of a particular science, which may be called the *Critique of Pure Reason.* For reason is the faculty which furnishes us with the principles of knowledge à priori. Hence, pure reason is the faculty which contains the principles of cognizing anything absolutely à priori. An Organon of pure reason would be a compendium of those principles according to which alone all pure cognitions à priori can be obtained. The completely extended application of such an organon would afford us a system of pure reason. As this, however, is demanding a great deal, and it is yet doubtful whether any extension of our knowledge be here possible, or if so, in what cases; we can regard a science of the mere criticism of pure reason, its sources and limits, as the *propædeutic* to a system of pure reason. Such a science must not be called a Doctrine, but only a Critique of Pure Reason; and its use, in regard to speculation, would be only negative, not to enlarge the bounds of, but to purify our reason, and to shield it against error—which alone is no little gain. I apply the term *transcendental* to all knowledge which is not so much occupied with objects as with the mode of our cognition of these objects, so far as this mode of cognition is possible à priori. A system of such conceptions would be called *Transcendental Philosophy*. But this, again, is still beyond the bounds of our present essay. For as such a science must contain a complete exposition not only of our synthetical *à priori*, but of our analytical *à priori* knowledge, it is of too wide a range for our present purpose, because we do not require to carry our analysis any farther than is necessary to understand, in their full extent, the principles of synthesis *à priori*, with which alone we have to do. This investigation, which we cannot properly call a doctrine, but only a transcendental critique, because it aims not at the enlargement, but at the correction and guidance of our knowledge, and is to serve as a touchstone of the worth or worthlessness of all knowledge *à priori*, is the sole object of our present essay. Such a critique is consequently, as far as possible, a preparation for an organon; and if this new organon should be found to fail, at least for a canon of pure reason, according to which the complete system of the philosophy of pure reason, whether it extend or limit the bounds of that reason, might one day be set forth both analytically and synthetically. For that this is possible, nay, that such a system is not of so great extent as to preclude the hope of its ever being completed, is evident. For we have not here to do with the nature of outward objects, which is infinite, but solely with the mind, which judges of the nature of objects, and, again, with the mind only in respect of its cognition *à priori*. And the object of our investigations, as it is not to be sought without, but altogether within ourselves, cannot remain concealed, and in all probability is limited enough to be completely surveyed and fairly estimated, according to its worth or worthlessness. Still less let the reader here expect a critique of books and systems of pure reason; our present object is exclusively a critique of the faculty of pure reason itself. Only when we make this critique our foundation do we possess a pure touchstone for estimating the philosophical value of ancient and modern writings on this subject; and without this criterion, the incompetent historian or judge decides upon and corrects the groundless assertions of others with his own, which have themselves just as little foundation.

Transcendental philosophy is the idea of a science, for which the Critique of Pure Reason must sketch the whole plan architectonically, that is, from principles, with a full guarantee for the validity and stability of all the parts which enter into the building. It is the system of all the principles of pure reason. If this Critique itself does not assume the title of transcendental philosophy, it is only because, to be a complete system, it ought to contain a full analysis of all human knowledge *à priori*. Our critique must, indeed, lay before us a complete enumeration of all the radical conceptions which constitute the said pure knowledge. But from the complete analysis of these conceptions themselves, as also from a complete investigation of those derived from them, it abstains with reason; partly because it would be deviating from the end in view to occupy itself with this analysis, since this process is not attended with the difficulty and insecurity to be found in the synthesis, to which our critique is entirely devoted, and partly because it would be inconsistent with the unity of our plan to burden this essay with the vindication of the completeness of such an analysis and deduction, with which, after all, we have at present nothing to do. This completeness of the analysis of these radical conceptions, as well as of the deduction from the conceptions *à priori* which may be given by the analysis, we can, however, easily attain, provided only that we are in possession of all these radical conceptions, which are to serve as principles of the synthesis, and that in respect of this main purpose nothing is wanting.

To the Critique of Pure Reason, therefore, belongs all that constitutes transcendental philosophy; and it is the complete idea of transcendental philosophy, but still not the science itself; because it only proceeds so far with the analysis as is necessary to the power of judging completely of our synthetical knowledge *à priori*.

The principal thing we must attend to, in the division of the parts of a science like this, is that no conceptions must enter it which contain aught empirical; in other words, that the knowledge *à priori* must be completely pure. Hence, although the highest principles and fundamental conceptions of morality are certainly cognitions *à priori*, yet they do not belong to transcendental philosophy; because, though they certainly do not lay the conceptions of pain, pleasure, desires, inclinations, etc. (which are all of empirical origin), at the foundation of its precepts, yet still into the conception of duty —as an obstacle to be overcome, or as an incitement which should not be made into a motive—these empirical conceptions must necessarily enter, in the construction of a system of pure morality. Transcendental philosophy is consequently a philosophy of the pure and merely speculative reason. For all that is practical, so far as it contains motives, relates to feelings, and these belong to empirical sources of cognition.

If we wish to divide this science from the universal point of view of a science in gen-

eral, it ought to comprehend, first, a *Doctrine of the Elements*, and, secondly, a *Doctrine of the Method* of pure reason. Each of these main divisions will have its subdivisions, the separate reasons for which we cannot here particularize. Only so much seems necessary, by way of introduction or premonition, that there are two sources of human knowledge (which probably spring from a common, but to us unknown root), namely, sense and understanding. By the former, objects are *given* to us; by the latter, *thought*. So far as the faculty of sense may contain representations *à priori*, which form the conditions under which objects are given, in so far it belongs to transcendental philosophy. The transcendental doctrine of sense must form the first part of our science of elements, because the conditions under which alone the objects of human knowledge are given must precede those under which they are thought.

CONCEPT OF FREEDOM *

The *will* is a kind of causality belonging to living beings in so far as they are rational, and *freedom* would be this property of such causality that it can be efficient, independently on[1] foreign causes *determining* it; just as *physical necessity* is the property that the causality of all irrational beings has of being determined to activity by the influence of foreign causes.

The preceding definition of freedom is *negative*, and therefore unfruitful for the discovery of its essence; but it leads to a *positive* conception which is so much the more full and fruitful. Since the conception of causality involves that of laws, according to which, by something that we call cause, something else, namely, the effect, must be produced (laid down); hence, although free-

* From Immanuel Kant, *Fundamental Principles of the Metaphysic of Ethics*, Thomas K. Abbott, translator. Longmans, Green & Co., Inc., New York, 1934.
[1] Note that the translator uses "on" with "independent" and its variants where we would expect "of."—Ed.

dom is not a property of the will depending on physical laws, yet it is not for that reason lawless; on the contrary it must be a causality acting according to immutable laws, but of a peculiar kind; otherwise a free will would be an absurdity. Physical necessity is a heteronomy of the efficient causes, for every effect is possible only according to this law, that something else determines the efficient cause to exert its causality. What else then can freedom of the will be but autonomy, that is the property of the will to be a law to itself? But the proposition: The will is in every action a law to itself, only expresses the principle, to act on no other maxim than that which can also have as an object itself as a universal law. Now this is precisely the formula of the categorical imperative and is the principle of morality, so that a free will and a will subject to moral laws are one and the same. . . .

It is not enough to predicate freedom of our own will, from whatever reason, if we have not sufficient grounds for predicating the same of all rational beings. For as morality serves as a law for us only because we are *rational beings*, it must also hold for all rational beings; and as it must be deduced simply from the property of freedom, it must be shown that freedom also is a property of all rational beings. It is not enough then to prove it from certain supposed experiences of human nature (which indeed is quite impossible, and it can only be shown *à priori*), but we must show that it belongs to the activity of all rational beings endowed with a will. Now I say every being that cannot act except *under the idea of freedom* is just for that reason in a practical point of view really free, that is to say, all laws which are inseparably connected with freedom have the same force for him as if his will had been shown to be free in itself by a proof theoretically conclusive.[1] Now I affirm that we must attribute to every rational being which has a will that it has also the idea of freedom and acts entirely under this idea. For in such a being we conceive a reason that is practical, that is, has causality in reference to its objects. Now we cannot possibly conceive a reason consciously receiving a bias from any other quarter with respect to its judgments, for then the subject would ascribe the determination of its judgment not to its own reason, but to an impulse. It must regard itself as the author of its principles independent on foreign influences. Consequently as practical reason or as the will of a rational being it must regard itself as free, that is to say, the will of such a being cannot be a will of its own except under the idea of freedom. This idea must therefore in a practical point of view be ascribed to every rational being.

We have finally reduced the definite conception of morality to the idea of freedom. This latter, however, we could not prove to be actually a property of ourselves or of human nature; only we saw that it must be presupposed if we would conceive a being as rational and conscious of its causality in respect of its actions, *i.e.*, as endowed with a will; and so we find that on just the same grounds we must ascribe to every being endowed with reason and will this attribute of determining itself to action under the idea of its freedom. . . .

As a rational being, and consequently belonging to the intelligible world, man can never conceive the causality of his own will otherwise than on condition of the idea of freedom, for independence on the determining causes of the sensible world (an independence which Reason must always ascribe to itself) is freedom. Now the idea of freedom is inseparably connected with the conception of *autonomy*, and this again with the universal principle of morality which is ideally the foundation of all actions of *rational* beings, just as the law of nature is of all phenomena. . . .

CATEGORICAL IMPERATIVE

Every rational being reckons himself *qua* intelligence as belonging to the world of understanding, and it is simply as an efficient

cause belonging to that world that he calls his causality a *will*. On the other side he is also conscious of himself as a part of the world of sense in which his actions which are mere appearances [phenomena] of that causality are displayed; . . . although on the one side I must regard myself as a being belonging to the world of sense, yet on the other side I must recognise myself as subject as an intelligence to the law of the world of understanding, *i.e.*, to reason, which con-

[1] I adopt this method of assuming freedom merely *as an idea* which rational beings suppose in their actions, in order to avoid the necessity of proving it in its theoretical aspect also. The former is sufficient for my purpose; for even though the speculative proof should not be made out, yet a being that cannot act except with the idea of freedom is bound by the same laws that would oblige a being who was actually free. Thus we can escape here from the onus which presses on the theory.

tains this law in the idea of freedom, and therefore as subject to the autonomy of the will: consequently I must regard the laws of the world of understanding as imperatives for me, and the actions which conform to them as duties.

And thus what makes categorical imperatives possible is this, that the idea of freedom makes me a member of an intelligible world, in consequence of which if I were nothing else all my actions *would* always conform to the autonomy of the will, but as I at the same time intuit myself as a member of the world of sense, they *ought* so to conform, and this *categorical* "ought" implies a synthetic *à priori* proposition, inasmuch as besides my will as affected by sensible desires there is added further the idea of the same will but as belonging to the world of the understanding, pure and practical of itself, which contains the supreme condition according to Reason of the former will; precisely as to the intuitions of sense there are added concepts of the understanding which of themselves signify nothing but regular form in general, and in this way synthetic *à priori* propositions become possible, on which all knowledge of physical nature rests. . . .

Extreme Limits of all Practical Philosophy

All men attribute to themselves freedom of will. Hence come all judgments upon actions as being such as *ought to have been done*, although they *have not been* done. However this freedom is not a conception of experience, nor can it be so, since it still remains, even though experience shows the contrary of what on supposition of freedom are conceived as its necessary consequences. On the other side it is equally necessary that everything that takes place should be fixedly determined according to laws of nature. This necessity of nature is likewise not an empirical conception, just for this reason, that it involves the notion of necessity and consequently of *à priori* cognition. But this conception of a system of nature is confirmed by

experience, and it must even be inevitably presupposed if experience itself is to be possible, that is, a connected knowledge of the objects of sense resting on general laws. Therefore freedom is only an Idea [Ideal Conception] of Reason, and its objective reality in itself is doubtful, while nature is a *concept* of the *understanding* which proves, and must necessarily prove, its reality in examples of experience.

There arises from this a dialectic of Reason, since the freedom attributed to the will appears to contradict the necessity of nature, and placed between these two ways Reason for *speculative purposes* finds the road of physical necessity much more beaten and more appropriate than that of freedom; yet for *practical purposes* the narrow footpath of freedom is the only one on which it is possible to make use of reason in our conduct; hence it is just as impossible for the subtlest philosophy as for the commonest reason of men to argue away freedom. Philosophy must then assume that no real contradiction will be found between freedom and physical necessity of the same human actions, for it cannot give up the conception of nature any more than that of freedom.

Nevertheless, even though we should never be able to comprehend how freedom is possible, we must at least remove this apparent contradiction in a convincing manner. For if the thought of freedom contradicts either itself or nature, which is equally necessary, it must in competition with physical necessity be entirely given up.

It would, however, be impossible to escape this contradiction if the thinking subject, which seems to itself free, conceived itself *in the same sense* or in *the very same relation* when it calls itself free as when in respect of the same action it assumes itself to be subject to the law of nature. Hence it is an indispensable problem of speculative philosophy to show that its illusion respecting the contradiction rests on this, that we think of man in a different sense and relation when we call him free, and when we regard him as subject to the laws of nature as being part and parcel of nature. It must therefore show that not only *can* both these very well co-exist, but that both must be thought *as necessarily united* in the same subject, since otherwise no reason could be given why we should burden reason with an idea which, though it may possibly *without contradiction* be reconciled with another that is sufficiently established, yet entangles us in a perplexity which sorely embarrasses Reason in its theoretic employment. This duty, however, belongs only to speculative philosophy, in order that it may clear the way for practical philosophy. The philosopher then has no option whether he will remove the apparent contradiction or leave it untouched; for in the latter case the theory respecting this would be *bonum vacans* into the possession of which the fatalist would have a right to enter, and chase all morality out of its supposed domain as occupying it without title. . . .

The claims to freedom of will made even by common reason are founded on the consciousness and the admitted supposition that reason is independent on merely subjectively determined causes which together constitute what belongs to sensation only, and which consequently come under the general designation of sensibility. Man considering himself in this way as an intelligence, places himself thereby in a different order of things and in a relation to determining grounds of a wholly different kind when on the one hand he thinks of himself as an intelligence endowed with a will, and consequently with causality, and when on the other he perceives himself as a phenomenon in the world of sense (as he really is also), and affirms that his causality is subject to external determination according to laws of nature. Now he soon becomes aware that both can hold good, nay, must hold good at the same time. For there is not the smallest contradiction in saying that a *thing in appearance* (belonging to the world of sense) is subject to certain laws, on which the very same *as a thing* or being *in itself* is independent; and that he must conceive and think of himself in this two-fold way, rests as to the first on the consciousness of him-

self as an object affected through the senses, and as to the second on the consciousness of himself as an intelligence, *i.e.*, as independent on sensible impressions in the employment of his reason (in other words as belonging to the world of understanding).

Hence it comes to pass that man claims the possession of a will which takes no account of anything that comes under the head of desires and inclinations, and on the contrary conceives actions as possible to him, nay, even as necessary, which can only be done by disregarding all desires and sensible inclinations. The causality of such actions lies in him as an intelligence and in the laws of effects and actions [which depend] on the principles of an intelligible world, of which indeed he knows nothing more than that in it pure reason alone independent on sensibility gives the law; moreover since it is only in that world, as an intelligence, that he is his proper self (being as man only the appearance of himself) those laws apply to him directly and categorically, so that the incitements of inclinations and appetites (in other words the whole nature of the world of sense) cannot impair the laws of his volition as an intelligence. Nay, he does not even hold himself responsible for the former or ascribe them to his proper self, *i.e.*, his will: he only ascribes to his will any indulgence which he might yield them if he allowed them to influence his maxims to the prejudice of the rational laws of the will. . . .

But Reason would overstep all its bounds if it undertook to *explain how* pure reason can be practical, which would be exactly the same problem as to explain *how freedom is possible*.

For we can explain nothing but that which we can reduce to laws, the object of which can be given in some possible experience. But freedom is a mere Idea (Ideal Conception), the objective reality of which can in no wise be shown according to laws of nature, and consequently not in any possible experience; and for this reason it can never be comprehended or understood, because we cannot support it by any sort of example or analogy. It holds good only as a necessary hypothesis of reason in a being that believes itself conscious of a will, that is, of a faculty distinct from mere desire (namely a faculty of determining itself to action as an intelligence, in other words, by laws of reason independently on natural instincts). Now where determination according to laws of nature ceases, there all *explanation* ceases also, and nothing remains but *defence*, i.e., the removal of the objections of those who pretend to have seen deeper into the nature of things, and thereupon boldly declare freedom impossible. We can only point out to them that the supposed contradiction that they have discovered in it arises only from this, that in order to be able to apply the law of nature to human actions, they must necessarily consider man as an appearance: then when we demand of them that they should also think of him *qua* intelligence as a thing in itself, they still persist in considering him in this respect also as an appearance. In this view it would no doubt be a contradiction to suppose the causality of the same subject (that is, his will) to be withdrawn from all the natural laws of the sensible world. But this contradiction disappears, if they would only bethink themselves and admit, as is reasonable, that behind the appearances there must also lie at their root (although hidden) the things in themselves, and that we cannot expect the laws of these to be the same as those that govern their appearances.

Bibliography

Texts

Critique of Pure Reason, 2d ed. Translated by N. K. Smith. New York: St. Martin's Press, Inc., 1933.

Critique of Practical Reason and Other Writings in Moral Philosophy. Translated and edited by L. W. Beck. Chicago: The University of Chicago Press, 1949.

Studies

Cassirer, H. W. *A Commentary on Kant's Critique of Judgement.* London: George Allen & Unwin, Ltd., 1938.

————. *Kant's First Critique: An Appraisal of the Permanent Significance of Kant's Critique of Pure Reason.* London: George Allen & Unwin, Ltd., 1955.

Smith, N. K. *A Commentary to Kant's 'Critique of Pure Reason,'* 2d ed. New York: St. Martin's Press, Inc., 1930.

10

Introduction

Georg Wilhelm Friedrich Hegel was born on August 27, 1770, in Stuttgart. In his early schooling he studied classical authors for ethics and mathematics. In 1788 he went to the University of Tübingen as a student of theology. Among his companions were men like Hölderlin and Schelling. With them he protested against the political and ecclesiastical inertia which he found about him. He then went to Bern and devoted himself to further intellectual pursuits, particularly to the study of the early records of Christianity. During this time, he wrote *A Life of Jesus Christ*.

In January of 1787, he took an academic position in Frankfurt, obtained through his friend Hölderlin. He turned his attention to questions of economics and government. His interest then returned to religion and its study from the viewpoint of natural reason as revealed in positive documents. Positive religion he regarded as imposed on the mind from without. At this point of his career, Hegel still held philosophy to be subject to religion. However, he was soon to take the view that philosophy is a higher mode of apprehending the infinite than even religion.

In 1801 Hegel arrived in Jena, where the romantic poets Tieck, Novalis, and Schlegel had made history with their works on mysticism and Fichte pursued the thoughts of Kant in a way regarded as new and daring. Hegel's friend Schelling was already a prominent philosopher, and Hegel soon attained a similar standing, as was obvious from the articles published by them separately and jointly in the *Critical Journal of Philosophy* during the years 1802–1803. After completing his habilitation work, much under the influence of Schelling's philosophy of nature, Hegel began lecturing on logic and metaphysics. His lectures were poorly attended. During this period (on the 14th of October, 1806, Napoleon was at Jena) Hegel published his *Phenomenology of Spirit* (1807). He then became the editor of a Bamberg newspaper and assumed directorship of the Aegidien Gymnasium (secondary school) in Nurnberg, remaining there until 1816. Hegel married Marie von Tucher, who was twenty-two years his junior. His married life was a happy one, and he had two sons. In 1812 his first two volumes of *Science of Logic* appeared, and a third volume was added in 1816. He was offered professorships at three universities and accepted the one at Heidelberg.

In 1818 Hegel accepted the chair of philosophy at Berlin, which had been vacant since the death of Fichte. In 1821 Hegel published *Foundations of the Philosophy of Law*.

During the thirteen-year period at Berlin, Hegel's lectures revolved largely around the topics of aesthetics, the philosophy of religion, and the philosophy of history. He became quite popular and his lectures now were attended by visitors from all parts of Germany and even from abroad.

In 1831 Hegel prepared a revision of his *Science of Logic*. In the fall he returned for the winter session at the University, and on November 14, after a one-day illness, he died of cholera. He was buried, in accordance with his wish, between Fichte and Solgar.

In the tradition of German speculative idealists like Fichte and Schelling, Hegel begins his philosophy with Idea, which is not a phenomenon of individual consciousness but the sum of reality. His philosophy is dynamic and dialectic, that is, the development of being through the thesis of being (in-itself), the antithesis of being (outside-itself), and the synthesis of being (for-itself). Logic treats the first phase as the science of the Idea in itself; philosophy of nature treats Idea outside itself; and philosophy of mind treats Idea returning to itself out of otherness. Thought, as the universal and absolute substance, is God, which evolves into the world and in human nature becomes conscious of itself. Nature and spirit are manifestation of the Absolute.

As a sample of this complex and difficult philosophy, about which Hegel is supposed to have remarked that not more than a dozen of his contemporaries understood it, some of his ideas on philosophy are presented in the following passage.

PHILOSOPHY, RELIGION AND HUMAN THOUGHT *

Philosophy misses an advantage enjoyed by the other sciences. It cannot like them rest the existence of its objects on the natural admissions of consciousness, nor can it assume that its method of cognition, either for starting or for continuing, is one already accepted. The objects of philosophy, it is true, are upon the whole the same as those of religion. In both the object is Truth, in that supreme sense in which God and God only is the Truth. Both in like manner go on to treat of the finite worlds of Nature and the human Mind, with their relation to each other and to their truth in God. Some *acquaintance* with its objects, therefore, philosophy may and even must presume, that and a certain interest in them to boot, were it for no other reason than this: that in point of time the mind makes general *images* of objects, long before it makes *notions* of them, and that it is only through these mental images, and by recourse to them, that the thinking mind rises to know and comprehend *thinkingly*.

But with the rise of this thinking study of things, it soon becomes evident that thought will be satisfied with nothing short of showing the *necessity* of its facts, of demonstrating the existence of its objects, as well as their nature and qualities. Our original acquaintance with them is thus discovered to be inadequate. We can assume nothing, and assert nothing dogmatically; nor can we accept the assertions and assumptions of others. And yet we must make

a beginning: and a beginning, as primary and underived, makes an assumption, or rather is an assumption. It seems as if it were impossible to make a beginning at all.

This *thinking study of things* may serve, in a general way, as a description of philosophy. But the description is too wide. If it be correct to say, that thought makes the distinction between man and the lower animals, then everything human is human, for the sole and simple reason that it is due to the operation of thought. Philosophy, on the other hand, is a peculiar mode of thinking —a mode in which thinking becomes knowledge, and knowledge through notions. However great therefore may be the identity and essential unity of the two modes of thought, the philosophic mode gets to be different from the more general thought which acts in all that is human, in all that gives humanity its distinctive character. And this difference connects itself with the fact that the strictly human and thought-induced phenomena of consciousness do not originally appear in the form of a thought, but as a feeling, a perception, or mental image—all of which aspects must be distinguished from the form of thought proper.

According to an old preconceived idea, which has passed into a trivial proposition, it is thought which marks the man off from the animals. Yet trivial as this old belief may seem, it must, strangely enough, be recalled to mind in presence of certain preconceived ideas of the present day. These ideas would put feeling and thought so far apart as to make them opposites, and would represent them as so antagonistic, that feel-

* From Georg Hegel, *The Logic of Hegel*. Translated by William Wallace. 1892. By permission of the Clarendon Press, Oxford.

ing, particularly religious feeling, is supposed to be contaminated, perverted, and even annihilated by thought. They also emphatically hold that religion and piety grow out of, and rest upon something else, and not on thought. But those who make this separation forget meanwhile that only man has the capacity for religion, and that animals no more have religion than they have law and morality.

Those who insist on this separation of religion from thinking usually have before their minds the sort of thought that may be styled *after-thought*. They mean 'reflective' thinking, which has to deal with thoughts as thoughts, and brings them into consciousness. Slackness to perceive and keep in view this distinction which philosophy definitely draws in respect of thinking is the source of the crudest objections and reproaches against philosophy. Man,—and that just because it is his nature to think,—is the only being that possesses law, religion, and morality. In these spheres of human life, therefore, thinking, under the guise of feeling, faith, or generalised image, has not been inactive: its action and its productions are there present and therein contained. But it is one thing to have such feelings and generalised images that have been moulded and permeated by thought, and another thing to have thoughts about them. The thoughts, to which after-thought upon those modes of consciousness gives rise, are what is comprised under reflection, general reasoning, and the like, as well as under philosophy itself.

The neglect of this distinction between thought in general and the reflective thought of philosophy has also led to another and more frequent misunderstanding. Reflection of this kind has been often maintained to be the condition, or even the only way, of attaining a consciousness and certitude of the Eternal and True. The (now somewhat antiquated) metaphysical proofs of God's existence, for example, have been treated, as if a knowledge of them and a conviction of their truth were the only and essential means of producing a belief and conviction

that there is a God. Such a doctrine would find its parallel, if we said that eating was impossible before we had acquired a knowledge of the chemical, botanical, and zoological characters of our food; and that we must delay digestion till we had finished the study of anatomy and physiology. Were it so, these sciences in their field, like philosophy in its, would gain greatly in point of utility; in fact, their utility would rise to the height of absolute and universal indispensableness. Or rather, instead of being indispensable, they would not exist at all.

The *Content*, of whatever kind it be, with which our consciousness is taken up, is what constitutes the qualitative character of our feelings, perceptions, fancies, and ideas; of our aims and duties; and of our thoughts and notions. From this point of view, feeling, perception, &c. are the *forms* assumed by these contents. The contents remain one and the same, whether they are felt, seen, represented, or willed, and whether they are merely felt, or felt with an admixture of thoughts, or merely and simply thought. In any one of these forms, or in the admixture of several, the contents confront consciousness, or are its *object*. But when they are thus objects of consciousness, the modes of the several forms ally themselves with the contents; and each form of them appears in consequence to give rise to a special object. Thus what is the same at bottom, may look like a different sort of fact.

The several modes of feeling, perception, desire, and will, so far as we are *aware* of them, are in general called ideas (mental representations): and it may be roughly said, that philosophy puts thoughts, categories, or, in more precise language, adequate *notions*, in the place of the generalised images we ordinarily call ideas. Mental impressions such as these may be regarded as the metaphors of thoughts and notions. But to have these figurate conceptions does not imply that we appreciate their intellectual significance, the thoughts and rational notions to which they correspond. Conversely, it is one thing to have thoughts and intelligent notions, and another to know what impressions, perceptions, and feelings correspond to them.

This difference will to some extent explain what people call the unintelligibility of philosophy. Their difficulty lies partly in an incapacity—which in itself is nothing but want of habit—for abstract thinking; *i.e.* in an inability to get hold of pure thoughts and move about in them. In our ordinary state of mind, the thoughts are clothed upon and made one with the sensuous or spiritual material of the hour; and in reflection, meditation, and general reasoning, we introduce a blend of thoughts into feelings, percepts, and mental images. (Thus, in propositions where the subject-matter is due to the senses—*e.g.* 'This leaf is green'—we have such categories introduced, as being and individuality.) But it is a very different thing to make the thoughts pure and simple our object.

But their complaint that philosophy is unintelligible is as much due to another reason; and that is an impatient wish to have before them as a mental picture that which is in the mind as a thought or notion. When people are asked to apprehend some notion, they often complain that they do not know what they have to think. But the fact is that in a notion there is nothing further to be thought than the notion itself. What the phrase reveals, is a hankering after an image with which we are already familiar. The mind, denied the use of its familiar ideas, feels the ground where it once stood firm and at home taken away from beneath it, and, when transported into the region of pure thought, cannot tell where in the world it is.

One consequence of this weakness is that authors, preachers, and orators are found most intelligible, when they speak of things which their readers or hearers already know by rote,—things which the latter are conversant with, and which require no explanation.

The philosopher then has to reckon with popular modes of thought, and with the objects of religion. In dealing with the ordinary modes of mind, he will first of all, as we saw, have to prove and almost to awaken the need for his peculiar method of knowledge. In dealing with the objects of religion, and with truth as a whole, he will have to show that philosophy is capable of apprehending them from its own resources; and should a difference from religious conceptions come to light, he will have to justify the points in which it diverges.

To give the reader a preliminary explanation of the distinction thus made, and to let him see at the same moment that the real import of our consciousness is retained, and even for the first time put in its proper light, when translated into the form of thought and the notion of reason, it may be well to recall another of these old unreasoned beliefs. And that is the conviction that to get at the truth of any object or event, even of feelings, perceptions, opinions, and mental ideas, we must think it over. Now in any case to think things over is at least to transform feelings, ordinary ideas, &c. into thoughts.

Nature has given every one a faculty of thought. But thought is all that philosophy claims as the form proper to her business: and thus the inadequate view which ignores the distinction stated [above], leads to a new delusion, the reverse of the complaint previously mentioned about the unintelligibility of philosophy. In other words, this science must often submit to the slight of hearing even people who have never taken any trouble with it talking as if they thoroughly understood all about it. With no preparation beyond an ordinary education they do not hesitate, especially under the influence of religious sentiment, to philosophise and to criticise philosophy. Everybody allows that to know any other science you must have first studied it, and that you can only claim to express a judgment upon it in virtue of such knowledge. Everybody allows that to make a shoe you must have learned and practised the craft of the shoemaker, though every man has a model in his own foot, and possesses in his hands the natural endowments for the operations required. For philosophy alone, it seems to be imagined, such study, care, and application are not in the least requisite.

This comfortable view of what is required for a philosopher has recently received corroboration through the theory of immediate or intuitive knowledge.

So much for the form of philosophical knowledge. It is no less desirable, on the other hand, that philosophy should understand that its content is no other than *actuality*, that core of truth which, originally produced and producing itself within the precincts of the mental life, has become the *world*, the inward and outward world, of consciousness. At first we become aware of these contents in what we call Experience. But even Experience, as it surveys the wide range of inward and outward existence, has sense enough to distinguish the mere appearance, which is transient and meaningless, from what in itself really deserves the name of actuality. As it is only in form that philosophy is distinguished from other modes of attaining an acquaintance with this same sum of being, it must necessarily be in harmony with actuality and experience. In fact, this harmony may be viewed as at least an extrinsic means of testing the truth of a philosophy. Similarly it may be held the highest and final aim of philosophic science to bring about, through the ascertainment of this harmony, a reconciliation of the self-conscious reason with the reason which *is* in the world,—in other words, with actuality.

In the preface to my Philosophy of Law, p. xix, are found the propositions:

What is reasonable is actual;
and, What is actual is reasonable.

These simple statements have given rise to expressions of surprise and hostility, even in quarters where it would be reckoned an insult to presume absence of philosophy, and still more of religion. Religion at least need not be brought in evidence; its doctrines of the divine government of the world affirm these propositions too decidedly. For their philosophic sense, we must pre-suppose intelligence enough to know, not only that God is actual, that He is the supreme actuality, that He alone is truly actual; but also, as regards the logical bearings of the question, that existence is in part mere appearance, and only in part actuality. In common life, any freak of fancy, any error, evil and everything of the nature of evil, as well as every degenerate and transitory existence whatever, gets in a casual way the name of actuality. But even our ordinary feelings are enough to forbid a casual (fortuitous) existence getting the emphatic name of an actual; for by fortuitous we mean an existence which has no greater value than that of something possible, which may as well not be as be. As for the term Actuality, these critics would have done well to consider the sense in which I employ it. In a detailed Logic I had treated amongst other things of actuality, and accurately distinguished it not only from the fortuitous, which, after all, has existence, but even from the cognate categories of existence and the other modifications of being.

The actuality of the rational stands opposed by the popular fancy that Ideas and ideals are nothing but chimeras, and philosophy a mere system of such phantasms. It is also opposed by the very different fancy that Ideas and ideals are something far too excellent to have actuality, or something too impotent to procure it for themselves. This divorce between idea and reality is especially dear to the analytic understanding which looks upon its own abstractions, dreams though they are, as something true and real, and prides itself on the imperative 'ought,' which it takes especial pleasure in prescribing even on the field of politics. As if the world had waited on it to learn how it ought to be, and was not! For, if it were as it ought to be, what would come of the precocious wisdom of that 'ought'? When understanding turns this 'ought' against trivial external and transitory objects, against social regulations or conditions, which very likely possess a great relative importance for a certain time and special circles, it may often be right. In such a case the intelligent observer may meet much that fails to satisfy the general requirements of right; for who is not acute enough to see a great deal in his own surroundings which is really far from being as it ought to be? But such acuteness is mistaken in the conceit that, when it examines these objects and pronounces what they ought to be, it is dealing with questions of philosophic science. The object of philosophy is the Idea: and the Idea is not so impotent as merely to have a right or an obligation to exist without actually existing. The object of philosophy is an actuality of which these objects, social regulations and conditions, are only the superficial outside.

Thus reflection—thinking things over—in a general way involves the principle (which also means the beginning) of philosophy. And when the reflective spirit arose again in its independence in modern times, after the epoch of the Lutheran Reformation, it did not, as in its beginnings among the Greeks, stand merely aloof, in a world of its own, but at once turned its energies also upon the apparently illimitable material of the phenomenal world. In this way the name philosophy came to be applied to all those branches of knowledge, which are engaged in ascertaining the standard and Universal in the ocean of empirical individualities, as well as in ascertaining the Necessary element, or Laws, to be found in the apparent disorder of the endless masses of the fortuitous. It thus appears that modern philosophy derives its materials from our own personal observations and perceptions of the external and internal world, from nature as well as from the mind and heart of man, when both stand in the immediate presence of the observer.

This principle of Experience carries with it the unspeakably important condition that, in order to accept and believe any fact, we must be in contact with it; or, in more exact terms, that we must find the fact united and combined with the certainty of our own selves. We must be in touch with our subject-matter, whether it be by means of our external senses, or, else, by our profounder mind and our intimate self-consciousness.—This principle is the same as that which has in the present day been termed faith, immediate knowledge, the revelation in the outward world, and, above all, in our own heart.

Those sciences, which thus got the name of philosophy, we call *empirical* sciences, for the reason that they take their departure from experience. Still the essential results which they aim at and provide, are laws, general propositions, a theory—the thoughts of what is found existing.

Bibliography

Texts

The Phenomenology of Mind. Translated by J. Baillie. London: G. Allen & Unwin, Ltd., 1931 (2d ed.)

Science of Logic. Translated by W. H. Johnston and L. C. Struthers. 2 vols. London: G. Allen & Unwin, Ltd., 1929. (This is the so-called "Greater Logic of Hegel.")

Studies

Caird, B. *Hegel.* London: W. Blackwood & Sons, 1883.

Stace, W. T. *The Philosophy of Hegel.* London: Dover Publications, 1924 (new edition, New York, 1955).

11

ARTHUR SCHOPENHAUER
1788–1860

Introduction

Born in 1788, Arthur Schopenhauer belonged to a business family which lived in Danzig and later in Hamburg. Relations within the family were not the happiest, though the material comforts of life were not lacking. After the early death of his father, instead of turning to business as a profession, Schopenhauer devoted himself to study. In 1820, he became a university lecturer at Berlin, where Hegel was teaching. In his lectures he could not compete with Hegel and finally gave up the university life and began to travel. From 1833 on, he lived as a writer in Frankfurt. Here he dedicated himself to a life which opposed the philosophy of the universities and manifested a strong core of resentment and pessimism which was evident in his personality, even in his early years. He considered himself misunderstood, persecuted, and abandoned by the world. It is said that he esteemed his poodle much more than he did men. Later in life he became one of the most widely read philosophers on the Continent. Schopenhauer had an outstanding gift of style. His main work is entitled *The World as Will and Idea.* He died in 1860.

Schopenhauer was influenced by Kant, Plato, and Buddhist philosophy. His philosophy, unlike Hegel's, is voluntaristic in that he explains the universe as "Will" unfolding itself in individuals. Will is not only a power of choice but also the blind unreasoning impulse toward self-preservation and the will-to-live. The world is the expression of Universal Will; individuals' wills produce their bodies as their phenomena. Will is seen in the indefatigably active forces of nature. In nature, animal, and man, the will-to-live is a combative impulse. Schopenhauer sees man pessimistically, describing him as evil, capable only of enjoying pain as positive feeling. Pleasure is but a temporary satisfaction. One man must be the "dust of the other." Escape from this bondage is had by the contemplation of art, a sympathetic attitude toward the disappearance of the illusion of individuality, and the substitution of the "will-to-let-live" for the "will-to-live." Such a point of view implies the oneness of nature; as a result of the "negation of the will-to-live," an indifference to self-preservation is fostered and the preservation of the race is engendered. This point of view suggests the state of nirvana in which passion, desire, conflict, and suffering are nonexistent. Some of Schopenhauer's thoughts are presented in the following passage, which even in translation reflects the gifted pen that he wielded.

PRIMACY OF THE WILL IN SELF-CONSCIOUSNESS *

The will, as the thing-in-itself, constitutes the inner, true, and indestructible nature of man; yet in itself it is without consciousness. For consciousness is conditioned by the intellect, and the intellect is a mere accident of our being, for it is a function of the brain. The brain, together with the nerves and spinal cord attached to it, is a mere fruit, a product, in fact a parasite, of the rest of the organism, in so far as it is not directly geared to the organism's inner work-

* From Arthur Schopenhauer, *The World as Will and Representation.* Reprinted by permission of The Falcon's Wing Press, Colorado. Copyright 1958.

ing, but serves the purpose of self-preservation by regulating its relations with the external world. On the other hand, the organism itself is the visibility, the objectivity, of the individual will, its image, as this image presents itself in that very brain (which in the first book we learned to recognize as the condition of the objective world in general). Therefore, this image is brought about by the brain's forms of knowledge, namely space, time, and causality; consequently it presents itself as something extended, successively acting, and material, in other words, operative or effective. The parts of the body are both directly felt and perceived by means of the senses only in the brain. In consequence of this, it can be said that the intellect is the secondary phenomenon, the organism the primary, that is, the immediate phenomenal appearance of the will; the will is metaphysical, the intellect physical; the intellect, like its objects, is mere phenomenon, the will alone is thing-in-itself. Then, in a more and more *figurative* sense, and so by way of comparison, it can be said that the will is the substance of man, the intellect the accident; the will is the matter, the intellect the form; the will is heat, the intellect light.

We will now first of all verify, and at the same time elucidate, this thesis by the following facts appertaining to the inner life of man. Perhaps, on this occasion, more will be gained for knowledge of the inner man than is to be found in many systematic psychologies.

1. Not only the consciousness of other things, i.e., the apprehension of the external world, but also *self-consciousness*, as already mentioned, contains a knower and a known, otherwise it would not be a *consciousness*. For *consciousness* consists in knowing, but knowing requires a knower and a known. Therefore self-consciousness could not exist if there were not in it a known opposed to the knower and different therefrom. Thus, just as there can be no object without a subject, so there can be no subject without an object, in other words, no knower without something different from this

that is known. Therefore, a consciousness that was through and through pure intelligence would be impossible. The intelligence is like the sun that does not illuminate space unless an object exists by which its rays are reflected. The knower himself, precisely as such, cannot be known, otherwise he would be the *known* of another knower. But as the *known* in self-consciousness we find exclusively the *will*. For not only willing and deciding in the narrowest sense, but also all striving, wishing, shunning, hoping, fearing, loving, hating, in short all that directly constitutes our own weal and woe, desire and disinclination, is obviously only affection of the will, is a stirring, a modification, of willing and not-willing, is just that which, when it operates outwards, exhibits itself as an act of will proper.[1] But in all knowledge the known, not the knower, is the first and essential thing, inasmuch as the former is the προτότυπος, the latter the ἔκτυπος.[2] Therefore in self-consciousness the known, consequently the will, must be the first and original thing; the knower, on the other hand, must be only the secondary thing, that which has been added, the mirror. They are related somewhat as the self-luminous is to the reflecting body; or as the vibrating strings are to the sounding-board, where the resulting note would then be consciousness. We can also consider the plant as such a symbol of consciousness. As we know, it has two poles, root and corona; the former reaching down into darkness, moisture and cold, and the latter up into brightness, dryness and

[1] It is remarkable that Augustine already knew this. Thus in the fourteenth book *De Civitate Dei*, c. 6, he speaks of the *affectiones animi* that in the previous book he brought under four categories, namely *cupiditas, timor, laetitia, tristitia*, and he says: *voluntas est quippe in omnibus, imo omnes nihil aliud, quam voluntates sunt: nam quid est cupiditas et laetitia, nisi voluntas in eorum consensionem, quae volumus? et quid est metus atque tristitia, nisi voluntas in dissensionem ab his, quae nolumus?*

"In them all [desire, fear, joy, sadness] the will is to be found; in fact they are all nothing but affections of the will. For what are desire and joy but the will to consent to what we want? And what are fear and sadness but the will not to consent to what we do not want?" [Tr.]

[2] "Prototype"; "copy," "ectype." [Tr.]

warmth; then as the point of indifference of the two poles where they part from each other close to the ground, the collum or root-stock (*rhizoma, le collet*). The root is what is essential, original, perennial, whose death entails the death of the corona; it is therefore primary. The corona, on the other hand, is the ostensible, that which has sprouted forth, that which passes away without the root dying; it is therefore the secondary. The root represents the will, the corona the intellect, and the point of indifference of the two, namely the collum, would be the *I*, which, as their common extreme point, belongs to both. This I is the *pro tempore* identical subject of knowing and willing, whose identity I call in my very first essay (*On the Principle of Sufficient Reason*) and in my first philosophical astonishment, the miracle κατ' ἐξοχήν.[3] It is the point of departure and of contact of the whole phenomenon, in other words, of the objectification of the will; it is true that it conditions the phenomenon, but the phenomenon also conditions it. The comparison here given can be carried even as far as the individual character and nature of men. Thus, just as usually a large corona springs only from a large root, so the greatest mental abilities are found only with a vehement and passionate will. A genius of phlegmatic character and feeble passions would be like succulent plants that have very small roots in spite of an imposing corona consisting of thick leaves; yet he will not be found. Vehemence of the will and passionate ardour of the character are a condition of enhanced intelligence, and this is shown physiologically through the brain's activity being conditioned by the movement communicated to it with every pulsation through the great arteries running up to the *basis cerebri.* Therefore an energetic pulse, and even, according to Bichat, a short neck are necessary for great activity of the brain. But the opposite of the above is of course found; that is, vehement desires, passionate, violent character, with weak intellect, in other words, with a small brain of inferior confor-

mation in a thick skull. This is a phenomenon as common as it is repulsive; it might perhaps be compared to the beet-root.

2. But in order not merely to describe consciousness figuratively, but to know it thoroughly, we have first to find out what exists in every consciousness in the same manner, and what therefore will be, as the common and constant element, that which is essential. We shall then consider what distinguishes one consciousness from another, and this accordingly will be the accidental and secondary element.

Consciousness is known to us positively only as a property of animal nature; consequently we may not, indeed we cannot, think of it otherwise than as *animal consciousness,* so that this expression is in fact tautological. Therefore what is always to be found in *every* animal consciousness, even the most imperfect and feeblest, in fact what is always its foundation, is the immediate awareness of a *longing,* and of its alternate satisfaction and non-satisfaction in very different degrees. To a certain extent we know this *a priori.* For amazingly varied as the innumerable species of animals may be, and strange as some new form of them, never previously seen, may appear to us, we nevertheless assume beforehand with certainty its innermost nature as something well known, and indeed wholly familiar to us. Thus we know that the animal *wills,* indeed even *what* it wills, namely existence, well-being, life, and propagation. Since we here presuppose with perfect certainty an identity with ourselves, we have no hesitation in attributing to it unchanged all the affections of will known to us in ourselves; and we speak positively and plainly of its desire, aversion, fear, anger, hatred, love, joy, sorrow, longing, and so on. On the other hand, as soon as we come to speak of phenomena of mere knowledge, we run into uncertainty. We do not venture to say that the animal conceives, thinks, judges, or knows; we attribute to it with certainty only representations in general, since without these its *will* could not be stirred or agitated in the ways previously

3 *"Par excellence."* [Tr.]

mentioned. But as regards the animals' definite way of knowing, and its precise limits in a given species, we have only indefinite concepts, and make conjectures. Therefore understanding between us and them is often difficult, and is brought about ingeniously only in consequence of experience and practice. Here, then, are to be found distinctions of consciousness. On the other hand, longing, craving, willing, or aversion, shunning, and not-willing, are peculiar to every consciousness; man has them in common with the polyp. Accordingly, this is the essential and the basis of every consciousness. The difference of its manifestations in the various species of animal beings depends on the different extension of their spheres of knowledge in which the motives of those manifestations are to be found. Directly from our own nature we understand all the actions and attitudes of animals that express stirrings and agitations of the will; and so to this extent we sympathize with them in many different ways. On the other hand, the gulf between us and them arises simply and solely from a difference of intellect. The gulf between a very intelligent animal and a man of very limited capacity is possibly not much greater than that between a blockhead and a genius. Therefore here also, the resemblance between them in another aspect, springing from the likeness of their inclinations and emotions and again assimilating both, sometimes stands out surprisingly, and excites astonishment. This consideration makes it clear that in all animal beings the *will* is the primary and substantial thing; the *intellect*, on the other hand, is something secondary and additional, in fact a mere tool in the service of the will, which is more or less complete and complicated according to the requirements of this service. Just as a species of animals appears equipped with hoofs, claws, hands, wings, horns, or teeth according to the aims of its will, so is it furnished with a more or less developed brain, whose function is the intelligence requisite for its continued existence. Thus the more complicated the organization becomes in the ascending series of animals, the more mani-

fold do its needs become, and the more varied and specially determined the objects capable of satisfying them, consequently the more tortuous and lengthy the paths for arriving at these, which must now all be known and found. Therefore, to the same extent, the animal's representations must also be more versatile, accurate, definite, and connected, and its attention more eager, more continuous, and more easily roused; consequently its intellect must be more developed and complete. Accordingly we see the organ of intelligence, the cerebral system, together with the organs of sense, keep pace with an increase of needs and wants, and with the complication of the organism. We see the increase of the *representing* part of consciousness (as opposed to the *willing* part) bodily manifesting itself in the ever-increasing proportion of the brain in general to the rest of the nervous system, and of the cerebrum to the cerebellum. For (according to Flourens) the former is the workshop of representations, while the latter is the guide and regulator of movements. But the last step taken by nature in this respect is disproportionately great. For in man not only does the power of representation in *perception*, which hitherto has existed alone, reach the highest degree of perfection, but the *abstract* representation, thinking, i.e., *reason* (*Vernunft*) is added, and with it reflection. Through this important enhancement of the intellect, and hence of the secondary part of consciousness, it obtains a preponderance over the primary part in so far as it becomes from now on the predominantly active part. Thus, whereas in the case of the animal the immediate awareness of its satisfied or unsatisfied desire constitutes by far the principal part of its consciousness, and indeed the more so the lower the animal stands, so that the lowest animals are distinguished from plants only by the addition of a dull representation, with man the opposite is the case. Intense as his desires may be, more intense even than those of any animal and rising to the level of passions, his consciousness nevertheless remains continuously and predominantly concerned and engrossed with representations and ideas. Undoubtedly this is mainly what has given rise to that fundamental error of all philosophers, by virtue of which they make thinking the essential and primary element of the so-called soul, in other words, of man's inner or spiritual life, always putting it first, but regard willing as a mere product of thinking, and as something secondary, additional, and subsequent. But if willing resulted merely from knowing, how could the animals, even the lowest of them, manifest a will that is often so indomitable and vehement, in spite of such extremely limited knowledge? Accordingly, since that fundamental error of the philosophers makes, so to speak, the accident into the substance, it leads them on to wrong paths from which there is no longer a way out. Therefore that relative predominance of the *knowing* consciousness over the *desiring*, and consequently of the secondary part over the primary, which appears in man, can in certain abnormally favoured individuals go so far that, in moments of supreme enhancement, the secondary or knowing part of consciousness is entirely detached from the willing part, and passes by itself into free activity, in other words, into an activity not stimulated by the will, and therefore no longer serving it. Thus the knowing part of consciousness becomes purely objective and the clear mirror of the world, and from this the conceptions of *genius* arise, which are the subject of our third book.

3. If we descend through the series of grades of animals, we see the intellect becoming weaker and weaker and more and more imperfect; but we certainly do not observe a corresponding degradation of the will. On the contrary, the will everywhere retains its identical nature, and shows itself as a great attachment to life, care for the individual and for the species, egoism and lack of consideration for all others, together with the emotions springing therefrom. Even in the smallest insect the will is present complete and entire; it wills what it wills as decidedly and completely as does man. The difference lies merely in *what* it wills, that

is to say, in the motives; but these are the business of the intellect. As that which is secondary and tied to bodily organs, the intellect naturally has innumerable degrees of perfection, and in general is essentially limited and imperfect. The *will*, on the other hand, as that which is original and the thing-in-itself, can never be imperfect, but every act of will is wholly what it can be. By virtue of the simplicity belonging to the will as the thing-in-itself, as the metaphysical in the phenomenon, its *essential nature* admits of no degrees, but is always entirely itself. Only its *stimulation or excitement* has degrees, from the feeblest inclination up to passion, and also its excitability, and thus its vehemence, from the phlegmatic to the choleric temperament. On the other hand, the *intellect* has not merely degrees of *excitement*, from sleepiness up to the mood and inspiration, but also degrees of its *real nature*, of the completeness thereof; accordingly, this rises gradually from the lowest animal which perceives only obscurely up to man, and in man again from the blockhead to the genius. The *will* alone is everywhere entirely itself, for its function is of the greatest simplicity; for this consists in willing and in not-willing, which operates with the greatest ease and without effort, and requires no practice. On the other hand, knowing has many different functions, and never takes place entirely without effort, which it requires for fixing the attention and making the object clear, and at a higher degree, also for thinking and deliberation; it is therefore capable of great improvement through practice and training. If the intellect holds out to the will something simple and perceptible, the will at once expresses its approval or disapproval. This is the case even when the intellect has laboriously pondered and ruminated, in order finally to produce from numerous data by means of difficult combinations the result that seems most in agreement with the interests of the will. Meanwhile, the will has been idly resting; after the result is reached, it enters, as the sultan does the divan, merely to express again its monotonous approval or disapproval. It is true that this can turn out different in degree, but in essence it remains always the same.

This fundamentally different nature of the will and the intellect, the simplicity and originality essential in the former in contrast to the complicated and secondary character of the latter, become even clearer to us when we observe their strange interplay within us, and see in a particular case how the images and ideas arising in the intellect set the will in motion, and how entirely separated and different are the roles of the two. Now it is true that we can already observe this in the case of actual events that vividly excite the will, whereas primarily and in themselves they are merely objects of the intellect. But, to some extent, it is not so obvious here that this reality as such primarily exists only in the intellect; and again, the change generally does not occur as rapidly as is necessary, if the thing is to be easily seen at a glance, and thus really comprehensible. On the other hand, both these are the case if it is mere ideas and fantasies that we allow to act on the will. If, for example, we are alone, and think over our personal affairs, and then vividly picture to ourselves, say, the menace of an actually present danger, and the possibility of an unfortunate outcome, anxiety at once compresses the heart, and the blood ceases to flow. But if the intellect then passes to the possibility of the opposite outcome, and allows the imagination to picture the happiness long hoped-for as thereby attained, all the pulses at once quicken with joy, and the heart feels as light as a feather, until the intellect wakes up from its dream. But then let some occasion lead the memory to an insult or injury suffered long ago, and anger and resentment at once storm through the breast that a moment before was at peace. Then let the image of a long-lost love arise, called up by accident, with which is connected a whole romance with its magic scenes, and this anger will at once give place to profound longing and sadness. Finally, if there occur to us some former humiliating incident, we shrivel up, would like to be swallowed up, blush with shame, and often try to divert and distract ourselves forcibly from it by some loud exclamation, scaring away evil spirits as it were. We see that the intellect strikes up the tune, and the will must dance to it; in fact, the intellect causes it to play the part of a child whom its nurse at her pleasure puts into the most different moods by chatter and tales alternating between pleasant and melancholy things. This is due to the fact that the will in itself is without knowledge, but the understanding associated with it is without will. Therefore the will behaves like a body that is moved, the understanding like the causes that set it in motion, for it is the medium of motives. Yet with all this, the primacy of the will becomes clear again when this will, that becomes, as we have shown, the sport of the intellect as soon as it allows the intellect to control it, once makes its supremacy felt in the last resort. This it does by prohibiting the intellect from having certain representations, by absolutely preventing certain trains of thought from arising, because it knows, or in other words experiences from the selfsame intellect, that they would arouse in it any one of the emotions previously described. It then curbs and restrains the intellect, and forces it to turn to other things. However difficult this often is, it is bound to succeed the moment the will is in earnest about it; for the resistance then comes not from the intellect, which always remains indifferent, but from the will itself; and the will has an inclination in one respect for a representation it abhors in another. Thus the representation is in itself interesting to the will, just because it excites it. At the same time, however, abstract knowledge tells the will that this representation will cause it a shock of painful and unworthy emotion to no purpose. The will then decides in accordance with this last knowledge, and forces the intellect to obey. This is called "being master of oneself"; here obviously the master is the will, the servant the intellect, for in the last instance the will is always in command, and therefore constitutes the real core, the being-in-itself, of man. In this respect Ἡγεμονιχόν [4] would be a fitting title for the *will;* yet again this title seems to apply to the *intellect,* in so far as that is the guide and leader, like the footman who walks in front of the stranger. In truth, however, the most striking figure for the relation of the two is that of the strong blind man carrying the sighted lame man on his shoulders.

The relation of the will to the intellect here described can further be recognized in the fact that the intellect is originally quite foreign to the decisions of the will. It furnishes the will with motives; but only subsequently, and thus wholly *a posteriori,* does it learn how these have acted, just as a man making a chemical experiment applies the reagents, and then waits for the result. In fact, the intellect remains so much excluded from the real resolutions and secret decisions of its own will that sometimes it can only get to know them, like those of a stranger, by spying out and taking unawares; and it must surprise the will in the act of expressing itself, in order merely to discover its real intentions. For example, I have devised a plan, but I still have some scruple regarding it; on the other hand, the feasibility of the plan, as regards its possibility, is completely uncertain, since it depends on external circumstances that are still undecided. Therefore at all events it is unnecessary for the present to come to a decision about it, and so for the time being I let

the matter rest. Now I often do not know how firmly I am already attached in secret to this plan, and how much I desire that it be carried into effect, in spite of the scruple; in other words, my intellect does not know this. But only let a favourable report reach me as to its feasibility, and at once there arises within me a jubilant, irresistible gladness, diffused over my whole being and taking permanent possession of it, to my own astonishment. For only now does my intellect learn how firmly my will had already laid hold of the plan, and how entirely it was in agreement therewith, whereas the intellect had still regarded it as entirely problematical and hardly a match for that scruple.

Bibliography

Texts

The World as Will and Idea, 5th ed. Translated by R. B. Haldane and J. Kemp. 3 vols. London: Kegan Paul, Trench, Trubner & Co., Ltd., 1906.

Selected Essays. Translated by E. B. Bax. London: G. Bell & Sons, Ltd., 1891.

Studies

Copleston, F. C., S.J. *Arthur Schopenhauer, Philosopher of Pessimism.* London: Burns & Oates, Ltd., 1946.

McGill, V. J. *Schopenhauer, Pessimist and Pagan.* New York: Brentano, 1931.

---

[4] "The principal faculty" (a Stoic term). [Tr.]

12

Introduction

John Henry Newman was born in Old Broad-street, London, England, on February 21, 1801. In the spring of 1808, he entered Ealing School. It was at this academy that Newman first developed his love for the classics. He was always shy and took little part in games, though he did ride. At this school he came under the influence of Rev. Walter Mayers who inspired in him interest in the study of dogma. Newman had spent most of his preschool days at Ham, near Richmond, where he lived with his grandmother and her daughter Elizabeth. In 1817, Newman went to Trinity College, Oxford and took his B.A. degree in 1820. He took his M.A. degree in 1823. In May, 1828, Newman was appointed by the Bishop of Oxford to Saint Mary's. In September of 1843 he resigned from Saint Mary's and six days later preached his last sermon there. On October 3, 1845, he resigned his fellowship and six days later (October 9) was received into the Roman Catholic Church by Father Dominic. A year and a half later he was ordained a priest by Cardinal Fransoni. In 1851 he was appointed rector of the Catholic University of Ireland, a position he held for some years. In the spring of 1879 he was created a car-dinal. He died on August 11, 1890, and was buried at Rednal.

Newman is considered by many primarily a theologian, by others, a literary genius, and by still others, a philosopher. It is because of his mode of philosophic reflection and the unique contributions to philosophical thought contained in his *Grammar of Assent* that Newman is considered here. The epistemological assumption necessary for an understanding of Newman's work would seem to be that not everything can be demonstrated and that faith is the alternative to a possible skepticism. Moreover, Newman has in mind the concrete, whole person, not an abstract intellect that deals with life realities. For Newman, "universal essences" were not very meaningful. Concrete fact was far more important. He leaned not on the deductive rationalism of the Schoolmen, but more on the inductive attitude of the nineteenth century. Overconcern for the universal led, he felt, to a neglect of the equally important concrete real. This principle of realism is apparent in his treatment of the real and notional consent. In the following passage Newman points out practical consequences of the notional and of the real assent.

NOTIONAL AND REAL ASSENT *

It appears from what has been said, that, though Real Assent is not intrinsically operative, it accidentally and indirectly affects practice. It is in itself an intellectual act, of which the object is presented to it by the imagination; and though the pure intellect does not lead to action, nor the imagination either, yet the imagination has the means, which pure intellect has not, of stimulating those powers of the mind from which action proceeds. Real Assent then, or Belief, as it may be called, viewed in itself, that is, simply as Assent, does not lead to action; but the images in which it lives, representing as they do the concrete, have the power of

* From John Henry Cardinal Newman, *An Essay in Aid of a Grammar of Assent*, 1947. By permission of David McKay Company, Inc., New York.

the concrete upon the affections and passions, and by means of these indirectly become operative. Still this practical influence is not invariable, nor to be relied on; for, given images may have no tendency to affect given minds, or to excite them to action. Thus, a philosopher or a poet may vividly realize the brilliant rewards of military genius or of eloquence, without wishing either to be a commander or an orator. However, on the whole, broadly contrasting Belief with Notional Assent and with Inference, we shall not, with this explanation, be very wrong in pronouncing that acts of Notional Assent and of Inference do not affect our conduct, and acts of Belief, that is, of Real Assent, do (not necessarily, but do) affect it.

I have scarcely spoken of Inference since my Introductory Chapter, though I intend, before I conclude, to consider it fully; but I have said enough to admit of my introducing it here in contrast with Real Assent or Belief, and that contrast is necessary in order to complete what I have been saying about the latter. Let me then, for the sake of the latter, be allowed here to say, that, while Assent, or Belief, presupposes some apprehension of the things believed, Inference requires no apprehension of the things inferred; that in consequence, Inference is necessarily concerned with surfaces and aspects; that it begins with itself, and ends with itself; that it does not reach as far as facts; that it is employed upon formulas; that, as far as it takes real objects of whatever kind into account, such as motives and actions, character and conduct, art, science, taste, morals, religion, it deals with them, not as they are, but simply in its own line, as materials of argument or inquiry, that they are to it nothing more than major and minor premises and conclusions. Belief, on the other hand, being concerned with things concrete, not abstract, which variously excite the mind from their moral and imaginative properties, has for its objects, not only directly what is true, but inclusively what is beautiful, useful, admirable, heroic; objects which kindle devotion, rouse the passions, and attach the affections; and thus it leads the way to actions of every kind, to the establishment of principles, and the formation of character, and is thus again intimately connected with what is individual and personal.

I insisted on this marked distinction between Beliefs on the one hand, and Notional Assents and Inferences on the other, many years ago in words which it will be to my purpose to use now. I quote them, because, over and above their appositeness in this place, they present the doctrine which I have been insisting, from a second point of view, and with a freshness and force which I cannot now command, and, moreover, (though they are my own, nevertheless, from the length of time which has elapsed since their publications,) almost with the cogency of an independent testimony.

They occur in a protest which I had occasion to write in February, 1841, against a dangerous doctrine maintained, as I considered, by two very eminent men of that day, now no more—Lord Brougham and Sir Robert Peel. That doctrine was to the effect that the claims of religion could be secured and sustained in the mass of men, and in particular in the lower classes of society, by acquaintance with literature and physical science, and through the instrumentality of Mechanics' Institutes and Reading Rooms, to the serious disparagement, as it seemed to me, of direct Christian instruction. In the course of my remarks is found the passage which I shall here quote and which, with whatever differences in terminology, and hardihood of assertion, befitting the circumstances of its publication, nay, as far as words go, inaccuracy of theological statement, suitably illustrates the subject here under discussion. It runs thus:—

"People say to me, that it is but a dream to suppose that Christianity should regain the organic power in human society which once it possessed. I cannot help that; I never said it could. I am not a politician; I am proposing no measures, but exposing a fallacy and resisting a pretence. Let Benthamism reign, if men have no aspirations;

but do not tell them to be romantic and then solace them with 'glory:' do not attempt by philosophy what once was done by religion. The ascendency of faith may be impracticable, but the reign of knowledge is incomprehensible. The problem for statesmen of this age is how to educate the masses, and literature and science cannot give the solution.

"Science gives us the grounds or premisses from which religious truths are to be inferred; but it does not set about inferring them, much less does it reach the inference —that is not its province. It brings before us phenomena, and it leaves us, if we will, to call them works of design, wisdom, or benevolence; and further still, if we will, to proceed to confess an Intelligent Creator. We have to take its facts, and to give them a meaning, and to draw our own conclusions from them. First comes knowledge, then a view, then reasoning, and then belief. This is why science has so little of a religious tendency; deductions have no power of persuasion. The heart is commonly reached, not through the reason, but through the imagination, by means of direct impressions, by the testimony of facts and events, by history, by description. Persons influence us, voices melt us, looks subdue us, deeds inflame us. Many a man will live and die upon a dogma: no man will be a martyr for a conclusion. A conclusion is but an opinion; it is not a thing which *is*, but which *we are 'quite sure about'*; and it has often been observed, that we never say we are sure and certain without implying that we doubt. To say that a thing *must* be, is to admit that it *may not* be. No one, I say, will die for his own calculations: he dies for realities. This is why a literary religion is so little to be depended upon; it looks well in fair weather; but its doctrines are opinions, and when called to suffer for them it slips them between its folios, or burns them at its hearth. And this again is the secret of the distrust and raillery with which moralists have been so commonly visited. They say and do not. Why? Because they are contemplating the fitness of things, and they live by the square, when they should

be realizing their high maxims in the concrete. Now Sir Robert Peel thinks better of natural history, chemistry, and astronomy than of such ethics; but these too, what are they more than divinity *in posse*? He protests against '*controversial* divinity:' is *inferential* much better?

"I have no confidence, then, in philosophers who *cannot help* being religious, and are Christians by *implication*. They sit at home, and reach forward to distances which astonish us; but they hit without grasping, and are sometimes as confident about shadows as about realities. They have worked out by a calculation the lie of a country which they never saw, and mapped it by means of a gazetteer; and, like blind men, though they can put a stranger on his way, they cannot walk straight themselves, and do not feel it quite their business to walk at all.

"Logic makes but a sorry rhetoric with the multitude; first shoot round corners, and you may not despair of converting by a syllogism. Tell men to gain notions of a Creator from His works, and, if they were to set about it (which nobody does) they would be jaded and wearied by the labyrinth they were tracing. Their minds would be gorged and surfeited by the logical operation. Logicians are more set upon concluding rightly, than on right conclusions. They cannot see the end for the process. Few men have that power of mind which may hold fast and firmly a variety of thoughts. We ridicule 'men of one idea;' but a great many of us are born to be such, and we should be happier if we knew it. To most men argument makes the point in hand only more doubtful, and considerably less impressive. After all, man is *not* a reasoning animal; he is a seeing, feeling, contemplating, acting animal. He is influenced by what is direct and precise. It is very well to freshen our impressions and convictions from physics, but to create them we must go elsewhere. Sir Robert Peel 'never can think it possible that a mind can be so constituted, that, after being familiarized with the wonderful discoveries which have been made in every part of experimental science, it can retire from such contemplations without more enlarged conceptions of God's providence, and a higher reverence for His name!' If he speaks of religious minds, he perpetrates a truism; if of irreligious, he insinuates a paradox.

"Life is not long enough for a religion of inferences; we shall never have done beginning, if we determine to begin with proof. We shall ever be laying our foundations; we shall turn theology into evidences, and divines into textuaries. We shall never get at our first principles. Resolve to believe nothing, and you must prove your proofs and analyze your elements, sinking farther and farther, and finding 'in the lowest depth a lower deep,' till you come to the broad bosom of scepticism. I would rather be bound to defend the reasonableness of assuming that Christianity is true, than demonstrate a moral governance from the physical world. Life is for action. If we insist on proofs for everything, we shall never come to action: to act you must assume, and that assumption is faith.

"Let no one suppose, that in saying this I am maintaining that all proofs are equally difficult, and all propositions equally debatable. Some assumptions are greater than others, and some doctrines involve postulates larger than others, and more numerous. I only say, that impressions lead to action, and that reasonings lead from it. Knowledge of premisses, and inferences upon them,— this is not to *live*. It is very well as a matter of liberal curiosity and of philosophy to analyze our modes of thought: but let this come second, and when there is leisure for it, and then our examinations will in many ways even be subservient to action. But if we commence with scientific knowledge and argumentative proof, or lay any great stress upon it as the basis of personal Christianity, or attempt to make man moral and religious by libraries and museums, let us in consistency take chemists for our cooks, and mineralogists for our masons.

"Now I wish to state all this as matter of fact, to be judged by the candid testimony of any persons whatever. Why we are so constituted that faith, not knowledge or argument, is our principle of action, is a question with which I have nothing to do; but I think it is a fact, and, if it be such, we must resign ourselves to it as best we may, unless we take refuge in the intolerable paradox, that the mass of men are created for nothing, and are meant to leave life as they entered it.

"So well has this practically been understood in all ages of the world, that no religion yet has been a religion of physics or of philosophy. It has ever been synonymous with revelation. It never has been a deduction from what we know; it has ever been an assertion of what we are to believe. It has never lived in a conclusion; it has ever been a message, a history, or a vision. No legislator or priest ever dreamed of educating our moral nature by science or by argument. There is no difference here between true religions and pretended. Moses was instructed not to reason from the creation, but to work miracles. Christianity is a history supernatural, and almost scenic: it tells us what its Author is, by telling us what He has done. . . .

Bibliography

Texts

Cardinal Newman's Works. 40 vols. New York: Longmans, Green & Co., Inc., 1874–1921. (Index by J. Rickaby.)

Studies

Cronin, J. F. *Cardinal Newman: His Theory of Knowledge.* Washington, D.C.: The Catholic University of America Press, 1935.

Rickaby, Joseph. *Index to the Works of J. H. Newman.* London: Longmans, Green & Co., Ltd., 1935.

Ward, Wilfred. *Life of Cardinal Newman.* 2 vols. London: Longmans, Green & Co., Ltd., 1912.

13

Introduction

John Stuart Mill, eldest son of James Mill, was born in London and received perhaps the most remarkable education a young man of his time had ever had. Though his father had intended that he teach the Benthamite philosophy of life, he developed a type of utilitarian philosophy very much his own.

In his early years he had been subjected to a rigid and intensive training under the guidance of his father. He had learned subjects such as Greek at the age of three. During these very early years, up to the age of twelve, he had been trained in and examined on many areas in the classics and in history, including Aristotelian logic. Thereafter he devoted his time to subjects such as political economy. Indeed, he was a precocious young man. It has been said that he was a quarter of a century ahead of his contemporaries.

Though he had planned to study law, he abandoned this idea and in 1822, entered the India House, where he achieved a position of prominence in the same fashion as had his father before him. In this position he had much time for intellectual endeavors and even found time to found a "Utilitarian Society" whose members were mostly Benthamites. During this time he wrote several articles for various newspapers and reviews on political and economic subjects. He also edited the Benthamite journal, *Rationale of Judicial Evidence.* Mill subsequently underwent a change of thought and relinquished his Benthamite way of thinking. At the same time he struggled with depressive thoughts and feelings. As he gradually emerged from his troubled condition, he realized the narrowness and insufficiency of the position of his father.

From the time of his recovery, young Mill attempted a more adequate and comprehensive presentation of utilitarian philosophy. As he grew in this direction, he became one of the leaders of liberalism among the intellectuals of England during the middle of the nineteenth century.

Among his more significant writings are *System of Logic* (1843), *The Principles of Political Economy* (1848), *On Liberty* (1859), *The Considerations on Representative Government* (1861), *Utilitarianism* (1863), *Examination of Sir William Hamilton's Philosophy* (1865), and *The Subjection of Women* (1869). His *Autobiography* appeared in 1873, and three essays, *Nature, The Utility of Religion,* and *Theism* were published posthumously in 1874.

The philosophy of Mill can be placed under the heading of *positivism,* a philosophical movement which had its roots in the works of Auguste Comte (1798–1857). Its main tenet is that only phenomena (appearances) are knowable as received by the external senses. This leaves little room for a philosophy built on introspection, deductive metaphysical reasoning, or such phenomena as moral experiences. Rather for Mill real or "positive" phenomena are only those having the "permanent possibility of sensation." Mill's philosophy reflects English empiricism and Humean psychologism in his effort to explain all psychological phenomena through the association of atomistic images. He does not admit a priori contents or forms of the mind. Mill showed considerable interest in logic; indeed, he is sometimes called "the father of inductive logic." His ethics are utilitarian and contain many criticisms which reflect the needs of the times. The following passage mirrors the unrest of the times and the ideas which heralded social reforms.

INDIVIDUALITY *

Such being the reasons which make it imperative that human beings should be free to form opinions, and to express their opinions without reserve; and such the baneful consequences to the intellectual, and through that to the moral nature of man, unless this liberty is either conceded, or asserted in spite of prohibition; let us next examine whether the same reasons do not require that men should be free to act upon their opinions—to carry these out in their lives, without hindrance, either physical or moral, from their fellow-men, so long as it is at their own risk and peril. This last proviso is of course indispensable. No one pretends that actions should be as free as opinions. On the contrary, even opinions lose their immunity when the circumstances in which they are expressed are such as to constitute their expression a positive instigation to some mischievous act. An opinion that corn-dealers are starvers of the poor, or that private property is robbery, ought to be unmolested when simply circulated through the press, but may justly incur punishment when delivered orally to an excited mob assembled before the house of a corn-dealer, or when handed about among the same mob in the form of a placard. Acts, of whatever kind, which, without justifiable cause, do harm to others, may be, and in the more important cases absolutely require to be, controlled by the unfavourable sentiments, and, when needful, by the active interference of mankind. The liberty of the individual must be thus far limited; he must not make himself a nuisance to other people. But if he refrains from molesting others in what concerns them, and merely acts according to his own inclination and judgment in things which concern himself, the same reasons which show that opinion should be free, prove also that he should be allowed, without molesta-

* From J. S. Mill, "On Liberty," in *Utilitarianism; On Liberty;* and, *Representative Government.* Everyman's Library. Reprinted by permission of E. P. Dutton & Co., Inc., New York, and J. M. Dent & Sons, Ltd., Publishers, London.

tion, to carry his opinions into practice at his own cost. That mankind are not infallible; that their truths, for the most part, are only half-truths; that unity of opinion, unless resulting from the fullest and freest comparison of opposite opinions, is not desirable, and diversity not an evil, but a good, until mankind are much more capable than at present of recognising all sides of the truth, are principles applicable to men's modes of action, not less than to their opinions. As it is useful that while mankind are imperfect there should be different opinions, so it is that there should be different experiments of living; that free scope should be given to varieties of character, short of injury to others; and that the worth of different modes of life should be proved practically, when any one thinks fit to try them. It is desirable, in short, that in things which do not primarily concern others, individuality should assert itself. Where, not the person's own character, but the traditions or customs of other people are the rule of conduct, there is wanting one of the principal ingredients of human happiness, and quite the chief ingredient of individual and social progress.

In maintaining this principle, the greatest difficulty to be encountered does not lie in the appreciation of means towards an acknowledged end, but in the indifference of persons in general to the end itself. If it were felt that the free development of individuality is one of the leading essentials of well-being; that it is not only a co-ordinate element with all that is designated by the terms civilisation, instruction, education, culture, but is itself a necessary part and condition of all those things; there would be no danger that liberty should be undervalued, and the adjustment of the boundaries between it and social control would present no extraordinary difficulty. But the evil is, that individual spontaneity is hardly recognized by the common modes of thinking as having any intrinsic worth, or deserving any regard on its own account. The majority, being satisfied with the ways of mankind as they now are (for it is they who make them what they are), cannot comprehend why those ways should not be good enough for everybody; and what is more, spontaneity forms no part of the ideal of the majority of moral and social reformers, but is rather looked on with jealousy, as a troublesome and perhaps rebellious obstruction to the general acceptance of what these reformers, in their own judgment, think would be best for mankind. Few persons, out of Germany, even comprehend the meaning of the doctrine which Wilhelm von Humboldt, so eminent both as a *savant* and as a politician, made the text of a treatise—that "the end of man, or that which is prescribed by the eternal or immutable dictates of reason, and not suggested by vague and transient desires, is the highest and most harmonious development of his powers to a complete and consistent whole;" that, therefore, "the object towards which every human being must ceaselessly direct his efforts, and on which especially those who design to influence their fellow-men must ever keep their eyes, is the individuality of power and development"; that for this there are two requisites, "freedom, and variety of situations"; and that from the union of these arise "individual vigour and manifold diversity," which combine themselves in "originality." [1]

Little, however, as people are accustomed to a doctrine like that of von Humboldt, and surprising as it may be to them to find so high a value attached to individuality, the question, one must nevertheless think, can only be one of degree. No one's idea of excellence in conduct is that people should do absolutely nothing but copy one another. No one would assert that people ought not to put into their mode of life, and into the conduct of their concerns, any impress whatever of their own judgment, or of their own individual character. On the other hand, it would be absurd to pretend that people ought to live as if nothing whatever had been known

[1] *The Sphere and Duties of Government,* from the German of Baron Wilhelm von Humboldt, pp. 11–13.

in the world before they came into it; as if experience had as yet done nothing towards showing that one mode of existence, or of conduct, is preferable to another. Nobody denies that people should be so taught and trained in youth as to know and benefit by the ascertained results of human experience. But it is the privilege and proper condition of a human being, arrived at the maturity of his faculties, to use and interpret experience in his own way. It is for him to find out what part of recorded experience is properly applicable to his own circumstances and character. The traditions and customs of other people are, to a certain extent, evidence of what their experience has taught *them;* presumptive evidence, and as such, have a claim to his deference: but, in the first place, their experience may be too narrow; or they may not have interpreted it rightly. Secondly, their interpretation of experience may be correct, but unsuitable to him. Customs are made for customary circumstances and customary characters; and his circumstances or his character may be uncustomary. Thirdly, though the customs be both good as customs, and suitable to him, yet to conform to custom, merely *as* custom, does not educate or develop in him any of the qualities which are the distinctive endowment of a human being. The human faculties of perception, judgment, discriminative feeling, mental activity, and even moral preference, are exercised only in making a choice. He who does anything because it is the custom makes no choice. He gains no practice either in discerning or in desiring what is best. The mental and moral, like the muscular powers, are improved only by being used. The faculties are called into no exercise by doing a thing merely because others do it, no more than by believing a thing only because others believe it. If the grounds of an opinion are not conclusive to the person's own reason, his reason cannot be strengthened, but is likely to be weakened, by his adopting it: and if the inducements to an act are not such as are consentaneous to his own feelings and character (where affection, or the rights of others, are not concerned) it is so much done towards rendering his feelings and character inert and torpid, instead of active and energetic.

He who lets the world, or his own portion of it, choose his plan of life for him, has no need of any other faculty than the ape-like one of imitation. He who chooses his plan for himself, employs all his faculties. He must use observation to see, reasoning and judgment to foresee, activity to gather materials for decision, discrimination to decide, and when he has decided, firmness and self-control to hold to his deliberate decision. And these qualities he requires and exercises exactly in proportion as the part of his conduct which he determines according to his own judgment and feelings is a large one. It is possible that he might be guided in some good path, and kept out of harm's way, without any of these things. But what will be his comparative worth as a human being? It really is of importance, not only what men do, but also what manner of men they are that do it. Among the works of man, which human life is rightly employed in perfecting and beautifying, the first in importance surely is man himself. Supposing it were possible to get houses built, corn grown, battles fought, causes tried, and even churches erected and prayers said, by machinery—by automatons in human form—it would be a considerable loss to exchange for these automatons even the men and women who at present inhabit the more civilised parts of the world, and who assuredly are but starved specimens of what nature can and will produce. Human nature is not a machine to be built after a model, and set to do exactly the work prescribed for it, but a tree, which requires to grow and develop itself on all sides, according to the tendency of the inward forces which make it a living thing.

It will probably be conceded that it is desirable people should exercise their understandings, and that an intelligent following of custom, or even occasionally an intelligent deviation from custom, is better than a blind and simply mechanical adhesion to it. To a certain extent it is admitted that our understanding should be our own: but there is not the same willingness to admit that our desires and impulses should be our own likewise; or that to possess impulses of our own, and of any strength, is anything but a peril and a snare. Yet desires and impulses are as much a part of a perfect human being as beliefs and restraints: and strong impulses are only perilous when not properly balanced; when one set of aims and inclinations is developed into strength, while others, which ought to co-exist with them, remain weak and inactive. It is not because men's desires are strong that they act ill; it is because their consciences are weak. There is no natural connection between strong impulses and a weak conscience. The natural connection is the other way. To say that one person's desires and feelings are stronger and more various than those of another, is merely to say that he has more of the raw material of human nature, and is therefore capable, perhaps of more evil, but certainly of more good. Strong impulses are but another name for energy. Energy may be turned to bad uses; but more good may always be made of an energetic nature, than of an indolent and impassive one. Those who have most natural feeling are always those whose cultivated feelings may be made the strongest. The same strong susceptibilities which make the personal impulses vivid and powerful, are also the source from whence are generated the most passionate love of virtue, and the sternest self-control. It is through the cultivation of these that society both does its duty and protects its interests: not by rejecting the stuff of which heroes are made, because it knows not how to make them. A person whose desires and impulses are his own—are the expression of his own nature, as it has been developed and modified by his own culture—is said to have a character. One whose desires and impulses are not his own, has no character, no more than a steam-engine has a character. If, in addition to being his own, his impulses are strong, and are under the government of a strong will, he has an energetic character. Whoever thinks that individuality of desires and impulses should not be encouraged to unfold itself, must maintain that society has no need of strong natures—is not the better for containing many persons who have much character—and that a high general average of energy is not desirable.

In some early states of society, these forces might be, and were, too much ahead of the power which society then possessed of disciplining and controlling them. There has been a time when the element of spontaneity and individuality was in excess, and the social principle had a hard struggle with it. The difficulty then was to induce men of strong bodies or minds to pay obedience to any rules which required them to control their impulses. To overcome this difficulty, law and discipline, like the Popes struggling against the Emperors, asserted a power over the whole man, claiming to control all his life in order to control his character—which society had not found any other sufficient means of binding. But society has now fairly got the better of individuality; and the danger which threatens human nature is not the excess, but the deficiency, of personal impulses and preferences. Things are vastly changed since the passions of those who were strong by station or by personal endowment were in a state of habitual rebellion against laws and ordinances, and required to be rigorously chained up to enable the persons within their reach to enjoy any particle of security. In our times, from the highest class of society down to the lowest, every one lives as under the eye of a hostile and dreaded censorship. Not only in what concerns others, but in what concerns only themselves, the individual or the family do not ask themselves—what do I prefer? or, what would suit my character and disposition? or, what would allow the best and highest in me to have fair play, and enable it to grow and thrive? They ask themselves, what is suitable to my position? what is usually done by persons of my station and pecuniary circumstances? or (worse still) what is usually done by persons of a station and circumstances superior to mine? I do not mean that they choose what is customary in prefer-

ence to what suits their own inclination. It does not occur to them to have any inclination, except for what is customary. Thus the mind itself is bowed to the yoke: even in what people do for pleasure, conformity is the first thing thought of; they like in crowds; they exercise choice only among things commonly done: peculiarity of taste, eccentricity of conduct, are shunned equally with crimes: until by dint of not following their own nature they have no nature to follow: their human capacities are withered and starved: they become incapable of any strong wishes or native pleasures, and are generally without either opinions or feelings of home growth, or properly their own. Now is this, or is it not, the desirable condition of human nature?

It is so, on the Calvinistic theory. According to that, the one great offence of man is self-will. All the good of which humanity is capable is comprised in obedience. You have no choice; thus you must do, and no otherwise: "whatever is not a duty, is a sin." Human nature being radically corrupt, there is no redemption for any one until human nature is killed within him. To one holding this theory of life, crushing out any of the human faculties, capacities, and susceptibilities, is no evil: man needs no capacity, but that of surrendering himself to the will of God: and if he uses any of his faculties for any other purpose but to do that supposed will more effectually, he is better without them. This is the theory of Calvinism; and it is held, in a mitigated form, by many who do not consider themselves Calvinists; the mitigation consisting in giving a less ascetic interpretation to the alleged will of God; asserting it to be his will that mankind should gratify some of their inclinations; of course not in the manner they themselves prefer, but in the way of obedience, that is, in a way prescribed to them by authority; and, therefore, by the necessary condition of the case, the same for all.

In some such insidious form there is at present a strong tendency to this narrow theory of life, and to the pinched and hidebound type of human character which it patronises. Many persons, no doubt, sincerely think that human beings thus cramped and dwarfed are as their Maker designed them to be; just as many have thought that trees are a much finer thing when clipped into pollards, or cut out into figures of animals, than as nature made them. But if it be any part of religion to believe that man was made by a good Being, it is more consistent with that faith to believe that this Being gave all human faculties that they might be cultivated and unfolded, not rooted out and consumed, and that he takes delight in every nearer approach made by his creatures to the ideal conception embodied in them, every increase in any of their capabilities of comprehension, of action, or of enjoyment. There is a different type of human excellence from the Calvinistic: a conception of humanity as having its nature bestowed on it for other purposes than merely to be abnegated. "Pagan self-assertion" is one of the elements of human worth, as well as "Christian self-denial." [2] There is a Greek ideal of self-development, which the Platonic and Christian ideal of self-government blends with, but does not supersede. It may be better to be a John Knox than an Alcibiades, but it is better to be a Pericles than either; nor would a Pericles, if we had one in these days, be without anything good which belonged to John Knox.

It is not by wearing down into uniformity all that is individual in themselves, but by cultivating it, and calling it forth, within the limits imposed by the rights and interests of others, that human beings become a noble and beautiful object of contemplation; and as the works partake the character of those who do them, by the same process human life also becomes rich, diversified, and animating, furnishing more abundant aliment to high thoughts and elevating feelings, and strengthening the tie which binds every individual to the race, by making the race infinitely better worth belonging to. In proportion to the development of his individuality, each person becomes more valuable to himself, and is therefore capable of being more valuable to others.

2 Sterling's *Essays*.

Bibliography

Texts

On Liberty. Edited with an introduction by Currin V. Shields. New York: The Liberal Arts Press, Inc., 1956.

Philosophy of Scientific Method. Edited with an introduction by Ernest Nagel. New York: Hafner Publishing Company, Inc., 1950.

Studies

Anschutz, Richard Paul. *The Philosophy of J. S. Mill*. Fair Lawn, N.J.: Oxford University Press, 1953.

Packe, Michael St. John. *The Life of John Stuart Mill*. With a preface by F. A. Hazek. New York: The Macmillan Company, 1954.

14 SÖREN KIERKEGAARD
1813–1855

Introduction

Sören Kierkegaard was born in Copenhagen on May 15, 1813. He was raised in a solidly pious Lutheran religious background. He went to the University of Copenhagen, where he matriculated in the faculty of theology but devoted his studies to philosophy, literature, and history. During this time, he became rather cynical and disillusioned and felt that philosophy, particularly of the Hegelian type, was not compatible with Christianity. In the spring of 1836, Kierkegaard seems to have had suicidal tendencies. In June of that year, he underwent a type of moral conversion or moral commitment. After the death of his father in 1838, he resumed his theological studies and in 1840 passed his examinations in theology. Though he was engaged to Regina Olsen, he broke the engagement, feeling he was unsuited for married life. In 1843 he published *Either/Or,* a work in which he manifested his existential approach to life and his rejection of the speculative Hegelian philosophy, which was then being taught in the universities. At this time two other works appeared: *Fear and Trembling* and *Repetition.* In 1844, there followed *Concept of Dread* and *Philosophical Fragments.* A year later there appeared *Stages on Life's Way,* and in 1846, *Concluding Unscientific Postscript.* Kierkegaard wrote under various pseudonyms, but his identity was well-known. At this time his reaction against the essentialism of the contemporaneous philosophies was marked by an increased return to reality and existence. One can say that his writings are more directly religious than philosophical, for it was his concern for religious living that drove him back to reality.

A new phase can be seen in Kierkegaard's works after 1848, at which time he had a religious experience, as he indicates in his *Journal.* About the same time, he composed *Christian Discourses, Point of View,* a work which was only published after his death. *Sickness unto Death* appeared in 1849. It became more and more evident in the works of Kierkegaard that he was attacking the Danish State Church because he felt it no longer deserved the name of Christian. Much controversy developed around the writings of Kierkegaard, and the question of an emasculated Christianity as an established church was a frequent topic of discussion. Kierkegaard died on November 4, 1855.

The individual and the crowd, dialectic stages of truth as subjectivity, the idea of existence, and the concept of dread are basic topics in Kierkegaard's existential philosophy. Because of his interest in the individual, Kierkegaard vigorously opposed the systematic philosophy of Hegel. His interest in the individual's vital concern for his own well-being and salvation shifted Kierkegaard's philosophic interest away from Hegelian essentialism to real, concrete existence. This attitude also caused him to reject the "objective" and abstract concern for truth for a subjective regard for truth in which the individual works through the aesthetic level of sense, impulse, and emotion; and through the ethical level of moral self-sufficiency to the religious level where man relates himself to God by faith—man wills his self—the self grounded transparently in the Power which constituted it. The attraction and repulsion of the unknown in the alarming possibility of freedom, and consequently of sin, produces dread. The same dread holds also for the good, e.g., for the sinner before he makes the leap of faith. Though primarily a religious thinker, Kierkegaard, like Newman, brought new emphasis to another dimension of truth—the subjective.

ON SUBJECTIVE TRUTH, INWARDNESS *

Whether truth is defined more empirically, as the conformity of thought and being, or more idealistically, as the conformity of being with thought, it is, in either case, important carefully to note what is meant by being. And in formulating the answer to this question it is likewise important to take heed lest the knowing spirit be tricked into losing itself in the indeterminate, so that it fantastically becomes a something that no existing human being ever was or can be, a sort of phantom with which the individual occupies himself upon occasion, but without making it clear to himself in terms of dialectical intermediaries how he happens to get into this fantastic realm, what significance being there has for him, and whether the entire activity that goes on out there does not resolve itself into a tautology within a recklessly fantastic venture of thought.

If being, in the two indicated definitions, is understood as empirical being, truth is at once transformed into a *desideratum*, and everything must be understood in terms of becoming; for the empirical object is unfinished and the existing cognitive spirit is itself in process of becoming. Thus the truth becomes an approximation whose beginning cannot be posited absolutely, precisely because the conclusion is lacking, the effect of which is retroactive. Whenever a beginning is *made*, on the other hand, unless through being unaware of this the procedure stamps itself as arbitrary, such a beginning is not the consequence of an immanent movement of thought, but is effected through a resolution of the will, essentially in the strength of faith. That the knowing spirit is an existing individual spirit, and that every human being is such an entity existing for himself, is a truth I cannot too often repeat; for the fantastic neglect of this is responsible for much confusion. Let no one misunderstand

* From Sören Kierkegaard, *Concluding Unscientific Postscript*, David F. Swenson, translator. By permission of Princeton University Press, Princeton, N. J. Copyright © 1941.

me. I happen to be a poor existing spirit like all other men; but if there is any lawful and honest manner in which I could be helped into becoming something extraordinary, like the pure I-am-I for example, I always stand ready gratefully to accept the gift and the benefaction. But if it can only be done in the manner indicated, by saying *ein zwei drei kokolorum,* or by tying a string around the little finger, and then when the moon is full, hiding it in some secret place—in that case I prefer to remain what I am, a poor existing human being.

The term "being," as used in the above definitions, must therefore be understood (from the systematic standpoint) much more abstractly, presumably as the abstract reflection of, or the abstract prototype for, what being is as concrete empirical being. When so understood there is nothing to prevent us from abstractly determining the truth as abstractly finished and complete; for the correspondence between thought and being is, from the abstract point of view, always finished. Only with the concrete does becoming enter in, and it is from the concrete that abstract thought abstracts.

But if being is understood in this manner, the formula becomes a tautology. Thought and being mean one and the same thing, and the correspondence spoken of is merely an abstract self-identity. Neither formula says anything more than that the truth is, so understood as to accentuate the copula: the truth *is*, i.e. the truth is a reduplication. Truth is the subject of the assertion, but the assertion that it is, is the same as the subject; for this being that the truth is said to have is never its own abstract form. In this manner we give expression to the fact that truth is not something simple, but is in a wholly abstract sense a reduplication, a reduplication which is nevertheless instantly revoked.

Abstract thought may continue as long as it likes to rewrite this thought in varying phraseology, it will never get any farther. As soon as the being which corresponds to the truth comes to be empirically concrete, the truth is put in process of becoming, and is again by way of anticipation the conformity of thought with being. This conformity is actually realized for God, but it is not realized for any existing spirit, who is himself existentially in process of becoming.

For an existing spirit *qua* existing spirit, the question of the truth will again exist. The abstract answer has significance only for the abstraction into which an existing spirit is transformed when he abstracts from himself *qua* existing individual. This can be done only momentarily, and even in such moments of abstraction the abstract thinker pays his debt to existence by existing in spite of all abstraction. It is therefore an existing spirit who is now conceived as raising the question of truth, presumably in order that he may exist in it; but in any case the question is raised by someone who is conscious of being a particular existing human being. In this way I believe I can render myself intelligible to every Greek, as well as to every reasonable human being. If a German philosopher wishes to indulge a passion for making himself over, and, just as alchemists and necromancers were wont to garb themselves fantastically, first makes himself over into a superrational something for the purpose of answering this question of the truth in an extremely satisfactory manner, the affair is no concern of mine; nor is his extremely satisfactory answer, which is no doubt very satisfactory indeed—when you are fantastically transformed. On the other hand, whether it is or is not the case that a German professor behaves in this manner, can be readily determined by anyone who will concentrate enthusiastically upon seeking guidance at the hands of such a sage, without criticism but seeking merely to assimilate the wisdom in a docile spirit by proposing to shape his own life in accordance with it. Precisely when thus enthusiastically attempting to learn from such a German professor, one would realize the most apt of epigrams upon him. For such a

speculative philosopher could hardly be more embarrassed than by the sincere and enthusiastic zeal of a learner who proposes to express and to realize his wisdom by appropriating it existentially. For this wisdom is something that the Herr Professor has merely imagined, and written books about, but never himself tried. Aye, it has never even occurred to him that this should be done. Like the custom clerk who writes what he could not himself read, satisfied that his responsibilities ended with the writing, so there are speculative philosophers who write what, when it is to be read in the light of action, shows itself to be nonsense, unless it is, perhaps, intended only for fantastic beings.

In that the question of truth is thus raised by an existing spirit *qua* existing, the above abstract reduplication that is involved in it again confronts him. But existence itself, namely, existence as it is in the individual who raises the question and himself exists, keeps the two moments of thought and being apart, so that reflection presents him with two alternatives. For an objective reflection the truth becomes an object, something objective, and thought must be pointed away from the subject. For a subjective reflection the truth becomes a matter of appropriation, of inwardness, of subjectivity, and thought must probe more and more deeply into the subject and his subjectivity.

But then what? Shall we be compelled to remain in this disjunction, or may we not here accept the offer of benevolent assistance from the principle of mediation, so that the truth becomes an identity of subject and object? Well, why not? But can the principle of mediation also help the existing individual while still remaining in existence himself to become the mediating principle, which is *sub specie aeterni*, whereas the poor existing individual is confined to the strait-jacket of existence? Surely it cannot do any good to mock a man, luring him on by dangling before his eyes the identity of subject and object, when his situation prevents him from making use of this identity, since he is in process of becoming in consequence of being an existing individual. How can it help to explain to a man how the eternal truth is to be understood eternally, when the supposed user of the explanation is prevented from so understanding it through being an existing individual, and merely becomes fantastic when he imagines himself to be *sub specie aeterni*? What such a man needs instead is precisely an explanation of how the eternal truth is to be understood in determinations of time by one who as existing is himself in time, which even the worshipful Herr Professor concedes, if not always, at least once a quarter when he draws his salary.

The identity of subject and object posited through an application of the principle of mediation merely carries us back to where we were before, to the abstract definition of the truth as an identity of thought and being; for to determine the truth as an identity of thought and object is precisely the same thing as saying that the truth *is*, i.e. that the truth is a reduplication. The lofty wisdom has thus again merely been absent-minded enough to forget that it was an existing spirit who asked about the truth. Or is the existing spirit himself the identity of subject and object, the subject-object? In that case I must press the question of where such an existing human being is, when he is thus at the same time also a subject-object? Or shall we perhaps here again first transform the existing spirit into something in general, and thereupon explain everything except the question asked, namely, how an existing subject is related to the truth *in concreto;* explain everything except the question that must in the next instance be asked, namely, how a particular existing spirit is related to this something in general, which seems to have not a little in common with a paper kite, or with the lump of sugar which the Dutch used to hang up under the loft for all to lick at.

So we return to the two ways of reflection; and we have not forgotten that it is an existing spirit who asks the question, a wholly individual human being. Nor can we forget that the fact that he exists is precisely what will make it impossible for him to proceed along both ways at once, while his earnest concern will prevent him from frivolously and fantastically becoming subject-object. Which of these two ways is now the way of truth for an existing spirit? For only the fantastic I-am-I is at once finished with both ways, or proceeds methodically along both ways simultaneously, a mode of ambulation which for an existing human is so inhuman that I dare not recommend it.

Since the inquirer stresses precisely the fact that he is an existing individual, then one of the above two ways which especially accentuates existence would seem to be especially worthy of commendation.

The way of objective reflection makes the subject accidental, and thereby transforms existence into something indifferent, something vanishing. Away from the subject the objective way of reflection leads to the objective truth, and while the subject and his subjectivity become indifferent, the truth also becomes indifferent, and this indifference is precisely its objective validity; for all interest, like all decisiveness, is rooted in subjectivity. The way of objective reflection leads to abstract thought, to mathematics, to historical knowledge of different kinds; and always it leads away from the subject, whose existence or non-existence, and from the objective point of view quite rightly, becomes infinitely indifferent. Quite rightly, since as Hamlet says, existence and non-existence have only subjective significance. At its maximum this way will arrive at a contradiction, and in so far as the subject does not become wholly indifferent to himself, this merely constitutes a sign that his objective striving is not objective enough. At its maximum this way will lead to the contradiction that only the objective has come into being, while the subjective has gone out; that is to say, the existing subjectivity has vanished, in that it has made an attempt to become what in the abstract sense is called subjectivity, the mere abstract form of an abstract objectivity. And yet, the objectivity which has thus come into being is, from the subjective point of view at the most, either an hypothesis or an approximation, because all eternal decisiveness is rooted in subjectivity.

However, the objective way deems itself to have a security which the subjective way does not have (and, of course, existence and existing cannot be thought in combination with objective security); it thinks to escape a danger which threatens the subjective way, and this danger is at its maximum: madness. In a merely subjective determination of the truth, madness and truth become in the last analysis indistinguishable, since they may both have inwardness.[1] Nevertheless, perhaps I may here venture to offer a little remark, one which would seem to be not wholly superfluous in an objective age. The absence of inwardness is also madness. The objective truth as such, is by no means adequate to determine that whoever utters it is sane; on the contrary, it may even betray the fact that he is mad, although what he says may be entirely true, and especially objectively true. I shall here permit myself to tell a story, which without any sort of adaptation on my part comes direct from an asylum. A patient in such an institution seeks to escape, and actually succeeds in effecting his purpose by leaping out of a window, and prepares to start on the road to freedom, when the thought strikes him (shall I say sanely enough or madly enough?): "When you come to town you will be recognized, and you will at once be brought back here again; hence you need to prepare yourself fully to convince everyone by the objective truth of what you say, that all is in order as far as your sanity is concerned." As he walks along and thinks about this, he sees a ball lying on the ground, picks it up, and puts it into the tail pocket of his coat. Every step he takes

[1] Even this is not really true, however, for madness never has the specific inwardness of the infinite. Its fixed idea is precisely some sort of objectivity, and the contradiction of madness consists in embracing this with passion. The critical point in such madness is thus again not the subjective, but the little finitude which has become a fixed idea, which is something that can never happen to the infinite.

the ball strikes him, politely speaking, on his hinder parts, and every time it thus strikes him he says: "Bang, the earth is round." He comes to the city, and at once calls on one of his friends; he wants to convince him that he is not crazy, and therefore walks back and forth, saying continually: "Bang, the earth is round!" But is not the earth round? Does the asylum still crave yet another sacrifice for this opinion, as in the time when all men believed it to be flat as a pancake? Or is a man who hopes to prove that he is sane, by uttering a generally accepted and generally respected objective truth, insane? And yet it was clear to the physician that the patient was not yet cured; though it is not to be thought that the cure would consist in getting him to accept the opinion that the earth is flat. But all men are not physicians, and what the age demands seems to have a considerable influence upon the question of what madness is. Aye, one could almost be tempted sometimes to believe that the modern age, which has modernized Christianity, has also modernized the question of Pontius Pilate, and that its urge to find something in which it can rest proclaims itself in the question: What is madness? When a *Privatdocent*, every time his scholastic gown reminds him that he ought to say something, says *de omnibus dubitandum est,* and at the same time writes away at a system which offers abundant internal evidence in every other sentence that the man has never doubted anything at all: he is not regarded as mad.

Don Quixote is the prototype for a subjective madness, in which the passion of inwardness embraces a particular finite fixed idea. But the absence of inwardness gives us on the other hand the prating madness, which is quite as comical; and it might be a very desirable thing if an experimental psychologist would delineate it by taking a handful of such philosophers and bringing them together. In the type of madness which manifests itself as an aberrant inwardness, the tragic and the comic is that the something which is of such infinite concern to the unfortunate individual is a particular fixation which does not really concern anybody. In the type of madness which consists in the absence of inwardness, the comic is that though the something which the happy individual knows really is the truth, the truth which concerns all men, it does not in the slightest degree concern the much respected prater. This type of madness is more inhuman than the other. One shrinks from looking into the eyes of a madman of the former type lest one be compelled to plumb there the depths of his delirium; but one dares not look at a madman of the latter type at all, from fear of discovering that he has eyes of glass and hair made from carpet-rags; that he is, in short, an artificial product. If you meet someone who suffers from such a derangement of feeling, the derangement consisting in his not having any, you listen to what he says in a cold and awful dread, scarcely knowing whether it is a human being who speaks, or a cunningly contrived walking stick in which a talking machine has been concealed. It is always unpleasant for a proud man to find himself unwittingly drinking a toast of brotherhood with the public hangman;. but to find oneself engaged in rational and philosophical conversation with a walking stick is almost enough to make a man lose his mind.

The subjective reflection turns its attention inwardly to the subject, and desires in this intensification of inwardness to realize the truth. And it proceeds in such fashion that, just as in the preceding objective reflection, when the objectivity had come into being, the subjectivity had vanished, so here the subjectivity of the subject becomes the final stage, and objectivity a vanishing factor. Not for a single moment is it forgotten that the subject is an existing individual, and that existence is a process of becoming, and that therefore the notion of the truth as identity of thought and being is a chimera of abstraction, in its truth only an expectation of the creature; not because the truth is not such an identity, but because the knower is an existing individual for whom the truth cannot be such an identity as long as he lives in time. Unless we hold fast to this,

speculative philosophy will immediately transport us into the fantastic realism of the I-am-I, which modern speculative thought has not hesitated to use without explaining how a particular individual is related to it; and God knows, no human being is more than such a particular individual.

If an existing individual were really able to transcend himself, the truth would be for him something final and complete; but where is the point at which he is outside himself? The I-am-I is a mathematical point which does not exist, and in so far there is nothing to prevent everyone from occupying this standpoint; the one will not be in the way of the other. It is only momentarily that the particular individual is able to realize existentially a unity of the infinite and the finite which transcends existence. This unity is realized in the moment of passion. Modern philosophy has tried anything and everything in the effort to help the individual to transcend himself objectively, which is a wholly impossible feat; existence exercises its restraining influence, and if philosophers nowadays had not become mere scribblers in the service of a fantastic thinking and its preoccupation, they would long ago have perceived that suicide was the only tolerable practical interpretation of its striving. But the scribbling modern philosophy holds passion in contempt; and yet passion is the culmination of existence for an existing individual—and we are all of us existing individuals. In passion the existing subject is rendered infinite in the eternity of the imaginative representation, and yet he is at the same time most definitely himself. The fantastic I-am-I is not an identity of the infinite and the finite, since neither the one nor the other is real; it is a fantastic rendezvous in the clouds, an unfruitful embrace, and the relationship of the individual self to this mirage is never indicated.

All essential knowledge relates to existence, or only such knowledge as has an essential relationship to existence is essential knowledge. All knowledge which does not inwardly relate itself to existence, in the reflection of inwardness, is, essentially viewed, accidental knowledge; its degree and scope is essentially indifferent. That essential knowledge is essentially related to existence does not mean the above-mentioned identity which abstract thought postulates between thought and being; nor does it signify, objectively, that knowledge corresponds to something existent as its object. But it means that knowledge has a relationship to the knower, who is essentially an existing individual, and that for this reason all essential knowledge is essentially related to existence. Only ethical and ethico-religious knowledge has an essential relationship to the existence of the knower.

Bibliography

Texts

A Kierkegaard Anthology. Edited by R. Bretall and translated by D. E. Swenson and W. Lowrie. Princeton, N.J.: Princeton University Press, 1946.

Studies

Collins, J., *The Mind of Kierkegaard.* Chicago: Henry Regnery Company, 1953.

Lowrie, W., *Kierkegaard.* Fair Lawn, N.J.: Oxford University Press, 1938.

15

Introduction

Friedrich Wilhelm Nietzsche was born on October 15, 1844, at Rocken in Prussian Saxony. Five years later, his father, a Lutheran pastor, died. Nietzsche was then raised in a family consisting of his mother, sister, grandmother, and two aunts. He went to the University of Bonn for one year before leaving for Leipzig, where he studied philology. By this time he had abandoned Christianity and had become a devotee of Schopenhauer's works. On the recommendation of his professor, Ritschl, Nietzsche was offered an academic appointment at the University of Basel, even before he had finished his doctoral work.

Nietzsche found enjoyable companionship in Richard Wagner, whom he visited at his villa on Lake Lucerne. In *Birth of Tragedy from the Spirit of Music*, which appeared in 1872, Nietzsche contrasted Greek culture before and after Socrates. He maintained that the contemporary German culture showed a strong resemblance to the Greek culture after Socrates and that it would not survive unless it were permeated with the spirit of Wagner. Though Wagner was appreciative of the book, scholars of Greek tragedy differed considerably with the views of Nietzsche. Nietzsche thereby lost credit in the world of classical scholarship. From 1873 to 1876 Nietzsche published several essays in which he attacked various professors for pursuing historical learning as a substitute for living culture. Though in 1867 Nietzsche had depicted Wagner as originating a rebirth of the Greek genius, about this time relations between Nietzsche and Wagner had already begun to grow cold. This marked the termination of the first phase of Nietzsche's development, dedicated mostly to a general consideration of human life and the meaning of culture.

In the second phase of his development,

Nietzsche attacked all accepted beliefs. His work *Human, All Too Human,* which appeared in three parts (1878–1879), is an attack upon metaphysics and an attempt to show that human experience must be explained not in terms of a metaphysical superstructure but rather in materialistic terms. At this time, in the spring of 1879, poor health and his own dissatisfaction led Nietzsche to resign his position at Basel. The next ten years he wandered throughout Europe seeking health cures. In 1881 he published *The Dawn of Day* in which he attacked the morality of self-renunciation and in 1882 published *Joyful Wisdom* in which he presented the idea of Christianity as hostile to life.

Between 1883 and 1885 the four-part work *Thus Spake Zarathustra* appeared in which he presented the doctrine of superman of the transevaluation of all values. This was the third phase of Nietzsche's thought. In 1886 there followed *Beyond Good and Evil* and then *Genealogy of Morals* (1887), which according to many is Nietzsche's greatest work.

In 1888 Nietzsche wrote a bitter attack on Wagner and followed this attack with a second one, which was published only after a nervous breakdown. His next work was *Ecce Homo*, a sort of autobiography. Extreme indications of mental instability were evinced by Nietzsche's exaggerated spirit of self-assertion. Psychological disturbance became more and more prominent, and in 1889 he was taken to a clinic in Basel. He never really recovered but went to Jena and then to his mother's home in Naumberg. After the death of his mother, he lived with his sister at Weimar. Nietzsche died on August 25, 1900.

The philosophy of Nietzsche might be classified as biological pragmatism. The principle of existence in this philosophy is the "will to power." Philosophy must strive to overthrow all existing values and value systems to help realize new values and ideals. One recognizes in these new values that the essence of life rests in an instinctive striving for power. All other realities, e.g., knowledge, are only good if they further self-affirmation, a sense of mastery, and the "will to power" in every natural expression of a fuller life. This expression of life will produce the "superman" who is uninhibited by a morality like Christianity, which is but a support for the weak and suffering. War, suffering, and misery are good since they eliminate weaklings. Nietzsche's views on morality are reflected in the following passage.

CONSCIENCE AND THE SOVEREIGN INDIVIDUAL *

The breeding of an animal that *can promise* —is not this just that very paradox of a task which nature has set itself in regard to man? Is not this the very problem of man? The fact that this problem has been to a great extent solved, must appear all the more phenomenal to one who can estimate at its full value that force of *forgetfulness* which works in opposition to it. Forgetfulness is no mere *vis inertiæ*, as the superficial believe, rather is it a power of obstruction, active and, in the strictest sense of the word, positive—a power responsible for the fact that what we have lived, experienced, taken into ourselves, no more enters into consciousness during the process of digestion (it might be called psychic absorption) than all the whole manifold process by which our physical nutrition, the so-called "incorporation," is carried on. The temporary shutting of the doors and windows of consciousness, the relief from the clamant alarms and excursions, with which our subconscious world of servant organs works in mutual co-operation and antagonism; a little quietude, a little *tabula rasa* of the consciousness, so as to make room again for the new, and above all for the more noble functions and functionaries, room for government, foresight, predetermination (for our organism is on an oligarchic model)—this is the utility, as I have said, of the active forgetfulness, which is a very sentinel and nurse of psychic order, repose, etiquette; and this shows at once why it is that there can exist no happiness, no gladness, no hope, no pride, no real *present*, without forgetfulness. The man in whom this preventative apparatus is damaged and discarded, is to be compared to a dyspeptic, and it is something more than a comparison—he can "get rid of" nothing. But this very animal who finds it necessary to be forgetful, in whom, in fact, forgetfulness represents a force and a form of *robust* health, has reared for himself an opposition-power, a memory, with whose help forgetfulness is, in certain instances, kept in check—in the cases, namely, where promises have to be made;—so that it is by no means a mere passive inability to get rid of a once indented impression, not merely the indigestion occasioned by a once pledged word, which one cannot dispose of, but an *active* refusal to get rid of it, a continuing and a wish to continue what has once been willed, an actual *memory of the will;* so that between the original "I will," "I shall do," and the actual discharge of the will, its *act*, we can easily interpose a world of new strange phenomena, circumstances, veritable volitions, without the snapping of this long chain of the will. But what is the underlying hypothesis of all this? How thoroughly, in order to be able to regulate the future in this way, must man have first learnt to distinguish between necessitated and accidental phenomena, to think casually, to see the distant as present and to anticipate it, to fix with certainty what is the end, and

* From Friedrich Nietzsche, *The Genealogy of Morals*, H. B. Samuel, translator. George Allen & Unwin, Ltd., London. Reprinted by permission of George Allen & Unwin, Ltd., London.

what is the means to that end; above all, to reckon, to have power to calculate—how thoroughly must man have first become *calculable, disciplined, necessitated* even for himself and his own conception of himself, that, like a man entering a promise, he could guarantee himself *as a future.*

This is simply the long history of the origin of *responsibility*. That task of breeding an animal which can make promises, includes, as we have already grasped, as its condition and preliminary, the more immediate task of first *making* man to a certain extent, necessitated, uniform, like among his like, regular, and consequently calculable. The immense work of what I have called, "morality of custom" (cf. *Dawn of Day*, Aphs. 9, 14, and 16), the actual work of man on himself during the longest period of the human race, his whole prehistoric work, finds its meaning, its great justification (in spite of all its innate hardness, despotism, stupidity, and idiocy) in this fact: man, with the help of the morality of customs and of social strait-waistcoats, was *made* genuinely calculable. If, however, we place ourselves at the end of this colossal process, at the point where the tree finally matures its fruits, when society and its morality of custom finally bring to light that to which it was only the means, then do we find as the ripest fruit on its tree the *sovereign individual*, that resembles only himself, that has got loose from the morality of custom, the autonomous "supermoral" individual (for "autonomous" and "moral" are mutually exclusive terms),—in short, the man of the personal, long, and independent will, *competent* to *promise*,—and we find in him a proud consciousness (vibrating in every fibre), of *what* has been at last achieved and become vivified in him, a genuine consciousness of power and freedom, a feeling of human perfection in general. And this man who has grown to freedom, who is really *competent* to promise, this lord of the *free* will, this sovereign—how is it possible for him not to know how great is his superiority over everything incapable of binding itself by prom-

ises, or of being its own security, how great is the trust, the awe, the reverence that he awakes—he "deserves" all three—not to know that with this mastery over himself he is necessarily also given the mastery over circumstances, over nature, over all creatures with shorter wills, less reliable characters? The "free" man, the owner of a long unbreakable will, finds in this possession his *standard of value:* looking out from himself upon the others, he honours or he despises, and just as necessarily as he honours his peers, the strong and the reliable (those who can bind themselves by promises),—that is, every one who promises like a sovereign, with difficulty, rarely and slowly, who is sparing with his trusts but confers *honour* by the very fact of trusting, who gives his word as something that can be relied on, because he knows himself strong enough to keep it even in the teeth of disasters, even in the "teeth of fate,"—so with equal necessity will he have the heel of his foot ready for the lean and empty jackasses, who promise when they have no business to do so, and his rod of chastisement ready for the liar, who already breaks his word at the very minute when it is on his lips. The proud knowledge of the extraordinary privilege of *responsibility*, the consciousness of this rare freedom, of this power over himself and over fate, has sunk right down to his innermost depths, and has become an instinct, a dominating instinct—what name will he give to it, to this dominating instinct, if he needs to have a word for it? But there is no doubt about it—the sovereign man calls it his *conscience.*

His conscience?—One apprehends at once that the idea "conscience," which is here seen in its supreme manifestation, supreme in fact to almost the point of strangeness, should already have behind it a long history and evolution. The ability to guarantee one's self with all due pride, and also at the same time to *say yes* to one's self—that is, as has been said, a ripe fruit, but also a *late* fruit: —How long must needs this fruit hang sour and bitter on the tree! And for an even longer period there was not a glimpse of such a fruit to be had—no one had taken it on himself to promise it, although everything on the tree was quite ready for it, and everything was maturing for that very consummation. "How is a memory to be made for the man-animal? How is an impression to be so deeply fixed upon this ephemeral understanding, half dense, and half silly, upon this incarnate forgetfulness, that it will be permanently present?" As one may imagine, this primeval problem was not solved by exactly gentle answers and gentle means; perhaps there is nothing more awful and more sinister in the early history of man than his *system of mnemonics*. "Something is burnt in so as to remain in his memory: only that which never stops *hurting* remains in his memory." This is an axiom of the oldest (unfortunately also the longest) psychology in the world. It might even be said that wherever solemnity, seriousness, mystery, and gloomy colours are now found in the life of the men and of nations of the world, there is some *survival* of that horror which was once the universal concomitant of all promises, pledges, and obligations. The past, the past with all its length, depth, and hardness, wafts to us its breath, and bubbles up in us again, when we become "serious." When man thinks it necessary to make for himself a memory, he never accomplishes it without blood, tortures and sacrifice; the most dreadful sacrifices and forfeitures (among them the sacrifice of the first-born), the most loathsome mutilation (for instance, castration), the most cruel rituals of all the religious cults (for all religions are really at bottom systems of cruelty)—all these things originate from that instinct which found in pain its most potent mnemonic. In a certain sense the whole of asceticism is to be ascribed to this: certain ideas have got to be made inextinguishable, omnipresent, "fixed," with the object of hypnotising the whole nervous and intellectual system through these "fixed ideas"—and the ascetic methods and modes of life are the means of freeing those ideas from the competition of all other ideas so as to make them "unforgettable." The worse memory man had, the

ghastlier the signs presented by his customs; the severity of the penal laws affords in particular a gauge of the extent of man's difficulty in conquering forgetfulness, and in keeping a few primal postulates of social intercourse ever present to the minds of those who were the slaves of every momentary emotion and every momentary desire. We Germans do certainly not regard ourselves as an especially cruel and hardhearted nation, still less as an especially casual and happy-go-lucky one; but one has only to look at our old penal ordinances in order to realise what a lot of trouble it takes in the world to evolve a "nation of thinkers" (I mean: *the* European nation which exhibits at this very day the maximum of reliability, seriousness, bad taste, and positiveness, which has on the strength of these qualities a right to train every kind of European mandarin). These Germans employed terrible means to make for themselves a memory, to enable them to master their rooted plebeian instincts and the brutal crudity of those instincts: think of the old German punishments, for instance, stoning (as far back as the legend, the millstone falls on the head of the guilty man), breaking on the wheel (the most original invention and speciality of the German genius in the sphere of punishment), dart-throwing, tearing, or trampling by horses ("quartering"), boiling the criminal in oil or wine (still prevalent in the fourteenth and fifteenth centuries), the highly popular flaying ("slicing into strips"), cutting the flesh out of the breast; think also of the evil-doer being besmeared with honey, and then exposed to the flies in a blazing sun. It was by the help of such images and precedents that man eventually kept in his memory five or six "I will nots" with regard to which he had already given his *promise*, so as to be able to enjoy the advantages of society—and verily with the help of this kind of memory man eventually attained "reason"! Alas! reason, seriousness, mastery over the emotions, all these gloomy, dismal things which are called reflection, all these privileges and pageantries of humanity: how dear is the price that they have exacted! How much blood and cruelty is the foundation of all "good things"!

Bad Conscience

But how is it that that other melancholy object, the consciousness of sin, the whole "bad conscience," came into the world? And it is here that we turn back to our genealogists of morals. For the second time I say —or have I not said it yet?—that they are worth nothing. Just their own five-spans-long limited modern experience; no knowledge of the past, and no wish to know it; still less a historic instinct, a power of "second sight" (which is what is really required in this case) —and despite this to go in for the history of morals. It stands to reason that this must needs produce results which are removed from the truth by something more than a respectful distance.

Have these current genealogists of morals ever allowed themselves to have even the vaguest notion, for instance, that the cardinal moral idea of "ought" originates from the very material idea of "owe"? Or that punishment developed as a *retaliation* absolutely independently of any preliminary hypothesis of the freedom or determination of the will?—And this to such an extent, that a *high* degree of civilisation was always first necessary for the animal man to begin to make those much more primitive distinctions of "intentional," "negligent," "accidental," "responsible," and their contraries, and apply them in the assessing of punishment. That idea—"the wrong-doer deserves punishment *because* he might have acted otherwise," in spite of the fact that it is nowadays so cheap, obvious, natural, and inevitable, and that it has had to serve as an illustration of the way in which the sentiment of justice appeared on earth, is in point of fact an exceedingly late, and even refined form of human judgment and inference; the placing of this idea back at the beginning of the world is simply a clumsy violation of the principles of primitive psychology. Throughout the longest period of human history punishment was *never* based

on the responsibility of the evil-doer for his action, and was consequently *not* based on the hypothesis that only the guilty should be punished;—on the contrary, punishment was inflicted in those days for the same reason that parents punish their children even nowadays, out of anger at an injury that they have suffered, an anger which vents itself mechanically on the author of the injury— but this anger is kept in bounds and modified through the idea that every injury has somewhere or other its *equivalent* price, and can really be paid off, even though it be by means of pain to the author. Whence is it that this ancient deep-rooted and now perhaps ineradicable idea has drawn its strength, this idea of an equivalency between injury and pain? I have already revealed its origin, in the contractual relationship between *creditor* and *ower*, that is as old as the existence of legal rights at all, and in its turn points back to the primary forms of purchase, sale, barter, and trade.

The realisation of these contractual relations excites, of course (as would be already expected from our previous observations), a great deal of suspicion and opposition towards the primitive society which made or sanctioned them. In this society promises will be made; in this society the object is to provide the promiser with a memory; in this society, so may we suspect, there will be full scope for hardness, cruelty, and pain: the "ower," in order to induce credit in his promise of repayment, in order to give a guarantee of the earnestness and sanctity of his promise, in order to drill into his own conscience the duty, the solemn duty, of repayment, will, by virtue of a contract with his creditor to meet the contingency of his not paying, pledge something that he still posesses, something that he still has in his power, for instance, his life or his wife, or his freedom or his body (or under certain religious conditions even his salvation, his soul's welfare, even his peace in the grave; so in Egypt, where the corpse of the ower found even in the grave no rest from the creditor—of course, from the Egyptian standpoint, this peace was a matter of particular importance). But especially has the creditor the power of inflicting on the body of the ower all kinds of pain and torture—the power, for instance, of cutting off from it an amount that appeared proportionate to the greatness of the debt;—this point of view resulted in the universal prevalence at an early date of precise schemes of valuation, frequently horrible in the minuteness and meticulosity of their application, *legally sanctioned* schemes of valuation for individual limbs and parts of the body. I consider it as already a progress, as a proof of a freer, less petty, and more *Roman* conception of law, when the Roman Code of the Twelve Tables decreed that it was immaterial how much or how little the creditors in such a contingency cut off, *"si plus minusve secuerunt, ne fraude esto."* Let us make the logic of the whole of this equalisation process clear; it is strange enough. The equivalence consists in this: instead of an advantage directly compensatory of his injury (that is, instead of an equalisation in money, lands, or some kind of chattel), the creditor is granted by way of repayment and compensation a certain *sensation of satisfaction*—the satisfaction of being able to vent, without any trouble, his power on one who is powerless, the delight *"de faire le mal pour le plaisir de la faire,"* the joy in sheer violence: and this joy will be relished in proportion to the lowness and humbleness of the creditor in the social scale, and is quite apt to have the effect of the most delicious dainty, and even seem the foretaste of a higher social position.

Bibliography

Texts

The Complete Works of Friedrich Nietzsche. Translated under the general editorship of O Levy. 18 vols. New York: Macmillan, 1909–1913.

Studies

Copleston, F. C., S.J. *Friedrich Nietzsche, Philosopher of Culture.* London: Burns & Oates Ltd., 1942.

Knight, A. H. J. *Some Aspects of the Life and Work of Nietzsche, and Particularly of His Connection with Greek Literature and Thought.* London: Cambridge University Press, 1933.

16

Introduction

Berdyaev was born in the Ukrainian capital of Kiev and educated in Russia. He was named professor of philosophy at the University of Moscow in 1917. One of Berdyaev's few consistencies was rebellion. He was imprisoned twice under the old Russian regime and twice under the new, banished to the North by czarist Russia, tried and threatened with permanent exile in Siberia, and finally deported in 1922 by the Bolsheviks. He went to Berlin where he founded an academy of religious philosophy; he next moved to Paris, which he made his home. He died on March 23, 1948, at Clamart, near Paris. He has been called "the Philo of our age" because he attempted the union of East and West, heralding the coming age of ecumenical civilization and world unity. He was an anarchist. He was a mystic. He was a fan-tastic humanist-eschatologist, and if this be a contradiction, it is one among many. For him, as later for Merleau-Ponty, denial of life's essential ambiguity became a fugue. Two major themes give continuity to Berdyaev's mystical anarchy: *freedom* and *person*. The human person was the absolute and ultimate value for Berdyaev, and freedom was his god. He revolted with a kind of mystical abandon against any limitation, whether political, moral, religious, or otherwise, that threatened freedom. Despite all this he was one of the most modest of men, yet always an aristocrat. He was a philosopher in the old sense of the word, loving wisdom wherever he met it. His perhaps undisciplined use of mythical and religious sources has not helped his current philosophical stature. In the following selections on person, love, and sex, he brings a needed spirit to conservative, academic thought.

MAN AS A PERSON *

Our conception of man must be founded upon the conception of personality. True anthropology is bound to be personalistic. Consequently it is essential to understand the relation between personality and individuality. Individuality is a naturalistic and biological category, while personality is a religious and spiritual one. I want to build up a personalistic but certainly not an individualistic system of ethics. An individual is part of the species, it springs from the species although it can isolate itself and come into conflict with it. The individual is produced by the biological genetic process; it is born and it dies. But personality is not generated, it is created by God. It is God's idea, God's conception, which springs up in eternity. From the point of view of the individual, personality is a task to be achieved. Personality is an axiological category. We say of one man that he is a personality, and of another that he is not, although both are individuals. Sometimes a psychologically and biologically remarkable individual may be devoid of personality. Personality is a wholeness and unity possessing absolute and eternal worth. An individual may be lacking in such wholeness and unity, he may be disintegrated, and everything in him may be mortal. Personality is the image and likeness

* From Nicolas Berdyaev, *The Destiny of Man*, pp. 54–58. Reprinted by permission of Harper & Row, Publishers, Incorporated, New York, and Geoffrey Bles, Ltd., London. Harper Torchbook.

of God in man and this is why it rises above the natural life. Personality is not a part of something, a function of the genus or of society: it is a whole comparable to the whole of the world. It is not a product of the biological process or of social organization; it cannot be conceived in biological or psychological or sociological terms. Personality is spiritual and presupposes the existence of a spiritual world. The value of personality is the highest hierarchical value in the world, a value of the spiritual order.

It is essential to bear in mind that the value of personality presupposes the existence of superpersonal values and is indeed constituted by them. Personality is the creator and the bearer of superpersonal values and this is the only source of its wholeness, unity and eternal significance. But this must not be taken to mean that personality has no intrinsic value or is merely a means for superpersonal values. It is itself an absolute and exalted value, but it can only exist in virtue of superpersonal values. In other words, the existence of personality presupposes the existence of God; its value presupposes the supreme value—God. If there is no God as the source of superpersonal values, personality as a value does not exist either; there is merely the individual entity subordinate to the natural life of the genus. Personality is *the* moral principle, and our relation to all other values is determined by reference to it. Hence the idea of personality lies at the basis of ethics. An impersonal system of ethics is a *contradictio in adjecto*. Ethics is to a great extent the theory of personality. Moral life is centred in the person and not in generalities. Personality is a higher value than the state, the nation, mankind or nature, and indeed it does not form part of that series.

The value and unity of personality does not exist apart from the spiritual principle. The spirit forms personality, enlightens and transfigures the biological individual and makes him independent of the natural order. Personality is certainly not an abstract norm or idea suppressing and enslaving the concrete, individual living being. The idea or ideal value of personality is the concrete fullness of life. The spiritual principle which constitutes personality does not imply a bloodless and abstract spiritualism. Conflict between good and evil or between any values can only exist for a person. Tragedy is always connected with the personality—with its awakening and its struggles. A personality is created by the Divine idea and human freedom. The life of personality is not self-preservation as that of the individual but self development and self-determination. The very existence of personality presupposes sacrifice, and sacrifice cannot be impersonal. Psychological individualism so characteristic of the nineteenth and twentieth centuries is the very reverse of personalism. Complete disintegration of personality, i.e. of the wholeness and unity of the self, is exemplified in the work of Proust. The self is broken up into elements, sensations and thoughts, the image and likeness of God disappear and everything is enveloped, as it were, in mental cobwebs. The refinement of a soul which ceases to be the bearer of superpersonal values, of the divine principle, leads to dissociation and disintegration. The refined soul needs a stern spirit to give it eternal worth and to hold it together in wholeness and unity.

M. Scheler has worked out an interesting theory of personality. His aim was to build up a purely personalistic system of ethics. Philosophical anthropology which must be the basis of ethics is very little developed, and M. Scheler is one of the few philosophers who have done something towards it. According to M. Scheler, man is a being who transcends himself and the whole of life.[1] We have already seen that Scheler regards man as undefinable biologically. The fundamental opposition is for him not that between man and animal, but between personality and organism, spirit and life. The dualism between spirit and life is essential to Scheler's view. He criticises with great subtlety the conception of autonomy in Kant,

[1] Scheler's view of personality is developed in the best of his works, *Der Formalismus in der Ethik und die materiele Werthethik.*

Fichte and Hegel and rightly says that it means the autonomy of impersonal spirit and not of personality. German idealism is unfavourable to the idea of personality and is not concerned with it.[2] Scheler tries to defend the personalistic view both of man and of God by distinguishing between personality and the self. The self presupposes something outside it, a not-self. But personality is absolute and does not presuppose anything outside itself. Personality is not a part of the world but is correlative to it.

There is no doubt that personality is a whole and not a part; it is a microcosm. Scheler wants to base his ethics on the value of personality, highest in the hierarchy of values. He means the value not of personality in the abstract but of the concrete individual person, unique and unreplaceable. This is an advance upon the normative legalistic ethics such as Kant's. But Scheler is wrong in saying that personality is self-contained. He maintains this in order to defend the faith in God as a Person, but he is mistaken. Personality from its very nature presupposes another—not the "not-self" which is a negative limit, but another person. Personality is impossible without love and sacrifice, without passing over to the other, to the friend, to the loved one. A self-contained personality becomes disintegrated. Personality is not the absolute, and God as the Absolute is not a Person. God as a Person presupposes His other, another Person, and is love and sacrifice. The Person of the Father presupposes the Persons of the Son and of the Holy Spirit. The Holy Trinity is a Trinity of Persons just because they presuppose one another and imply mutual love and intercommunion.

On another plane the personality of God and of man presuppose each other. Personality exists in the relation of love and sacrifice. It is impossible to conceive of a personal God in an abstract monotheistic way. A person cannot exist as a self-contained

and self-sufficient Absolute. Personalistic metaphysics and ethics are based upon the Christian doctrine of the Holy Trinity. The moral life of every individual person must be interpreted after the image of the Divine Tri-unity, reversed and reflected in the world. A person presupposes the existence of other persons and communion between them. Personality is the highest hierarchical value and never is merely a means. But it does not exist as a value apart from its relation to God, to other persons and to human society. Personality must come out of itself, must transcend itself—this is the task set to it by God. Narrow self-centredness ruins personality.

The individual is correlative to the genus, the person is correlative to society. A person presupposes other persons and their intercommunion; an individual presupposes the existence of the genus. He is nurtured by the genus and is as mortal as the genus. Personality, however, does not share the destiny of the genus but is immortal. The complexity of man lies in the fact that he is both an individual, a part of the genus, and a person, a spiritual being. The individual in his biological self-assertion and self-centredness may sever himself from the life of the genus, but this alone never leads to the affirmation of personality, its growth and expansion. Hence Christian ethics is personalistic, but not individualistic. The narrow isolation of personality in modern individualism is the destruction and not the triumph of personality. Hardened selfhood—the result of original sin—is not personality. It is only when the hardened selfhood melts away and is transcended that personality manifests itself.

The struggle that takes place within the genus is for the self-assertion of the individual and not of personality. The individual's struggle for existence and power within the genus has nothing to do with the value of personality. The struggle for personality and its value is spiritual and not biological. In that struggle man inevitably comes into conflict with society, for metaphysically he is a social being. . . .

---

[2] G. Gurvitch in his interesting book, *Fichtes System der konkreten Ethik*, tries to interpret Fichte in the spirit of personalism.

LOVE AND SEX *

The solution lies in love, in erotic and friendly love; for love is intimately related to the personality and is the means by which the Ego emerges from its self-sufficiency in quest of another Ego as opposed to another impersonal or collective Self. But the Ego is only an embryonic personality; to become one in reality, it must commune with the Thou and the We. It is this communion of personalities longing to be reflected in one another which confirms the personality. The Ego's reserve is an expression of its solitude and isolation. It is its way of protecting itself from the social and objective world. The Ego's essential need is communion with the Thou, but it is in constant danger of being confronted with the object. As a result, it adopts a defensive attitude to shield its consciousness from the brutal contact with things. Thus, although its enforced solitude is a phase in the personality's development towards self-consciousness, it is a phase that must be transcended. But objectification, the building up of an impersonal world, is not a means of achieving this end. We shall therefore have to consider more particularly the problem of the personality. . . .

A real communion, a real triumph over solitude, can only occur when the Ego identifies itself with the Thou, as in the case of love and friendship. The same is equally true of knowledge. The Ego's contact with an object or society is not sufficient to banish solitude; it must commune with the Thou and the We. Because knowledge is invariably concerned with the *general*, the abstract and the universal, it tends to overlook the individual, the singular and the personal. But when the union of the Ego with the Thou is also a communion, its universal results acquire a greater validity precisely because they are based upon the individual, the singular and the personal. The true affirmation of individuality is to be found in

what is universal and concrete rather than in what is general and abstract. Solitude can, indeed, be overcome when the universal and the general dominate the particular and the singular, but only at the cost of the total suppression of the Ego and, consequently, of the Thou. But in terms of Existential philosophy, knowledge is primarily concerned with the Ego and the Thou; it is essentially personalist. In fact, it is important not to submerge solitude in impersonal generality, but to transcend it by the agency of the personality. By emancipating itself from the yoke of society, of a logical and social community, knowledge could make its thought supra-logical.

To triumph over solitude is to *transcend* the Ego in the sphere of intellectual or emotional life. But the Ego has two different ways of transcending itself: by identifying itself with an object or a general principle and by entering into communion with the Thou. There is certainly a positive value in the act by which the Ego emerges into the objective world in the process of instituting society or of elaborating the general principles and concepts indispensable to communication, but the world of this transcendence is a degraded, disrupted and circumscribed world. The light of the *Logos* is reflected even in the general principle inherent in objective knowledge, but this reflection is a mere glimmer in an otherwise opaque world in which the human Ego is but a slave. Thus the problem of knowledge is rich in contradictions and antinomies, as is shown in its contingent problems of communion, of time and of the personality. Objective processes succeed in achieving a merely superficial reconciliation of these contradictions; in reality, the progress of objective knowledge only helps to multiply them. The idea of God is the only solution capable of effectively resolving these often intolerable contradictions. God, according to the masterly definition of Nicolas of Cusa, is precisely the *coincidentia oppositorum*.

---

* From Nicolas Berdyaev, *Solitude and Society*. Geoffrey Bles, Ltd., London, 1938. Reprinted by permission of Geoffrey Bles, Ltd., London.

The nature of knowledge is conjugal; it supposes a duality; it cannot be the exclusive product either of the object or of the peculiar agency of the subject. For this reason, solitude can be overcome only by a cognitive act based upon true love; for there can be no real union with the general, but only with another Ego, with the Thou. The conjugal essence of knowledge is theandric; it has both a human and a divine aspect. The effect of objective processes is to eliminate both these elements, and to substitute in their place impersonal and general principles. The inherent difficulty of knowledge consists in transcending this impersonal and general state, so as to achieve the conjugal union of personalities. But it may happen that the Ego, in its pursuit of knowledge, fails to triumph over solitude, and is obliged to seek union in other ways. The knowledge I have in mind comprehends not merely the academic learning of savants and philosophers, but also the experience of everyday communal life, which is especially open to the tyranny of general principles and of social imitation.

Sex is one of the chief causes of human solitude. Man is a sexual being, that is, half a being,[1] divided and incomplete, aspiring to be complete. Sex brings about a profound division of the Ego, which is by nature bisexual, both male and female, androgynous. Thus man's endeavour to overcome solitude through communion is primarily an endeavour to overcome the isolation caused by sex, to achieve reunion in sexual integrity. Its very existence implies separation, want, longing, and the desire to identify oneself with another. But the physical union of the sexes, which puts an end to sexual desire, is not in itself sufficient to banish solitude. Indeed, it may only intensify man's sense of solitude. Another result of sexual union may also help to precipitate the Ego into the objective world, because sex is a natural phenomenon situated in the objective world. Marriage and the family are its social conse-

[1] The original Russian word for *sex* means both *sex* and *half.*

quences. As a biological and social phenomenon, sexuality is objective, and therefore incapable of completely allaying solitude. The biological union of the sexes and the institution of the family may, indeed, to a certain degree allay and diminish the sense of solitude, but they are unable permanently to vanquish it. . . .

Love and friendship are man's only hope of triumphing over solitude. Love is, indeed, the best way of achieving this end, for it brings the Ego in contact with the Other Self, with another Ego in which it is truly reflected. This is the communion of one personality with another. An impersonal love, which is not concentrated on any individual image, does not deserve to be called love. Rozanov spoke of this kind of love as "glass love." It is very likely a perverted form of Christian love. Friendship, too, has a personalist and erotic foundation. The personality and love are intimately related, for *love transforms the Ego into a personality.* Only love can effect that complete fusion with another being which transcends solitude. The pursuit of knowledge cannot achieve this unless it be inspired by love. The disintegrating and demoniac aspect of sexual life may also manifest itself in love; for the materialization of human existence in the objective world tends to make love a tragic and moral experience. The objective world, that of biology and of society, cannot suffer the idea of authentic love and its disdain for both natural and social laws. This love is only concerned with the extra-natural order wherein solitude is eliminated. And that accounts for its intimate relationship with death.

We are once more confronted with duality. Sexual communication may take place within the framework of society and of social institutions, but it is powerless to achieve true communion or to vanquish solitude. The sexes may also unite in an extra-social community of love, and thus really overcome solitude. In the social and objective world, however, sexual union is the prelude to a tragic destiny, to a mysterious alliance with death. Dualism is insurmountable within the limits of the natural world. It comprehends, however, the principle of transcendence without which there can be no achievement of the authentic life or escape from the limitations of a circumscribed world. Transcendence is the very essence of love. Man is impelled towards it by his poignant sense of solitude in an ice-bound world of objects and by his need of communion with the Other Self. But such is the metaphysical mystery inherent in sexuality that even the very height of passion, a love as overwhelming as that of Tristan and Iseult, fails to banish completely the sense of sexual solitude and longing. A demoniac element of hostility persists between the lovers. Thus the ultimate triumph over solitude may be regarded as the realization of the image of a perfect androgyne. But this in its turn implies the transfiguration of nature. It is therefore true to say that the problem of solitude is most acutely felt in the sphere of sexuality.

Communism eliminates this problem by identifying the Ego with the social collective, and by substituting a collective consciousness for the personal one. The Ego's existence is definitely objectified in the process of social construction. Hence the importance which communism assigns to eugenics, to the mechanism and technical aspects of sex, in short, to the negation of personal love. Such a system of farmyard breeding is intended to stifle sexual longing and its inherent sense of solitude. The *erotic* aspect of human life is sacrificed to the economic and technical aspects. The same tendency is apparent in the German racial doctrine, which attempts to solve objectively an essentially extra-social and existential problem. But there is nothing novel in this: the same negation of personal love and the same conception of sexual life are to be found in the teachings of certain doctors of the Church. Sexual life has two fundamental aspects: firstly, it forms a part of the Ego's inner existence, as well as of that of the human destiny and of the human personality; but it remains in constant tragic conflict with the hostile objective world of society

and of the family. Secondly, it is based on a racial urge which impels it to assume objective and social forms. That is also true of the Will to power which, though intimately related to man's innermost destiny, has the effect of plunging him into the social and objective world. The rule of power or of might only extends to the objective world and is incapable of triumphing over solitude. Thus the destiny of a Caesar or a Napoleon is perforce a tragic one.

Religion implies a relationship: it may be defined as an attempt to overcome solitude, to release the Ego from its seclusion, to achieve community and intimacy. Its very essence associates it with the mystery of Being, with Being itself. But only God is capable of overcoming solitude: religion only implies a relationship, and, as such, can only be secondary and transitory. Transcendence and plenitude, as well as the purpose of existence, are only manifest in God. There is a tendency to overlook the fact that God is the primary consideration, that religion can prove an obstacle to man's communication with God.[2] Man's relations to God as historically manifest in religion, are not free from a certain element of objectification. When religion becomes a mere social and objective manifestation, the sense of solitude fails to be ontologically transcended; if that sense is diminished, it is due to the Ego's immersion in the objective world and society, even though that world be called the Church. Transcendence can only take place if the relationship between the Ego and the divine world is rooted in the inner life, in the Church-community as opposed to the Church-society. It follows that our affirmation of an inherent duality, of any opposition between the Spirit and nature, between freedom and necessity, between existence, or primary life, and objectivity, holds equally true of religion as well as of knowledge and sexual life. . . .

[2] Karl Barth notes this very clearly, and that is the positive aspect of his theology. He is more convincing in his *Römerbrief* than in his dogmatic philosophy.

MAN AS A SEXED BEING *

The problem of sex is of fundamental importance to anthropology. Man is a sexual being, and sexual polarity is characteristic of human nature. Sex is not a function of the human organism but a quality of it as a whole and of every cell which composes it. Rozanov always maintained this, and Freud has shown it to be true. Man is not only a sexual but a bisexual being, combining the masculine and the feminine principle in himself in different proportions and often in fierce conflict. A man in whom the feminine principle was completely absent would be an abstract being, completely severed from the cosmic element. A woman in whom the masculine principle was completely absent would not be a personality. The masculine principle is essentially personal and anthropological. The feminine principle is essentially communal and cosmic. It is only the union of these two principles that constitutes a complete human being. Their union is realized in every man and every woman within their bisexual, androgynous nature, and it also takes place through the intercommunion between two natures, the masculine and the feminine. In the fallen world a cosmic struggle is going on between the masculine and the feminine principles: the two not only seek union but also wage a war against each other like deadly enemies. This is due to the polarity of human nature. . . .

The strong feeling of the central position of the problem of sex is characteristic of our epoch, as well as a deep desire to comprehend the elements of sex. It is as though sex had suddenly come into notice, something

* From Nicolas Berdyaev, *The Destiny of Man*, pp. 61–62. Reprinted by permission of Harper & Row, Publishers, Incorporated, New York. Geoffrey Bles, Ltd., London. Harper Torchbook. And from Nicolas Berdyaev, *The Meaning of the Creative Act*, pp. 180–183. Copyright 1955 by Harper & Row, Publishers, Incorporated, New York. Reprinted by permission of Harper & Row, Publishers, Incorporated, New York, and YMCA Press, Paris.

secret had become known. Man's concept and feeling for the world depends on sex. Sex is the source of being; the polarity of sex is the foundation of creation. The sense of being, its intensity and its colouring, has its roots in sex. With ever increasing acuity men begin to recognize, scientifically, philosophically and religiously, that sexuality is not a special, differentiated function of the human being, that is diffused throughout his whole being, penetrates all his cells and determines the whole of his life. To-day we cannot separate sex from the whole of life: we cannot assign to it only the importance of a special function of the organism. Sex is vastly broader and deeper than that which we are accustomed to call the sexual function in a specific sense. The specific sex function is itself the result of the differentiation of some sort of general, pre-sexual life. We cannot draw a sharp line scientifically between the normal and natural in sex and the abnormal and unnatural. This boundary line has been drawn not by the natural order of things but by general social morality, in which there is always very much of the conditional. From the philosophical viewpoint, we should do away with the category of "naturalness" as a criterion of good and evil. The "normal" and "natural" sexual function is the product of the differentiation of sex-life, outflowing through the whole physical and spiritual being of man. It is quite possible to say that man is a sexual being, but we cannot say that man is a food-digesting being. Man's sexual nature cannot be placed on the same level with other functions of his organism, even the most essential; such as the circulation of the blood. In man's sexuality we perceive the metaphysical roots of his being. Sex is the meeting-point of two worlds in the human organism. In this point of sex is hidden the secret of being. We cannot escape from sex. We may leave aside the differentiated function of sex, we may deny or conquer this "natural" function. But in this case man's sexual function is only transferred—and man still remains a sexual being. . . .

It would be a fatal error to identify sex with the sexual act, as is often done. A denial of the sexual act is not denial of sex. And a too-ardent refusal of the sexual act is an ardent evidence of sex in man. Weakness or lack of interest in the sexual act is no proof of the weakness of sex in a man, for the sex-energy flowing out through man's whole being may have many expressions and take many directions. When it is said that a man has conquered sex in himself by the power of spiritual creativeness, this formula is only the surface of the phenomenon. In such a case sex has not been overcome, but sex energy has merely been given another direction—it is directed towards creativity.

In general the importance of the sexual act for sex-life as a whole must not be exaggerated. Sex-life is possible, even much more intense, without the sexual act. The sexual act, the sexual function, is conquerable, but sex is unconquerable. Asceticism can only transpose sexual energy, give it another direction, but it cannot conquer sex. Sex is related not to some part, but to the whole man. Sex is not merely one of many sides of man—it includes and determines the whole. Whatever way man turns, he is followed everywhere by sex-energy, and this leaves its stamp on all his activities. In everything we find the cross-section of sex. In knowledge itself there is an element of masculine activity and feminine passivity. Sex is related to the very secret of man's being and hence it has remained the element most shrouded in mystery. In all ages men have felt the uncanny relationship of sex with birth and death and hence it could never be considered by men as a special function (an important function but still less important than eating, for instance). . . . Sex is a cosmic force and may be comprehended only in the cosmic aspect.

From the fact that a person is identified either as a man or as a woman, it is clear that sex is an element diffused through all man's being and not a differentiated function. If sex is an infirmity, then it is an organic infirmity, not a functional infirmity of man's whole organism, physical and metaphysical. Sex is not only the point of contact of two worlds in man, but also the point of contact between man and the cosmos, microcosmos and macrocosmos. Man is joined with the cosmos first of all by sex. In sex we have the source of man's true connection with the cosmos and of his servile dependence. The categories of sex, male and female, are cosmic categories not merely anthropological categories. . . . In the realm of sex, people with racial consciousness, both religious men and positivists, are concentrated on the sexual act itself and on its consequences, and fail completely to see the universal significance of sex, as well for the whole man as for the whole cosmos. The secret of sex is not at all the sexual act, performed either for virtuous child-begetting or for perverted enjoyment. First of all, we cannot believe that the sexual act was ever indulged in, anywhere or by anyone in the world, solely for the virtuous purpose of begetting children. . . .

The mystery of sex is revealed only in love. But there is no sphere of life where there reigns such inert conservatism and such conditional hypocrisy as in that of sexual love. The most extreme revolutionaries are very often conservative when the question of love arises. The revolutionary consciousness is encountered most rarely in the sphere of sex and love, although here it should be the most radical, I would even say the most religious. The socially minded and learned radicals and revolutionaries think only of the social and physiological ordering of sex—they never go any deeper. Love is wiped off the worldly account-books and turned over to the poets and the mystics. When these "Christians" or positivists speak of sex, do they recall the love of Tristan and Isolde, of Romeo and Juliet, the love which was sung by the Provençal troubadours or by Dante? Neither their theology nor their science, neither their morals nor their sociology, see in love a world-problem. We can say how Christian theology and ethics, scientific biology and sociology react to the sexual act, but how they consider love is unknown. The old racially-conceived theology and science cannot even know love.

Bibliography

Texts

Solitude and Society. London: Geoffrey Bles, Ltd., 1938.

Slavery and Freedom. London: Geoffrey Bles, Ltd., 1944.

Freedom and the Spirit. London: Geoffrey Bles, Ltd., 1935.

Christian Existentialism: A Berdyaev Anthology. Selected and translated by Donald A. Lowrie. London: George Allen & Unwin, Ltd., 1965.

The Destiny of Man. New York: Harper & Row, Publishers, Incorporated, 1959.

Dream and Reality. London: Geoffrey Bles, Ltd., 1950.

Meaning of the Creative Act. New York: Harper & Row, Publishers, Incorporated, 1955.

Studies

Clark, O. F. *Introduction to Berdyaev*. London: Geoffrey Bles, Ltd., 1950.

Lowrie, D. A. *Rebellious Prophet: A Life of Nicolai Berdyaev*. New York: Harper & Row, Publishers, Incorporated, 1960.

Vallon, M. A. *An Apostle of Freedom: Life and Teachings of Nicolas Berdyaev*. New York: Philosophical Library, Inc., 1960.

17

MAX SCHELER
1874–1928

Introduction

Max Scheler was born in Munich in 1874. He studied under Rudolph Eucken and the Neo-Kantian Otto Liebmann. He first lectured as a *Privatdozent* in Jena. He afterwards lectured at the University of Munich and in 1919, in Cologne. In 1928 he went to his next post in Frankfurt, where he died before being able to resume teaching.

Scheler cannot be evaluated simply as a follower of Husserl because he did not meet Husserl until after he had completed his formal education and had begun teaching in Jena. Scheler was one of the four original coeditors of Husserl's yearbook for philosophy and phenomenological research along with Adolph Reinach, Alexander Pfänder, and Moritz Geiger.

Scheler has been called the most brilliant German thinker of his day. He was a man of passion, a Faustian man. He was an intuitive genius, considered by many Husserl's equal or at least second to none but him. Not until Heidegger's emergence in the mid-twenties did any single person so dazzle the German philosophical scene; no other individual did so much to spread phenomenology beyond Germany, especially into Spain and France.

Baptized a Catholic as a boy, Scheler drifted away from Catholicism; subsequently, he formally rejoined the Catholic Church and remained a Catholic for six years, only to leave the church once more in 1922. His philosophy of religion, influenced by his great love for St. Augustine, earned him the name "the Catholic Nietzsche."

The basic criticism of Scheler's work today is that it is a wealth of brilliant insights inadequately grounded and developed. On one occasion Husserl called Scheler's phenomenology "fool's gold."

Scheler's main concern is ethics; the heart of his ethics is *value*, and the supreme value is *person*. Metaphysics and ethics are based on a philosophical anthropology: What is man? To answer this question he turned to phenomenology, not so much as a system or step-by-step method, but as an attitude and spirit of experiencing which would help in an intuitive penetration of the given and of the world of relationships between persons and values.

Scheler developed an ethics around *value* rather than *oughtness*, a theory that his most important associate at Munich, Dietrich von Hildebrand, developed as the concept of adequate value *response*. Scheler distinguishes a hierarchy of values, from vital values to pleasure values to spiritual values to religious values. His phenomenology of feeling, which distinguishes mere moods from feelings of value to which he ascribes genuine cognitive content, is a new contribution to psychology.

The soul of Scheler's philosophy is his *personalism*. For Scheler, *community* is the *primordial* given; the *self* and the *other* are given only after a process of differentiation within this original community. Scheler's concept of community and his unique view of love as a creative transformation of the lover (rather than the one loved) through his orientation toward the ever greater potential of enhancing value in the loved one, is shown in part in the following selections.

COMMUNITY *

It is impossible to form any judgment about concrete questions of community without

* From Max Scheler, *On the Eternal in Man*, pp. 373–377. Copyright by Harper & Row, Publishers, Incorporated, New York.

touching on the fundamental questions, What is the *nature* of community? To what ends do its essential forms exist?

The first underlying proposition from which we must proceed is this: man, the finite personal spirit (and only *as* such), does not live a communal life with other finite personal spirits from pure accident and only *de facto* (for, say, historical reasons or prompted by his positive knowledge of nature). No; it is inherent in the *eternal, ideal nature* of an intelligent person that all its existence and activity as a spirit is *ab origine* just as much an outward-conscious, co-responsible, communal reality as a self-conscious, self-responsible, individual reality. The being of a man is just as originally a matter of being, living and acting "together" as a matter of existing for himself. Notice that this statement is divided not by a hair-splitting nuance but by an immeasurable chasm from this other one: "All men of which we have knowledge through personal experience or historical documents lived or live in a community." The first expresses an eternal and essential truth which is definitive *per se* and implies an essential necessity. The second expresses a contingent experience which like all such may be severely limited or more comprehensive but can never be complete and definitive. All that is established from contingent experience can also be undone by fresh contingent experience. Even the logical subjects of the two propositions are quite different in substance and scope. The first is true of *all possible finite spiritual beings,* even those outside our earthly ken (*e.g.* the angelic host) or hidden from us now (*e.g.* the souls of the dead). In so far as they exist—and we believe they exist—they live in community. But one may go further: the first proposition is true and the second, in its strict sense, is wholly untrue. It is simply not true at all that every man known in history lived in community with other men. There have been Robinson Crusoes—recluses, hermits, solitaries, anchorites of all kinds. But it is the Robinson Crusoe who can help us to clarify the implications of *our* proposition. It implies that the conscious experience of *"belonging"* to a community, of being a "member" of it, was present even in him, present just as originally as his individual "I"-feeling or self-awareness. It implies that awareness

of membership is a characteristic even of persons living in such isolation, and that the *mental intention* in the direction of community exists quite independently of whether it finds or does not find fulfillment in the subject's contingent sensory experience of other men (via sight and other forms of apprehension)—and, further, irrespective of the number or kind of "other" men. Even a hypothetical spiritual-corporeal being who had never been conscious of his fellows via the senses would ascertain his membership of a community, his "belonging," precisely on account of a positive awareness that a whole class of intentions in his *essential* nature was craving and *not finding fulfilment*—all types of loving (love of God, of one's neighbour, etc.), promising, thanking, entreaty, obedience, serving, ruling and so on. Hence this imaginary being would not say, "I am alone—alone in infinite space and infinite time; I am alone in the world, I belong to no community," but he would tell himself: "I do not know the *actual* community to which I know that I belong—I must look for it—but I *know* that I do belong to one." This, not the (nevertheless) half-true platitude that men normally live in nations, States, etc., is what the great proposition of the Stagirite means: ἄνθρωπος ζῷον πολιτικόν. Man, *i.e.* the vehicle of the rational psychic power, is a *communal* creature. *Where there is an "I" there is a "we,"* or "I" *belong* to a "we."

But we may also say: Just as man *knows* himself to be from the beginning a member of a universal community, a community with a measureless realm of rational spirits like himself, so, as a rational spiritual being, he is *objectively* and originally oriented toward that community and realm. He is spiritually thus determined no less originally than in his physical aspect. Community, of course, is implicit in the creature of flesh and blood by reason of his very origin in the mother's womb, if not by virtue of dependence on her love and care, with its corresponding instincts of complementary mother-child love; this is not to mention his endowment with organs which direct him to the other sex and with gregarious instincts corresponding to this arrangement. Nevertheless, the spiritual rational community is no mere development from the natural biological community. One should not think that man loses his essential sociability as he lives more in the spirit. Thinkers like Darwin and Spencer make a great mistake when they suppose that *all* human community "evolved" or can be derived from the natural biological community to be found, as "animal societies," even in subhumanity, and when in consequence they explain all non-sensual love, sacrifice, sense of obligation, conscience and repentance as mere refinements and developments of the psychic powers holding the animal herd together.

The spiritual and personal community of man exists in its own right and has its own origin. In both right and origin it is superior to the biological community. Its origin is as divinely spiritual as its right is divinely sanctioned.

The great importance of this becomes apparent as soon as we add a *second* proposition to our first. Because we have an awareness, as original as the self-awareness with which it is inextricably associated, of our organic membership in a universal community of spiritual beings, one which we cannot disregard, we have at the centre of our souls an urgent need and limitless pressure of spirit to *transcend* in thought, and aspire beyond in loving desire, not only our solitary, naked self but every one of the historically actual and sensually visible communities to which we belong; this implies in effect, when rationally determined, an urge to regard *every* actual community in its turn as the "organ" of a still broader, more comprehensive and higher community of spirits. There is nothing clearer or surer to our hearts and minds than this: *not one* of these earthly communities (family, municipality, State, nation, circle of friends, etc.), would ever quite suffice to satisfy the demands of our reason and hearts, no matter what degree of perfection it might attain in history. But since all communities of this kind are communities not only of spirits but also of *per-*

sons, this (in principle) boundless urge and the demand of reason for ever richer, more universal and higher community find only in *one* idea their possible conclusion and perfect satisfaction—the idea of communion of love and spirit with an infinite spiritual person who at the same time is the origin, founder and sovereign Lord of all possible spiritual communities as of all actual communities on earth. Just as certain kinds of love are implanted in the *nature* of our spiritual existence—kinds differentiated from the outset, before casual experience of their correlative objects, as emotional acts which demand fulfilment (love, for example, of children, parents, home, country)—so there is also a *supreme* kind of love, love of *God*, which we already feel and possess before we have a clear intellectual conception of the supreme being. That is why Pascal can say to God, "I would not seek thee, if thou hadst not already found me." We are equally clear in heart and mind that their intentions can be entirely fulfilled and satisfied only by this supreme and final union of love and reason in God, and that we are unable to envisage correctly the communities in which we know ourselves involved, unable to see them in a *true* light, until we are conscious of them against the *divine background* of this supreme and final community of all spiritual beings—until we see their shape against the illumination which only community with the personal God projects. In that community alone do peace and rest attend the endless questing of heart and mind beyond all finite visible communities: *Inquietum cor nostrum* (said Augustine) *donec requiescat in te*. It is in and through *God* that for the first time we are truly *bound in spirit* to one another. This is exactly the meaning of the "first" and "greatest" commandment (Mark 12.30-31), which merges self-sanctification and love of one's neighbour in their common root, the love of God. There are various kinds of natural evidence of God's existence. Every theme and thread of Creation, when we follow it, leads us back to God; we have only to imagine it protracted into infinity according to the law of being which governs the finite section known to us. All threads meet simultaneously in him. But here I should like to draw your attention to the existence of another independent and original evidence of the supreme being, which arises *solely* from the idea of a community of personal, spiritual beings. This "sociological proof" of God, though it coincides with the goal of all the others, does not depend on them for logical support. Today it is perhaps unduly neglected.

Thus, if the natural light of the mind tells us that *all* community (on earth as in heaven) is directly or indirectly founded in God, that in him all true community has directly or (through intermediary creative causes) indirectly its origin, highest lawgiver, judge, lord and governor, the same light also tells us this: each individual is not responsible solely for his own character and conduct, responsible through his conscience before his Lord and creator, but each individual (likewise every comparatively restricted community) is also responsible to God—as originally as for self—for everything of moral bearing in the character and proceedings of the larger corporate selves of which he is an integral part. That is the *third* principle in the doctrine of community. For if community is more than a historically fortuitous, earthly co-operation of intelligent bodies, resting on artificial and arbitrary man-made contracts, if it necessarily proceeds from the *project* and divine, constructive intention of *one intelligent heart and mind*, if in the range of its ideal conception it embraces the suprasensual *ab origine*, including its very Lord and creator, the centre of all things—and if this central divinity is all that vouches for the sanctity of contracts, the possibility of truly binding reciprocal promises—then *from the outset* each one of us must be responsible for all, not only for himself (though he is that too!). Each and every one of us, then, is co-responsible for the collective guilt and collective merit which accrue to his community as a unit and integer, not as an "aggregate" of the individuals called its "members."

From that you may see how perverted is the doctrine (introduced by Epicurus, later a basis for all "liberal" theories of society up to Kant) which attempts to base the nature and existence of human community on human *contracts*, whether by imputing an origin in actual treaties or by contending that the legitimacy of every society must be decided by regarding it "as if" it rested on contracts. For every contract presupposes a common standard incumbent upon both contracting parties, and this standard can only derive from a third party *"in whose eyes"* the contract is binding or not binding; again, the legitimate assumption of a promise on the part of a promise-receiver presupposes the co-responsibility of this receiver for the legitimacy of the promise which he is to assume.

This third great principle of ethics and religion is the principle of religious moral reciprocity or *moral solidarity*. It does not mean something which is universally obvious —that wherever, or only where, we have consciously assumed a definite obligation, or know for sure, positively, that we were conscious participants and "co-efficients" in an action, we have a share of the ensuing responsibility. Neither does it mean simply that when we are confronted by the guilt of others we would do better to think of our own guilt than to pass judgment on theirs. No; what it means is that we should feel ourselves truly co-responsible in *all* guilt. It means therefore that from the very beginning—even where the magnitude or extent of our actual participation are not clearly in view before our mind's eye—we must answer to the living God for *all* rise and fall in the moral and religious condition of the *collective whole* of the moral world, which is an intrinsically solidary unit.[1] Whatever precise or imprecise knowledge we may possess concerning our share of moral causation, its nature, extent, etc., merely shows to our inner self, which already knows itself origi-

[1] Whether we are in a leading or serving position in the community in question is a matter which determines only the degree (not the fact) of our responsibility.

nally co-responsible, the direction and degree in which we may also *judge* ourselves co-responsible. But it is not this knowledge alone which *creates* this co-responsibility as a *quality* of our persons. Even if we were able to place it in the endlessly intricate context of all the moral and religious action, reaction and interaction of men and souls, this knowledge could never set before our mental eye the full extent of what our conduct has indirectly added to us or subtracted from us in the way of collective merit and collective guilt. There is no moral gesture so trivial that does not radiate, like the splashing stone, an infinity of ripples—circles soon lost to the naked eye. But if a physicist can pursue the tremor beyond this natural barrier—how much farther can God the omniscient pursue the moral repercussion! *If* no impediments intervene, A's love of B not only awakens B's reciprocal love of A but stirs a natural growth of *general,* life-warming love in B's responding heart; hence B's love of C and D; and so the flood rolls on within the moral universe, from C and D to E and F *ad infinitum.* But the same is true of hatred, injustice, unchastity and all kinds of sin. Each one of us has been a partner in an immensity of actions good and bad, things of which he has—and *can* have—no inkling, but for which he nevertheless stands co-responsible before God. . . .

LOVE AND PERSONALITY *

There are types of value which are essentially related to personality as their vehicle, and which can only attach to a person; "virtues," for example, are values of this type. But in addition to this there is the value of the person as such, i.e. as that which essentially possesses these virtues. *Love for the value of persons,* i.e. for the person as a reality mediated in personal value, is *moral love* in the full sense of the term. I have given a detailed analysis of the concept of personality in another work.[1] Here I only wish to emphasize that the love which has moral value is not that which pays loving regard to a person for having such and such qualities, pursuing such and such activities, or for possessing talents, beauty or virtue; it is that love which incorporates these qualities, activities and gifts into its object, because they belong to that *individual person.* And it is therefore the only love that is "absolute," since it is unaffected by the possibility that these qualities and activities may change.[2]

Wherever we encounter the individual we meet with an *ultimate* which cannot be manufactured in any way out of features, qualities, activities, etc. Conversely, in that very mode of discernment which alone discloses the individual, it is always the features, qualities and activities which retain a merely abstract and general character, so long as we do not know the individual to whom they belong. It is characteristic, however, of individual personality that we only become acquainted with it *in* and *through* the act of loving, and that its value as an individual is likewise only disclosed in the course of this act. Being an "object" of love represents, as it were, the only objective status wherein personality has existence and can therefore be manifested. Hence the utterly misguided "rationalism" of seeking to account for one's love for an individual person in any such terms as those relating to his qualities, acts, achievements or disposi-

* From Max Scheler, *The Nature of Sympathy.* Routledge & Kegan Paul, Ltd., London, 1954. Reprinted by permission of Routledge & Kegan Paul, Ltd., London.
[1] Cf. the chapters "Zur theoretischen Auffassung der Person überhaupt" and "Die Person in ethischen Zusammenhängen" in **Der Formalismus in der Ethik.**

[2] The point was brought out clearly long ago by Aristotle, in the profound chapter on Friendship in his Nichomachean Ethics.

tions. Indeed the very attempt to do so has the effect of bringing the phenomenon of individual personal love sharply home to us. For we always find out in the process, that we can imagine every single one of these details to be altered or absent, without being a whit the more able, on that account, to leave off loving the person concerned. We also realize that if we consider these qualities and activities separately, and add up our liking for each of them, their total value for us is nothing like enough to justify our love of the person. There is always a surplus we cannot account for (The same thing also applies in hatred, of course.) Moreover, the curious inconstancy of the reasons we are accustomed to offer ourselves in justification of our love for somebody, is a further indication that all such reasons are merely trumped-up after the event, and that none of them provides the real explanation.

How else then, is personality disclosed to us in love? Let us begin by getting this much clear: love is the most personal of attitudes, but a thoroughly *objective* one none the less, in the sense that in it we are "objective" insofar as we free ourselves (in an unaccustomed fashion), from bondage to our own interests, wishes and ideas; but for all this the element of the personal in man can *never be disclosed to us as an "object."* Persons cannot be objectified, in love or any other genuine act, not even in cognition. Personality is that unity of substance, baffling observation and eluding analysis, which the individual experiences as inherent in all the acts he performs; no "object" therefore, let alone a "thing." That part of others which does present itself objectively to me is never more than (1) the physical body; (2) its corporeal unity; (3) the self and the (vital) "soul" belonging to it. And the same applies to everyone in respect of himself. The person of another can only be disclosed to me by my *joining in the performance* of his acts, either cognitively, by "understanding" and vicarious "re-living," or morally, by "following in his footsteps." The moral core of the personality of Jesus, for example, is revealed to one man only: His disciple. This is the only path which can lead to such a disclosure. It may be vouchsafed to a disciple who knows nothing of an "historical" kind about Jesus, nothing of His outward life, or even of His historical existence; for even to be *aware* of oneself *as* a disciple, which naturally implies an awareness of one's master as having an historical existence, is already a different thing from *being* a disciple. The theologian, on the other hand, for all his knowledge of Jesus' career (including His inner life), is forever precluded by his office from any such insight; it necessarily transcends his field of view. A thing which is continually forgotten by the learned theological intellectualism of our day!

The values attaching to the physical, the corporeal and the mental can all be given us objectively, and may even be so given in the process of loving those who possess them. But this does not apply to purely personal values, i.e. the value of the personality itself. So long as we continue to "objectify" someone in any way, his personality eludes our grasp, and only its trappings remain. Admittedly, we can still have love in an objective sense for the non-moral values of a personality itself, as an intellect for example, or an artistic force, for these we can grasp by reliving them in ourselves. But we can never grasp the purely moral value of a person in this way, for it is carried, in principle, only by his act of love. Hence this ultimate moral value of a personality is only disclosed to us when we associate ourselves with its own act of love. In order to elicit this moral value in our original, we must love what he loves, and love it *with* him. There is but one other case in which we may receive an "objective" impression, not of the person as such, but of the self, and receive it by other means than those of discerning it immediately by way of expressive phenomena. Wherever the person loved is felt by us to be far more exalted than we are, it is noticeable how we seize hold of his personal existence by associating ourselves in his own acts of self-love and then scrutinizing the content given in these concomitant acts.

It is this type of loving participation, namely in the love with which God loves Himself, which Brentano has recently claimed, in his book on Aristotle, to be already discernible in the Metaphysics; and which some of the mystics and schoolmen refer to as "*amare Deum in Deo.*" But we are also familiar with the corresponding state of affairs at the human level. It can happen, under certain circumstances, that we love a man more than he loves himself. Thus many people who hate themselves, are in fact loved, though any conjoint participation in their acts of self-hatred ought to mean "hating them." Yet these are cases in which a man's self-hatred may dissolve at the implied reproach of one who loves him and whom he loves in return: viz. "that he ought not to hate a thing so, when the other, who loves him, is so very fond of it." But so long as a man has love for himself, rather than hatred, the act of "joining in" with such self-love is certainly *one* of the forms which other people's love for him may assume.

Bibliography

Texts

An English translation of Scheler's most important work, *Der Formalismus in der Ethik und die materiale Wertethik* (French translation: *Le formalisme en éthique et l'éthique matérielle des valeurs.* Translated by Maurice de Gandillac. Paris: Gallimard, 1955) is being prepared by Manfred Frings.

The Nature of Sympathy. London: Routledge & Kegan Paul, Ltd., 1954.

Philosophical Perspectives. Boston: Beacon Press, 1958.

On the Eternal in Man. New York: Harper & Row, Publishers, Incorporated, 1960.

Ressentiment. New York: Free Press of Glencoe, 1961.

Man's Place in Nature. New York: Noonday Books, Farrar, Straus & Giroux, Inc., 1961.

Studies

Frings, M. *Max Scheler: A Concise Introduction into the World of a Great Thinker.* Pittsburgh: Duquesne University Press, 1965.

Ranly, E. W. *Scheler's Phenomenology of Community.* The Hague: Martinus Nijhoff, 1966.

Buber, M. "The Philosophical Anthropology of Max Scheler." *Philosophy and Phenomenological Research,* vol. 6 (1946), pp. 307–321; see also Buber's *Between Man and Man.* London: Fontana, 1963, chap. 5, sec. 2.

Schutz, A. "Scheler's Theory of Intersubjectivity and the General Thesis of the Alter Ego." *Philosophy and Phenomenological Research,* vol. 2 (1942), pp. 323–347; also in A. Schutz, *Collected Papers.* The Hague: Martinus Nijhoff, 1962, vol. I, pp. 150–179.

———. "Max Scheler's Epistemology and Ethics." *Review of Metaphysics,* vol. 9 (1957), pp. 304–314, 486–501.

Becker, H., and **H. O. Dahlke.** "Max Scheler's Sociology of Knowledge." *Philosophy and Phenomenological Research,* vol. 2 (1942), pp. 310–322.

Spiegelberg, H. *The Phenomenological Movement.* The Hague: Martinus Nijhoff, vol. I (1965), pp. 228–270.

Philosophy Today (Scheler Number), vol. 12 (1968).

18

MARTIN BUBER
1878–1965

Introduction

Martin Buber was born in Vienna and spent his youth in Lemberg in Galicia at the home of his grandfather, the Hebrew scholar Salomon Buber, from whom he absorbed the religious wisdom of Hassidism. The intense mystical faith and piety of his Jewish world encountered the world of European modern enlightenment when he returned to Austria in 1898 to study philosophy, the Kantian and Neo-Kantian philosophy of the day. He studied also at the universities of Berlin, Leipzig, and Zurich, with such teachers as Wilhelm Dilthey, Georg Simmel, Sigmund Freud, Ernst Mach, Wilhelm Wundt, and Carl Stumpf, Husserl's most important predecessor after Franz Brentano. He acquired a deep and rich background in philosophy, art, literature, psychology, and sociology. He was influenced very early by existentialist thought, not only in Kierkegaard and Nietzsche but apparently also in Husserl's phenomenology with its emphasis on time and on the personal standpoint in observing human experience. He was twenty years old when he joined the Zionist movement; he saw it as a cultural movement and was for a time a leader of a group of young artists and writers in Prague and Vienna; he was the editor of two Zionist journals, *Welt* and *Der Jude*. Buber's conception of a cultural Zionism conflicted with legalistic, moralistic, and political Zionism, and he turned to more scholarly goals after breaking with the group.

In 1923 he became professor of the philosophy of religion at the University of Frankfurt; this was also the year that his most famous work, *I and Thou*, was published. Between 1928 and 1938 he wrote the studies *Between Man and Man*, which can be considered the sequel to *I and Thou*, although there are good reasons for reading it first. There is no question that Buber's work ranks among the most significant and creative in our day. He has been unique in reaching the ordinary reader, so much so that a major slick magazine found him very much "in" and created for him the rather original classification of "hip religion." At the same time his impact on the scholarly world. of theology, philosophy, education, sociology, and psychiatry has been immeasurable.

Buber's central theme is *person*, the value of persons as distinguished from things, a doctrine he learned from the great Judaic tradition and also from Kant and his teachers. But in Buber the dynamics of *dialogue*, of the different kinds of *presence* that a person has to another person, received memorable expression. His understanding of person is a theory of *relation*, of the realm of the between, i.e., of what happens between men in interpersonal encounter. The kind of relation is indicated by the word a person uses, *Thou* or *It*, so that you and I emerge as persons only in the I-Thou relation.

PERSON AS ACTUATED THROUGH RELATION *

To man the world is twofold, in accordance with his twofold attitude.

The attitude of man is twofold, in accord-ance with the twofold nature of the primary words which he speaks.

The primary words are not isolated words, but combined words.

The one primary word is the combination *I–Thou*.

The other primary word is the combination

* From Martin Buber, *I and Thou*. Charles Scribner's Sons, New York. Reprinted with the permission of Charles Scribner's Sons, New York.

I–It; wherein, without a change in the primary word, one of the words *He* and *She* can replace *It*.

Hence the *I* of man is also twofold.

For the *I* of the primary word *I–Thou* is a different *I* from that of the primary word *I–It*.

Primary words do not signify things, but they intimate relations.

Primary words do not describe something that might exist independently of them, but being spoken they bring about existence.

Primary words are spoken from the being.

If *Thou* is said, the *I* of the combination *I–Thou* is said along with it.

If *It* is said, the *I* of the combination *I–It* is said along with it.

The primary word *I–Thou* can only be spoken with the whole being.

The primary word *I–It* can never be spoken with the whole being.

There is no *I* taken in itself, but only the *I* of the primary word *I–Thou* and the *I* of the primary word *I–It*.

When a man says *I* he refers to one or other of these. The *I* to which he refers is present when he says *I*. Further, when he says *Thou* or *It*, the *I* of one of the two primary words is present.

The existence of *I* and the speaking of *I* are one and the same thing.

When a primary word is spoken the speaker enters the word and takes his stand in it.

The life of human beings is not passed in the sphere of transitive verbs alone. It does not exist in virtue of activities alone which have some *thing* for their object.

I perceive something. I am sensible of something. I imagine something. I will something. I feel something. I think something. The life of human beings does not consist of all this and the like alone.

This and the like together establish the realm of *It*.

But the realm of *Thou* has a different basis.

When *Thou* is spoken, the speaker has no thing for his object. For where there is a thing there is another thing. Every *It* is bounded by others; *It* exists only through being bounded by others. But when *Thou* is spoken, there is no thing. *Thou* has no bounds.

When *Thou* is spoken, the speaker has no *thing;* he has indeed nothing. But he takes his stand in relation.

It is said that man experiences his world. What does that mean?

Man travels over the surface of things and experiences them. He extracts knowledge about their constitution from them: he wins an experience from them. He experiences what belongs to the things.

But the world is not presented to man by experiences alone. These present him only with a world composed of *It* and *He* and *She* and *It* again.

I experience something.—If we add "inner" to "outer" experiences, nothing in the situation is changed. We are merely following the uneternal division that springs from the lust of the human race to whittle away the secret of death. Inner things or outer things, what are they but things and things!

I experience something.—If we add "secret" to "open" experiences, nothing in the situation is changed. How self-confident is that wisdom which perceives a closed compartment in things, reserved for the initiate and manipulated only with the key. O secrecy without a secret! O accumulation of information! It, always It!

The man who experiences has not part in the world. For it is "in him" and not between him and the world that the experience arises.

The world has no part in the experience. It permits itself to be experienced, but has no concern in the matter. For it does nothing to the experience, and the experience does nothing to it.

As experience, the world belongs to the primary word *I–It*.

The primary word *I–Thou* establishes the world of relation.

The spheres in which the world of relation arises are three.

First, our life with nature. There the relation sways in gloom, beneath the level of speech. Creatures live and move over against us, but cannot come to us, and when we address them as *Thou*, our words cling to the threshold of speech.

Second, our life with men. There the relation is open and in the form of speech. We can give and accept the *Thou*.

Third, our life with spiritual beings. There the relation is clouded, yet it discloses itself; it does not use speech, yet begets it. We perceive no *Thou*, but none the less we feel we are addressed and we answer—forming, thinking, acting. We speak the primary word with our being, though we cannot utter *Thou* with our lips.

But with what right do we draw what lies outside speech into relation with the world of the primary word?

In every sphere in its own way, through each process of becoming that is present to us we look out toward the fringe of the eternal *Thou;* in each we are aware of a breath from the eternal *Thou;* in each *Thou* we address the eternal *Thou*. . . .

If I face a human being as my *Thou*, and say the primary word *I–Thou* to him, he is not a thing among things, and does not consist of things.

Thus human being is not *He* or *She*, bounded from every other *He* and *She*, a specific point in space and time within the net of the world; nor is he a nature able to be experienced and described, a loose bundle of named qualities. But with no neighbour, and whole in himself, he is *Thou* and fills the heavens. This does not mean that nothing exists except himself. But all else lives in *his* light.

Just as the melody is not made up of notes nor the verse of words nor the statue of lines, but they must be tugged and dragged till their unity has been scattered into these many pieces, so with the man to whom I say *Thou*. I can take out from him the colour of his hair, or of his speech, or of his goodness. I must continually do this. But each time I do it he ceases to be *Thou*.

And just as prayer is not in time but time in prayer, sacrifice not in space but space in sacrifice, and to reverse the relation is to abolish the reality, so with the man to whom I say *Thou*. I do not meet with him at some time and place or other. I can set him in a particular time and place; I must continually do it: but I set only a *He* or a *She*, that is an *It*, no longer my *Thou*.

So long as the heaven of *Thou* is spread out over me the winds of causality cower at my heels, and the whirlpool of fate stays its course.

I do not experience the man to whom I say *Thou*. But I take my stand in relation to him, in the sanctity of the primary word. Only when I step out of it do I experience him once more. In the act of experience *Thou* is far away.

Even if the man to whom I say *Thou* is not aware of it in the midst of his experience, yet relation may exist. For *Thou* is more than *It* realises. No deception penetrates here; here is the cradle of the Real Life. . . .

—What, then, do we experience of *Thou*?
—Just nothing. For we do not experience it.
—What, then, do we know of *Thou*?
—Just everything. For we know nothing isolated about it any more.

The *Thou* meets me through grace—it is not found by seeking. But my speaking of the primary word to it is an act of my being, is indeed *the* act of my being.

The *Thou* meets me. But I step into direct relation with it. Hence the relation means being chosen and choosing, suffering and action in one; just as any action of the whole being, which means the suspension of all partial actions and consequently of all sensations of actions grounded only in their particular limitation, is bound to resemble suffering.

The primary word *I–Thou* can be spoken only with the whole being. Concentration and fusion into the whole being can never take place through my agency, nor can it ever take place without me. I become through my relation to the *Thou*; as I become *I*, I say *Thou*.

All real living is meeting.

The relation to the *Thou* is direct. No system of ideas, no foreknowledge, and no fancy intervene between *I* and *Thou*. The memory itself is transformed, as it plunges out of its isolation into the unity of the whole. No aim, no lust, and no anticipation intervene between *I* and *Thou*. Desire itself is transformed as it plunges out of its dream into the appearance. Every means is an obstacle. Only when every means has collapsed does the meeting come about.

In face of the directness of the relation everything indirect becomes irrelevant. It is also irrelevant if my *Thou* is already the *It* for other *I's* ("an object of general experience"), or can become so through the very accomplishment of this act of my being. For the real, though certainly swaying and swinging, boundary runs neither between experience and non-experience, nor between what is given and what is not given, nor yet between the world of being and the world of value; but cutting indifferently across all these provinces it lies between *Thou* and *It*, between the present and the object.

The present, and by that is meant not the point which indicates from time to time in our thought merely the conclusion of "finished" time, the mere appearance of a termination which is fixed and held, but the real, filled present, exists only in so far as actual presentness, meeting, and relation exist. The present arises only in virtue of the fact that the *Thou* becomes present.

The *I* of the primary word *I–It*, that is, the *I* faced by no *Thou*, but surrounded by a multitude of "contents," has no present, only the past. Put in another way, in so far as man rests satisfied with the things that he experiences and uses, he lives in the past, and his moment has no present content. He

has nothing but objects. But objects subsist in time that has been.

The present is not fugitive and transient, but continually present and enduring. The object is not duration, but cessation, suspension, a breaking off and cutting clear and hardening, absence of relation and of present being.

True beings are lived in the present, the life of objects is in the past.

Appeal to a "world of ideas" as a third factor above this opposition will not do away with its essential twofold nature. For I speak of nothing else but the real man, of you and of me, of our life and of our world—not of an *I*, or a state of being, in itself alone. The real boundary for the actual man cuts right across the world of ideas as well.

To be sure, many a man who is satisfied with the experience and use of the world of things has raised over or about himself a structure of ideas, in which he finds refuge and repose from the oncome of nothingness. On the threshold he lays aside his inauspicious everyday dress, wraps himself in pure linen, and regales himself with the spectacle of primal being, or of necessary being; but his life has no part in it. To proclaim his ways may even fill him with well-being.

But the mankind of mere *It* that is imagined, postulated, and propagated by such a man has nothing in common with a living mankind where *Thou* may truly be spoken. The noblest fiction is a fetish, the loftiest fictitious sentiment is depraved. Ideas are no more enthroned above our heads than resident in them; they wander amongst us and accost us. The man who leaves the primary word unspoken is to be pitied; but the man who addresses instead these ideas with an abstraction or a password, as if it were their name, is contemptible.

In one of the three examples it is obvious that the direct relation includes an effect on what confronts me. In art the act of the being determines the situation in which the form becomes the work. Through the meeting that which confronts me is fulfilled, and enters the world of things, there to be endlessly active, endlessly to become *It*, but also endlessly to become *Thou* again, inspiring and blessing. It is "embodied"; its body emerges from the flow of the spaceless, timeless present on the shore of existence.

The significance of the effect is not so obvious in the relation with the *Thou* spoken to men. The act of the being which provides directness in this case is usually understood wrongly as being one of feeling. Feelings accompany the metaphysical and metapsychical fact of love, but they do not constitute it. The accompanying feelings can be of greatly differing kinds. The feeling of Jesus for the demoniac differs from his feeling for the beloved disciple; but the love is the one love. Feelings are "entertained": love comes to pass. Feelings dwell in man; but man dwells in his love. That is no metaphor, but the actual truth. Love does not cling to the *I* in such a way as to have the *Thou* only for its "content," its object; but love is *between I* and *Thou*. The man who does not know this, with his very being know this, does not know love; even though he ascribes to it the feelings he lives through, experiences, enjoys, and expresses. Love ranges in its effect through the whole world. In the eyes of him who takes his stand in love, and gazes out of it, men are cut free from their entanglement in bustling activity. Good people and evil, wise and foolish, beautiful and ugly, become successively real to him; that is, set free they step forth in their singleness, and confront him as *Thou*. In a wonderful way, from time to time, exclusiveness arises—and so he can be effective, helping, healing, educating, raising up, saving. Love is responsibility of an *I* for a *Thou*. In this lies the likeness—impossible in any feeling whatsoever—of all who love, from the smallest to the greatest and from the blessedly protected man, whose life is rounded in that of a loved being, to him who is all his life nailed to the cross of the world, and who ventures to bring himself to the dreadful point—to love *all men*.

Let the significance of the effect in the third example, that of the creature and our contemplation of it, remain sunk in mystery. Believe in the simple magic of life, in service in the universe, and the meaning of that waiting, that alertness, that "craning of the neck" in creatures will dawn upon you. Every word would falsify; but look! round about you beings live their life, and to whatever point you turn you come upon being. . . .

Spirit in its human manifestation is a response of man to his *Thou*. Man speaks with many tongues, tongues of language, of art, of action; but the spirit is one, the response to the *Thou* which appears and addresses him out of the mystery. Spirit is the word. And just as talk in a language may well first take the form of words in the brain of the man, and then sound in his throat, and yet both are merely refractions of the true event, for in actuality speech does not abide in man, but man takes his stand in speech and talks from there; so with every word and every spirit. Spirit is not in the *I*, but between *I* and *Thou*. It is not like the blood that circulates in you, but like the air in which you breathe. Man lives in the spirit, if he is able to respond to his *Thou*. He is able to, if he enters into relation with his whole being. Only in virtue of his power to enter into relation is he able to live in the spirit. . . .

The fundamental difference between the two primary words comes to light in the spiritual history of primitive man. Already in the original relational event he speaks the primary word *I–Thou* in a natural way that precedes what may be termed visualisation of forms —that is, before he has recognised himself as *I*. The primary word *I–It*, on the other hand, is made possible at all only by means of this recognition—by means, that is, of the separation of the *I*.

The first primary word can be resolved, certainly, into *I* and *Thou*, but it did not arise from their being set together; by its nature it precedes *I*. The second word arose from the setting together of *I* and *It*: by nature it comes after *I*. . . .

Only brief glimpses into the context in time of the two primary words are given us by primitive man, whose life, even if it could be made fully accessible, can represent only as it were allegorically that of the real early man. We receive fuller knowledge from the child.

Here it becomes crystal clear to us that the spiritual reality of the primary words arises out of a natural reality, that of the primary word *I–Thou* out of natural combination, and that of the primary word *I–It* out of natural separation.

The ante-natal life of the child is one of purely natural combination, bodily interaction and flowing from the one to the other. Its life's horizon, as it comes into being, seems in a unique way to be, and yet again not to be, traced in that of the life that bears it. For it does not rest only in the womb of the human mother. Yet this connexion has such a cosmic quality that the mythical saying of the Jews, "in the mother's body man knows the universe, in birth he forgets it," reads like the imperfect decipherment of an inscription from earliest times. And it remains indeed in man as a secret image of desire. Not as though his yearning meant a longing to return, as those suppose who see in the spirit—confusing it with their intellect—a parasite of nature, when it is rather (though exposed to diverse illnesses) nature's best flower. But the yearning is for the cosmic connexion, with its true *Thou*, of this life that has burst forth into spirit.

Every child that is coming into being rests, like all life that is coming into being, in the womb of the great mother, the undivided primal world that precedes form. From her, too, we are separated, and enter into personal life, slipping free only in the dark hours to be close to her again; night by night this happens to the healthy man. But this separation does not occur suddenly and catastrophically like the separation from the bodily mother; time is granted to the child to exchange a spiritual connexion, that is, *relation*, for the natural connexion with the world that he gradually loses. He has stepped out of the glowing darkness of chaos into the cool light of creation. But he does not possess it yet; he must first draw it truly out, he must make it into a reality for himself, he must find for himself his own world by seeing and hearing and touching and shaping it. Creation reveals, in meeting, its essential nature as form. It does not spill itself into expectant senses, but rises up to meet the grasping senses. That which will eventually play as an accustomed object around the man who is fully developed, must be wooed and won by the developing man in strenuous action. For no *thing* is a ready-made part of an experience; only in the strength, acting and being acted upon, of what is over against men, is anything made accessible. Like primitive man the child lives between sleep and sleep (a great part of his waking hours is also sleep) in the flash and counter-flash of meeting.

The primal nature of the effort to establish relation is already to be seen in the earliest and most confined stage. Before anything isolated can be perceived, timid glances move out into indistinct space, towards something indefinite; and in times when there seems to be no desire for nourishment, hands sketch delicately and dimly in the empty air, apparently aimlessly seeking and reaching out to meet something indefinite. You may, if you wish, call this an animal action, but it is not thereby comprehended. For these very glances will after protracted attempts settle on the red carpet-pattern and not be moved till the soul of the red has opened itself to them; and this very movement of the hands will win from a woolly Teddy-bear its precise form, apparent to the senses, and become lovingly and unforgettably aware of a complete body. Neither of these acts is experience of an object, but is the correspondence of the child—to be sure only "fanciful"—with what is alive and effective over against him. (This "fancy" does not in the least involve, however, a "giving of life to the universe": it is the instinct to make everything into *Thou*, to give relation to the universe, the instinct which completes out of its own richness the living effective action when a mere copy or symbol of it is given in what is over against him.) Little, disjointed, meaningless sounds still go out persistently into the void. But one day, unforeseen, they will have become conversation—does it matter that it is perhaps with the simmering kettle? It is conversation. Many a movement termed reflex is a firm trowel in the building up of the person in the world. It is simply not the case that the child first perceives an object, then, as it were, puts himself in relation with it. But the effort to establish relation comes first —the hand of the child arched out so that what is over against him may nestle under it; second is the actual relation, a saying of *Thou* without words, in the state preceding the word-form; the thing, like the *I*, is produced late, arising after the original experiences have been split asunder and the connected partners separated. In the beginning is relation—as category of being, readiness, grasping form, mould for the soul; it is the *a priori* of relation, *the inborn Thou*.

The inborn *Thou* is realised in the lived relations with that which meets it. The fact that this *Thou* can be known as what is over against the child, can be taken up in exclusiveness, and finally can be addressed with the primary word, is based on the *a priori* of relation.

In the instinct to make contact (first by touch and then by visual "touch" of another being) the inborn *Thou* is very soon brought to its full powers, so that the instinct ever more clearly turns out to mean mutual relation, "tenderness." But the instinct to "creation," which is established later (that is, the instinct to set up things in a synthetic, or, if that is impossible, in an analytic way— through pulling to pieces or tearing up), is also determined by this inborn *Thou*, so that a "personification" of what is made, and a "conversation," take place. The development of the soul in the child is inextricably bound up with that of the longing for the *Thou*, with the satisfaction and the disappointment of this longing, with the game of his experiments and the tragic seriousness of his perplexity. Genuine understanding of this phenomenon, which is injured by every attempt

to lead it back into more confined spheres, can only be promoted if, during its observation and discussion, its cosmic and metacosmic origin is kept in mind. For it reaches out from the undivided primal world which precedes form, out of which the bodily individual who is born into the world, but not yet the personal, actualised being, has fully emerged. For only gradually, by entering into relations, is the latter to develop out of this primal world.

Through the *Thou* a man becomes *I*. That which confronts him comes and disappears, relational events condense, then are scattered, and in the change consciousness of the unchanging partner, of the *I*, grows clear, and each time stronger. To be sure, it is still seen caught in the web of the relation with the *Thou*, as the increasingly distinguishable feature of that which reaches out to and yet is not the *Thou*. But it continually breaks through with more power, till a time comes when it bursts its bonds, and the *I* confronts itself for a moment, separated as though it were a *Thou*; as quickly to take possession of itself and from then on to enter into relations in consciousness of itself.

Only now can the other primary word be assembled. Hitherto the *Thou* of relation was continually fading away, but it did not thereby become an *It* for some *I*, an object of perception and experience without real connexion—as it will henceforth become. It became rather an *It*, so to speak, for itself, an *It* disregarded at first, yet waiting to rise up in a new relational event. Further, the body maturing into a person was hitherto distinguished, as bearer of its perceptions and executor of its impulses, from the world round about. But this distinction was simply a juxtaposition brought about by its seeing its way in the situation, and not an absolute severance of *I* and its object. But now the separated *I* emerges, transformed. Shrunk from substance and fulness to a functional point, to a subject which experiences and uses, *I* approaches and takes possession of all *It* existing "in and for itself," and forms in conjunction with it the other primary word. The man who has become conscious of *I*, that is, the man who says *I–It*, stands before things, but not over against them in the flow of mutual action. Now with the magnifying glass of peering observation he bends over particulars and objectifies them, or with the field glass of remote inspection he objectifies them and arranges them as scenery, he isolates them in observation without any feeling of their exclusiveness, or he knits them into a scheme of observation without any feeling of universality. The feeling of exclusiveness he would be able to find only in relation, the feeling of universality only through it. Now for the first time he experiences things as sums of qualities. From each relational experience qualities belonging to the remembered *Thou* had certainly remained sunk in his memory; but now for the first time things are for him actually composed of their qualities. From the simple memory of the relation the man, dreaming or fashioning or thinking, according to his nature, enlarges the nucleus, the substance that showed itself in the *Thou* with power and gathered up in itself all qualities. But now also for the first time he sets things in space and time, in causal connexion, each with its own place and appointed course, its measurability and conditioned nature.

The *Thou* appears, to be sure, in space, but in the exclusive situation of what is over against it, where everything else can be only the background out of which it emerges, not its boundary and measured limit. It appears, too, in time, but in that of the event which is fulfilled in itself: it is not lived as part of a continuous and organised sequence, but is lived in a "duration" whose purely intensive dimension is definable only in terms of itself. It appears, lastly, simultaneously as acting and as being acted upon—not, however, linked to a chain of causes, but, in its relation of mutual action with the *I*, as the beginning and the end of the event. This is part of the basic truth of the human world, that only *It* can be arranged in order. Only when things, from being our *Thou*, become our *It*,

can they be co-ordinated. The *Thou* knows no system of co-ordination.

But now that we have come so far, it is necessary to set down the other part of the basic truth, without which this would be a useless fragment—namely, a world that is ordered is not the world-order. There are moments of silent depth in which you look on the world-order fully present. Then in its very flight the note will be heard; but the ordered world is its indistinguishable score These moments are immortal, and most transitory of all; no content may be secured from them, but their power invades creation and the knowledge of man, beams of their power stream into the ordered world and dissolve it again and again. This happens in the history both of the individual and of the race.

To man the world is twofold, in accordance with his twofold attitude.

He perceives what exists round about him —simply things, and beings as things; and what happens round about him—simply events, and actions as events; things consisting of qualities, events of moments; things entered in the graph of place, events in that of time; things and events bounded by other things and events, measured by them, comparable with them: he perceives an ordered and detached world. It is to some extent a reliable world, having density and duration. Its organisation can be surveyed and brought out again and again; gone over with closed eyes, and verified with open eyes. It is always there, next to your skin, if you look on it that way, cowering in your soul, if you prefer it so. It is your object, remains it as long as you wish, and remains a total stranger, within you and without. You perceive it, take it to yourself as the "truth," and it lets itself be taken; but it does not give itself to you. Only concerning it may you make yourself "understood" with others; it is ready, though attached to everyone in a different way, to be an object common to you all. But you cannot meet others in it. You cannot hold on to life without it, its reliability sustains you; but should you die in it, your grave would be in nothingness.

Or on the other hand, man meets what exists and becomes as what is over against him, always simply a *single* being and each thing simply as being. What exists is opened to him in happenings, and what happens affects him as what is. Nothing is present for him except this one being, but it implicates the whole world. Measure and comparison have disappeared; it lies with yourself how much of the immeasurable becomes reality for you. These meetings are not organised to make the world, but each is a sign of the world-order. They are not linked up with one another, but each assures you of your solidarity with the world. The world which appears to you in this way is unreliable, for it takes on a continually new appearance; you cannot hold it to its word. It has no density, for everything in it penetrates everything else; no duration, for it comes even when it is not summoned, and vanishes even when it is tightly held. It cannot be surveyed, and if you wish to make it capable of survey you lose it. It comes, and comes to bring *you* out; if it does not reach you, meet you, then it vanishes; but it comes back in another form. It is not outside you, it stirs in the depth of you; if you say "Soul of my soul" you have not said too much. But guard against wishing to remove it into your soul—for then you annihilate it. It is your present; only while you have it do you have the present. You can make it into an object for yourself, to experience and to use; you must continually do this—and as you do it you have no more present. Between you and it there is mutual giving: you say *Thou* to it and give yourself to it, it says *Thou* to you and gives itself to you. You cannot make yourself understood with others concerning it, you are alone with it. But it teaches you to meet others, and to hold your ground when you meet them. Through the graciousness of its comings and the solemn sadness of its goings it leads you away to the *Thou* in which the parallel lines of relations meet. It does not help to sustain you in life, it only helps you to glimpse eternity.

The world of *It* is set in the context of space and time.

The world of *Thou* is not set in the context of either of these.

The particular *Thou*, after the relational event has run its course, *is bound* to become an *It*.

The particular *It*, by entering the relational event, *may* become a *Thou*.

These are the two basic privileges of the world of *It*. They move man to look on the world of *It* as the world in which he has to live, and in which it is comfortable to live, as the world, indeed, which offers him all manner of incitements and excitements, activity and knowledge. In this chronicle of solid benefits the moments of the *Thou* appear as strange lyric and dramatic episodes, seductive and magical, but tearing us away to dangerous extremes, loosening the well-tried context, leaving more questions than satisfaction behind them, shattering security—in short, uncanny moments we can well dispense with. For since we are bound to leave them and go back into the "world," why not remain in it? Why not call to order what is over against us, and send it packing into the realm of objects? Why, if we find ourselves on occasion with no choice but to say *Thou* to father, wife, or comrade, not say *Thou* and mean *It*? To utter the sound *Thou* with the vocal organs is by no means the same as saying the uncanny primary word; more, it is harmless to whisper with the soul an amorous *Thou*, so long as nothing else in a serious way is meant but *experience* and *make use of*.

It is not possible to live in the bare present. Life would be quite consumed if precautions were not taken to subdue the present speedily and thoroughly. But it is possible to live in the bare past, indeed only in it may be a life be organised. We only need to fill each moment with experiencing and using, and it ceases to burn.

And in all the seriousness of truth, hear this: without *It* man cannot live. But he who lives with *It* alone is not a man.

Bibliography

Texts

I and Thou. New York: Charles Scribner's Sons, 1958.

Between Man and Man. London: Fontana, 1963.

Paths in Utopia. Boston: Beacon Press, 1958.

The Knowledge of Man. New York: Harper & Row, Publishers, Incorporated, 1965.

Daniel. New York: Holt, Rinehart and Winston, Inc., 1964.

Pfuetze, P. *Self, Society, Existence*. New York: Harper & Row, Publishers, Incorporated, 1961.

Smith, R. G. *The Thought of Martin Buber*. Shorne, Kent: Ridgeway House, 1947.

Smith, R. G. *Martin Buber*. Richmond: John Knox Press, 1967.

Wood, R. E. *Martin Buber's Ontology*. Evanston, Ill.: Northwestern University Press, 1969.

Marcel, G. "Martin Buber's Philosophical Anthropology," in *Searchings*. Westminster, Md.: The Newman Press, 1967, pp. 73–92.

Beek, M. A. and J. Weiland. *Martin Buber: Personalist and Prophet*. Westminster, Md.: The Newman Press, 1968.

Streiker, L. D. *The Promise of Buber*. Philadelphia: J. B. Lippincott Company, 1969.

19

Introduction

Teilhard de Chardin was born on May Day in the castle of Sarcenot in Auvergne, grew up on an ancient vineyard estate near Clermont-Ferrand, studied at the Jesuit *collège* at Villefranche-sur-Saône, and at eighteen, after passing his baccalaureate, entered the Jesuit novitiate at Aix-en-Provence on March 20, 1899. After classical studies at Laval and philosophy in Jersey, he taught physics and chemistry in Cairo. Next came theological studies in Sussex. All during these fifteen years, Teilhard had been deepening his competence in geology, anthropology, and paleontology. He served as a stretcher-bearer in World War I and was decorated with the Médaille Militaire for heroism and the Cross of the Légion d'honneur. After the war he returned to the Sorbonne in Paris and completed his doctoral studies under Marcellin Boule in 1922. He continued teaching at the Catholic University of Paris, while also lecturing at other schools in Paris with great success, until 1923, when he went to China on a paleontology mission.

On his return to Paris he found that some of his ideas on *"transformisme"* in primate evolution were under criticism, and he was advised to restrict his energies more specifically to paleontology. Thus he began, at the age of forty-two, a new period of intense and productive research. He returned to China in 1926, was appointed adviser to the National Geological Survey of China in 1929, became a member of the Citroen-Haardt Expedition across Chinese Turkestan and Mongolia in 1931 and 1932, and participated in and directed expeditions in 1934 to Szechwan, and in 1935 and 1936, to India and Burma. He also did field work in Somaliland, Ethiopia, and Java and other parts of Indonesia. In 1938 he completed *The Phenomenon of Man.* After twenty years he returned to Paris and a year later, preparing for an expedition to South Africa, suffered a severe heart attack, which forced him to delay the trip two years. While in Paris he was elected a Membre de l'Institut, named to the Académie des Sciences, and made Director of the National Research Center of France. In 1951, under the auspices of the Wenner-Gren Foundation, he moved to New York, where, except for trips to Africa in 1953 and Paris in 1954, he remained until his death on April 10, 1955. His research in anthropogenesis, based on human paleontology and physical anthropology, formed the scientific foundation for his ideas on evolution, a theory of evolving psychosocial hyperpersonalism based on evidence of convergence in biological evolution.

The thought of Teilhard is complex. As an inadequate but logical guide to the beginner, the following key concepts are presented.

Teilhard adopts the phenomenological approach insofar as he intends to describe and analyze the phenomenon of man as a scientist would any other phenomenon; by way of simplification this means observation of the *whole* of humanity from the *outside* rather than of the *individual* from *internal* evidence. From this global vantage point, *evolution* appears as a primary given, and the problem becomes one of understanding what is happening in evolution in order to learn where man is going. In the discovery of the patterns, the *structures*, and especially the *interrelationships* existing *and coming to be* in the universe, certain *trends* can be identified. Evidence indicates that evolution is a "law" of the universe, that *evolution has not ceased* but is still, even now, going on. The universe, and man along with it as in it and part of it, is *still evolving* and in a *definite direction*. Evidence further indicates that just as the ascent from inorganic physical simplicity to complexity prepared for and "called" for unification and integration as needs for survival against disintegration, dissolution, and destruction, and just as from this organization life emerged, so also, after gradually increased complexity, *consciousness* emerged as another actuation of the potential latent in the dynamic universe of energized matter. Consciousness had had to wait for certain favorable prerequisite conditions to exist before it could emerge and evolve from a latent or dormant state to an actuality. Then, after the prerequisites of even greater complexity and greater organizational convergence, unification, and integration were fulfilled, consciousness broke the bonds of closed individuality and the *human* emerged. As communication further advanced the ever-converging sociocultural complexity, it became possible for the truly *personal* to emerge with the social. Teilhard finds evidence that this trend of convergence toward person has not ceased. The survival of a newly evolved or emerged high level of *organized* complexity was always in danger of dissolution into lower constituent elements. A disintegrating force is like a cancer, out for its "own good" at the expense and eventual destruction of its host—and ultimately of itself. Likewise, the achievement of personhood and the perseverance of the *personal* mode of organization against regression to a lower,

previously surpassed level of evolution, are conditioned by the emergence of the *hyperpersonal* mode of organization. Contemporary man has finally begun to be aware of the directionality of evolution and has become "evolution conscious of itself." He is faced today with the option of freely assenting to the "wisdom of nature," i.e., to the still partially latent dynamic thrust of that energy-charged matter, or incarnate energy, which Teilhard can now call love. He can thereby actuate that latent potential for hyperpersonal unity, or he can choose to buck the tide of evolution and abort the birth of the still-evolving hyperpersonal level of human potentiality. The latter will eventually mean complete destruction of the human and personal in man. And global nuclear war, with mutual annihilation, will mean the end of life itself. Thus man's freedom is not absolute, i.e., freedom to choose the hyperperson or not. Evolution is a sort of irreversible, noncyclic, "material ecumenism of the universe" and shares the mystery of free commitment in general, in that we, the total community of contemporary man, are most free when we assent to take the reins and consciously direct the energy of the evolving universe, which energy in man is named love, toward the ultimate "Omega" point. The following selections are concerned with the role of love and energy in this task.

LOVE AS ENERGY *

In any domain—whether it be the cells of a body, the members of a society or the elements of a spiritual synthesis—*union differentiates*. In every organised whole, the parts perfect themselves and fulfil themselves. Through neglect of this universal rule

* From Pierre Teilhard de Chardin, *The Phenomenon of Man.* By permission of Harper & Row, Publishers, Incorporated, New York, and William Collins Sons & Co., Ltd., New York, and Éditions Du Seuil.

many a system of pantheism has led us astray to the cult of a great All in which individuals were supposed to be merged like a drop in the ocean or like a dissolving grain of salt. Applied to the case of the summation of consciousnesses, the law of union rids us of this perilous and recurrent illusion. No, following the confluent orbits of their centres, the grains of consciousness do not tend to lose their outlines and blend, but, on the contrary, to accentuate the depth and incommunicability of their *egos*. The more "other" they become in conjunction, the more they find themselves as "self." How could it be otherwise since they are steeped in Omega? Could a centre dissolve? Or rather, would not its particular way of dissolving be to super-centralise itself?

Thus, under the influence of these two factors—the essential immiscibility of consciousness, and the natural mechanism of all unification—the only fashion in which we could correctly express the final state of a world undergoing physical concentration would be as a system whose unity coincides with a paroxysm of harmonised complexity. Thus it would be mistaken to represent Omega to ourselves simply as a centre born of the fusion of elements which it collects, or annihilating them in itself. By its structure Omega, in its ultimate principle, can only be a *distinct Centre radiating at the core of a system of centres;* a grouping in which personalisation of the All and personalisations of the elements reach their maximum, simultaneously and without merging, under the influence of a supremely autonomous focus of union.[1] That is the only picture which emerges when we try to apply the notion of collectivity with remorseless logic to a granular whole of thoughts.

And at this point we begin to see the motives for the fervour and the impotence which accompany every egoistic solution of life. Egoism, whether personal or racial, is quite rightly excited by the idea of the element ascending through faithfulness to life, to the extremes of the incommunicable and the exclusive that it holds within it. It *feels* right. Its only mistake, but a fatal one, is *to confuse individuality with personality.* In trying to separate itself as much as possible from others, the element individualises itself; but in doing so it becomes retrograde and seeks to drag the world backwards towards plurality and into matter. In fact it diminishes itself and loses itself. To be fully

ourselves it is in the opposite direction, in the direction of convergence with all the rest, that we must advance—towards the "other." The goal of ourselves, the acme of our originality, is not our individuality but our person; and according to the evolutionary structure of the world, we can only find our person by uniting together. There is no mind without synthesis. The same law holds good from top to bottom. The true ego grows in inverse proportion to "egoism." Like the Omega which attracts it, the element only becomes personal when it universalises itself.[2]

There is, however, an obvious and essential proviso to be made. For the human particles to become really personalised under the creative influence of union, they must not—according to the preceding analysis—join up together anyhow. Since it is a question of achieving a synthesis of centres, it is centre to centre that they must make contact and *not otherwise.* Thus, amongst the various forms of psychic inter-activity animating the noosphere, the energies we must identify, harness and develop before all others are those of an "intercentric" nature, if we want to give effective help to the progress of evolution in ourselves.

Which brings us to the problem of love.

We are accustomed to consider (and with what a refinement of analysis!) only the sentimental face of love, the joy and miseries it causes us. It is in its natural dynamism and its evolutionary significance that I shall be dealing with it here, with a view to determining the ultimate phases of the phenomenon of man.

Considered in its full biological reality, love—that is to say the affinity of being with being—is not peculiar to man. It is a general property of all life and as such it embraces, in its varieties and degrees, all the forms

[1] It is for this central focus, necessarily autonomous, that we shall henceforward reserve the expression "Omega Point."

[2] Conversely, it only universalises itself properly in becoming super-personal. There is all the difference (and ambiguity) between the true and the false political or religious mysticisms. By the latter man is destroyed; by the former he is fulfilled by "becoming lost in the greater than himself."

successively adopted by organised matter. In the mammals, so close to ourselves, it is easily recognised in its different modalities: sexual passion, parental instinct, social solidarity, etc. Farther off, that is to say lower down on the tree of life, analogies are more obscure until they become so faint as to be imperceptible. But this is the place to repeat what I said earlier when we were discussing the *"within* of things." If there were no internal propensity to unite, even at a prodigiously rudimentary level—indeed in the molecule itself—it would be physically impossible for love to appear higher up, with us, in "hominised" form. By rights, to be certain of its presence in ourselves, we should assume its presence, at least in an inchoate form, in everything that is. And in fact if we look around us at the confluent ascent of consciousnesses, we see it is not lacking anywhere. Plato felt this and has immortalised the idea in his *Dialogues*. Later, with thinkers like Nicolas of Cusa, mediaeval philosophy returned technically to the same notion. Driven by the forces of love, the fragments of the world seek each other so that the world may come to being. This is no metaphor; and it is much more than poetry. Whether as a force or a curvature, the universal gravity of bodies, so striking to us, is merely the reverse or shadow of that which really moves nature. To perceive cosmic energy "at the fount" we must, if there is a *within* of things, go down into the internal or radial zone of spiritual attractions.

Love in all its subtleties is nothing more, and nothing less, than the more or less direct trace marked on the heart of the element by the psychical convergence of the universe upon itself.

This, if I am not mistaken, is the ray of light which will help us to see more clearly around us.

We are distressed and pained when we see modern attempts at human collectivisation ending up, contrary to our expectations and theoretical predictions, in a lowering and an enslavement of consciousness. But so far how have we gone about the business of unification? A material situation to be pre-

served; a new industrial field to be opened up, better conditions for a social class or less favoured nations—those are the only and very mediocre grounds on which we have so far tried to get together. There is no cause to be surprised if, in the footsteps of animal societies, we become mechanised in the very play of association. Even in the supremely intellectual act of science (at any rate as long as it remains purely speculative and abstract) the impact of our souls only operates obliquely and indirectly. Contact is still superficial, involving the danger of yet another servitude. Love alone is capable of uniting living beings in such a way as to complete and fulfil them, for it alone takes them and joins them by what is deepest in themselves. This is a fact of daily experience. At what moment do lovers come into the most complete possession of themselves if not when they say they are lost in each other? In truth, does not love every instant achieve all around us, in the couple or the team, the magic feat, the feat reputed to be contradictory, of "personalising" by totalising? And if that is what it can achieve daily on a small scale, why should it not repeat this one day on world-wide dimensions?

Mankind, the spirit of the earth, the synthesis of individuals and peoples, the paradoxical conciliation of the element with the whole, and of unity with multitude—all these are called Utopian and yet they are biologically necessary. And for them to be incarnated in the world all we may well need is to imagine our power of loving developing until it embraces the total of men and of the earth.

It may be said that this is the precise point at which we are invoking the impossible. Man's capacity, it may seem, is confined to giving his affection to one human being or to very few. Beyond that radius the heart does not carry, and there is only room for cold justice and cold reason. To love all and everyone is a contradictory and false gesture which only leads in the end to loving no one.

To that I would answer that if, as you

claim, a universal love is impossible, how can we account for that irresistible instinct in our hearts which leads us towards unity whenever and in whatever direction our passions are stirred? A sense of the universe, a sense of the *all*, the nostalgia which seizes us when confronted by nature, beauty, music —these seem to be an expectation and awareness of a Great Presence. The "mystics" and their commentators apart, how has psychology been able so consistently to ignore this fundamental vibration whose ring can be heard by every practised ear at the basis, or rather at the summit, of every great emotion? Resonance to the All—the keynote of pure poetry and pure religion. Once again: what does this phenomenon, which is born with thought and grows with it, reveal if not a deep accord between two realities which seek each other; the severed particle which trembles at the approach of "the rest"?

We are often inclined to think that we have exhausted the various natural forms of love with a man's love for his wife, his children, his friends and to a certain extent for his country. Yet precisely the most fundamental form of passion is missing from this list, the one which, under the pressure of an involuting universe, precipitates the elements one upon the other in the Whole— cosmic affinity and hence cosmic direction. A universal love is not only psychologically possible; it is the only complete and final way in which we are able to love.

But, with this point made, how are we to explain the appearance all around of us of mounting repulsion and hatred? If such a strong potentiality is besieging us from within and urging us to union, what is it waiting for to pass from potentiality to action? Just this, no doubt: that we should overcome the "anti-personalist" complex which paralyses us, and make up our minds to accept the possibility, indeed the reality, of some *source* of love and *object* of love at the summit of the world above our heads. So long as it absorbs or appears to absorb the person, the collectivity kills the love that is trying to come to birth. As such the collectivity is essentially unlovable. That is where philanthropic systems break down. Common sense is right. It is impossible to give oneself to anonymous number. But if the universe ahead of us assumes a face and a heart, and so to speak personifies itself,[3] then in the atmosphere created by this focus the elemental attraction will immediately blossom. Then, no doubt, under the heightened pressure of an infolding world, the formidable energies of attraction, still dormant between human molecules, will burst forth.

The discoveries of the last hundred years, with their unitary perspectives, have brought a new and decisive impetus to our sense of the world, to our sense of the earth, and to our human sense. Hence the rise of modern pantheism. But this impetus will only end by plunging us back into super-matter unless it leads us towards someone.

For the failure that threatens us to be turned into success, for the concurrence of human monads to come about, it is necessary and sufficient for us that we should extend our science to its farthest limits and recognise and accept (as being necessary to close and balance space-time) not only some vague future existence, but also, as I must now stress, the radiation *as a present reality* of that mysterious centre of our centres which I have called Omega.

HUMAN UNANIMISATION *

How depressing is the spectacle of the scattered human mass! A turbulent ant-hill of separate elements whose most evident characteristic, excepting certain limited cases of

---

* From Pierre Teilhard de Chardin, *The Future of Man*. By permission of Harper & Row, Publishers, Incorporated, New York, and William Collins Sons & Co., Ltd., New York, and Éditions du Seuil.

[3] Not, of course, by becoming a person, but by charging itself at the very heart of its development with the dominating and unifying influence of a focus of personal energies and attractions.

deep affinity (married couples, families, the team, the mother country) seems to be one of mutual repulsion, whether between individuals or groups. Yet we nurse in the depths of our hearts the conviction that it could be otherwise, that the chaos and disorder are "against nature" inasmuch as they prevent the realisation, or delay the coming, of a state of affairs which would multiply as though to infinity our human powers of thought, feeling and action.

Is the situation really desperate, or are there reasons for believing, despite appearances to the contrary, that Mankind as a whole is not only capable of unanimity but is actually in process of becoming unanimised? Do there exist, in other words, certain planetary energies which, overcoming the forces of repulsion that seem to be incurably opposed to human harmony, are tending inexorably to bring together and organise upon itself (unbelievable though this may seem) the terrifying multitude of milliards of thinking consciousnesses which forms the "reflective layer" of the earth?

My object here is to show that such energies do exist.

They are of two kinds: forces of compression, which by external and internal determinisms bring about a first stage of enforced unification; and subsequently forces of attraction, which through the action of internal affinity effect a genuine unanimisation by free consent.

Let us look in turn at these two processes which so pervade the human atmosphere that, like light and air, we tend to ignore them, although they envelop us so closely that no act of ours can escape them.

1 Enforced Unification: or the Geographical and Mental Curvature of Compression

a. *The Geographical Curvature.* Biologically speaking the human zoological group is developing on a closed surface. More exactly, since although the world population has already virtually filled the continents to saturation-point it shows no sign of levelling out but continues to increase at an ever-growing rate, the group behaves as though it were developing in a world that is shrinking, so that it becomes ever more tightly compressed upon itself.

The first and obvious effect of this ethnic compression is to bring bodies together. But the growing density of human matter, however material its origin, is also having a profound effect on human souls. In order to adapt itself in a vital sense to the increasing pressure, to survive and live in comfort, the multitude of thinking beings reacts naturally by arranging itself as well as possible, economically and technologically, upon itself. This automatically compels it to be constantly *inventing* new systems of mechanical equipment and social organisation. In other words it is forced to reflect; and this causes it to reflect a little more upon itself —to turn inward, that is to say, and further develop in itself those qualities which are specifically and in a higher sense human.

It is a profoundly instructive and mysterious phenomenon. The human mass is spiritually warmed and illumined by the iron grip of planetary compression; and the warming, whereby the rays of individual interaction expand, induces a further increase, in a kind of recoil, of the compression which was its cause . . . and so on, in a chain-reaction of increasing rapidity.

Out of this there arises first an irresistible grouping principle which, in its impact on the intelligence, almost automatically overrules the egoistical and mutually repulsive tendencies of the individual.

But that is not all: for to this first geographical compression there is rapidly added a tightening effect, due this time to the emergence and influence of a curvature which is not mechanical but *mental*, and which I must now explain.

b. *The Mental Curvature.* In the "humanising" chain of events which we have described, the mind, which at first seemed to be no more than a "device" for confronting and resisting planetary compression, is swiftly transformed into a "reason" of exist-ence. We think first in order to survive, and then we live in order to think: such is the fundamental law of anthropogenesis which emerges. But Thought, once it is let loose, displays an extraordinary power of self-pro-traction and extension, as though it were an independent organism which, being once born, cannot be restrained from growing and propagating itself and absorbing everything into its network. All history bears witness to the fact that nothing has ever been able to prevent an idea from growing and spreading and finally becoming universal. The reflec-tive, psychic environment which surrounds us is so constituted that we cannot remain in it without moving forward; and we cannot advance except by drawing closer and rub-bing shoulders with one another. It is as though all our individual strivings after truth soared upward into a mental "cupola" whose closed walls inexorably compel our minds to mingle!

An enforced coalescence of all Thought in the sum total of itself . . .

The increasingly apparent growth, over-riding the monstrous and chaotic human dispersal which so distresses us, of this force of auto-unification emerging from the psychic energies released by our technico-social mastery of the earth: this surely is a guarantee that, within our universe, the im-pulse of totalisation must eventually triumph over the impulses of dispersal.

But on one condition. Under the influence of economic forces and the intellectual reasons invoked to break down the barriers behind which our egotism shelters, there must emerge, since this alone can be com-pletely unanimising, the sense of a single, fundamental aspiration.

2 Free Unification through Attraction. A point of Universal Convergence on the Horizon

Despite the compulsions, both geographical and psychic, which oblige men to live and think in an ever closer community, they do not necessarily love each other the more on that account. The two greatest scientists in the world, being preoccupied with the same problem, may none the less detest each other. This is a sad fact of which we are all aware, and because of this separation of head and heart we are bound to conclude that, however social necessity and logic may impel it from behind, the human mass will only become thoroughly unified under the influence of some form of *affective* energy which will place the human particles in the happy position of being unable to love and fulfil themselves individually except by con-tributing in some degree to the love and fulfilment of all; to the extent, that is to say, that all are equal and integral parts of a single universe that is vitally converging. A "pull," in other words, must be born of the "push." But amid the politico-social crisis which now besets us, have we valid, objec-tive reasons for believing in the possibility of this hopeful state of affairs, even to the point of discerning its first indications?

I believe we have, on the following grounds.

If we look for the principal outcome, "Result No. 1," of the ineluctable unification of our scientific intelligence during the past century, we must quickly perceive that the gain consists far less in our securing control of any particular source of natural energy than in the general awakening of our con-sciousness to the vast and extreme organ-icity of the universe as a whole, considered in terms of its internal forces of develop-ment. We see more clearly with every in-crease in our knowledge that we are, all of us, participants in a process (Cosmogenesis culminating in Anthropogenesis) upon which our ultimate fulfilment—one might even say, our beatification—obscurely depends. And whence can it arise, this accumulation of evidence that the extreme point of each of us (our ultra-ego, it might be termed) coincides with some common fulfilment of the evolutionary process, a common super-ego, except out of the principle of attraction which we have postulated as being necessary to bring together the rebellious seeds of our

⸱individualities, uniting them from within and unanimising them at the heart?

Thus, superimposed on the twofold tightening action of what I have called the geometrical and mental curvature of the human earth—superimposed yet *emanating* from them—we have a third and final unifying influence brought to bear in regulating the movements of the Noosphere, that of a destiny that is supremely attractive, the same for all at the same time. A total community of desire, which makes of it a third force as planetary in its dimensions as the other two, but operating, no matter how irresistibly, in the manner of a seduction—that is to say, by free consent.

It would be premature to assert that this new force as yet plays any very explicit part in the course of political or social events. Yet may we not claim, observing the precipitate growth of democracies and totalitarian regimes during the past hundred and fifty years, that it is the *Sense of Species*, which for a time seemed to have vanished from human hearts, dispelled in some sort by the growth of Reflection, that is now gradually resuming its place and reasserting its rights over narrow individualism? Sense of Species interpreted in the new, grand human manner: not, as formerly, a shoot which merely seeks to prolong itself until it bears its fruit, but the fruit itself, gathering and growing upon itself in the expectation of eventual ripeness.

But if the hope of this maturing of the Species, and the belief in its coming, are to illumine and truly unanimise our hearts, we must endow it with certain positive attributes. It is here that opinions are divided.

Those who think on Marxist lines believe that all that is necessary to inspire and polarise the human molecules is that they should look forward to an eventual state of *collective* reflection and sympathy, at the culmination of anthropogenesis, from which all will benefit through *participation:* as it were, a vault of intermingled thoughts, a closed circuit of attachments in which the individual will achieve intellectual and affective wholeness to the extent that he is one with the whole system.

But in the Christian view only the eventual appearance, at the summit and in the heart of the unified world, of an autonomous centre of congregation is structurally and functionally capable of inspiring, preserving and fully releasing, within a human mass still spiritually dispersed, the looked-for forces of unanimisation. By this hypothesis only a veritable *super-love*, the attractive power of a veritable "super-being," can of psychological necessity dominate, possess and synthesise the host of earthly loves. Failing such a centre of universal coherence, not metaphorical or theoretical but *real*, there can be no true union among totalised Mankind, and therefore no true substance. A world culminating in the Impersonal can bring us neither the warmth of attraction nor the hope of irreversibility (immortality) without which individual egotism will always have the last word. A veritable *Ego* at the summit of the world is needed for the consummation, without confounding them, of all the elemental *egos* of Earth . . . I have talked of the "Christian view," but this idea is gaining ground in other circles. Was it not Camus who wrote in *Sisyphe*, "If Man found that the Universe could love he would be reconciled"? And did not Wells, through his exponent the humanitarian biologist Steele in *The Anatomy of Frustration*, express his need to find, above and beyond humanity, a "universal lover"?

Let me recapitulate and conclude.

Essentially, in the twofold irresistible embrace of a planet that is visibly shrinking, and Thought that is more and more rapidly coiling in upon itself, the dust of human units finds itself subjected to a formidable pressure of coalescence, far stronger than the individual or national repulsions that so alarm us. But despite the closing of this vice nothing seems finally capable of guiding us into the natural sphere of our inter-human affinities except the emergence of a powerful field of internal attraction, in which we shall find ourselves caught *from within*. The rebirth of the Sense of Species, rendered virtually inevitable by the phase of compressive and totalising socialisation which we have now entered, affords a first indication of the existence of such a field of unanimisation and a clue to its nature.

Nevertheless, however efficacious this newly born faith of Man in the ultra-human may prove to be, it seems that Man's urge towards *Some Thing* ahead of him cannot achieve its full fruition except by combining with another and still more fundamental aspiration—one from above, urging him towards *Some One*.

Bibliography

Texts

The Phenomenon of Man. New York: Harper & Row, Publishers, Incorporated, 1961.

The Divine Milieu. New York: Harper & Row, Publishers, Incorporated, 1960.

The Future of Man. New York: Harper & Row, Publishers, Incorporated, 1964.

Hymn of the Universe. New York: Harper & Row, Publishers, Incorporated, 1965.

Studies

Francoeur, R. *The World of Teilhard.* Baltimore: Helicon, 1961.

Rabut, O. *Teilhard de Chardin: A Critical Study.* New York: Sheed & Ward, Inc., 1961.

Raven, C. E. *Teilhard de Chardin: Scientist and Seer.* New York: Harper & Row, Publishers, Incorporated, 1962.

20

Introduction

Jacques Maritain was born on November 18, 1882, and pursued his first philosophical studies at the Sorbonne under Henri Bergson. In 1905, at the time of his agrégation in philosophy, he was a convinced Bergsonian. In 1906, after his conversion to Catholicism, he felt the need of finding a philosophy more reconcilable to his religious persuasion. He turned to Thomas Aquinas and has become in the eyes of many the leading living Thomist, even if he has perhaps found it difficult to recognize himself in the different identities his followers have projected upon him, ranging from conservative Thomism to authentic existentialism.

His first important work was a critical confrontation of Bergsonism and Thomism. His numerous works since then have established his leadership in orthodox Thomism. He has written in almost all branches of philosophy, such as logic; epistemology; metaphysics; æsthetics; and moral, social, and political philosophy. He has also written on natural theology. Although many of his works offer contributions to a philosophy of man, he has not worked out a specific philosophical anthropology. Maritain's other contributions are to biography, cultural criticism, religion, philosophy of science, and spirituality. He has taught at several universities in the United States, such as Columbia, Chicago, Princeton, and Yale.

Orthodox Thomism has come to mean an academic philosophy innocent of scholarly attempts to effect an *aggiornamento* with the help of contributions from contemporary non-Thomist sources, e.g., existentialism, phenomenology, and linguistic analysis. In the highly critical discussion of phenomenology in his major work, *The Degrees of Knowledge,* Maritain rejects Husserl's transcendental idealism (as indeed did most of Husserl's own following), but does not see this as ruling out phenomenology as such; in fact, Maritain singles out the neglected work of Alexander Pfänder (leader of the Munich Circle) as deserving much more attention than it has been given previously.

Maritain's epistemology has been criticized for ceaselessly attempting to guarantee the value of conceptual knowledge and its ability to attain real existence by appealing to an abstractive intuition of being. Much of Maritain's early work, including his study of Aquinas and especially his theory of intuition, is best understood when seen in the light of his disagreement with Bergson, whose philosophy Maritain rejected after studying Aquinas. Maritain has been a pioneer in his attempt to use the texts of Aquinas as a basis for a modern theory of man as a person and a theory of the social nature of man. The following selections stand on their own, however, independent of such radical considerations.

MAN AS A PERSON IN SOCIETY *

Perhaps the most apposite approach to the philosophical discovery of personality is the

* From Jacques Maritain, *The Person and the Common Good.* Reprinted with the permission of Charles Scribner's Sons, New York. Copyright 1947 Charles Scribner's Sons, New York. Reprinted also with the permission of Geoffrey Bles, Ltd., London.

study of the relation between personality and love.

"Not the person but only its qualities do we love," Pascal has said. This is a false statement, and exhibits in Pascal a trace of the very rationalism against which he strove to protect himself. Love is not concerned with qualities. They are not the object of our love. We love the deepest, most substantial and hidden, the most *existing* reality of the beloved being. This is a metaphysical center deeper than all the qualities and essences which we can find and enumerate in the beloved. The expressions of lovers are unending because their object is ineffable.

Love seeks out this center, not, to be sure, as separated from its qualities, but as one with them. This is a center inexhaustible, so to speak, of existence, bounty and action; capable of giving and of *giving itself*; capable of receiving not only this or that gift bestowed by another, but even another self as a gift, another self which bestows itself. This brief consideration of love's own law brings us to the metaphysical problem of the person. For love is not concerned with qualities or natures or essences but with *persons*.

"Thou art *thyself*," says Juliet "though not a Montague . . . Romeo, doff thy name, and for thy name, which is not part of thee, take all myself."

To bestow oneself, one must first exist; not indeed, as a sound, which passes through the air, or an idea, which crosses the mind, but as a thing, which subsists and exercises existence for itself. Such a being must exist not only as other things do, but eminently, in self-possession, holding itself in hand, master of itself. In short, it must be endowed with a spiritual existence, capable of containing itself thanks to the operations of the intellect and freedom, capable of superexisting by way of knowledge and of love. For this reason, the metaphysical tradition of the West defines the person in terms of independence, as a reality which, subsisting spiritually, constitutes a universe unto itself, a relatively independent whole within the great whole of the universe, facing the transcendent whole which is God. For the same reason, this tradition finds in God the sovereign Personality whose existence itself consists in a pure and absolute super-existence by way of intellection and love. Unlike the concept of the individuality of corporeal things, the concept of personality is related not to matter but to the deepest and highest

dimensions of being. Its roots are in the spirit inasmuch as the spirit holds itself in existence and superabounds in existence. Metaphysically considered, personality is, as the Thomistic School rightly asserts, "subsistence," the ultimate achievement by which the creative influx seals, within itself, a nature face to face with the whole order of existence so that the existence which it receives is *its own* existence and *its own* perfection. Personality is the subsistence of the spiritual soul communicated to the human composite. Because, in our substance, it is an imprint or seal which enables it to possess its existence, to perfect and give itself freely, personality testifies to the generosity or expansiveness in being which an incarnate spirit derives from its spiritual nature and which constitutes, within the secret depths of our ontological structure, a source of dynamic unity, of unification from within.

Personality, therefore, signifies interiority to self. And because it is the spirit in man which takes him, in contrast to the plant and animal, beyond the threshold of independence properly so called, and of interiority to oneself, the subjectivity of the person has nothing in common with the isolated unity, without doors or windows, of the Leibnizian monad. It requires the communications of knowledge and love. By the very fact that each of us is a person and expresses himself to himself, each of us requires communication with *other* and *the others* in the order of knowledge and love. Personality, of its essence, requires a dialogue in which souls really communicate. Such communication is rarely possible. For this reason, personality in man seems to be bound to the experience of affliction even more profoundly than to the experience of creative effort. The person is directly related to the absolute. For only in the absolute is it able to enjoy its full sufficiency. Its spiritual homeland is the whole universe of the absolute and of those indefectible goods which are as the pathways to the absolute Whole which transcends the world.

Finally, we turn to religious thought for

the last word and find that the deepest layer of the human person's dignity consists in its property of resembling God—not in a general way after the manner of all creatures, but in a *proper* way. It is the *image of God*. For God is spirit and the human person proceeds from Him in having as principle of life a spiritual soul capable of knowing, loving and of being uplifted by grace to participation in the very life of God so that, in the end, it might know and love Him as He knows and loves Himself. . . .

There is not in me one reality, called my individual, and another reality, called my person. One and the same reality is, in a certain sense an individual, and, in another sense, a person. Our whole being is an individual by reason of that in us which derives from matter, and a person by reason of that in us which derives from spirit. Similarly, the whole of a painting is a physico-chemical mixture by reason of the coloring stuff of which it is made, and the whole of it is a work of beauty by reason of the painter's art.

Of course, material individuality is not something evil in itself. Obviously as the very condition of our existence, it is something good. But it is precisely as related to personality that individuality is good. Evil arises when, in our action, we give preponderance to the individual aspect of our being. For although each of our acts is simultaneously the act of ourselves as an individual and as a person, yet, by the very fact that it is free and involves our whole being, each act is linked in a movement towards the supreme center to which personality tends, or in a movement towards that dispersion into which, if left to itself, material individuality is inclined to fall.

It should be noted here that man must realize through his will that of which his nature is but the sketch. In terms of a commonplace—and a very profound one—which goes back to Pindar, man must become what he is. And this he must do at a sorrowful cost and with formidable risks. He himself, in the moral order, must win his liberty and his personality. In other words, as observed above, his action can follow the bent either

of personality or of material individuality. If the development occurs in the direction of material individuality, it will be orientated towards the detestable ego whose law is *to grasp* or absorb for itself. At the same time personality, as such, will tend to be adulterated and to dissolve. But if the development occurs in the direction of spiritual personality, man will be orientated towards the generous self of the heroes and saints. Thus, man will be truly a person only in so far as the life of the spirit and of liberty reigns over that of the senses and passions.

Here we are confronted with the crucial problem of the education of man. There are some who confound the person with the individual. To effectuate the development of personality and the freedom of expansion to which it aspires, they reject all asceticism; these would have the tree bear fruit without having been pruned. Instead of self-fulfilment, the man, thus educated, achieves only dispersion and disintegration. The heart becomes atrophied and the senses exacerbated, or else all that is most human in man recoils in a vacuum veiled in frivolity.

Others misunderstand the distinction between the individual and the person; they mistake it for a separation. These believe that there are two separate beings in each of us, the one—the individual, the other—the person. Their motto is: "Death to the individual, long live the person!" The pity is that, in killing the individual, they also kill the person. The *despotic* conception of the progress of the human being is no whit better than the *anarchistic* conception. Its ideal seems to be first, remove the heart—painlessly if possible—then replace it with the heart of an angel. The second is by far the more difficult operation, and succeeds more rarely. Instead of the authentic person, exhibiting the mysterious visage of the Creator, a mask appears, the austere mask of the Pharisee.

It is the interior principle, namely, nature and grace, which matters most in the education and progress of the human being, just as it is an inner principle which matters most in organic growth. Our instruments are simply the aids; our art is but the servant and cooperator of this interior principle. The whole function of this art is to prune and to trim—operations in which both the individual and the person are interested—in such wise that, within the intimacy of the human being, the gravity of individuality diminishes and that of true personality and its generosity increases. Such an art, to be sure, is difficult. . . .

Personality tends by nature to communion. This frequently misunderstood point should be emphasized. For the person requires membership in a society in virtue both of its dignity and its needs. Animal groups or colonies are called societies only in an improper sense. They are collective wholes constituted of mere individuals. Society in the proper sense, human society, is a society of persons. A city worthy of the name is a city of human persons. The social unit is the person.

But why is it that the person, as person, seeks to live in society? It does so, first, because of its very perfections, as person, and its inner urge to the communications of knowledge and love which require relationship with other persons. In its radical generosity, the human person tends to overflow into social communications in response to the law of superabundance inscribed in the depths of being, life, intelligence and love. It does so secondly because of its needs or deficiencies, which derive from its material individuality. In this respect, unless it is integrated in a body of social communications, it cannot attain the fullness of its life and accomplishment. Society appears, therefore, to provide the human person with just those conditions of existence and development which it needs. It is not by itself alone that it reaches its plenitude but by receiving essential goods from society.

Here the question is not only of his material needs, of bread, clothes and shelter, for which man requires the help of his fellowmen, but also, and above all, of the help which he ought to be given to do the work of reason and virtue, which responds to the specific feature of his being. To reach a certain degree of elevation in knowledge as well as a certain degree of perfection in moral life, man needs an education and the help of other men. In this sense, Aristotle's statement that man is by nature a political animal holds with great exactitude: man is a political animal because he is a rational animal, because reason requires development through character training, education and the cooperation of other men, and because society is thus indispensable to the accomplishment of human dignity.

There is a correlation between this notion of the *person* as social unit and the notion of the *common good* as the end of the social whole. They imply one another. The common good is common because it is received in persons, each one of whom is as a mirror of the whole. Among the bees, there is a public good, namely, the good functioning of the hive, but not a common good, that is, a good received and communicated. The end of society, therefore, is neither the individual good nor the collection of the individual goods of each of the persons who constitute it. Such a conception would dissolve society as such to the advantage of its parts, and would amount to either a frankly anarchistic conception, or the old disguised anarchistic conception of individualistic materialism in which the whole function of the city is to safeguard the liberty of each; thus giving to the strong full freedom to oppress the weak.

The end of society is the good of the community, of the social body. But if the good of the social body is not understood to be a common good of *human persons*, just as the social body itself is a whole of human persons, this conception also would lead to other errors of a totalitarian type. The common good of the city is neither the mere collection of private goods, nor the proper good of a whole which, like the species with respect to its individuals or the hive with respect to its bees, relates the parts to itself alone and sacrifices them to itself. It is the good *human* life of the multitude, of a multitude of persons; it is their communion in good living. It is therefore common to both *the whole and the parts* into which it flows back and which, in turn, must benefit from it. Unless it would vitiate itself, it implies and requires recognition of the fundamental rights of persons and those of the domestic society in which the persons are more primitively engaged than in the political society. It includes within itself as principal value, the highest access, compatible with the good of the whole, of the persons to their life of person and liberty of expansion, as well as to the communications of generosity consequent upon such expansion. If, as we intend to emphasize later, the common good of the city implies an intrinsic ordination to something which transcends it, it is because it requires, by its very essence and within its proper sphere, communication or redistribution to the persons who constitute society. It presupposes the persons and flows back upon them, and, in this sense, is achieved in them.

Thus, that which constitutes the common good of political society is not only: the collection of public commodities and services—the roads, ports, schools, etc., which the organization of common life presupposes; a sound fiscal condition of the state and its military power; the body of just laws, good customs and wise institutions, which provide the nation with its structure; the heritage of its great historical remembrances, its symbols and its glories, its living traditions and cultural treasures. The common good includes all of these and something much more besides—something more profound, more concrete and more human. For it includes also, and above all, the whole sum itself of these; a sum which is quite different from a simple collection of juxtaposed units. (Even in the mathematical order, as Aristotle points out, 6 is not the same as $3 + 3$.) It includes the sum or sociological integration of all the civic conscience, political virtues and sense of right and liberty, of all the activity, material prosperity and spiritual riches, of unconsciously operative hereditary wisdom, of moral rectitude, justice, friendship, happiness, virtue and heroism in the individual lives of its members. For these things all are, in a certain measure, *communicable* and so revert to each member, helping him to perfect his life and liberty of person. They all constitute the good human life of the multitude.

Bibliography

Texts

The Degrees of Knowledge. New York: Charles Scribner's Sons, 1959.

The Person and the Common Good. New York: Charles Scribner's Sons, 1947.

The Range of Reason. New York: Charles Scribner's Sons, 1952.

Creative Intuition in Art and Poetry. New York: Pantheon Books, a Division of Random House, Inc., 1953.

True Humanism. London: Geoffrey Bles, Ltd., 1947.

Man and the State. Chicago: The University of Chicago Press, 1951.

Moral Philosophy. New York: Charles Scribner's Sons, 1964.

Bergsonian Philosophy and Thomism. New York: Philosophical Library, Inc., 1955.

An Introduction to Philosophy. London: Sheed & Ward, Ltd., 1930.

Preface to Metaphysics. New York: Sheed & Ward, Inc., 1939.

Existence and the Existent. New York: Pantheon Books, a Division of Random House, Inc., 1948.

Studies

Evans, J. *Jacques Maritain: The Man and His Achievement.* New York: Sheed & Ward, Inc., 1963.

Fecher, C. *The Philosophy of Jacques Maritain.* Westminster, Md.: The Newman Press, 1953.

Van Riet, G. *Thomistic Epistemology.* St. Louis: B. Herder Book Co., 1963, vol. I, pp. 315–340.

21

Introduction

Karl Jaspers was born on February 20, 1883, in Oldenburg, near the North Sea coast. His father studied law and later became the director of a bank. After a somewhat trying Gymnasium training, during which he more than once clashed with school authorities because he balked at blind obedience to unreasonable orders and customs, Jaspers began by studying law in Heidelberg and Munich, and then took up the study of medicine in Berlin, Göttingen, and Heidelberg. He passed his state medical exams in 1908, received his M.D. in 1909, and became a volunteer research assistant in the Psychiatric Hospital of Heidelberg University.

In 1913 he had completed his first major book, *General Psychopathology*, a pioneer work in the field; it met with enthusiastic approval, and several offers of positions came his way from major figures, among whom was Kraepelin in Munich. Jaspers preferred to stay at Heidelberg, but there was no opening in the department. In order to stay and await an opening, he reluctantly decided to join the philosophy faculty as an assistant professor of psychology, a move he later recognized as fortunate and wise.

In 1921 he became a full professor. He was still at Heidelberg, despite continued offers from other universities, when in December, 1931, he published his first major work in philosophy, three volumes entitled simply *Philosophy*. During the decade from 1921 to 1931 he published nothing that had been written since his appointment as full professor. This fact added to his being something of a renegade (as an M.D., not a Ph.D.) on the philosophy faculty. The situation was further aggravated by friction with Heinrich Rickert, who was head of the department, and by a fatiguing organic illness that was his since childhood. These were difficult years. In 1937, because of his sharp criticism of racism and extreme nationalism, he was stripped of his post by the Nazi regime. With the American occupation in 1945 he returned to Heidelberg once more. In 1948 he accepted a professorship at the University of Basel, his last position.

Jaspers has been assigned by some the first place among the philosophers of existence as the originator of the movement. He rejects the term existentialism because it suggests a school, but he is included in every study of existentialism. And although he says in his *Philosophical Memoir* of 1953: "As a method I adopted and retained Husserl's phenomenology—which he initially called 'descriptive psychology'—discarding only its refinement to essence perception. . . . Phenomenology became a research method," still he cannot be and is not included among phenomenological philosophers. It was precisely with his transition from psychiatry to philosophy that he dropped phenomenology as a method.

For Jaspers, becoming authentically human means becoming *Existenz* rather than mere *Dasein*. This transition is the actualization of a personal potential. In certain extreme situations (death, illness, suffering), a man can face the possibility of loss or threat of loss of his being; in these moments he can transcend individual differences between men to see others as having community with him, as sharing a common destiny with him. Communication is the affirmation of this community, the enactment of ties and bonds between persons. Writing in his seventieth year he could say: "From my school days on, the question of *communication* between human beings was to me the basic question of our life. Man can only come to himself with his fellow man." In the following selection Jaspers relates his existential philosophy to the difficulty of becoming a genuine person in contemporary society.

MAINTENANCE OF SELFHOOD IN
THE CONTEMPORARY SITUATION *

The modality of human existence is the pre-supposition of everything. Apparatus may be perfected as much as you please, but if men of the right sort are lacking, it is of no avail. If man is not to be allowed to founder in the mere persistence of life, it may seem essential that in his consciousness he shall be confronted with Nothingness, he must recall his origin. Whereas at the outset of his historical course he was in danger of being physically annihilated by the natural forces, now his very being is menaced by a world he has himself established. Though upon another level than in the unknown beginnings of his development, his whole being is again at stake.

Neither an exuberant joy of life nor yet a resolute endurance of Nothingness can save him. Both are doubtless indispensable as temporary refuges in time of trouble; but they do not suffice.

If man is to be himself, he needs a positively fulfilled world. When his world has fallen into decay, when his ideas seem to be dying, man remains hidden from himself so long as he is not able to discover on his own initiative the ideas that come to meet him in the world.

But with the self-existence of the individual there begins that which then for the first time realises itself to become a world. Even though this should seem to have become hopeless in an unspiritual life-order, there remains in man as a pure possibility that which has momentarily receded out of sight. If to-day we ask in our despair what is still left for us in this world, to every one there comes the answer: 'That which you are, because you can.' The mental situation to-day compels man, compels every individual, to fight wittingly on behalf of his true essence. He must either maintain it or lose

it according to the way in which he becomes aware of the foundation of his being in the reality of his life.

The present moment seems to be one which makes extensive claims, makes claims it is almost impossible to satisfy. Deprived of his world by the crisis, man has to reconstruct it from its beginnings with the materials and presuppositions at his disposal. There opens to him the supreme possibility of freedom, which he has to grasp even in face of impossibility, with the alternative of sinking into nullity. If he does not pursue the path of self-existence, there is nothing left for him but the self-willed enjoyment of life amid the coercions of the apparatus against which he no longer strives. He must either on his own initiative independently gain possession of the mechanism of his life, or else, himself degraded to become a machine, surrender to the apparatus. He must, through communication, establish the tie between self and self, in full awareness that here everything turns upon loyalty or disloyalty; and in default of this his life will be utterly despiritualised and become a mere function. He must either advance to the frontier where he can glimpse his Transcendence, or else must remain entangled in the disillusionment of a self that is wholly involved in the things of the world. The demands made of him are such as assume him to have the powers of a titan. He must meet these demands, and must see what he is capable of in the way of self-development; for, if he fails to do so, there will remain for him nothing but a life in which he will have the advantages neither of man nor of beast.

It boots nothing to complain that too much is being laid upon the individual, and that circumstances ought to be altered. Effective work upon environing conditions can only arise out of the modality of selfhood. I am unfaithful to my own possibilities when I await from a change of circumstances

---

* From Karl Jaspers, *Man in The Modern Age*, Routledge & Kegan Paul, Ltd., London, 1951, 2d ed. Eden and Cedar Paul, translators. Reprinted by permission of the publishers.

what I can do on my own initiative. I shirk my task when I impose upon another what is incumbent on myself; and this other can only thrive when I myself become all that I am capable of being.

Against the World or in the World

The first sign of awakening circumspection in the individual is that he will show a new way of holding himself towards the world. Selfhood or self-existence first arises out of his being against the world in the world.

The first step leads out of the world into solitude. Self-existence which, in the negative resolve for self-renunciation, fails to grasp any world-existence, consumes itself in possibility. It can only speak in order to question things. To create unrest is its element. This method of Kierkegaard's, which was inevitable as a phase in the transition, would become insincere if a man firmly established on his own foundations were to promote unrest for others. Any one who, while carrying on an occupation, takes a positive grasp of life, who acts as a teacher, has a family, lives in a world of historical and scientific knowledge because he finds this more relevant, has abandoned the path of the unworldliness of negative resolve. He cannot wish to snatch the ground from under the feet of others without showing them the ground on which he himself stands.

The second path leads into the world, but only by way of the possibility of the first path. For philosophising self-existence cannot stand fast in its world with unquestioning satisfaction.

To-day, when the envelopment of all life in the apparatus can no longer be helped, when life has become an enterprise in which the great majority of persons are workers and employees, it is futile to expect a profession or means of livelihood in which one will be independent of others. Participation in the community of interests and of labour of all those who pursue the same occupation or practise the same means of earning a liveli-

hood, a participation that will safeguard one's own life subject to externally imposed purposes and conditions, is now unavoidable. There are, of course, still vestiges of comparatively independent enclaves, relics of the past, which it may be well to preserve, whenever they are found, as precious possibilities handed down from antiquity and capable of disclosing an irreplaceable type of human existence; but for almost all it is now inevitable to work in a joint enterprise or to perish. The question is how to live in such an enterprise.

Ambiguously alluring is the possibility of setting oneself exclusively against the world. He only can sincerely renounce it who condemns himself to suffer shipwreck in face of all realisation. For if, while trying to turn to the best account a favourable economic situation life offers him, he nevertheless keeps himself to himself utterly apart from the world, he sinks into a vacancy in which he still remains a prey to the world; he becomes insincere in his flight from the world which, while railing against it, he only eludes in order, through negating it, to count still as being.

The reality of the world cannot be evaded. Experience of the harshness of the real is the only way by which a man can come to his own self. To play an active part in the world, even though one aims at an impossible, an unattainable goal, is the necessary pre-condition of one's own being. What we have to endeavour, therefore, is to live at harmony with the powers of this world without being absorbed by them. The enterprise in its restriction to the region of the indispensable retains its preponderance, a solidarised attempt to further the provision of the elementary necessaries of human life for all remaining the field of activity for the individual likewise—the individual participating in this work because all are engaged in it in order to make life possible. But the ethos of this labour also contains the dread of self-existence.

The degradation of the field of labour to become merely relative would seem to annul one's pleasure in using one's energies; and yet it is the existence of man to be able to persist in this jejune activity without any paralysis of the will-to-do. For selfhood is only possible in virtue of this tension, thanks to which, instead of merely juxtaposing two vital domains, we try to bring it about that one shall be fulfilled with the other, even though a universally valid form of unification as the only desirable life for all be impossible. Thus we have to live, as it were, upon a narrow mountain ridge, falling away on one side into the mere enterprise, or, on the other, into a life devoid of reality side by side with the enterprise.

The significance of entering into the world constitutes the value of philosophy. True, philosophy is not an instrument, and still less is it a talisman; but it is awareness in the process of realisation. Philosophy is the thought with which or as which I am active as my own self. It is not to be regarded as the objective validity of any sort of knowledge, but as the consciousness of being in the world.

Technical Sovereignty, Primary Will-to-know, Unconditioned Ties

The entry of the selfhood into its world is to be contemplated in its possible trend. From the technical, the road leads by way of the primary will-to-know to the unconditioned ties.

(a) Everyday complications of a technicised world make it necessary for me to master these complications in the environment accessible to me. The relationship to things has been transformed; as a further remove there remain, in their indifference, nothing more than transferable functions; technique has divorced man from the immediate present. The new task is, with the methods of technical realisation, to come once again into the direct presence of human existence as regards all things in the world. The new presupposition of intensified possibilities must be pressed into our service. The rationalisation of the means of life, including a rationalised distribution of our

time and a rationalised economising of our energies, must restore to every individual (in virtue likewise of his own spontaneous effort) the possibility of being thoroughly contemporary; so that he can reflect about, so that he can allow to ripen, so that he can enter into genuine contact with, the things which are his own. The new possibility is not merely an objectively secure engrossment with the purposive mechanical realisation of the material conditions of life, but the attainment thereby of a freedom that shall enable us to rise superior to all material considerations.

Wherever the realm of technique has been conquered, man's enthusiasm concerning discoveries that make him the originator of a transformation of the world, that make him, so to say, a second great architect of the world, is the privilege of those who have advanced to the limits of the attainable.

Where technique is being utilised, the appropriate attitude is a restriction to the necessary minimum of effort, the economising of time, deliberate movements which waste no energy. Notwithstanding the apparently bewildering complication of the technical world, there becomes possible a peculiar tranquillity which dominates the objective conditions of life and the vital activities of the doer. Obedience to the laws of orderly functioning, in which people are trained from childhood upward, provides free space for selfhood as well.

The world of technique seems destructive to the natural world. People complain that life has become unnatural. Artificial technique, which in the course of its development has had to put up with much ugliness and has had to accept a severance from nature, might in the end provide a more effective access to nature in general. Modern man is able to enjoy the sunshine and the play of the elements with a new awareness of them. Technique supplies the possibility of a life which can be passed in any part, in many parts, of the geographical world; of a life wherein it has become increasingly possible to enjoy light and air and all their manifestations. Since everything has become close and accessible, the limits of the home have been greatly expanded. Thanks to this conquest of nature there has increased a true delight in nature undefiled, which the activities of my body enable me to attain to, enjoy, and ardently perceive as lord of the senses five. Insofar as I avail myself and expand this revelation in the environment directly vouchsafed to me, and insofar as I keep my feet firmly planted upon the ground (using the revelation as no more than one of the technical instruments to bring me into closer contact with the universal mother), I am enabled—in these artificially created possibilities—not merely to see the cipher of nature more distinctly, but also to read it better.

Technicisation is a path along which we have no choice but to advance. Any attempt to retrace our steps would mean that life would be rendered increasingly difficult until it would become impossible. Invective is of no use here; we have to overcome. The world of technique, therefore, must be taken as a matter of course; so much so that all which goes on within it must lie almost outside the field of active attention. As contrasted with the need that all our activities must be more successfully grounded upon advanced technique, we have to cultivate our awareness of the non-mechanisable to the pitch of infallibility. To render the world of technique absolute would be destructive of selfhood, and therefore our sense of the value of technical achievement must be permeated with a new significance.

(b) The system whereby the elementary necessaries of human life are provided, demands knowledge only for utilitarian purposes. Selfhood in knowledge, on the other hand, is a primary will to know. Here we are concerned with a longing for knowledge for its own sake. If I accept utility as the ultimate standard of knowledge, I surrender my own selfhood therein. But if knowledge be pursued for its own sake, in the pursuit I achieve self-awareness.

Utilitarian knowledge is only possible as an outcome of that genuine knowledge which undergoes segregation and contemplates itself as something set apart in the world of the cogently valid and actual. Consequently, even in the technical life-order, a decisive sense for the modality of the known is only trustworthy where there is a selfhood which sets limits. In default of this, there arises a confusion of the known and the imaginary. If rationally cogent knowledge be rendered absolute, all being is contemplated as lying within the realm of technique, with the result of a misunderstanding that gives rise to the superstition of science, and ere long to every sort of superstition. For under such conditions man can neither cognise in a trustworthy fashion nor yet be truly himself, seeing that science can only comprehend that which it itself primarily is.

The future lies where the tension of the modalities of knowledge is maintained. In such conditions, special knowledge would still be illuminated by being, and philosophy would be fulfilled by the singularity of the world. Selfhood is the supreme instrument of knowledge, an instrument which indeed supplies vision only according to the degree in which it takes cognisance of the world, but also only insofar as it itself remains active. Life becomes for the individual the responsibility of the human being aware of himself as being, and, in addition and simultaneously, the experiment of the knower. What man does investigatively, purposively, and constructively, is (regarded in its entirety) the road of endeavour on which he discovers his destiny and the manner in which he becomes aware of being.

(c) But life as mere life, the life that proceeds in a succession of passing moments until it comes to its term, has no destiny; for it, time is no more than a series, remembrance is indifferent; the present (having no continuity with the future) is nothing more than a momentary enjoyment or a momentary failure to achieve enjoyment. Man wins destiny only through ties: not through coercive ties imposed on him as an impotent creature by great forces that lie without; but by ties freely comprehended which he makes his own. Such ties hold his life together, so that it is not frittered away but becomes the ctuality of his possible existence. Then emembrance discloses to him its indelible oundations; and the future reveals to him he region wherein he will be held account-ıble for what he does to-day. Life grows ndefinitely vast. From moment to moment, ıe has his epoch, his realisation, his ma-:urity, his possibility. Selfhood exists as a life which wishes to become an aggregate, and as such secures valid ties only through the doer.

The melting away of historical intercon-ıexıuııs uıılıı they become a mere heap of individuals replaceable at will as functions in the apparatus, tends to disintegrate man into the brief perspective of the contemporary present. Interconnexion is then purely relative; it is forfeitable, no more than temporary, and the unconditioned is regarded as a merely unconcrete emotionalism. Amid this positivism, the sense of chaos grows. That is why, to-day, people are continually demanding new ties, arc in search of authority and of ecclesiastical faith. But even though time can work wonders, genuine ties cannot be artificially established; they must be freely engendered by the individual in community life. If the demand for ties is nothing more than a demand for an artificial order in obedience to authority and written law, the real task is being evaded, the upshot being that the unconditioned becomes impossible and freedom is paralysed. Man, therefore, is faced by two alternatives. Either he must seek to calm his self-forgetful life by a return to authoritative forms which can sanctify the apparatus for supplying the elementary needs of human life; or else, as an individual, he must grasp the very foundations by building upon which an exclusive unconditioned always determines life.

He alone can remain sincere in the world who lives by means of something genuinely acquired which he can only get by way of ties. Revolt against objective ties, therefore, as purely negational, is insincere, culminates in an eternal chaos, and is apt to persist when the purpose of the revolt no longer obtains: it is only sincere, it is only true, as the struggle of freedom for breathing-space; is justified only by the energy of an endeavour to form ties.

Historical Immersion

He only who freely enters into ties is thereby endowed with the power of revolting despairingly against himself. The unfulfillable and yet only task left for contemporary man as man, has been, in the face of Nothingness, to find the true path at his own risk, the path on which life will once more become a whole, notwithstanding all its dispersal in the restlessness of prevailing commotions. As in the days of the mythical heroes of antiquity, everything seems thrust back upon the individual.

But what is requisite is that a man, in conjunction with other men, should merge himself in the world as a historically concrete entity, so that, amid the universal homelessness, he may win for himself a new home. His remoteness from the world sets him free to immerse his being. This remoteness is not achieveable by an intellectualist abstraction, but only through a simultaneous getting into touch with all reality. The immersion is not a visible act of one who plumes himself on it, but is effected in a tranquil unconditionedness. Remoteness from the world gives an inward distinction; but immersion, on the other hand, awakens all that is human in selfhood. The former demands self-discipline; but the latter is love.

True, this historical immersion, which the unconditionedness of possible existence can achieve in virtue of ties, is not to be effected in accordance with any prescription; we can only speak of it as an appeal. It is to be encountered in the energy of veneration, as concentration in occupational work, and as exclusively in erotic love.

The energy of veneration holds firmly to the standard of what man is and can be, sustaining itself by the contemplation of great historical figures. It does not admit that what is thus disclosed to it can perish from out the world. It is loyal to whatever has been effective in its self-becoming as tradition. It comprehends that out of which its being has grown in the particular person in whose shadow it first became aware of itself; and it persists as a pious affection which never wanes. Remembrance preserves for it as an absolute claim that which no longer has any real existence in the world. Even though what the individual now encounters in life seems almost always to lack value and distinction, and even though disillusionment be heaped upon disillusionment, still he has to preserve as far as may be the standard of his own essence, to find indications for his path amid the dispersed embers of the true, and to become certain where it is that man is really man.

Work and nothing but work performed day after day will, when performed, sink forthwith into the fathomless abysses of oblivion. But it will become a manifestation of selfhood when it is actively performed under the impulsion of long views, when he who does the work works constructively, with his mind concentrated upon the continuity of his will to work and upon his awareness of its trend. Even if he be unable to escape the curse of unemployment, or if his labour power be perforce applied to ends against which his inner being revolts, still there remains to him the standard of his own essence, the question how far, even in this last poverty, he can by his own activity still achieve a nearness to things; and there endures a possibility hard to fulfil, a truth never to be demanded from others, namely the recognition, 'Although I am an anvil, as a hammer I can consummate what I must suffer.'

Exclusiveness in the love of the sexes binds two human beings together unconditionally for the whole of their future. It is unfathomably rooted in the decision which links the self to this fidelity at the moment when it really became aware of itself through the other. The negative renunciation of polygamous eroticism is the outcome of a positive which, as contemporary love, is only sincere when it includes the whole of life; and the negative determination not to squander oneself is the outcome of an uncompromising readiness for this loyalty on the part

of a possible selfhood. Without strictness in erotic matters, there is no selfhood; but eroticism becomes first truly human through the exclusiveness of unconditional ties. When desire breathes a flattering tale, when some inward monitor seems to tell us that the charm of erotic fulfilment and individual happiness are only to be found in a succession of diversified sexual experiences, the standard of true humanhood remains in the power we have to refrain from stooping to this lure, and to refuse our recognition to the demands of uncontrolled nature.

Veneration is, as it were, the foundation of selfhood; occupational activity is its possible realisation in the world; and exclusive love of an individual or an unconditional readiness for such love is the sincerity of the spirit of selfhood, without which we lapse into invincible brutalism.

Every search for the unconditioned makes man, so to say, unnatural in his severity towards himself; for the genuineness of a being that is historically irreplaceable is associated with an immense exercise of self-restraint, with a vigorous control of the will. He only who uses an unbending force of self-discipline, sustained by an urgent feeling for the possibility of true fulfilment, walks along the road proper to man as man —a road primarily entered upon under the coercion of objective authority, but now deliberately and freely chosen by the self become aware of its own responsibility.

This liberty in historical immersion, unconditioned, is, as far as the real life of the masses is concerned, associated with the existence of the authority of spiritual powers. The tension between freedom and authority is of such a kind that each would become annulled were it not for the existence of the other; liberty becoming chaos, and authority becoming despotism. Selfhood, therefore, cherishes the conservative forces against which, at one time, it had to come into its own as an individual. It wants the tradition which, for all spiritual life, is solidly embodied only in authoritative figures. Although there is no freedom in the Church, the Church, nonetheless, is a necessary condition of such liberty as is at any time attainable. It preserves the extent of spiritual value, a feeling for the inexorability of transcendental reality, the urgency of the claims which the transcendental makes upon man. Great would be the dangers attendant upon its unnoted decay to become part of the mass-apparatus in tacit alliance with unfaith and with the consequent loss of that which it still possesses competent to function once again as a source of freedom.

Man's Nobility

The question whether human worth be still possible is identical with the question whether human nobility be still possible. There is no longer any question of aristocracy in the form of the rule of a minority of persons who hold their privileged position merely in virtue of inheritance, of a stratum which is uplifted above the crowd by power, possessions, education, and a realised cultural ideal; of those who regard their dominion as the best thing for the community, and whose dominion is accepted as best by the masses. Seldom indeed could any such dominion remain for long a true aristocracy, a genuine rule by the best. Even though for a brief space an aristocracy which held its position upon sociological or biological grounds has done great work, it soon decays into the enforced rule of a minority of persons who, themselves constituting a mass, come to display the typical lineaments of the mass, namely decision by majorities, hatred of any outstanding individuals, a demand for equality, the relentless isolation or exclusion of any notable peculiarities which are not characteristic of the crowd, the persecution of the pre-eminent. Aristocracy as the dominion of a minority-mass arrogates to itself, to all who belong to this ruling minority, qualities which are but sociological substitutes for the true nobility of human existence. If again and again such an aristocracy has created a unique spiritual world, this has been owing to its origin from a true nobility and to a long-lasting process of self-education.

Sociologically there will perhaps continue to exist powerful strata, but they will be barbaric. The problem of human nobility to-day is how we are to rescue the reality of the best, who constitute a very small minority.

Such an aristocracy cannot hold itself aloof from the world, cannot realise its true self through the cultivation of personal life inspired by a romantic love for the past. It would be nothing more than the artificial segregation of a group putting forward unwarrantable claims, unless it were deliberately and with a full exercise of the conscious will to participate in the vital conditions of the epoch, wherein, in fact, its being is rooted.

The best in the sense of the nobility of human existence are not merely the talented who might be cultivated by selection, are not racial types whose existence might be determined by anthropological canons, are not persons of genius who have created works altogether out of the common—but, among all of these, are persons who are themselves, in contradistinction to those who feel in themselves a mere vacancy, who recognise no cause for which to fight, who are in flight from themselves.

To-day there is beginning the last campaign against the nobility. Instead of being carried on upon a political and sociological plane, it is conducted in the realm of mind. People would gladly turn the course of developments backward; would check that unfolding of personality which was regarded as fundamental to times which, though recent, are already forgotten. The urgency of the problem how we are best to care for the mass-man who is not willing to stand firmly on his own feet, has led to a revolt of the existential plebeianism in each one of us against the selfhood which the Godhead (though concealed) demands from us. The possibility that the individual shall come to his own self in the course of his destiny is to be definitively destroyed. The instincts of the masses make common cause—as they have often done before, but now more dangerously than ever—with religio-ecclesiastical and politico-absolutist instincts, to furnish a consecration for the universal level-ing-down in the mass-order.

This revolt is directed against what is truly noble in man. Earlier revolts, political re-volts, could succeed without ruining man; but this revolt, were it to be successful, would destroy man. For not merely during recent centuries but throughout historical times since the days of the Jewish prophets and the Greek philosophers, human existence has been shown to depend upon that which nowadays we term individuality or personal-ity. Whatever we call it, it is objectively incomprehensible, is the always unique and irreplaceable modality of selfhood.

Solidarity

When men are huddled together like dust in a heap, reality and certainty exist where friends are true friends in the factual com-munication of their manifestations and in the solidarity of personal loyalty.

What frees us from solitude is not the world, but the selfhood which enters into ties with others. Interlinkage of self-existent persons constitutes the invisible reality of the essential. Since there is no objective criterion of trustworthy selfhood, this could not be directly assembled to form influential groups. As has been well said: 'There is no trust (no organised association) of the per-sons who are the salt of the earth.' That is their weakness, inasmuch as their strength can only inhere in their inconspicuousness. There is among them a tie which does not take the form of any formal contract, but is stronger than any national, political, par-tisan, or social community, and stronger than the bonds of race. Never direct and immediate, it first becomes manifest in its consequences.

The best gift the contemporary world can give us is this *proximity* of self-existent human beings. They are, in fact, themselves the guarantee that being exists. In the world are to be found the figures of those who have influenced me as reality; not the transient creatures who were mere acquaint-ances, but the enduring personalities who made me aware of myself. There no longer exists a pantheon, but there is a place set apart in the imagination for the remem-brance of genuine human beings, of those whom we have to thank for being what we are. The persons who are decisive for us are, primarily, not those who are merely known as the 'great men' of history; but these great ones in proportion as they have been, so to say, reincarnated in the living who have exerted an effective influence upon us. The latter are for us (who have confident assur-ance of their proximity) enduring though unexacting—without idolisation and without propaganda. They are not conspicuous among those who are recognised by the masses of the public and by them regarded as the persons who count, and yet it is upon them that the proper course of affairs depends.

True nobility is not found in an isolated being. It exists in the interlinkage of inde-pendent human beings. Such are aware of their duty to discover one another, to help one another onward wherever they encounter one another, and to be ever ready for com-munication, on the watch, but without im-portunacy. Though they have entered into no formal agreement, they hold together with a loyalty which is stronger than any formal agreement could give. This solidarity extends even to an enemy when selfhood comes into genuine opposition with selfhood. Thus there is realised that which, for instance, might exist in political parties across all diver-gencies as a solidarity of the best—palpable even when it does not come to open expres-sion because there is no occasion for it or because its development is obstructed by the chances of the situation.

The solidarity of these persons has to be distinguished from the universally arising preferences dependent upon sympathy and antipathy; from the peculiar attractive force which all mediocrities exercise on one an-other because it is congenial to them to be among those who do not make lofty de-mands; and from the feeble but persistent and passive holding together of the many against the few. Whereas all of these latter categories feel themselves more secure because they exist as and encounter one another as masses and deduce their rights from mass-power, the solidarity of the self-existent is infinitely more assured in its personal trustworthiness even so far as the unobjectified and unobjectifiable minutiæ of behaviour are concerned, but is rendered insecure in the world by the weakness due to the comparatively small number of such persons and to the uncertainty of their contacts. The others, those of the mass-categories, have dozens of men as friends who are not really friends; but a member of the élite is lucky if he has but one friend.

The nobility of the self-existent spirit is widely scattered, the individuals that combine to form it being separated by great intervals. One who enters that nobility does not elect himself to it by an act of judgment, but enters it through the realisation of his own being. The unity of this dispersed élite is like the Invisible Church of a *corpus mysticum* in the anonymous chain of the friends from among whom, here and there, and through the objectivity of individual activities, one selfhood is revealed to another and perhaps distant selfhood. In this immaterial realm of mind there are, at any moment, a few indwellers who, entering into close proximity, strike flame out of one another by the intimacy of their communication. They are the origin of the loftiest soaring movement which is as yet possible in the world. They alone constitute true human beings.

Nobility and Politics

The masses first enter into movement thanks to leaders who tell them what they (the masses) want. Minorities make history. But it is improbable to-day that the masses would retain their veneration for an aristocracy even though they should recognise that the members of this aristocracy form a body of persons who have a right to rule. No doubt it is needful that to-day all those who, owing to the lack of true selfhood, are unable to think sincerely, should nevertheless acquire and busy themselves with the

grammar of thought. But the masses, having in this way learned a little, having in this way come to participate a little in thought, are continually eager to participate in political action.

The question therefore arises how a minority put into power by the momentary assent of the masses is to fashion for itself the instruments of authority whereby then, even when assent is withdrawn, it can maintain its dominion in order to impress upon the mass-man the desired stamp, though the mass-man has no true self and does not know what he really wants. Exclusive minorities, aware of their own nobility, may join forces in order to seize power in a State, doing so under the name of the vanguard, of the most advanced, of those endowed with the most energetic wills, or as the retainers of a great leader, or on the ground of privileges of blood. They range themselves like the sects of old days, exerting a vigorous selection upon their own ranks, imposing high demands, exercising strict control. They feel themselves to be an élite, striving to preserve themselves as such after acquiring power, and for this purpose training up a younger generation of successors who are to perpetuate their authority. Nevertheless, even though in their origination the energy of selfhood as the nobility of man may have played a part and may continue to play a part in the most decisive individuals, the generality of such a ruling caste soon becomes a new and by no means aristocratic mass as a minority. There seems to be really no hope—in an epoch when the influence of the mass-man is decisive—that the nobility of human existence shall persist in the form of a ruling minority.

It follows, therefore, that the problem of nobility versus the masses is no longer a specifically political problem. The two, of course, still appear as antitheses in political argumentation, but it is only the words that are the same as of old, for the things signified are heterogeneous—whether an organised minority rules in defiance of the larger masses, or the nobility works anonymously in the mass-order: whether an unjustified and therefore intolerable form of rule becomes definitively established, or whether the nobility of human existence finds scope for realisation.

False Claim to Nobility

Since nobility is manifested only in the soaring movement wherein being strives to realise itself, nobility cannot furnish its own predicate. It is not a species to which one belongs and another does not belong, but man at large in the possibility of his uplift. Because we are prone to find our satisfaction in mere life, the energy of the soaring movement is always confined to a few, but even in them not definitively so confined. They are not the representatives of the masses as the climax of mass-being, but, rather, their obscure reproach. Only as misunderstood do they become known to the masses.

The notion of equality, as apart from a mere metaphysical primary possibility, and as considered in relation to the actual life of man, is inveracious, and is therefore almost always silently rejected. The physiognomically repulsive in demeanour and aspect, hateful laughter, detestable self-satisfaction, unworthy plaintiveness, the emotional conviction that one is strong only in association with the masses—he alone who feels in tune with the base can fail to be repelled by such things. No man can contemplate his image in the mirror without some perplexity or dismay; and the more vigorously he aspires, the more sensitive will he be to the presence of other than aspiring elements in himself. The masses are to be recognised insofar as they serve, achieve, look upward towards the impulse of a possible ascent; this meaning, insofar as they themselves are that which the few are to a much more decisive degree. It is not man as an instance of life, but man as possible existence, who is worthy to be loved—as the nobility potentially present in every individual.

But if the nobility in man wishes to understand itself as a definite life and wishes to choose itself, it fortifies itself. Genuine nobility is anonymous in the form of man's claim on himself, whereas spurious nobility is a pose and the making of claims on others.

In answer, therefore, to the question whether an aristocracy is possible to-day, we can only appeal to the man who moots this question, to his own self. This is the spiritual campaign which goes on in every individual, unless he be palsied once for all.

The Philosophical Life

The nobility of human existence may be termed the philosophical life. He is ennobled who is tinged by the sincerity of a faith. One, indeed, who leaves to an authority that which he can only be himself, forfeits his nobility; but one who has trust in the Godhead does not lose himself, for he experiences the truth of his soaring movement as a movement of the finite self-existence even in failure—a truth thanks to which all that happens to him in the world cannot be anything more than he is himself.

It is primarily a matter of tradition that nobility of this sort is still demanded. We cannot achieve everything in outward activity; and as far as inward activity at the centre of human things is concerned what is needed is a word which is not an empty word but can be the awakening of that which is yet to come. The word undergoes transformation, but is the secret clue by which true human existence feels its way into the coming time. As the philosophical life, this human existence (without which the soul is lacking to the objective reality of life in the world) is the ultimate significance of philosophical thought. In it alone is systematic philosophy tested and confirmed.

Man's future resides in the modality of his philosophical life. This is not to be regarded as a prescription in accordance with which he has to guide himself, nor yet as an ideal type towards which he has to converge. The philosophical life is not, speaking generally, a unique thing, identical for all. It is like a star-shower, a myriad meteors, which, knowing not whence they come nor whither they go, shoot through life. The individual will join in the movement, to however small an extent, through the soaring of his self-existence.

The Situation of the Selfhood

Man does not arrive at an end of his development; it is an essential part of his being that, as time goes on, he should perpetually change in the progress towards an ever new destiny. From the outset, each of his configurations in the world which, for the time, he has brought into being, bears within it the germs of its own ruin.

After history has driven him out of one form of life into the next, out of one awareness of his being into another, he can remember having passed from the previous phase to the present one, but it seems to him as if he could advance no farther along the road. Never since the beginning of his days does man seem to have realised that he is faced by Nothingness, and that it is incumbent upon him through his remembrance of the past to carve out a new path for himself.

To-day, although the possibilities of an expansion of life have become immeasurable, we feel ourslves to be in so narrow a strait that our existential possibility is deprived of its breadth. Since this has been generally realised, a sense of despair has affected human activity (or, as regards those who do not realise it, an unconsciousness)— a sense of despair which, objectively regarded, might just as well herald an end as a beginning.

Man cannot evade this situation, cannot return to forms of consciousness which are unreal because they belong to the days of the past. He might tranquillise himself in the self-forgetful pleasures of life, fancying himself to have gone back to nature in the peace of timelessness. But one day iron reality would again confront him and paralyse him.

For the individual, thrust back into his own nudity, the only option to-day is to make a fresh start in conjunction with the other individuals with whom he can enter into a loyal alliance. The stirring reports of the way in which, during the last phases of the Great War when our western front was crumbling, here and there some of our men stood firm, and, as self-sacrificing individuals, effected what no command could have made them do, actually and at the last moment safeguarding the soil of the fatherland against destruction and storing up for German memories a consciousness of invincibility—these reports disclose an otherwise scarcely attained reality as a symbol of contemporary possibilities. Here was the first human existence which, in the face of Nothingness, in face of destruction, was able to realise, no longer its own world, but a world which would belong to future generations.

If we term the condition of those confronted with Nothingness 'unfaith', then the energy of the selfhood in unfaith engenders an inward activity which promotes a soaring movement in face of that which is hidden from sight. This energy scorns to shift on to objective causes that which must spring from internal freedom or fail of its effect. It regards itself as called to the highest, and lives in the tension of a cogency, in a forcible revolt against mere life, in the pliability of the relative, in the patience of one who has the capacity for waiting, in the exclusiveness of a historical tie. It knows that it is failing, and, in the act of failure, reads the cipher of being. It is the faith which is grounded in philosophy, the faith which, enabling each individual that succumbs to hand on the torch to another, unceasingly regenerates itself.

No term can be set to this movement. Perpetually it enables us to see what man is or can be. In every moment wherein a human being moves forward on his path under the spur of the unconditioned, there is in time that which annihilates time.

The past cannot tell him how he is to conduct himself. Though illuminated by the light of a remembered past, he has to decide for himself. At length it becomes clear to him what his mental situation is; in what vesture he becomes aware and assured of being; what he unconditionally wants; to whom, in the extant situation, he is to turn, and whose voice, speaking to him in the inner man, he shall listen to.

Unless he draws from these sources, the world remains for him mere enterprise. If his being is to become a true world, the man who, in community life, is to give himself up to a whole must first of all grasp himself.

Self-existence or selfhood is the condition in default of which the world as the reality of human activity, a reality permeated by an ideal, is no longer possible. Because selfhood exists only in unity with the being of the time, it is still resolutely determined to live only in this same time even though it should find itself in conflict therewith. Every act of its realisation becomes the germ, however small, of the creation of a new world.

Bibliography

Texts

Philosophy, Vol. I (1969), Vol. II (1970). Chicago: The University of Chicago Press.

Man in the Modern Age. London: Routledge & Kegan Paul, Ltd., 1952.

The Perennial Scope of Philosophy. New York: Philosophical Library, Inc., 1949.

Way to Wisdom. New Haven, Conn.: Yale University Press, 1951.

Existentialism and Humanism. New York: Moore, 1952.

Reason and Existence, New York: Noonday Books, Farrar, Straus & Giroux, Inc., 1955.

Reason and Anti-reason in Our Time. New Haven, Conn.: Yale University Press, 1952.

Philosophy and the World. Chicago: Henry Regnery Company, 1963.

Philosophy of Existence. Philadelphia: University of Pennsylvania Press, 1971.

Studies

Wallraff, C. F. *Karl Jaspers*. An Introduction to His Philosophy. Princeton, N.J.: Princeton University Press, 1970.

Grabau, R. F. "Karl Jaspers: Communication Through Transcendence," in G. A. Schrader (ed.), *Existential Philosophers: Kierkegaard to Merleau-Ponty*. New York: McGraw-Hill Book Company, 1967, pp. 109–160.

Schrag, C. O. *Existence, Existenz, and Transcendence: An Introduction to the Philosophy of Karl Jaspers*. Pittsburgh: Duquesne University Press, 1971.

Allen, E. *The Self and Its Hazards: A Guide to the Thought of Karl Jaspers*. New York: Philosophical Library, Inc., 1951.

Collins, J. *The Existentialists*. Chicago: Henry Regnery Company, 1952, chap. 3.

Tymieniecka, A. T. *Phenomenology and Science in Contemporary European Thought*. New York: Noonday Books, Farrar, Straus & Giroux, Inc., 1962, pp. 63–80.

Schilpp, P. A. (ed.). *The Philosophy of Karl Jaspers*. New York: Tudor Publishing Company, 1957.

22

MARTIN HEIDEGGER
1889–

Introduction

Martin Heidegger was born into an old Catholic family in the town of Messkirch in Baden, where his father was the sexton of St. Martin's Church. After attending the Gymnasium in Constance, Heidegger entered the seminary and, briefly, the Jesuit order, to study for the priesthood. His first philosophy book, given to him by one of his teachers, a priest at the Gymnasium (who was later to become the archbishop of Freiburg), was a doctoral dissertation on the meanings of Being in Aristotle. It was by Franz Brentano, a former priest, forerunner of the phenomenological movement, and teacher of Carl Stumpf and Edmund Husserl. Somehow that work must have made an indelible impression on the young Heidegger. The unifying theme of his entire philosophical corpus and of his life itself has ever remained the question of the meanings of Being. Heidegger soon left the Jesuits, but not the Church, and went to study philosophy under Heinrich Rickert in Freiburg, completing his Ph.D. work in 1913 and being admitted as a *Privatdozent* (lecturer) in Freiburg in 1915. The subject of his thesis and first published book was Duns Scotus' doctrine of categories and meanings (1916).

Heidegger's lectures soon began to bring him success and reputation. His several articles and books had begun to establish him as a scholar in his own right. These facts make it clear that he cannot be seen merely as a disciple of Husserl, who came to Freiburg as a full professor in 1916. Heidegger was twenty-seven (Husserl fifty-seven) when he became Husserl's assistant. By 1923, when he went from Freiburg to Marburg as a full professor himself, his reputation was already considerable, even before the sensation created by his major work. It was at Marburg in 1927 (the same year Gabriel Marcel's *Metaphysical Journal* appeared) that he "completed" and published *Sein und Zeit* (*Being and Time*) as a contribution to Husserl's phenomenological *Jahrbuch* (and dedicated to him). In 1929 he was elected Husserl's successor to the chair of philosophy at Freiburg, having already been designated by Husserl as his choice. He remained there until 1946, serving also as *Rektor* (president) from May, 1933 (when he joined the Nazi party) until February, 1934 (and these ten months have for some outweighed the other seventy-eight years). Since 1946, with occasional seminars and addresses, he has lived alone with his wife in his small ski hut on top of a mountain, near the little town of Todtnau in the Black Forest, not far from Freiburg.

Heidegger's writing has continued to the present, revealing both unity and evolution. Estimations of his significance range from calling him the greatest living philosopher to calling his work meaningless linguistic nonsense, and sometimes he is dismissed unheard because of his political stand or lack of it.

The style and content of the so-called "later" Heidegger has tended toward that of a mystic, passionately searching, first in man and then in man's words, for what he clearly has not yet found and which he therefore has consistently described in negative terms which are themselves witnesses of his failure in the continuing search. The only positive term Heidegger has for his goal is "Being," which he has, over the years of his search, sometimes identified as "truth," a hiding truth never given without some concealment, and as "presence," a hiding presence revealing itself freely and in its own good time. Heidegger's greatest sorrow is that man has given up the search and forgotten to search for Being. He has one by one rejected the names existentialist, metaphysician, ontologist, and even philosopher. For him thinking is now meditation, a lonely way, a leap. His increasingly mystic approach, mainly through the poet, who "names the holy," as well as his objection to being called an atheist, suggests reservations on the truth of his calling Nietzsche (of all unlikely candidates): "the last German philosopher who passionately sought God." From such remarks it would seem that Heidegger's relationship to theology can offer an important clue to understanding his philosophy. Nevertheless, against the suggestion that, for Heidegger, Being = God, stands his denial of any such pantheistic equation. Heidegger prefers to see his philosophical search for Being, as he said in 1960, as paralleling the nonphilosophical search for God. As philosophical thinking is to Being, so theological thinking is to God. The total Heideggerian corpus remains, in content, philosophy. What bridges beyond his philosophical content is his methodology, a hermeneutics of Being, i.e., a meditative listening to Being's self-revealing words—words that call for a response. To try to find Being again really

means actively to let Being freely continue to reveal itself as it has in the past, does in the present, and will in the future. It is to let Being's past self-revelations, especially in the privileged form of language, bring Being up to an encounter in the present through a kind of retrieval of the unsaid behind the words spoken in the past. Then out of this encounter, in the present, with Being retrieved from the past, comes a response opening out toward the future. Heidegger's emphasis on language as the "house of Being" suggests affinities, in principle at least, with the philosophical school of linguistic analysis as well as with the theological concepts of textual exegesis.

These are difficult points worth further study. The following selections, although chosen for their content, cannot avoid exemplifying Heidegger's controversial method and style as well.

PHILOSOPHICAL ANTHROPOLOGY AS THE SCIENCE OF MAN AND THE FOUNDATION OF PHILOSOPHY *

"The whole interest of my reason, whether speculative or practical, is concentrated in the three following questions:

1
What can I know?
2
What ought I do?
3
What may I hope?" [1]

These three questions, however, are those with which the three disciplines of true metaphysics, i.e., *metaphysica specialis*, are concerned. Man's knowledge is con-

cerned with nature, with that which is actually given in the broadest sense of the term (cosmology); man's activity concerns his personality and freedom (psychology); finally, man's hope is directed toward immortality as bliss, as union with God (theology).

These three fundamental interests do not determine man as a natural being but as a "citizen of the world." They constitute the object of philosophy as a "matter of world citizenship," that is, they define the domain of philosophy. Hence, Kant states in the introduction to his course of lectures on logic wherein he develops the concept of philosophy in general: "The field of philosophy as pertaining to world citizenship can be reduced to the following questions:

1
What can I know?

---

* By permission from Heidegger, M., *Kant and the Problem of Metaphysics*, James S. Churchill, translator. Indiana University Press, Bloomington, Ind., 1962.
[1] Kant, *Critique of Pure Reason* A 804, B 832f., NKS, p. 635.

2
What should I do?
3
What may I hope?
4
What is man?" ²

Here, a fourth question is added to the three previously cited. But when we consider that *psychologia rationalis* as a discipline of *metaphysica specialis* already treats of man, are we not constrained to believe that this fourth question relative to man is only superficially added to the other three and is, therefore, superfluous.

However, Kant does not simply add this fourth question to the other three, for he says: "Basically, all these can be classified under anthropology, since the first three are related to the last." ³

With this, Kant states unequivocally the real result of the laying of the foundation of metaphysics. The attempt to repeat the laying of the foundation also receives thereby a clear indication of the task involved. To be sure, Kant mentions anthropology only in a very general way. However, in the light of what has been said above, it seems true beyond a doubt that only a philosophical anthropology can undertake the laying of the foundation of true philosophy, i.e., *metaphysica specialis*. Is it not necessary to conclude, therefore, that a repetition of the Kantian laying of the foundation pursues as its specific task the development of a "philosophical anthropology" and hence that the idea of such an anthropology must be determined beforehand?

**The Idea of a
Philosophical Anthropology**

What does a philosophical anthropology include? What is anthropology in general and how does it become philosophical? "Anthropology" denotes the science of man. It comprises all the information that can be ob-

tained about the nature of man as a being composed of a body, a soul, and a mind. The domain of anthropology includes not only those given verifiable properties which distinguish the human species from plants and animals but also man's latent abilities and the differences of character, race, and sex. And inasmuch as man not only appears as a natural being but also as a being that acts and creates, anthropology must also seek to know what man as an active being can and should "make of himself." His powers and obligations depend finally on certain basic attitudes which man as such is always capable of adopting. These attitudes are called *Weltanschauungen* and the "psychology" of these includes the whole of the science of man.

Since anthropology must consider man in his somatic, biological, and psychological aspects, the results of such disciplines as characterology, psychoanalysis, ethnology, pedagogic psychology, the morphology of culture, and the typology of *Weltanschauungen* must converge in it. Hence, the content of such a science is not only vast but also fundamentally heterogeneous because of basic differences in the manner of formulating questions, the necessity of justifying the results acquired, the mode of presentation of the facts, the form of communication, and finally the essential presuppositions [of each of the component disciplines]. Insofar as all of these differences and, in certain respects, the totality of the essent as well can be related to man and thus classified under anthropology, anthropology becomes so comprehensive that the idea of such a science loses all precision.

Anthropology today, therefore, is not only the name of a discipline; the term denotes a fundamental tendency characteristic of the present position of man with regard to himself and to the totality of the essent. According to this tendency, a thing is known and understood only when it receives an anthropological explanation. Today, anthropology not only seeks the truth concerning man but also claims to have the power of deciding the meaning of truth as such.

² *Works* (Cass.), VIII, p. 343.
³ *Ibid.*, p. 344.

No other epoch has accumulated so great and so varied a store of knowledge concerning man as the present one. No other epoch has succeeded in presenting its knowledge of man so forcibly and so captivatingly as ours, and no other has succeeded in making this knowledge so quickly and so easily accessible. But also, no epoch is less sure of its knowledge of what man is than the present one. In no other epoch has man appeared so mysterious as in ours.[4]

However, is not the very fact that the problems of anthropology are characterized by this breadth and uncertainty conducive to the formation of a philosophical anthropology and to the encouragement of its further development? With the idea of a philosophical anthropology do we not acquire that discipline in which the whole of philosophy must be concentrated?

Several years ago, Max Scheler said of philosophical anthropology: "In a certain sense, all the central problems of philosophy can be reduced to the question of man and his position and metaphysical situation within the totality of Being, the world, and God."[5] But Scheler also saw, and with great clarity, that the many determinations relative to the essence of man cannot be simply packed together, as it were, in a common definition. "Man is so broad, motley, and various a thing that the definitions of him all fall a little short. He has too many sides."[6] This is why Scheler's efforts, which in his last years became more intense and more fruitful, were directed not only to the attainment of a unitary idea of man but also to the working out of the essential difficulties and complications connected with this task.[7]

Perhaps the fundamental difficulty of a philosophical anthropology lies not in the problem of obtaining a systematic unity insofar as the essential determinations of this multifarious being, man, are concerned, but in the concept of anthropology itself. This is a difficulty which even the most abundant and "spectacular" knowledge can no longer explain away.

How, then, does an anthropology become philosophical? Is it only because its knowledge acquires a degree of generality which differentiates it from empirical knowledge, although we are never able to determine precisely the degree of generality at which knowledge stops being empirical and becomes philosophical?

Certainly, an anthropology may be said to be philosophical if its method is philosophical, i.e., if it is pursued as an inquiry into the essence of man. In this case, anthropology strives to distinguish the essent we call man from plants, animals, and every other type of essent, and by this delimitation it attempts to bring to light the specific essential constitution of this particular region of the essent. Philosophical anthropology then becomes a regional ontology of man, coordinated with other ontologies with which it shares the whole domain of the essent. Thus understood, philosophical anthropology cannot be considered without further explication as the center of philosophy; above all, this last pretension cannot be based on the internal problematic of this anthropology.

It is also possible for anthropology to be philosophical if, as anthropology, it determines either the objective of philosophy or its point of departure or both at once. If the objective of philosophy lies in the development of a *Weltanschauung*, then anthropology must define the "position of man in the cosmos." And if man is accepted as that essent which, in the order of establishing an absolutely certain knowledge, is absolutely the first given and the most certain, then it is inevitable that, following the plan of a philosophy thus conceived, human subjectivity be placed at the very center of the problem. The first task is compatible with the second, and both, as modes of anthropological inquiry, can avail themselves of the method and the results of a regional ontology of man.

4 Cf. Max Scheler, *Die Stellung des Menschen im Kosmos*, 1928, p. 13f.
5 Cf. *Zur Idee des Menschen, Abhandlungen und Aufsätze*, Vol. I (1915), p. 319. In the second and third editions, the volumes have been published under the title *Vom Umsturz der Werte*.
6 *Ibid.*
7 Cf. *Die Stellung des Menschen im Kosmos*.

But just these diverse possibilities of defining the philosophical character of an anthropology are sufficient in themselves to show the indeterminateness of this idea. This indeterminateness is increased if one takes into account the diversity of the empirical-anthropological knowledge on which, at least in the beginning, every philosophical anthropology relies.

As natural and self-evident as the idea of a philosophical anthropology may appear in spite of its ambiguity, and as irresistible as the urge to reaffirm it may be in spite of these objections, still it is inevitable that "anthropologism" in philosophy will always be combated. The idea of philosophical anthropology is not only insufficiently determined, its role within philosophy as a whole remains obscure and indecisive.

The reason for these deficiencies is to be found in the limitations inherent in the idea of a philosophical anthropology. This discipline has not been explicitly justified with respect to the essence of philosophy but only with respect to the object and point of departure of philosophy as seen from without. Thus, the delimitation of this idea ends by reducing anthropology to a kind of dumping-ground for all basic philosophical problems. It is obvious that this way of considering anthropology is both superficial and, from the standpoint of philosophy, highly questionable.

But even if, in a certain sense, anthropology gathers to itself all the central problems of philosophy, why may these be reduced to the question: What is man? Is this reduction possible only if someone decides to undertake it or, on the contrary, must these problems lead back to this question? And if the latter is true, what is the basis of this necessity? Is it perhaps that the central problems of philosophy have their source in man, not only in the sense that man propounds them but also that in their intrinsic content they bear a relation to him? In what respect do all central philosophical problems find their abode in the essence of man? And, in general, which problems are essential and wherein lies their center? What is the meaning of the expression "to philosophize" if the philosophical problematic is such that it finds its abode and its center in the essence of man? . . .

It is now a matter of asking why the three questions—1. What can I know? 2. What should I do? 3. What may I hope?—"admit of being related" to the fourth? Why can "all these be classified under anthropology"? What do these three questions have in common? In what respect are they one and, hence, capable of being reduced to the fourth? How must this fourth question itself be formulated in order to include the other three and sustain them in its unity?

The most profound interest of human reason forms the connecting link between these three questions. In them are brought into question a power, a duty, and a hope of human reason.

Where there is a question concerning a power and one delimits its possibilities, there is revealed at the same time a non-power [Nicht-Können]. An omnipotent being need not ask, "What am I able to do?", i.e., "What am I not able to do?" Not only does such a being have no need to ask such a question; it is contrary to its nature to be able to ask it. This not-being-able is not a deficiency but the absence of all deficiency and all "negativity." Whosoever asks, "What am I able to do?" betrays thereby his own finitude. And whosoever is concerned in his innermost interests by such a question reveals a finitude in his innermost nature.

When an obligation is brought into question, the being who raises the question hesitates between a "yes" and a "no," thus finding himself tormented by the question of what he should do. A being fundamentally concerned with his duty understands himself through a not-yet-having-fulfilled, so that he is driven to ask himself what he should do. This not-yet of the fulfillment of something still indeterminate reveals a being who, because his duty is his most intimate interest, is basically finite.

Whenever a hope is brought into question, it is a matter of something which can be granted or denied to the one who asks. What is asked for is such that it can be expected or not expected. All expectation, however, reveals a privation, and if this privation involves the most intimate interest of human reason then the latter is affirmed to be essentially finite.

Thus, not only does human reason betray its finitude by these questions, but also its innermost interest is concerned with this finitude. It is not a question of eliminating the power, the obligation, and the hope in order to evade the finitude but, conversely, it is a question of becoming certain of this finitude in order to hold oneself in it.

Hence, finitude is not merely an acci-dental property of human reason; the fini-tude of human reason is finitization [*Ver-endlichung*], i.e., "concern" [*Sorge*] about the ability to be finite.

It follows that human reason is not finite only because it propounds these three ques-tions, but, on the contrary, it propounds these three questions because it is finite and so radically finite, indeed, that in its rationality this finitude itself is at stake. It is because these three questions concern this unique [object], i.e., finitude, that their relation admits of being established to the fourth question: What is man?

PHENOMENOLOGY OF THE PERSONAL AND THE IMPERSONAL: THE "I" AND THE "THEY" AS HUMAN EXISTENTIALS *

The Dasein-with of Others and Everyday Being-with

The answer to the question of the "who" of everyday Dasein is to be obtained by analys-ing that kind of Being in which Dasein main-tains itself proximally and for the most part. Our investigation takes its orientation from Being-in-the-world—that basic state of Da-sein by which every mode of its Being gets co-determined. If we are correct in saying that by the foregoing explication of the world, the remaining structural items of Being-in-the-world have become visible, then this must also have prepared us, in a way, for answering the question of the "who."

In our "description" of that environment which is closest to us—the work-world of the craftsman, for example,—the outcome was that along with the equipment to be found when one is at work [in Arbeit], those Others for whom the "work" ["Werk"] is destined are "encountered too." If this is ready-to-hand, then there lies in the kind of Being which belongs to it (that is, in its involve-ment) an essential assignment or reference

* From Martin Heidegger, *Being and Time*. SCM Press, London, 1962. Reprinted by permission of SCM Press.

to possible wearers, for instance, for whom it should be "cut to the figure." Similarly, when material is put to use, we encounter its producer or "supplier" as one who "serves" well or badly. When, for example, we walk along the edge of a field but "out-side it," the field shows itself as belonging to such-and-such a person, and decently kept up by him; the book we have used was bought at So-and-so's shop and given by such-and-such a person, and so forth. The boat anchored at the shore is assigned in its Being-in-itself to an acquaintance who un-dertakes voyages with it; but even if it is a "boat which is strange to us," it still is in-dicative of Others. The Others who are thus "encountered" in a ready-to-hand, environ-mental context of equipment, are not some-how added on in thought to some Thing which is proximally just present-at-hand; such "Things" are encountered from out of the world in which they are ready-to-hand for Others—a world which is always mine too in advance. In our previous analysis, the range of what is encountered within-the-world was, in the first instance, narrowed down to equipment ready-to-hand or Nature present-at-hand, and thus to entities with a character other than that of Dasein. This restriction was necessary not only for the purpose of simplifying our explication but above all because the kind of Being which belongs to the Dasein of Others, as we encounter it within-the-world, differs from readiness-to-hand and presence-at-hand. Thus Dasein's world frees entities which not only are quite distinct from equipment and Things, but which also—in accordance with their kind of Being *as Dasein* themselves— are "in" the world in which they are at the same time encountered within-the-world, and are "in" it by way of Being-in-the-world. These entities are neither present-at-hand nor ready-to-hand; on the contrary, they are *like* the very Dasein which frees them, in that *they are there too, and there with it.* So if one should want to identify the world in general with entities within-the-world, one would have to say that Dasein too is "world."

Thus in characterizing the encountering of *Others*, one is again still oriented by that Dasein which is in each case one's own. But even in this characterization does one not start by marking out and isolating the "I" so that one must then seek some way of getting over to the Others from this isolated subject? To avoid this misunderstanding we must notice in what sense we are talking about "the Others." By "Others" we do not mean everyone else but me—those over against whom the "I" stands out. They are rather those from whom, for the most part, one does *not* distinguish oneself—those among whom one is too. This Being-there-too [Auch-dasein] with them does not have the ontological character of a Being-present-at-hand-along "with" them within a world. This "with" is something of the character of Dasein; the "too" means a sameness of Being as circumspectively concernful Being-in-the-world. "With" and "too" are to be understood *existentially*, not categorically. By reason of this *with-like* [mithaften] Being-in-the-world, the world is always the one that I share with Others. The world of Dasein is a *with-world* [Mitwelt]. Being-in is *Being-with* Others. Their Being-in-themselves

within-the-world is *Dasein-with* [Mitdasein].

When Others are encountered, it is not the case that one's own subject is *proximally* present-at-hand and that the rest of the subjects, which are likewise occurrents, get discriminated beforehand and then apprehended; nor are they encountered by a primary act of looking at oneself in such a way that the opposite pole of a distinction first gets ascertained. They are encountered from out of the *world*, in which concernfully circumspective Dasein essentially dwells. Theoretically concocted "explanations" of the Being-present-at-hand of Others urge themselves upon us all too easily; but over against such explanations we must hold fast to the phenomenal facts of the case which we have pointed out, namely, that Others are encountered *environmentally*. This elemental worldly kind of encountering, which belongs to Dasein and is closest to it, goes so far that even one's *own* Dasein becomes something that it can itself proximally "come across" only when it *looks away* from "Experiences" and the "centre of its actions," or does not as yet "see" them at all. Dasein finds "itself" proximally in *what* it does, uses, expects, avoids—in those things environmentally ready-to-hand with which it is proximally *concerned*.

And even when Dasein explicitly addresses itself as "I here," this locative personal designation must be understood in terms of Dasein's existential spatiality. In interpreting this we have already intimated that this "I-here" does not mean a certain privileged point—that of an I-Thing—but is to be understood as Being-in in terms of the "yonder" of the world that is ready-to-hand—the "yonder" which is the dwelling-place of Dasein as *concern*.

W. von Humboldt has alluded to certain languages which express the "I" by "here," the "thou" by "there," the "he" by "yonder," thus rendering the personal pronouns by locative adverbs, to put it grammatically. It is controversial whether indeed the primordial signification of locative expressions is adverbial or pronominal. But this dispute loses its basis if one notes that locative adverbs have a relationship to the "I" *qua* Dasein. The "here" and the "there" and the "yonder" are primarily not mere ways of designating the location of entities present-at-hand within-the-world at positions in space; they are rather characteristics of Dasein's primordial spatiality. These supposedly locative adverbs are Dasein-designations; they have a signification which is primarily existential, not categorical. But they are not pronouns either; their signification is prior to the differentiation of locative adverbs and personal pronouns: these expressions have a Dasein-signification which is authentically spatial, and which serves as evidence that when we interpret Dasein without any theoretical distortions we can see it immediately as "Being-alongside" the world with which it concerns itself, and as Being-alongside it spatially— that is to say, as desevering and giving directionality. In the "here," the Dasein which is absorbed in its world speaks not towards itself but away from itself towards the "yonder" of something circumspectively ready-to-hand; yet it still has *itself* in view in its existential spatiality.

Dasein understands itself proximally and for the most part in terms of its world; and the Dasein-with of Others is often encountered in terms of what is ready-to-hand within-the-world. But even if Others become themes for study, as it were, in their own Dasein, they are not encountered as person-Things present-at-hand: we meet them "at work," that is, primarily in their Being-in-the-world. Even if we see the Other "just standing around," he is never apprehended as a human-Thing present-at-hand, but his "standing-around" is an existential mode of Being —an unconcerned, uncircumspective tarrying alongside everything and nothing [Verweilen bei Allem und Keinem]. The Other is encountered in his Dasein-with in the world.

The expression "Dasein," however, shows plainly that "in the first instance" this entity is unrelated to Others, and that of course it can still be "with" Others afterwards. Yet one must not fail to notice that we use the term "Dasein-with" to designate that Being for which the Others who are [die seienden

Anderen] are freed within-the-world. This Dasein-with of the Others is disclosed within-the-world for a Dasein, and so too for those who are Daseins with us [die Mitdaseienden], only because Dasein in itself is essentially Being-with. The phenomenological assertion that "Dasein is essentially Being-with" has an existential-ontological meaning. It does not seek to establish ontically that factically I am not present-at-hand alone, and that Others of my kind occur. If this were what is meant by the proposition that Dasein's Being-in-the-world is essentially constituted by Being-with, then Being-with would not be an existential attribute which Dasein, of its own accord, has coming to it from its own kind of Being. It would rather be something which turns up in every case by reason of the occurrence of Others. Being-with is an existential characteristic of Dasein even when factically no Other is present-at-hand or perceived. Even Dasein's Being-alone is Being-with in the world. The Other can *be missing* only *in* and *for* a Being-with. Being-alone is a deficient mode of Being-with; its very possibility is the proof of this. On the other hand, factical Being-alone is not obviated by the occurrence of a second example of a human being "beside" me, or by ten such examples. Even if these and more are present-at-hand, Dasein can still be alone. So Being-with and the facticity of Being with one another are not based on the occurrence together of several "subjects." Yet Being-alone "among" many does not mean that with regard to their Being they are merely present-at-hand there alongside us. Even in our Being "among them" they are *there with* us; their Dasein-with is encountered in a mode in which they are indifferent and alien. Being missing and "Being away" [Das Fehlen und "Fortsein"] are modes of Dasein-with, and are possible only because Dasein as Being-with lets the Dasein of Others be encountered in its world. Being-with is in every case a characteristic of one's own Dasein; Dasein-with characterizes the Dasein of Others to the extent that it is freed by its world for a Being-with. Only so far as one's own Dasein has the essential structure of

Being-with, is it Dasein-with as encounterable for Others.

If Dasein-with remains existentially constitutive for Being-in-the-world, then, like our circumspective dealings with the ready-to-hand within-the-world (which, by way of anticipation, we have called "concern"), it must be Interpreted in terms of the phenomenon of *care;* for as "care" the Being of Dasein in general is to be defined. Concern is a character-of-Being which Being-with cannot have as its own, even though Being-with, like concern, is a *Being towards* entities encountered within-the-world. But those entities towards which Dasein as Being-with comports itself do not have the kind of Being which belongs to equipment ready-to-hand; they are themselves Dasein. These entities are not objects of concern, but rather of *solicitude.*

Even "concern" with food and clothing, and the nursing of the sick body, are forms of solicitude. But we understand the expression "solicitude" in a way which corresponds to our use of "concern" as a term for an *existentiale.* For example, "welfare work" ["Fürsorge"], as a factical social arrangement, is grounded in Dasein's state of Being as Being-with. Its factical urgency gets its motivation in that Dasein maintains itself proximally and for the most part in the deficient modes of solicitude. Being for, against, or without one another, passing one another by, not "mattering" to one another —these are possible ways of solicitude. And it is precisely these last-named deficient and Indifferent modes that characterize everyday, average Being-with-one-another. These modes of Being show again the characteristics of inconspicuousness and obviousness which belong just as much to the everyday Dasein-with of Others within-the-world as to the readiness-to-hand of the equipment with which one is daily concerned. These Indifferent modes of Being-with-one-another may easily mislead ontological Interpretation into interpreting this kind of Being, in the first instance, as the mere Being-present-at-hand of several subjects. It seems as if only negligible variations of the same kind of Being

lie before us; yet ontologically there is an essential distinction between the "indifferent" way in which Things at random occur together and the way in which entities who are with one another do not "matter" to one another.

With regard to its positive modes, solicitude has two extreme possibilities. It can, as it were, take away "care" from the Other and put itself in his position in concern: it can *leap in* for him. This kind of solicitude takes over for the Other that with which he is to concern himself. The Other is thus thrown out of his own position; he steps back so that afterwards, when the matter has been attended to, he can either take it over as something finished and at his disposal, or disburden himself of it completely. In such solicitude the Other can become one who is dominated and dependent, even if this domination is a tacit one and remains hidden from him. This kind of solicitude, which leaps in and takes away "care," is to a large extent determinative for Being with one another, and pertains for the most part to our concern with the ready-to-hand.

In contrast to this, there is also the possibility of a kind of solicitude which does not so much leap in for the Other as *leap ahead* of him [ihm *vorausspringt*] in his existentiell potentiality-for-Being, not in order to take away his "care" but rather to give it back to him authentically as such for the first time. This kind of solicitude pertains essentially to authentic care—that is, to the existence of the Other, not to a *"what"* with which he is concerned; it helps the Other to become transparent to himself *in* his care and to become *free for* it.

Solicitude proves to be a state of Dasein's Being—one which, in accordance with its different possibilities, is bound up with its Being towards the world of its concern, and likewise with its authentic Being towards itself. Being with one another is based proximally and often exclusively upon what is a matter of common concern in such Being. A Being-with-one-another which arises [entspringt] from one's doing the same thing as someone else, not only keeps for the most part within the outer limits, but enters the mode of distance and reserve. The Being-with-one-another of those who are hired for the same affair often thrives only on mistrust. On the other hand, when they devote themselves to the same affair in common, their doing so is determined by the manner in which their Dasein, each in its own way, has been taken hold of. They thus become *authentically* bound together, and this makes possible the right kind of objectivity [die rechte Sachlichkeit], which frees the Other in his freedom for himself.

Everyday Being-with-one-another maintains itself between the two extremes of positive solicitude—that which leaps in and dominates, and that which leaps forth and liberates [vorspringend-befreienden]. It brings numerous mixed forms to maturity; to describe these and classify them would take us beyond the limits of this investigation.

Just as *circumspection* belongs to concern as a way of discovering what is ready-to-hand, solicitude is guided by *considerateness* and *forbearance*. Like solicitude, these can range through their respective deficient and Indifferent modes up to the point of *inconsiderateness* or the perfunctoriness for which difference leads the way.

The world not only frees the ready-to-hand as entities encountered within-the-world; it also frees Dasein, and the Others in their Dasein-with. But Dasein's ownmost meaning of Being is such that this entity (which has been freed environmentally) is Being-in in the same world in which, as encounterable for Others, it is there with them. We have interpreted worldhood as that referential totality which constitutes significance. In Being-familiar with this significance and previously understanding it, Dasein lets what is ready-to-hand be encountered as discovered in its involvement. In Dasein's Being, the context of references or assignments which significance implies is tied up with Dasein's ownmost Being—a Being which essentially can have no involvement, but which is rather that Being *for the sake of which* Dasein itself is as it is.

According to the analysis which we have now completed, Being with Others belongs to the Being of Dasein, which is an issue for Dasein in its very Being. Thus as Being-with, Dasein "is" essentially for the sake of Others. This must be understood as an existential statement as to its essence. Even if the particular factical Dasein does *not* turn to Others, and supposes that it has no need of them or manages to get along without them, it *is* in the way of Being-with. In Being-with, as the existential "for-the-sake-of" of Others, these have already been disclosed in their Dasein. With their Being-with, their disclosedness has been constituted beforehand; accordingly, this disclosedness also goes to make up significance—that is to say, worldhood. And, significance, as worldhood, is tied up with the existential "for-the-sake-of-which." Since the worldhood of that world in which every Dasein essentially is already, is thus constituted, it accordingly lets us encounter what is environmentally ready-to-hand as something with which we are circumspectively concerned, and it does so in such a way that together with it we encounter the Dasein-with of Others. The structure of the world's worldhood is such that Others are not proximally present-at-hand as free-floating subjects along with other Things, but show themselves in the world in their special environmental Being, and do so in terms of what is ready-to-hand in that world.

Being-with is such that the disclosedness of the Dasein-with of Others belongs to it; this means that because Dasein's Being is Being-with, its understanding of Being already implies the understanding of Others. This understanding, like any understanding, is not an acquaintance derived from knowledge about them, but a primordially existential kind of Being, which, more than anything else, makes such knowledge and acquaintance possible. Knowing oneself [Sichkennen] is grounded in Being-with, which understands primordially. It operates proximally in accordance with the kind of Being which is closest to us—Being-in-the-world as Being-with; and it does so by an acquaintance with that which Dasein, along with the

Others, comes across in its environmental circumspection and concerns itself with— an acquaintance in which Dasein understands. Solicitous concern is understood in terms of what we are concerned with, and along with our understanding of it. Thus in concernful solicitude the Other is proximally disclosed.

But because solicitude dwells proximally and for the most part in the deficient or at least the Indifferent modes (in the indifference of passing one another by), the kind of knowing-oneself which is essential and closest, demands that one become acquainted with oneself. And when, indeed, one's knowing-oneself gets lost in such ways as aloofness, hiding oneself away, or putting on a disguise, Being-with-one-another must follow special routes of its own in order to come close to Others, or even to "see through them" ["hinter sie" zu kommen].

But just as opening oneself up [Sichoffenbaren] or closing oneself off is grounded in one's having Being-with-one-another as one's kind of Being at the time, and indeed *is* nothing else but this, even the explicit disclosure of the Other in solicitude grows only out of one's primarily Being with him in each case. Such a disclosure of the Other (which is indeed thematic, but not in the manner of theoretical psychology) easily becomes the phenomenon which proximally comes to view when one considers the theoretical problematic of understanding the "psychical life of Others" ["fremden Seelenlebens"]. In this phenomenally "proximal" manner it thus presents a way of Being with one another understandingly; but at the same time it gets taken as that which, primordially and "in the beginning," constitutes Being towards Others and makes it possible at all. This phenomenon, which is none too happily designated as *"empathy"* [*"Einfühlung"*], is then supposed, as it were, to provide the first ontological bridge from one's own subject, which is given proximally as alone, to the other subject, which is proximally quite closed off.

Of course Being towards Others is ontologically different from Being towards Things which are present-at-hand. The entity which is "other" has itself the same kind of Being as Dasein. In Being with and towards Others, there is thus a relationship of Being [Seinsverhältnis] from Dasein to Dasein. But it might be said that this relationship is already constitutive for one's own Dasein, which, in its own right, has an understanding of Being, and which thus relates itself towards Dasein. The relationship-of-Being which one has towards Others would then become a Projection of one's own Being-towards-oneself "into something else." The Other would be a duplicate of the Self.

But while these deliberations seem obvious enough, it is easy to see that they have little ground to stand on. The presupposition which this argument demands—that Dasein's Being towards an Other is its Being towards itself—fails to hold. As long as the legitimacy of this presupposition has not turned out to be evident, one may still be puzzled as to how Dasein's relationship to itself is thus to be disclosed to the Other as Other.

Not only is Being towards Others an autonomous, irreducible relationship of Being: this relationship, as Being-with, is one which, with Dasein's Being, already is. Of course it is indisputable that a lively mutual acquaintanceship on the basis of Being-with, often depends upon how far one's own Dasein has understood itself at the time; but this means that it depends only upon how far one's essential Being with Others has made itself transparent and has not disguised itself. And that is possible only if Dasein, as Being-in-the-world, already is with Others. "Empathy" does not first constitute Being-with; only on the basis of Being-with does "empathy" become possible: it gets its motivation from the unsociability of the dominant modes of Being-with.

But the fact that "empathy" is not a primordial existential phenomenon, any more than is knowing in general, does not mean that there is nothing problematical about it. The special hermeneutic of empathy will have to show how Being-with-one-another and Dasein's knowing of itself are led astray and obstructed by the various possibilities of Being which Dasein itself possesses, so that a genuine "understanding" gets suppressed, and Dasein takes refuge in substitutes; the possibility of understanding the stranger correctly presupposes such a hermeneutic as its positive existential condition. Our analysis has shown that Being-with is an existential constituent of Being-in-the-world. Dasein-with has proved to be a kind of Being which entities encountered within-the-world have as their own. So far as Dasein *is* at all, it has Being-with-one-another as its kind of Being. This cannot be conceived as a summative result of the occurrence of several "subjects." Even to come across a number of "subjects" [einer Anzahl von "Subjekten"] becomes possible only if the Others who are concerned proximally in their Dasein-with are treated merely as "numerals" ["Nummer"]. Such a number of "subjects" gets discovered only by a definite Being-with-and-towards-one-another. This "inconsiderate" Being-with "reckons" ["rechnet"] with the Others without seriously "counting on them" ["auf sie zählt"], or without even wanting to "have anything to do" with them.

One's own Dasein, like the Dasein-with of Others, is encountered proximally and for the most part in terms of the with-world with which we are environmentally concerned. When Dasein is absorbed in the world of its concern—that is, at the same time, in its Being-with towards Others—it is not itself. *Who* is it, then, who has taken over Being as everyday Being-with-one-another?

Everyday Being-one's-self and the "They"

The *ontologically* relevant result of our analysis of Being-with is the insight that the "subject character" of one's own Dasein and that of Others is to be defined existentially —that is, in terms of certain ways in which one may be. In that with which we concern ourselves environmentally the Others are encountered as what they are; they *are* what they do [sie *sind* das, was sie betreiben].

In one's concern with what one has taken hold of, whether with, for, or against, the Others, there is constant care as to the way one differs from them, whether that difference is merely one that is to be evened out, whether one's own Dasein has lagged behind the Others and wants to catch up in relationship to them, or whether one's Dasein already has some priority over them and sets out to keep them suppressed. The care about this distance between them is disturbing to Being-with-one-another, though this disturbance is one that is hidden from it. If we may express this existentially, such Being-with-one-another has the character of *distantiality* [*Abständigkeit*]. The more inconspicuous this kind of Being is to everyday Dasein itself, all the more stubbornly and primordially does it work itself out.

But this distantiality which belongs to Being-with, is such that Dasein, as everyday Being-with-one-another, stands in *subjection* [*Botmässigkeit*] to Others. It itself *is* not; its Being has been taken away by the Others. Dasein's everyday possibilities of Being are for the Others to dispose of as they please. These Others, moreover, are not *definite* Others. On the contrary, any Other can represent them. What is decisive is just that inconspicuous domination by Others which has already been taken over unawares from Dasein as Being-with. One belongs to the Others oneself and enhances their power. "The Others" whom one thus designates in order to cover up the fact of one's belonging to them essentially oneself, are those who proximally and for the most part *"are there"* in everyday Being-with-one-another. The "who" is not this one, not that one, not oneself [man selbst], not some people [einige], and not the sum of them all. The "who" is the neuter, *the "they"* [*das Man*].

We have shown earlier how in the environment which lies closest to us, the public "environment" already is ready-to-hand and is also a matter of concern [mitbesorgt]. In utilizing public means of transport and in making use of information services such as the newspaper, every Other is like the next. This Being-with-one-another dissolves one's own Dasein completely into the kind of Being of "the Others," in such a way, indeed, that the Others, as distinguishable and explicit, vanish more and more. In this inconspicuousness and unascertainability, the real dictatorship of the "they" is unfolded. We take pleasure and enjoy ourselves as *they* [*man*] take pleasure; we read, see, and judge about literature and art as *they* see and judge; likewise we shrink back from the "great mass" as *they* shrink back; we find "shocking" what *they* find shocking. The "they," which is nothing definite, and which all are, though not as the sum, prescribes the kind of Being of everydayness.

The "they" has its own ways in which to be. That tendency of Being-with which we have called "distantiality" is grounded in the fact that Being-with-one-another concerns itself as such with *averageness*, which is an existential characteristic of the "they." The "they," in its Being, essentially makes an issue of this. Thus the "they" maintains itself factically in the averageness of that which belongs to it, of that which it regards as valid and that which it does not, and of that to which it grants success and that to which it denies it. In this averageness with which it prescribes what can and may be ventured, it keeps watch over everything exceptional that thrusts itself to the fore. Every kind of priority gets noiselessly suppressed. Overnight, everything that is primordial gets glossed over as something that has long been well known. Everything gained by a struggle becomes just something to be manipulated. Every secret loses its force. This care of averageness reveals in turn an essential tendency of Dasein which we call the "levelling down" [*Einebnung*] of all possibilities of Being.

Distantiality, averageness, and levelling down, as ways of Being for the "they," constitute what we know as "publicness" ["die Offentlichkeit"]. Publicness proximally controls every way in which the world and Dasein get interpreted, and it is always right —not because there is some distinctive and primary relationship-of-Being in which it is related to "Things," or because it avails

itself of some transparency on the part of Dasein which it has explicitly appropriated, but because it is insensitive to every difference of level and of genuineness and thus never gets to the "heart of the matter" ["auf die Sachen"]. By publicness everything gets obscured, and what has thus been covered up gets passed off as something familiar and accessible to everyone.

The "they" is there alongside everywhere [ist überall dabei], but in such a manner that it has always stolen away whenever Dasein presses for a decision. Yet because the "they" presents every judgment and decision as its own, it deprives the particular Dasein of its answerability. The "they" can, as it were, manage to have "them" constantly invoking it. It can be answerable for everything most easily, because it is not someone who needs to vouch for anything. It "was" always the "they" who did it, and yet it can be said that it has been "no one." In Dasein's everydayness the agency through which most things come about is one of which we must say that "it was no one."

Thus the particular Dasein in its everydayness is *disburdened* by the "they." Not only that; by thus disburdening it of its Being, the "they" accommodates Dasein [kommt . . . dem Dasein entgegen] if Dasein has any tendency to take things easily and make them easy. And because the "they" constantly accommodates the particular Dasein by disburdening it of its Being, the "they" retains and enhances its stubborn dominion.

Everyone is the other, and no one is himself. The *"they,"* which supplies the answer to the question of the *"who"* of everyday Dasein, is the *"nobody"* to whom every Dasein has already surrendered itself in Being-among-one-other [Untereinandersein].

In these characters of Being which we have exhibited—everyday Being-among-one-another, distantiality, averageness, levelling down, publicness, the disburdening of one's Being, and accommodation—lies that "constancy" of Dasein which is closest to us. This "constancy" pertains not to the enduring Being-present-at-hand of something, but rather to Dasein's kind of Being as Being-with. Neither the Self of one's own Dasein nor the Self of the Other has as yet found itself or lost itself as long as it is [seiend] in the modes we have mentioned. In these modes one's way of Being is that of inauthenticity and failure to stand by one's Self. To be in this way signifies no lessening of Dasein's facticity, just as the "they," as the "nobody," is by no means nothing at all. On the contrary, in this kind of Being, Dasein is an *ens realissimum*, if by "Reality" we understand a Being with the character of Dasein.

Of course, the "they" is as little present-at-hand as Dasein itself. The more openly the "they" behaves, the harder it is to grasp, and the slier it is, but the less is it nothing at all. If we "see" it ontico-ontologically with an unprejudiced eye, it reveals itself as the "Realest subject" of everydayness. And even if it is not accessible like a stone that is present-at-hand, this is not in the least decisive as to its kind of Being. One may neither decree prematurely that this "they" is "really" nothing, nor profess the opinion that one can Interpret this phenomenon ontologically by somehow "explaining" it as what results from taking the Being-present-at-hand-together of several subjects and then fitting them together. On the contrary, in working out concepts of Being one must direct one's course by these phenomena, which cannot be pushed aside.

Furthermore, the "they" is not something like a "universal subject" which a plurality of subjects have hovering above them. One can come to take it this way only if the Being of such "subjects" is understood as having a character other than that of Dasein, and if these are regarded as cases of a genus of occurrents—cases which are factually present-at-hand. With this approach, the only possibility ontologically is that everything which is not a case of this sort is to be understood in the sense of genus and species. The "they" is not the genus to which the individual Dasein belongs, nor can we come across it in such entities as an abiding characteristic. That even the traditional logic fails us when confronted with these

phenomena, is not surprising if we bear in mind that it has its foundation in an ontology of the present-at-hand—an ontology which, moreover, is still a rough one. So no matter in how many ways this logic may be improved and expanded, it cannot in principle be made any more flexible. Such reforms of logic, oriented towards the "humane sciences," only increase the ontological confusion.

The "they" is an existentiale; and as a primordial phenomenon, it belongs to Dasein's positive constitution. It itself has, in turn, various possibilities of becoming concrete as something characteristic of Dasein [seiner daseinsmässigen Konkretion]. The extent to which its dominion becomes compelling and explicit may change in the course of history.

The Self of everyday Dasein is the *they-self*, which we distinguish from the *authentic Self*—that is, from the Self which has been taken hold of in its own way [eigens ergriffenen]. As they-self, the particular Dasein has been *dispersed* into the "they," and must first find itself. This dispersal characterizes the "subject" of that kind of Being which we know as concernful absorption in the world we encounter as closest to us. If Dasein is familiar with itself as they-self, this means at the same time that the "they" itself prescribes that way of interpreting the world and Being-in-the-world which lies closest. Dasein is for the sake of the "they" in an everyday manner, and the "they" itself Articulates the referential context of significance. When entities are encountered, Dasein's world frees them for a totality of involvements with which the "they" is familiar, and within the limits which have been established with the "they's" averageness. *Proximally*, factical Dasein is in the with-world, which is discovered in an average way. *Proximally*, it is not "I," in the sense of my own Self, that "am," but rather the Others, whose way is that of the "they." In terms of the "they," and as the "they," I am "given" proximally to "myself" [mir "selbst"]. Proximally Dasein is "they," and for the most part it remains so. If Dasein discovers the world in its own way [eigens] and brings it close, if it discloses to itself its own authentic Being, then this discovery of the "world" and this disclosure of Dasein are always accomplished as a clearing-away of concealments and obscurities, as a breaking up of the disguises with which Dasein bars its own way.

With this Interpretation of Being-with and Being-one's-Self in the "they," the question of the "who" of the everydayness of Being-with-one-another is answered. These considerations have at the same time brought us a concrete understanding of the basic constitution of Dasein: Being-in-the-world, in its everydayness and its averageness, has become visible.

Bibliography

Texts

Kant and the Problem of Metaphysics. Bloomington, Ind.: Indiana University Press, 1962.

Being and Time. London: SCM Press, 1962.

"Remembrance of the Poet," "Hölderlin and Essence of Poetry," "On the Essence of Truth," and "What Is Metaphysics?"—all in W. Brock (ed.), *Existence and Being.* Chicago: Henry Regnery Company, 1949.

The Question of Being. New York: Twayne, 1958.

An Introduction to Metaphysics. New Haven, Conn.: Yale University Press, 1958.

Discourse on Thinking. New York: Harper & Row Publishers, Incorporated, 1966.

What Is Philosophy? New Haven, Conn.: College & University Press, Services, Inc., n.d.

Studies

Collins, J. *The Existentialists.* Chicago: Henry Regnery Company, 1952, chap. 5.

Langan, T. *The Meaning of Heidegger.* New York: Columbia University Press, 1958.

Richardson, W. *Heidegger: Through Phenomenology to Thought.* The Hague: Martinus Nijhoff, 1963.

Spiegelberg, H. *The Phenomenological Movement.* The Hague: Martinus Nijhoff, 1965, 2d ed., vol. 1, pp. 271–357.

Thévenaz, P. *What Is Phenomenology?* Chicago: Quadrangle Books, 1962, pp. 53–67.

Tymieniecka, A. T. *Phenomenology and Science in Contemporary European Thought.* New York: Noonday Books, Farrar, Straus & Giroux, Inc., 1962, pp. 117–137.

Vycinas, V. *Earth and Gods.* The Hague: Martinus Nijhoff, 1961.

Harries, K. "Martin Heidegger: The Search for Meaning," in G. A. Schrader (ed.), *Existential Philosophers: Kierkegaard to Merleau-Ponty.* New York: McGraw-Hill Book Company, 1967, pp. 161–208.

Schmitt, R. *Martin Heidegger on Being Human.* An Introduction to *Sein und Zeit.* New York: Random House, Inc., 1969.

Versényi, L. *Heidegger, Being and Truth.* New Haven, Conn.: Yale University Press, 1965.

Frings, M. S. (ed.). *Heidegger and the Quest for Truth.* Chicago: Quadrangle Books, 1968.

Rahner, K. "Introduction to the Concept of Existential Philosophy in Heidegger," in *Philosophy Today,* vol. 13 (1969), pp. 126–137.

23

Introduction

Gabriel Marcel was the only child of a highly cultivated agnostic Catholic father who served for a time as French Minister in Stockholm and later as director of fine arts at the Bibliothèque National and at the National Galleries. His mother died when he was four, and he was brought up by her sister, who, though converted to Protestantism, nevertheless remained an agnostic. Marcel describes his childhood and youth as privileged, free, and refreshed with frequent travel, but cramped, fettered, and filled with hateful recollections of the "abstract and inhuman school system." The clash of his free personal life with the object-oriented school years seems to have been decisive for his later inclinations toward the theater as a privileged form of expression (he has published fifteen of his twenty dramas), toward music (which he has called his "true vocation"), and against systematizing expression in philosophy. His personality can be felt as a powerful presence in his writings and provides their strongest and perhaps their sole claim to a unifying principle. Marcel recognized this early. After trying to reduce his diaries to some system, he gave it up as impossible, doing so chiefly because it ran against the grain of his temperament and his whole personality rebelled. He then published his *Metaphysical Journal,* just as he had written it, in 1927, the year of Heidegger's *Being and Time.* Much later, when delivering the Gifford Lectures in 1949 and 1950, he again attempted with limited·success to present his major themes systematically. And thus we witness something unique in the history of philosophy: Marcel giving his Jesuit friend Roger Troisfontaines his blessing to work from the latter's outline of his thought and asking him to prepare its comprehensive exposition. This Troisfontaines did in *De l'existence à l'être,* which appeared in two volumes in 1952.

Profiting from the lesson of such attempts, we can perhaps be content to mention some of these major themes without trying to impose any necessarily arbitrary sequence.

The *primordial given* for Marcel's phenomenology of man is not the Cartesian "I think" nor the existentialist "I exist" but the incarnate interpersonal "we are." Philosophical anthropology begins as social anthropology: existence is coexistence. Marcel, in his famous phenomenology of being and having, opened and explored a theme later taken up by Sartre and Merleau-Ponty, that of the body as a content of experience. Here the theme is human existence as an ambiguous incarnation in a body. Existence and embodiment do not coincide, however. One's relationships to oneself and one's body are ambiguous, an ambiguity that language both reveals and witnesses when we try to describe those relationships in terms of *being and having.* Another original theme which Marcel has pioneered in existentialist philosophy is *engagement* or *commitment,* considered not as an accidental determination but as an "existential," a term meaning an essential structure of human nature. It is closely related to one of Marcel's best-known themes, *participation:* man is no mere bystander, onlooker, or spectator in the world, but is inserted in being, most primordially through *perception.* One of the richest areas of phenomenological study advanced by Marcel is *encounter,* as contrasted with mere meeting. Encounter can be seen initially as prepersonal meeting. It is in the loving encounter that the potential is actualized. Encounter, then, as the locus of the interpersonal "we," precedes differentiation into the personal "I" and the personal "Thou." Encounter is thus the creative source of personhood in the sense of being the relationship requisite for the actualization of what would otherwise remain merely latent human potentialities. It is what Alfred

Schutz would call the "face to face" relationship of consociates which can result in the "We-relationship." Some characteristics of this interpersonal behavior are *availability* (*disponibilité*), *creative fidelity*, and re-*sponse* to the other's *appeal* (*invocation*) based on *hope*, expressed by a *promise*, and productive of a special way by which persons can "belong" to one another. Some of these themes appear in the following selection.

ENGAGEMENT AND AVAILABILITY AS INTERPERSONAL EXISTENTIALS *

If we forget, as I think we should, the theories and definitions of philosophy in order to learn all we can from direct experiences, we are led to the conclusion that the act which establishes the *ego*, or rather by which the *ego* establishes itself, is always identically the same: it is this act which we must try to grasp without allowing ourselves to be led astray by the fictitious speculations which throughout human history have been accumulating in this field. I think that we should employ current forms of ordinary language which distort our experiences far less than the elaborate expressions in which philosophical language is crystallised. The most elementary example, the closest to earth, is also the most instructive. Take, for instance, the child who brings his mother flowers he has just been gathering in the meadow. "Look," he cries, "I picked these." Mark the triumph in his voice and above all the gesture, simple and rapid enough, perhaps, which accompanies his announcement. The child points himself out for admiration and gratitude: "It was I, I who am with you here, who picked these lovely flowers, don't go thinking it was Nanny or my sister; it was I and *no one else.*" This exclusion is of the greatest importance: it seems that the child wants to attract attention almost materially. He claims enthusiastic praise, and it would be the most calamitous thing in the world if by mistake it was bestowed on someone who did not deserve it. Thus the child draws attention to himself, he offers himself to the other in order to receive a special tribute. I do not believe it is possible to insist too much upon the presence of the other, or more exactly others, involved in the statement: "It is I who . . ." It implies that "There are, on the one hand, those who are excluded about whom you must be careful not to think, and, on the other, there is the *you* to whom the child speaks and whom he wants as a witness."

The same affirmation on the part of an adult would be less openly advertised; it would be enveloped in a halo of false modesty where the complexities of the game of social hypocrisy are discernible. Think of the amateur composer who has just been singing an unknown melody in some drawing-room. People exclaim: "What is that? Is it an unpublished song by Fauré?" etc. "No, as a matter of fact, it is my own . . ." etc. If we leave on one side, as we should, all the elaborations of social convention, we shall recognise the fundamental identity of the act. The difference has only to do with the attitude adopted or simulated regarding the expected tribute.

To go on with our analysis, we observe that this ego here before us, considered as a centre of magnetism, cannot be reduced to certain parts which can be specified such as "my body, my hands, my brain"; it is a global presence—a presence which gains glory from the magnificent bouquet which I myself have picked, which I have brought you; and I do not know whether you should admire more the artistic taste of which it is a proof or the generosity which I have shown in giving it to you, I, who might so easily have kept it for myself. Thus the beauty of

* From Gabriel Marcel, *Homo Viator*, pp. 13–26, 1962. Reprinted by permission of Harper & Row, Publishers, Incorporated, New York, Harper Torchbooks, and M. Fernand Aubier, Paris.

the object is in a fashion reflected upon me, and if I appeal to you, then, I repeat, I do so as to a qualified witness whom I invite to wonder at the *whole* we form—the bouquet and I.

But we must not fail to notice that the admiration which I expect from you, which you give me, can only confirm and heighten the satisfaction I feel in recognising my own merits. Why should we not conclude from this that the *ego here present* certainly involves a reference to someone else, only this other someone is treated as a foil or amplifier for my own self-satisfaction.

"But," you will object, "self-satisfaction, self-confidence, self-love: all this takes for granted a self already established which it is necessary to define." I think that here we must be careful not to fall into a trap of language. This pre-existent *ego* can only be postulated, and if we try to describe it, we can only do so negatively, by way of exclusion. On the other hand it is very instructive to give a careful account of the act which establishes what I call myself, the act, for instance, by which I attract the attention of others so that they may praise me, maybe, or blame me, but at all events so that they notice me. In every case *I produce* myself, in the etymological sense of the word, that is to say I put myself forward.

Other examples bring us to the same conclusion. Let us keep to the level of a child's experience. A little stranger stretches out his hand to take the ball which I have left on the ground; I jump up; the ball is mine. Here again the relationship with others is at the root of the matter, but it takes the form of an order: *Do not touch.* I have no hesitation in saying that the instantaneous claiming of our own property is one of the most significant of our experiences. Here again I "produce" myself. I warn the other person that he must conform his conduct to the rule I have given him. It can be observed without any great subtlety that the sense of possession was already implicit in the previous examples, only it was possession of a virtue rather than a thing. Here, however, more clearly than just now, the *ego* is seen as a

global and indefinable presence. I, here before you, possess the ball, perhaps I might consent to lend it to you for a few moments, but you must quite understand that it is I who am very kindly lending it to you and that, in consequence, I can take it back from you at any minute if I so wish; I the despot, I the autocrat.

I have used the term presence several times; now I will try as far as possible to define what I mean by it. Presence denotes something rather different and more comprehensive than the fact of just being there; to be quite exact one should not actually say that an object is present. We might say that presence is always dependent on an experience which is at the same time irreducible and vague, the sense of existing, of being in the world. Very early in the development of a human being this consciousness of existing, which we surely have no reason to doubt is common also to animals, is linked up with the urge to make ourselves *recognised* by some other person, some witness, helper, rival or adversary who, whatever may be said, is needed to integrate the self, but whose place in the field of consciousness can vary almost indefinitely.

If this analysis as a whole is correct, it is necessary to see what I call my *ego* in no way as an isolated reality, whether it be an element or a principle, but as an *emphasis* which I give, not of course to the whole of my experience, but to that part of it which I want to safeguard in a special manner against some attack or possible infringement. It is in this sense that the impossibility of establishing any precise frontiers of the *ego* has been often and rightly pointed out. This becomes clear as soon as one understands that the *ego* can never be thought of as a portion of space. On the other hand, it cannot be repeated often enough that, after all, the self is *here, now;* or at any rate there are such close affinities between these facts that we really cannot separate them. I own that I cannot in any way conceive how a being for whom there was neither a here nor a now could nevertheless appear as "I." From this it follows paradoxically enough that the emphasis of which I have spoken cannot avoid tending to conceive of itself as an enclosure, that is to say as exactly the thing it is not; and it is only on deeper reflection that it will be possible to detect what is deceptive in this localisation.

I spoke of an enclosure, but it is an enclosure which moves, and what is even more essential, it is vulnerable: *a highly sensitive enclosure.* The incomparable analyses of Meredith in *The Egoist* would fit in very naturally here. Nobody, perhaps, has ever gone so far in the analysis of a susceptibility for which the term self-love is manifestly incomplete. Actually, this susceptibilty is rooted in anguish rather than in love. Burdened with myself, plunged in this disturbing world, sometimes threatening me, sometimes my accomplice, I keep an eager lookout for everything emanating from it which might either soothe or ulcerate the wound I bear within me, which is my *ego*. This state is strikingly analogous to that of a man who has an abscess at the root of his tooth and who experiments cautiously with heat and cold, acid and sugar, to get relief. What then is this anguish, this wound? The answer is that it is above all the experience of being torn by a contradiction between the all which I aspire to possess, to annex, or, still more absurd, to monopolise, and the obscure consciousness that after all I am nothing but an empty void; for, still, I can affirm nothing about myself which would be really myself; nothing, either, which would be permanent; nothing which would be secure against criticism and the passage of time. Hence the craving to be confirmed from outside, by another; this paradox, by virtue of which even the most self-centred among us looks to others and only to others for his final investiture.

This contradiction is constantly appearing here. Nowhere does it show up in greater relief than in the attitude which our everyday language so aptly terms pose. The *poseur* who seems only to be preoccupied with others is in reality entirely taken up with himself. Indeed, the person he is with only interests him in so far as he is likely to form a favourable picture of him which in turn he will receive back. The other person reflects him, returns to him this picture which he finds so enchanting. It would be interesting to find out what social climate is most favourable for posing, and what on the other hand are the conditions most likely to discourage it. It might generally be said that in a virile atmosphere posing is unmasked immediately and made fun of. At school or in barracks the *poseur* has practically no chance of success. A consensus of opinion is almost certain to be formed against him, his companions see through him at once, each one of them accuses him of infringing a certain implicit pact, that of the little community to which he belongs. It is not easy to formulate it exactly, but it is a distinct perception of the incompatibility between a certain reality in which each one participates and this play-acting which degrades and betrays it. On the other hand, the more artificial, unreal and, in a certain sense, effeminate the environment, the less the incompatibility will be felt. This is because in such circles everything depends upon opinions and appearances, from which it follows that seduction and flattery have the last word.

Now, posing is a form of flattery, a manner of paying court while seeming to obtrude oneself. Beneath it all we invariably find self-love and, I might add, pretension. This last, by its very ambiguity, is particularly instructive. To pretend is not only to aspire or to aim high, it is also to simulate, and actually there is simulation in all posing. To realise this we only need to recall what affectation is in all its forms. From the moment that I become preoccupied about the effect I want to produce on the other person, my every act, word and attitude loses its authenticity; and we all know what even a studied or affected simplicity can be.

Here, however, we must note something of capital importance. From the very fact that I treat the other person merely as a means of resonance or an amplifier, I tend to consider him as a sort of apparatus which I can, or think I can, manipulate, or of which I can dispose at will. I form my own ideas of him and, strangely enough, this idea can become a substitute for the real person, a shadow to which I shall come to refer my acts and words. The truth of the matter is that to pose is always to pose before oneself. "To play to the gallery . . . ," we are accustomed to say, but the gallery is still the self. To be more exact, we might say that the other person is the provisional and as it were accessory medium, through which I can arrive at forming a certain image, or idol of myself; the work of stylisation by which each of us fashions this image might be traced step by step. This work is helped by social failure as much as by success. When he who poses is scoffed at by his companions, he decides, more often than not, that he has to do with imbeciles and shuts himself up with jealous care in a little private sanctuary where he can be alone with his idol.

Here we are in line with the merciless analyses to which the anti-romantics have subjected the cult of the *ego*. "But," you may ask, "should we not take care not to go too far? Is there not a normal condition of the *ego* which should not be confused with its abnormalities or perversions?" The question is a very delicate one. It must in no way be mistaken for a problem of technical philosophy, with which we are not dealing here and which involves the question of the very existence of a superior principle of unity which guides our personal development. What concerns us here is only to know under what conditions I become conscious of myself as a person. It must be repeated that these conditions are essentially social. There is, in particular, every reason to think that the system of perpetual competition to which the individual is subjected in the world of to-day cannot fail to increase and exasperate this consciousness of the *ego*. I have no hesitation in saying that if we want to fight effectively against individualism in its most harmful form, we must find some way of breaking free from the asphyxiating atmosphere of examinations and competition in which our young people are struggling. "I must win, not you! I must get above you!"

We can never insist enough upon how the real sense of fellowship which shows itself in such striking contrast among any team worthy of the name, has been rendered weak and anaemic by the competitive system. This system does in fact encourage each one to compare himself with his neighbour, to give himself a mark or a number by which he can be measured against him. Moreover, we must notice a thing which is essential in our argument: such a system, which makes self-consciousness or, if you prefer to call it so, self-love ten times worse, is at the same time the most depersonalising process possible; for the thing in us which has real value cannot be judged by comparison, having no common measure with anything else. Unfortunately, however, it seems as though people have taken a delight in accumulating every possible confusion concerning this point, and I have no hesitation in saying that the responsibilities of those who claim to celebrate the cult of the individual are overwhelming. Maybe there is no more fatal error than that which conceives of the *ego* as the secret abode of originality. To get a better idea of this we must here introduce the wrongly discredited notion of gifts. The best part of my personality does not belong to me. I am in no sense the owner, only the trustee. Except in the realm of metaphysics, with which we are not dealing to-day, there is no sense in enquiring into the origin of these gifts. On the other hand, it is very important to know what my attitude should be with regard to them. If I consider myself as their guardian, responsible for their fruitfulness, that is to say if I recognise in them a call or even perhaps a question to which I must respond, it will not occur to me to be proud about them and to parade them before an audience, which, I repeat, really means myself. Indeed, if we come to think of it, there is nothing in me which cannot or should not be regarded as a gift. It is pure fiction to imagine a pre-existent self on whom these gifts were bestowed in virtue of certain rights, or as a recompense for some former merit.

This surely means that I must puncture

the illusion, infinitely persistent it is true, that I am possessed of unquestionable privileges which make me the centre of my universe, while other people are either mere obstructions to be removed or circumvented, or else those echoing amplifiers, whose purpose is to foster my self-complacency. I propose to call this illusion moral egocentricity, thus marking clearly how deeply it has become rooted in our very nature. In fact, just as any notions we may have of cosmography do not rid us from the immediate impression that the sun and stars go round the earth, so it is not possible for us to escape completely here below from the preconceived idea which makes each one tend to establish himself as the centre around which all the rest have no other function but to gravitate. It is equally true that this idea or prejudice, no matter how becomingly it may be adorned in the case of great egoists, appears, when we come down to a final analysis, to be merely another expression of a purely biological and animal claim. Moreover, the ill-starred philosophies which, particularly in the nineteenth century, attempted to justify this position not only marked a retrogression as far as the secular wisdom of civilised humanity was concerned, but, it cannot be disputed for a moment, have directly helped to precipitate mankind into the chaos where it is struggling at the present time.

Does it, however, follow that this *egolatry*, this idolatry of the self, must necessarily be met by a rationalistic and impersonal doctrine? Nothing, I believe, would be farther from the truth. Whenever men have tried to put such a doctrine into practice we must own that it has proved itself extremely disappointing. To be more exact, such an experiment has never been and never could be effective. Actually it is of the very essence of this doctrine that it cannot be really put into practice, except perhaps by a few theorists who are only at ease among abstractions, paying for this faculty by the loss of all real contact with living beings, and, I might add, with the great simplicities of existence. For the immense majority of human beings, the entities which such a rationalism claims to set up as the object of everybody's reverent attention are only shams behind which passions incapable of recognising themselves take cover. It has been given to our generation, as to that of the end of the eighteenth century and that of the Second Empire, not only to observe but to suffer the disastrous effects of the sin of the ideologists. This consists, above all perhaps, of infinitely intensifying the inner-falsehood, of thickening the film which is interposed between a human being and his true nature until it is almost impossible to destroy it.

Moreover, this same point will enable us to understand the most characteristic elements in what to-day is commonly accepted as the meaning of the term "person." Nowadays, the individual allows himself, legitimately enough, to be likened to an atom caught up in a whirlwind, or, if you wish, a mere statistical unit; because most of the time he is simply a specimen among an infinity of others, since the opinions, which he thinks are his own, are merely reflections of the ideas accepted in the circles he frequents and handed round in the press which he reads daily. Thus he is only, as I have had occasion to write, an anonymous unit of that anonymous entity "one." But he almost inevitably has the illusion that his reactions are authentic, so that he *submits*, while all the time he imagines he is taking action. It is, on the contrary, in the nature of a person to face any given situation directly and, I should add, to make an effective decision upon it. But, it may be asked, is not this the *ego* appearing once more? I think not. Let us understand each other. There could naturally be no question of conceiving of the person as of something distinct from that other thing, the *ego*; as if they were in separate compartments. Such an idea would be completely fictitious. We must go further. The person cannot be regarded as an element or attribute of the *ego* either. It would be better to say that it is something compelling, which most certainly takes its birth in what appears to me to be mine, or to be me myself, but this compelling force only becomes conscious of itself when it becomes a reality. It can thus in no way be compared with a slight desire. Let us say that it is of the order of "I will" and not of "I would like. . . ." I claim to be a person in so far as I assume responsibility for what I do and what I say. But to whom am I responsible, to whom do I acknowledge my responsibility? We must reply that I am conjointly responsible both to myself and to everyone else, and that this conjunction is precisely characteristic of an engagement of the person, that it is the mark proper to the person. We will not stay any longer among abstractions where there is always a risk of becoming imprisoned by words. Supposing that I wish or feel bound to put a certain person on his guard against someone else. I decide to write him a letter to this effect. If I do not sign my letter I am still as it were moving in a realm of play, of pastimes, and I might readily add mystification; I reserve to myself the possibility of denying my action; I deliberately maintain my position in a zone as it were halfway between dreams and reality, where self-complacency triumphs, the chosen land of those who, in our time, have made themselves the champions of the gratuitous act. From the moment that I sign my letter, on the contrary, I have taken on the responsibility for it, that is to say I have shouldered the consequences in advance. I have created the irrevocable not only for the other person but for myself. Of my own free will I have brought into existence new decisions which will bear upon my own life with all their weight. This, of course, does not exclude the possibility that it was a reprehensible, perhaps even a criminal action to write the letter. There is nevertheless a radical difference of quality, or more exactly of weight, between this action and that of writing a letter without signing it. Let us repeat that I tend to establish myself as a person in so far as I assume responsibility for my acts and so behave as a real being (rather than a dreamer who reserves the strange power of modifying his dreams, without having to trouble whether this modification has any repercussions in the hypothetical outside world in which everybody else dwells). From

the same point of view we might also say that I establish myself as a person in so far as I really believe in the existence of others and allow this belief to influence my conduct. What is the actual meaning of *believing* here? It means to realise or acknowledge their existence in itself, and not only through those points of intersection which bring it into relation with my own.

Person — engagement — community — reality: there we have a sort of chain of notions which, to be exact, do not readily follow from each other by deduction (actually there is nothing more fallacious than a belief in the value of deduction) but of which the union can be grasped by an act of the mind. It would be better not to call this act by the much abused term of intuition, but by one which on the contrary is too little used—that of synopsis, the act by which a group is held together under the mind's comprehensive gaze.

As I hinted just now, one cannot strictly say that personality is good in itself, or that it is an element of goodness: the truth is much more that it controls the existence of a world where there is good and evil. I should be inclined to think that the *ego*, so long as it remains shut up within itself, that is to say the prisoner of its own feelings, of its covetous desires, and of that dull anxiety which works upon it, is really beyond the reach of evil as well as of good. It literally has not yet awakened to reality. Indeed, it is to be wondered whether there does not exist an infinite number of beings for whom this awakening has never truly taken place. There is no doubt that direct judgment cannot be applied to such beings. I would go further: it seems to me that each of us, in a considerable part of his life or of his being, is still unawakened, that is to say that he moves on the margin of reality like a sleep-walker. Let us say that the *ego*, as such, is ruled by a sort of vague fascination, which is localised, almost by chance, in objects arousing sometimes desire, sometimes terror. It is, however, precisely against such a condition that what I consider the essential characteristic of the person is opposed, the characteristic, that is to say, of availability (*disponibilité*).

This, of course, does not mean emptiness, as in the case of an available dwelling (*local disponible*), but it means much rather an aptitude to give oneself to anything which offers, and to bind oneself by the gift. Again, it means to transform circumstances into opportunities, we might even say favours, thus participating in the shaping of our own destiny and marking it with our seal. It has sometimes been said of late, "Personality is vocation." It is true if we restore its true value to the term vocation, which is in reality a call, or more precisely the response to a call. We must not, however, be led astray here by any mythological conception. It depends, in fact, on me whether the call is recognised as a call, and, strange as it may seem, in this matter it is true to say that it comes both from me and from outside me at one and the same time; or rather, in it we become aware of that most intimate connection between what comes from me and what comes from outside, a connection which is nourishing or constructive and cannot be relinquished without the ego wasting and tending towards death.

Perhaps we might make this clearer by pointing out that each of us from the very beginning, appears to himself and to others as a particular problem for which the circumstances, whatever they may be, are not enough to provide a solution. I use the term problem absolutely against my will, for it seems to be quite inadequate. Is it not obvious that if I consider the other person as a sort of mechanism exterior to my own *ego*, a mechanism of which I must discover the spring or manner of working, even supposing I manage to take him to pieces in the process, I shall never succeed in obtaining anything but a completely exterior knowledge of him, which is in a way the very denial of his real being? We must even go further and say that such a knowledge is in reality sacrilegious and destructive, it does no less than denude its object of the one thing he has which is of value and so it *degrades him effectively*. That means—and there is nothing which is more important to keep in view

—that the knowledge of an individual being cannot be separated from the act of love or charity by which this being is accepted in all which makes of him a unique creature or, if you like, the image of God. There is no doubt that this expression borrowed from the language of religion renders more exactly than any other the truth I have in view at the moment. It is, however, none the less necessary to remember that the truth can be actively misunderstood by each one of us at any time and that there will always be something in experience which seems to provide an argument for him who, following in the footsteps of the cynics of all time, claims to reduce his fellows to little machines whose every movement it is only too easy for him to examine and even to regulate according to his fancy.

It must be understood that these observations are just as directly applicable to the relationship which binds me to myself, the manner in which it is given me to apprehend my own being. It is indeed a fact that I also can conceive of myself as a pure piece of mechanism and make it my chief business to control the machine as well as possible. From the same standpoint, I can regard the problem of my life purely as a problem of tangible results. All that is perfectly consistent. The simplest reflection, however, shows that this mechanism must inevitably serve some purpose which I am at liberty to choose and which is recognised and established as a purpose by my own act. We know from experience, however, that this act can remain practically unsuspected by the very one who has made it. If, indeed, I passively accept a group of regulations which seem to be imposed upon me by the circle to which I belong by birth, by the party to which I have allowed myself to be attached without any genuine thought on my part, everything goes on as though I were really nothing but an instrument, a mere cog in the wheel, as if, in short, the supreme human gift of free action had been refused me. Nevertheless, on reflection we see that all the time this presupposes the act by which the person has failed to recognise himself, or more exactly, has alienated that which alone could confer the dignity which is proper to his nature.

What then is this principle which it is given him thus to fail to recognise or on the contrary to guard and promote? It is easy to discover it if we penetrate the meaning of the notion of availability to which I referred a little way back. The being who is ready for anything is the opposite of him who is occupied or cluttered up with himself. He reaches out, on the contrary, beyond his narrow self, prepared to consecrate his being to a cause which is greater than he is, but which at the same time he makes his own. Here, moreover, it is the order of creation, of power, and of creative fidelity which is borne in upon us. We go wrong when we confuse creating with producing. That which is essential in the creator is the act by which he places himself at the disposal of something which, no doubt in one sense depends upon him for its existence, but which at the same time appears to him to be beyond what he is and what he judged himself capable of drawing directly and immediately from himself. This obviously applies to the case of the artist and to the mysterious gestation which alone makes the appearance of a work of art possible. It is not necessary to insist on this. We must remember, however, that the creative process, though less apparent, is none the less effective wherever there is personal development of any kind. Only here what the person has to create is not some work in a way outside himself and capable of assuming an independent existence, it is his own self in very truth. How can we help seeing that the personality is not to be conceived of apart from the act by which it creates itself, yet at the same time this creation depends in some way upon a superior order? It will seem to the person that sometimes he invents the order, sometimes he discovers it, and reflection will moreover show that there is always a continuity between the invention and the discovery, and that no line of demarcation as definite as that ordinarily accepted by common sense can be established between the one and the other.

If this is so, it must be seen that the personality cannot in any way be compared to an object of which we can say *it is there*, in other words that it is given, present before our eyes, that it is part of a collection of things which can, of their essence, be counted, or again, that it is a statistical unit which can be noted in the calculations of a sociolgist employing the methods of an engineer. Or again, if we no longer consider things from outside but from within, that is to say from the point of view of the person himself, it does not seem that strictly speaking he can say "I am" of himself. He is aware of himself far less as a being than as a desire to rise above everything which he is and is not, above the actuality in which he really feels he is involved and has a part to play, but which does not satisfy him, for it falls short of the aspiration with which he identifies himself. His motto is not *sum* but *sursum*.

We must be on our guard here. It certainly would not do to underestimate the danger of a certain romanticism which belongs to every age. This consists of systematically depreciating that which is, in favour of some vaguely imagined and wished-for possibility, of which the transcendent appeal seems to be bound up with the fact that it is not and perhaps never can be fully realised. There can be no question here of an aspiration of that kind, for such an aspiration really springs from the *ego* and not from the personality, it is still a mere form of self-complacency. Here, and indeed everywhere as I see it, the necessity for incarnation must be given an important place. What I have been trying to say is that the personality is only realised in the act by which it tends to become incarnate (in a book, for instance, or an action or a complete life), but at the same time it is of its very essence never to fix itself or crystallise itself finally in this particular incarnation. Why? Because it participates in the inexhaustible fullness of the being from which it emanates. There lies the deep reason for which it is impossible to think of personality or the personal order without at the same time thinking of that which reaches beyond them both, a supra-

personal reality, presiding over all their initiative, which is both their beginning and
their end.

Bibliography

Texts

Metaphysical Journal. Chicago: Henry Regnery Company, 1952.

Being and Having. London: Fontana, 1965.

Homo Viator. New York: Harper & Row, Publishers, Incorporated, 1962.

The Philosophy of Existentialism. New
York: Philosophical Library, Inc., 1956.

The Mystery of Being. Chicago: Henry Regnery Company, 1960.

Man against Mass Society. Chicago: Henry
Regnery Company, 1952.

The Decline of Wisdom. New York: Philosophical Library, Inc., 1955.

Creative Fidelity. New York: Farrar, Straus
& Giroux, Inc., 1964.

*The Existential Background of Human
Dignity*. Cambridge, Mass.: Harvard University Press, 1963.

Searchings. Westminster, Md.: The Newman
Press, 1967.

Philosophical Fragments 1909–1914. Notre
Dame, Ind.: University of Notre Dame Press,
1965.

Royce's Metaphysics. Chicago: Henry Regnery Company. 1956.

Studies

Collins, J. *The Existentialists*. Chicago:
Henry Regnery Company, 1952, chap. 4.

Gallagher, K. *The Philosophy of Gabriel
Marcel*. New York: Fordham University Press,
1962.

Miceli, V. *Ascent to Being: Gabriel Marcel's
Philosophy of Communion*. New York: Desclée, 1965.

Spiegelberg, H. *The Phenomenological
Movement*. The Hague: Martinus Nijhoff,
1965, 2d ed., vol. 2, pp. 421–444.

Tymieniecka, A. T. *Phenomenology and Sci-
ence in Contemporary European Thought*.
New York: Noonday Books, Farrar, Straus &
Giroux, Inc., 1962, pp. 82 ff.

Zaner, R. *The Problem of Embodiment:
Some Contributions to a Phenomenology
of the Body*. The Hague: Martinus Nijhoff,
1964, part 1.

Keen, S. *Gabriel Marcel*. Richmond: John
Knox Press, 1967.

van Ewijk, T. J. M. *Gabriel Marcel*. New
York: Deus, 1965.

Ballard, E. G. "Gabriel Marcel: The Mystery
of Being," in G. A. Schrader (ed.), *Existential Philosophers: Kierkegaard to Merleau-
Ponty*. New York: McGraw-Hill Book Company, 1967, pp. 209–259.

O'Malley, J. B. *The Fellowship of Being:
An Essay on The Concept of Person in
the Philosophy of Gabriel Marcel*. The
Hague: Martinus Nijhoff, 1966.

24

Introduction

Alfred Schutz was born in Vienna and studied law and the social sciences there under Ludwig von Mises, Othmar Spann, Hans Nelsen, and Friedrich von Wieser. From the very beginning he combined the interests, perspectives, and skills of a sociologist, a psychologist, a musicologist, and a philosopher, and later, those of a phenomenologist. He brought these varied perspectives into focus in his attempt to understand the world of interpersonal relationships. From Wilhelm Dilthey he learned that knowledge of the human world of intersubjectivity, especially as history records its manifestations in the genesis and evolution of cultures, cannot be gained through causal explanations as is done in the physical sciences. Heinrich Rickert had offered analyses of this methodological difference between the physical and social sciences, and Max Weber had developed the doctrine of ideal types. With these resources Schutz first attacked the problem of methodology itself and then turned his energies to the establishment of a solid philosophical basis for a methodology of the sciences of man. During this time he also drew concepts from Henri Bergson and from Edmund Husserl's transcendental phenomenology.

After twelve years of research and of putting his methodology to use, in 1932 he published his major work, *Der sinnhafte Aufbau der sozialen Welt: Eine Einleitung in die verstehende Soziologie,* in which he stressed, as the title suggests, that interpretive sociology's goal is to understand not merely the *objective* meaning of social action, but the meaning which the actor bestows on his action, i.e., the meaning it has *for him.*

In 1932 Husserl, much impressed by this work, invited Schutz to Freiburg, where he was to return frequently, although he declined Husserl's request that he become his assistant. The Nazi occupation of Austria forced him to leave for Paris, where he remained for over a year before making his home in the United States in July, 1939. It was Marvin Farber, student of Husserl at Freiburg in 1923 and 1924 and his pioneer American interpreter and critic, who in 1939 took the initiative in having Schutz called on to join the establishment of the International Phenomenological Society and to become a member of the editorial board of the society's journal, *Philosophy and Phenomenological Research.* Schutz was appointed lecturer and then professor in the Graduate School of Political and Social Science at the New School for Social Research in New York. There he rejoined two other European "refugees" (The New School was formerly called "the University in Exile") and eminent students of Husserl, Dorion Cairnes and Aron Gurwitch. Until his death in 1959, Schutz continued his phenomenological studies in dialogue with thinkers in Europe as well as in the United States, including William James and the American sociologists W. I. Thomas and G. H. Mead.

Schutz's ultimate goal was a systematic phenomenology of the social world in all its interpersonal relationships. This phenomenology was based on the world of working in daily life and the commonsense world that Husserl called the *Lebenswelt,* the world of the "natural attitude." Schutz's approach was predicated on the thesis that *action* rather than perception is the proper starting point for the social sciences. Action holds methodological primacy for the social sciences because perception, when understood to mean scientific observation (the traditional methodology for the natural sciences), reaches only overt conduct. But this is only a fraction of total behavior. Persons are more than elements in the scientist's field of observation. A person can be understood *as* a person only when considered as one who defines a situation by his actions. A person is a subjectivity who preinterprets his own actions. Understanding a person can, therefore, be accomplished only by grasping the *meaning* an act has *for the person acting*. A philosophical anthropology, a theory or hypothesis of man's nature, is, of course, implied here. Schutz's work contains, however, only scattered suggestions of his final theory of man. Apparently that the-

sis was a rejection, after years of trying, of all attempts to derive intersubjectivity from transcendental subjectivity and was a recognition of intersubjectivity as itself a primordial given. This conclusion is important for comparison with, and confirmation of, the French phenomenologists, because Schutz rigorously pursued his own approach and methodology within sociology as validly as within philosophy.

PHENOMENOLOGY OF THE WE-EXPERIENCE AND THE STRUCTURE OF THE INTERPERSONAL WORLD *

I Social Reality within Reach of Direct Experience

1 The Face-to-face Situation and the "Pure" We-relation

I experience a fellow-man directly if and when he shares with me a common sector of time and space. The sharing of a common sector of time implies a genuine simultaneity of our two streams of consciousness: my fellow-man and I grow older together. The sharing of a common sector of space implies that my fellow-man appears to me in person as he himself and none other. His body appears to me as a unified field of expressions, that is, of concrete symptoms through which his conscious life manifests itself to me vividly. This temporal and spatial immediacy are essential characteristics of the face-to-face situation. The specific style and the structure of social relations and of social interaction which occur in face-to-face situations are decisively influenced by these characteristics.

We shall first consider the way in which a face-to-face situation becomes constituted. In order to become aware of such a situation, I must consciously pay attention to a fellow-

man, to a human being confronting me in person. We shall term this awareness *Thou-orientation*. Since a face-to-face situation presupposes this orientation, we shall now describe the features of the latter.

The Thou-orientation is the general form in which any particular fellow-man is experienced in person. The very fact that I recognize something within the reach of my direct experience as a living, conscious human being constitutes the Thou-orientation. In order to preclude misunderstandings, it must be emphasized that the Thou-orientation is not a judgement by analogy. Becoming aware of a human being confronting me does not depend upon an imputation of life and consciousness to an object in my surroundings by an act of reflective thought. The Thou-orientation is a prepredicative experience of a fellow being. In this experience I grasp the existence of a fellow-man in the actuality of a particular person who must be present here and now. The Thou-orientation presupposes the presence of the fellow-man in temporal and spatial immediacy. The essential feature of the Thou-orientation is the recognition that a fellow-man *is* before me; the orientation does not presuppose that I know what are precisely the particular characteristics of that fellow-man. The formal concept of the Thou-orientation refers to the "pure" experience of another Self as a human being, alive and conscious, while the

* From Alfred Schutz, *Collected Papers*, vol. II. The Hague, Martinus Nijhoff, 1964. Reprinted by permission of the publisher.

specific content of that consciousness remains undefined. Of course, I never have such a "pure" experience of another Self. I always confront a particular fellow-man, living his particular life and having his own particular thoughts. The Thou-orientation is therefore not "pure" in fact but is always actualized in different degrees of concreteness and specificity.

The Thou-orientation is either one-sided or reciprocal. It is onesided if I turn to you, but you ignore my presence. It is reciprocal if I am oriented to you, and you, in turn, take my existence into account. In that case a social relation becomes constituted. We shall define this relation formally as the "pure" We-relation, knowing fully that in fact a We-relation is always filled with "content," that is, that the "pure" We-relation, in analogy to the "pure" Thou-orientation, is actualized in different degrees of concreteness and specificity. An illustration may help to clarify this point. If you and I observe a bird in flight my "bird-flight observations" are a sequence of experiences in my own mind just as your "bird-flight observations" are experiences in your mind. Neither you nor I, nor any other person, can say whether my experiences are identical with yours since no one can have direct access to another man's mind. Nevertheless, while I cannot know the specific and exact content of your consciousness, I do know that you are a living human being, endowed with consciousness. I do know that, whatever your experiences during the flight of the bird, they were contemporaneous with mine. Furthermore, I may have observed movements of your body and expressions of your face during these moments, interpreting them as indications of your attentiveness to the bird's flight. Therefore, I may coordinate the event "bird-flight" not only with phases of my own consciousness but also with "corresponding" phases of your consciousness. Since we are growing older together during the flight of the bird, and since I have evidence, in my own observations, that you were paying attention to the same event, I may say that *we* saw a bird in flight.

I am born into a world which is inhabited by others who will confront me in face-to-face situations. My experiences of particular fellow-men as well as my knowledge that there are other human beings—only some of whom I have experienced directly as fellow-men—originate in this a priori given by my birth. Scheler [1] rightly maintains that the We-experience forms the basis of the individual's experience of the world in general. The difficult question of the *transcendental* constitution of this experience and of the experience of the alter ego cannot be pursued here. By assuming the *mundane* existence of other Selves we may turn to the description of the origin of experiences of fellow-men in the We-relation.

I "participate" in the conscious life of another Self only when I am engaged in a concrete We-relation, face to face with a fellow-man. If you speak to me, for example, I understand the objective sign-meaning of the words. But, since I "participate" in the step-by-step constitution of your speaking experiences in the contemporaneity of the We-relation, I may also apprehend the subjective configuration of meaning in which the words stand for you. But the process by which I apprehend the subjective configuration of meaning in which my fellow-man's experiences stand for him must not be confused with the We-relation proper. The words of my fellow-man are primarily signs in an objective context of meaning. They are also indications for the subjective context in which any experience, including speaking, stands for him. But the process by which I apprehend his conscious life is necessarily a process in my own conscious life. It is I who interpret the words as signs in an objective meaning context and as indications of his subjective intentions. The very fact that I can do so, however, presupposes my experience of the other Self as a fellow-man who shares experiences with me in the ongoing community of space and time; it presupposes the "pure" We-relation.

[1] *Die Wissensformen und die Gesellschaft,* Leipzig, 1926, II. "Erkenntnis und Arbeit," p. 475f.

The stream of concrete experiences which fills the We-relation with "content" bears a strong similarity to the manifold and continuous stream of my own consciousness. There is one fundamental difference. My own stream of consciousness is interior, it is "pure" duration. The We-relation, however, consists not only in the community of time, that is, in the synchronization of two interior streams of duration; it consists also in the community of space, that is, the bodily and thus exterior presence of a fellow-man face to face with me. Hence, the experience of a fellow-man in a We-relation is, strictly speaking, also "mediate": I apprehend his conscious life by interpreting his bodily expressions as indications of subjectively meaningful processes. Yet, among all self-transcending experiences the We-relation most closely resembles the inward temporality of my stream of consciousness. In that sense we may say that I experience my fellow-man "directly" in a We-relation.

My experience of the fellow-man is direct as long as I am straightforwardly engaged *in* the We-relation, that is, as long as I participate in the common stream of *our* experiences. If I think and reflect *about* our experience, this directness is broken. I must interrupt my straightforward engagement in the We-relation. In a manner of speaking, I must step outside the face-to-face situation. While I was engaged in the We-relation, I was busy attending to you; in order to think about it, I must break off the immediate rapport between us. Before I can reflect about our common experience its vivid phases, in which we were jointly engaged, must have come to a stop. Straightforward engagement in the We-relation is possible only in the ongoing experiences of a face-to-face situation, while reflection is ex post facto. It begins after the concrete We-relation has come to an end.

The retrospective grasp of past common experiences may be clear and distinct or confused and unsharp. The more I am involved in reflecting upon the common experience, the less directly do I live it and the remoter is the living, concrete human

being who is my partner in the We-relation. The fellow-man whom I experience directly while I am busily engaged in our common experience becomes a mere object of my thought as I begin to reflect about us.

2 Social Relations in the Face-to-face Situation

The foregoing description of the pure We-relation will provide a useful basis for the analysis of the We-relation as a concrete social relation in face-to-face situations. We found that the pure We-relation is constituted in the reciprocal Thou-orientation; that the latter, in its pure form, consists in the mere awareness of the existence of a fellow-man before me; and that it consequently does not necessarily involve a grasp of the specific traits of that fellow-man. In a concrete social relation, however, this is precisely what is involved.

Obviously, the extent of my knowledge of the traits which characterize my partners in different social relations varies considerably. In the pure We-relation I apprehend only the existence of a fellow-man and the fact that he is confronting me. For a concrete social relation to become established, however, I must also know how he is oriented to me. In face-to-face situations I gain knowledge of this specific aspect of my partner's conscious life by observing the concrete manifestations of his subjective experiences in the common stream of the We-relation. Hence, we may say that concrete social relations in face-to-face situations are founded upon the pure We-relation. Not only is the latter logically prior to the former in the sense that it contains the essential features of any such social relation; the grasp of the specific traits of the partner which is an element of concrete social relations presupposes the community of space and time which characterizes the pure We-relation. The pure We-relation may be thus also considered as a formal concept designating the structure of concrete social relations in the face-to-face situation.

This point becomes clear if one considers

the fact that no specific *"pure"* experiences correspond to the pure We-relation. The participant in an ongoing We-relation apprehends this relation only in the shared experiences which refer, by necessity, to the specific partner confronting him. The essential features of the pure We-relation can be seen in reflection, after the concrete We-relation has come to an end; they are experienced only in the variety of its actualizations.

Having discussed the connection between the pure We-relation and the concrete We-relation, we must now describe the various actualizations of the latter and show how it differs from all other social relations. The experiences which go on concretely in the We-relation are differentiated in several ways. I do not experience partners in all We-relations with equal intensity, nor am I equally intimate with them. Furthermore, my partners appear to me in different perspectives which exercise a certain amount of constraint upon my experiences of the partner. Finally, in the We-relation I may be turned attentively to my partner's experiences, i.e., to his conscious processes and subjective motivations, or I may be only remotely interested in these, concentrating instead on his overt acts and expressions. The concrete actualizations of the We-relation are determined by these factors; within the temporal and spatial immediacy given by the face-to-face situation these factors bestow a higher or lower degree of "directness" upon the experiences in the We-relation. An example may illustrate this point.

Both sexual intercourse and a casual conversation are instances of the We-relation in which the partners are face-to-face. Yet what a difference in the degree of directness which characterizes the experiences in these relations! Very different depth-levels of the conscious life of the partners are involved. Intensity and degree of intimacy vary radically. But not only *my* experiences *in* these relations differ in all the aforementioned aspects. We may say that differences in the "degree of directness" are characteristics of the We-relation proper.

With the discussion of the relative directness of social relations we touch upon a problem of basic significance for the understanding of the constitution of social reality and subjective experience. We shall be obliged to take up this problem again when describing the transition from the direct experience of fellow-men in face-to-face situations to the experience of social reality transcending this situation. At present we must hold to the analysis of the characteristics peculiar to social relations in the face-to-face situation.

We found earlier that in the face-to-face situation the conscious life of my fellow-man becomes accessible to me by a maximum of vivid indications. Since he is confronting me in person, the range of symptoms by which I apprehend his consciousness includes much more than what he is communicating to me purposefully. I observe his movements, gestures and facial expressions, I hear the intonation and the rhythm of his utterances. Each phase of my consciousness is co-ordinated with a phase of my partner's. Since I perceive the continuous manifestations of my partner's conscious life I am continuously attuned to it. One highly important consequence of this state of affairs is the fact that my partner is given to me more vividly and, in a sense, more "directly" than I apprehend myself. Since I "know" my past, I "know" myself in infinitely greater detail than anyone else. Yet this is knowledge in retrospect, in reflection; it is not direct and vivid experience. Hence, while I am straightforwardly engaged in the business of life, my own self is not present to me in an equally wide range of symptoms as is a fellow-man whom I confront in the Here and Now of a concrete We-relation.

In the face-to-face situation I have immediate experience of my fellow-man. But as I confront my fellow-man, I bring into each concrete situation a stock of preconstituted knowledge which includes a network of typifications of human individuals in general, of typical human motivations, goals, and action patterns. It also includes knowledge of expressive and interpretive schemes, of objective sign-systems and, in particular, of the vernacular language. In addition to such general knowledge I have more specific information about particular kinds and groups of men, of their motivations and actions. If I formerly had direct experience of this particular fellow-man now confronting me, I may, of course, fall back upon the highly specialized information sedimented in these experiences. In the ongoing experiences of the We-relation I check and revise my previous knowledge about my partner and accumulate new knowledge about him. Thereby my general stock of knowledge also undergoes a continuous modification. My experience of a fellow-man in the We-relations thus stands in a multiple context of meaning: it is experience of a human being, it is experience of a typical actor on the social scene, it is experience of this particular fellow-man, and it is experience of this particular fellow-man in this particular situation, Here and Now.

As I look at you in the community of space and time I have direct evidence that you are oriented to me, that is, that you experience what I say and do, not only in an objective context of meaning but also as manifestations of my conscious life. I know that the same goes for you, and that you refer your experiences of me back to what you grasp of my experiences of you. In the community of space and time our experiences of each other are not only coordinated but also reciprocally determined by continuous cross-reference. I experience myself through you, and you experience yourself through me. The reciprocal mirroring of Selves in the partners' experience is a constitutive feature of the We-relation in face-to-face situations. Since, however, the We-relation and the partner in it are not grasped reflectively but directly experienced, the multifaceted reflections of the Self in the mirror of the other Self are not separately brought to consciousness. My experience of the ongoing phases of my own conscious life and my experience of the coordinated phases of your conscious life is unitary: experience in the We-relation is genuinely shared.

This is a significant fact for the structure not only of social relations but also of social interaction in face-to-face situations: I am in a position to witness your projects and to observe their fulfillment or frustration in the course of your actions. Outside an ongoing We-relation I may calculate the objective chances of success for another man's projected goals by drawing upon my stock of knowledge about social reality, and I may interrupt, as it were, an ongoing We-relation in order to do so. But only in the ongoing We-relation may I directly apprehend the outcome of my partner's plans by witnessing the course of his action.

I am inclined, in general, to assign to fellow human beings a world which corresponds to the world as I experience it myself. In the We-relation I do so with infinitely greater confidence because, as we saw, the world within the reach of my fellow-man coincides with mine. I may assume not only that the table in front of me is the same table which is in front of you but also that your experiences of this table correspond to mine. Therefore, I am always able to check the adequacy of the schemata by which I interpret your utterances and expressions by pointing to an object in the world within our common reach. This is an eminently important circumstance in the building up of my stock of knowledge and for my practical adjustment to social reality. Having verified the assumption that you interpret your experience in a way which for all practical purposes is roughly identical with mine, at least with respect to objects in our common environment, I have some justification for generally correlating my interpretive schemes with your expressive schemes.

The community of environment and the sharing of experiences in the We-relation bestows upon the world within the reach of our experience its intersubjective, social character. It is not my environment nor your environment nor even the two added; it is an intersubjective world within reach of our common experience. In this common experience the intersubjective character of the world in general both originates and is continuously confirmed.

The community of the world within reach of our experiences in the We-relation enables me to verify constantly the results of my interpretation of other men's experiences. The fellow-man face to face with me can be always interrogated. Hence I apprehend not only how he interprets his own experiences, that is, what meaning his experiences have for him. We may say that the realization of the correspondence and divergence of the meaning of our experiences originates in the We-relation. We already pointed out that my stock of knowledge, in so far as it refers to that particular fellow-man, and men in general, is constantly verified, corrected, and extended in the We-relation.

My own experiences, too, undergo a certain modification in the We-relation, and the same holds good for my partner. Neither he nor I attend to our respective experiences without awareness of the Other. I realize that my experiences interlock with his and necessarily refer to them. The cross-reference of the partners' experiences in a We-relation has especially important consequences for the structure of social interaction in face-to-face situations. I generally impute a set of genuine "because" and "in-order-to" motives to anybody to whom my actions are directed. In this I rely on my stock of knowledge, which contains typifications of fellow-men in terms of typical sets of invariant "because" and "in-order-to" motives. While a provisional imputation of such motives to others characterizes all social action, interaction in face-to-face situations is privileged in that the motives of a partner in a We-relation are more directly accessible to the actor than the motives of others. It must be noted, however, that the general structure of motivational reciprocity remains the same. In projecting my own action I take account of my fellow-man by fancying—that is to say, rehearsing—likely courses of his future conduct in terms of the invariant motives which I impute to him. My partner's actual conduct then either confirms, approximates, or frustrates my expec-

tations. The project of my action is thus always oriented to my partner by anticipations of his future conduct. But in face-to-face situations, in consequence of the continuous reciprocal modification of experience by the partner in the We-relation, I may "participate" in the constitution of the motives in my partner's conscious life. I am in a position to place your present experiences into an "in-order-to" context by interpreting them as antecedents of your future conduct. At the same time, I may place your present experiences into a "because" context by interpreting them as consequences of your past experiences. My grasp of another man's motives generally orients my action addressed to him; in a We-relation I grasp my fellow-man's motives in the particular fashion just described. I witness the constitution of motivational configurations in my partner's conscious life, then I witness his reactions to my conduct; and I am present when my "in-order-to" motives become the "because" motives of his actions, and so forth. I always grow older between the rehearsing of the conduct of another man to whom my action is addressed and his actual conduct. But if I have addressed an action to a fellow-man, to a partner in a We-relation, I have not grown older alone; we have grown older together. Since we are jointly engaged in our common experiences, I "participate" in the projection and realization of his plans. Social interaction, characterized in all its forms by an interlocking of the actors' motives, gains an outstanding feature if it occurs in face-to-face situations. The motivational configuration of the actions of my fellow-man, as well as his overt conduct, is integrated into the *common* experience of the We-relation.

Direct Observations

Our description of social relations in the face-to-face situation revealed the structure of this situation in its fundamental form. We shall now consider a modification of this situation in which I confront a fellow-man, but the fellow-man does not take my presence into account or is not aware of my presence at all. For the social sciences the most important version of this situation is that in which I am the observer of the conduct of a fellow-man. The analysis of observation and of the observer is indispensable for an understanding of the procedures by which the social sciences gather knowledge about social reality.

The social relations in the face-to-face situation are characterized by reciprocity of the Thou-orientations of the two partners. If I am merely observing, my Thou-orientation is, of course, onesided. My observation is conduct oriented to him, but his conduct need not be oriented to me. The question then arise how I am able to apprehend his conscious life.

In order to answer this question, we may begin by recapitulating those features of the We-relation which also apply to a mere observer. For the observer, too, the body of the Other is a field of direct expression. He, too, may take his observations as expressions that indicate the Other's conscious processes. Words, signs of any kind, and gestures and movements can be interpreted by the observer as standing in a subjective configuration of meaning for the individual observed. The observer may apprehend in a unitary and integrated manner both the manifestations of the Other's conscious processes and the step-by-step constitution of the processes thus manifested. This is possible because he witnesses the Other's ongoing experiences in synchrony with his own interpretations of the Other's overt conduct in an objective context of meaning. The bodily presence of the Other offers to the partner in the We-relation as well as to the observer a maximum of vivid symptoms. The world which is within reach of the observer is congruent with the world within reach of the observed person. There is thus a certain chance that the experiences of the world within reach on the part of the observed person roughly coincide with the corresponding experiences of the observer. But the observer cannot be certain that this is really the case. As long as he remains a mere

observer, he is not in a position to verify his interpretation of the Other's experiences by checking them against the Other's own subjective interpretations. And yet, the facility with which the observer can transform himself into a partner in a face-to-face social relation places him in a privileged position relative to the collection of knowledge about social reality. The observed individual can become a fellow-man who may be questioned, while a mere contemporary is not within my reach Here and Now, and a predecessor is, of course, forever beyond interrogation.

In consequence of the fact that as an observer I am one-sidedly oriented to the individual observed, the subjective context in which his experiences are meaningful to me is not co-ordinated with the subjective context in which my experiences are meaningful to him. Hence there is not the multifaceted reflexion of mirror-images, characteristic of the We-relation, which enables me to identify my experiences with his.

The observer is oriented to the Other but does not act upon him. Therefore, his motives do not interlock with the observed person's; the observer cannot project his "in-order-to" motives on the assumption that they will become "because" motives of the Other. The overt conduct of the observed individual does not offer adequate clues to the question whether and how his course of action is fulfilling his subjective projects. Perhaps the observer cannot even say whether the observed fragments of overt conduct constitute an action in the pursuit of a projected goal or whether they are mere behavior.

Since the observer who is interested in the observed individual's motives cannot apprehend these motives as directly as could a partner in a We-relation, he must proceed by one of the following three ways: First, he may remember from his own past experience a course of action similar to the one observed and recall its motive. By matching a given course of action with a given pattern of "because" and "in-order-to" motives, he will ascribe to the individual the motives which he, the observer, might have if only he were performing this action himself. The identification of one's own hypothetical motives with the Other's real motives may be immediate, i.e., it may occur in the course of the Other's ongoing action, or it may take place in a retrospective interpretation of the observed event. Second, if the observer does not find some rule of thumb for the interpretation of the observed course of action in his *own* experience, he may yet find in his general stock of knowledge typifications of the observed individual from which he may derive a typification of the observed individual's typical motives. A complete stranger to our society, let us say, who walked through a lecture hall, a courtroom, and a place of worship would observe in all three places situations that seem roughly alike. Yet, he would be unable to say much, if anything, about the motives of the overt conduct that he observed. If, however, the observer knew from previous experience that here a teacher, there a judge, and there a priest is performing his official duties, he would be able to deduce their typical "because" and "in-order-to" motives from that segment of his stock of knowledge which referred to typical teachers, judges, and priests.

Third, if the observer possesses no knowledge at all about the observed individual, or insufficient knowledge about the type of individual involved, he must fall back upon an inference from "effect to cause." This means that, in observing an accomplished act and its results, he assumes that this particular accomplished act and these results, were, indeed, the "in-order-to" motive of the actor.

These different ways of understanding the motives of individuals under observation do not have the same likelihood of being correct. Aside from the adequacy of one's stock of knowledge concerning typical motivations of typical individuals, the interpretation of other men's "in-order-to" motives will be the more dubious the farther it stands from the vivid context of a We-relation. The information, for example, that the individual one sees speaking to an assembly is a priest does not allow with certainty the conclusion that

he is preaching a sermon. To impute to someone an "in-order-to" motive on the basis of an observed accomplished act is even more uncertain. That act may indeed have completely failed to achieve the goal projected by the actor. One's grasp of genuine "because" motives, on the other hand, does not suffer much by the fact that one is merely an observer rather than a partner in a We-relation. Both the observer and the partner in a face-to-face social relation must try to reconstruct, ex post facto, the experiences which motivated the Other before he embarked on a given course of action. With respect to this task which depends on one's "objective" knowledge, the partner's position in a We-relation is not privileged.

The observation of social relations is more complicated, to be sure, than the observation of individual conduct, yet it proceeds according to the same basic principles. The observer must again draw upon his stock of knowledge about social relations in general, this particular social relation, and the partners involved in it. The observer's scheme of interpretation cannot be identical, of course, with the interpretive scheme of either partner in the social relation observed. The modifications of attention which characterize the attitude of the observer cannot coincide with those of a participant in an ongoing social relation. For one thing, what he finds relevant is not identical with what they find relevant in the situation. Furthermore, the observer stands in a privileged position in one respect: he has the ongoing experiences of *both* partners under observation. On the other hand, the observer cannot legitimately interpret the "in-order-to" motives of one participant as the "because" motives of the other, as do the partners themselves, unless the interlocking of motives becomes explicitly manifested in the observable situation.

II The World of Contemporaries as a Structure of Typifications

1   The Transition from Direct to Indirect Experience of Social Reality

In the analysis of the We-relation we found that in face-to-face situations fellow-men are experienced on different levels of intimacy and in different degrees of directness. Within the temporal and spatial immediacy given by the face-to-face situation itself we found differences in the degree of directness which characterize the experience of another Self to be constitutive traits of the concrete We-relation proper. We saw that no matter how indifferent and uninvolved we may be in relation to a particular concrete fellow-man (e.g., a stranger in the subway), the face-to-face experience is essentially direct.

The stratification of attitudes by degrees of intimacy and intensity extends into the world of mere contemporaries, i.e., of Others who are not face-to-face with me, but who co-exist with me in time. The gradations of experiential directness outside the face-to-face situation are characterized by a decrease in the wealth of symptoms by which I apprehend the Other and by the fact that the perspectives in which I experience the Other are progressively narrower. We may illustrate this point by considering the stages by which a fellow-man confronting me becomes a mere contemporary. Now we are still face-to-face, saying goodbye, shaking hands; now he is walking away. Now he calls back to me; now I can still see him waving to me; now he has disappeared around a corner. It is impossible to say at which precise moment the face-to-face situation ended and my partner became a mere contemporary of whom I have knowledge (he has, probably, arrived at home) but no direct experience. The gradations of directness can be also illustrated by the series ranging from a conversation face-to-face, to a conversation by phone, to an exchange of letters, to a message transmitted by a third party. Both examples show a progressive decrease in the wealth of symptoms by which I experience my partner and a progressive narrowing of the perpectives in which my partner appears to me. While we may legitimately distinguish between direct and indirect experiences of social reality, we must realize that these are polar concepts between which exist many concrete transitional forms.

In the routine of everyday life the problem underlying the transition from face-to-face situations to the world of mere contemporaries do not, as a rule, become visible. In the routine of everyday life we fit both our own conduct and the conduct of our fellow-man into a matrix of meaning which transcends the Here and Now of present experience. Hence, the attribute of present directness or indirectness of a social relation seems irrelevant to us. The deeper reason for this circumstance lies in the fact that a face-to-face experience of a fellow-man retains its constitutive traits even after I cease to see my fellow-man in person. The ongoing direct experience becomes a past direct experience. As a rule we see no reason why a fellow-man who was a partner in a concrete We-relation, with whom we interacted, whom we have loved or hated, should turn into something "different" merely because he happens to be absent at the moment. We still love him or hate him, as the case may be, and nothing in the routine of everyday life compels us to notice that our experience of him underwent a significant structural modification.

Careful description reveals, however, that such a modification does occur. The recollection of a fellow-man in a face-to-face situation indeed contains the constitutive traits of that situation, and these are structurally different from those which characterize an attitude, or an act of consciousness generally, which is oriented to a mere contemporary. In the face-to-face situation the fellow-man and I were partners in a concrete We-relation. He was present in person, with a maximum of symptoms by which I could apprehend his conscious life. In the community of space and time we were attuned to one another; his Self reflected mine; his experiences and my experiences formed a common stream, *our* experience; we grew older together. As soon as my fellow-man leaves, however, my experience of him undergoes a transformation. I know that he is in some Here and Now of his own, and I know that his Now is contemporaneous with mine, but I do not participate in it, nor do I share his Here. I know that my fellow-man has grown older since he left me, and, upon reflection, I know that, strictly speaking, he has changed with each additional experience, with each new situation. But all this I fail to take into account in the routine of everyday life. I hold on to the familiar image I have of you. I take it for granted that you are as I have known you before. Until further notice I hold invariant that segment of my stock of knowledge which concerns you and which I have built up in face-to-face situations, that is, until I receive information to the contrary. But then this is information about a contemporary to whom I am oriented as a mere contemporary and not as a fellow-man. It is a contemporary, of course, whom I experienced directly before, about whom I have more specific knowledge, gained in the shared experiences of past We-relations, than about others who are and always were mere contemporaries.

In this connection we must discuss the nature of those social relations which, according to Weber [2] are characterized by the "probability of the repeated recurrence of the behavior which corresponds to its subjective meaning, behavior which is an understandable consequence of the meaning and hence expected." Customarily we consider marriage or friendship as predominantly face-to-face relations that contain experiences of a high degree of directness. We are wont to do so, as we pointed out earlier, because of a general tendency to consider an action or a sequence of actions in a framework of larger units irrespective of whether the actors themselves have or have not integrated their actions—i.e., the projects of their actions—into such units. Closer scrutiny resolves the pretended unity of a marriage or a friendship into a manifold sequence of situations. In some of these situations, "marriage" or "friendship" was a

face-to-face social relation, in others it was a social relation among mere contemporaries. Taking the terms in their precise sense, these social relations are indeed not continuous—but they are recurrent. Let us investigate then what the participants in a social relation of this type, e.g., two friends, mean when they speak of their friendship:

First, A, speaking of his friendship with B, may be thinking of a series of past face-to-face social relations with B. These past We-relations with B evidently constitute a series rather than an uninterrupted span. In this recollection A finds both solitary phases of his past experience as well as phases involving We-relations with individuals other than B.

Second, above and beyond concrete We-relations involving B, A may mean that his conduct or some aspect of his conduct is oriented by the fact that there is such a man, B, or, more specifically, that it is oriented by some aspects of B's expected future conduct. Thus, A has an attitude involving B as a (mere) contemporary, and he stands with B in a social relation which is a social relation among (mere) contemporaries. A's actions in this relation are oriented by B as he imagines B's reactions to his conduct. Whereas actions *interlock* in a concrete We-relation, they are just *oriented* reciprocally in a social relation that involves (mere) contemporaries. Thus, we find that social relations between the two friends as (mere) contemporaries are interposed in a discontinuous series of concrete We-relations between them. Third, A may refer to the fact that a face-to-face social relation with B is always restorable—technical hindrances being left out of account—and that he is confident that B will participate as a friend in future We-relations in a manner congruent with the We-relations that A and B experienced in the past.

In the foregoing we concerned ourselves with transitions from face-to-face situations to situations involving mere contemporaries. Thereby we investigated a border province lying between the domain of directly experienced social reality and the indirectly ex-

[2] Max Weber, *The Theory of Social and Economic Organization*, New York, 1947, p. 119.

perienced world of contemporaries. The closer we approach the latter, the lower the degree of directness and the higher the degree of anonymity which characterizes my experience of others. Accordingly, the broader world of contemporaries itself contains various strata: My partners in former We-relations who are now mere contemporaries but who are restorable to face-to-face situations; partners in the *former* We-relations of my *present* partner in a We-relation who are potentially accessible to my direct experience (your friend whom I have not met yet); contemporaries of whom I have knowledge and whom I am to meet shortly (Professor X whose books I have read and with whom I have an appointment in the near future); contemporaries of whose existence I am aware, as reference points for typical social functions (post office employees involved in the processing of my letters); collective social realities which are known to me by their function and organization while their personnel remains anonymous—although I could, under certain circumstances, gain direct personal experience of the individuals in question (the House of Lords); collective social realities which are by their very nature anonymous and of which I consequently cannot gain direct personal experience under any circumstances; objective configurations of meaning which are instituted in the world of my contemporaries and which are essentially anonymous in character (the Articles of the Constitution, the rules of French grammar); and finally, artifacts in the broadest sense, which testify to some subjective meaning-context of some unknown person, i.e., the sense which the artifact "had" for its creator, user, beholder, etc. All these strata of the large domain of indirectly experienced social reality are characterized, in a graduated series, by different degrees of anonymity and by transitions from relative nearness to direct experience to absolute detachment from it.

2 The Contemporary as
    an Ideal Type and
    the They-relation

Whereas I experience fellow-men *directly* in the temporal and spatial immediacy of a face-to-face situation, this immediacy is lacking in my experience of mere contemporaries. Contemporaries are not present in person, *but I do know of their co-existence with me in time:* I know that the flux of their experiences is simultaneous with mine. This knowledge, however, is necessarily indirect. Hence, the contemporary is not a Thou in the pregnant sense that this term has in a We-relation. These terms describe the social topography of my Here and Now, whose contents are, of course, continuously changing. The reference point is always my present experiences. A mere contemporary may be a former fellow-man, and I may be counting on meeting him again face-to-face in a recurrent pattern. Yet the structure of the experiences involved differs radically. The Other who is a mere contemporary is not given to me *directly* as a unique particular Self. I do not apprehend his Selfhood in straightforward prepredicative experience. I do not even have an immediate experience of the Other's *existence*. I can only experience the Other in acts of inference by which I judge that the Other is such rather than otherwise, by imputing to him certain typical attributes. *Whereas I experience the individual Thou directly in the concrete We-relation, I apprehend the contemporary only mediately, by means of typifications.* In order to clarify this point we shall investigate various kinds of such mediating typifications by which I apprehend a contemporary.

One way by which my experience of contemporaries can become constituted is by derivation from previous immediate experiences of contemporaries in face-to-face situations. We have already investigated this mode of constitution and found that the knowledge gained directly of a fellow-man in a We-relation is maintained as valid—until further notice—even after the fellow-man moved out of the face-to-face situation. The act by which I apprehend the former fellow-man as a contemporary is thus a typification in the sense that I hold invariant my previously gained knowledge, although my former fellow-man has grown older in the meantime and must have necessarily gained new experiences. Of these experiences I have either no knowledge or only knowledge by inference or knowledge gained through fellow-men or other indirect sources.

Another mode by which experiences of contemporaries are constituted turns out to be merely a variant of the one previously mentioned. Contemporaries whom I apprehend as former fellowmen of my present partner in a We-relation are also experienced mediately, by following the example of my partner in holding invariant *his* former direct experiences of a particular person. Hence, I cannot even fall back upon my own direct experiences of that person but must first interpret the communications of my partner about his former direct experiences and then join him in holding invariant his knowledge about that particular contemporary.

These modes of constitution refer to everything we know of contemporaries through the mediation of our *own* past, direct as well as indirect experiences of Others and to everything we know through the mediation of the past experiences of Others, communicated to us directly as well as anonymously. It is abundantly clear that all such knowledge of contemporaries points back to, and is legitimized by, an originary direct experience of a fellowman. But I can also gain knowledge about my contemporary social world in other ways than the one just cited. My experiences of things and events in physical reality, of objects manufactured by men, of tools and artifacts, of cultural objects, institutions and action patterns, too, refer to the world of my contemporaries (or point back to the world of my predecessors, a circumstance which we shall discuss later). This is so because I can always interpret them as testimony to the conscious life of human beings who produced and used these tools and artifacts, who adhered to these institutions, performed these actions. Such interpretations are by their very nature derivative. They consist of inferences based on and mediated by my experiences of fellowmen, either of particular fellow-men or of fellow-human beings in general. Face-to-face

with a fellow-man I witnessed in simultaneity with my own ongoing conscious life the step-by-step constitution of his conduct, of experiences meaningful to him, that resulted in an accomplished act, artifact, tool, etc. Now I interpret an accomplished act, artifact, tool, etc., as a pointer to such subjective step-by-step processes. Without original experiences of this kind, objects and events in the outer world would be nothing but material things and physical processes without any reference to a human world.

My experiences of contemporaries are thus necessarily derivative and indirect. Nevertheless, it is obvious that I can be oriented to mere contemporaries as I can be oriented to fellowmen. These orientations, too, may range from mere attitudes to social action and social interaction. In analogy to the concept of Thou-orientation we shall subsume all conscious acts oriented to contemporaries under the concept, They-orientation.

In contrast to the way I experience the conscious life of fellowmen in face-to-face situations, the experiences of contemporaries appear to me more or less *anonymous* processes. The object of the They-orientation is my knowledge of social reality in general, of the conscious life of other human beings in general, regardless of whether the latter is imputed to a single individual or not. The object of the They-orientation is *not* the existence of a concrete man, *not* the ongoing conscious life of a fellow-man which is directly experienced in the We-relation, *not* the subjective configuration of meaning which I apprehend if experiences of a fellow-man constitute themselves before my eyes. My knowledge of contemporaries stands by its very nature in an *objective context of meaning*. Only *post hoc* may I append interpretations which refer back to a subjective meaning configuration, a point to which we shall return later when describing the constitution of personal ideal types. My knowledge of the world of contemporaries is typical knowledge of typical processes. Fundamentally, I leave it undecided in whose consciousness such typical processes are occurring. Detached as they are from a subjective configuration of meaning, such proc-esses—typical experiences of "someone"—*exhibit the idealization: "again and again"*, i.e., of typical anonymous repeatability.

The unity of the mere contemporary is originally built up in the unity of *my* experi-ence, more precisely, in a synthesis of my interpretations of the Other's experiences. It is not constituted in my direct experience of the unity of *his* ongoing conscious life in the Here and Now of a concrete Thou. Through this synthesis of my interpretations of the typical experiences of a more or less anony-mous contemporary I apprehend him as a *personal ideal type*.

It should be clearly recognized that the more complete the substitution of a series of complex, interlocking, and interdependent objective meaning contexts for a subjective configuration of meaning, the more anony-mous will be the object of my They-orienta-tion. Our analysis has shown that the syn-thesis of the interpretations by which I know my contemporaries as ideal types does not apprehend the unique Self of a human being in his vivid present. It is an act of thought that holds invariant some typical attribute of fellow-human beings and dis-regards the modifications and variations of that attribute "in real life," i.e. when em-bedded in the ongoing experiences of a con-crete and unique individual. Hence, *the per-sonal ideal type merely refers to, but is never identical with, a concrete Other or a plurality of Others*.

This point will be illustrated by a few examples. If I drop a letter into the mailbox, I act in the expectation that certain con-temporaries of mine (post office employees) will adequately interpret the wish I signified by writing out an address, attaching a stamp, etc., and will in fact carry it out. The expec-tation which oriented my action was not directed to specific concrete individuals but to the genus "post office employees." Max Weber pointed out that the acceptance of money as legal tender depends on the sub-jective chance that other contemporaries will also accept these tiny physical objects as means of payment. This, too, is an example of a They-orientation referring to the typical conduct of typical contemporaries. If I per-form or refrain from performing some deter-minate act in order to avoid the intervention of certain people with badges and uniforms —to adduce another of Weber's examples—that is to say, if I orient my conduct to the law and its enforcement agencies, I stand in a social relation with my contemporaries, personified according to ideal types, i.e., in a They-relation.

In these examples I have acted with the expectation that certain determinate kinds of conduct are likely on the part of others: postal clerks, individuals involved in mone-tary transactions, policemen. I have a certain attitude toward them: I reckon with them when I plan my actions, in short, I am in a social relation with them. But my partners in these relations do not appear as concrete and specific individuals. They appear as instances of the genus "postal clerk," "user of the currency," "policeman." I ascribe to them specific patterns of conduct, specific functional performances. They are relevant for me as contemporaries only so far as they are typical performers of such functions, that is, as ideal types. In the They-relation I draw upon my stock of knowledge accord-ing to which there are "people" who are "typical" clerks, policemen, etc., and who do "typical" things *as* clerks, policemen, etc. I do not care how they "feel" about being clerks and doing police work, how, in other words, they experience their (ongoing) con-duct in a subjective context of meaning. For me, their performances stand basically in an objective context of meaning. In the They-relation my partners are not concrete and unique individuals, but *types*.

This essential feature of the experience of contemporaries should not lead one to the false conclusion that one apprehends the conduct of others by typification only in rela-tion to the world of contemporaries. It is true that the experience of contemporaries is *always* in the form of typifications, but the same holds for the apprehension of the world of predecessors. Furthermore, since knowledge of typical patterns of action and of personal ideal types constitutes part of one's stock of knowledge about social reality in general, typifications of this kind are also used in the experience of partners in the concrete We-relation, i.e., of the unique individual face-to-face with me. Consequently, *ideal types serve also as schemes of interpretation for that domain of social reality which is experienced directly.* However, there is an important difference: in the concrete We-relation the typifying schemata are swept along and modified by the unique Thou apprehended in the immediacy of a shared vivid present. The typifying schemata are, so to speak, formal models without content, matched against the concrete fellow-man and thereby deprived of their status as mere typifications. We shall illustrate this point with an example.

I am face-to-face with several fellow-men. Their experiences appear to me as an undivided and unbroken sequence of events in their conscious life. But the "They" with which I am face-to-face can be always resolved into a Thou and Thou and Thou in such manner that I can join with each Thou in a concrete We-relation. If, for example, I am observing three fellow-men playing cards, I can direct my attention to each of the players. In the Thou-orientation I can apprehend the way in which this particular individual is attending to the business at hand, the subjective context of meaning within which he places this business, etc., a context which will vary from player to player. But, as a detached observer. I can also transpose, as it were, the situation from the vivid present into the typified world of contemporaries. I draw upon my stock of knowledge and say: They are playing a game of rummy. Statements of this kind refer to the conscious life of the individual players only in so far as the typical performance "card-playing" is co-ordinated with a sequence of ongoing experiences for each player. These, it may be assumed, stand in a subjective context of meaning for him. But thereby I merely postulate that if, indeed, he is playing rummy, his conduct must be oriented by the rules of the game. This postulate is, of course, generally applicable to people who play rummy, any time, anywhere, and is by no means restricted to the three persons in front of me. No concrete

experience of A is identical with any concrete experience of B or C since it belongs to the conscious life of one specific individual at a specific moment of his biography. The concrete experience is unique and cannot be repeated. It is neither identical nor even commensurable with any real experience of B. *The typical—and only the typical—is homogeneous.* Only in so far as I disregard the unique individuals A and B and C and say, "They" are playing cards, do I recognize in them an example of the anonymous genus "card-player." By typifying them I have performed an interpretive act of thought which bestowed anonymity upon A, B, and C.

The objective matrix of meaning which originated in the construction of typical experiences of typical contemporaries, coordinated with typical performances, may be retranslated into subjective configurations of meaning. I apply the typifications which are part of my stock of knowledge to concrete fellow-men in face-to-face situations. I apprehend the fellow-men as individuals "like others" of a designated type. At the same time, these fellow-men, as partners in a We-relation, are experienced directly. Therefore, they are "people like others" and yet unique individuals, endowed with a conscious life which goes on before my eyes.

Bibliography

Texts

Collected Papers, Vol. 1, *The Problem of Social Reality*, 1962; Vol. 2, *Studies in Social Theory*, 1964; Vol. 3, *Studies in Phenomenological Philosophy*, 1966. The Hague: Martinus Nijhoff.

The Phenomenology of the Social World. Evanston, Ill.: Northwestern University Press, 1967.

Studies

Natanson, M. "Introduction" in A. Schutz *Collected Papers*, Vol. 1, pp. xxv–xlvii, also H. van Breda "Preface," in *ibid.*, pp.vi–xiii.
Tymieniecka, A. T. *Phenomenology and Science in Contemporary European Thought.* New York: Noonday Books, Farrar, Straus & Giroux, Inc., 1960, pp. 104 ff.

25

Introduction

Karl Rahner was born in the university town of Freiburg-im-Breisgau in the southwest corner of Germany on March 5, 1904, a little more than a decade before Heidegger (in 1915) and Husserl (in 1916) came there to make Freiburg one of the two or three most important centers of modern existential and phenomenological philosophy, and a little 'ess than a decade before Husserl published 1is epoch-making *Ideas Concerning a Pure Phenomenology and Phenomenological Philosophy* (1913). It was the year when Jaspers was studying medicine at Heidelberg, Marcel was enduring the last of his *Lycée* imprisonment in France, Heidegger was finishing at the Gymnasium and about to begin his brief tenure as a seminarian and Jesuit, and Teilhard de Chardin was studying philosophy on an island in the English Channel.

In 1922 Rahner decided to become a Jesuit, as his older brother Hugo had before him. After three years of philosophical studies at Pullach, Germany, two years of teaching at the Jesuit college in Feldkirch, Austria, and four years of theological studies at Valkenburg in the Netherlands, where he was ordained a priest in 1932, Rahner returned to Freiburg in 1934 for two years of study in philosophy under Heidegger. It was during these two years that Rahner wrote his first major philosophical work, *Geist in Welt* (*Spirit in the World*) a metaphysics of human cognition. In 1937 he was appointed lecturer in dogmatic theology at the University of Innsbruck, Austria. War ended this in 1938. During the Nazi occupation of Austria and through the war years he did pastoral work in Vienna and in a small village in Bavaria. During this time he published his second philosophical work, *Hörer des Wortes*, on the foundation of a philosophy of religion. Besides being his only strictly philosophical books, these two works were also really his last books. His 2,040 publications between 1924 and 1969 (this number includes reviews by him and translations of him) have been mainly articles (for journals and lexicons) and short monographs (e.g., the series *Questiones Disputatae*).

In 1948 Rahner returned to the University of Innsbruck as professor of dogmatic theology and of the history of dogma. He remained there until 1964, when he took Romano Guardini's chair on the philosophical faculty of the University of Munich as professor of Christian anthropology and the philosophy of religion, while also serving as a theologian at the Second Vatican Council.

Rahner's entire orientation as a scholar has been service to modern, contemporary man, a commitment rooted in the consciousness of the obligation all men have to be of some service to one another. If his calling and his concept of the ultimate goal of service have made his philosophy theocentric, the same orientation has made his theology anthropocentric. This concern for the relationship of human persons to the divine led him first to work out a philosophical anthropology which then became the foundation and motivation for a theological anthropology. He began in *Geist in Welt* with a study of human behavior as man's nature in action, of human activity considered as man's self-expression and self-revelation. Some of man's activities were common also to animals, to life, and to active things in general. But two were proper to man and therefore promised a better understanding of man than other activities. One was human cognition and the other, volition. *Human* cognition was shown in language and scientific and cultural creativity. Volition was man's real though limited self-determinability as shown in responsibility and commitment. Rahner focused on cognition as the activity offering a privileged access to the human nature that is its source. He found human cognition to be, on the one hand, an act by which man is in the world and outside or *absent* and at a distance from *himself*. Absence from self thereby made possible *presence to* some perceived *other* while still *remaining* oneself in the act. He found it, on the other hand, to be an act by which man is *present to himself* and able to distinguish himself from whatever nonself appears on what is experienced as an apparently unlimited horizon of possibility. This horizon is not really experienced clearly or in itself, as one would an object, but as an unobjectified and unobjectifiable *anticipation*. To experience something *as* limited or to recognize limitation as such is already to transcend it cognitively, to be by anticipation on the other side of that limit. Otherwise the thing would fill the horizon, whereas it never does. This horizon is that toward which man is by nature oriented and facing, so that he transcends, with a kind of momentum carrying him right on by and beyond them, all the beings that one by one stand out silhouetted, profiled, and bounded within its unbounded expanse. Rahner suggests that we name that whereby man in his cognitive act is *absent* (or distinct) *from self and present* (or identical) *with other*, "sense," "body," "matter," or "*world*," and name that whereby man is *present* (or identical) *with self and absent* (or distinct)

from other, "*spirit*." Man's cognitive acts, therefore, reveal his essence as a "worlded" spirit, a materialized or incarnate spirit. As *incarnate*, man is dependent on his senses, on the world, and on matter. As *spirit*, he transcends the senses, the world, and matter. Man is both: man as incarnate spirit is dependent transcendence and transcending dependence. Man depends at every instant on sense, matter, and world while, and though, transcending it; and he transcends it only while, and though, dependent on it.

From this concept of man Rahner bridges from philosophical anthropology to theological anthropology through a philosophy of religion which shows that since man is an incarnate *spirit*, i.e., a *spirit* in the world, he is by nature an unlimited openness and therefore not a priori an impossible recipient of revelation. And he shows that as an *incarnate* spirit, i.e., a spirit in the *world*, man is by nature temporal and historical, and therefore any such revelation must happen and be sought for in human history: man is he who listens for and to the Word (*Hörer des Wortes*).

In style and vocabulary Rahner shows the influence of Heidegger. His two books were written during and immediately following his study under Heidegger at Freiburg. It is no surprise therefore to find his influence in the content as well.

THE NATURE OF TRUTH *

The reflections that we are going to make can be grouped into three equal parts. If we express ourselves in Thomist terms, these are: I—The judgment; II—The light of the agent intellect; III—God, pure being, pure thought. And if we adopt Hegelian terminology, corresponding to the three parts of his *Phenomenology of Spirit*, we would have:

* By permission of Karl Rahner, "Truth in St. Thomas Aquinas," *Revista Portuguesa de Filosofia*, vol. 7, pp. 353–370, 1951. Andrew Tallon, translator.

consciousness (Bewusstsein); self-consciousness (Selbstbewusstsein); absolute spirit.

The first part imposes itself upon our consideration because St. Thomas believed that for man truth exists only in the judgment; the second, because for St. Thomas the judgment is not passive reception of an impression but active, creative synthesis, realized between the transcendental "a priori" of the spirit (the light of the agent intellect) and sense experience; the third imposes itself as well because St. Thomas recognizes, corresponding to the truth of the judgment, the ontological truth of being itself, an interior luminosity of being in the measure in which it is being, luminosity which has its full realization, its first and original norm, in Absolute Being, which is absolute Spirit.

I The Judgment. "Truth consists in the adequation of knowledge with its object . . ." even according to Kant in the Critique of Pure Reason.¹ Nor should it cause wonder that in the Thomist metaphysics of the essence of truth the same statement be the point of departure and, if we wish, the definition of truth: adæquatio rei et intellectus.²

At bottom, however, such a definition is only a preliminary sketch, or rather a description of what we already know when we begin to investigate what truth is. The same thing happens with this question as happens with all truly metaphysical questions: it is a question about known being and, by that very fact, about the always uncomprehended.

Indeed, what do we wish to affirm when we say that truth is encountered in the adequation between thought and object? What do "thinking," "being," and "adequating" properly mean? How can all this, reciprocally, be in agreement? It is evident that we will be able to comprehend this basic definition perfectly, a definition otherwise so well known, only if we comprehend each of its elements according to their origin and if we comprehend them precisely with the meaning they have in this statement in which we find them united.

As for what we should think of the intellect, we find a first indication in that statement of St. Thomas in which he affirms that the judgment is the seat of human truth. Now it is clear that according to the common thought of men, what is identified with the thing is the content of the judgment and not the judicative act as such: illud quod intellectus intelligendo dicit et cognoscit, oportet esse rei adaequatum . . . non

operatio qua id dicit.³ Such an intelligible content which, at least in certain circumstances, claims to be true, is for St. Thomas only the judgment and not the simple concept, i.e., what he calls the simplex apprehensio or incomplexum. Therefore, for the end we have in view, it is of major importance to emphasize clearly the essentials of the Thomist doctrine with respect to the judgment. A judgment is not, for St. Thomas, the simple union of concepts, as such, in order thus to form a more concrete concept. Such a concretizing synthesis (Heidegger calls it predicative synthesis) is, according to St. Thomas, still an incomplexum, for example the definition. For there really to be a judgment, and, by that very fact, truth, more is required; what is required is a relation of this concretizing synthesis with the thing as it is in itself—a comparatio vel applicatio ad rem per affirmationem vel negationem.

This affirmative or objectifying synthesis (through which alone exists a complex, a judgment), which we could also call, with Heidegger, "veritative" synthesis, is then the constitutive element of the judgment. By that very fact it is also the constitutive element of truth, if this affirmative synthesis is de facto realized. It is proper to note, moreover, that the subject and the predicate do not perform the same function in the sentence. In this way analysis reveals the Thomist doctrine of the concretizing synthesis: the objective concept of the predicate is referred, by the affirmative synthesis, to the thing as it is in itself (which is designated by the subject of the enunciation) in such a way that the affirmative synthesis is as much a condition of the possibility of the concretizing synthesis as vice versa.

Truth exists, then, for St. Thomas, only in such a judgment. Indeed, only in it exists the affirmative and objectifying relation of the known and conceptual content, to the thing in itself.⁴ This thing, as such, is inde-

¹ Critique of Pure Reason, B 83.
² Cf I, qu. 21, a. 2c; De Ver., qu. 1, a. 1 c., etc.

³ C. Gentes, I. 59.
⁴ I.e.: "Indeed, the relation (a relation that is affirmative and objectifying) of the content (a content that is known and conceptual) to the thing in

pendent of anyone's psychic perception of it; from it the judgment draws its value, for the concretizing synthesis of the judgment is no more than the intellectual reproduction of the synthesis that objectively exists between a subject (*hypokeimenon*) and a quiddity (quidditas, forma, etc.): synthesis, by means of which the subject is determined.

How does the subject know, however, in uttering a judgment that in its relative reproduction of the objective synthesis it succeeds in really attaining a perfect adequation? It is clear that it cannot be thought "a priori" (at least in general) in a comparison of the thing known in the judgment with the thing in itself.

To understand St. Thomas' opinion on this point, more than anything else we have to remember that according to Aquinas the judgment as well as the concept contains a double element: one is the sense element, the other is the intellectual (i.e. imagination, the sense element, and concept, the intellectual, insofar as concept is based on the spontaneity of the intellect, as we could say with Kant). St. Thomas would willingly subscribe to Kant's statement: "thoughts without content are hollow, images without concepts are blind." [5]

What Kant says here St. Thomas subsumes under the general heading of the necessary conversion (i.e. "turning," or, perhaps better, "permanent turnedness" [Tr.]) of spontaneous thought to the phantasm. [6] For St. Thomas, as for Kant, there are no intuitions that are not sensitive. And as for sense intuition, with respect to its truth, its certainty, and its metaphysical essence, we will say just in passing that according to St. Thomas the sensibility as such, in attaining concrete being, attains it in its own reality. The "impression engraved in the receptivity of our consciousness" is, simultaneously and in strict identity, a reality of the sensible object itself and of the sensibility as such.

This realism, apparently ingenuous, is nevertheless profoundly metaphysical. Indeed, it proceeds from a conception of the sensibility that is a metaphysico-ontological one, and not merely an empirico-sensualistic one. This latter conception would consist in conceiving the senses as mere instruments of perception, in the manner of a camera, while the former conception, on the contrary, originates in the conception of a limited receptive intuition of the singular as such which is represented in itself. Thus it comprehends at its roots the metaphysical concept of the material, i.e., of the materiality of the thing that is represented, and of the materiality, or sensibility, of receptive intuitive knowledge.

Unfortunately it is not possible to develop this transcendental deduction of the sensibility that belongs necessarily to a finite receptive intuition. We can only affirm, although it be somewhat unphilosophical to do so, that for St. Thomas the apprehension of certain determinations of the material object in its very entity, through sense, includes no contradiction. For him the metaphysical essence of the affecting of one material being by another equally material being (contrary to the common interpretation) consists in a reality of the agent being strictly identical with a reality of the patient. Let us imagine now that this determination, as such, of the patient, becomes conscious. In this case, since the patient we are dealing with is sensibility, a determination of the agent as such also becomes consciously perceived. If anyone were to insist on saying that according to obvious experience what we experience directly by the senses (sensible qualities) can exist only in sense experience itself, St. Thomas would respond: the determination of a being (say, "A"), although it belongs to it only insofar as it is acting on the patient ("B"), does not fail, because of that, to be a determination of that same being ("A"). It produces that determination as simultaneously its own and the patient's. This position admitted, ample room remains for the physical and metaphysical aspects of the problem. On one hand, physics will answer the question that belongs to it: what

itself exists only in the judgment." The *relation of content* to *thing* exists only in *judgment.*—Tr.
[5] *Critique of Pure Reason,* B 75.
[6] I, qu. 84, a. 7.

the determinations of the material being are, determinations that are proper to it independently of the reality that affects the sensible thing insofar as this reality affects the sensibility.

On the other hand, prior to the physical question and independently of it, it is possible to resolve the metaphysical question: how is it that cognition can attain another being in its own reality, in a receptive way? Indeed, such a question, of itself, ought to be resolved antecedently to and independently of physics: antecedently, because notwithstanding the critique of the appearances that this question performs, it already presupposes, of itself, and necessarily, a world distinct from external cognition, and, by that fact, it presupposes a cognition that already attained the external object; and independently, even though the physical question judges that such sense cognition experientially apprehends nothing but the subjective impression itself. Besides, in this supposition there should be a real distinction between cognition and the thing known. It is a matter of finite experience of the sensibility —of a finite experience provoked by a finite being, as it is in itself, and which is manifested in itself. Now because it is a matter of this experience, because it is a question of a cognition in which the object is the sensible thing in its very sensible phenomenality, the reason is perfectly self-evident why, according to St. Thomas, sense cognition, as such, cannot be false, nor, strictly speaking, true.[7] Purely passive conscious acceptance—Hegel would say consciousness (Bewusstsein) without self-consciousness (Selbstbewusstsein), and Kant would say receptivity without spontaneity—permits, in its passivity, the object to introduce itself into the receptivity of the senses of the one knowing and thus show itself as it is; but this passivity deprives the sensibility of the power to distinguish itself from its impression and from the object, and to pronounce upon it as it is in itself. The sensibility always experiences a true reality, but cannot enunciate it through a judgment. It is therefore strictly impossible for it as such to be true or false.

It possesses the objects partially, but at the same time loses itself in vacuous and unordered particularities. Where such a sensibility exists in unity of consciousness simultaneously with a spontaneous spiritual cognition, as happens in man, this still sublogical evidence of the object, although it reveals itself by itself in the sensibility, can naturally have a certain importance for grounding truth; but, by itself, it grounds only the truth of the material content of a particular judgment. However, the formal structure of this judgment—and with more reason the structure and the content of universal judgments and especially of metaphysical judgments—cannot be grounded in the evidence of sense perception.

II The Light of the Agent Intellect. Therefore, if we ask in what the truth of the judgment is founded, since this is more than pure passive acceptance of an impression of the particular sensible object as such, we arrive, in St. Thomas as well as in all the great metaphysicians of knowledge, from Plato to Hegel, at a principle of truth prior to the sense impression. St. Thomas does not see such a principle, in the line of Plato, Plotinus, Augustine, Bonaventure, Malebranche, in an objective "a priori," which, as a second realm of objects immediately accessible to man, transcends the particular objects apprehended by the senses, but, in the line of Aristotle, Kant, and Hegel, he sees it in a formal "a priori" of the spontaneous spirit itself. That is to say, that principle does not have truth objectively seen as idea, God, light from God, etc., for its basis; its basis, speaking in the manner of St. Thomas, is in the light of the intelligence itself, which informs, objectifies, conceptualizes, and judges the data from sense cognition.

A transcendental deduction of this formal "a priori" of the intelligence in the Thomist sense can be made in different ways. We could, with St. Thomas, investigate the apri-

[7] *De Ver.* qu. I, a. 11.

oristic conditions of the possibility of conceptualizing the singular object sensibly apprehended. It is in this way that St. Thomas ordinarily conceives the notion of spontaneity of the intelligence (of the *intellectus agens,* as he calls it, supported by an Aristotelian notion) and of its essential structure.

We could also investigate, according to the mind of St. Thomas, the condition of the possibility of what St. Thomas calls *"reditio subjecti in seipsum,"* which is the distinctive attitude of spirit in relation to all other infra-intellectual beings, and which we could call, in modern terms and in the language of Hegel, self-consciousness (Selbstbewusstsein). It becomes possible for the knower to loose himself from sense experience, to keep himself free above it, in the exteriorization (which occurs in the ambiance of the sense impression, judging it as true) which is necessary in order for him to know himself in himself as opposed to the world, or, according to Heidegger's terminology, in order to be "existence" (Dasein). Since we have to face this total problem in the perspective of the certainty of truth, we wish at least to make allusion to another path that is most directly related with this same question. The certainty of the truth of any judgment that may have no relation with the evidence of sense perception is effected, according to St. Thomas, by a return to the first principles. These occupy the first place *in via inventionis,* and the thinking subject turns to them in the verification of his judgments, *resolvendo.*[8] We do not intend here to penetrate further into the content of the first principles. We only note that St. Thomas did not consider them simply in the order of formal logic; he considered them also in the ontological order, that is, as apodictic and metaphysical principles that claim to be necessary and simply valid for every being. In what then is this certainty of the truth of these first principles founded?

Evidently it is not a question of establishing them through reasoning by a syllogism. They have to be seen as evident in them-

selves: *dicendum quod omnis scientia habetur per aliqua principia per se nota et per consequens visa.*[9] They are *"per se nota,"* as St. Thomas often says. It is no doubt licit to express ourselves this way. But to interpret this Thomist justification of truth correctly is precisely to know what this evidence means.

The evidence of first principles is not the vision of a *given,* as if a thing in itself, although non-existent, were to present itself to the mind, as if a sentence, for example, were to present itself to the spirit and become seen in its objective ideality. St. Thomas does not know sentences in themselves, "values," "ideas in themselves." He rejects all that absolutely. For him there exists no objective realm of ideal essences absolutely independent of the existent being: i.e. no two realms, one of being and one of knowability.

The hypothesis of a vision of ideas objective in themselves (of which theory Thomas Aquinas was acquainted from Plato and Saint Augustine) should lead logically to ontologism, to intuition of absolute being in itself. Now St. Thomas rejects this "a priori" theory for theological motives as well as for motives based on the Aristotelian metaphysics of cognition. Nor does Aquinas admit the evidence of the conceptual data in itself, as if the intrinsic intelligibility of the intelligible content of singular concepts of the subject and predicate of the first principles as such could establish the value of these principles relatively to being in itself.

This thesis of classical pre-Kantian rationalism of the 17th and 18th centuries would also have had an adversary in St. Thomas, as in fact it had in Kant. For that matter he already refuted it, and for the same motives as Kant, i.e., the ontological argument for the existence of God. This argument would be valid according to the presuppositions of classical rationalism, and, for that matter, not only in Leibniz and Wolff, but also, in the medieval equivalent of this rationalism (although verified in a way more objectively

8 I, qu. 79, a. 8 c. etc.

9 I-II qu. I, a. 5c.

mystical and a little ontologistic), in Saint Anselm, Saint Albert the Great, Giles of Rome, Thomas of Strasbourg, Saint Bonaventure, etc. The evidence, no doubt existent, of the conception of different concepts that necessarily must be made relative to the first principles, only has ontological value if the ontological meaning of these concepts is known. This can be verified by considering the ontological argument and its respective refutation. St. Thomas, however, affirms purely and simply that it is not evident from such meaning, for we are in a field in which concepts outstrip the concrete sense experience of the singular and are not only a mere indication of the same. These universal concepts, which ground the first principles, present themselves to man in a perception of sensibly experienced singular things: it is in this sense—and only in this sense—that the universal metaphysical concepts are abstracted from the singular object that ultimately is apprehended by the senses. In this manner St. Thomas is Aristotelian and not Platonic. This Aristotelianism of his would be very poorly understood if from it we would want to conclude precipitously that the ontological value of metaphysical concepts is adequately founded, for St. Thomas, on the particular sensible objects as such. St. Thomas is totally convinced that the singular as such can express only something of itself, and that many singulars, experienced as such, can ground only a universality of empirical, indicative, and merely assertive propositions, but never the metaphysical universality of concepts that would be required in order to ground an apodictic universality and validity of the metaphysical propositions of the first principles.

In order to ground this universality of metaphysical ideas, a principle is needed that precedes the individual, i.e., an "a priori" principle; and, as such, according to what we have said already, it is not admitted by St. Thomas as objective or for itself alone (for it can only be a formal "a priori" principle of the spontaneous spirit itself); St. Thomas calls it *lumen intellectus agentis*. This light is the "a priori" form under which

the spontaneity of the spirit perceives the material sensible; for that very reason St. Thomas calls for the matter of the intelligible from within the sense of impression.

This same light informs the material sensible, thus constructing the "intelligible in act," synthesis between the material sensible and the "a priori" principle of the spirit. This aprioristic form, under which the sensible element is apprehended, is, in the Thomist metaphysics of knowledge, ontologically no more than the dynamic movement of the intellect toward the absolute totality of objects that are accessible to human intellect as such: the *tendentia in objectum formale adaequatum intellectus* as it is expressed in Thomist language.

Because it is apprehended in this dynamic tendency of the intellect, which Hegel would call "appetite" (Begierde), the particular sensible thing is known as finite, i.e., as incapable, in its limitation, of filling up the space of this dynamism. Because of this comparing the particular thing to the absolute and ideal term of knowledge, the particular thing appears as existent (concrete being) in relation to Being, and because of that as "such," as a finite individual, corresponding to which, because of its finitude, there are other possibles as objects of still another possible experience. By knowing the particular thing this way, the universal is known at the same time, and vice versa. Transcendence relative to all the possible objects of knowledge appears thus as a transcendental condition for the possibility of abstraction and therefore of judgment, i.e., of comprehension of something, *as* something; such a transcendence is also the transcendental condition for *reditio completa*, i.e., for self-consciousness.

Now in the first place, the problem arises of the ambit of this transcendence of the horizon of possible objects of human knowledge, transcendence which manifested itself by the first light of the agent intellect. Here St. Thomas separates himself from Kant. For Kant, transcendence of reason and of its formal "a priori" does not of itself extend beyond the field of the imagination, i.e., of sense intuition. In Thomist terminology, for Kant the *objectum formale* of human intellect is the *ens principium numeri*, the *ens materiale*, the *existent* that brings with itself matter as intrinsic principle, matter which is for St. Thomas the metaphysical reason for the formation of space and time. Aquinas however thinks another way: intellect's transcendence is directed simply toward being, outstrips the domain of the sensibility, thus manifesting a knowledge of being as such, and grounding therefore the possibility of metaphysics in its human specificity.

To carry out the transcendental deduction of this ambit here would delay us too long. Let us be content to indicate the works of J. Maréchal, which are without doubt the best explanation of the problem of Kant according to the spirit of St. Thomas. It is necessary, however, in our study, to note the following: this manifestation of the domain of a metaphysics that outstrips the sensibility and includes all being, even according to St. Thomas, is not realized by means of a certain direct intuition of metaphysical being, in the sense of classical rationalism or of ontologism. For St. Thomas it is realized in another way, and it is precisely this that the deduction of this ambit of transcendence would have to show. For St. Thomas the affirmation of this ambit and that of the knowledge of being that with it, and only with it, is affirmed and manifested (especially in the ultimate and most formal structures), belongs to the transcendental conditions for the possibility of objective and judicative knowledge of a spirit conscious of itself relative to the objects of sense intuition. In other words: it must be shown that transcendence, as condition that makes judicative and aprioristic knowledge of the objects of the intuitive world possible, must be a transcendence that outstrips this world and therefore is affirmed as such in all finite cognition. Once this transcendental deduction has been made—we omit it here—the condition is fulfilled by which Kant himself is ready to recognize a metaphysics. Judicative knowledge of the world—of the physical,

as Kant says—does not offer an immediate vision of the metaphysical, but contains implicitly, as condition for its own possibility, the affirmation of transcendental being and of its ultimate structures.

In St. Thomas these structures are not immediately and formally affirmed by the categories—these categories also belong, according to St. Thomas, primarily to material being—but affirmed before, by what St. Thomas calls the transcendental determination of being. These are for St. Thomas the primitive categories of metaphysical being. It is from these metaphysical concepts that the first principles are formed, that are valid therefore for being as such, and for that reason are valid also for the being of immediate sense experience.

Now we can indicate more exactly the nature of the evidence of first principles to which St. Thomas reduces the certainty of all our true judgments. And an objection cannot be made on the basis of experimental sense evidence, for this, as such, is not of itself alone in any way a judgment, and therefore also is not a true judgment.

The evidence of judgments is based ultimately on the first principles. These are essentially metaphysical, i.e., intrinsically valid relative to being as such. The legitimacy of this claim of value is not known through an evidence of the thing that is affirmed and that emanates from the thing itself. This would suppose either a possibility of comparing the idea with the metaphysical object in itself, and therefore would suppose a metaphysical intuition, or would be equivalent to confusing the idea with the existent object in itself.

The evidence of first principles is prior to the objective vision of what man affirms in all the judgments he formulates in his knowledge of the world; the metaphysical value of these principles and that of this affirmation is implicitly the "a priori" condition for the possibility of knowledge of the world. With the same necessity with which man judges, he also affirms the metaphysical value of the "a priori" structures of being as such, structures which he places and affirms jointly in his transcendental "a priori."

And since an existential suspension (*epoché*) of his judicative relation to the world is simply impossible for man, he necessarily and implicitly affirms these metaphysical principles; and he would, in his thought, commit an offense against the principle of contradiction (since this is a formal law of thought), if he were to deny or doubt explicitly the ontological laws of being implicitly affirmed. Human evidence of metaphysical principles is not based ultimately then on an identity of concepts, as such, conceived on the basis of evidence (such principles are also "a priori" synthetic in a Thomist metaphysics of knowledge, of course), but rather on the evidence of the formal logical contradiction between one's implicit affirmation and explicit negation of the value of those principles. For whoever might be in the condition of being able to realize a metaphysical and existential suspension (*epoché*) of the judgement as such (to doubt is also to judge), the metaphysical principles would cease to have value; but, at the same moment, such a person would cease to be what he affirms himself to be in every action: limited spirit, "existence" (in the modern sense of existential philosophy).

Given this conception of the evidence of limited human knowledge, one clearly comprehends that the Thomist metaphysics of knowledge cannot be censured by saying that its theory of the adequation of truth is based on the ingenuous supposition of the comparison of the thing in itself with the thing insofar as known, in the way we would know the adequation. In sense knowledge, explained strictly in accord with Thomism, such an objection has no foundation, because object known and object in itself are strictly the same thing. In what it says in respect to metaphysical objects and their evidence, this objection is vain, because such evidence for limited knowledge is not founded on the thing in itself but on the "a priori" of the intellect. Therefore in no way is there made "a priori" the attempt of a comparison. This attempt is itself based on a failure to comprehend what spirit is, for it is in spirit that truth originally has its native land.

The little importance that St. Thomas "a priori" attributes to the attempt of a comparison between the object in itself and the apprehended object is indeed manifest from the fact that he writes in the *De Veritate* [10] that truth exists in the intellect by means of the judgment about the thing in itself. However, this truth, this proportion of the judicative act to the thing (*proportio ad rem*), is not known, in the ultimate analysis, by a reflection, by a look at the thing itself, as perhaps we would hope, but by a reflection of the intellect upon itself. We do not intend to give here a precise interpretation of this text of St. Thomas, on which an immense amount has already been written. Let us say, in order to terminate this second part, only that the transcendental reflection upon the conditions for the possibility of knowledge, i.e. upon the *natura intellectus*, as St. Thomas expresses it, and of which we have been treating above, is precisely, according to our way of looking at it, what St. Thomas, in the place cited, calls the *supra seipsum reflecti* of the intellect.

Truth is, therefore, in each particular case, a judgment upon the object in itself; and because the judgment is an affirmative and "veritative" synthesis, truth grounds our first metaphysical principles of being, which are the foundation that sustains individual judgments. However, these principles are grounded in a formal "a priori" of the spirit, in the *lumen intellectus*. Its value is known, because its implicit affirmation as transcendental condition for the possibility of objects of knowledge as such is known.

In this way we also see what truth meant for St. Thomas in this degree of that self-consciousness which is always necessarily joined to true judgments. For man, truth is only in the judgment. The judgment supposes abstraction and self-consciousness. Both are possible solely thanks to the transcendental "a priori" of spirit, which opens on the horizon of being as such. In this way a *particular* true judgment relative to a concrete being is possible only in an implicit, though formal, judgment of being as such,

[10] Cf. especially qq. 1–9.

and by means of that judgment, i.e., in a comprehension of being as such; and therefore, in the ultimate analysis, it is an implicit affirmation of the pure being of God himself. *Omnes cognoscentes implicite cognoscunt Deum in quolibet cognito.* Truth is only possible in the presence of being as such.

III Pure Being and Pure Thought. Nevertheless, we have not yet arrived at the end. The heart of the metaphysico-Thomist notion of truth is still lacking. We said that for St. Thomas truth in the human judgment supposes essentially a formal "a priori" principle in the understanding itself that judges, as condition for the possibility of truth, what is implicitly there to be affirmed; and truth is precisely a judgment of the thing as it is in itself. Because of this, spirit brings with itself the ultimate and most formal metaphysical structure of its possible objects. Spirit should therefore be affirmed as structure of its objects, i.e., of being as such and in itself. Substantially, this means only the affirmation of a radical unity of being and knowing, for it is only on this hypothesis that the value of the formal "a priori" of spirit, relative to being, can be justified. That is primarily to say that by the fact of man's affirming in every judgment the value of its transcendental "a priori" (and with it the first principles of being as such), he affirms also the intrinsic intelligibility of the existent as such: *quidquid est intelligi potest.*[11]

Moreover, it is further affirmed that any existent, as a possible object of knowledge, has an intrinsic orientation toward knowledge and a possible knower; this orientation is a determination given to every existent together with the essence of the being. Therefore being and knowing must possess a certain radical unity, or, as St. Thomas says, be *unius generis;* this is an axiom that evidently applies primarily to Pure Being and then to other beings in the measure that they are, and are not affected by non-being, i.e., by prime matter.

Indeed, the essentially necessary correla-

tivity of the two can be founded ultimately only in a radical unity of both. This means that being and knowing are correlatives, because they are radically the same thing. Pure Being and pure Knowing are the same thing and we call him God. A limited existent knows and is known to himself in the measure in which he is analogically being. Only thus, finally, is the ultimate metaphysical understanding of knowledge and therefore of the notion of truth awakened, and is truth revealed in its profound sense. If being and knowing (pure being, absolutely, and an existent, in the measure in which it is being) form a radical unity, knowing can consist, in the ultimate analysis, only in possessing an object intentionally present [i.e., being intentionally in the presence of an object.—Tr.]. Knowing can be conceived only as the self-presence of the existent to itself, i.e., as the internal luminosity of being relative to itself, or again as the identity in being between knowing and being which primarily knows itself, primarily knower and primarily known. True knowledge is, therefore, fundamentally the indubitable self-presence of being to itself. Knowledge and truth are intentional thought representative of something different from the knower, because this knower, divided in its finitude (i.e. divided by being internally affected by non-being), is not everything, and is therefore unable to know everything beforehand, through an interiorly illuminated self-possession.

Despite everything, to know, because it means to extend oneself and "disperse oneself" over objects, is always to take possession of oneself, which is the beginning and end of knowledge; and the degree of possibility of this conscious return to oneself is, for St. Thomas, the essential indication of the degree of potency of being that belongs to an existent. [12]

Since for Aquinas knowledge is true because it comprehends being in general in the measure in which it is at the same time, and necessarily, an opening of the being itself of the subject that is knowing, we can

[11] C. *Gentes,* II, 98

[12] C. *Gentes,* IV, 11.

affirm, in modern terminology, that true knowledge is also always an existential task of man. Indeed, the more man draws back toward himself and becomes more present to himself, the more he places himself in the presence of being as such.

Once it is seen that knowledge is a self-presence of being, in a radical unity, we should be able to comprehend easily what ontological truth is for St. Thomas. It would be the same thing as emphasizing the essential coordination of ontological truth and logical truth. Any existent is interiorly illuminated to itself, i.e., possesses itself with itself through the object of logical truth, in the measure in which it is being; and this is ultimately the reason why it is knowable, why it is capable of being an object of knowledge, and therefore ontologically true.

Because of this, in God (pure being) logical and ontological truth are absolutely identified.

We may end here with a brief summary:

First, truth is having present with oneself the thing in itself in the judgment, which is a relation of synthesis that concretizes two ideas about the same object.

Second, truth is perceived because humanly it exists only in the judgment; it is always based on a transcendental "a priori" of a formal nature. In this "a priori," on the one hand, are affirmed the most formal structures of being as such, and this affirmation introduces the ultimate human foundation of truth in the intelligible necessity with which it is affirmed implicitly in every judgment; on the other hand, this transcendental "a priori" is the transcendental condition for the possibility of self-consciousness. For that reason we can say that truth is possible only in self-consciousness. To encounter truth is always also for spirit to return to itself.

Third, truth is therefore, in its profoundest sense, the interior clarity, the intelligibility that belongs "ipso facto" to an existent in the measure in which it is being; it is the self-presence of being with itself, in such a way that pure being and pure thought are the same thing,—absolute spirit, in

whose presence we find ourselves through the transcendence of our spirit. And, since there is truth only where there is transcendence of being as such, the most hidden cause of every truth and what at the same time actuates all truth, is one alone: GOD.

By way of conclusion: the most personal and at the same time the most metaphysical existential can be expressed for us in the well known verses of St. Thomas: *Adoro te devote latens deitas, quae sub his figuris vere latitas.* Everything is an appearance of God who in the appearance is ever revealed and ever hidden.

Bibliography

Texts

Spirit in the World. New York: Herder and Herder, Inc., 1968.

Hearers of the Word. New York: Herder and Herder, Inc., 1969.

On the Theology of Death. New York: Herder and Herder, Inc., 1965.

Hominisation. London: Burns & Oates Ltd., 1965.

"Introduction to the Concept of Existential Philosophy in Heidegger," *Philosophy Today,* vol. 13 (1969), pp. 126–137.

Studies

Roberts, L. *The Achievement of Karl Rahner.* New York: Herder and Herder, Inc., 1967.

John, H. J. *The Thomist Spectrum.* New York: Fordham University Press, 1966, pp. 167–179.

Tallon, A. "Rahner and Personization," *Philosophy Today,* vol. 14 (1970), pp. 44–56.

―――. "Spirit, Matter, Becoming: Karl Rahner's *Spirit in the World (Geist in Welt)*", *Modern Schoolman,* vol. 48 (1971), pp. 151–165.

Baker, K. "Rahner: The Transcendental Method." *Continuum,* vol. 2 (1964), pp. 51–59.

McCool, G. "The Philosophy of the Human Person in Karl Rahner's Theology." *Theological Studies,* vol. 22 (1961), pp. 537–562.

America, (Special Issue), vol. 123 (Oct. 31, 1970).

26

Introduction

Jean-Paul Sartre was born in Paris in 1905 into a family of mixed Catholic and Protestant background. He lost his father at an early age and went to live with his grandparents at La Rochelle, beginning even then to show his literary productivity by publishing two short stories in 1923 while still a student at the *Lycée*. In 1924 he returned to Paris for four years of philosophical studies at the Ecole Normale Supérieure of the University of Paris. After passing his agrégation examinations, he went to Le Havre to teach at the Lycée, later going to the Lycée Henri IV. In November, 1933, he went to Berlin as a research scholar under a fellowship of the Institut Français de Berlin, remaining there until July, 1934, mainly studying the German phenomenologists, especially Husserl. He did not turn to Heidegger in depth until 1939. Returning to France he next taught philosophy at the Lycée Condorcet, wrote four studies on imagination and the emotions, and in 1938 published *Nausea*. This "novel" made Sartre a spectacular literary success and paved the way for his philosophical success. In 1939 he joined the French Army. He was held prisoner for nine months by the Germans in 1940, was released in 1941 for medical reasons, and spent the next four years as an active member of the resistance movement, while teaching philosophy at the Lycée Condorcet and, in 1943, publishing his most important work, *Being and Nothingness*, subtitled *An Essay in Phenomenological Ontology*. It was a tome of 722 packed pages begun thirteen years before, in 1930. Shortly afterward Sartre put aside teaching and has devoted himself since to writing in philosophy and other areas. Since 1945, when the new monthly review *Les Temps modernes* was launched, Sartre has almost without interruption been its editor. He is apparently still working on a book (or series of books, by now) announced over twenty years ago as *L'Homme*, concerned with the moral perspectives of his ontology. In 1965 he published an autobiographical essay entitled *The Words*.

Sartre's main concern is *freedom*. Freedom is the motif in all his work. As he means it, freedom is best understood as an experience of the human *consciousness* that is in contrast and conflict with experiencing a *thing*. Sartre's often paradoxical analysis of the nature and structures of consciousness makes up almost half of *Being and Nothingness;* a detailed study of the relationships between people, especially as to the role of the body, makes up the larger part of the second half. The last part of the book takes up freedom and responsibility. In his attempt to reconcile freedom and things, subject and object, consciousness and being, Sartre's habit of overstatement, combined with his tendency to view only one side of a phenomenon and not consider alternative interpretations, leads him to identify free consciousness with "the nothing," because consciousness sets itself off against Being and does so by an act of negation. Sartre identifies consciousness, the source of the act of negation, with the nothing. Of course it is true that in consciousness the knower distinguishes himself from the known, but this is not a pure negation. To say something is "existing elsewhere" or is "other" is not to say "not existing," but only to recognize both a presence and a distancing non-identity with the consciousness. Since for Sartre consciousness is a negation of Being which cannot exist without Being, perfect consciousness is, therefore, logically incompatible with perfect Being. God, then, as defined in such terms, is an impossible self-contradiction. It is paradoxical also that Sartre's language in the famous dictum "Existence precedes essence" can mean either that free consciousness, now identified with this existence, is some basic raw material or energy for creativity which man has "by nature," or that a man's "essence" or character and his "authenticity" or "bad faith" are the result of how he uses this energy in his free choices and acts.

Other theses Sartre treats have previously been seen, e.g., the *intentionality* of consciousness, *engagement* as the essentially incarnate nature of consciousness, and *tran-scendence* as the act resulting from the essentially incomplete and unsatisfied nature of consciousness, drawing it outside itself. We have also previously encountered the "gaze" or stare, considered as the basic experience of social existence and seen as a conflict, and the role of the body, especially as consciously experienced in interpersonal relations.

The following selection takes up Sartre's major theme, *responsible freedom*.

FREEDOM AND RESPONSIBILITY *

In our attempt to reach to the heart of freedom we may be helped by the few observations which we have made on the subject in the course of this work and which we must summarize here. In the first chapter we established the fact that if negation comes into the world through human-reality, the latter must be a being who can realize a nihilating rupture with the world and with himself; and we established that the permanent possibility of this rupture is the same as freedom. But on the other hand, we stated that this permanent possibility of nihilating what I am in the form of "having-been" implies for man a particular type of existence. We were able then to determine by means of analyses like that of bad faith that human reality is its own nothingness. For the for-itself, to be is to nihilate the in-itself which it is. Under these conditions freedom can be nothing other than this nihilation. It is through this that the for-itself escapes its being as its essence; it is through this that the for-itself is always something other than what can be *said* of it. For in the final analysis the for-itself is the one which escapes this very denomination, the one which is already beyond the name which is given to it, beyond the property which is recognized in it. To say that the for-itself has to be what it

is, to say that it is what it is not while not being what it is, to say that in it existence precedes and conditions essence or inversely according to Hegel, that for it "Wesen ist was gewesen ist"—all this is to say one and the same thing: to be aware that man is free. Indeed by the sole fact that I am conscious of the causes which inspire my action, these causes are already transcendent objects for my consciousness; they are outside. In vain shall I seek to catch hold of them; I escape them by my very existence. I am condemned to exist forever beyond my essence, beyond the causes and motives of my act. I am condemned to be free. This means that no limits to my freedom can be found except freedom itself or, if you prefer, that we are not free to cease being free. To the extent that the for-itself wishes to hide its own nothingness from itself and to incorporate the in-itself as its true mode of being, it is trying also to hide its freedom from itself.

The ultimate meaning of determinism is to establish within us an unbroken continuity of existence in itself. The motive conceived as a psychic fact—*i.e.*, as a full and given reality—is, in the deterministic view, articulated without any break with the·decision and the act, both of which are equally conceived as psychic givens. The in-itself has got hold of all these "data"; the motive provokes the act as the physical cause its effect; everything is real, everything is full.

* From Jean-Paul Sartre, *Being and Nothingness*, 1956, reprinted by permission of the Philosophical Library © 1956.

Thus the refusal of freedom can be conceived only as an attempt to apprehend oneself as being-in-itself; it amounts to the same thing. Human reality may be defined as a being such that in its being its freedom is at stake because human reality perpetually tries to refuse to recognize its freedom. Psychologically in each one of us this amounts to trying to take the causes and motives as *things*. We try to confer permanence upon them. We attempt to hide from ourselves that their nature and their weight depend each moment on the meaning which I give to them; we take them for constants. This amounts to considering the meaning which I gave to them just now or yesterday —which is irremediable because it is *past* —and extrapolating from it a character fixed still in the present. I attempt to persuade myself that the cause *is* as it was. Thus it would pass whole and untouched from my past consciousness to my present consciousness. It would inhabit my consciousness. This amounts to trying to give an essence to the for-itself. In the same way people will posit ends as transcendences, which is not an error. But instead of seeing that the transcendences there posited are maintained in their being by my own transcendence, people will assume that I encounter them upon my surging up in the world; they come from God, from nature, from "my" nature, from society. These ends ready made and pre-human will therefore define the meaning of my act even before I conceive it, just as causes as pure psychic givens will produce it without my even being aware of them.

Cause, act, and end constitute a *continuum*, a *plenum*. These abortive attempts to stifle freedom under the weight of being (they collapse with the sudden upsurge of anguish before freedom) show sufficiently that freedom in its foundation coincides with the nothingness which is at the heart of man. Human-reality is free because it *is not enough*. It is free because it is perpetually wrenched away from itself and because it has been separated by a nothingness from what it is and from what it will be. It is free, finally, because its present being is itself a

nothingness in the form of the "reflection-reflecting." Man is free because he is not himself but presence to himself. The being which is what it is can not be free. Freedom is precisely the nothingness which *is made-to-be* at the heart of man and which forces human-reality *to make itself* instead of *to be*. As we have seen, for human reality, to be is to *choose oneself*; nothing comes to it either from the outside or from within which it can *receive or accept*. Without any help whatsoever, it is entirely abandoned to the intolerable necessity of making itself be— down to the slightest detail. Thus freedom is not *a* being; it is *the being* of man—*i.e.*, his nothingness of being. If we start by conceiving of man as a plenum, it is absurd to try to find in him afterwards moments or psychic regions in which he would be free. As well look for emptiness in a container which one has filled beforehand up to the brim! Man can not be sometimes slave and sometimes free; he is wholly and forever free or he is not free at all.

These observations can lead us, if we know how to use them, to new discoveries. They will enable us first to bring to light the relations between freedom and what we call the "will." There is a fairly common tendency to seek to identify free acts with voluntary acts and to restrict the deterministic explanation to the world of the passions. In short the point of view of Descartes. The Cartesian will is free, but there are "passions of the soul." Again Descartes will attempt a physiological interpretation of these passions. Later there will be an attempt to instate a purely psychological determinism. Intellectualistic analyses such as Proust, for example, attempts with respect to jealousy or snobbery can serve as illustrations for this concept of the passional "mechanism." In this case it would be necessary to conceive of man as simultaneously free and determined, and the essential problem would be that of the relations between this unconditioned freedom and the determined processes of the psychic life: how will it master the passions, how will it utilize them for its own benefit? A wisdom which comes from ancient times—the wisdom of the Stoics—will teach us to come to terms with these passions so as to master them; in short it will counsel us how to conduct ourselves with regard to affectivity as man does with respect to nature in general when he obeys it in order better to control it. Human reality therefore appears as a free power besieged by an ensemble of determined processes. One will distinguish wholly free acts, determined processes over which the free will has power, and processes which on principle escape the human-will.

It is clear that we shall not be able to accept such a conception. But let us try better to understand the reasons for our refusal. There is one objection which is obvious and which we shall not waste time in developing; this is that such a trenchant duality is inconceivable at the heart of the psychic unity. How in fact could we conceive of a being which could be *one* and which nevertheless on the one hand would be constituted as a series of facts determined by one another—hence existents in exteriority—and which on the other hand would be constituted as a spontaneity determining itself to be and revealing only itself? *A priori* this spontaneity would be capable of no action on a determinism already *constituted*. On what could it act? On the object itself (the present psychic fact)? But how could it modify an in-itself which by definition is and can be only what it is? On the actual law of the process? This is self-contradictory. On the antecedents of the process? But it amounts to the same thing whether we act on the present psychic fact in order to modify it in itself or act upon it in order to modify its consequences. And in each case we encounter the same impossibility which we pointed out earlier. Moreover, what instrument would this spontaneity have at its disposal? If the hand can clasp, it is because it can be clasped. Spontaneity, since by definition it is *beyond reach* can not in turn *reach*; it can produce only itself. And if it could dispose of a special instrument, it would then be necessary to conceive of this as of an intermediary nature between

free will and determined passions—which is not admissible. For different reasons the passions could get no hold upon the will. Indeed it is impossible for a determined process to act upon a spontaneity, exactly as it is impossible for objects to act upon consciousness. Thus any synthesis of two types of existents is impossible; they are not homogeneous; they will remain each one in its incommunicable solitude. The only bond which a nihilating spontaneity could maintain with mechanical processes would be the fact that it *produces itself by an internal negation directed toward these existents.* But then the spontaneity will exist precisely only in so far as it denies concerning itself that it is these passions. Henceforth the ensemble of the determined πάθος will of necessity be apprehended by spontaneity as a pure transcendent; that is, as what is necessarily *outside*, as what *is not* it. This internal negation would therefore have for its effect only the dissolution of the πάθος in the world, and the πάθος would exist as some sort of object in the midst of the world for a free spontaneity which would be simultaneously will and consciousness. This discussion shows that two solutions and only two are possible: either man is wholly determined (which is inadmissible, especially because a determined consciousness—*i.e.*, a consciousness externally motivated—becomes itself pure exteriority and ceases to be consciousness) or else man is wholly free.

But these observations are still not our primary concern. They have only a negative bearing. The study of the will should, on the contrary, enable us to advance further in our understanding of freedom. And this is why the fact which strikes us first is that if the will is to be autonomous, then it is impossible for us to consider it as a *given* psychic fact; that is, in-itself. It can not belong to the category defined by the psychologist as "states of consciousness." Here as everywhere else we assert that the state of consciousness is a pure idol of a positive psychology. If the will is to be freedom, then it is of necessity negativity and the power of nihilation. But then we no longer can see why autonomy should be preserved for the will. In fact it is hard to conceive of those holes of nihilation which would be the volitions and which would surge up in the otherwise dense and full web of the passions and of the πάθος in general. If the will is nihilation, then the ensemble of the psychic must likewise be nihilation. Moreover—and we shall soon return to this point—where do we get the idea that the "fact" of passion or that pure, simple desire is not nihilating? Is not passion first a project and an enterprise? Does it not exactly posit a state of affairs as intolerable? And is it not thereby forced to effect a withdrawal in relation to this state of affairs and to nihilate it by isolating it and by considering it in the light of an end—i.e., of a non-being? And does not passion have its own ends which are recognized precisely at the same moment at which it posits them as non-existent? And if nihilation is precisely the being of freedom, how can we refuse autonomy to the passions in order to grant it to the will?

But this is not all: the will, far from being the unique or at least the privileged manifestation of freedom, actually—like every event of the for-itself—must presuppose the foundation of an original freedom in order to be able to constitute itself as will. The will in fact is posited as a reflective decision in relation to certain ends. But it does not create these ends. It is rather a mode of being in relation to them: it decrees that the pursuit of these ends will be reflective and deliberative. Passion can posit the same ends. For example, if I am threatened, I can run away at top speed because of my fear of dying. This passional fact nevertheless posits implicitly as a supreme end the value of life. Another person in the same situation will, on the contrary, understand that he must remain at his post even if resistance at first appears more dangerous than flight; he "will stand firm." But his goal, although better understood and explicitly posited, remains the same as in the case of the emotional reaction. It is simply that the methods of attaining it are more clearly conceived; certain of them are rejected as dubious or

inefficacious, others are more solidly organized. The difference here depends on the choice of means and on the degree of reflection and of making explicit, not on the end. Yet the one who flees is said to be "passionate," and we reserve the term "voluntary" for the man who resists. Therefore the question is of a difference of subjective attitude in relation to a transcendent end. But if we wish to avoid the error which we denounced earlier and not consider these transcendent ends as pre-human and as an *a priori* limit to our transcendence, then we are indeed compelled to recognize that they are the temporalizing projection of our freedom. Human reality can not receive its ends, as we have seen, either from outside or from a so-called inner "nature." It chooses them and by this very choice confers upon them a transcendent existence as the external limit of its projects. From this point of view—and if it is understood that the existence of the *Dasein* precedes and commands its essence —human reality in and through its very upsurge decides to define its own being by its ends. It is therefore the positing of my ultimate ends which characterizes my being and which is identical with the sudden thrust of the freedom which is mine. And this thrust is an *existence;* it has nothing to do with an essence or with a property of a being which would be engendered conjointly with an idea.

Thus since freedom is identical with my existence, it is the foundation of ends which I shall attempt to attain either by the will or by passionate efforts. Therefore it can not be limited to voluntary acts. Volitions, on the contrary, like passions are certain subjective attitudes by which we attempt to attain the ends posited by original freedom. By original freedom, of course, we should not understand a freedom which would be *prior* to the voluntary or passionate act but rather a foundation which is strictly contemporary with the will or the passion and which these *manifest*, each in its own way. Neither should we oppose freedom to the will or to passion as the "profound self" of Bergson is opposed to the superficial self; the for-itself is wholly selfness and can not have a "profound self," unless by this we mean certain transcendent structures of the psyche. Freedom is nothing but the *existence* of our will or of our passions in so far as this existence is the nihilation of facticity; that is, the existence of a being which is its being in the mode of having to be it. We shall return to this point. In any case let us remember that the will is determined within the compass of motives and ends already posited by the for-itself in a transcendent projection of itself toward its possibles. If this were not so, how could we understand deliberation, which is an evaluation of means in relation to already existing ends?

If these ends are already posited, then what remains to be decided at each moment is the way in which I shall conduct myself with respect to them; in other words, the attitude which I shall assume. Shall I act by volition or by passion? Who can decide except me? In fact, if we admit that circumstances decide for me (for example, I can act by volition when faced with a minor danger but if the peril increases, I shall fall into passion), we thereby suppress all freedom. It would indeed be absurd to declare that the will is autonomous when it appears but that external circumstances strictly determine the moment of its appearance. But, on the other hand, how can it be maintained that a will which does not yet exist can suddenly decide to shatter the chain of the passions and suddenly stand forth on the fragments of these chains? Such a conception would lead us to consider the will as a *power* which sometimes would manifest itself to consciousness and at other times would remain hidden, but which would in any case possess the permanence and the existence "in-itself" of a property. This is precisely what is inadmissible. It is, however, certain that common opinion conceives of the moral life as a struggle between a will-thing and passion-substances. There is here a sort of psychological Manichaeism which is absolutely insupportable.

Actually it is not enough to will; it is necessary to will to will. Take, for example, a given situation: I can react to it emotion-

ally. We have shown elsewhere that emotion is not a physiological tempest; [1] it is a reply adapted to the situation; it is a type of conduct, the meaning and form of which are the object of an intention of consciousness which aims at attaining a particular end by particular means. In fear, fainting and cataplexie [2] aim at suppressing the danger by suppressing the consciousness of the danger. There is an *intention* of losing consciousness in order to do away with the formidable world in which consciousness is engaged and which comes into being through consciousness. Therefore we have to do with magical behavior provoking the symbolic satisfactions of our desires and revealing by the same stroke a magical stratum of the world. In contrast to this conduct voluntary and rational conduct will consider the situation scientifically, will reject the magical, and will apply itself to realizing determined series and instrumental complexes which will enable us to resolve the problems. It will organize a system of means by taking its stand on instrumental determinism. Suddenly it will reveal a technical world; that is, a world in which each instrumental-complex refers to another larger complex and so on. But what will make me decide to choose the magical aspect or the technical aspect of the world? It can not be the world itself, for this in order to be manifested waits to be discovered. Therefore it is necessary that the for-itself in its project must choose being the one by whom the world is revealed as magical or rational; that is, the for-itself must as a free project of itself give to itself magical or rational existence. It is responsible for either one, for the for-itself can *be* only if it has chosen itself. Therefore the for-itself appears as the free foundation of its emotions as of its volitions. My fear *is* free and manifests my freedom; I have put all my freedom into my fear, and I have chosen myself as fearful in this or that cir-

[1] *Esquisse d' une théorie phénoménologique des émotions*, Hermann, 1939. In English, *The Emotions: Outline of a Theory*. Tr. by Bernard Frechtman. Philosophical Library, 1948.
[2] A word invented by Preyer to refer to a sudden inhibiting numbness produced by any shock. Tr.

cumstance. Under other circumstances I shall exist as deliberate and courageous, and I shall have put all my freedom into my courage. In relation to freedom there is no privileged psychic phenomenon. All my "modes of being" manifest freedom equally since they are all ways of being my own nothingness. . . .

The essential consequence of our earlier remarks is that man being condemned to be free carries the weight of the whole world on his shoulders; he is responsible for the world and for himself as a way of being. We are taking the word "responsibility" in its ordinary sense as "consciousness (of) being the incontestable author of an event or of an object." In this sense the responsibility of the for-itself is overwhelming since he is the one by whom it happens that *there is* a world; since he is also the one who makes himself be, then whatever may be the situation in which he finds himself, the for-itself must wholly assume this situation with its peculiar coefficient of adversity, even though it be insupportable. He must assume the situation with the proud consciousness of being the author of it, for the very worst disadvantages or the worst threats which can endanger my person have meaning only in and through my project; and it is on the ground of the engagement which I am that they appear. It is therefore senseless to think of complaining since nothing foreign has decided what we feel, what we live, or what we are.

Furthermore this absolute responsibility is not resignation; it is simply the logical requirement of the consequences of our freedom. What happens to me happens through me, and I can neither affect myself with it nor revolt against it nor resign myself to it. Moreover everything which happens to me is *mine*. By this we must understand first of all that I am always equal to what happens to me *qua* man, for what happens to a man through other men and through himself can be only human. The most terrible situations of war, the worst tortures do not create a non-human state of things; there is no non-human situation. It is only through fear,

flight, and recourse to magical types of conduct that I shall decide on the non-human, but this decision is human, and I shall carry the entire responsibility for it. But in addition the situation is *mine* because it is the image of my free choice of myself, and everything which it presents to me is *mine* in that this represents me and symbolizes me. Is it not I who decide the coefficient of adversity in things and even their unpredictability by deciding myself?

Thus there are no *accidents* in a life; a community event which suddenly bursts forth and involves me in it does not come from the outside. If I am mobilized in a war, this war is *my* war; it is in my image and I deserve it. I deserve it first because I could always get out of it by suicide or by desertion; these ultimate possibles are those which must always be present for us when there is a question of envisaging a situation. For lack of getting out of it, I have *chosen* it. This can be due to inertia, to cowardice in the face of public opinion, or because I prefer certain other values to the value of the refusal to join in the war (the good opinion of my relatives, the honor of my family, *etc.*). Anyway you look at it, it is a matter of a choice. This choice will be repeated later on again and again without a break until the end of the war. Therefore we must agree with the statement by J. Romains, "In war there are no innocent victims." [3] If therefore I have preferred war to death or to dishonor, everything takes place as if I bore the entire responsibility for this war. Of course others have declared it, and one might be tempted perhaps to consider me as a simple accomplice. But this notion of complicity has only a juridical sense, and it does not hold here. For it depended on me that for me and by me this war should not exist, and I have decided that it does exist. There was no compulsion here, for the compulsion could have got no hold on a freedom. I did not have any excuse; for as we have said repeatedly in this book, the peculiar character

[3] J. Romains: *Les hommes de bonne volonté*, "Prélude à Verdun."

of human-reality is that it is without excuse. Therefore it remains for me only to lay claim to this war.

But in addition the war is *mine* because by the sole fact that it arises in a situation which I cause to be, and that I can discover it there only by engaging myself for or against it, I can no longer distinguish at present the choice which I make of myself from the choice which I make of the war. To live this war is to choose myself through it and to choose it through my choice of myself. There can be no question of considering it as "four years of vacation" or as a "reprieve," as a "recess," the essential part of my responsibilities being elsewhere in my married, family, or professional life. In this war which I have chosen I choose myself from day to day, and I make it mine by making myself. If it is going to be four empty years, then it is I who bear the responsibility for this.

Finally, as we pointed out earlier, each person is an absolute choice of self from the standpoint of a world of knowledges and of techniques which this choice both assumes and illumines; each person is an absolute upsurge at an absolute date and is perfectly unthinkable at another date. It is therefore a waste of time to ask what I should have been if this war had not broken out, for I have chosen myself as one of the possible meanings of the epoch which imperceptibly led to war. I am not distinct from this same epoch; I could not be transported to another epoch without contradiction. Thus *I am* this war which restricts and limits and makes comprehensible the period which preceded it. In this sense we may define more precisely the responsibility of the for-itself if to the earlier quoted statement, "There are no innocent victims," we add the words, "We have the war we deserve." Thus, totally free, undistinguishable from the period for which I have chosen to be the meaning, as profoundly responsible for the war as if I had myself declared it, unable to live without integrating it in *my* situation, engaging myself in it wholly and stamping it with my seal, I must be without remorse or regrets as

I am without excuse; for from the instant of my upsurge into being, I carry the weight of the world by myself alone without anything or any person being able to lighten it.

Yet this responsibility is of a very particular type. Someone will say, "I did not ask to be born." This is a naive way of throwing greater emphasis on our facticity. I am responsible for everything, in fact, except for my very responsibility, for I am not the foundation of my being. Therefore everything takes place as if I were compelled to be responsible. I am *abandoned* in the world, not in the sense that I might remain abandoned and passive in a hostile universe like a board floating on the water, but rather in the sense that I find myself suddenly alone and without help, engaged in a world for which I bear the whole responsibility without being able, whatever I do, to tear myself away from this responsibility for an instant. For I am responsible for my very desire of fleeing responsibilities. To make myself passive in the world, to refuse to act upon things and upon Others is still to choose myself, and suicide is one mode among others of being-in-the-world. Yet I find an absolute responsibility for the fact that my facticity (here the fact of my birth) is directly inapprehensible and even inconceivable, for this fact of my birth never appears as a brute fact but always across a projective reconstruction of my for-itself. I am ashamed of being born or I am astonished at it or I rejoice over it, or in attempting to get rid of my life I affirm that I live and I assume this life as bad. Thus in a certain sense I *choose* being born. This choice itself is integrally affected with facticity since I am not able not to choose, but this facticity in turn will appear only in so far as I surpass it toward my ends. Thus facticity is everywhere but inapprehensible; I never encounter anything except my responsibility. That is why I can not ask, "*Why* was I born?" or curse the day of my birth or declare that I did not ask to be born, for these various attitudes toward my birth—*i.e.*, toward the *fact* that I realize a presence in the world—are absolutely nothing else but ways of assuming this birth in full responsibility and of making it *mine*. Here again I encounter only myself and my projects so that finally my abandonment—*i.e.*, my facticity—consists simply in the fact that I am condemned to be wholly responsible for myself. I am the being which *is* in such a way that in its being its being is in question. And this "is" of my being *is* as present and inapprehensible.

Under these conditions since every event in the world can be revealed to me only as an *opportunity* (an opportunity made use of, lacked, neglected, *etc.*), or better yet since everything which happens to us can be considered as a *chance* (*i.e.*, can appear to us only as a way of realizing this being which is in question in our being) and since others as transcendences-transcended are themselves only *opportunities* and *chances*, the responsibility of the for-itself extends to the entire world as a peopled-world. It is precisely thus that the for-itself apprehends itself in anguish; that is, as a being which is neither the foundation of its own being nor of the Other's being nor of the in-itselfs which form the world, but a being which is compelled to decide the meaning of being —within it and everywhere outside of it. The one who realizes in anguish his condition as *being* thrown into a responsibility which extends to his very abandonment has no longer either remorse or regret or excuse; he is no longer anything but a freedom which perfectly reveals itself and whose being resides in this very revelation. But as we pointed out at the beginning of this work, most of the time we flee anguish in bad faith.

Bibliography

Texts

Nausea. Norfolk, Conn.: New Directions, 1949.

The Emotions: Outline of a Theory. New York: Philosophical Library, Inc., 1948.

Search for a Method. New York: Alfred A. Knopf, Inc., 1963.

Psychology of Imagination. New York: Philosophical Library, Inc., 1948.

The Transcendence of the Ego. New York: Noonday Books, Farrar, Straus & Giroux, Inc., 1957.

The Flies. New York: Vintage Books, Random House, Inc., 1947.

No Exit. New York: Vintage Books, Random House, Inc., 1947.

Being and Nothingness. New York: Philosophical Library, Inc., 1956.

Existentialism. New York: Philosophical Library, Inc., 1947.

Situations. New York: Philosophical Library, Inc., 1965.

Studies

Desan, W. *The Tragic Finale.* New York: Harper & Row, Publishers, Incorporated, 1954.

————. *The Marxism of Jean-Paul Sartre.* Garden City, N.Y.: Anchor Books, Doubleday & Company, Inc., 1965.

Collins, J. *The Existentialists.* Chicago: Henry Regnery Company, 1952, chap. 2.

Gurwitch, A. "A Non-egological Conception of Consciousness." *Philosophy and Phenomenological Research*, vol. 1 (1941), pp. 325–338.

Natanson, M. *A Critique of Jean-Paul Sartre's Ontology.* Lincoln, Nebr.: University of Nebraska Press, 1951.

Schutz, A. "Sartre's Theory of the Alter Ego." *Philosophy and Phenomenological Research,* vol. IX (1948), pp. 181–199; also in A. Schutz, *Collected Papers.* The Hague: Martinus Nijhoff, 1962, vol. 1, pp. 180–203.

Spiegelberg, H. *The Phenomenological Movement.* The Hague: Martinus Nijhoff, 1965, vol. 2, pp. 445–515.

Thévenaz, P. *What Is Phenomenology?* Chicago: Quadrangle Books, 1962, pp. 67–83.

Zaner, R. *The Problem of Embodiment: Some Contributions to a Phenomenology of the Body.* The Hague: Martinus Nijhoff, 1964, part II.

McBride, W. L. "Jean-Paul Sartre: Man, Freedom, and *Praxis*," in G. A. Schrader (ed.), *Existential Philosophers: Kierkegaard to Merleau-Ponty.* New York: McGraw-Hill Book Company, 1967, pp. 261–329.

27

STEPHAN STRASSER
1905–

Introduction

Stephan Strasser was born in Austria and first studied there at the University of Vienna and later at the University of Dijon in France. During the war he was at the University of Louvain in Belgium and worked at the Husserl Archives which are kept at the Higher Institute of Philosophy. He served as the able editor of the first volume of the definitive posthumous edition of Edmund Husserl's works (*Husserliana*). This first volume was the German version of the *Cartesian Meditations* (*Cartesianische Meditationen und Pariser Vorträge*) and was published in German in 1950 and in English in 1960. The original text actually went back to Husserl's lectures given in Paris at the Sorbonne in 1929 and was first published in French in 1931.

After the war Strasser taught at Louvain until 1947, when he went to the University of Nijmegen in Holland. He has been teaching there ever since, except for 1956, when he was visiting professor at Duquesne University. The Nijmegen University catalog (*Gids*) lists his first two courses as "Philosophical Psychology and Anthropology" and "Phenomenological Anthropology." He is a member of the faculties of philosophy and the social sciences. These brief notices, taken together with the titles of two of his books available in English (*The Soul in Metaphysical and Empirical Psychology and Phenomenology and the Human Sciences*), aptly indicate Strasser's main concern. His goal is a true science of man that uses phenomenology not as a self-sufficient science, but as a descriptive method that draws on all the human sciences in order to provide the bases for an interpretation of man as nature and as person. Some may feel that philosophy would lose its identity in the midst of such a complex of sciences. Others may feel that it already has, so that one does little in giving the new name, "a scientific phenomenological philosophy," to what philosophers are doing today. Still others may feel that certain theses, such as those on man's soul, are inaccessible to this method. In the selections that follow, Strasser rigorously applies the method of phenomenological description followed by metaphysical interpretation, and meets these challenges.

THE METAPHYICS OF "BEING AND HAVING" AND THE CONCEPT OF THE SOUL *

The Characteristics of "Having." Manifestly, that from which my personal existence in all its fullness unfolds itself must be ascribed to the realm of what I *am* and not to that of what I *have*. What is the difference between these two metaphysical categories? For the answer to this question we may refer to the profound considerations of the well-known existentialist Gabriel Marcel. He writes as follows:

☐ Ultimately, everything is reduced to the distinction between what one has and what one is. Only it is extraordinarily difficult to express this in a conceptual form. Yet it must be possible to do it. What one has evidently presents a certain exteriority with respect to the one who has. Nevertheless this

* By permission of Duquesne University Press, From Stephan Strasser, *The Soul in Metaphysical and Empirical Psychology* (second impression). Duquesne University Press, Pittsburgh, Pa., 1962.

exteriority is not absolute. In principle, what one has are things or that which can be assimilated to things, and to the precise extent that such an assimilation is possible. I am able to *have* in the strict sense of the term only something which has to a certain extent an existence that is independent of me; nay, the fact of being possessed by me is added to other properties, qualities, etc. belonging to the thing I have. I have only that of which I can dispose in some way and within certain limits; in other words, [I have only] to the extent that I can be considered as a force endowed with powers. Only that which one has can be transmitted.[1]

So, according to Marcel, the essential characteristics of "having" are the following:

1
The object of my "having" exists independently of me, at least to a certain extent.

2
It exhibits with respect to me a certain exteriority and foreignness.

3
I am able to have everything to the extent that it has the character of an object (we intentionally widen here Marcel's description of "that which can be assimilated to things, and to the precise extent that such an assimilation is possible").

4
Within certain limits, I can dispose of everything I "have."

5
According to Marcel, I can cede to another only that which I have. We would like to formulate this characteristic somewhat more carefully and positively by saying: in principle, I can get rid of what I have.

I Do Not "Have" My Own Ego. It is evident that this phenomenological description of the reality which in general can become the object of my "having" does not at all apply to my primordial ego. We may say even

that *a priori* none of the five enumerated characteristics can be a property of my "ego-source" or my soul. My soul is not foreign to me or independent of me, because it is the metaphysical *principium fontale*, the fountain head, of my personal subsistent being. My soul, moreover, does not have the mode of being of an object, for I cannot "dispose" of it or get rid of it since it is precisely the soul which makes possible all my acts of "disposing" and getting rid of.

On the other hand, we must admit that because of the third essential characteristic I am in principle able to "have," at least intentionally, i.e. in the way of a "filling of an empty intention," [2] everything in so far as it has the character of an object. But, as we have shown definitely, my soul does not have the mode of being of an object; therefore, it cannot be something which I can "have" in any way. However, there is something which I have, namely the psychical phenomena. Thus it follows that my soul is not a lived event of consciousness, not a psychical datum, not an element resulting from the dissection of psychical phenomena, not a structure consisting of psychical elements. It is manifest therefore that we must not seek for a solution of our problem in the direction of "having," but in the direction of "being." Contrary to everyday usage of language, we therefore assert: my soul is not *my* soul because I "have" it. My "ego-source," my originating ego, *my soul is that which primarily I am.*

The same result may be reached in another way. To Marcel's analysis of the essence of "having" we may add a sixth eidetic point, which can be formulated as follows: *a priori* I can "have" an endless number of relatively subsistent beings, but *a priori I can "be" only a single subsistent being.*

We do not have to examine here how this *a-priori* is connected with general metaphysical truths, insofar as it gives expression to the absolute value of the principle of

---

[1] *Être et Avoir*, Paris, 1935, p. 225.

[2] German: *Erfüllungsbewusstsein.* In Husserl's terminology a purely formal assumption without concrete content is called "empty." The intention is "filled" when it obtains a material content (Tr.).

ens et unum, being and unity. Our statement is immediately evident because of its eidetic character. However, we would like to add the following remark. The data of consciousness always present themselves concretely in the plural. They belong to the objects which I am able to "have" in the above-indicated sense. So the temptation is great to attempt to construct somehow a "psychical ego" out of the manifoldness of the psychical phenomena. But any such attempt will inevitably meet the same difficulties which stopped Hume.

Hume's Error.   The critics of Hume have accurately gauged his error and sharply condemned it. Konstantin Österreich, for instance, is quite correct in asserting:

□ The explanation of Hume's mistake is that he looked in consciousness for the ego as a separate, independent, and isolated content which somehow stands in the same line as all other contents. But the ego does not do that. It stands outside the line.[3]

However, it is easier to criticize Hume than positively to solve the anthropological problem raised by him. It is not sufficient to speak in this connection of "wholeness," "structure," or "gestalt." From a metaphysical view point such an answer does not solve the question. The view, for instance, that the ego is to be considered as a complex of "gestalts" satisfies philosophers no more than the theory of "bundles" or "collections" of the English sceptic himself. Fundamentally Hume speaks the strict truth when he says that "we have no impression of self or substance, as something simple and individual."[4] The only suitable answer here is: do not look among your "impressions," your "ideas," or any contents of consciousness whatsoever which you have. Pay attention to the fact that you *are*. What you have is always a plurality; what you are is

necessarily an identical self-subsistent unity. And this is precisely what we mean when we speak of "substance."

The only methical attitude which will safeguard us from Hume's typical error in our search for the soul is not to start from physiological, psychological or sociological facts. The only possibility to stay outside the "line" mentioned by Österreich is not to join the line. In other words, whoever looks for the essence of the soul must primarily try to investigate what he *is*. One who does not investigate directly his existence does not look for the essence of the soul but for something else.

I Am Primarily Soul.   This elementary truth may be expressed also in this way. That which I am primordially, i.e. in such a way that no exteriority, foreignness, disposability, plurality and real composition breaks its existential immediacy, that is my soul, my spiritual soul. We have called it the "ego-source," because the soul is that which I am primarily. In other words, I am spiritual soul inasmuch as I am myself absolutely.[5]

This statement applies to the dynamic aspect of my primordial life as ego just as well as to that of its identity. Precisely as "originating" ego I am the same at every moment of my existence; and precisely as "ego-source" I am another at every moment of my life. Metaphysically this fact can be explained only through the metaphenomenal relationship of two transcendental principles —namely, the "principle of self-subsistency" and the "principle of accidentality."[6] The

---

[3] *Die Phänomenologie des Ich*, vol. I, Leipzig, 1910, pp. 11 f.
[4] *Treatise of Human Nature*, Oxford, 1896, vol. I, appendix, pp. 633 f.

[5] The expression "I am primarily soul," which we have used repeatedly in this connection must not be confused with the more or less Platonic theses "I am only a soul" or "As soul, I have a complete being." In the subsequent investigations we will have an opportunity to inquire in what sense I am also essentially my body.
[6] With these expressions we want to indicate the meaning of the Thomistic concepts of substance and accidents, which are free from all physicalism. To prevent another source of misunderstandings, we will distinguish hereafter also between the self-subsistent being, the "being-in-subsistence" (the *substantia* as *id quod*) and the "principle of self-subsistency" (the *substantia* as *id quo*). In an analogous way, we want to distinguish the "accidental being" and the "principle of accidentality."

following text of Gerard Verbeke seems very appropriate to explain the ontological structure with respect to the egological realm.

☐ My *whole* being has a dynamic character. As a self-subsistent being *and* as an accidental being I am constantly modified. But this cannot be explained through the principle of self-subsistency but only through the principle of accidentality.

My *whole* being has a character of permanence. As a self-subsistent being *and* as an accidental being I am always the same. But this cannot be explained through the principle of accidentality but only through the principle of self-subsistency.[7]

These expressions correctly indicate the metaphysical structure and at the same time are phenomenologically justified.

It is a misuse of the traditional categories when one claims that the self-subsistent being is found by detaching from it what is accidental being in it. It is likewise doing violence to metaphysics when with Theodor Lipps one claims that the psychical data are the empirically observable accidents of an otherwise unknown substantial support. As de Raeymaeker emphasizes, "What is given in experience is the real, particular being, and not its accidents."[8] If we want to apply this truth to our egological problem, we will have to say: I *am* the self-subsistent being and I *am* the accidental being. I *am* also the "accidents," namely, insofar as I, the self-subsisting being, am at the same time of a dynamic nature. I *am* they and therefore I do not *have* them, not even in the form of psychical phenomena which can be grasped intentionally.

What, then, are, metaphysically speaking, the contents of consciousness, psychical facts, objects of inner experience? What is that which is spoken of by the introspective psychologist? What is the basis of his idea of the soul? . . .

EXPERIENCE OF THE RETROVERTED ACT AS STARTING POINT FOR THE PHENOMENOLOGY OF THE HUMAN SPIRIT-SOUL

What in general is required that I may be able to form a concept which is concerned with my concrete being and essence as ego? What makes it *a priori* possible for me to arrive at egological statements? What condition must be fulfilled before there is such a possibility?

The answer to this question is without ambiguity. To make such judgments *I must be a priori capable of performing acts of which I myself am in some way the source and the object.* This is a fact which has not yet actually been doubted by anyone. Whoever would attempt to doubt the truth of this statement, would come in contradiction with the reality of his own existence. Anyone who were to assert: I cannot perform actions of which I myself am the object, proves precisely by this negative judgment regarding

himself that he is very well capable of it. Accordingly, our statement presents itself as primordially evident, i.e. any attempt to deny it leads to the reappearance of the structural relation itself which it is supposed to deny.[9]

However, the scope of this primordially evident statement must be very carefully examined. It is not unintentionally that we have formulated it with so much discretion. We may not assert without any further ado: I am the *sole* source and the *sole* object of my "retroverted" acts.[10]

It is not even evident in the ordinary sense of the term. Immediately open to under-

[7] *Noten by de cursus van Metaphysica,* Louvain, 1945/46.

[8] *The Philosophy of Being,* p. 177.
[9] Cf. the author's "Beschouwingen over het vraagstuk der apodicticiteit," *Tydschrift voor philosophie,* 1946, pp. 226 ff.
[10] The author uses here and in other passages the terms *rückgerichtet, ichgerichtet* and *rückzielend,* which I have rendered by "retroverted," "directed to the ego," and "retro-directed." Translator's note.

standing is only that the act which "aims" is in a certain sense my act and that my own activity is to some extent exercised upon myself. But for the time being I do know neither whether I am the sole source of this activity nor whether I am its sole recipient. Special analyses would be needed to obtain clarity in this point.

"Retroverted" Acts and Reflection. A second remark is connected with this. Acts of the kind described above are often called *reflective acts.* This term, which is derived from the Latin *reflectere* indicates a kind of "turning back," "bending oneself backwards," "bending backwards over oneself." As we will see, it is not unintentionally that in the philosophical tradition especially thought and the activities of consciousness are indicated as reflective. The term "reflection" is accompanied by the idea of "bending oneself over oneself in thought," "thinking of oneself," "becoming conscious of oneself." But provisionally we do not yet know what consciousness, thought, etc. are, for we have put these ideas "between brackets." Moreover, it is not yet clear to us whether and to what extent the idea contained in the term "reflection" is applicable to our activities. For this reason we prefer to speak of acts that are *"directed to the ego," "retroverted,"* or *"retro-directed."* With these terms we want to indicate the phenomenological appearance of the structural relation that there is something in the act which originates in me and something which reverts to me.[11]

Obviously, in this way our considerations are bound to encompass a much wider area. The expression "acts turned towards the ego" in the above-described sense embraces also such activities as "looking at oneself," "moving oneself," "washing oneself," etc. The essential difference between "looking at

oneself" and "thinking about oneself" is not immediately evident. In the present phase of our studies we will not be able to clarify the distinction without making use of concepts that have not yet been justified. We will therefore consider actions turned towards the ego in their entirety and ask ourselves whether in spite of their diversity they have certain common traits. Is it possible for such disparate phenomena as "looking at oneself" and "thinking about oneself" to show common characteristics? Do they obey definite essential laws? A phenomenological analysis will show that this really is the case.

Phenomenology of "Retroverted" Activities

A retroverted act is an act of which somehow *I* am the source and at the same time the recipient. I am the reality from which the act goes out, i.e. its subject, and at the same time the reality upon which the act is exercised, i.e. its object. In a mysterious way I am divided without ceasing to be a unity. Something in me functions as subject pole and something else as object pole. We must now subject to a closer examination this ego which is the source and the recipient of retroverted acts.

The Unity of the Subject Pole. The subject pole, as we notice immediately, is always identically the same ego. When I say "I look at myself," "I wash myself," "I think of myself," the term "I" indicates the author of all these activities, who remains all the time the same. The activities may be very numerous, extremely variable and diversified; yet their variation and manifoldness does not impair the identity of their source. In this respect there is no difference between acts turned towards the ego and acts whose orientation is directed towards the "world." Without hesitation, I will say, for instance, that I have washed myself, dressed myself and gone out, without anyone being in doubt whether the subject of the washing and dressing be the same as that of the going out. Manifestly, it is one and the same ego

[11] We do not want to dispute the right of others, especially Thomists, to use a different terminology. Yet the question must be asked whether the limitation of the problem to absolute categories does not result in an oversimplification. In our opinion, the *"reditio completa,"* the complete return, of St. Thomas points to the possibility in principle of a *"reditio incompleta,"* an incomplete return.

pole which turns sometimes to its surroundings and sometimes to its own person. Even when the immediate support of the activity is a definite organ, we do not doubt for even a single moment that the action itself goes out from the subject as such. No one will get the idea of saying "my hands wash me," or "my legs move me," but it appears to be evident to us that *I* wash myself and that *I* move myself. The stream of activities goes out from me and in its course runs through different channels—including my own members and organs. My hands do not wash me, but *I* wash myself *with* my hands; my feet do not move me, but *I* move myself *with* my feet. We believe that we know this "I" already. It is the familiar, simple, everyday ego from which spring my being and my acting; it is the ego of undivided subsistence, the numerically identical subject pole; briefly, it is the primordial ego. Accordingly, for the time being we say that *the subject of retroverted activities is always "I," the identical primordial ego.*

The Plurality of the Object Pole. A wholly different picture is presented by the object pole of retroverted acts. Here the matter is not so simple. To give an approximate description of it we will have to draw attention to a whole series of essential characteristics.

In the first place, we notice that here we have to do with a plurality of object poles. The immediate object of "I move myself" can be identified only in part with that of "I wash myself"; and the object of "I think of myself" seems to be still more extended. The multiplicity of the various object poles forces itself upon us. Sometimes their mutual relationship can be considered as a partial or total inclusion of one in the other; sometimes one object pole is "outside" or "alongside" the other. The object of "I brush my teeth" is not included in that of "I wash myself" and vice versa. These objects therefore present, at least with respect to my retrodirected activities, a certain independence of each other. Later this relative independence will have to be characterized more closely. Provisionally, we may limit ourselves

to this statement: When I consider myself as the object of actual or possible retrodirected activities, I discover in myself something which at first I did not even suspect—namely, an aspect of multiplicity. I become aware of the fact that the numerically identical subject pole is faced with a plurality of different object poles. *I am a unity insofar as I perform an act, and I am a plurality insofar as these acts are exercised upon myself.* We do not yet know how this phenomenological condition must be explained, but later we will see that a great difficulty lies concealed here.

The Foundation of This Plurality. If we try to find on what this aspect of plurality is founded, we will soon discover a certain mutual exteriority of the object poles. One is not the other; one is *at a distance* from the other; one is *outside* the other. This being-at-a-distance assumes sometimes the mode of a spatio-temporal distance, and at other times that of a purely temporal dispersion. As L. van der Horst remarks, "when I turn my regard to my interior, I find *contents of consciousness* which are at a distance from each other." [12] For instance, the idea of writing an article which I had yesterday is not the same as that which I have today. I have modified or perhaps even given up my intention to treat the matter in this or that way. Let us suppose that I really have come back upon my decision to treat the problem in *this* way. This fact does not reduce my first plan to nothing, for in a sense it continues to exist "alongside" my new plan. I can still recall it; I can compare it with my new thoughts; I can confirm or come back upon my change of plan; etc. Briefly, my former plan still constitutes a possible object pole. However, the term "former" expresses that it is no longer actual and thus indicates a temporal distance. Again, we can see in a sense which is not just figurative but *analogous* that one object pole is not the other; one is at a certain "dis-

12 "Tijd onder psychologisch aspect," *Tijdschrift voor Psychologie*, vol. 3, 1948, p. 337.

tance" from the other; in a sense, one is foreign to the other. Thus *the "originating" ego which is always and wholly present to itself is faced by a plurality of object poles which are dispersed in a spatio-temporal and temporal way.*

The Objectivisable Ego as Multiple Unity

A further precision of the foregoing statements remains necessary. These statements should not be understood as if we consider the ego, insofar as it can become the object of retroverted acts, as a plurality and mutual exteriority of elements without any further qualification. In this respect we must carefully distinguish the situation which exists on the part of the subject from the one which characterizes the objectivisable ego. At once it seems evident that I as the performer of my acts am always the same, undivided, numerically identical subject. But the same cannot be said of the object-ego, for *retroverted acts do not reach me immediately but only mediately.* Everyday language clearly expresses this. Certainly, it is no accident that we usually say "I shave myself," and not "my hand shaves me," while on the other hand we may say also "I shave my beard," but not "I shave myself in the area of the beard." What I want to indicate by the words "my beard" is not, at least not primarily, a possessive relationship, for I do not possess my limbs and organs in the same way as I possess three or four pairs of shoes. By putting "my" before "beard" I want to express this: the retroverted activity of shaving is exercised immediately upon the beard, but insofar as this beard belongs to my per-

son, i.e. insofar as it is *my* beard, the activity concerns me in a mediate way. This assertion applies universally to all egological object-poles. No matter how numerous and diverse they may be, how clearly they reveal that they are outside one another and diverse, they all share in the unity of the primordial ego. In this sense the beard I shave is "my" beard; the representation I form is "my" representation; and the decision I came back upon is still "my" decision. The immediate objects of my retroverted acts are sometimes *this* and sometimes *that;* they are divided, ordered and arranged now in a spatio-temporal way and then in a purely temporal respect. But what I reach in this way is always *my* object poles. Thus the plurality and dispersion of my retroverted acts is limited and contained by the unity of my primordial ego. What I attain immediately with my retroverted acts is diverse realities that are "outside" and "alongside" one another, but the mediate recipient of all these acts is I myself as their anonymous ontological center. Accordingly, we may characterize the phenomenological situation as follows. *As subject pole I am a unity, and as object pole I am a plurality in a unity, a "unitas multiplex,"* i.e., as we will say from now on, a multiple unity (W. Stern). Here again, it is manifest that a great conceptual difficulty lies hidden behind these words. However, provisionally we will limit ourselves to the description and analysis of what is given in itself. Phenomenologically speaking, the object-ego appears divided into many diverse realities, although, on the other hand, these realities are connected and united into a whole. . . .

PHENOMENOLOGY OF THE HUMAN PERSON AS EGO, AUTHOR OF ACTS

The Non-ego in the Ego. Let us now return to the problem which was our starting point. The multiplicity of mutually distinct real or possible temporal objects allows us to

make these objects the terms of retro-directed acts of knowing and willing. On the other hand, this plurality of distinct realities which present different profiles in a temporal perspective is not given to me at once. We encounter here the phenomenon of mutability, distance and foreignness, and, as we have seen, this phenomenon is genuinely analogous to "worldly" phenomena of the same order. Here again we have to say: if I am the self-exploring ego which tries to arrive at a sharp delimitation of temporal objects and to retain them unchanged in its grasp, then I am not the ego which gives rise to the kaleidoscopic variations of temporal and emotional perspectives, to the ceaseless changing, the fading and blending of innumerable nuances. Insofar as my cognitive act has to overcome these resistances, it is struggling against "worldly" obstacles. Here too, I encounter the non-ego in the ego. My endeavor to know myself does not remain wholly "in" me; there is always something of it which is directed to the realm of the "world."

Something analogous applies to the ego-directed acts of willing. They also encounter a particular resistance, which does not seem to originate "properly" in me. When, for example, I want to "pull myself together" for a certain purpose, I have the impression that my task consists in trying to overcome the non-ego in the ego. This is a well-known familiar experience. Accordingly, our retro-directed effort always and necessarily meets in ourselves something of the "world" and "worldly" laws that are foreign to the ego.

Quasi-objective Reality. It is time, however, to characterize somewhat the objects of retro-directed acts, for obviously the categories *subjective-objective, immanent-transient, and primordial-reflective* are not sufficient to give an adequate description of the facts. We ask ourselves therefore what these peculiar objects are which belong to the ego, but also to the non-ego. What shall we call something which is no more an object of an *agere* than of a *facere*? What sort of beings are these realities which constitute a plurality, but also a multiple unity? realities which reveal themselves somehow as self-subsistent, but only in a relative sense? realities which possess a certain foreignness and

strangeness to the ego, but not the same foreignness and strangeness as the things and beings of the surrounding world? A term is needed to characterize this special mode of being which is proper to me insofar as I am the object of retro-directed acts. Manifestly, this mode of being lies midway between the domain of *agere* and that of *facere*. It cannot be considered as either immanent or transient, but shows certain features of both. In many respects it seems to be "worldly," yet it cannot be simply ascribed to the "world." It is clear that I am never an object for myself in the same sense as another being or thing; nevertheless with my retro-directed acts I do not reach my primordial ego immediately. I am for myself an as-it-were-object, an as-if-object, an almost-object, or, as we shall say it from now on, a *quasi-object*. Accordingly, all concrete intentional poles of my real or possible retroverted acts are quasi-objects. As "originating" ego I have with them a quasi-objective relationship.

Characterization of the Subject Pole of Retro-directed Acts

The Dependence of the Ego on the "World" in its Retroverted Acts.   We will now raise the question whether within the framework of a metaphysics of finite being the subject of retroverted acts can be considered as their absolute source. An examination of the question shows that this is not the case. The ego is not the absolutely creative source of retro-directed acts. All the time it is forced to seek support, aid and complementation in the realm of objects and quasi-objects. Activities such as looking at oneself, washing oneself, moving oneself, etc. are possible only in a surrounding world, a living space, and with the aid of "worldly" objects. Even the apparently pure act of thinking of oneself cannot be performed without the ego appealing continually to objects and quasi-objects. When I think of myself, I try to form an image of myself in the form of a synthesis, made of all kinds of impressions, representations, thoughts, etc. In addition, I have apprehended myself in all these representations and thoughts as a personal and social ego in function of my corporeity, my surroundings, my fellow men. If, for example, I take the resolution "to improve myself," I will do so because of an experience, an occurrence, or an advice, which ultimately are an experience in the world, an occurrence in a social situation, an advice of another being. We must therefore admit that for all our retro directed acts we count on a contribution from the non-ego. Thus I am not the one and only foundation from which my retroverted acts originate. To indicate their origin with greater precision I will have to say: I bring them forth insofar as I am enmeshed in quasi-objects and objects. Of course, as primordial ego I am the true source of these acts, but not without the necessary relations I have to non-ego realities. Accordingly, I am the original author of my retroverted acts, but not in a sovereign way.

Man Is a Relatively Immanent Being. Therefore, in this way also we arrive at the conclusion that retro-directed acts are not of a truly immanent nature. True, there is always something in them which goes out from me, and something which returns to me. But we must not forget the correlated truth that in every retro-directed act there is also something which goes out from the "world," and something which returns to it. Clearly, concrete man is no more a closed monad than he is a simple moment in a steady flow of development. He is neither *actor,* doer, nor *factor,* maker. The expression *"sese movet,"* he moves himself, cannot be applied to him in the strict sense; likewise, the cosmological principle *"quidquid movetur ab alio movetur,"* whatever is in motion is moved by another, does not apply to him without qualification. The performer of retro-directed acts stands somewhere midway between these two absolute categories. To a certain extent, he shows himself closed, yet in a way which allows a measure of receptivity. He unites self-suf-

ficiency with want; his independence is mixed with dependence. How these contradictions can be reconciled we do not yet know. Provisionally we restrict ourselves to the statement that man as the performer of retro-directed acts must be considered as an *imperfect interiority,* a *relatively immanent being.*

Quasi-objective Processes

The phenomena which characterize the quasi-objective ego are extraordinarily complicated and offer many aspects. Our description would be one-sided if this complexity were not taken into consideration. So to complete our analyses we will have to discuss the quasi-objective processes.

Processes on the Borderline of the Ego. Till the present we have considered the world of quasi-objects exclusively from the intentional standpoint of the ego. This could give rise to the impression that these objects are purely passive. This, however, is not the case. The primordial ego is not always the immediate support of all activity. Of course, as we have pointed out before, it is true that *"I walk with my legs"* and that no one will assert "my legs walk." But, on the other hand, it cannot be denied that everyone says "my heart beats" and not "I beat with my heart." Here we have an event whose origin cannot be simply identified with the primordial ego. It is only insofar as this heart is *my* heart that this mysterious activity also somehow belongs to me.

We have to do here with certain automatic processes. The heart beats whether I want it or not. Its dynamism takes its course independently of my will and knowledge. On the other hand, however, this dynamism has a quasi-objective character; I do not face it in the same way as the ticking of my watch. The heart is capable, for instance, of expressing something of myself, which the ticking of my watch cannot do. Yet even this expressive function of the heart beat escapes my will and usually also my knowledge. In this sense I must consider these automatic processes as belonging to the non-ego in the ego. Undoubtedly, such "self-activated" processes exhibit a great foreignness and exteriority; they lie, so to speak, at the outskirts of the ego. Yet they do not simply belong to the realm of "worldly" phenomena. I exist *also* in the beating of my heart and also in the thousands of mysterious functions and processes described by the physiologist, the biologist, the chemist, etc. Generally, however, I exist "in them" only in a very mediate way. By its very nature the quasi-objective process belongs to the realm that is most remote from the ego.

Nothing authorizes us to assume that the domain of physiology is the only one in which we encounter quasi-objective dynamism. The empirical psychologist is accustomed to come across analogous phenomena. As everyday experience shows, often temporal objects also obey their own laws. To give a few examples, something I want to recall does not come to my mind, but when I *no longer* think of it, I suddenly know it again; a chain of associations takes a course which I do not like, but when I try to get rid of them, I do not succeed; an emotion, affective state, or passion "dominates me." Something of which I am not simply the source by its own spontaneous action determines my whole personal life.

These Processes Are Not Suitably Described by "Passivity." This is the reason why a quasi-objective process is often called passivity. The expressions *"passio," "affectio," "trahi,"* etc. point in this direction, as well as Husserl's qualification of the associative process as a "passive synthesis." But the question must be asked whether this terminology is suitable. Something which takes part in considerable—often even violent—dynamic processes may not be simply disposed of as passivity. To the contrary, in their own way, associative syntheses, the structural formation of the contents of my memory, the fit of passion, etc. are expressions of activity just as much as the beating of my heart. Only this type of activity

is not immediately, and generally not in its totality, *my* activity.

Quasi-objective Processes and Retroverted Acts. Nevertheless, I exist *also* in the quasi-objective process. It can even happen that I exist *only* in it. In conditions such as unconsciousness, sleep, dreams and hypnosis the quasi-objective functions take over. Of course, the primordial ego is still at work, but it does not rise above the level of its connection with quasi-objects and objects. So when we spoke of the ability we have of detaching ourselves from the quasi-objects and of facing as subjects the quasi-objective process, we were not concerned with an actual possibility but with a possibility in principle. *In principle* I am capable of making all quasi-objects the object of retro-directed acts. Whether and to what extent I *de facto* make use of this essential possibility is something for the empirical psychologist and the physiologist to decide.

Accordingly, there is no question here of a sphere of passivity, but of a domain in which the ego seems to border upon the non-ego. I am the origin of these processes, but in such a mediate way that I experience them almost as "happening" to me. It is in this sense that we call them quasi-objective processes.

Definition of the Concept "My Body"

"My Body" Is the Whole of Quasi-objects. A first contribution to the elucidation of the above-described egological situation can perhaps be given by a more precise determination of the concept *"my body."* Starting from our analyses of retro-directed acts we may say that my body is *the whole of my real and possible concrete quasi-objects.* In other words, everything which concretely can be the object of a retro-directed act belongs to the phenomenal domain of corporeity. My body therefore is characterized by this that *a priori* it can become a quasi-object for me with respect to all its levels, organs and structures. Evidently, this con-

cept of the body includes much that usually is classified as belonging to the realm of the psychical. However, we do not worry about this deviation from customary terminology, which will be justified later.

I Neither Simply "Have" Nor "Am" My Body. This conceptual definition may be completed with another, for which the way has been prepared above. . . . My body is the reality which I have and am. Better, it is the totality of all realities which I do not have in the absolute sense because I am they, and those which I am not absolutely because I have them.[13] Let us recall the essential characteristics of "having" described by Gabriel Marcel. Why do these characteristics not apply in the absolute sense to my body? Why do the various parts of my body, my limbs and organs, present a mutually *restricted* independence, a *lesser* exteriority, a *limited* diversity? Why can I "dispose" of them only within certain limits? Why can I not simply "set aside" my body? Obviously, the reason is that I am *also* this body. That "in" which I exist cannot be really independent and foreign with respect to me; I cannot "dispose" of it as I want; I cannot "get rid" of it without putting my very existence in jeopardy. In other words, my body with all its different levels, organs and structures is neither an object nor a complex of objects. On the other hand, it is *not simply* "I myself." The mode of being of my body appears to lie midway between "being" and "having," in the same way as it constitutes the transition from being-subject to being-object, from being-as-ego to "disposable" being.

My Body Is Quasi-objectively. The preceding characterization of my body is to a large extent negative. Perhaps we may complement this description in a more positive way as follows. My body is the extension of my "originating" ego in the direction of the "world." It is the bridge which connects the

ego with "worldly" things and beings. It is the continuation of my subjectivity in the realm of the objectivisable. It is the link between what *a priori* I can only be and what *a priori* I can only have. · All this may be summarized succinctly in the formula: the mode of being of my body is quasi-objective.

First Reflection on the Metaphysical Contrast: "My Body"—"My Soul"

The Inner Tension of the Ego. We are now sufficiently prepared to express conceptually, at least in a provisional way, the inner tension of our personal life, which constituted our starting point. The preceding descriptions indicate essential characteristics of our total existence as human persons. They are no constructural hypotheses, fancies or speculative flights of the mind. Nevertheless, one would be inclined to consider them such, for what we have discovered in our investigation is a series of contradictory statements.

Summarizing briefly the most important ones, we have successively asserted the following—

1
I am a subject, and I exist "in" my quasi-objects.

2
I am numerically *one* being, and I am a plurality in a unity.

3
I am simple and I am a plurality of relatively independent, juxtaposed and mutually external quasi-objects.

4
My retro-directed acts have their origin in me and these same acts originate in the "world."

5
I am the recipient of my retro-directed acts, and the "world" receives these acts.

The last two contradictory pairs of statements may be formulated also in this way:

[13] Cf. H. Plessner, *Lachen und Weinen*, Arnhem, 1941, p. 39: Man "neither *is* nor *has* merely a body."

I am an immanent being and I am not an immanent being.

6
I execute acts, and I offer resistance to these acts.

The Non-simplicity of the Ego. We are faced here with a series of contradictory judgments all of which are valid at the same time and with respect to the same object—namely, my ego. These judgments, moreover, are made from one and the same standpoint, which is that of my concrete retro-directed act. Finally all these judgments are based upon genuine phenomenological evidences. If we do not want to end in absurdities, we will have to make up our mind and admit: *I am not simple;* I am "composed." How this composition has to be conceived I do not yet know. I know only that in my human existence the modes of being of two realities reveal themselves. These realities I call, in deference to a very old and venerable tradition, *"my body"* and *"my spiritual soul."*

The Explanation of My Contradictory Character. In the light of this distinction we can explain the contradictory character of our affirmations as follows. I am body insofar as I exist "in" my quasi-objects. As a body, I am a plurality in a unity. Insofar as I am body, I consist of a plurality of relatively independent, juxtaposed, and mutually external quasi-objects. As body, I am relatively immanent. Insofar as I am body, I offer resistance to my own acts.

Opposite this series of judgments we place another contrasting series. Insofar as I am spiritual soul, I am subject. As spiritual soul, I am unique and simple. My life as spiritual soul runs its course in genuine immanence. My spiritual soul is the source of all my acts.

Some of these points will have to be more fully explained. But first we must make a remark of fundamental importance.

Metaphysical Consequences

Because of My Spiritual Soul I Am Primordially an Ego. If our preceding analyses are correct, the difference between "my spiritual soul" and "my body" is essential and irreducible. It is quite possible for one part of my body to take over the functions of another part, but it is unthinkable that my body or a part of it, say, a finely tuned organ, take over the place of my soul. Without any further comment this conclusion follows clearly from our analyses. The reason is that my body with all its members, organs and structures has essentially a quasi-objective character. Thus my body can exist only insofar as it is a *quasi-object for me.* In other words, my body with all its parts must necessarily be a "body-for-me," a "body by means of which I . . ." Briefly, it can be only "my embodiment." Thus my body is unthinkable without something which is the subject with respect to all real and possible quasi-objects of this body. This is the aprioristic condition under which the existence of an ego is possible in the world. In every person therefore there must be something which cannot be changed into a quasi-object, something which in principle does not function as the pole of intentional acts, something which does not appear to me as just a fact among other facts. *In the emphasis given to this partial truth lies the indisputable merit of those metaphysicists* who since Kant, as we have tried to show above, have influenced modern thought about the spiritual ego. It should be clear now also in what consists the error committed by these philosophers. The reality which makes us spiritual beings, patently is not a super-individual "general consciousness," a non-human transcendental ego, a person in Scheler's sense. To characterize this reality we do not need anything else than the concept of the spiritual soul, provided that we take care to safeguard it from false interpretations. Above all, we must emphasize therefore that the spiritual soul is not the object of the research of empirical psychology; that the soul does not appear to us as a "detached" entity among other "detached" entities; that the soul therefore does not function as an object or quasi-object with respect to ego-directed thinking or willing. Because of my spiritual soul I am primordially an ego; and in it lies the basis for the condition which makes possible all the data, facts and states which interest the empirical psychologist, the psychiatrist, the sociologist, etc.

My Spiritual Soul Is the Principle of My Existence as an Ego.   Perhaps this metaphysical thesis may be completed by the following considerations. The relation of my soul to my body is essentially irreversible. Otherwise man would not be essentially different from other more or less closed physical, chemical, or biological systems. What makes such a "multiple unity" into an ego or person is precisely the subjective element which does not belong to the organized multiple unity. In other words, just as it is impossible to be the son of one's father and at the same time this father himself, so also one and the same reality cannot be the body of something and at the same time that which is embodied in it. For this reason we say that *this relationship is irreversible.* From this irreversibility flow the above-mentioned relationships. If my body is essentially a *"quasi-object for . . .,"* my soul cannot be a *"quasi-object for . . ."* But in that case we must admit also that my soul is not the object of explicit intentional self-knowledge, not a phenomenon among other phenomena, not an object to be treated by the psychologist or the psychiatrist. Here lies the reason also why all objectivistic efforts to understand man as the resultant of certain physiological, biological, psychological, or sociological facts must necessarily fail. It is impossible in principle to explain man as any kind of a "system of equilibrium." The result of any effort to do it anyhow, is inevitably a manikin, a robot, a machine in the Cartesian sense, but never a person. What is always lacking is precisely the principle of absolute egological being, which we have called the spiritual soul. My spiritual soul is that which distinguishes me from a biological system; it is the ultimate reason why I am more than just a phase in a cosmic process of evolution. Briefly, my spiritual soul is the principle of my existence as an ego.

"My Soul" Is Not an Abstract Aspect of My Ego.   From this it follows that what I call my spiritual soul does not represent an abstract aspect of my personal existence.[14] The proof of this assertion does not seem difficult. Abstraction is possible only where we have to do with one or more concretely given data. This applies also when there is question of different degrees of abstraction. Even the most complex system of abstraction is ultimately based upon the solid foundation of concrete facts. Such a concrete datum is, for instance, the phenomenon "my body." Reflecting on my body I can abstract, for example, from its color, shape and weight, and form the universal concept of "one's own body." I can eliminate also the aspect of animation and thus change "my body" into the general concept of "corpse." But I cannot abstract from my spiritual soul. Evidently, the condition under which an abstractive act is possible is not fulfilled—namely, that the reality to be abstracted be something given. For, as we have seen, my spiritual soul is not a fact among facts, but that through which facts are facts. In other words, I am capable of abstracting from every particular reality, but unable to grasp adequately in a universal concept the principle of my own existence.[15] No matter what I think, represent to myself, or imagine, I will always be this unique individual existence which is "there," together with the represented, thought, or imagined object, as the one to whom these objects "appear." Whether I think of the origin of the terrestrial globe or the air traffic in the year 2000, I am always "there with it" as the singular ego. Somehow I am present, not as a human being with two

[14] Even recently, Alexis Carrel claimed: "In reality, the body and the soul are views taken of the same object by different methods, abstractions obtained by our reason from the concrete unity of our being. The antithesis of matter and mind represents merely the opposition of two kinds of techniques." *Man, the Unknown,* New York, 7th ed., 1935, p. 118.
[15] Undoubtedly, we cannot do without an inadequate conceptual symbol of the reality which cannot be grasped objectively. However, such a symbol is not introduced because of an intentional consciousness of contents, but only because of a "directional" consciousness.

hands and two feet, not as the person called by this or that name, who is the father of a family and a citizen of this State. I am present neither as a personal nor as a social ego, but as the anonymous and primordial ontological center, i.e. as the subject which faces the different objects and quasi-objects in an objective or quasi-objective way. This is also the mysterious reason why in Husserl's philosophy, after all kinds of reductions—whether they are called psychological, phenomenological or transcendental-phenomenological—there always remains an irreducible ego for which the reduced reality is a phenomenon. The "last spectator" necessarily escapes from every kind of "world nihilation." [16] What has been described here as the ultimate subject is manifestly nothing else than the *principium fontale*, the fountain spring, of my personal being, i.e., my soul. I cannot leave my soul out of consideration, because my soul is that which considers. I cannot "raise" it to universality, because for me the soul represents a center of the universe which cannot be compared with anything else. In other words, my soul is not a possible object of abstractive thinking. My soul is for me the unique and incomparable reality through which *my* being is rooted in being *itself*. . . .[17]

PHENOMENOLOGY OF THE HUMAN PERSON AS EMBODIED

The Embodied Ego as Unqualified Unity and as Multiple Unity

How is it possible for me to be at the same time an irreducible subject and an ordered whole of quasi-objects? How can I exist as unqualified unity and as multiple unity and yet be only one person? In raising such questions one comes face to face with the problem of the unity of body and soul.

One could answer that soul and body are partial substances, and that it is only the one man who is composed of these partial substances who possesses complete being. However, in such an answer the terms "part," "whole" and "to compose" are given a fourth meaning which is entirely different; and if no attention is drawn to this fact, one cannot fail to give rise to false ideas.

I, Turned toward the World. For this reason we ask ourselves whether it would not be better to present things in such a way as an analysis of my existence makes them appear. This analysis shows that I am a being among other beings, an ego in the midst of a universe of beings. No matter how different the interpretations are which various philosophers have given to this primordial situation, it is this situation which remains the starting point of every concrete metaphysics of being. Whoever reflects upon man and his existence cannot escape from taking into consideration two elementary truths, which are usually combined in a single statement: "I am, but not alone"; "I—open to the world"; "I—and you." In innumerable passages of his unpublished manuscripts Husserl speaks of an ego which by means of thought, feeling, sense of value, action, etc. inserts itself into the previously given

[16] However, it seems wholly illicit to us to conclude from this to an ontological priority of the ego which cannot be "placed between brackets" with respect to world, reality and being, or even to attribute to it "constituent" (i.e. creative) forces. Let us not forget that even this "last" subject is an ego which "discovers" its existence in the midst of the universe of being. Therefore, it is a finite, contingent and limited being. We may speak here only of a metaphysical relationship between ego and world, a relationship which must inevitably be thought by a being endowed with a finite intellect.

[17] By this we do not deny that the *distinction* between my body and my soul is based upon acts of abstraction. The immediate datum is obviously man in his concrete unity. The distinction can be made only insofar as we, as it were, "eliminate by abstraction" everything which in the immediately given personal unity is not soul. Here again the irreversibility of the body-soul relationship shows itself.

world. Let us give the name of *existential movement* or *existential "turning toward"* to the act by which every subject, in virtue of an essential necessity, turns towards the world, the vital or social surroundings.

Care must be taken, however, not to lose sight of a fundamental fact—namely, that for man the world is primordially a material world. This does not mean that I am locked up in a world consisting of extended things. In my view of the world other egos, persons and their personal life play a decisive role. These other egos I understand immediately, without having to pierce through the armor of lifeless matter. I understand them immediately as *besouling spiritual acts, acts which besoul matter.* In an analogous way I grasp *immediately* also the products of social, cultural and artistic life as manifestations of spiritual persons in matter. Thus besouled matter is not at all a wall separating us, but rather a mediator between you and me; it is the support of personal animation and "spiritualization" (*"Begeistung,"* Husserl). I grasp the other immediately (and not by an analogous process of reasoning) as embodied person, because I myself am a body-soul unity. Notwithstanding the fact that its importance can hardly be overestimated, the relationship "I—you" is not the absolutely first datum of philosophical anthropology. Before being able to have a personal relation to other human persons, I myself must first exist as embodied person.[18] The primordial problem therefore is the problem of embodiment.

Embodiment. It is intentionally that we speak here of the *problem of embodiment.* My embodiment is not an event that occurred at a definite moment. It must not be explained as if God "infused" my soul into a body. Rather, my incarnation consists in this that I as spirit have been created in a transcendental relation to a situation in 'the material cosmos which demands a soul, and it is in this that consists the creation of the

individual soul. Embodiment, therefore, is not an historical fact; it is a mode of being which, as long as I live, I do not cease to realize. Because I have been created with this transcendental relation, I can obtain my ontological fullness only as an ego which *embodies itself continually.*

In metaphysical terms, what is the meaning of this essential relation to the material cosmos? What is it to be embodied? Manifestly, it means that I make participate in my self-subsistent being, and this of necessity, things which are not " 'in themselves.' They are not persons but things, elements of the constant evolution of the universe," in which "the 'distinct from every other' is never found perfectly realized."[19] In other words, they are material relatively self-subsistent realities. By virtue of an essential necessity (*"per se"*) it belongs to me to raise "worldly" things and elements to a higher mode of being by forcing them to participate in my existential movement. For it belongs to the definition of my originating ego "to communicate to corporeal matter the 'to be' in which it itself subsists."[20] In order to reach the fullness of its being, my soul must be able to animate; it must penetrate the material world surrounding it; it must unite with itself in existential unity the material elements that possess sufficient *"ordinabilitas."* As St. Thomas expresses it, the soul "has a natural aptitude and inclination to be united with the body."[21] Accordingly, I am soul insofar as I have a respect to a material world; and I am body insofar as this respect is realized in me. As such, I am a single being.

Continuous Embodiment. We just spoke of "making things participate." This actively causing to participate manifests itself, for example, in the processes of integration and disintegration described in the preceding pages. We may even say that what we have called the "originating ego" is experienced

---

[18] Obviously, this "before" must not be taken in a genetico-psychological sense, but ontologically.

[19] Louis de Raeymaeker, *The Philosophy of Being,* p. 243.
[20] St. Thomas, *Summa theol.*, p. I, q. 76, a. 1, *ad* 5.
[21] *Loc. cit.*, *ad* 6.

by me primarily as the primordial driving force of my besouling and formative act. I am the constant source of the existential movement, and my body is its prolongation in the direction of the world. Maurice Merleau-Ponty is right when he writes:

☐ The union of body and soul is not sealed by an arbitrary decree between two external terms, of which one is object and the other subject. This union is brought about at every moment in the existential movement.[22]

This thought requires a more detailed explanation. In order to be able to exist as originating spiritual ego in a material world, I am obliged continually to bridge the gap separating me from the material world around me; and this means that I must continually embody myself. Between me as soul and the world of things there must always be an intermediary which is neither soul nor thing, but a besouled thing.

Moreover, I have to exist in a plurality of quasi-objects to find a passage to the unlimited plurality of "worldly" objects. I have to surround myself with concentric circles of members that are "outside" and "alongside" one another in order to obtain a foothold in a world of infinitely dispersed "parts outside parts." I have to live also in an orderly series of dynamic processes, which allow me to adapt myself to the ceaseless changes of cosmic formations. To maintain myself in the material world it is not sufficient for me to be "with myself"; I must also be "with" the material world, open and receptive to its values and non-values. From this it follows that in a material universe I can live only as an imperfect interiority.

Conclusion. All this is contained in the mystery of my embodiment, which is the ontological foundation of all forms of my human existence. In accordance with our analyses, we may summarize it briefly as follows. I am spirit, but existentially I am not a self-sufficient spirit. This means that

[22] *Phénomenologie de la perception,* 2nd ed., Paris, 1945, p. 105.

I am a besouling spirit which animates matter, a spirit-soul. As such, I am primordially oriented in my being towards a world of material (or materialized) realities. For I can reach the fullness of my being only if I exist in a way that corresponds with my natural lack of fullness. My mode of being therefore must be that of a *self-embodying spirit.* This means that I am spirit *and* bridge between spirit and matter. I exist *primordially* as spiritual ego and I exist *also* in my body. I am spirit-soul and I am also the matter which I besoul immediately. Thus, as an embodied person, I am a duality, a plurality, and at the same time a unity. . . .

Now I want to know to what extent I am the source of my acts. To what extent does the surrounding world participate in the realization of retro-directed activity, and to what extent do I participate in it? How are we to distinguish in principle between the act that flows *immediately* from me and the quasi-objective occurrence which belongs to me *only indirectly*? How am I to know that anything at all depends on me and me alone? By what right do I speak of an originating ego when I cannot even prove in a philosophically exact way that a single action originates in me and in me alone? . . .

From a methodological viewpoint it may perhaps be justified to start from a *provisional* concept of the soul and to presuppose that the soul is spiritual. In doing so we make use of the same liberty as the geographer who in order not to have to face all difficulties at the same time at first describes the apparent motion of the sun around the earth. In the same way, for methodical reasons, we have characterized the soul as the principle of self-subsistence, unity, order, and active orientation to the world; briefly, as the principle of my existential movement. Now, however, it is no longer merely a question of the soul as the metaphysical foundation of a vital orientation, but, as was mentioned in the first part of this book, we are concerned with the spiritual soul as the source of genuine deeds. If we want to reveal its permanent presence, we will have to show it as the egological reality which is no longer biologically conditioned by the world surrounding it, but based upon itself. Obviously, the method followed thus far is not suitable for this purpose. To reach it we will have to follow a different road. . . .

Reflective Reduction

To isolate this reality by abstraction we will apply the method of reflective reduction, i.e. we will reduce our whole concrete being as persons till we arrive at something which we are forced to consider unconditionally as a subject. We eliminate everything that possesses the character of a thing in order to penetrate to the egological reality with respect to which the members are members. . . .

PHENOMENOLOGY OF THE HUMAN SPIRIT-SOUL

Method to be Followed. Our starting point may seem perhaps to be somewhat formalistic. The ego which resisted our reductive elimination was the understanding ego, the ego which knows by intellectual insights and wills deliberately. It was the ego of the Platonic "phronesis." [23] We must now try to seize this "fact" as an essential relation. However, in order not to go beyond the realm of the clearly and distinctly known, we choose as the object of our analysis an *act of judgment* as the prototype of intellectual understanding, and a decision as the exemplar of deliberate willing. We eliminate all psychological complications that can arise in them. Thus we assume that the intellectual or volitional act in question is performed after the manner of unqualified affirmation and that it is performed without any distraction, for any deviation from this "classical" case would make our analyses very complex without in the least altering their results. Phenomenologically, we can now make the following assertion: as long as we remain in the sphere of "phronesis" there is no possibility of a regress in reflective acts that are based upon one another. Evidently, *it is impossible to arrive by way of reflec-*

tion *"behind"* our *"being in the presence of being."* We will prove this statement by means of concrete analyses.

Concrete Analysis in the Speculative Order. Let us assume that I make the judgment p regarding one or the other objective state of affairs. Obviously, it will then be impossible for me to formulate at the same time another judgment q whose object is the truth of p. What is striking here is that we are able to reflect immediately upon a judgment that has already been made, but not upon the judgment that is actually made now.

To illustrate this somewhat, let us assume that I want to know how much is two and three. Once I have understood that $2 + 3 = 5$ and have come to the conviction: "It is so; two and three is five," I will be able to confirm or correct, renew or reject this judgment in a subsequent act. But what cannot co-exist in me is, on the one hand, the conviction p "two and three is five" and, on the other, the thought q "my conviction that two and three is five is false." But where a negation is impossible there can likewise be no question of an affirmation. For, if my judgment q were positive, if it would be "Yes, it is true that two and three is five," and would coincide in time with p, then we would not have to do with two different judgments. There would be no mutual distinction between p and q, and therefore they would

[23] Cf. *Phaedo*, 79d. This term will be used here in the Platonic sense and not in that of Aristotle. It means the inclination and ability to view the eternal and unchangeable ideas, or in modern terms, the capacity of grasping universal and necessary truths.

have to be considered as identical. Briefly, an explicit judgment evaluating the judgment I am *actually* making is impossible. I am able to make the *"pensée pensée,"* the "thought thought" the object of a retro-directed act, but the *"pensée pensante,"* the "thinking thought" is not an intentional object with respect to itself. A regress to infinity is impossible here, for the simple reason that the *first* retrogressive step is impossible.

Concrete Analysis in the Practical Order. The practical sphere allows analogous observations. I am not capable of making decision r and at the same time decision s whose object is the correctness of r. Again, we must say that, once the decision is made, I certainly am capable of confirming, completing, correcting, or reversing it in a subsequent act of will. But unthinkable is an actual decision r and a likewise actual resolution s having as its content: "I reverse r because it is not a fortunate decision." If, however, s and r would be simultaneous decisions having the same content, they would of necessity coincide in a single act of will, i.e. they would be identical. Briefly, our *"volonté voulue,"* our "willed will" is at our disposal as a quasi-object, but not our *"volonté voulante,"* our "willing will." Our actual conviction that something is really so or is really good is not a quasi-object of simultaneous ego-directed acts. We are faced here with ultimate, irreducible data, data which, no matter how paradoxical it may sound, are characterized by the fact that they are never "given" in the strict sense of the term, data that are never objective data for us. . . .

Care must be taken, however, to prevent a misunderstanding leading to grave consequences. When we assert that our strictly spiritual acts do not allow any simultaneous reflection upon themselves, this concept may seem to remind us of a kind of "unconscious spirit." As a matter of fact, the idea of unconscious though spiritual functions plays a very important role in the systems of certain analytic psychologists, especially that of Carl G. Jung.[24] How it is possible for a psychologist and psychiatrist to adopt such a position is something we will see in the course of our subsequent discussions. But as of now we must emphasize that Frankl's concept of the "spiritual" needs to be critically examined. For, according to the view commonly accepted by the greatest thinkers of ancient times, the Middle Ages, and the modern period, one of the essential characteristics of the mind is to be present with itself in thinking and willing, to be "a source that thinks itself" (Karl Rahner). A mind which does not know anything of itself, which is blind for its own spiritual being, in other words, an "unconscious mind," is something wholly unspiritual.

In Spiritual Acts Self-observation Is Impossible. This shows itself clearly in the spiritual acts we have analyzed. In them "all self-observation and self-consideration" is actually impossible, but—and this is to be noted carefully—only because it is *unnecessary.* In other words, the spiritual cannot "come" to itself because it *is* already present with itself. So in our language the expressions "impossible," "incapable," "not able" do not indicate a limitation, deficiency or defect, but on the contrary are the negative aspect of a fullness, a power, a richness. Thus *an intentional reflection of my internal light upon itself is impossible because it is meaningless, and by virtue of my innermost nature I do not do what is meaningless.* In other words, the spiritual light shines in the darkness, but it does not throw a single ray upon itself. It is "unable" to do so because it is useless, meaningless, and

[24] While it is true that Jung does not explicitly use the term "unconscious spiritual" it will not escape the careful reader of his works that the unconscious, as described by Jung, possesses specifically spiritual qualities. A reality which is capable of producing "thoughts," discovering "objective truths," conceiving and communicating "ideas," including that of God, must be called spiritual in accordance with the universally recognized usage of this term. But according to Jung these abilities belong to the unconscious, namely the "collectively unconscious." Cf. Jung, *Über die Psychologie des Unbewuszten,* 5th ed., Zurich, 1953, pp. 120, 122, 123.

therefore incompatible with the nature of spiritual light. In the spirit of this comparison we may say: as a being which thinks and acts according to evident understanding, I am fully present with myself and do not need to "reflect upon myself" in order to know that I am.

I Am the Understanding of My Primordial Convictions. From this it follows, on the other hand, that I do not "have" my primordial convictions of truth and value in the same way as I have a lively imagination or a feeling of pain. I *am* my understanding of unconditioned values and ultimate truths. In my intimate aspiration to meaningful existence I am in an absolute way present to myself. I *am* the man who has taken this decision, who has freely chosen *this* and freely rejected *that,* the man who is "pervaded" by the truth of this and the falsity of that. There is nothing that is more myself than this my primordial being present with being. In scholastic terminology, it is the unfolding and ramification of my primary act of being in secondary acts of self-perfection. In my free search of meaning, and the taking of position regarding reality implied by this, in my free decisions, and the implied views of values which determine my decisions— considered not as a "system" or a "world view," but only insofar as they actually "live" in me—I am present with myself. No foreignness, exteriority or disposability is conceivable here; here I am alone in complete intimacy with myself, inescapably responsible for myself. For this reason it is in these acts of "considering to be true" and "holding to be valuable" that we have to see the specifically human feature, as well as the most personal essential characteristic, of my existential orientation. . . .

The Spiritual Ego as Interiority of Consciousness

First Characteristic

Spiritual Ego Is Unqualifiedly Subsistent. The question here is to establish first of all that our spiritual ego is not merely relatively self-subsistent but *unqualifiedly self-subsistent.* By this we mean that in order to be able to exist the soul does not need any material surrounding world as its support. For its existence it does not need the help of objects or quasi-objects. True, the spiritual soul is essentially related to a material world. To realize its full perfection the soul is obliged by its very nature to become embodied and to impose the law of its essence upon relatively self-subsistent material elements. But it is the spiritual reality which gives the form that raises the mode of being to a higher level. This reality is the "entelechy" of all organic functions, the beginning and end of all vital developments. Thus in opposition to material realities we must consider this soul as unqualifiedly subsistent.

Second Characteristic

The Spiritual Soul Is a Simple Unity. Our spiritual soul is a *simple unity.* It is not a complex, an ordered whole consisting of parts, elements, or members which are connected in one respect but not in another. In my spiritual life I am myself in an undivided and indivisible way, no matter what I do or what is done to me. From this it follows that I can metaphysically interpret my spiritual being and activities only as a transcendental relation between my self-subsistence and my accidents. For in every moment of my existence I am one and the same ego, and in every moment of my existence I am another ego. For instance, I am now convinced of "this" and then of "that"; now I want this and then I want that. My tendency to knowing and my desire for values fill me fully; yet at the same time they vary ceaselessly. They exclude the simultaneous occurrence of any divergent conviction or opposite tendency.

I Am My Spiritual Soul. It is important to emphasize that all this is valid with respect to the domain of "phronesis." As soon as we fasten our attention on the sphere of the besouled body, on the sphere of the not-wholly-understood and the not-really-willed, we notice immediately the inner tensions described at the beginning of this book. Then, for instance, I can "see" a stick half immersed in water as broken, yet "know" that it is not broken. I can also consciously tend to something, and at the same time struggle against it in my "subconscious." I am then convinced *somewhere* that S is *p*, i.e. that S is good, but at the same time I think *elsewhere* that S is not *p*, i.e. that S is not good. In my transcendental life there is no room for such a "somewhere" and "elsewhere" which can be explained physiologically or psychologically.[25] Here I am an ego which in an undivided way every time makes a decision with respect to a truth or a value. As a transcendental being, I coincide always and fully with myself, and yet am always another. This situation can be described neither within the framework of a positive science nor in an aprioristic theory of order. A purely metaphysical explanation has to be sought. To interpret these phenomenological data we have to admit the metaphenomenal relationship of a principle of subsistence with a principle of becoming. It is only the mutual penetration of these two principles which makes possible the reality of the soul as one and subsistent. Accordingly, there is no question here of a hypothetical substance which would be the unknown support of its known accidents. I am my spiritual soul as a self-subsistent reality, and at the same time as an accidental reality. I am this soul in a primordial way—for this soul is the source of my existence.

Third Characteristic

Authentic Interiority. In this way we arrive at a third and very important essential characteristic. We are now in a position to show that my existence as an ego has its foundation in an authentic interiority.

25 Thomas Aquinas remarks "the fact that man wants not to covet and yet covets occurs because of the disposition of the body by which the sense appetite is prevented from totally following the command of reason." *Summa theol.*, I–II, q. 17, a. 7, *ad* 1.

To clarify this difficult concept we may perhaps make use of our theory of order. In describing the higher forms of order we were able to conclude that there exists in them a certain solidarity between the members of an ordered whole. Each member is to a certain extent present with respect to the other; each member, as it were, "feels" what the other is and does; each member collaborates in a definite way with the others. This is the reason why the organic whole is relatively more closed and independent with respect to its vital surroundings. On the other hand, notwithstanding the remarkable collaboration of structure and organs, there is in the biological sphere a spatio-temporal or purely temporal dispersion, a fragmentation of the total act in different functions, a division of energy over several centers.

Let us now pass over from the besouled body to the spiritual ego as such. In this spiritual reality we find no absence at all of the one with respect to the other, no mutual foreignness, no inner tension. Perfect unity rules here, in the sense of perfect presence of the whole relative to the whole. This unity therefore does not have the characteristics of primitivity, such as that of a lump, or of poverty, as that of a point. This spiritual unity is infinitely more rich and at the same time more intimate than that of the most differentiated organism. In the realm of the spiritual there is evidently no limited solidarity of one member with one or more others, but a complete availability of the whole for the whole. Everything is comprised here in a single act which refers to itself and is its own foundation. This mode of being can be characterized only as an *active presence of the spirit with itself*. This follows from our preceding analyses, for if in my inner self I would face myself as a stranger, an unknown reality, a being with its own will, I would here also be subject to the law of dispersion, i.e. to the law of matter. Evidently, this is not the case. On the contrary, as a spiritual ego, I am not "outside" myself, not "alongside" myself, not "opposite to" myself, but in myself, *present* with myself, *grasping* myself.

"*Perfect Reflection.*" All these expressions, of course, are based upon metaphors borrowed from imperfect immanence. The very idea of immanence itself in its absolute meaning is likewise essentially inadequate and therefore linguistically and conceptually capable only of improper expression. This use of metaphors may give rise to serious misunderstandings. Therefore, it is important to emphasize that when interiority of consciousness is described as "perfect reflection," or as "*reditio completa*," complete return, one should carefully avoid imagining this reflection as a retro-directed or ego-directed act. There is no question here either of a subject pole which "bends backwards" or of an object pole over which the subject pole "bends"; likewise, there is no question of either a subject ego which "returns" or of an object ego to which the subject ego "returns." [26] The very terms "subject" and "object" are even no longer quite suitable here. For the "*reditio completa*" is not a mirrored reflection of oneself, nor is interiority of consciousness a "mirroring consciousness." It is important to note this, for spiritual immanence is often described as follows: "I think and insofar as thinking I think myself." Even in Thomas Aquinas we find expressions echoing this idea. He says, for instance, that "perceiving its act, the soul understands itself whenever it understands something." [27] However, it should not be forgotten that for St. Thomas "to understand" has another meaning with respect to "itself" than as directed to "something." The act of presence with itself is the basis of every form of consciousness. But this spiritual self-possession is no objective self-knowledge, no "introspection" in the sense of psychology. As Maurice Pradines remarks very correctly, "A conscious being is not a being that looks at itself in a mirror, but a being that possesses itself." [28] Moreover, the empirical sciences offer a wealth of arguments for the correctness of this view. It is very well possible to be a "rational animal" without possessing objective self-knowledge. It may be sufficient to point here to the case of consciousness in children and primitive men. Ethnologists tell us that primitive men are not conscious of themselves, that they do not conceive of themselves as subjects, and that their own existence appears to them as that of a thing among things. It would, however, be more correct to say that they do not possess any *explicit* self-knowledge. They are so fascinated by the spectacle of their surrounding world that they never arrive at the idea of making a quasi-object pole of the content of their lived events. Nevertheless, they possess the primordial spiritual presence with themselves which makes it possible for them to grasp themselves as identical self-subsistent beings among other beings, and these other beings as others. This proves that we must not conceive "understanding oneself" as a retro-directed act, as a reflecting upon oneself, but as an existential presence with the self which, even when it is not conceptually explicated, makes it possible for the subject to affirm himself throughout the inexhaustible multiplicity of lived experiences. [29]

"*To Understand Something.*" In "understanding something," on the other hand, I am directed as a subject to an object. Here rules the typical subject-object tension; here we find that relation which nowadays goes by the name of "intentional." "Understanding something" therefore is a "tending to," a conscious grasping and spiritual embrace of a "worldly" object or a quasi-object. However, even this understanding owes its clarity and "illuminating" character to the interiority conscious of itself from which it comes forth. But primordial self-consciousness is not a second act based upon a pre-

[26] When Thomas Aquinas characterizes the spiritual presence with oneself as a "returning to one's essence by a complete return," he emphasizes at the same time that "to return to one's essence is nothing else than that a being subsists in itself." *Summa theol.*, I, q. 14, a. 2, *ad* 1.
[27] *Summa theol.*, I, q. 93, a. 7, *ad* 4.
[28] *Traité de Psychologie générale*, 2nd ed., Paris, 1946, vol. I, p. 7.
[29] Cf. A. Dondeyne, "Idealisme of Realisme?", *Tijdschrift v. Philosophie*, vol. 3 (1941), pp. 607 f.

ceding act. With Fernand Van Steenberghen we would prefer to characterize it as follows.

☐ Self-consciousness is not, at least at first, a distinct act in opposition to the knowledge of the object. Rather it is the same act in so far as it is transparent to itself.[30]

So we must interpret the above-quoted text of Thomas Aquinas in this way. I am originally in a cognitive relation to myself, and this primordial knowing is the foundation of all my particular acts of knowledge. As a spiritual ego, I am with myself, and this spiritual presence with myself makes it possible for me to be present with the other in a knowing and understanding way, in an act of spiritual directedness (an intentional act).

Psychological Self-knowledge. We may complete these considerations with the remark that psychological self-knowledge does not have the "thinking thought" as its object but the "thought thought." This self-knowledge therefore can begin only when acts of consciousness have passed from the stage of actuality to that of quasi-objectivity. Accordingly, psychological self-knowledge requires a special theoretical act which is based upon a preceding act that is no longer fully actual. When as psychologists we revert intentionally to our own temporal members, we succeed within limits in explicating our implicit presence with ourselves in true judgments, which, however, are necessarily inadequate. It is in this sense that Thomas Aquinas remarks regarding self-knowledge:

☐ The act by which the intellect understands a stone is different from the act by which it understands that it understands the stone.[31]

This view of St. Thomas is fully in accordance with the phenomenological data. Edmund Husserl, for instance, describes objective self-knowledge as follows:

☐ First of all, one must realize that every "reflection" has the character of a modification of consciousness, and this modification is of such a nature that in principle every consciousness can experience it. One may speak here of modification insofar as every reflection essentially proceeds from certain changes in attitude which cause a certain change in a pre-given lived event or datum of lived experience hitherto possessed unreflectingly. This modification affects the very mode of the consciousness or object of consciousness reflected upon. [32]

Merleau-Ponty likewise asserts:

☐ No particular thought reaches us in the heart of our thinking; such a thought is not conceivable without another thought as its witness.[33]

He complements this idea as follows:

☐ What is considered to be the thought of the thought, as pure self-perception, is not yet thought and needs to be revealed.[34]

Thus Merleau-Ponty also admits a primordial self-consciousness, a "confused grasp of originating subjectivity on itself," [35] which, however, is contained only implicitly in every particular act of consciousness. To make this self-consciousness explicit and grasp it in an objective synthetic judgment a second act is required which testifies regarding the first act that is no longer fully actual.

"I Will My Willing." It is in this sense also that we must interpret the formula "I will my willing." For if the first and second willing did not have a very different meaning, this sentence would be meaningless. The

---

[30] *Epistemology*, New York, 1949, p. 103.
[31] *Summa theol.*, I, q. 88, a. 4, *ad* 2. Cf. the very profound and extensive study of P. H. J. Walgrave regarding the problem of "Zelfkennis en innerlijke ervaring by St. Thomas," *Tijdschrift v. Philosophie*, vol. 9 (1947), pp. 1–62.
[32] *Ideen zu einer reinen Phänomenologie . . .*, p. 458.
[33] *Phénoménologie de la Perception*, 2nd ed., Paris, 1945, p. 458.
[34] *Op. cit.*, p. 462.
[35] *Op. cit.*, p. 463.

best way to show this is by means of a fully concrete situation. Let us assume that we are in a restaurant and answer the waiter's question as to what we desire by saying "We desire our desire." If the waiter were very intelligent, he would reply: "You desire your desire; therefore you desire nothing." This conclusion would be wholly valid, because the subject desire and the object desire effectively neutralize each other. For this reason we prefer to express the profound thought which does not receive justice in the above-mentioned formula in the following way. All our particular acts of will are grounded in a primordial willing. This primordial willing, however, is not a conscious tendency to "this" or a desire of "that." On the contrary, it represents my original self-affirmation as a "striving" spirit, which in all my intentional acts of willing is particularized and directed to special poles. In other words, as a striving spirit I am present with myself, and this makes it possible for me to strive in an act of interior directedness after the other as other, knowing it, valuing it, and loving it.

Fourth Characteristic

Transcendence of the "World." Finally, we would like to indicate a fourth fundamental difference between genuine and imperfect interiority. We have characterized relative immanence by saying that something of the being comes from the surrounding world, and something of it returns to the surrounding world. Hence the flux which is the characteristic phenomenon of vital interiority. The flux and reflux takes place in such a way that what at a given moment is more valuable, higher ranking, more finely differentiated, more forceful remains in the being. For the organism derives all the valuable elements which it needs for its formation and conservation from its surroundings. For this reason it lives fully turned to the external. Even the primitive man and the little child appear wholly absorbed in the spectacle of the world; they are, so to speak, magnetically attracted by all these moving,

multicolored, sonorous, desirable, or frightening things. But with respect to man the situation is different. Because as a transcendental being he is directed to being itself, he has by his very nature a firm and lasting anchorage, so that he is more than just a ripple on the stream of life, more than a "worldly" situation, more than a nodal point of vital connections. He does, therefore, not have to expect all his values from the world and his surroundings. He is able to reflect upon his spiritual nature and to discover in himself spiritual values. Of course, it is another question whether he does it in the form of explicit and conceptual reflection. Thanks to his interiority of consciousness man is primordially a bearer of values in the material world. He does not receive all his values from his surroundings, and especially not those values which are decisive with respect to his full self-development. Not everything and certainly not the best of what he needs for his self-development comes from the cosmos. Therefore, we may conclude that not everything, and especially not the best of him will return to the cosmos.

To possess a spiritual interiority therefore means to have within oneself one's own foundation as a being that grasps values and realizes them. It means to be a primordially knowing and primordially willing being in an existential unity. These are the essential characteristics which make man a self-subsistent being endowed with a spirit or, in the words of perennial philosophy, a person.

Bibliography

Texts

The Soul in Metaphysical and Empirical Psychology. Pittsburgh: Duquesne University Press, 1962.

Phenomenology and the Human Sciences: A Contribution to a New Scientific Ideal. Pittsburgh: Duquesne University Press, 1963.

The Idea of Dialogal Phenomenology. Pittsburgh: Duquesne University Press, 1969.

28

MAURICE MERLEAU–PONTY
1907–1961

Introduction

Maurice Merleau-Ponty, a Catholic by birth, was born in La Rochelle in Normandy. He was educated in the French *lycées* and later studied philosophy at the Ecole Normale Supérieure (University of Paris). There he met the more precocious Sartre, who, though only two years older, would have a long and impressive list of publications by the time Merleau-Ponty's first book appeared in 1942. In fact it was Sartre who introduced him to the work of Edmund Husserl in 1935 after returning from his two years of research study of German philosophy and psychology in Berlin (on a fellowship from the Institut Français de Berlin). Merleau-Ponty certainly acted on this suggestion with considerable industry, studying not only Husserl's published work but also his later unpublished manuscripts kept at the Catholic University of Louvain in Belgium.*

It was not until 1942 that Merleau-Ponty's first book, *The Structure of Behavior*, appeared, although it was in the making long before, probably being completed by 1938. In 1945 he published his major work, *Phenomenology of Perception*. In this same year he and Sartre cofounded the review

Les Temps modernes, although he never allowed his name to appear on its masthead with Sartre's, no doubt for political reasons. Most of Merleau-Ponty's writing after this was essays, later collected and published in books.

After teaching at the Lycée de Saint Quentin, the Université de Lyon, and the Sorbonne, he was in 1952 appointed to the chair of philosophy at the Collège de France. He was the youngest man ever to be named to this prestigious position once held by such men as Henri Bergson, Edouard Le Roy, Louis Lavelle, and Etienne Gilson. He remained there until his premature death at fifty-four on May 4, 1961.

It is still too soon to try to summarize Merleau-Ponty's thought, but certain major themes are clear from his two most important books. One of the first is that philosophy, like man, is *engagée*, i.e., *involved* in and *committed* to the world, and has no choice about "getting involved" or not. It is a search, an activity of man who is essentially incarnate within the world; it is committed to action, especially social and even political action. In Merleau-Ponty's words, "It is easier to write books than to live."

Taking a theme from Marcel and developing it with brilliance combined with the solid scientific care and treatment it still needed from someone more used to academic discipline and at home with system than Marcel, Merleau-Ponty attempted to work out a phenomenology of man's being-present-within-the-world (*être-au-monde*). His first book, *The Structure of Behavior*, was really a prolegomenon to this task. It showed, through a critical though sympathetic and painstaking analysis of behaviorist and Gestalt psychologies, that a new starting point is needed which takes a clue from the best of Gestalt psychology and pursues it

* Belgium has become something of an international center for historical research in phenomenology since the Franciscan Herman Van Breda rescued the complete Husserl manuscripts from Freiburg four months after Husserl's death there in 1938. Van Breda was there in search of materials for his doctoral thesis on Husserl. He subsequently set up the Husserl Archives at Louvain, and the manuscripts are being edited and published under the general title *Husserliana*. A dozen volumes had appeared by 1970, while another Louvain series, *Phänomenologica*, also published under the patronage of the Archives, has produced over thirty volumes. *Phänomenologica* include historical, critical, and original studies by many authors. The already large and excellent series from Duquesne University and the growing series from Northwestern University, although they both consist mainly of translations, also belong to this family.

through use of phenomenology in the hope of overcoming the persistent error of a Cartesian dualism and of reuniting subject and object, man and world. This dualism is at the root of all those divisions that keep man from unity on every level of experience, including harmony in social and political life and even in religious, theological, philosophical, and scientific goals. Its forms are numerous: idealism versus materialism, realism versus rationalism versus naturalism, solipsism versus collectivism, "rugged individualism" versus "enlightened socialism," incarnationalism versus eschatologism, *vita activa* versus *vita contemplativa*, physical (natural, mathematical) sciences versus social (human, divine) sciences, racism and nationalism versus evolutionary humanism, determinism versus responsible freedom, and so on like a litany of Babel whose unifying theme is disunity, an increasingly conscious suicidal trend so universal as to constitute genocide.

The philosophical starting point against this dualism was suggested by Husserl's concept of the *Lebenswelt*, the world perceived before distorted by religious, philosophical, and scientific presuppositions, prejudices, interpretations, additions, and subtractions, or at least methodically freed from them. In practice this means a description of experience before trying to explain it. This description is phenomenology's role. Any explanatory hypotheses that experience may force on man then become inductions based on perception of the relations between man and his world. Thus Merleau-Ponty's second work, his *Phenomenology of Perception*, is really a phenomenology of the perceived world as related to man, the perceiver, rather than a phenomenology of the action itself of perception. Perception has primacy over other human actions and behavior because it is conscious and given first to us before anything like a methodic doubt, no matter how sophisticated, or any other arbitrary preunderstanding or explanation is interposed between experience and description of experience. Perception has a kind of organic primordiality in the manner in which

it makes us present within the world, as though our bodies and sense precede us there and are always already there in and of the world, as we realize we are also, since they are ourselves. Merleau-Ponty emphasizes ambivalence, maintaining that the experienced is only in part intelligible and that the intelligible can only in part be experienced. Thus doubt in the face of possible illusion can be overcome only by believing against the risk and committing oneself to action. Freedom emerges, therefore, as a reality conditioned by being experienced by a person who has, with at least some responsibility, adopted a particular style of life, a style that inclines him toward values consonant with it, and who always exercises choice within a particular incarnate situation. Any attempt to identify the influence of the situation and distinguish it from that of responsible freedom participates in the same ambiguity as all human existence.

But Merleau-Ponty's most important theme remains man's incarnate social nature: unprejudiced perception overcomes dualism in the experienced continuity of my active body with the world and especially with other persons and their bodies. The one original structure, the one primordial common ground is *presence*, of which the perceiver and the world (the subject and the object) are subsequent abstractions and distinguishable as two constituent elements by abstraction. It is contrary to the experienced phenomenon of presence to create the false problem of first being a closed consciousness, hermetically sealed in a sensor-equipped body-island, trying to establish contact with an outside world. My body *is* world, jointly part of the total system "world." And my body is myself incarnate. A phenomenology of my body discovers that it is myself and my possibility of taking varying perspectives of the perceivable but also in my actuality of already always being in certain perspectives by nature, one of which is our mutual coexistence in an interpersonal world. The following selections develop some of these themes.

PHENOMENOLOGY OF EMBODIMENT *

In its descriptions of the body from the point of view of the self, classical psychology was already wont to attribute to it "characteristics" incompatible with the status of an object. In the first place it was stated that my body is distinguishable from the table or the lamp in that I can turn away from the latter whereas my body is constantly perceived. It is therefore an object which does not leave me. But in that case is it still an object? If the object is an invariable structure, it is not one *in spite of* the changes of perspective, but *in* that change or *through* it. It is not the case that everrenewed perspectives simply provide it with opportunities of displaying its permanence, and with contingent ways of presenting itself to us. It is an object, which means that it is standing in front of us, only because it is observable: situated, that is to say, directly under our hand or gaze, indivisibly overthrown and re-integrated with every movement they make. Otherwise it would be true like an idea and not present like a thing. It is particularly true than an object is an object only in so far as it can be moved away from me, and ultimately disappear from my field of vision. Its presence is such that it entails a possible absence. Now the permanence of my own body is entirely different in kind: it is not at the extremity of some indefinite exploration; it defies exploration and is always presented to me from the same angle. Its permanence is not a permanence in the world, but a permanence from my point of view. To say that it is always near me, always there for me, is to say that it is never really in front of me, that I cannot array it before my eyes, that it remains marginal to all my perceptions, that it is *with* me. It is true that external objects too never turn one of their sides to me without

hiding the rest, but I can at least freely choose the side which they are to present to me. They could not appear otherwise than in perspective, but the particular perspective which I acquire at each moment is the outcome of no more than physical necessity, that is to say, of a necessity which I can use and which is not a prison for me: from my window only the tower of the church is visible, but this limitation simultaneously holds out the promise that from elsewhere the whole church could be seen. It is true, moreover, that if I am a prisoner the church will be restricted, for me, to a truncated steeple. If I did not take off my clothes I could never see the inside of them, and it will in fact be seen that my clothes may become appendages of my body. But this fact does not prove that the presence of my body is to be compared to the *de facto* permanence of certain objects, or the organ compared to a tool which is always available. It shows that conversely those actions in which I habitually engage incorporate their instruments into themselves and make them play a part in the original structure of my own body. As for the latter, it is my basic habit, the one which conditions all the others, and by means of which they are mutually comprehensible. Its permanence near to me, its unvarying perspective are not a *de facto* necessity, since such necessity presupposes them: in order that my window may impose upon me a point of view of the church, it is necessary in the first place that my body should impose upon me one of the world; and the first necessity can be merely physical only in virtue of the fact that the second is metaphysical; in short, I am accessible to factual situations only if my nature is such that there are factual situations for me. In other words, I observe external objects with my body, I handle them, examine them, walk round them, but my body itself is a thing which I do not observe: in order to be able to do so, I should need the use of a second body which itself would

* From Maurice Merleau-Ponty, *Phenomenology of Perception*, Routledge & Kegan Paul, Ltd., London, 1965, 2d ed. Colin Smith, Translator. Reprinted by permission of Routledge & Kegan Paul, Ltd., and Humanities Press.

be unobservable. When I say that my body is always perceived by me, these words are not to be taken in a purely statistical sense, for there must be, in the way my own body presents itself, something which makes its absence or its variation inconceivable. What can it be? My head is presented to my sight only to the extent of my nose end and the boundaries of my eye-sockets. I can see my eyes in three mirrors, but they are the eyes of someone observing, and I have the utmost difficulty in catching my living glance when a mirror in the street unexpectedly reflects my image back at me. My body in the mirror never stops following my intentions like their shadow, and if observation consists in varying the point of view while keeping the object fixed, then it escapes observation and is given to me as a simulacrum of my tactile body since it imitates the body's actions instead of responding to them by a free unfolding of perspectives. My visual body is certainly an object as far as its parts far removed from my head are concerned, but as we come nearer to the eyes, it becomes divorced from objects, and reserves among them a quasi-space to which they have no access, and when I try to fill this void by recourse to the image in the mirror, it refers me back to an original of the body which is not out there among things, but in my own province, on this side of all things seen. It is no different, in spite of what may appear to be the case, with my tactile body, for if I can, with my left hand, feel my right hand as it touches an object, the right hand as an object is not the right hand as it touches: the first is a system of bones, muscles and flesh brought down at a point of space, the second shoots through space like a rocket to reveal the external object in its place. In so far as it sees or touches the world, my body can therefore be neither seen nor touched. What prevents its ever being an object, ever being "completely constituted"[1] is that it is that by which there are objects. It is neither tangible nor visible in so far as it is that which sees

and touches. The body therefore is not the nondescript one among external objects and simply having the peculiarity of always being there. If it is permanent, the permanence is absolute and is the ground for the relative permanence of disappearing objects, real objects. The presence and absence of external objects are only variations within a field of primordial presence, a perceptual domain over which my body exercises power. Not only is the permanence of my body not a particular case of the permanence of external objects in the world, but the second cannot be understood except through the first: not only is the perspective of my body not a particular case of that of objects, but furthermore the presentation of objects in perspective cannot be understood except through the resistance of my body to all variation of perspective. If objects may never show me more than one of their facets, this is because I am myself in a certain place from which I see them and which I cannot see. If nevertheless I believe in the existence of their hidden sides and equally in a world which embraces them all and co-exists with them, I do so in so far as my body, always present for me, and yet involved with them in so many objective relationships, sustains their co-existence with it and communicates to them all the pulse of its duration. Thus the permanence of one's own body, if only classical psychology had analysed it, might have led it to the body no longer conceived as an object of the world, but as our means of communication with it, to the world no longer conceived as a collection of determinate objects, but as the horizon latent in all our experience and itself ever-present and anterior to every determining thought.

The other "characteristics" whereby one's own body were defined were no less interesting, and for the same reasons. My body, it was said, is recognized by its power to give me "double sensations": when I touch my right hand with my left, my right hand, as an object, has the strange property of being able to feel too. We have just seen that the two hands are never simultaneously in the relationship of touched and touching to each

---

[1] Husserl, *Ideen*. T. II (unpublished.)

other. When I press my two hands together, it is not a matter of two sensations felt together as one perceives two objects placed side by side, but of an ambiguous set-up in which both hands can alternate the rôles of "touching" and being "touched." What was meant by talking about "double sensations" is that, in passing from one rôle to the other, I can identify the hand touched as the same one which will in a moment be touching. In other words, in this bundle of bones and muscles which my right hand presents to my left, I can anticipate for an instant the integument or incarnation of that other right hand, alive and mobile, which I thrust towards things in order to explore them. The body catches itself from the outside engaged in a cognitive process; it tries to touch itself while being touched, and initiates "a kind of reflection" [2] which is sufficient to distinguish it from objects, of which I can indeed say that they "touch" my body, but only when it is inert, and therefore without ever catching it unawares in its exploratory function.

It was also said that the body is an affective object, whereas external things are from my point of view merely represented. This amounted to stating a third time the problem of the status of my own body. For if I say that my foot hurts, I do not simply mean that it is a cause of pain in the same way as the nail which is cutting into it, differing only in being nearer to me; I do not mean that it is the last of the objects in the external world, after which a more intimate kind of pain should begin, an unlocalized awareness of pain in itself, related to the foot only by some causal connection and within the closed system of experience. I mean that the pain reveals itself as localized, that it is constitutive of a "pain-infested space." "My foot hurts" means not: "I think that my foot is the cause of this pain," but: "the pain comes from my foot" or again "my foot has a pain." This is shown clearly by the "primitive voluminousness of pain" formerly spoken of by psychologists. It was therefore recog-

nized that my body does not present itself as the objects of external impressions do, and that perhaps even these latter objects do no more than stand out against the affective background which in the first place throws consciousness outside itself.

Finally when the psychologists tried to confine "kinaesthetic sensations" to one's own body, arguing that these sensations present the body's movements to us globally, whereas they attributed the movements of external objects to a mediating perception and to a comparison between successive positions, it could have been objected that movement, expressing a relationship, cannot be felt, but demands a mental operation. This objection, however, would merely have been an indictment of their language. What they were expressing, badly it is true, by "kinaesthetic sensation," was the originality of the movements which I perform with my body: they directly anticipate the final situation, for my intention initiates a movement through space merely to attain the objective initially given at the starting point; there is as it were a germ of movement which only secondarily develops into an objective movement. I move external objects with the aid of my body, which takes hold of them in one place and shifts them to another. But my body itself I move directly, I do not find it at one point of objective space and transfer it to another, I have no need to look for it, it is already with me—I do not need to lead it towards the movement's completion, it is in contact with it from the start and propels itself towards that end. The relationships between my decision and my body are, in movement, magic ones.

If the description of my own body given by classical psychology already offered all that is necessary to distinguish it from objects, how does it come about that psychologists have not made this distinction or that they have in any case seen no philosophical consequence flowing from it? The reason is that, taking a step natural to them, they chose the position of impersonal thought to which science has been committed as long as it believed in the possibility of separat-

2 Husserl, *Méditations cartésiennes*, p. 81.

ing, in observation, on the one hand what belongs to the situation of the observer and on the other the properties of the absolute object. For the living subject his own body might well be different from all external objects; the fact remains that for the unsituated thought of the psychologist the experience of the living subject became itself an object and, far from requiring a fresh definition of being, took its place in universal being. It was the life of the "psyche" which stood in opposition to the real, but which was treated as a second reality, as an object of scientific investigation to be brought under a set of laws. It was postulated that our experience, already besieged by physics and biology, was destined to be completely absorbed into objective knowledge, with the consummation of the system of the sciences. Thenceforth the experience of the body degenerated into a "representation" of the body; it was not a phenomenon but a fact of the psyche. In the matter of living appearance, my visual body includes a large gap at the level of the head, but biology was there ready to fill that gap, to explain it through the structure of the eyes, to instruct me in what the body really is, showing that I have a retina and a brain like other men and like the corpses which I dissect, and that, in short, the surgeon's instrument could infallibly bring to light in this indeterminate zone of my head the exact replica of plates illustrating the human anatomy. I apprehend my body as a subject-object, as capable of "seeing" and "suffering," but these confused representations were so many psychological oddities, samples of a magical variety of thought the laws of which are studied by psychology and sociology and which has its place assigned to it by them, in the system of the real world, as an object of scientific investigation. This imperfect picture of my body, its marginal presentation, and its equivocal status as touching and touched, could not therefore be *structural* characteristics of the body itself; they did not affect the idea of it; they became "distinctive characteristics" of those *contents* of consciousness which make up our representation of the body: these contents are consistent, affective and strangely duplicated in "double sensations," but apart from this the representation of the body is a representation like any other and correspondingly the body is an object like any other. Psychologists did not realize that in treating the experience of the body in this way they were simply, in accordance with the scientific approach, shelving a problem which ultimately could not be burked. The inadequacy of my perception was taken as a *de facto* inadequacy resulting from the organization of my sensory apparatus; the presence of my body was taken as a *de facto presence* springing from its constant action on my receptive nervous system; finally the union of soul and body, which was presupposed by these two explanations, was understood, in Cartesian fashion, as a *de facto union* whose *de jure* possibility need not be established, because the fact, as the starting point of knowledge, was eliminated from the final result. Now the psychologist could imitate the scientist and, for a moment at least, see his body as others saw it, and conversely see the bodies of others as mechanical things with no inner life. The contribution made from the experiences of others had the effect of dimming the structure of his own, and conversely, having lost contact with himself he became blind to the behaviour of others. He thus saw everything from the point of view of universal thought which abolished equally his experience of others and his experience of himself. But as a psychologist he was engaged in a task which by nature pulled him back into himself, and he could not allow himself to remain unaware to this extent. For whereas neither the physicist nor the chemist are the objects of their own investigation, the psychologist *was himself*, in the nature of the case, the fact which exercised him. This representation of the body, this magical experience, which he approached in a detached frame of mind, was himself; he lived it as he thought it. It is true that, as has been shown,[3] it was not enough for him to be a

3 Guillaume, *L' Objectivité en Psychologie.*

psyche in order to know this, for this knowledge, like other knowledge, is acquired only through our relations with other people. It does not emerge from any recourse to an ideal of introspective psychology, and between himself and others no less than between himself and himself, the psychologist was able and obliged to rediscover a preobjective relationship. But as a psyche speaking of the psyche, he *was* all that he was *talking* about. This history of the psyche which he was elaborating in adopting the objective attitude was one whose outcome he already possessed within himself, or rather he was, in his existence, its contracted outcome and latent memory. The union of soul and body had not been brought about once and for all in a remote realm; it came into being afresh at every moment beneath the psychologist's thinking, not as a repetitive event which each time takes the psyche by surprise, but as a necessity that the psychologist knew to be in the depths of his being as he became aware of it as a piece of knowledge. The birth of perception from the "sense-data" to the "world" was supposed to be renewed with each act of perception, otherwise the sense-data would have lost the meaning they owed to this development. Hence the "psyche" was not an object like others: it had done everything that one was about to say of it before it could be said; the psychologist's being knew more about itself than he did; nothing that had happened or was happening according to science was completely alien to it. Applied to the psyche, the notion of fact, therefore, underwent a transformation. The *de facto* psyche, with its "peculiarities," was no longer an event in objective time and in the external world, but an event with which we were in internal contact, of which we were ourselves the ceaseless accomplishment or upsurge, and which continually gathered within itself its past, its body and its world. Before being an objective fact, the union of soul and body had to be, then, a possibility of consciousness itself and the question arose as to what the perceiving subject is and whether he must be able to experience

a body as his own. There was no longer a fact passively submitted to, but one assumed. To be a consciousness or rather *to be an experience* is to hold inner communication with the world, the body and other people, to be with them instead of being beside them. To concern oneself with psychology is necessarily to encounter, beneath objective thought which moves among ready-made things, a first opening upon things without which there would be no objective knowledge.

The cultivation of habit as a rearrangement and renewal of the body image presents great difficulties to traditional philosophies, which are always inclined to conceive synthesis as intellectual synthesis. It is quite true that what brings together, in habit, component actions, reactions and "stimuli" is not some external process of association.[4] Any mechanistic theory runs up against the fact that the learning process is systematic: the subject does not weld together individual movements and individual stimuli but acquires the power to respond with a certain type of solution to situations of a certain general form. The situations may differ widely from case to case, and the response movements may be entrusted sometimes to one operative organ, sometimes to another, both situations and responses in the various cases having in common not so much a partial identity of elements as a shared significance. Must we then see the origin of habit in an act of understanding which organizes the elements only to withdraw subsequently?[5] For example, is it not the case that forming the habit of dancing is discovering, by analysis, the formula of the movement in question, and then reconstructing it on the basis of the ideal outline by the use of previously acquired movements, those of walking and running? But before the formula of the new dance can incorporate certain elements of general motility, it must first have had, as it

[4] See, on this point, *La Structure du Comportement*, pp. 125 and ff.
[5] As Bergson, for example, thinks when he defines habit as "the fossilized residue of a spiritual activity"

were, the stamp of movement set upon it. As has often been said, it is the body which "catches" (*kapiert*) and "comprehends" movement. The cultivation of habit is indeed the grasping of a significance, but it is the motor grasping of a motor significance. Now what precisely does this mean? A woman may, without any calculation, keep a safe distance between the feather in her hat and things which might break it off. She feels where the feather is just as we feel where our hand is." If I am in the habit of driving a car, I enter a narrow opening and see that I can "get through" without comparing the width of the opening with that of the wings, just as I go through a doorway without checking the width of the doorway against that of my body.[7] The hat and the car have ceased to be objects with a size and volume which is established by comparison with other objects. They have become potentialities of volume, the demand for a certain amount of free space. In the same way the iron gate to the Underground platform, and the road, have become restrictive potentialities and immediately appear passable or impassable for my body with its adjuncts. The blind man's stick has ceased to be an object for him, and is no longer perceived for itself; its point has become an area of sensitivity, extending the scope and active radius of touch, and providing a parallel to sight. In the exploration of things, the length of the stick does not enter expressly as a middle term: the blind man is rather aware of it through the position of objects than of the position of objects through it. The position of things is immediately given through the extent of the reach which carries him to it, which comprises besides the arm's own reach the stick's range of action. If I want to get used to a stick, I try it by touching a few things with it, and eventually I have it "well in hand," I can see what things are "within reach" or out of reach of my stick. There is no question here of any quick esti-

mate or any comparison between the objective length of the stick and the objective distance away of the goal to be reached. The points in space do not stand out as objective positions in relation to the objective position occupied by our body; they mark, in our vicinity, the varying range of our aims and our gestures. To get used to a hat, a car or a stick is to be transplanted into them, or conversely, to incorporate them into the bulk of our own body. Habit expresses our power of dilating our being in the world, or changing our existence by appropriating fresh instruments.[8] It is possible to know how to type without being able to say where the letters which make the words are to be found on the banks of keys. To know how to type is not, then, to know the place of each letter among the keys, nor even to have acquired a conditioned reflex for each one, which is set in motion by the letter as it comes before our eye. If habit is neither a form of knowledge nor an involuntary action, what then is it? It is knowledge in the hands, which is forthcoming only when bodily effort is made, and cannot be formulated in detachment from that effort. The subject knows where the letters are on the typewriter as we know where one of our limbs is, through a knowledge bred of familiarity which does not give us a position in objective space. The movement of her fingers is not presented to the typist as a path through space which can be described, but merely as a certain adjustment of motility, physiognomically distinguishable from any other. The question is often framed as if the perception of a letter written on paper aroused the representation of the same letter which in turn aroused the representation of the movement needed to strike it on the machine. But this is mythological language. When I run my eyes over the text set before me, there do not occur perceptions which stir up representations,

[6] Head, *Sensory disturbances from cerebral lesion*, p. 188.
[7] Grünbaum, *Aphasie und Motorik*, p. 395.

[8] It thus elucidates the nature of the body image. When we say that it presents us immediately with our bodily position, we do not mean, after the manner of empiricists, that it consists of a mosaic of 'extensive sensations'. It is a system which is open on to the world, and correlative with it.

but patterns are formed as I look, and these are endowed with a typical or familiar physiognomy. When I sit at my typewriter, a motor space opens up beneath my hands, in which I am about to "play" what I have read. The reading of the word is a modulation of visible space, the performance of the movement is a modulation of manual space, and the whole question is how a certain physiognomy of "visual" patterns can evoke a certain type of motor response, how each "visual" structure eventually provides itself with its mobile essence without there being any need to spell the word or specify the movement in detail in order to translate one into the other. But this power of habit is no different from the general one which we exercise over our body: if I am ordered to touch my ear or my knee, I move my hand to my ear or my knee by the shortest route, without having to think of the initial position of my hand, or that of my ear, or the path between them. We said earlier that it is the body which "understands" in the cultivation of habit. This way of putting it will appear absurd, if understanding is subsuming a sense-datum under an idea, and if the body is an object. But the phenomenon of habit is just what prompts us to revise our notion of "understand" and our notion of the body. To understand is to experience the harmony between what we aim at and what is given, between the intention and the performance—and the body is our anchorage in a world. When I put my hand to my knee, I experience at every stage of the movement the fulfilment of an intention which was not directed at my knee as an idea or even as an object, but as a present and real part of my living body, that is, finally, as a stage in my perpetual movement towards a world. When the typist performs the necessary movements on the typewriter, these movements are governed by an intention, but the intention does not posit the keys as objective locations. It is literally true that the subject who learns to type incorporates the key-bank space into his bodily space.

The example of instrumentalists shows even better how habit has its abode neither in thought nor in the objective body, but in the body as mediator of a world. It is known [9] that an experienced organist is capable of playing an organ which he does not know, which has more or fewer manuals, and stops differently arranged, compared with those on the instrument he is used to playing. He needs only an hour's practice to be ready to perform his programme. Such a short preparation rules out the supposition that new conditioned reflexes have here been substituted for the existing sets, except where both form a system and the change is all-embracing, which takes us away from the mechanistic theory, since in that case the reactions are mediated by a comprehensive grasp of the instrument. Are we to maintain that the organist analyses the organ, that he conjures up and retains a representation of the stops, pedals and manuals and their relation to each other in space? But during the short rehearsal preceding the concert, he does not act like a person about to draw up a plan. He sits on the seat, works the pedals, pulls out the stops, gets the measure of the instrument with his body, incorporates within himself the relevant directions and dimensions, settles into the organ as one settles into a house. He does not learn objective spatial positions for each stop and pedal, nor does he commit them to "memory." During the rehearsal, as during the performance, the stops, pedals and manuals are given to him as nothing more than possibilities of achieving certain emotional or musical values, and their positions are simply the places through which this value appears in the world. Between the musical essence of the piece as it is shown in the score and the notes which actually sound round the organ, so direct a relation is established that the organist's body and his instrument are merely the medium of this relationship. Henceforth the music exists by itself and through it all the rest exists. [10] There is here no place for

[9] Cf. Chevalier, *L'Habitude*, pp. 202 and ff.
[10] 'As though the musicians were not nearly so much playing the little phrase as performing the rites on which it insisted before it would consent

any "memory" of the position of the stops, and it is not in objective space that the organist in fact is playing. In reality his movements during rehearsal are consecratory gestures: they draw affective vectors, discover emotional sources, and create a space of expressiveness as the movements of the augur delimit the *templum*.

The whole problem of habit here is one of knowing how the musical significance of an action can be concentrated in a certain place to the extent that, in giving himself entirely to the music, the organist reaches for precisely those stops and pedals which are to bring it into being. Now the body is essentially an expressive space. If I want to take hold of an object, already, at a point of space about which I have been quite unmindful, this power of grasping constituted by my hand moves upwards towards the thing. I move my legs not as things in space two and a half feet from my head, but as a power of locomotion which extends my motor intention downwards. The main areas of my body are devoted to actions, and participate in their value, and asking why common sense makes the head the seat of thought raises the same problem as asking how the organist distributes, through "organ space," musical significances. But our body is not merely one expressive space among the rest, for that is simply the constituted body. It is the origin of the rest, expressive movement itself, that which causes them to begin to exist as things, under our hands and eyes. Although our body does not impose definite instincts upon us from birth, as it does upon animals, it does at least give to our life the form of generality, and develops our personal acts into stable dispositional tendencies. In this sense our nature is not long-established custom, since custom presupposes the form of passivity derived from nature. The body is our general medium for having a world. Sometimes it is restricted to the actions

necessary for the conservation of life, and accordingly it posits around us a biological world; at other times, elaborating upon these primary actions and moving from their literal to a figurative meaning, it manifests through them a core of new significance: this is true of motor habits such as dancing. Sometimes, finally, the meaning aimed at cannot be achieved by the body's natural means; it must then build itself an instrument, and it projects thereby around itself a cultural world. At all levels it performs the same function which is to endow the instantaneous expressions of spontaneity with "a little renewable action and independent existence." [11] Habit is merely a form of this fundamental power. We say that the body has understood, and habit has been cultivated when it has absorbed a new meaning, and assimilated a fresh core of significance.

To sum up, what we have discovered through the study of motility, is a new meaning of the word "meaning." The great strength of intellectualist psychology and idealist philosophy comes from their having no difficulty in showing that perception and thought have an intrinsic significance and cannot be explained in terms of the external association of fortuitously agglomerated contents. The *Cogito* was the coming to self-awareness of this inner core. But all meaning was *ipso facto* conceived as an act of thought, as the work of a pure *I*, and although rationalism easily refuted empiricism, it was itself unable to account for the variety of experience, for the element of senselessness in it, for the contingency of contents. Bodily experience forces us to acknowledge an imposition of meaning which is not the work of a universal constituting consciousness, a meaning which clings to certain contents. My body is that meaningful core which behaves like a general function, and which nevertheless exists, and is susceptible to disease. In it we learn to know that union of essence and existence which we shall find again in perception generally, and which we shall then have to describe more fully.

to appear.' (Proust, *Swann's Way*, II, trans. C. K. Scott Moncrieff, Chatto & Windus, p. 180.)
'Its cries were so sudden that the violinist must snatch up his bow and race to catch them as they came.' (Ibid., p. 186.)

[11] Valéry, *Introduction à la Méthode de Léonard de Vinci, Variété*, p. 177.

FREEDOM

What then is freedom? To be born is both to be born of the world and to be born into the world. The world is already constituted, but also never completely constituted; in the first case we are acted upon, in the second we are open to an infinite number of possibilities. But this analysis is still abstract, for we exist in both *at once*. There is, therefore, never determinism and never absolute choice, I am never a thing and never bare consciousness. In fact, even our own pieces of initiative, even the situations which we have chosen, bear us on, once they have been entered upon by virtue of a state rather than an act. The generality of the "rôle" and of the situation comes to the aid of decision, and in this exchange between the situation and the person who takes it up, it is impossible to determine precisely the "share contributed by the situation" and the "share contributed by freedom." Let us suppose that a man is tortured to make him talk. If he refuses to give the names and addresses which it is desired to extract from him, this does not arise from a solitary and unsupported decision: the man still feels himself to be with his comrades, and, being still involved in the common struggle, he is as it were incapable of talking. Or else, for months or years, he has, in his mind, faced this test and staked his whole life upon it. Or finally, he wants to prove, by coming through it, what he has always thought and said about freedom. These motives do not cancel out freedom, but at least ensure that it does not go unbuttressed in being. What withstands pain is not, in short, a bare consciousness, but the prisoner with his comrades or with those he loves and under whose gaze he lives; or else the awareness of his proudly willed solitude, which again is a certain mode of the *Mit-Sein*. And probably the individual in his prison daily reawakens these phantoms, which give back to him the strength he gave to them. But conversely, in so far as he has committed himself to this action, formed a bond with his comrades or adopted this morality, it is because the historical situation, the comrades, the world around him seemed to him to expect that conduct from him. The analysis could be pursued endlessly in this way. We choose our world and the world chooses us. What is certain, in any case, is that we can at no time set aside within ourselves a redoubt to which being does not find its way through, without seeing this freedom, immediately and by the very fact of being a living experience, take on the appearance of being and become a motive and a buttress. Taken concretely, freedom is always a meeting of the inner and the outer —even the prehuman and prehistoric freedom with which we began—and it shrinks without ever disappearing altogether in direct proportion to the lessening of the *tolerance* allowed by the bodily and institutional data of our lives. There is, as Husserl says, on the one hand a "field of freedom" and on the other a "conditioned freedom"; [12] not that freedom is absolute within the limits of this field and non-existent outside it (like the perceptual field, this one has no traceable boundaries), but because I enjoy immediate and remote possibilities. Our commitments sustain our power and there is no freedom without some power. Our freedom, it is said, is either total or non-existent. This dilemma belongs to objective thought and its stable-companion, analytical reflection. If indeed we place ourselves within being, it must necessarily be the case that our actions must have their origin outside us, and if we revert to constituting consciousness, they must originate within. But we have learnt precisely to recognize the order or phenomena. We are involved in the world and with others in an inextricable tangle. The idea of situation rules out absolute freedom at the source of our commitments, and equally, indeed, at their terminus. No commitment, not even commitment in the Hegelian State, can make me

---

12 Fink, *Vergegenwätigung und Bild*, p. 285.

leave behind all differences and free me for anything. This universality itself, from the mere fact of its being experienced, would stand out as a particularity against the world's background, for existence both generalizes and particularizes everything at which it aims, and cannot ever be finally complete.

The synthesis of *in itself* and *for itself* which brings Hegelian freedom into being has, however, its truth. In a sense, it is the very definition of existence, since it is effected at every moment before our eyes in the phenomenon of presence, only to be quickly re-enacted, since it does not conjure away our finitude. By taking up a present, I draw together and transform my past, altering its significance, freeing and detaching myself from it. But I do so only by committing myself somewhere else. Psychoanalytical treatment does not bring about its cure by producing direct awareness of the past, but in the first place by binding the subject to his doctor through new existential relationships. It is not a matter of giving scientific assent to the psychoanalytical interpretation, and discovering a notional significance for the past; it is a matter of reliving this or that as significant, and this the patient succeeds in doing only by seeing his past in the perspective of his co-existence with the doctor. The complex is not dissolved by a non-instrumental freedom, but rather displaced by a new pulsation of time with its own supports and motives. The same applies in all cases of coming to awareness: they are real only if they are sustained by a new commitment. Now this commitment too is entered into in the sphere of the implicit, and is therefore valid only for a certain temporal cycle. The choice which we make of our life is always based on a certain givenness. My freedom can draw life away from its spontaneous course, but only by a series of unobtrusive deflections which necessitate first of all following its course—not by any absolute creation. All explanations of my conduct in terms of my past, my temperament and my environment are therefore true, provided that they be regarded not as separable contributions, but as moments of my total being, the significance of which I am entitled to make explicit in various ways, without its ever being possible to say whether I confer their meaning upon them or receive it from them. I am a psychological and historical structure, and have received, with existence, a manner of existing, a style. All my actions and thoughts stand in a relationship to this structure, and even a philosopher's thought is merely a way of making explicit his hold on the world, and what he is. The fact remains that I am free, not in spite of, or on the hither side of, these motivations, but by means of them. For this significant life, this certain significance of nature and history which I am, does not limit my access to the world, but on the contrary is my means of entering into communication with it. It is by being unrestrictedly and unreservedly what I am at present that I have a chance of moving forward; it is by living my time that I am able to understand other times, by plunging into the present and the world, by taking on deliberately what I am fortuitously, by willing what I will and doing what I do, that I can go further. I can pass freedom by, only if I try to get over my natural and social situation by refusing, in the first place, to take it up, instead of using it as a way into the natural and human world. Nothing determines me from outside, not because nothing acts upon me, but, on the contrary, because I am from the start outside myself and open to the world. We are *true* through and through, and have with us, by the mere fact of belonging to the world, and not merely being in the world in the way that things are, all that we need to transcend ourselves. We need have no fear that our choices or actions restrict our liberty, since choice and action alone cut us loose from our anchorage. Just as reflection borrows its wish for absolute sufficiency from the perception which causes a thing to appear, and as in this way idealism tacitly uses that "primary opinion" which it would like to destroy as opinion, so freedom flounders in the contradictions of commitment, and fails to realize that, without the roots which it thrusts into the world, it would not be freedom at all. Shall I make this promise? Shall I risk my life for so little? Shall I give up my liberty in order to save liberty? There is no theoretical reply to these questions. But there are these *things* which stand, irrefutable, there is before you this person whom you love, there are these men whose existence around you is that of slaves, and *your* freedom cannot be willed without leaving behind its singular relevance, and without willing freedom *for all*. Whether it is a question of things or of historical situations, philosophy has no function other than to teach us once more to see them clearly, and it is true to say that it comes into being by destroying itself as separate philosophy. But what is here required is silence, for only the hero lives out his relation to men and the world. "Your son is caught in the fire; you are the one who will save him. . . . If there is an obstacle, you would be ready to give your shoulder provided only that you can charge down that obstacle. Your abode is your act itself. Your act is you. . . . You give yourself in exchange. . . . Your significance shows itself, effulgent. It is your duty, your hatred, your love, your steadfastness, your ingenuity. . . . Man is but a network of relationships, and these alone matter to him." [13]

[13] A. de Saint-Exupéry, *Pilote de Guerre*, pp. 171 and 174.

Bibliography

Texts

The Structure of Behavior. Boston: Beacon Press, 1963.

Phenomenology of Perception. London: Routledge & Kegan Paul, Ltd., 1965. 2d ed.

The Primacy of Perception. Evanston, Ill.: Northwestern University Press, 1964.

Sense and Non-sense. Evanston, Ill.: Northwestern University Press, 1964.

Signs. Evanston, Ill.: Northwestern University Press, 1964.

In Praise of Philosophy. Evanston, Ill.: Northwestern University Press, 1963.

The Visible and the Invisible. Evanston, Ill.: Northwestern University Press, 1968.

Humanism and Terror. Boston: Beacon Press, 1969.

Themes from the Lectures at the Collège de France 1952–1960. Evanston, Ill.: Northwestern University Press, 1970.

Studies

Barral, M. *The Phenomenology of the Body in Merleau-Ponty.* Pittsburgh: Duquesne University Press, 1965.

Kwant, R. *The Phenomenological Philosophy of Merleau-Ponty.* Pittsburgh: Duquesne University Press, 1963.

Spiegelberg, H. *The Phenomenological Movement.* The Hague: Martinus Nijhoff, 1965, 2d ed., vol. 2, pp. 516–562.

Thévenaz, P. *What Is Phenomenology?* Chicago: Quadrangle Books, 1962, pp. 83–92.

Zaner, R. *The Problem of Embodiment: Some Contributions to a Phenomenology of the Body.* The Hague: Martinus Nijhoff, 1964, part III.

Langan, T. *Merleau-Ponty's Critique of Reason.* New Haven, Conn.: Yale University Press, 1966.

Rabil, A. *Merleau-Ponty: Existentialist of the Social World.* New York: Columbia University Press, 1967.

O'Neill, J. *Perception, Expression, and History: The Social Phenomenology of Merleau-Ponty.* Evanston, Ill.: Northwestern University Press, 1970.

Carr, D. *"Maurice Merleau-Ponty: Incarnate Consciousness,"* in G. A. Schrader (ed.), *Existential Philosophers: Kierkegaard to Merleau-Ponty.* New York: McGraw-Hill Book Company, 1967, pp. 369–429.

29

JOHN PETERS
1909–1961

Introduction

John Peters was born in the Netherlands in 1909 and studied philosophy at Angelicum College in Rome and at the Institut Supérieur de Philosophie of the University of Louvain in Belgium. In 1946 he became professor of philosophy at the University of Nijmegen in the Netherlands. In 1962 he was to come to Duquesne University as a visiting professor but died a few months before at the age of fifty-two. Little else is available beyond these meager biographical data. His only book in English (and it is a translation) is a tome of over 500 pages whose title, *Metaphysics: a Systematic Survey*, hardly does it justice. It is much more than a metaphysics.

It encompasses a philosophy of nature, a philosophy of knowledge (which is not the traditional epistemology), a philosophy of man, and a philosophy of God. It further lays the groundwork for a moral philosophy by a study of the social and historical nature of man. As a systematic work it has the merit of order and clarity. As a survey it succeeds in offering some of the best contemporary European thought on the whole range of philosophic concern, almost none of which is yet available in English. The following selections take up themes too often neglected in academic textbook philosophy and introduce new themes calling for considerable rethinking in the light of recent continental advances.

HUMAN KNOWING AS PARTICIPATION *

We can approach the essence of knowing by reflecting on the pre-knowledge of what it is to know that is contained in the exercise of the cognitive act. For, strictly speaking, we do not know something until we know that we know it and thus in a way know what it is to know.

For this reason sense experiences, in which consciousness in the strict sense is lacking, may be called cognitive acts only in a degraded, analogous sense, as a kind of participation in understanding. Likewise, the perceptive observing of the fact that something is or is this way or that way is a diminished way of knowing as compared with the insight into, and understanding of the reason or ground why it has to be or has to be this

way. To know in the strict and proper sense is to understand a being in its truth, i.e., in its interconnection with everything else in *being*.

The Antinomy of Immanence and Transcendence. Man's mode of knowing manifests itself as a special subject-object relationship. It is immediately directed to the other beings facing the subject and only reflexively to the being who knows. Idealism and phenomenalism attempt to explain the origin of the object either wholly or partially by means of the subject's spontaneity. Empiricism and realism, on the other hand, have to explain how the cognitive act of finite man can extend also to the other beings in such a way that these beings are noetically in him. For, man is not these other beings because they are ontically outside him and opposed to him. Isn't it an antinomy if we

* By permission of Duquesne University Press. From John A. Peters, *Metaphysics, a Systematic Survey*, Duquesne University Press, Pittsburgh, Pa., 1963.

have to accept that the object is, on the one hand, transcendent to the knower and, on the other immanent in him?

"Physical" and "Intentional" Modes of Being. Intellectual knowledge is directed to being as it is in itself; therefore, this being has to become immanent in the knower and, consequently, to know the other being means to become the other *as other.*

To explain how the knower can become the other as other, a distinction is made between the mode in which the being is in itself and its mode of *being* in the knower. The object, so it is said, is in itself in a material way, but in the intellect it is immaterially, i.e., when it is in itself, matter limits the form to the concrete and individual, but in the intellect the form is stripped of the limitations of matter and thus becomes abstract and universal. Accordingly, the knower becomes the other in an immaterial way.

This becoming-the-other of the knower is explained through the production of the *concept.* Although this concept is a thought produced by the action of the intellect and, therefore, strictly an immanent object, nevertheless, it is also essentially a re-presentation of the being as it is in itself because it is similar to it and as a *cognitive* image refers to it.

Thus a twofold way of *being* is distinguished:

1

The "physical" mode of *being*, which the object has as it is in itself, i.e., as being in the real world around us and also in the realm of the possible, to which our cognitive acts are directed.

2

The "intentional" mode of *being*, which the object has precisely insofar as it is represented by the concept in the intellect. The cognitive presence of the object to the subject is a presence by means of an "intention" —i.e., the concept, which as immanent terminus originates in the intellect but nevertheless is essentially directed to the object as it is in itself and therefore transcendent to the subject.[1]

Insufficiency of this View. As long as the concept and the being to which this concept refers are placed in *opposition* to each other, it is impossible to explain why we do not know first our concepts but the being as it is in itself. This being itself has to be immanent in us, for what is not immanent in the knower is not known.

A certain identity of concept and being, therefore, is required. This identity is found in considering the concept not according to the mode of *being* it has as something belonging to the intellect, but according to its intelligible content, for according to this content it is a *likeness* of the subject in itself.

However, likeness is not a sufficient explanation. For similarity says both agreement and difference. By means of likeness it is possible to explain how I know the being precisely insofar as the concept is similar to this being. But it cannot explain how I can know this being precisely insofar as it differs from the concept, i.e., according to the mode of *being* it has in itself as a physical being, and how, as happens in judgment, I see my concept *as* (or *as not*) more or less adequately resembling or agreeing with "that which is as it is in itself." Therefore, the difference also must be immanent in me. But how? By means of another concept? And so on to infinity?

To escape from this difficulty, the concept is said not to be an ordinary sign, i.e., not something which has to be known first before

---

[1] Generally speaking, intention means the dynamic directedness of one being to another being in view of its perfection. In this sense every finite activity is intentionally directed to its object. Especially of knowing and loving is it said that they contain their object in themselves in an intentional way. Accordingly, intentional is whatever is connected with immanent acts as the expression of their directedness; for example, concept, representation, word, gesture, symbol, sign, and even all behavior and cultural products. In a special sense intention means the tendential directedness to a purpose to be attained by the use of certain means. In this sense it is usually opposed to "execution."

it can give us knowledge of something else. The concept is not an instrumental sign but a formal sign, something which, without having to be known first, immediately makes something else known. It is not first in itself and then in addition refers to something else, but its whole being consists in being-a-sign-of, in referring to.[2]

Nevertheless, even this reply does not settle the problem of how we know objects. For the sign remains distinct from the signified, it has a mode of being (to be a sign) which the signified does not have; consequently, it does not explain how we could know the signified according to its own mode of *being*, distinct from that of the sign, as long as only the sign is immanent in the knower.

The Essence of Knowing. Thus, we have to maintain that the being, as it is in itself, according to its *own* mode of *being*, is immanent in the knower. The knower in the act of knowing *is* the known in the act of being known. Knowing can never be understood by means of an intentionality "taken by itself," but has to be conceived as the *identity of an act with an act.*

The identity of an act with an act, however, is not in the first place that of one act with another act, for such an identity can only be relative, but is the identity of an act with itself. Let us see what this identity means.

A material being is to some extent identified with the form through which it is "such," but it is only here-and-now "such." The form by itself does not constitute the essence of this being, but is united with a limiting principle of mutability and multiplication. It is given to matter, estranged from itself, it is "with matter" and not in perfect self-identity "with itself." And, although the form in itself is a principle of intelligibility, *as* a material-

ized form, it is not actually intelligible but only potentially.

If, on the other hand, a form by its very nature is not a form-of-matter but by itself constitutes the essence, the form is "with itself." The immaterial being is essentially not a bi-unity of matter and form, but the non-composed unity of a form with itself.

This immanence of the immaterial form as essential act in and with and for itself, in active identity with itself, this being-interior-to-itself is the essence of knowing—it is the coincidence of the knower and the known in a single act without any opposition.

Although we are unable to express knowing in any other way than by means of the opposition of the knower and the known and then declaring that the two are identical, the subject-object relationship does not pertain to the essence of knowing *as* knowing. The same is *a fortiori* true of the subject-object relationship in which the object is a different and opposite being. To know is not to stumble on something, to touch something or to catch something opposite us. Such expressions are imperfect representations arising from the sensitive experiences of touching, hearing, and seeing.

To know is to be oneself in pure inner activity, in immanence of *being*, which is the highest and most proper mode of being-oneself or identity. Accordingly, "to know" and "to be" should not be conceived as two spheres which are first distinguished and then brought together in a kind of intentional connection by means of a representation or cognitive image. They are an original unity, and where this unity is present in all its purity, there knowing is perfectly present.

Both one-sided idealism and one-sided realism tend to concentrate on the problem of the subject-object relationship and forget that "to be" expresses identity, and therefore in its perfection includes to-be-known and to-be-knowing in unity.

Participation and Knowing. If to know is to be self-illuminating for oneself, the transparence of the self for the self, self-consciousness (expressed by the term "I"), and

2 Cf. John of St. Thomas, *Cursus Philosophicus, Logica,* tr. II, q. 22, a. 1–2; *De anima,* q. 4, a. 1; q. 6, a. 2–3; q. 10, a. 2; q. 11, a. 1–2. J. Maritain, *Les degrés du savoir,* pp. 769–819. For a critique, see D. M. de Petter, "Intentionaliteit en identiteit," *Tijdschrift v. Philosophie,* vol. 2 (1940), pp. 515–550.

if, on the other hand, to know is also an active identity with *all* that is, as it is—for whatever is, is intelligible—then pure knowing will be an infinite openness of knowing to *being* and of *being* to knowing, a reciprocal openness which is all-embracing self-consciousness.

The question arises, however, how a *finite* knower would be possible and especially a knower who is primarily directed to the *other* as an object? The reply is that *participation* is possible, i.e., a knower who in a finite way participates in the intimacy of knowing and being-known which of itself is infinite. The analogous grades of cognitive participation are the grades of participation in the actuality of *being* according to a greater or lesser immateriality. Wherever, therefore, "to know" is realized in a particularized way, the reason for the particularization will be that the identity of the knowing being and the being-to-be-known is not perfect, so that there remains a duality or opposition of these two within the immanence of the cognitive act. This limited immanence or *merely relative identity*, in which the knower and the known as subsistent beings do not wholly coincide with actual knowing and actual being-known, finds expression in intentionality as immanent directedness of a subject to a transcendent object by means of a cognitive image.

The Imperfection of Man's Knowledge. Against the background of an absolute ideal of knowing that coincides with the fullness of life and the fullness of *being*, the imperfection of man's cognitive act reveals itself in its intentionality.

First of all, on the one hand, the all-embracing horizon of *being* has already manifested itself to some extent to man, who in his pre-predicative awareness of *being* is "in a way all things." Otherwise, how could he know that he does not know everything knowable and even that he does not totally know anything at all?

On the other hand, this infinite openness is a dynamic infinity. With the growth of his knowledge, man becomes also increasingly aware of it that he does not yet know everything; hence man's process of knowing in time remains always both extensively and intensively perfectible and is never finished. Every immanence of the already-known is essentially an intentional directedness to the not-yet-known.

Secondly, man is not his act of cognition, for his cognitive transition from being-in-potency to being-in-act implies the distinction of essence, power, and activity. Consequently, his *being* is prior to his actually-being-known-by-himself, his consciousness: he experiences that he himself is and does not know his *being* down to its deepest ground. Even in finite self-knowledge, therefore, there is a distinction between the known as it is in itself and the known precisely as it is known. Because of this inadequacy, self-knowledge has to be expressed in a word, concept, or cognitional image which does not wholly coincide with the ego and contains an intentional directedness to the ego as a not-yet-revealed mystery.

Thirdly, man becomes actually conscious of his self-presence only by means of reflection on the cognitive act in which he perceives the *other* beings with which he is interconnected in the course of his life. But this perception itself of objects is likewise deficient, for it can take place only by means of the sense experience of their external appearance at a certain moment of time and from a certain spatial perspective. What is already known about the object is provisionally synthesized in a representation or cognitional image, in whose structure memory, imagination, and the formation of concepts play a role, and this inner reconstruction is referred to the object through the judgment. However, since the object *as a being* in itself is immanent to the cognitive act in pre-predicative experience, prior to any analysis, the judgment is able to realize that the abstractly-general predicates fall short. Thus it can become the starting point and basis of new experiences and concepts, of inductive and deductive reasoning processes.

Finally, even our apodictic insights into the universal and into essential relationships are inadequate, for they presuppose abstraction. We know, however, there must be concretely-general "specific ideas" which give rise to individual possibilities of realization. For this reason our universal concepts and judgments reveal an intentional directedness to the overcoming of abstract univocity in analogous knowledge, which synthetically unites both the similarity and the difference of beings.

However, it is precisely this absolute synthesis of beings in unqualified *being* which we approach in the most inadequate way, for we approach it in the form of judgments about being as being and, therefore, by means of analogous concepts, from which we cannot derive the particular modes of *being*. We are unable to place ourselves on the viewpointless "standpoint" of the absolute. Nevertheless, the absolute origin of all beings is present in a way in our perspective as soon as we affirm of any being whatsoever that it *is*. Accordingly, despite everything, there is in us a certain immanence of "everything that is," as it comes forth from its source. This immanence, however, is potential and becomes actual only through the intentional movement of our knowledge from the factual, the many, the finite, and the mutable to their source. . . .

COMMUNICATION AS OPENNESS, TRUSTING SURRENDER AND FAITH

Human Interiority. Man's interiority in its *self-consciousness* transcends the interconnection of sensory impression and motor expression. Although the active self-presence of the subject is very imperfect because it is reached by means of the perception of objects, nevertheless man experiences that the horizon of his consciousness is not the limited horizon of perceptible objects but the all-embracing horizon of *being*, which no longer is a horizon.

This infinite openness, through which man can see the truth and goodness of his objects in their finiteness and relativity, is the foundation of his freedom to take a stand in his own way with respect to every object.

Insofar as every man in his self-consciousness and self-responsibility encompasses the whole of all beings to some extent, i.e., insofar as he is a spiritual person, he is no longer only a besouled body which through interaction with its surroundings exteriorizes its inner feelings in movements. The distinction as well as the necessary interconnection between interior and exterior, between within and without, disappear on the higher level of spiritual interiority, which is all-embracing.

Nevertheless, human beings remain distinct even as spiritual persons, not because one is here and the other there, but because each one is related in his own original way to "everything," each one is his own microcosmos with his own vision and evaluation of all beings in their *being*.

Of course, this "mentality," which is grounded in the individual essence of each man, is still in an incipient stage, it has not yet reached full clarity, is usually still estranged from itself and not yet free from contradiction. Nevertheless, it is for each one his own intimacy of thinking, loving, and deciding. The others do not have in any way immediate access to this personal domain through perception, even though it is true that the different perspectives of all are directed to the same all-embracing horizon.

Self-communication. Despite this lack of immediate perceptibility, there is in every person, precisely because being-a-person means universal openness, orientation to knowledge of the personal interiority of others. But this orientation to the other object-as-a-*subject* can be filled only from the other subject itself insofar as this subject makes itself known, reveals itself, in free *communication*.

Accordingly, with respect to the other's interiority, being-known undergoes a radical change. This change, however, has been gradually prepared on the level of the vegetative and the psychical through their expressive movement. While purely corporeal beings do not in any way control their knowability, the spiritual being freely disposes of its knowability. Its being-known is based on a free act of imparting knowledge, and the act of taking knowledge depends on this free act.

Thus, spiritual interiority is a domain which does not lie passively open to the observer or exteriorizes itself of necessity. Intimate personal life reveals itself only if the person actively shows it in freedom, if he lets himself be known through self-communication by bearing witness to the other about that of which he is the sole immediate witness and to which no one else has immediate access—namely, his subjectivity.

Its Conditions. Every being is knowable as a being. However, the higher the mode of its *being*, i.e., the more it is immanent to itself, the more conditions have to be fulfilled on the part of both the object known and the knowing subject if the truth is to be reached. Truth is no longer equally accessible to all.

For knowledge of spiritual beings it is required, on the part of the being known, that this being *reveal* itself, and this revelation is a free act. On the part of the knower, it is necessary that he *believe* in this revelation, and this believing likewise is a free act.

To believe, in the strict sense of the term, is a mode of knowing which does not rely on the experience and insight of the knowing subject himself, but on the testimony of another subject who communicates his experiences and insights. Faith, therefore, is an indirect way of acquiring certainty regarding a truth.

If intersubjective faith is to possess a critically justified cognitive value, two conditions must be met:

1
The other should know through experience or insight that of which he bears witness. He must be or have been present to the cognitive object.

2
There must be agreement between the content of his cognitive act and the content of his communication, between his thinking and speaking.

Intellectual and moral trustworthiness, therefore, are decisive for the truth value of the communication. To be able to believe in what someone says, we have to believe first in him who speaks as a witness of the truth.

Thus faith is an intellectual act having a moral aspect. It is an attitude of surrender to the freedom of another, an appeal to his freedom, asking him to speak as he thinks. It is an act of trust in him, based on the conviction that he deserves this trust.

Trusting Surrender. From what we have seen it follows that it is impossible to arrive at knowledge of the other's spiritual interiority unless the knower:

1
recognizes the other as an autonomous person;

2
respects the other's freedom to reveal himself or to conceal himself; for, if against the other's will he wants to force access, the other will close himself; therefore, knowledge of the other has to be accepted as a gift coming from the initiative of the subject to be known;

3
assents to the communication even before he has even heard it; for faith aims at the communication's content only by means of trust in the communicator.

If these conditions are fulfilled, it will become possible for a subject to acquire knowledge of what is directly accessible only to another subject, to enter into the other's spiritual interiority and from there to see, as it were through the eyes of the other subject, the beings as they can be seen only from the viewpoint of the other subject. To believe is the road to enlargement of knowledge by means of communicating with another knower.[3]

The Justification of Faith.   The trusting surrender on which the knowledge of faith is ultimately based must be justified. For a person has, in addition to the possibility of revealing or concealing himself, also the possibility of truthfully or untruthfully revealing himself. Moreover, there are limits to the reliability of the communication because of the finiteness and bodily character of the communicator. Not being pure self-consciousness, the communicator cannot know himself adequately; he, too, has only a limited insight, obtained by means of acts and attitudes directed to objects, into the deeper motives of his life and the origin of his acts from his individual essence.

The justification of the trust one has in another differs according to the grades of intimacy of the communication. Because self-knowledge is obtained by means of the subject's orientation to objects, self-communication likewise will take its course through communication of the subject's vision on objects.

If the communication of a person refers to objects which the other could reach also without the testimony of the other, or if the truth of his testimony can be verified through convergence of witnesses, then it will be sufficient that the probable trustworthiness of the witness be confirmed by our general knowledge of men. Life in society is based on such probabilities.

If, however, there is a question of a person's genuine internal self-communication concerning objects having a central significance precisely for this person, so that indirect verification is not easy or even impossible, then the past actions of this person may be able to offer some reason to trust him. Ultimately, however, this criterion falls short, and the full understanding of the self-communication depends on a *personal affective inclination* which is no longer justiable through general considerations. Nevertheless, this inclination does not mean that one blindly accepts whatever the other says. Precisely because this inclination is directed to the true welfare and the development of the other's essential potentialities, it accepts also the deficiency of his self-knowledge, his self-communication, and even of his trustworthiness, and attempts to know him, through and in spite of his defective communication, even better perhaps than he explicitly knows himself. In this way faith in the other can contribute to bringing him, as it were, to himself. . . .

[3] Cf. A. Brunner, *Glaube und Erkenntnis,* München, 1951; J. Mouroux, *Le croix en toi,* Paris, 1949.

MAN AS AN INCARNATE, SOCIAL, MORAL, HISTORICAL, AND IMMORTAL PERSON

By Nature Man is a Spiritual-material Person

Man is a Subsistent Being.   In his perceptive and active dealings with the beings around him man is conscious of his own *being:* he is "I" for himself, the conscious bearer, origin, and purpose of perceptions and action.

In his perceptions and actions he knows also that he is an organic living being, for he knows that his vegetative processes are his. And he knows about his being spatially and temporally in a definite place and at a definite moment, for the material events occurring in, and affecting his body concern him and pertain to him, albeit in a different way than his conscious acts.

Next, through memory and expectation he knows that he is the same "I" who unfolds himself in a plurality of successive acts.

Finally, he ascribes to himself a life of

imagination and representation, of understanding and thinking, of desiring, wanting, and willing.

All these different activities and passivities originate from the same "I" in diverse ways—as wholly unconscious, sensitively experienced or intellectually conscious—and are supported by this "I." They are interconnected, influence and condition one another.

Accordingly, man is aware of himself as one being, in the primary sense of being—namely, a *subsistent* being or supposit, which underlies the plurality of powers and the changing accidental activities and passivities.

Material-Spiritual Character of Man. This one human being is certainly corporeal, vegetatively and sensitively living. His essence, therefore, must be composed of determinable prime matter and a determining essential form. This essential form is the formal principle of both man's organic corporeal being and his vegetative and sensitive life. Viewed in this last respect, as the dynamic principle of life animating a body, the essential form is called "soul."

This one human being, however, is also intellectually knowing and willing. The intellectual activities of life are of a wholly proper nature and rise above all vital activities based on being-corporeal. For in their orientation to objects they are not limited to the material being appearing here and now, but possess a transcendental openness to everything that is, as it is—to the true, the good, and the beautiful, as such. Because human knowing and loving aim at the *being* or beings, albeit in a very imperfect way, and because outside being nothing is, man has in his intellectual powers an infinity of horizon, transcending the material—he is "in a way everything."

Activity and object, however, are proportioned to each other. Therefore, the activities also which are directed to the supra-material must be supra-material in their subjective mode of *being*. They cannot be intrinsically organic activities, as sense experience and sense appetite are, no matter how much the exercise of these activities is conditioned by sense experience and sense appetite.

We give the name "spiritual activities" to activities which, because of their all-embracing openness for the *being* of beings, are supra-material. These activities must originate from spiritual powers. And these spiritual powers, in their turn, must emanate from a spiritual principle of essence which is intrinsically independent of corporeal being.

Insofar, however, as a form transcends the limitation of being-here-and-now in space and time, it may not be conceived as merely the form of individuating matter. For a material form constitutes the individual essence only in conjunction with matter and limits the "to be" of the being to this or that specific mode of being-material. The "to be" of man, on the other hand, insofar as it is the root of the spiritual activities of understanding and willing, is a spiritual "to be." It is the "to be" of a being which can know about *being,* which in an infinite openness is knowingly and lovingly related to unqualified *being.* Accordingly, insofar as the form is an essential principle of such a being-spiritual, it is not a form limited by matter but a subsistent, supra-spatial and supra-temporal form.

Must we assume, then, that there are two formal principles in man: one through which he is spiritual, and the other through which he is here and now corporeal, vegetative, and sensitive? Such an assumption would militate against the unity of man, for one and the same being which thinks and wills also senses and experiences, moves and nourishes itself. But a single being has only one essential form. Therefore, the many human powers must flow from a single formal principle. The spiritual principle is also the first formal principle of vegetative life and sense life: by virtue of an essential necessity, man's "spirit" fulfills the role of "soul" with respect to the organic living body.

Accordingly, man is a being whose essence is a unity composed of spirit, which as soul is first form, and prime matter. The implication of this assertion is that man is a spiritual being of such a nature that he is corporeally living because of his being-spiritual, and that he is actuated to his being corporeally living through a spiritual principle. Although considered in itself the human spirit has "to be" as its "own to be," nevertheless, in order to attain self-realization through its actions, this spirit has to be an animating principle.[4]

Man as a Person The individual man is a single subsistent being, i.e., neither a non-autonomous part nor a property or attribute of a whole, but a being which "itself is in itself" and makes "to be" its own according to the essential mode in which it participates in *being*. This appropriation of *being* consists in the modification which the essence exercises with respect to *being*.

Subsistence, however, is an analogous concept, which can be realized in higher and lower modes. Man is subsistent in a much higher way than all other living and sensing beings. For he is the supposit of a rational nature, i.e., a self-conscious and free-willing, and therefore self-determining nature. His subsistence, then, does not mean only that he appropriates "to be" according to a mode which is wholly determined by his essence and according to activities which in given conditions flow of necessity from the essence as nature. His subsistence means that he appropriates "to be" according to a mode which, albeit determined by his essence, leaves him the liberty to interpret this essence in his activities by the judgment of his reason and to realize his essence according to this interpretation. He himself is responsible for the explicitation of his essence; he is the master of his acts insofar as they arise from reason and will. Thus in his free

actions he appropriates "to be" in a higher way than beings which do not have a free nature.

We speak of *person* with respect to a being which is subsistent in such an eminent way that it is capable of making itself be, of being the free origin of its own *being*. To be a person is the highest mode of being-subsistent. The person, therefore, is the highest and most eminent of all subsistent beings and may even be said to be properly and really a being in the full sense of the term. All sub-personal beings are imperfectly themselves and imperfectly subsistent, they do not dispose of their *being* because they are neither conscious nor free. The person, on the other hand, has a very special relation to *being* for to the extent that he is a person his *being* is essentially to-be-active, self-determination or "auto-position."

If we call a man a person,[5] we indicate that he has a spiritual nature which makes him not merely be a subsistent part of the material universe, individuated through "here-and-now," but also causes him to transcend and comprehend this universe through his powers of intellectual knowledge and love; consequently, he is capable of consciously and freely taking a position with respect to particular beings, including himself insofar as he is material, vegetative, and sensitive, or insofar as his own natural inclinations are concerned.

Insofar as man is a person, he is a whole that exists of itself, *in* itself, and for itself, a being that can *make itself be* in an original, unrepeatable way, determined by itself through acts for which it itself is responsible.[6]

[4] Concerning the difficult problem of the relation between *psyche* and *nous* in Aristotle (*de Anima*, bk. III cc. 4–5), see F. Nuyens, *L'évolution de la psychologie d'Aristote*, Louvain, 1948. For St. Thomas Aquinas' view of the soul, see *Summa theol.*, p. 1, qq. 75–76 and especially the extensive and masterly explanations of *De spiritualibus creaturis* and *De anima*. See also Stephan Strasser, *The Soul in Metaphysical and Empirical Psychology*, Pittsburgh, 2nd impr., 1961.

[5] Concerning the concept of person, see P. Ellerbeck, "Functie en inhoud van de term persoon in de psychologie"; J. Peters, "De plaats van de persoon in de hedendaagse philosophie"; D. M. de Petter, "Het persoon-zijn onder thomistisch-metaphysische belichting"; all in *Verslag der 13e Alg. Verg. v. d. Ver. v. Thomist. Wijsb.*, Nijmegen, 1948.
[6] The term "person" originally meant "mask," and consequently also role, character, function, dignity. It soon received the concrete meaning of indicating the rational and free, individual subsistent being. The formal-abstract term "personality" is used in several senses:

Man, however, is only a finite person. He is not absolute freedom, but merely possesses the power for actions which are distinct from his essence and flow from it as from a free nature that nevertheless is a nature. He is determined in many ways; his freedom consists in giving meaning to these determinations. Man is an embodied person, a spiritual being which is essentially material, a transcendental directedness to the *being* of beings *from* a definite situation in the spatio-temporal world.

The Embodied Person as Subject of Morality. Only the person is a subject of morality, but not the person as person— for freedom as freedom is its own norm— but the finite and embodied person. For the acts of such a person are not wholly autonomous, but normalized by the necessary purpose of his nature. Although this nature is essentially one, it is complex in its aspects, as appears when we consider the many powers emanating from it. This nature is spiritual and as such directed to the all-

1 In its purest form it means that through which a being is a person, that through which a being can freely appropriate "to be" to itself.
2 Thus it came to mean also the characteristic of being a person.
3 Concretely, personality means someone who through free self-determination has become "himself" in a striking way. Sometimes it is used in a neutral and more psychological sense in reference to someone who in his essence and actions reveals himself steadfast despite the change of his own moods, the opinion of others, and the variable situation. More appropriately and in an ethical sense, it indicates one who does the good and approximates his ideal essence in full freedom, from an interior affective inclination, without tension between his various powers.
4 In a less correct usage, "personality" means the power to recognize oneself as the same perduring being. In this sense there is sometimes question of a "split personality" (Th. Ribot).
5 Still less appropriate is the use of the term for the concretely given whole of capacities and inclinations which characterizes an individual or class with respect to affective life and will and distinguishes it from others (K. Schneider's psychopathic personality). The aspect of self-determination, which is clearly present in the concept of person, has disappeared almost completely in this usage of the term.

embracing *being* of beings, but it is also sensitive, vegetative, and material and therefore limited and determined. Accordingly, the norms will refer to the *hierarchy* of the various powers and their acts, they will prescribe that the "natural" order of values be maintained in the free acts. In other words, they will order the person to behave in accord with his personal dignity, i.e., as a rational being, in every situation in which he finds himself through his complex nature.

For the material, vegetative, and sensitive powers and inclinations emanate from nature as material dispositions for the spiritual, but the spiritual powers are the formal and final causes of the material. Therefore, man's natural inclinations, as a subsistent being to self-preservation, as a living being to nutrition, growth, and reproduction, as a sensitive being to sense pleasure and the avoidance or conquest of whatever is an obstacle, must be kept in order by reason and raised to being instruments and concrete expressions of the universal good of man as a spiritual person. They are the "matter" of moral virtues, as they are also the "matter" of freedom.

The moral process of becoming man, of becoming "what one is," is a process of order, of mutual compenetration and integration of the various aspects of being-man. It is a spiritualization of the corporeal or also an embodiment of the spiritual.

Man as a Person is Naturally Social

The Meaning of "Social." Every finite subsistent being by virtue of its essence, properties, activities and passivities, refers to all other beings by relations of agreement and difference, of exercising influence and being influenced. This being-together of beings expresses itself more particularly in the dealings which living beings, and especially sensitive beings, have with their surroundings.

However, just as man because of his spiritual nature is subsistent in an eminent way, so also has he an eminent relationship to the other beings through his intellectual powers of understanding and loving—in a kind of immanence he "is in a way everything."

Above all other relationships which man as a person has naturally, we must place his relations to fellow men who, like him, through their spiritual nature are free persons. Before the level of man is reached, relations are not relations in the full sense. Insofar as man by his very nature is directed to such interhuman relations, we speak of his social nature—the term "social" being derived from the Latin *socius*, companion.

In a degraded sense of "social" one could attribute a certain social instinct to animals insofar as some animals for their self-realization need to live together with others of their species, to which they owe their lives or with which they band together for a shorter or longer time to secure food, security, or reproduction.

Man, who is less self-sufficient than animals, depends more and longer on others of his species. The utilization of the world through technique, labor, and economy is at once collaboration with fellow human beings, and in this collaboration the useful result is increased through specialization and commerce. Although higher cultural life, as it manifests itself in beauty, art, and science, is a matter of eminently personal activity, it too is no less essentially a social affair which runs its course in the interchange of spiritual goods. Language, which alongside the hand and tools is the instrument *par excellence* of human activity, and which because of its signifying function is indispensable for the development of the person even in his most personal thought, is accepted from the forebears, modified, and transmitted to the descendants. Thus from his very birth man lives in a world that is already shaped and named by human beings, he lives in a cultural milieu that is essentially social.

Personal Social Relationships. Man, however, does not only *need* fellow human beings in order to search his own natural good. The proper and primary sense of the social nature of man *as a person* is that man is related to the others *as persons*, as subsistent beings whose self-realization is a purpose in itself and who may not be used by others as *pure* means. Man is naturally orientated to *personal* relationships.

Persons possess a closed subsistence but, precisely because of this, also universal openness: through knowledge they are related to the other in his individual originality without losing themselves. "True" knowledge of fellow men begins by acknowledging that they are persons. It is only when they have been recognized as such that affirmative or negative affective attitudes follow, such as to esteem or despise, to love or to hate, to seek or to flee, to hope or to fear, to bear with or to be angry, to envy or not to envy.

These intellectual and affective attitudes are the foundation of *social acts* in which human beings reciprocally meet and speak to one another about other beings or about themselves in the indicative, optative, or imperative moods, questioning and replying, warning and exhorting, requesting and counseling, begging and commanding, obeying and resisting.

In this social intercourse persons can manifest the sentiments which they have for one another. They are capable of responding to these sentiments in reciprocal affective acts, all of which imply either something of hatred or something of love.[7] When there is mutually expressed affectionateness, a personal bond arises, which can vary from an initial rather general benevolence through all levels of friendship to strictly personal love.

On the basis of social acts and actual affective expressions there may arise more permanent relationships of one human being *to* another, and if they are reciprocated, also

---

[7] Cf. J. van Boxtel, *Herstel der liefde in de sociale wijsbegeerte*, Nijmegen, 1948. Concerning the distinction between affective attitudes, social acts, personal bonds, permanent relations, societies, etc., see D. von Hildebrand, *Metaphysik der Gemeinschaft*, Augsburg, 1955. See also A. Oldendorff, *De psychologie van het sociale leven*, Utrecht, 1953; Chre. Barendse, "Intersubjectief verkeer en lichamelijkheid," *Lichamelijkheid*, Utrecht, 1951, pp. 85–119.

permanent relationships *between* human beings. In some cases the subjects of these relationships have been given special names; for instance, we speak of man and wife, relatives, friends, colleagues, parents and children, teacher and pupil.[8]

Moral Social Obligation. The first moral duty flowing from man's social nature as a person is the recognition that every other human being, no matter who he is, is a fellow man, an "other ego," an intellectual and moral person, at least in capacity and vocation.

This recognition, which implies a certain initial benevolence, has to be maintained and developed in our dealings with our fellow man. It is the foundation of all social virtues, and first of all of justice. The explicitation of this initial benevolence in friendship and love for some human beings with whom we find ourselves connected by special bonds or with whom we freely bind ourselves is the crown and the purpose of the social virtues.

Seen in this light, the self-realization of a being whose mode of *being* is a being-together implies a certain loving dedication to others. For this reason the concrete norms of morality do not explicitly speak of self-love, but of our relationship to fellow human beings. It is only through the practice of faith, hope and charity toward the others, as determined by the bond flowing from the spatio-temporal situation which we have accepted or freely chosen, that man becomes what he should be—more himself by means of a more intimate participation in the mode of *being* of the others.

What has been *ontically* stated regarding the tendency of every being to *self-realization* through activity is, therefore, ethically

understood in a more profound sense for man as a person when we say: "A finite personal being becomes more himself according as he enters more in true *communication* with others, by including the true well-being of fellow persons in his own well-being and taking care of it in the same way." Thus we understand better that subsistence and relativity do not exclude but rather include each other.

Person and Society. The fact that man as a person is by nature social has still another meaning—namely, that he is essentially connected with societies, which transcend the individual. The habitual relationships between human beings under certain conditions give rise to objective wholes, each of which presents itself as if it were one being. Relations exist *between* persons, and a society *contains* persons, as its members. By means of analogy with individual persons, the society is the subject of activities, attitudes, and relations. It presents itself, therefore, as an ordered unity of persons,[9] having a quasi-substantial essence and existence, quasi-proper powers, acts and activities.

The question must be raised whether man's being-a-person does not exclude that he can be a means for something else, so that he cannot be a non-subsistent part of a greater subsistent whole. Is his being-a-person not in contradiction with his membership in a society?

The reply is in the negative if one does not conceive the unity of a society as the absolute unity of a single subsistent being, but as the relative unity of many subsistent beings. Although in language and concept we attribute a quasi-subsistence to a society of persons, when we investigate the conditions under which such a quasi-subsistence is possible, we find that the many individual persons are considered precisely insofar as they are together and collaborate in orderly

---

[8] In their social acts men influence one another *as persons*. There is question here of a special and eminent form of efficient causality, which is closely connected with final exemplary causality: it proposes to the other's freedom a purpose to be attained, and moves him by means of motives freely accepted by him. This kind of causality is exemplified by human authority, for such authority is not an external compulsion.

[9] Concerning society as a "moral" unity of order, see Angelinus, *Wijsgerige gemeenschapsleer*, Nijmegen, 1949, pp. 55–87; F. Tellegen, *De Gemeenschap*, I–II, Roermond, n. d.

fashion to one and the same purpose. Thus not the society itself is the ultimate subject of powers and acts, but the persons composing it in their mutual relations. If, then, we substantialize society in speech, we merely use a concise form of expression to indicate the many ultimate subjects insofar as their thinking, willing, and acting run their course in connection with the thinking, willing, and acting of the others. The personal pronoun "we" indicates each "I" in its polar reference to the other "I's". The society, therefore, is nowhere else really present than in each of the persons and as a network of relations. However, it is present in each of the members in a different way, according to the place which this member occupies as one of the many poles or terms of the network.

Natural and Free Societies. Two fundamental kinds of society may be distinguished, although concrete societies will usually have something of both types.

First of all, the social relations themselves may be essential for the self-realization of the person. In such a case living-together is sought for its own sake, precisely as living-together, as social communication and mutual enrichment. The purpose of such a society of *life* coincides with the very purpose of each person taken separately. The society aims at making each person attain his natural good in active and passive communication with his fellow men.

Secondly, social relationships may be directed to the attainment of a purpose which for each of the members is a "means" to his personal self-realization. In the production and distribution of these useful means a norm is imposed by the harmony of mutual interests and by the requirements of the *utilitarian* society itself as a quasi-subsistent being, directed to self-preservation and self-development. The production of the useful goods has to be regulated by mutual consent, which is arrived at either in consultation with the interested parties or by following the directives of a few bearers of

authority. The possession also of these goods must be divided according to the merits and needs of the members. This coordination limits the individual in his freedom both to produce such goods and to appropriate what is produced or discovered.

By nature man is a member of the all-embracing society of human beings. This society, however, is too vast to act as a unit; the rights which it confers and the duties which it imposes are no others than the above-mentioned moral relations of man to man. The membership of this all-embracing society, therefore, has its intermediary in the membership of societies with smaller numbers, which as particular centers of relations can present themselves to other persons and other societies.

By nature man holds membership in the limited society of the family in which he is born and raised and the nation to which he belongs through descent, language and customs. To reach its welfare, the family needs to live in a broader organization, so that in this sense the family is not a "perfect" society. Hence we may say that man is by his very nature directed also to "civic" societies, such as the village, city, region, state, federation, and commonwealth, which contain more members and therefore make it possible to arrive at greater specialization and a broader satisfaction of needs. However, such societies are less naturally given with human nature itself than are family and nation in this sense that their limits and organizations depend more on the free will of the members, as this will manifests itself in human history. The first, but not the only, task of a civic society is to create a positive order of law.

Finally, marriage is also a natural society in a very fundamental sense. For its essence and purpose lie anchored in the very nature of human beings as man and woman. On the other hand, contrary to the society of the family at least insofar as the children are concerned, every individual marriage bond depends for its origin on the free self-determination of the partners.

Alongside the natural societies, there are also free societies, such as unions, associations, groups, parties, fraternities, etc. While the purpose of the natural societies is determined by human nature itself, that of free organizations is established by positive human decisions. Although it is true that the rise of free societies is in line with man's social nature, nevertheless, the concrete individual free organizations arise only through being freely established by man. The entrance also in an existing free organization is an act of self-determination.

Man as a Person is Naturally Historical

Conscience and Man's Temporal Dispersion. As a spiritual nature, human nature is the same in all men, insofar as all human natures by virtue of their reason are directed to truth, goodness and beauty. But human nature is different in each one, insofar as each views the same absolute from a different perspective. The particular standpoint in question is determined by each one's individual essence as the original mode in which he is man.

Because man, as a spirit-in-matter, is the transition between individuation through form and individuation through matter, each one's spiritual nature cannot be understood without its relation to the corporeal and individual. It is only from his "situation," conditioned by place and time in the material world, from sense experience, sense feelings and sensitive desires, that man comes to intellectual acts.

Thus each man's individual nature is a limited participation in unqualified being-man. Nevertheless, each one is called to realize the ideal of being-man in his own original way.

Man cannot obtain knowledge of his individual destiny by a simple deduction from the general moral norms contained in synderesis. Likewise, this destiny is not known to him through a clear and permanent intuition of his individual nature and its capa-

cities. For he is a temporal being which developes in a process of becoming. His life is dispersed through the ages of youth, adulthood and decline. Even his freedom is temporalized, it is not always capable of everything, but only of one thing after another. Man arrives at self-knowledge through reflection on his particular acts, but his individual nature reveals itself only in changing conditions. Thus the demands of this nature are not always equally strong or concerned with the same object.

The *judgment of conscience* which expresses what is demanded of man here and now and which is the norm of the individual action has to take into consideration man's present situation.

All this, however, does not mean that the judgment of conscience is not guided by the general and absolute norms of synderesis. On the contrary, for, temporal as he is, by means of memory and expectation and especially through his intellectual knowledge, man knows about his temporality. In this way it is possible for him to reduce the dispersion of his life to a certain unity. He is capable of accepting the past deliberately and of giving it a meaning freely by means of his decisions about the future. This unification of past and future takes place when man, reflecting on the past, discovers his supra-temporal spiritual nature as transcending the changing acts and in the light of this discovery judges the present situation.

Man's Historical Character. We do not use the term "historical" with respect to every being that is in time or for every event. A being is correctly spoken of as "historical" if to some extent it is capable of comprehending its temporal becoming as a unity and, consequently, able to orientate this becoming from the standpoint of supratemporal and absolute purposes and norms. An event is spoken of as historical if it is a free act pertaining to such a being which realizes itself in time and nevertheless transcends time.

Man, therefore, is naturally historical, for

his individual spiritual nature, on the one hand, is normalized by what is true, good, and beautiful in itself,[10] but on the other, it has to unfold this orientation to the absolute in a plurality of successive, individual acts which occur in changing situations.

Especially man's life as a social being is historical. Even societies and communities which are quasi-subsistent, pass through a period of evolution, and in this process their quasi-self-knowledge, their judgments about their own essence, purpose, and means, is not always equally perfect. It is within such societies having a common mentality or "spirit" that the life-story of the individual persons unrolls. The judgment of his conscience regarding what his own individual nature demands of him here and now will have to take into account also the place he occupies in the historical development of the different societies of which he is a member.

Man, then, cannot simply derive the norm of conscience from the norms of general human nature. He needs the experience of his historical course of life, both as individual and as member of society, to discover what his supra-temporal individual nature demands of him at every moment. The passage from the general to the particular is made by means of prudence, which implies an evaluation of the situation in the light and under the impulse of the first moral principles.

However, it would be erroneous to think that the judgments of conscience can come into conflict with the absolute general norms. On the contrary, the conclusions of prudence are implicitly contained in the general norms. It is only because of our imperfect knowledge of human nature and its orientation to its purpose that we are not simply capable of intuitively surveying the consequences which the principles contain under certain conditions and have to make use of a process of prudent reasoning. This reasoning process, however, is led by the general norms, and only in the estimations of prudence does the fullness contained in the absolute norms reveal itself. We may even say that the more the general norms assume a concrete shape in virtues, in the life of sentiments and will itself, the more man will more or less intuitively discover the particular in the general and, "connaturally" in tune with the norm, "feel" what his individual nature demands of him as man here and now. The virtuous man finds in his ordered inclination itself the rational norm of the individual acts to be done in changing time.

Man as a Person Has an Eternal Destiny

Man Transcends the Temporal. Man is an historical being because, despite his temporal character, he transcends this temporality to some extent through his spiritual nature, which is directed to the atemporal, the ever-actual and ever-present, the "to be" of beings. Although every temporal dispersion in past and future must be conceived as a kind of participation in absolute presence or eternity, man participates in eternity in a much higher way than subhuman material beings. What is meant by this higher mode of participating in eternity? [11]

Man is born and dies. His course of life is encompassed by a time in which he did not yet live and in which he will no longer live as this material person among the material beings of this world. As this spiritual person, however, he transcends all moments of time to some extent, for *all* temporal beings, no matter when they were or will be, somehow fall within the perspective of his all-embracing openness as a spirit. But if this is so, his "to be" also, insofar as it is spiritual, must escape the corruptibility of everything temporal.

Man's Nature and Immortality. It is possible for philosophical reflection to render

---

[10] What is true, good, and beautiful in itself, as such has neither past nor future but is simply actual and present.

[11] Concerning immortality, see A. Marc, *Psychologie réflexive*, vol. 2, pp. 311–342.

the statement acceptable that man's general desire for immortality is based on, and arises from human nature itself. In such a reflection we must keep in mind that man's essence is constituted by a spiritual principle, which as "soul" is the first form of the body, and by prime matter. The spiritual soul, however, *as* spiritual, is a subsistent form and, as such, is raised above the limitation to the here-and-now of place and time. This subsistent form is not intrinsically dependent on the body in its "to be," although it communicates its "to be" to this body in substantial unity. Therefore, although man's death means the cessation of the formal actuating influence which the spiritual soul exercises as soul of the organic body, it does not mean that the spiritual soul ceases to be precisely insofar as it is a subsistent form. Moreover, it is unthinkable that the spiritual soul itself would "die." As a subsistent form, it does not have any capacity for essential change, for becoming something else, because such a possibility arises only from a being's composition of matter and form.

Different Forms of Duration. As soon as one admits that man has a spiritual soul, he has to admit also that this spiritual soul has a higher mode of duration than the temporality implied by corruptibility. However, it is not possible for us to seize and express in adequate concepts the soul's supra-temporality as a higher participation in absolute presence or eternity. We say that with respect to his spiritual soul man has a supra-temporal destination and that, as far as this spiritual soul is concerned, "after" death man "continues to exist" in an "eternal life." But we should beware of conceiving this immortality as an "existence without end" in the *same* temporal process which character-izes material beings and man himself in his bodily *being*. The "after-existence" and "persistence" should not be conceived as a *longer* but as a *higher* form of "duration," as a self-presence which is not divided by temporal dispersion.

As far as the positive content of this eternal life is concerned and the question of how man in his spiritual soul can live a life of knowing and loving without actually turning to sense experience, imagination, and sensitive tendencies, we are faced with a philosophical "mystery" which our thought simply has to accept but cannot of itself fathom.

On the other hand, we are able to assert that the day in which man on his temporal road to self-realization makes his free moral acts harmonize or disharmonize with the integral purpose of his integral nature is decisive for the question whether or not he will attain his supra-temporal destiny and his ultimate happiness.[12]

Bibliography

Text

Metaphysics: A Systematic Survey. Pittsburgh, Pa.: Duquesne University Press, 1963.

[12] Some philosophers have thought that the spiritual soul, as a subsistent form, pre-exists prior to its formal influence on the human body and that for some reason or other, e.g., to expiate a fault, it is united with the body. Such a pre-existence, however, is not acceptable, once it is admitted that soul and body constitute a substantial unity and that the spiritual soul is *essentially* the soul of a body and therefore related to prime matter. For the individuation of such a soul would not be intelligible without the relationship to the corporeal. When the unity of the spiritual soul and the body is thus strongly emphasized, it has to be admitted that the spiritual soul, even when "after" the death of the body it "continues to exist," retains a certain bond with the bodily temporal life to which it owes its individuation.

30

PAUL RICOEUR
1913–

Introduction

Though born but five years later than Merleau-Ponty and eight years after Sartre, Paul Ricoeur is at present thought of as one of the "younger" important European philosophers. Without being an "existential phenomenologist" in the sense Luijpen has given this term, he is best approached as a philosopher whose concerns are those of the "existentialists," such as Jaspers and Marcel, and whose method is that of phenomenology, especially as understood through Husserl, its founder. This vulnerable generalization is based on Ricoeur's major published works. His first major influence was Marcel, his second Jaspers; his first book (with Mikel Dufrenne) was a study of Jaspers (*Karl Jaspers et la philosophie de l'existence*, 1947), his second a comparison of Marcel and Jaspers (*Gabriel Marcel et Karl Jaspers*, 1948). In 1950 his translation, with introduction and commentary, of Husserl's *Ideen I* appeared. Also in 1950 appeared the first of three volumes of Ricoeur's major original work, *Philosophy of the Will*, the first volume (which is Part I) bearing the title *The Voluntary and the Involuntary*, Part II being entitled *Finitude and Culpability*.

Ricoeur's chief concern, reminiscent of Marcel's broken world (*monde cassé*), is man as a broken unity (*unité brisée*), and the task he sees as his own is that of regaining that unity, of reuniting man with himself, with his body, and with his world through a new philosophy of man not so much from the usual viewpoint of man as consciousness and cognition but from the less common viewpoint of man as volition and freedom. His method begins with phenomenology in order to end in ontology. It might be called, after Marcel, "hyperphenomenology" or, perhaps better, phenomenology plus hermeneutic, description plus interpretation.

In *Philosophy of the Will* man's "faulted" being is the theme. Man's existential fault (*faute existentielle*) or faultiness (his finitude) shows itself especially in his passions, which account for his brokenness and call for transcendence (recalling an important term of Jaspers's), necessary for the ultimate restitution of unity. It is possible to see Ricoeur's *Philosophy of the Will* as his attempt to do for volition, in his own way, what Merleau-Ponty did for perception, in his way. The work may also be seen as a view of freedom as affirmation in contrast to Sartre's view of freedom as negation. But perhaps the chief merit of the first volume is the focus on freedom as self-appropriation and self-determination, whereby the subject enacts himself, becomes himself, in deciding and simultaneously accepting responsibility for his projection of himself, as willed body, or incarnate will, into action. In the following selection Ricoeur presents this theme.

PHENOMENOLOGY OF FREEDOM AS SELF-DETERMINATION *

* From Paul Ricoeur, *Freedom and Nature: The Voluntary and The Involuntary*. Northwestern University Press, Evanston, Ill., 1966. Erazim V. Kohák, translator. Reprinted by permission of the publisher.

The Imputation of Myself: "Se Decider"—Making Up My Mind

"Je Me Décide": I Make Up *My* Mind

This reference of the decision to myself poses difficult problems. In what sense do I designate myself in designating a project, and say "It is *I who will do*, am doing, have done"? [1]

1

We must readily admit that we are not always aware of this reference: most of the time I am so involved in what I will that I do not notice myself willing; I have neither the need nor the occasion for laying a claim to my act and claiming authorship in one sense or another. Then isn't this self-reference always superadded to the voluntary act, and doesn't it even alter it profoundly, by inverting the centrifugal direction of consciousness turned toward the project and substituting for it an altogether different act, reflexive in character, which deflects the thrust of consciousness?

2

This uncertainty makes it necessary to relate the self-referential judgment, "it is I who . . . ," to a self-reference which is more basic than all judgment: relating looking *at* oneself to a determination *of* oneself. How is reflection already implied in the action of the self on itself which is contemporaneous with the decision?

3

These difficult analyses must lead us to the most obscure regions of metaphysical questions concerning the *power-of-being* which the *power-of-doing* inevitably leads us to raise.

The Reflexive Judgment: It Is I Who . . .

Descartes had not the least doubt that self-consciousness was an inherent characteristic of thought: "It is so self-evident that it is I

[1] The method of experimental introspection used by Michotte and Prüm ("Le Choix volontaire et ses antécédents immédiats," *Arch. de Psych.*, vol. X [December, 1910], well highlights this consciousness of "it is myself who . . . ," connected with the consciousness of "designating," of "turning oneself towards"; cf. pp. 132–34 and 187–298 of extracts from transcript.

who doubt, who understand and who desire that nothing need be added to explain it" (*Second Meditation*). In the last analysis, Descartes surely is not wrong: a certain presence to myself must covertly accompany all intentional consciousness. We should form an oversimplified idea of this objective intention of consciousness if we considered reflection a secondary, alien act. But on the other hand, the explicit judgment "it is I who . . ." is not such an immediate self-presence clinging to the very thrust of consciousness. What then is the character of the project which makes it *available for* the distended apperception in which I impute the act to myself?

Let us start with situations in which self-affirmation is explicit and attempt to work our way back to the conditions which make it possible, as they are contained in any decision.

I form the consciousness of being the author of my acts in the world and, more generally, the author of my acts of thought, principally on the occasion of my contacts with an other, in a social context. Someone asks, who did that? I rise and reply, I did. Response—responsibility. To be responsible means to be ready to respond to such a question. But I can anticipate the question and lay a claim to responsibility which the other could neither note nor contest. Self-affirmation can then have the vainglorious overtone of self-satisfaction which calls on the other to attest and applaud; it is the other who certifies me as myself. Or again, rivalry, jealousy, harsh comparison, etc., present my consciousness of myself with a passionate orchestration whose difficult exegesis we shall have to undertake later.

And yet we sense that the other introduces nothing external but only evokes, by special revelatory power, that aptitude for imputing my acts to myself which is embedded even in my least reflexive acts. Life with the other might as well be our common dream, our analogous self-loss in the anonymous "they." Thus self-affirmation is a gesture of going out, of showing oneself, of bringing oneself to the fore and confronting oneself. "They" do not respond to the question, "who thinks so, who is making this noise?" because "they" is no-one. Some one must stand out of the mass in which each —or all—hide. In contrast with the "one," "I" take my act on myself, I assume it.[2]

All these expressions—to wake up, to take hold of oneself, to go forth, to show oneself, to confront—make self-consciousness appear as a breaking away: but I break away from others, since they are no-one, only as I break away from myself, inasmuch as I am alienated from myself, that is, surrendered to the others who are no-one. We need to seek the sources of self-consciousness in consciousness itself, with regard to which the others are no more than an occasion, an opportunity, but also a danger and a trap.

Now in waking up from anonymity I discover that I have no means of self-affirmation other than my acts themselves. "I" am only an aspect of my acts, the subject pole of my acts.[3] I have no means of affirming myself on the fringes of my acts. This is what the feeling of responsibility reveals to me.

Besides, it is after the fact, and in a situation of guilt, that reflection appears to itself as an articulation of a connection between the agent and the act which is more fundamental than all reflection. It is I who have done this. I accuse myself, and in accusing myself retrace the vestiges of my signature on the act. *Accusare:* to designate as the cause. At this stage we shall neglect the minor undertones of this consciousness wounded by itself; we shall forget the sting, the consciousness of fall and of indebtedness. An assurance irrupts in the heart of my affliction: the self is in its acts. As Nabert

masterfully analyzed it, awareness of the fault opens the limits of my act and shows me an evil self at the roots of an evil act.[4]

But perhaps we can also capture this very feeling of responsibility which after the fact is reflected in a guilty conscience, and capture it directly in its thrust towards the act. Sometimes, in serious circumstances, when everyone shrinks back, I step forward and say, I take charge of these men, of this job. Here the feeling of responsibility, in the moment of commitment, crowns the highest self-affirmation and most decided exercise of control over a zone of reality for which I make myself responsible. It carries the double emphasis of myself and of the project. He who is responsible is prepared to respond for his acts, because he posits an equation of the will: this action is myself.

Now we are about to perceive a basic self-relation which is neither a reflected judgment nor a retrospective observation, but is implied in intentionality, in the projecting of the project.

Let us try to take up the analysis of the project once more and to discover there what sets off a possible reflection.

Prereflexive Imputation of Myself

The task of our analysis is to elaborate an aspect of the project which we might call the prereflexive imputation of myself. This implies a self-reference which is not yet self-observation, but rather a certain way of relating oneself or of behaving with respect to oneself, a non-speculative or, better, non-observant, way. It is an implication of the self rigorously contemporaneous with the very act of decision which in some sense is an act with reference to the self. This implication of the self must contain the germ of the possibility of reflection, contain the willing available to the *judgment* of responsibility, "it is I who. . . ."

French expresses this double and indivisible relation to the self and to the object

[2] G. Marcel, "The Ego and Its Relation to Others," in *Homo Viator*, trans. Crauford (Chicago, 1951), pp. 13 f.; *Creative Fidelity*. trans. Rosthal (New York, 1964), re the act and the person, cf pp. 104–20.

[3] In this sense Husserl says that apart from its implication in its acts the self is not "a proper object of research": "if we abstract away its ways of relating itself [Beziehungsweisen] and behaving [Verhaltungsweisen], it is absolutely destitute of eidetic components and has not even any content which we could make explicit; it is in itself and for itself indescribable, pure Ego and nothing else," *Ideas*, § 80.

[4] Jean Nabert, *Éléments pour une éthique* (Paris, 1943), p. 6.

of an intention by transitive verbs of pronominal form: "je *me* décide à . . ." (I decide to or I make up *my* mind), "je *me* souviens à . . ." (I remember . . .), "je *me* représent" (I imagine), "je *me* rejouis de . . ." (I rejoice at).[5] For the moment let us neglect the diversity of self-relation implied in these expressions, themselves diverse—this must be linked to the diversity of intentional relation. It is already apparent that this self-reference, whatever it may be, is not isolable from reference to the project, to whatever is represented, remembered, or rejoiced over. The self is not complete in itself. In particular it does not will itself in a void, but in its projects. I affirm myself in my acts. This is precisely what the feeling of responsibility teaches us: this action is myself.

But how is this possible?

As our point of departure we need to take an aspect of the project which we have stressed above—to decide is to designate a personal action. The "myself" figures in the project as that which will do and that which can do. I project my own self into the action to be done. Prior to all reflection about the self which I project, the myself summons itself, it inserts into the plan of action to be done; in a real sense it becomes *committed*. And, in becoming committed, it binds itself: it constrains its future appearance. It throws itself ahead of itself in posing itself as the object, as a direct complement of the project. In projecting myself thus, I objectify myself in a way, as I objectify myself in a signature which I will be able to recognize, identify as mine, as my sign.

Thus it is clear that the entire initial implication of myself is not a conscious relation or an observation. I behave actively in relation to myself, I determine *myself*. Once again French usage throws light on the

situation: to determine my conduct is to determine myself—se *déterminer*. Prereflexive self-imputation is active not observational.

But in this aspect decision is not, strictly speaking, available to explicit reflection. In effect there is always a subject "I," projecting and not projected. We could say that the more I determine myself as the grammatical object, as he who does, the more I forget myself as he from whom, here and now, as from grammatical subject, issues the determination of the self-projected as the agent who will realize the project.

This initial analysis of the prereflexive self has to be completed by an inseparable second analysis: all acts carry with them a vague awareness of their subject-pole, their place of emission. This awareness does not suspend the direction of perceiving, imagining, or willing towards the object. Specifically in the acts which French expresses with reflexive constructions there is a juncture of the vague consciousness of being subject and of the subject as object, involved in the project, which takes place prior to all reflexive dissociation. A primordial identification resists the temptation to exile my self into the margins of its acts: an identification of the projecting and the projected myself. I am the myself which now wills (and projects) just as I am he who will do (and is projected). "This action is myself" means that there are no two selves, one projecting and one in the project; I affirm myself as the subject precisely in the object of my willing.

This difficult dialectic can also be clarified otherwise: the presence of the subject in his acts is likewise not a content of reflection in that it remains a presence of a subject. Distended reflection tends to make it an object of judgment: the feeling of responsibility orients this in some respects inevitable objectification in the direction of the specfic objectification of the project. I meet myself in my project, I am involved in my project, the project of myself by myself. Self-consciousness is thus at the basis of the identity which is prior to judgment and conditions it, a presence of *projecting*

---

[5] Similar construction occurs in other languages, as in German [*sich* entscheiden, *sich* erinnern, *sich* freuen] or in Czech [rozhodnouti *se*, těsiti *se*, pamatovati *se*], and is by no means peculiar to French or other romance languages. Unfortunately, except in circumlocutions [I make up *my* mind] or for emphasis [I made myself do it] it is not made explicit in English construction.—Trans.

subject and *projected* myself. We can understand reflexive judgment precisely by starting out with this prereflexive imputation of myself in my projects.[6]

We frequently imagine reflection as a turning about of consciousness which is at first outside of itself, then returns into itself and suspends its outward orientation. This forces us to regard consciousness turned towards the other as unconscious of itself and self-consciousness as corroding the consciousness which is directed towards something other than itself. Re-flection becomes retrospection, disastrous for the pro-ject.

This scheme misses what is essential, the awareness of that practical reference to myself which is the very root of reflection. Explicit reflection, in the distended form of the judgment "it is I who . . . ," only raises a more primitive affirmation of myself to the dignity of discourse, a judgment which projects itself in the plan of an action. It makes the practical prereflexive affirmation thematic.

At the same time, reflection derives all its meaning as a moment of an interior dialectic by which I alternately accentuate myself and the project, exalting the one by the other. Nor is the consideration of responsibility anything else. But it is false to assume that self-consciousness is inherently disruptive. Auguste Comte in particular is mistaken about the meaning of introspection.

[6] Bradley, "The Definition of Will," Part II, *Mind* (1903), pp. 145 ff., tends to avoid this idea of imputation in which he sees a snare of substantialism and voluntarism; he makes the identification of myself with the idea the sole criterion of volition. The idea which my self *produces, changes*—briefly, the idea of an *agency*—appears to him to employ a suspect causality. (Bradley agrees, to be sure, that once execution has begun, the idea of change, in actualizing itself, in turn changes by its impact my perception of myself—my self which is one with the idea which transforms the actual; I modify reality equally.) If we remember to distinguish causality and imputation of my self in its acts, there is no reason to oppose this *identification* of the self with the project with the *action of the self on itself*, on the condition that we note that in its prereflexive form this determination of the self is effected "in" the project of the action itself.—Completed by his "On Mental Conflict and Imputation," *Mind* (1902), p. 289.

In a great number of acts, awareness of myself is involved as an active ferment of the very thrust of consciousness towards its object. All the acts in which I "take a stand" (in relation to a reality, a fiction, a memory, or a project) are susceptible of being confirmed rather than changed by a more explicit self-consciousness. These are the acts which French expresses by reflexive constructions, se *souvenir* (to remember), se *représenter* (to imagine), se *décider* (to decide). In all these acts an action on oneself is already involved in the movement which carries consciousness towards the past, the unreal, or the project; it is only stressed in the explicit judgment of which the judgment of responsibility is typical. It is a mistake to consider only the acts in which consciousness is dissipated and alienated, as anger and the passions in general; as soon as the passions inject themselves into emotion, I am beside myself, not in the sense that I turn towards another thing, but rather in the sense that I am deprived of myself, a victim of. . . . Self-consciousness is the decisive moment of taking hold of myself which opens up a high vision of freedom: in a flash of light, the alienation is suspended. Besides, emotion and passion are not the only examples of possessed or fascinated consciousness of which self-consciousness would become aware if it could enter the light of freedom: inauthentic consciousness, lost in the impersonal "they," provides another example. Thus when self-consciousness is relatively alienated, as in passion or in the "they," it constitutes a dialectic of rejection. On the other hand, it constitutes a dialectic of confirmation when consciousness is relatively its own mistress, as in the act of "taking a stand."

Still it remains true that, separated from this internal dialectic, reflexive judgment uproots itself from living, practical affirmation and becomes pure observation and self-satisfaction. It is the fate of self-consciousness to corrupt itself in all the cases in which it becomes pure observer. As it does so, it in fact suspends consciousness directed towards an action and towards the other in general. It is in contrast with this uprooted consciousness that consciousness, considered in its thrust towards the other, can be said to be forgotten by the self. Descartes calls this forward leap "generosity."

Later we shall consider the drift by which self-affirmation becomes complaisant observation. Faithful to our methodological rule, we shall here suspend the wanderings of consciousness fascinated by the Self and by Nothing, and we shall conceive of a self-affirmation, available for reflection, which is the common keyboard of innocent love of myself and of that fascinated self-consciousness. In this pure description follows the discourse of the Serpent: "Am I not who you are/this complaisance which rises/in your soul as it loves itself?/Finally, I am thanks to it/to that inimitable tang/which you find only in yourself!" [7]

Consciousness and
Its Power of Being

Self-determination involved in the determination of a project leads us to the meaning of the word "possible" which we have reserved for the conclusion of our analysis of the possibility envisioned in the project. Am I who introduces possibilities into the world not ultimately myself possible? [8]

We shall approach this problem of the capacity for being inherent in the being which wills obliquely, starting with the foregoing analyses. Furthermore this can best be

[7] Valéry, "Ébauche du serpent," *Poésies* (Paris, 1936), p. 165. (Trans. Kohák.)

[8] Cf. Karl Jaspers' analyses of possible existence which is "that which comports itself actively in relation to the self," *Philosophie* (Berlin, 1932), II, 35. But it is Heidegger who has gone furthest in this direction. "That entity which in its Being has this very Being as an issue, comports itself towards its Being as its most authentic possibility. In each case Dasein *is* its possibility and it 'has' this possibility, but not just as a property" (*Being and Time*, p. H.42). Commenting on Being "as an issue" [*es geht um*] in this passage, Heidegger here shows "self-projective Being towards its own-most potentiality-for-being" (*ibid.*, p. H.191; trans. Macquarrie). Cf. primarily J.–P. Sartre, *Being and Nothingness*, trans. Barnes (New York, 1950), Part II, chap. 1, and Part IV, chap. 1.

examined in a context far removed from the context of pure description and will have to be taken up anew when all the other elements of the doctrine of choice shall have been put in their place.

We shall be guided by two methodological rules. First of all we shall have to begin with our prereflexive and active self-imputation rather than with explicit reflection: in particular, an unpremeditated consideration which would start with the spell or anxiety of power of being seems more likely to mislead the analysis than to aid it. The second rule: it is necessary to uncover the most primitive possibility of myself, which I launch within myself in making up *my* mind. This is the easiest analysis because it still refers to our analysis of the project. In effect, for a responsible being, that is, a being who *commits himself* in the project of an action which he at the same time recognizes as his, determining *oneself* is still one with determining his gesture *in the world*. We can thus search out what possibility of *myself* is simultaneous with the possibility of *action* opened up by the project. By this second means we shall avoid bringing prematurely into consideration the anxiety which is present not only on the level of rejection, but also on the level of engagement, at the dizzying edges of determination of the self and of the project. Thus we shall place ourselves on the prereflexive level of a will which makes the leap, which pro-jects the project.

Yet we could ask whether possibility still applies to my own self when I resolve *on something*? Does not the pro-jecting of the project separate me from potency by raising me to the level of act? Does not the reflexive form of the French expression, *"me déterminer,"* "to resolve myself," throw any light on this? In binding *myself,* as by an oath or a promise, is not all indetermination extinguished and all possibility with it?

And yet, as the analysis of anxiety will presently show, the possibility of indecision can be clarified only by a more basic possibility which I bring about by my very decision. We have started our description of decision by describing the project, that is, the object of decision, rather than by reflecting on the self who decides, in order to restrain the awareness that the will is first of all a thrust, a pro-ject, a leap—that is, an act, a "generosity." Now we have seen that the project *opens up* possibilities in the world by the very commitment which binds it. As long as I do not project anything, I do not chart possibilities within the actual. Our description of the project thus leads us to seek first of all those of my possibilities which I *open up* by deciding rather than those which I *lose* by it.

In deciding, I not only put an end to an antecedent confusion, but I also initiate a way for being what I am. This way is my "to be"—*a-venir*, future—and my possibility entailed by the project of my self. In what respect am I thus possible by starting with my own decision? First with respect to bodily gestures which would fulfill this possibility. To decide is to project a potential *myself* as the theme of proposed conduct for the body to follow. The possible which I am, in projecting a possible action, consists of a claim I make on my body. This possibility of myself is thus related to the capacity which the project both evokes and encounters in the body. It is the capacity for acting, insofar as my body's future is first possible before being actual (while in another respect the actual always precedes the possible, as awareness of the involuntary recognizes).

But I am also possible in another sense: in relation not only to my body's future reality, but also to the reality of my life-span and of decisions which I shall make in due time. Each decision I make uncovers a possible future, opens up some ways, closes others, and determines the outlines of new areas of indetermination offered as a possible course for subsequent decision. The possibility constituted within me by the project is thus always prior to myself as physical ability for realizing it and the subsequent capacity for deciding.

Such is my own covertly reflexive possibility which I initiate each time I form a project. It means that what I shall be is not

already given but depends on what I shall do. My possible being depends on my possible doing.

Thus it should be apparent that the capacity of which we speak is not the bare potency of the metaphysicians—the undetermined "hyle"—which, at least logically, precedes the act. The first capacity we encounter is the capacity which an act opens up before itself. With respect to this capacity, indetermination understood as indecision is impotence.

Then reflection enters in, and with it mounting anxiety.

We have said that reflection can be in the first place a moment in the dialectic of the intercourse between the project and myself. What becomes of my capacity for being when I reflect on my responsibility along these lines? Its meaning still does not change: it is only stressed, together with the possibility of the project. As I am able to do I am also able to be. The moment of recoil leads me back to a stronger consciousness *of* the projected action. The more I commit myself and the more I am able to do, the more I am possible. I cannot affirm my potency for being unless I confirm it with acts. My possibility is in the first place my exercised ability.

It seems to me completely mistaken to tie the experience of freedom to madness and dread. The experience of *exercised* freedom is free from anxiety and acquires the dramatic character which contemporary literature often attributes to it only under the condition of a profound alteration (which we shall examine later). The "generosity" which Descartes teaches is free of anxiety. The opposition of my being to the being of things, powerfully reinforced by my awareness of my own capacity for being, can very well move in the joyous mood which Descartes evokes in the *Treatise on Passions* and in his *Letters*. A thing is here, located, and determined by what is not itself, while freedom is not located, does not become aware of itself, does not discover itself as being already here until I observe it. It creates itself in doing and affirms itself to the extent to which it does—it is being which determines itself. Its potential being is not at all a gaping abyss, it is the actual task which freedom is for itself in the moment *in which it constitutes itself* by the decision it makes.

Bibliography

Texts

Philosophy of the Will, Part I, *The Voluntary and the Involuntary*, Evanston, Ill.: Northwestern University Press, 1966; Part II, *Finitude and Culpability*, Vol. I, *Fallible Man*, Chicago: Henry Regnery Company, 1965; Vol. II, *The Symbolism of Evil*, New York: Harper & Row, Publishers, Incorporated, 1967.

History and Truth. Evanston, Ill.: Northwestern University Press, 1965.

Husserl: An Analysis of His Phenomenology. Evanston, Ill.: Northwestern University Press, 1967.

Studies

Spiegelberg, H. *The Phenomenological Movement.* The Hague: Martinus Nijhoff, 1965, 2d ed., vol. 2, pp. 563–579.

31

WILLIAM A. LUIJPEN
1922–

Introduction

William Luijpen was born in the Netherlands, joined the Augustinian order, and pursued his first philosophical studies at the Angelicum College in Rome and then at the Sorbonne in Paris. The decisive contact in his training came when he next went to the Higher Institute of Philosophy at the University of Louvain in Belgium and to the University of Freiburg in Germany, two of the most important centers of contemporary philosophy in the world. There he studied the major representatives of phenomenology and of existential philosophy. Returning to the Netherlands, he joined the faculty of philosophy at the Augustinian college in Eindhoven. In 1960 and 1964 he was extremely successful as visiting professor of philosophy at Duquesne University, one of the two or three most important centers in the United States to have begun to show the influence of phenomenology and of existential themes in its school of philosophy, and even more in its school of psychology.

Luijpen's main concern has been a complete rethinking of the major questions about man and about God on the basis of contemporary philosophy. In 1952, he published *The Experience of Existence and Theology*, and then, after seven years of research, in 1959 he published *Existential Phenomenology*, translated in 1960. In 1965 his next work appeared in English, *Phenomenology and Atheism*, the basis of one of his courses at Duquesne in 1964. This was followed in 1965 by *Phenomenology and Metaphysics*.

Luijpen does not consider the great source works in phenomenology and existentialist thought as mere contributions to some already existing body of philosophical "dogmas," a set of theses to be protected and nourished with irrevocable allegiance. He does not even consider them as simply the raw material for a new synthesis to be arrived at through a critical analysis which tries first to find the common ground in all diversity, classify the divergences in relation to it, and then construct the synthesis. Rather he engages in a personal dialogue with each source on its *own* ground and in its own terms, with the goal certainly not of rote memorizing nor even of mere understanding in order to follow articulately, but of arriving at his own relatively independent rethinking of the perennial questions with the help of others who have done the same. It is his view that, to be authentic, each person must do this on his own. To do less is no search for wisdom, no invitation to commitment, but a waste of time, a bad survey of other people's contradictory answers to questions nobody is asking anymore. In the selections that follow, you may and should question his reading of the sources he chooses. Nothing quoted or referred to is intended as an "argument." No philosopher is an oracle proclaiming truths applicable to all men. A philosopher who publishes is also a writer, and writers write for their own reasons while readers read for theirs. There is a cause of the existence of disagreeing "schools" or movements which is also the cause of the existence of *any* "school" or movement; namely, that an authentic philosopher puts one man, himself, in his writing, while the reader tends to look for and recognize another man, *himself*, in his reading. Insofar as human nature is everywhere basically the same, agreement is possible. Insofar as no two men are exactly alike, disagreement is possible. The conclusion is not despair of reaching truth but relocation of truth to where it really is. The truth is social. It is neither in you nor in me but in us, which means primordially in the interpersonal world of *action*, where living with and loving life and one another precedes philosophizing and writing about it. Luijpen explores the themes of encounter and love in the following selection.

LOVE AS "STANDPOINT" OF THE KNOWING PERSON *

Love, as a standpoint of the knowing subject, is not so much of importance when there is question of knowing things as when man tries to understand his fellow-man. True, even with respect to things, the terms "to love" and "to like" are often used and, when the terms apply in this context, an unmistakably selective influence must be attributed to "love" as a standpoint. Nevertheless, it should be evident that there is question here only of love in a less strict sense. Used in its proper sense, the term always refers to intersubjectivity and indicates a specific attitude of a subject toward a subject.

The understanding of man, of what goes on in him, of the meaning of his behavior in various situations, has always been the fundamental aim of anyone who in any situation wanted to proceed "psychologically." The different schools of scientific psychology may, and even should, be viewed as attempts to pursue ordinary "lived" psychology in a more rigorous fashion. This purpose justifies whatever is undertaken in psychology provided that the undertaking is viewed as a participation in, and a contribution to a task whose accomplishment can never be fully satisfactory. However, more is involved than this impossibility of ever being fully satisfied with the attainments of scientific psychology.

As was pointed out by Buytendijk, even under the most favorable conditions scientific psychology will not be able to proceed beyond understanding the facticity of the man whom it attempts to know.[1] As soon as there is question of a human being in distress, of the aid one would like to give him or of the advice one would like to offer, scientific psychology falls short of what is needed.[2] Or, to express it more accurately, in such conditions the psychologist "feels" his insufficiency, because the strictly personal in his fellow man—which is what is at issue here—never does find expression in scientific psychology.

Perhaps one would be inclined to conclude immediately that, consequently, it will be meaningless even to attempt to obtain such knowledge. Such a conclusion, however, would be premature, for *de facto* man cannot dispense with this knowledge, or rather, he will always act as if he did possess knowledge of what is strictly personal.

Love and Knowledge of the Strictly Personal. Buytendijk thinks that this kind of knowledge is really attainable. "This knowledge of man," he says, "can never be acquired unless it be of someone for whom we *care*. This definition of the correct attitude and relationship to the person whom we *want* to know is considered correct and wholly uncontested outside the realm of science. It is Binswanger who has convincingly shown that even in psychology knowledge of a human being is possible only by means of what he calls the *objectivity of love*—which is nothing else than what in daily life is called 'heart-to-heart' knowledge." [3] It is striking that Buytendijk uses here the term "attitude." If we may understand this term as expressing Husserl's *Einstellung*,[4] we find ourselves immediately in well-known territory. At the same time it should be apparent why scientific psychology *has to* fall short.

By means of certain psycho-diagnostic models, of typological and characteriological schemata, the scientific psychologist asks the man whom he wants to know a *definite* question, to which only a *definite* reply can be expected. His concepts and schemata in-

---

* By permission of Duquesne University Press. From William A. Luijpen, *Existential Phenomenology* (fourth impression), Duquesne University Press, Pittsburgh, Pa., 1965.

[1] Buytendijk, "De waarde van de roman voor de psychologische kennis en de psychologische vorming," *Tijdschrift voor Philosophie*, vol. XI (1949), pp. 351–360.

[2] Cf. Buytendijk, *op. cit.*, p. 353.
[3] Buytendijk, *op. cit.*, p. 355.
[4] We have consistently rendered this term by "attitude." Tr.

dicate a certain attitude, to which corresponds a certain profile of the person who the other human being is. Although this profile is a *real* profile, it is only *one* aspect of him. Moreover, psychological "determinations" such as introvert, extrovert, frustrated, neurotic, sentimental, etc., always express only the "determination" of a person, i.e., his facticity. What this facticity means for this person the psychologist will understand only if he has at least some insight into the *person himself* as the source of meaning, into his subjectivity and freedom. This knowledge is possible only as a knowing from "heart-to-heart." Such a knowledge "means that we not only know a man's qualities, his character, and his ethical structure, but have also met him in the freedom of his decisions." [5]

To understand a human being is more than to express his facticity. For man is the unity-in-opposition of subjectivity and facticity. Although scientific psychology may go very far in its determination of this facticity, an insight into the subjectivity of a human being presupposes love.

As was mentioned above, the insufficiency of scientific psychology is "felt" especially when there is question of a human being in

distress, of the aid one would like to give him, or of the advice one would like to offer.[6] The reason is that effective aid or sound advice to a person presupposes not only an understanding of his facticity but also an insight into, and an appeal to his potentialities as *his* potentialities. The scientifically trained psychologist also knows that facticity is never purely facticity, i.e., that the unity-in-opposition of subjectivity and facticity leaves the subject a certain latitude—namely, the latitude of what he is capable of becoming (*Seinkönnen*). For man is essentially a project. However, to be able to help and offer advice, it is not sufficient that one knows "in general" about this latitude. It is not even enough to know that *this* facticity "in general" permits the development of this or that possibility. The crucial point is to establish whether or not *this* possibility really is the possibility of this human being. This means that I have to know the *individual* through whom a general possibility is a *real* possibility—namely, as *his* possibility. But "to know the essence and orientation of a concrete human being is possible only by participating in the self-project of his being." [7] Such a participation is called love. . . .

PHENOMENOLOGY OF INTERSUBJECTIVITY: THE ROLE OF THE BODY IN ENCOUNTER

My World as Our World.   Does man have anything to do with those living beings which he calls men? The reply cannot be given at once, but gradually develops when I attempt to think the man I am without the others. I am a being-in-the-world, but the worldly meanings of my world constantly refer to other human beings. The letter which I write refers to its addressee; the pen I use refers to the supplier who has to make his living from his sales. A boat at anchor refers to travellers; the mountains and forests which

I admire refer to the architect for whom they mean stone and wood, i.e., construction materials. The system of close and distant meanings which owes its origin in part also to my existence is permeated, therefore, with actual and possible meanings of which I am not the origin. My world refers to origins of meanings which are not my existence. Nevertheless, these meanings are not "nothing-for-me." They are meanings also for me, albeit in another sense than for other exist-

[6] D. J. van Lennep, *Gewogen-bekeken-ontmoet in het psychologisch onderzoek*, 's-Gravenhage, 1949.
[7] Buytendijk, *op. cit.*, p. 356.

[5] Buytendijk, *op. cit.*, p. 356.

ences. My world, therefore, apparently is not exclusively *my* world, and your world is not only *yours,* but the world of existence is our world (*die Welt des Daseins ist Mitwelt* [8]).

Man and world, however, constitute a unity of reciprocal implication. Therefore, that the world-for-other-existences has meaning also for me means that my existence is a co-existence with other existences. My presence in the world is a *co*-presence; my encounter with the world is *our* encounter; my world is *our* world.

A priori speaking, it is not certain that this co-presence indicates an essential structural aspect of being-man. Man is essentially in-the-world; his being-in-the-world is an *existentiale,* an essential structural aspect of being-man. It is impossible, therefore, to conceive man without the world. When the bond between man and world is broken, man is no longer. This break is inevitable—death—and after it at any rate it is no longer possible to speak of being-man. Whatever I may be after death, I will not be a man. Accordingly, I am not first a man and then enter or do not enter into the world. Being-in-the-world is not added to my being-man because there just happens to be a world. My being-man *is* a being-in-the-world.[9] To think away the world means to think away man.

Is Co-existence an Essential Aspect of Being-man? Obviously, in this phase of our investigation it is not permissible to appeal to arguments which are without any immediate relationship to the reason why above existence was described as co-existence. Existence, we said, is co-existence because my world reveals itself as *our* world (*Mitwelt*). But could this not simply be the consequence of the fact that there happen to be other men? If the answer would be in the affirmative, the affirmation of existence as co-existence would not imply much more than establishing a fact—much as one establishes that a man has two arms and two

ears. Man cannot be thought as man without the world, but he can be conceived without two ears. Would perhaps the same have to be said about man's co-existence? Heidegger neglects to investigate this possibility thoroughly and considers co-existence as an *existentiale,* as an essential structural aspect of existence. Sartre attacks Heidegger on this point and refuses to agree with him. He reproaches him for simply passing from an empirical observation to the affirmation of an essential structural aspect. Binswanger leaves Heidegger's description for what it is [10] and remarks that one cannot find in Heidegger what is most proper to being-human—namely, "the loving togetherness of Me and You."

Of course, it would be possible to point with Binswanger to situations showing that man has more dealings with his fellow man than were indicated above. Later we shall analyze these situations. At present, however, we are concerned with the question whether or not the fact that my world must be called our world is more than a fact, whether or not this co-existence is an essential structural aspect of human existence. When Heidegger replies in the affirmative to this question, he surreptitiously appeals to arguments which presuppose a co-existence in a much more profound sense. He puts forward reasons which are not derived from the fact that my world is our world, although it is precisely on this ground that existence is called co-existence. Heidegger points out that precisely the deficient modes of co-existence reveal existence as co-existence. For instance, he says, the experience of being-alone is possible only on the ground of a more original being-together. I can "miss" another only if my being is a being-together. The possibility of being-alone, the fact that I can "miss" another, reveals a more original togetherness.

Of course, the point is hardly debatable. However, the togetherness which I "miss" when I feel "alone" contains more than the

[8] Heidegger, *Sein und Zeit,* p. 118.
[9] Heidegger, *op. cit.,* p. 54.

[10] L. Binswanger, *Grundformen und Erkenntnis menschlichen Daseins,* Zurich, 1953, p. 267.

co-existence to which Heidegger concludes on the ground of the fact that my world is our world. Even when I am alone and miss the other, the ship refers to the traveller, and the book to the supplier. My existence, then, is still co-existence, yet I feel "alone." Being-alone, therefore, is not a deficient mode of *this* co-existence. When I am alone and miss the other, there reveals itself the possibility and the necessity of a mode of co-existing which has a richer content than the being-together in the world spoken of above. Accordingly, the deficient modes of this more profound mode of co-existing do not "prove" that being-together in the world is an essential structural aspect of human existence. But they show that *several dimensions* must be distinguished in co-existence.

The Body as Intermediary

The Other's Accessibility to Me. Whether or not our being-together in the world has to be called an *existentiale*, it certainly is evident that the meaning of the world for the other is accessible to me. This implies that the other himself is accessible to me. The letter which I write may be for me a material question of pen, paper, and communication, but for the other it may be the biggest fear and nightmare of his life. *His* fear and nightmare, however, are meanings also for me, they are accessible to me. Perhaps I have already taken these meanings into account when I wrote the letter. This would mean that I take the other into account and, therefore, that he is not concealed from me but accessible to me.

In daily life this situation is accepted as quite normal. Everyone admits that the patient is accessible to the doctor, the customer to the salesman, the student to the teacher. The thief is not concealed from the policeman who surprises him in the act, and a naughty boy is not concealed from his mother when she catches him.

The philosopher has to respect this unconcealedness and accessibility. He does not have the right to explicitate co-existence in such a way that it is reduced to nothing

or that its reality can no longer be conceived as reality. His function merely is to express this co-existence. He has to proceed in the same way in this explicitation as he does in explicitating the perception of a worldly thing, where his function is to describe this perception. Let us say that I perceive a "deliciously fragrant" apple. When it becomes apparent that the idea of the physical causality exercised by means of stimuli does not give us an insight into this perception,[11] i.e., that this idea does not allow us to conceive the possibility of perceiving a "deliciously fragrant" apple, then the philosopher will have to drop the idea of physical causality as the "explanation" of perception as it occurs and will have to retain his perception.[12] In daily life this procedure is considered quite normal. There was a time, however, when scientific circles judged it very abnormal to assume that I really smell delicious apples and really see green grass. They preferred to start from physico-chemical stimuli or from physiologically described organs and thus no longer attained to perception.[13] Existential phenomenology, however, is sensitive for what in daily life is accepted as quite normal. It officially forces doors open, or rather, it points to open doors and invites man to enter through them.[14] . . :

Encounter with the Other as the Other. It is not all necessary to appeal to reasoning from analogy or to theories of *Einfühlung* in order to explain the presence of the other as the other, for the encounter with the other directly and immediately distinguishes itself from the encounter with a mere thing. In this encounter the other reveals himself directly as the other, as not-a-thing, as a conscious-being-in-the-world.[15] It is the other in person whom I see shaking with fear or whom

[11] Merleau-Ponty, *Phénoménologie de la perception*, pp. 18–19.
[12] J. H. v. d. Berg and J. Linschoten, *Persoon en wereld*, Utrecht, 1953, pp. 251–253.
[13] A. de Waelhens, "La phénoménologie du corps," *Revue philosophique de Louvain*, 1950, pp. 374–382.
[14] Cf. H. C. Rümke, *Psychiatrie*, vol. I, Amsterdam, 1954, p. 148.
[15] Cf. Merleau-Ponty, *Sens et non-sens*, p. 187.

I hear sighing under the burden of his cares. I feel his cordiality in his handshake, in his soft-spoken voice, in the benevolence of his looks. Those too who hate me or are indifferent toward me, who find my company boring, who fear, despise, or mistrust me, those who want to console, tempt, blame, persuade, or amuse me are in person present to me. The look of such a one, his gesture, his words, his attitude, etc. are always *his* look, gesture, words, or attitude. He is in person directly and immediately present to me.

The presence of a thing, on the other hand, manifests itself quite differently. The way in which a rolling rock approaches me differs from that of an angry policeman. My desk does not groan under my elbows, my pen does not give me a hurt look when I use it wrongly, I do not blame an apple for falling on my head, and I do not expect to be congratulated on my birthday by my dog.

Accordingly, I have to accept the unconcealedness, the direct presence of the other as the other, as an original fact. Any "proof" is wholly superfluous, because this presence is immediately evident, and any attempt to make this presence acceptable appears to presuppose that the other is present to me.

"My" Body Is Not "a" Body

The preceding considerations, however, do not remove all difficulties. The other may be present to me through his look, his gesture, his attitude, his speech, etc., but his look, gesture, attitude, etc. are bodily realities. Is it not true, then, that it is *only the body* of the other which is present to me and comes into contact with me?

Again Cartesian Dualism. When the question is raised in this way, all the consequences of Cartesian dualism threaten to return. "Only the body" and not the conscious other, says the question. This presupposes that it is possible to speak about "the body alone." Such a presupposition appears to be of a Cartesian origin. Descartes had divorced consciousness and body from each other and described the body as a machine. Only from this Cartesian viewpoint

is it possible to speak of "the body alone." Such a view, however, is an explicitation that does not take into consideration the mode in which my body is given to me— namely, as "mine." The consequences of such a faulty standpoint are funest for, if I no longer think of my body as "mine," I no longer conceive my "self" as being corporeally-in-the-world. In his explicitation of the meaning of the human body Descartes omits precisely the most important aspect —namely, that the body is a *human* body. The body is properly human only in the indivisible unity which man is, just as an organ is an organ only in the totality of the organism. The body is *my* body only in its participation in the conscious *self*. According to Descartes' description the body is always only "a" body, i.e., a body pertaining to the immense group of bodies. *My* body, however, is *mine* through its mysterious reference to *me*, to the conscious *self* with which it has fused. My body has even grown so much into one with me that in some cases I do not hesitate to speak of "me" when I mean my body. I say, for instance, that I wash myself, move myself, watch myself. This "myself" means my body.

Physiology and My Body. My body, therefore, is not the body described by physiology or drawn by anatomy. The body which occurs in anatomy, biology, and physiology is merely "a" body. These sciences describe the body as a thing in the world. Their descriptions are based upon the observations of men of science, but they do not explicitate my perception of my body as mine. My hand reveals itself as mine when I try to grasp an object; my feet manifest themselves as mine when I carefully place them on the steps of a steep staircase; my eyes disclose themselves as mine when I let my gaze travel over the world. My hands with which I grasp do not belong to the system of seizable things, such as my pen, my shoes, and my pack of cigarettes. My feet do not belong to the world that can be walked upon, and my eyes do not pertain to the visible world. They reveal themselves as meanings which lie on the side of the subject which I am. These meanings cannot be found in a text book of anatomy or physiology, because "I" do not occur in such books.

My Body Is Not a Mere Instrument. For the same reason my body is not an instrument, as a hammer and a microscope are instruments. Instruments are extensions of my body but, if I consider my body as an instrument, of which body is my body an extension? My body cannot be an instrument, for it is my body, for it is fused with the conscious self which I am.

My Body Is Not the Object of "Having." It is not possible to apply to my body what, according to Marcel, can be said of the object of "having." I "have" a car, a pen, a book. In this "having" the object of the "having" reveals itself as an exteriority. There is a distance between me and what I "have." What I "have" is to a certain extent independent of me.[16] I can dispose of it or give it away without ceasing to be what I am—a man.[17] The same cannot be asserted of my body, at least not without so many restrictions that "having" is deprived of its strict sense. My body is not so far removed from my conscious self as is the ashtray on my desk. Likewise, my body is not something external to me like my car. I cannot dispose of my body or give it away as I dispose of money or give away my golf clubs. All this stems from the fact that my body is not "a" body but *my* body, not in the same way as my golf clubs are mine, but in such a way that my body *embodies* me.

My Body Is Not Isolated from Me. Accordingly, there can never be question of the body "alone" if this term is supposed to indicate an isolated body, a body which would stand apart from the conscious self but nevertheless be *my* body. The conscious self "informs" the body, i.e., it permeates the body with the *forma*, the form-giving actuality of the self,[18] through which the body is "mine." Reversely, I have to admit that my body is the embodiment of the conscious self, and that this self is an embodied self.[19]

It is true, of course, that the glance, the gesture, the attitude, speech, etc. of the other are bodily realities. However, the other's body is "his" body and, therefore, the glance, gesture, attitude, and speech are also "his" glance, gesture, attitude, and speech. The contact, then, with "his" body is not a contact with "only a body," with "a" body, for "a" body is not "his" body.[20] Accordingly, I encounter the other as the other, as a subject, when he looks at me with love, hatred, or indifference, when he throws me a gesture, when he assumes a threatening attitude, when he addresses me in speech, for his body is the embodiment of his subjectivity.

The Other's Body as Intermediary in His Encounter. We have previously pointed out that the meaning of the world-for-the-other is accessible to me—the world is our world. This world's accessibility implies the accessibility and unconcealedness of the other for me. I experience the fact of this unconcealedness in the encounter with the other. I myself am in the world, and in my world I encounter the other. In this encounter the other reveals himself directly as the other, I distinguish him immediately from worldly things,[21] I discern in him a source of sense and meaning, another exist-

---

[16] This independence does not mean that in "having" there is question of a thing-in-itself. For there is always question of my "having" and its object, which reveals itself to me as independent of me to a certain extent.

[17] Cf. Marcel, *Journal métaphysique*, p. 301.

[18] Not all members of my body and their functions participate equally in the formative actuality of the self. There are different levels of this "information," but they do not concern us here. Cf. Stephen Strasser, The *Soul in Metaphysical and Empirical Psychology*, Pittsburgh, 1957, pp. 123–126.

[19] We mention the embodiment of the self here only insofar as it is required to understand the meaning of immediate presence to the other as the other.

[20] Cf. Marcel, *Journal métaphysique*, pp. 325–329.

[21] Heidegger uses different terms to indicate the distinction of man's relationships to the worldly thing and to the other. To the worldly thing I am related in an attitude of *Besorgen*. My relation to the other is called *Fürsorge*. "Das Seiende zu dem sich das Dasein als Mitsein verhält, hat aber nicht die Seinsart des zuhandenen Zeugs, es ist selbst Dasein. Dieser Seiende wird nicht besorgt, sondern steht in der Fürsorge." *Sein und Zeit*, p. 121.

ence, because his body is the embodiment of his subjectivity.

In a certain sense, therefore, I may say that the other's body functions as an intermediary in my encounter with the other. For it is through his body that the other occurs in my world and, because I am in the world, the other must occur in my world if I am to meet him.

There is still another sense in which the other's body acts as intermediary in the encounter with my fellow man. His body not only makes direct contact possible, but also makes me participate in his world and makes it possible for me to enter into his world. Marcel's explicitations of "having" excellently serve to clarify this statement. I do not "have" my body in the same way as I have a car. Nevertheless, in a certain sense we may say that I do "have" my body—namely, insofar as the subject which I am "is" not my body. Although the conscious self and my body imply each other, although the conscious self has insolubly fused with my body, nevertheless I "am" not my hands, my face, my seeing, my hearing. There is a certain non-identity, a certain distance, between me and my body. In a sense, I can dispose of my body and give it away. In the supposition that I "am" my body, I am a thing and wholly immersed in a world of mere things. But then the conscious self is reduced to nothing and, consequently, also my body as "mine," as well as the world as "mine." Accordingly, I neither "am" my body nor "have" it. My body is precisely mid-way between these two extremes. It constitutes the transition from the conscious self to the worldly object. It is the mysterious reality which grafts me on things, secures my being-in-the-world, involves me in the world, and gives me a standpoint in the world.

Entering the Other's World through His Body. The direct contact with the other involves me also in his world through his body. When I am seated alongside the driver in a car, I enter through his body and its extension—the car—into the meanings which for him are possessed by the road, the countryside, the hills, narrow passes, bridges, etc.

If I become nervous because of the great speed, the driver enters into the meaning which the narrow bridge we are crossing has for me. When I watch a carpenter at work, I am through his bodily being involved in his world, and the meanings which saw, hammer, and nails have for him reveal themselves to me. I place myself in the meaning which my garden and trees have for the urchins whom I see crawling in through the hedge. The words my friend uses in describing distant countries which I have never visited transfer me into his world. Through his words I enter into his world, and his world becomes meaningful to me—his world becomes my world, our world.

The Body as Intermediary of the Other's Concealedness. Although the body is intermediary between me and the other, between the other and me, between his world and me, and between my world and him, not everything is said when this mediacy has been expressed. The other as the other is unconcealed from me, but nevertheless he is not totally transparent to me. The other never appears to me in perfectly lucid clarity. This should not be surprising, for not even I myself am transparent to myself. This "not even" indicates a kind of disappointment, a disappointment with the reality which I myself am. This disappointment befalls the phenomenologist when he experiences that Descartes' clear and distinct ideas are artificial constructs which do not occur but are mere abstractions. Who am I and what am I? I am present to myself, unconcealed from myself, I do not escape from myself. But I am also absent, concealed, and escaping from myself. The other also is concealed from me. Who are you and what are you?

The body not only is an intermediary in the encounter with the other, but at the same time also means a possibility for the other to hide from me, to withdraw from me. I too am able to conceal myself. Man is capable of simulation with respect to his fellow man, he can feign, dissemble, and lie. The body again is the intermediary. Nevertheless, it is precisely in this mode of self-concealment that man's unconcealedness before man is affirmed. Self-concealment is possible only on the basis of unconcealedness.

We Exist Together. Descartes' *Cogito*, then, means the negation of a phenomenological evidence which imposes itself irresistibly. I am not consciousness of my consciousness, locked up in myself, isolated from my body, from the world, and from the other. Through *my* body I am in the world, which appears to be our world and, therefore, my existing is an existing-together, a coexistence. The philosophy of "I think" has to be replaced by that of "we exist."

It goes without saying that this "we" shows many forms and contains a multitude of possibilities which still have to be investigated. Nevertheless one point should be clear: the encounter with the other reveals the other to me as "not a thing," but as existence, as a source of sense and meaning. Because the other is not a thing, he is my companion and, therefore, I can speak of "we." A thing does not accompany me.

It is important to emphasize this point, because we could easily become victims of our own terminology. To indicate the reciprocal implication of man and the world, we have made use of the terms "encounter" and "presence." When there is question of the other as the other, these same terms are used again. However, they have now a wholly different meaning, for the other reveals himself precisely as a meaning that differs from the thing. It is to stress this difference of meaning that we use the terms *companion* and *to accompany*. The encounter with the other, his presence, reveals the other to me as "like-me-in-the-world"—a meaning which I never perceive in the encounter with things. Because the other is "like-me-in-the-world," he is my "companion-in-the-world." [22]

The same remarks apply to the term "dialogue." I am a dialogue with the world, because what I am is unthinkable without the world, and because my world is not without me. A dialogue cannot be conceived without both participants. However, the way in which the other takes part in the dialogue when I encounter him differs radically from that in which a worldly thing replies to my questions. The other answers me as another self; he replies to me as I myself reply to his questioning, which is something no thing can do.

Finally, we must draw attention to a certain one-sidedness of our explicitation and compensate for it. Too much emphasis has been given to "I," to "like-me," to "my" companion. Why is the other "my" companion? Am I not "his" companion? Who are the others? Are they perhaps the rest of mankind, from which I set myself apart? By what right would I "first" affirm myself and "next" the others as the mass above which I raise myself? Evidently, the others are precisely those from whom I do *not* set myself apart, but among whom I "also" am. We exist together.

The Manifold Forms of "We." Probably many years will have to pass before positive sociology and social psychology will manage to indicate in a fairly satisfactory way the many forms which this "we" can assume. This should not surprise us if we keep in mind that man can act toward his fellow man in numerous different ways. "We" means a relationship of the "I" to another "I," a "You," and it should be evident that this relationship differs constantly, for instance, when there is question of working together, taking a drink together, travelling together, having an accident together, etc. The "we" experienced in a trade-union differs from that in a military barrack or in a monastery; the "we" of a hospital ward is not the same as that of a boys' camp, a hockey club, a lecture hall audience, or a movie theatre. Examples can be multiplied almost endlessly, so that it will really be very difficult to bring some order in this diversity of forms. [23]

[22] According as we penetrate more profoundly into the possibilities of interhuman relationships, the term "companion" will show a shift of meaning, as is also the case with the terms "encounter" and "presence." For the way in which the other accompanies me can be very diverse. For instance, the other with whom I go through life may love, neglect, or hate me. He is my companion, but this term can have many meanings.

[23] Cf., e.g., M. Nédoncelle, *Vers une philosophie de l'amour*, Paris, 1946, pp. 125–138.

The same situation occurs here with respect to this "we" as we previously met regarding the meanings of my world. My world is an extraordinarily complex system of nearby and remote meanings which are correlated with my more actual or less actual standpoints. Every effort to absolutize a certain standpoint, to consider it as the only or even the only possible standpoint, makes a real concept of my world impossible. Yet the tendency to absolutize a certain viewpoint and a certain meaning, for instance, that of physics and chemistry, is difficult to control. This tendency is an impoverishment of man's being and a constant threat of total blindness for everything which cannot be classified under certain categories, such as those of the physical sciences.

Different Levels of Co-existence.   The realization that absolutizing leads to impoverishment and blindness exhorts us to be very prudent when there is question of recognizing the multiformity of co-existence. It is necessary to see that this multiformity can occur on different levels. Thus, for instance, one may speak of human relations in the family, the school, the factory, the office, in youth organizations, in the armed forces, in medical services, in pastoral care. These relations could be described, and one could try to discover the rules governing the fundamental forms of human interrelationships, as is done, for example, by Josef Pieper.[24] That is the task of the sociologist. It is possible also, on the other hand, to observe, as is done by Rutten,[25] that in the many changes which have occurred in human relationships we "have suffered a loss in true humanity," [26] that we have been deprived of "intimate values which make man rich in a definitely human sense." [27] In that case one is no longer concerned with the actual sociological forms of co-existence, but with the conditions on which human relationships deserve

to be called *human* in the full sense of the term. For these relationships can also be *inhuman.*

Thus it appears that the multiformity of co-existence lies on different levels. We are aware of it that, regardless of the sociological form of co-existence,[28] we always come closer to or retreat from an *ideal* of co-existence which at the same time is an ideal of authentically being human. If in a labor organization, in a factory, all employees are perfectly attuned to one another, so that the purpose of their organization—the product—is perfectly realized, one could perhaps speak of a perfect form of co-existence from the sociological point of view. Nevertheless, it remains possible and even is very probable that these sociologically perfect human relationships are inhuman.[29]

Sociological and Anthropological Forms of Co-existence.   Thus there is good reason for making a distinction between sociological forms of co-existence and those forms which from now on we shall call anthropological. In any sociological form it is possible for man to be authentically man, less man, or inhuman. This thought supposes, of course, that man is not as an ash tray or a cabbage *is,* but that man's being is a "having-to-be" (*zu sein,* Heidegger; *avoir à être,* Sartre).

Just as sociologists search for the basic forms of co-existence from a definite standpoint, so also anthropologists, although their aim is different. In the present chapter we will limit ourselves to these fundamental anthropological forms. We will name them here without making an attempt to justify the classification. They are hatred, indifference, love, and justice.

It is not possible to speak in a true-to-life way about love or justice in general unless

[24] Cf. Josef Pieper, *Grundformen socialer Spielregeln,* Frankfurt a. M., n. d.
[25] Cf. F. J. Th. Rutten, *Menselijke verhoudingen,* Bussum, 1955.
[26] Cf. Rutten, *op. cit.,* p. 11.
[27] Cf. Rutten, *op. cit.,* p. 46.

[28] We do not want to argue here whether or not the term "sociological" is correct. Our intention should be sufficiently clear.
[29] We abstract here from the fact that, where the relationships are *inhuman,* it is usually impossible to speak of a perfect labor organization and a perfect realization of its purpose. This is the reason why even people who want merely to safeguard economic interests are concerned with the *human* character of their labor organization.

one realizes that, to use ethical terminology, they are not concerned with *commandments*, at least not if "commandments" are understood as laws without a foundation in man but imposed upon him from without. Once they are understood in this way, it is no longer possible to make it clear that man *ought* to love and to be just, in the sense in which people always desire to understand this "ought"—namely, as a *demand of our being*, as something *required by being-man*, as an internal "ought" in opposition to all extrinsically imposed command. Love and justice are modes of being-man, insofar as being-man is characterized by *zu sein*, by

avoir à être, by "having-to-be." Hatred and indifference likewise are modes of being-man, but in the sense that they are modes in which man *ought not* to realize himself.

This classification is not a division into four disparate modes. Hatred, indifference, love, and justice do not lie outside one another like marbles, wigs, courts of law, and cloud banks. Here also one should keep in mind that they are modes of being-man, or rather, modes in which one and the same concrete man can and does realize himself. It could even be said that all four are always real in this concrete man, but that the emphasis falls on one of them. . . .

PHENOMENOLOGY OF LOVE, AS ACTIVE LEANING, AS APPEAL-RESPONSE DIALOGUE, AND AS CREATIVE

Encounter

If nothing else was possible than the "we" of indifference, the term "encounter" could not have the genuinely human meaning that is attributed to it. In the genuinely human sense "encounter" is filled with an affection of which there is no trace in the "we" of indifference. Used in this genuinely human sense, the term indicates a kind of participation in the personal existence of the other for whom I care. This is precisely what is missing in the "we" of indifference. If there were only the "we" of indifference, the encounter with human beings would not have much more meaning than the meeting of certain qualities. But there are cases in which it is apparent that more than such a meeting is experienced. . . .

We may speak of such an encounter when a boy leads a blind man across the road, when a total stranger goes out of his way to show me the road, when a soldier deprives himself of something to give comfort to the prisoner whom he leads away. Loving also in the encounter—let us suppose so at least —of the young man who realizes that he is called to go through life together with "this" girl. But, we must ask, what is the proper

character of the loving encounter and what are the conditions in which it develops into love?

Love as Active Leaning

The loving encounter always presupposes the appeal of the other to my subjectivity. A call goes out from him, embodied in a word, a gesture, a glance, a request. His word, gesture, glance, or request mean an invitation to me whose true meaning is difficult to express in words. No matter, however, in what form the appeal of the other is embodied, it always implies an invitation to transcend myself, to break away from my preoccupation with myself and my fascinated interest in myself.

Self-centeredness. The compulsive way in which I am centered upon myself and mine makes it clear why I have such difficulty in understanding the true appeal of the other to me. For, to *see* a certain reality, I need more than eyes. To understand the meaning of the other's appeal to me I need a certain attitude, and this attitude implies that I have broken away to some extent from my preoccupation with myself. One who is full of pride or cupidity sees nothing. For the appeal of the other has nothing violent about it, it is not brutal, not bent on conquest, it does not jolt me, and deliberately leaves open the possibility of refusal. It does not present itself as a demand, for it is too humble to demand anything. For this reason it is possible that I will not understand this appeal. If I am fully occupied with myself, if I am absorbed in my occupations, obsessed by my thoughts and desires, I will not understand the other's appeal. If I am fully absorbed in myself, I know *a priori* that I am excused, no matter what the request may be, even though I may not explicitly realize that I have this conviction. Excused from everything, I am insensible to every appeal.

In daily life I am accustomed to playing a role. I am a physician, a middle class citizen, a teacher, a priest, an intellectual, or a laborer. As a judge I face the delinquent, as a teacher the student, as a physician the sick, as a priest the sinner. But who are they —those delinquents, students, sick, and sinners? They are those who address an appeal to me. Yet I will not understand their appeal if I identify myself with the role I have to play. Such an identification would mean a pre-occupation with myself which closes me to any appeal of the other to me.

What the Other's Appeal Is Not. Is it possible to make the appeal in question more clearly explicit? Perhaps it will be easier to begin by indicating how the appeal should not be understood. It may not be conceived as the other's attractiveness because of any of his corporeal or spiritual qualities. Such attractive qualities could perhaps invite me and draw me to a "being-with-the-other"—but can we speak of love here? Would love be impossible if the other's qualities are not attractive? Would love have to cease when the other's qualities cease to be attractive? At most, qualities may give rise to a kind of enamoredness, in which the desire to be "with" the other is inherent— but is love not rather the firm will to be "for" the other? As long as only the other's qual-

ities speak either positively or negatively to me, my reply will only be a reply to a "he" or a "she." If, however, one really loves, he is aware of it that the qualities or merits of the other are of little importance; they fall into the background to make room for what the other is over and above a certain facticity, over and above an inventory file card.

Likewise, the other's appeal to me may not be understood as being identical with any explicit request. A request could be explicitated as the expression and presentation of a *de facto* situation for which provisions have to be made. But this *is* not the other's appeal, as may be evident from the fact that, even when I satisfy the other's request materially, he may still go away "dissatisfied." He departs "dissatisfied," because he realizes that my heart was not in it when I did or gave what he wanted, that I spoke to him or received him only in a casual way, that he disturbed me, that "he was too much bother for me," that I was absent-minded and distracted. I satisfied his request and, nevertheless, he is "dissatisfied." Why? Because his appeal to me is more than his explicitly formulated request. The other does not merely *make* a request, he "is" also an appeal.

"Be with Me." Accordingly, understanding the other's appeal to me ties in not with his facticity but rather with what the other is over and above his facticity—namely, a subjectivity. His subjectivity itself is the appeal that is addressed to me. It is a plea that I participate in his subjectivity. Marcel endeavors to express this plea in words: "Be with me." It is the call of the other to go out beyond the confines of myself, to support, strengthen and, as it were, increase his subjectivity by participating in it.

Break with Self-centeredness. If the other's call, "Be with me," is to be understood by me, it is necessary that I shall have already somewhat broken away from and conquered my fascination with myself. On the other hand, however, it is precisely the appeal of the other which makes it possible for me to liberate myself from myself. The other's appeal reveals to me an entirely new, perhaps wholly unsuspected dimension of my existence. Who am I? Am I not more than the sum total of my objective qualities? Am I not more than a file card full of predicates? Am I not more than the role I play? Certainly, my being-human is richer. I am not identical with my facticity, I am a subjectivity, called to give again and again meaning to my facticity in free self-realization. I am not a thing in the-world, but I am a project-in-the-world, called to realize myself in the world and to make the world a human world.

The awareness of this calling, however, is merely a *provisional insight*. For the encounter with the other, his appeal to me, reveals an entirely new dimension of my subjectivity. I am called to realize myself in the world, but *for you*. The encounter with you reveals to me my destiny as destiny-for-you. Through you I understand the meaninglessness of my egoism and self-centeredness, which would fatally tempt me to lock myself up in myself and in my world. Yielding to this temptation would mean that I would miss my destiny.

Affection as Reply to the Other's Appeal. The other's appeal and my awareness of my destiny require that I reply. I realize, however, that the reply must be adapted to the call, "Be with me." A piece of information, a crust of bread, or a bit of money are not the answer that is requested of me. On the contrary, I am aware that they may be means to buy off the proper answer which I owe the other. "Be with me" is his request. It is a call upon my being, an appeal to be together. "Be satisfied if I give you what I have," I could reply. But such a reply would be the meaning possessed by tending the other a crust of bread or a coin. It would mean that I lock myself up again in myself, in my world, and hope that the other will never again disturb me. I remain alone, and the other stays "far away."

When the other's appeal does not originate from his facticity, the proper answer to his appeal is not primarily connected with any determined facticity. It is for this reason that the true meaning of my being-destined-for-the-other is so difficult to define. The appeal *is* not an explicit request, and the reply *is* not the material satisfaction of a desire. Sometimes even the refusal to satisfy a certain request may be the only way of really loving the other. The reply to the other's appeal is a reply to his subjectivity. As an embodied subject, the other is a source of meaning and of new meaning, and he gives unceasingly in his freedom meaning and new meaning to his facticity. As a subject, as another I, as a "selfhood," he freely goes through the world, he makes his history, he goes to meet his destiny. His appeal to me means an invitation to will his subjectivity, to offer him the possibility to exist, to consent to his freedom, to accept, support and share in it. My affirmative reply to his appeal is known as *"affection."*

Implications of My Reply to His Appeal. As it is used in the preceding context, there is little danger that the term "affection" will be misunderstood. In the ordinary usage of language, however, from which it has been borrowed, there is a certain ambiguity. It very often means a kind of sentimental indulgence which has nothing to do with love. The truth of this assertion should be immediately evident from the preceding considerations and from the nature of indulgence. Indulgence means a kind of openness to and compliance with the arbitrariness that can be implied in the other's explicit or implicit desires. But it is not at all certain that my openness to this arbitrariness really means an active participation in the other's subjectivity. Love wants the other's subjectivity, his free self-realization, but this implies that love refuse, precisely because it is love, whatever could impede or destroy the other's possibility of self-realization.

This thought has still another implication. The loving leaning to the other does not only refuse to show itself open to the other's arbitrariness, but also contains always, in the background, at least an implicit awareness of the destiny proper to the other's subjectivity. As a source of meaning and direction, the other's subjectivity means a searching for, and partial finding of his way in the world, and to the extent that he finds his way, he realizes himself, i.e., goes forward toward his destiny. The other's subjectivity is not an isolated *Cogito,* separated from his body and from his world. The other exists; he is bodily in the world; as an embodied I-in-the-world he accomplishes his being-human. I am called to love him as such and not as anything else.

This call implies that I will his bodily being and that I will his world for him. Otherwise my love would be an illusion. The man who loves his fellow man cares for his body, is concerned with what he needs for his material life, builds hospitals, constructs roads, harnesses rivers and seas, establishes traffic rules, builds schools and prisons—all to make it possible for the other to attain to *self*-realization in the world. Bodily being and the world are the facticity which for the other constitutes the starting point from which he sets forth to freely realize his possibilities and those of his world. It is in the world that he gives meaning and direction to his existence, that he goes forward to his destiny. But what is this destiny? It is not possible that I have no opinion about it. Even the conviction that the other has no destiny is a mode of thinking about his destiny.

Love and Happiness. This destiny may be called in a most general way "happiness." We abstract here from what exactly happiness is and from that in which it consists. Perhaps it is absolute freedom, perhaps material possessions, perhaps knowledge, virtue, or the possession of God. Whatever opinion I hold regarding happiness, it should be evident that my idea of it will exercise influence on, and give an orientation to my affection for the other. Through my affection I will his subjectivity, but this subjectivity is a searching for his way in the world onward to his destiny. My affection, therefore, will open certain worldly roads to him, but also close others—namely, those which would not bring

him closer to his destiny.[30] There are, for instance, subjects who long for the day when they will be able to make the entire world one huge concentration camp. Others would like to poison youth or kill off the incurably sick and the insane. Effective love of our fellow man owes it to itself to oppose such desires wherever it is possible.

This duty incumbent on love is the reason why true love, i.e., love which is effective and takes action and which is not conceived as a sentimental feeling, is so often misunderstood. Conceived as a sentimental feeling, as being fascinated by the other's qualities, love will show itself as an illusion, as being nothing of true love. But if love is effectively ready to open certain worldly roads to happiness and to close others, it is often interpreted as an attempt to dominate the other, as a means to overcome him and hold him in subjection. Of course, it cannot be denied that sometimes a man will tend to control his fellow man in this fashion. I can try to control the other completely, but it would mean that I reduce him to a thing and destroy his subjectivity, the project of the world which he is. In such a case there can be no question of love.[31] The effectiveness of love, however, has nothing to do with domineering or tyrannizing the other. In this connection it may be pointed out that love is modest and reserved, i.e., has an immense respect for the other's subjectivity. This respect is so essential that its absence would destroy love.[32]

Disinterestedness of Love. Is love, then,

[30] This is expressed in the classical definition of love as "to will good for someone else."
[31] It happens sometimes that parents attempt to control their children completely to make them play the "role" which they themselves have chosen for them. For instance, quite a few boys and girls have to remember all the time that they are the "parson's son," the "bank-director's daughter," or "better-class children."
[32] Heidegger also speaks about respect for the other's subjectivity and freedom. Being authentically human, as conceived by Heidegger, lets the other be what he is. For Heidegger, however, it does not include participation in the other's subjectivity, but rather the abstention from this participation because the other is destined for death anyhow. Cf. *Sein und Zeit,* p. 264.

concerned only with the other? It would be going too far to reply in the affirmative, for in love I am concerned also with myself. However, this could easily be misunderstood. We are still speaking here of love as an active leaning to the other, and not about the legitimate desire to *be loved* by the other. Insofar as my own subjectivity is an appeal to the other's being, a call to participate in my subjectivity, love is concerned with myself. This, however, is not the point. What is to be considered here is that even in love as the active leaning to the other I am to a certain extent concerned with myself. But, the point is, in what sense?

Since love wants the other's freedom, it is in a way defenseless. It places a limitless trust in the other and thus delivers itself to him. This trust implies an appeal of the lover to the beloved. The trust which love shows, the defenselessness which it displays, themselves are a call upon the love of the beloved. Love is not wholly concerned only with the other.

Once more, it is easier to state what this appeal of love to the beloved is *not* than to explicitate its meaning immediately in a positive way. The appeal of love to the beloved is not the will to draw in some way advantage from the affection for the other. It is impossible for the lover to aim at his own promotion or career and at the same time to keep his love pure. A sick person who would discover that the nurse caring for him in such a "loving" way does so exclusively in order to become head-nurse as soon as possible or to receive an eternal reward in heaven does not think that he is really loved.

Likewise, the appeal of love to the beloved does not mean that the lover wants to compel, dominate, or possess the other. Love wants the other's freedom. It does not suffice for love that the other *de facto* takes a certain way through the world, not even if this way is a good and safe way from the viewpoint of the destiny of human freedom. What love wants is that the other *himself* choose *this* safe way and avoid *that* dangerous path.

Self-realization and Love.   Sincerely being

at the other's disposal, therefore, implies that I renounce the temptation to promote myself in loving the other and the possibility of dominating the other. However, love contains still another aspect of self-denial, which is more difficult to seize. In love I destine myself for the other, but I vaguely realize that I also go forward to my own destiny. Even if I have never heard of any doctrine regarding man's destiny, I experience that in love I am on the road to the achievement of my manhood. Man's being is paradoxical in more than one way. As we pointed out previously, man is a subject, a being who exists for himself, a presence to himself, a self-controlling being. Man is an I, a selfhood. But he is a selfhood only in being fused with the non-I. Man is the paradox of immanence and transcendence (Dondeyne). This paradoxical aspect of man is put even in sharper relief by love. Love is the ready availability of my subjectivity, its belonging to the subject which the other is. But in giving and surrendering myself, it is revealed to me what my selfhood really is. My real self is the available self. Is, then, the appeal of love to the other perhaps the request to offer me the possibility of achieving my own manhood?

We are touching here the eternal question whether or not a fully disinterested love is possible. Is it possible for man to will something without willing it for his own sake? This question is especially important with respect to love, because *at the least* love wants the other's benefit.

We are of the opinion that it is impossible for man to love his fellow man in such a way that his love will not *de facto* be for the benefit of the lover himself. It is not possible for man to forego the fact that love, as active leaning to the other, is equally immediately the achievement of his own being, conceived as *zu sein*. This, however, does not mean that the achievement of one's own manhood is what love aims at, that this achievement is the motive why man loves. The opposite is true. In love man goes forward to his destiny, he finds the fulfilment of his manhood, on condition that this fulfilment be *not* the motive of his love. If the other were to thank me for my affection, and I would wave these thanks aside by saying that what I was interested in was the achievement of my own manhood, the other would immediately conclude that he was not really loved. For, ultimately, I would have been aiming at my own "career."

Love as the Appeal to the Other's Freedom. The appeal of love to the beloved can be correctly understood only when one sees that willing the subjectivity, the freedom, of the other cannot be fruitful unless the other ratifies this will through his consent. Love does not want to compel; it cannot even compel without ceasing to be love. For this reason love is in a sense helplessly surrendered to the other. Love wants the other's freedom and, therefore, becomes fruitful only through the free consent of the other. But the lover *cannot will* that his love be not understood, not accepted, and without fruit. Hence it appeals to the beloved, and this appeal we may explicitate as the request: "Accept that I be at your disposal." Even when love is obliged to close certain roads through the world for the beloved, it cannot want otherwise than that the beloved *himself* avoid these roads. It is not sufficient for love to make it materially impossible for the other to enter certain roads. This insufficiency is contained in its refusal to compel the beloved. The appeal of love to the beloved, then, means the request that the beloved *himself* see that *this* road and *not that* one will lead his subjectivity to its destiny. The request, "Accept that I be at your disposal," means, "See for yourself and realize your own happiness in freedom." The only fruit which love may hope for is that the other exist.[33]

The Creativity of Love

The "You." All the lines which gradually become visible in the explicitation of love converge on one point—the "you." It is always the "you" which is at stake in love and, when the "you" is not the point at issue, love loses its authenticity or is even fully destroyed. Thus love becomes possible only when I am sensitive to the other's subjectivity and no longer consider the other as the sum total of qualities, not even of very noble and perfect qualities. Thus what love wants is the other's subjectivity, and not my own promotion, career, or perfection, and still less my domination of the other. All this may be pithily expressed by saying that the motive of my love is "you." I love you, because you are you, because you are who you are. I love you, because you are lovable, but you are lovable because you are you.

The Meaning of You in Love. This "you" does not have the neutral meaning of "another self," of a "subjectivity like my subjectivity," which is disclosed to me in each and every encounter with a human being. *A fortiori* it is not the hateful subjectivity of the other who, as Sartre thinks, wants to murder me. Finally, it is not the "you" of indifference, for which above we have reserved the term "he."

The "you" of which there is question here is a "you-for-whom-I-care." This expression, however, says almost nothing unless the reality it represents is vividly in my mind. The meaning of this "you" is given to me in experience, taken in the broad sense, it is accessible to me as presence on condition that I love the other. Accordingly, there is no possibility at all that this "you" would ever be discovered by experience, in the sense of the physical sciences, just as it is like-

[33] One may ask whether love implies *per se* reciprocity. Insofar as my love is fruitful only through the other's "yes," the question has to be answered in the affirmative. If I love the other, I cannot will that he does not accept my ready availability. In this sense, then, it is true that in love "not everything turns around the other." "Liebe, in der sich 'alles nur um Dich dreht', is ebensowenig sich-selbst mehrend und zehrt sich ebenso an ihrem eigenen Feuer auf, wie Lieben in der sich 'alles

um Mich dreht'." L. Binswanger, *Grundformen und Erkenntnis menschlichen Daseins*, Zurich, 1953, p. 121. That "not everything turns around the other," however, really means for Binswanger that love is not love unless I am loved with the same intense love with which I myself love. It seems to us that this thesis, which Binswanger presupposes from the very first page of his book, is very debatable.

wise impossible that one would be able to account by means of scientific experience for the difference between a dead man and a murdered man. As far as the experience of the physical sciences is concerned, only that is real which can be expressed in terms of quantity. With respect to the "you," nothing can be understood in terms of quantity— just as in the case of a murdered man as murdered. To express it in phenomenological language, the viewpoint of the subject co-constitutes the objective meaning which reveals itself present in experience. Knowledge is the encounter of a subject with an object, a dialogue in which both take part and in which the questioned reality is oriented in its replies by the questions of the questioning subject.

The experience of the physical sciences, because of its own particular attitude, reveals to me nothing of the "you-for-whom-I-care." Likewise, the reality of this you is not disclosed by an objectivistic psychology which holds fast to the enumeration of psychical qualities or the description of the other's character, temperament, aptitude, inclinations, deviations, etc. An objectivistic psychology discovers the other's subjectivity as "a filled-out questionnaire," as a "he." Of course, we do not want to claim that love is capable only of a subjectivistic judgment of the other and, therefore, unable to observe that the other is stupid, rude, and immature. The very opposite is true. Love, however, refuses to reduce the other to a series of predicates, and it is precisely love which makes the lover clear-sighted for what the other is over and above his qualities.

The statement that the "you" of love is a "you-for-whom-I-care" merely establishes a fact. However, after all the preceding considerations it may be possible to realize to a certain extent the implications of this fact and at the same time perhaps to find a way to penetrate more profoundly into the true nature of love, considered as the active leaning to the other.[34] Most of the emphasis

---

[34] The reader may have noticed that, to prevent misunderstanding, we have intentionally and systematically excluded the phenomenological data of reciprocal love from our analysis.

will have to fall upon the "active" character of the leaning. We would like to conceive this "active" character as creativity.

Making the Other Be.   As we pointed out previously, the truth of every judgment is founded on a more profound truth—namely, the *aletheia*, the unconcealedness of reality for the knowing subject. This unconcealedness, however, presupposes the unveiling activity of the subject, by virtue of which reality is reality in the full sense of the term, viz., appearing reality. Knowledge, therefore, always is an encounter in which the subject "lets" reality be, respects and accepts its character as reality. This "letting-be" of reality by knowledge is not purely active but also passive, for it implies respect for, and acceptance of what reality is. Only when reality is respected and accepted, will knowledge be objective. Objective knowledge lets reality be-for-man, makes reality itself appear. The spontaneity or activity of the knowing subject, accordingly, is very limited precisely because of the sensitivity or passivity implied by knowing. Knowledge of reality cannot be called creativity.

The active aspect, implied by the existing subject which is not purely knowing but acting, distinguishes itself clearly from the active aspect found in knowledge. To do carpentry work is more than being sensitive and open to reality. The same applies to artistic labor. It is meaningful to call such activity of the subject "creative," although this term is used here in a less strict sense. In carpentry work and in artistic labor I do not merely "let" reality be, but I also "make" it be. I create a *new* meaning. By way of analogy with this "making-be" we would like to call the loving encounter, as active leaning to the other, "creative," although the creativity of love differs from that of the above-described actions. In and through love I "make" the other be.

Encounter and Making the Other Be.   If one realizes that not only the loving encounter, but any encounter with the other "makes" the other be, a first step will have been made toward the understanding of the preceding view of love. The loving encounter is only a special way of "making" the other be. Every encounter does the same, but in a way which is determined by the nature of the encounter in question. Examples should make this evident. They show that I "make" the other be and that he "makes" me be. This reciprocity offers no difficulty, because every encounter is reciprocal.

Let us take as a first example an encounter between two school-boys which ends in a fight. At first, John and Pete are quite friendly. They romp a bit and try to surpass each other in little tricks. John's every little trick calls for a counter-trick from Pete, which John in his turn tries to parry. At a given moment one of John's blows is unexpectedly hard. Pete thinks that it was intentional and protests. John vigorously defends himself against this accusation, but Pete feels insulted by his tone and assumes a threatening pose. John thinks that he is already under attack. The first brutal blow falls and, before either of them realizes what the situation is, the friendly encounter has degenerated into a fight.

On several occasions we have called the encounter a dialogue, in the broadest sense of the term. Two partners participate in a dialogue, two conscious beings contribute their part. But at the end of the dialogue it is no longer possible to determine what came from one and what from the other.[35] John and Peter are first "rompers," then "quarrelers," and finally "fighters." But they are these things "through" each other. They "make" each other be, as romping, as quarreling, and as fighting.

I Am Not "Alone" in My Mode of Being. As the preceding example suggests, man rarely if ever realizes that he makes the other be and that the other makes him be. Nevertheless, it is simply impossible to think of a mode of being or of behavior in which I am fully "alone," in which the other and the encounter with the other do not count.

If I want to think of myself as a reality, I will have to include the other, for he has contributed and still contributes to the reality which I am. I have to think of my own reality as come forth from the other, as nourished and educated by the other, as speaking the language of the other. And if I do not do this, I think of myself as a phantom, a demi-god, or the hero of a fanciful tale, but not as reality. I am a New Yorker through New Yorkers, an American through Americans, a philosopher through philosophers, a Christian through Christians, a smoker through smokers, etc. A mother is really a mother through her child, a sick person is genuinely sick only when he has visitors,[36] a German is a real German only when he is with other Germans, an outcast is a real outcast only when the others hate him. An asocial family is completely asocial only when society abandons or excludes it, a cute little button-nose is a cute little button-nose only when others notice it,[37] baldhead is a real baldhead only when he is called so by others, a Jew is really a Jew only when there are anti-Semites, and a youth is a real youth only through a girl.[38]

An Objection. We realize that these examples should be formulated with considerably more differentiation, for otherwise they are open to all kinds of objections. However, to avoid making this section too long, we have to risk this simplification. On the other hand, objections to the examples could easily show that they are misunderstood. It could easily happen that they miss the point. For instance, one could say that a Jew is a Jew even when there are no anti-Semites, that a sick man is sick even when he is not visited, and that a baldhead is a baldhead even if he is not called by that name.

The objector, however, would be mistaken. He presupposes that being a Jew is purely a biological matter, that a sick man is sick

[35] Cf. Kwant, "Het begrip 'ontmoeting' in de phanomenologische Wijsbegeerte," *Gawein,* vol. IV (1955), pp. 9–20.

[36] Cf. J. H. van den Berg, *Psychologie van het ziekbed.* Nijkerk, 1954, p. 14.
[37] Cf. F. J. J. Buytendijk, *Ontmoeting der sexen,* Utrecht-Antwerpen, 1952, p. 7.
[38] Cf. E. de Greeff, *Notre Destinée et nos Instincts,* Paris, 1945, pp. 157–158.

just as a cabbage is spoiled, and that a baldhead is bald just as a billiard ball is smooth. This assumption does not take into consideration the human aspect of being a Jew, being ill, or being bald. A baldhead is not bald just as a billiard ball is smooth, because a baldhead as a subject is related to his bald pate, has awareness of it, takes a standpoint with respect to it, and can make use of it. The being of man is a *human* being, because of his relatedness to being,[39] which is an understanding of being.[40] Man is the being who in his being is concerned with this being itself. Applied to the example, this means that the reality of a bald head is distinct from the smoothness of a billiard ball because the baldhead is a subjectivity who gives meaning to the facticity in question. But the sense he gives to it depends to a large extent upon the way others treat him. A baldhead is really a baldhead only when the others call him so.

When we disregard the inaccuracies in the formulation of the examples, the essential elements will reveal themselves at once. In the encounter I am the bearer of a being-for-the-other, which is at the same time a being-through-the-other. Once again, Sartre's analysis of the hateful stare could serve as a splendid illustration, because it shows how the violence of hatred can be wholly destructive of the other's subjectivity. However, our present aim is to penetrate more profoundly into the creative force of love, to discover the specific nature of love's power to make-the-other-be.

Accordingly, we ascribe a kind of "influence" to love. Let us point out at once that we are not thinking here of influence in a causalistic sense. There can be no question of reducing the active reality of love to the efficacy of a unilateral, determining "cause" in the scientific sense of the term. The reason is that such a set of concepts would not make it possible for us to realize what love is in its genuine form. Such concepts do not express the reality of love as it is ac-

cessible in "lived experience" to reflecting consciousness. There is more in love than the concepts of physical causality are capable of expressing. This should be evident at once if the essential aspects of love are called to mind. Appeal, destiny, being-at-the-other's disposal, self-denial, and acceptance indicate a reality which includes consciousness, reciprocity, and freedom. They are precisely the denial of a unilateral, determining, causalistic influence and therefore cannot be "explained" by it.

Analysis of Being-loved.   Perhaps there is no better way to arrive at some understanding of love's creativity than the phenomenological analysis of being-loved. What is the meaning of love, understood as the active leaning of the other toward me? What does the other "make" me be when he loves me?

As was pointed out, every encounter with the other "makes" me be. Love, however, "makes" me be in a way which no other encounter realizes. Through the encounter with New Yorkers I am a New Yorker, through the encounter with smokers I am a smoker, through that with philosophers I am a philosopher, etc. These modes of encounter result in a certain facticity or determination, which in the course of the encounter, as it were, adheres to me and makes me "determinable." A kind of sedimentation takes place through which ultimately all kinds of predicates expressing my factual being can be predicated of me. Social psychology investigates this matter. However, I am not identical with my facticity; I am a subjectivity, and for this subjectivity my factual being is the starting point for the realization of possibilities which are contained in my facticity. I am freedom. Now it is the loving encounter, love as the other's active leaning which makes me free, "makes" my subjectivity be, and enables me to realize myself.

Of course, we do not mean that without the other's love I would not be a subjectivity. But being a subjectivity can have all kinds of meanings. It may point to the fact that I am not a thing, even when my freedom is strangled or crushed by any force whatso-

39 Cf. Heidegger, *Sein und Zeit.* p. 12.
40 Cf. Heidegger, *op. cit.*, p. 14.

ever. It may indicate also a lived fullness of manhood, by which every obstacle is changed into a value, and man affirms himself as the king of creation. The term "subjectivity" can cover an entire gamut of meanings, and this should be kept in mind if we are to understand the creativity of love.

The other's loving leaning toward me "makes" my subjectivity be, insofar as the other by means of his affection participates mysteriously in my subjectivity, aids and favors it, so that I no longer plan my manhood and go forward to my destiny "alone" but "together" with the other. The other's love gives me to myself if this being-myself is understood as a kind of fullness of being.[41] The reality of this creativity is uncontrovertably experienced by anyone who receives genuine love. But it reveals itself most strikingly in the pedagogical situation if this situation is as it ought to be. By means of the educator's love the educated child or adult is, as it were, raised above himself; through the "power" of the educator's love obstacles lose their invincibility and the educated child or adult becomes "master of the situation," capable of self-realization on a level which he would never have reached if he had been left "alone." [42]

Creativity of Love.   The awareness of no longer being "alone" is perhaps the most eloquent witness of love's creativity. Love creates a "we," a "together" which is experienced as wholly different from the "we" of any other encounter whatsoever. The "we" of love can be expressed only—if it can be expressed at all—in terms of "fullness," "fulfillment," and "happiness." The other's love "makes" me be authentically human, "makes" me be happy.

My world, likewise, is "re-created" by the other's love,[43] for this world is a correlate of my self-realizing subjectivity. Through his love the other participates in my subjectivity and, therefore, also in my world. By means of his affection he wants me to have my world, so that the world shows itself to me in its mildest way and becomes accessible to me without offering resistance.[44] Through the other's love my world becomes my *Heimat*, my country; through it I feel at home in my world, and love it.[45] Children whose parents are unfeeling psychopaths are destined to come in touch only with the harshest meanings of the world. For them the world is pure resistance, and from their earliest youth inspires them to protest and hostility.[46] Without love the world is hell for man.[47]

At the same time it becomes crystal clear that the creative influence of love may not be conceived in a causalistic way. For the creative affection of the lover remains without results until the beloved accepts this affection. The "yes" of the beloved ratifies the affection and makes it fruitful. Whoever loves the other, wants his subjectivity, his freedom, his transcendence. Therefore, he cannot will but that the other *freely* consent to the love offered to him, for this love is precisely the willing of the beloved's *freedom*. Once again, the pedagogical situation is particularly illustrative of this point. The educator is fully aware of the fact that his love is not understood if the one who is being educated simply does what he tells him because the educator is in a controlling position. His love is fruitful only when the other "chooses" in favor of his education. Accordingly, the "influence" of love is not "causal," but it is a mysterious exchange from subject to subject.

There is only one word to express what love is—grace.[48] I can only say "yes" to it.

---

[41] "Who cannot say to his friend or beloved: 'You have given yourself to me, I have received my soul from your hands.' " Gustave Thibon.

[42] This idea is the starting point of Carl Rogers' "client centered therapy." Cf. J. Nuttin, *Psychoanalyse en spiritualistische opvatting van de mens*, Utrecht-Antwerpen, 1952, pp. 111–127.

[43] Max Picard, *Die unerschütterliche Ehe*, Erlenbach-Zürich, 1942, pp. 13–25.

[44] "Nil homini amicum sine homine amico." St. Augustine.

[45] "Seit ich in Deiner Liebe ein Ruhen und Bleiben habe, ist mir die Welt so klar und so lieb." Goethe.

[46] See Bunuel's film "Los Olvidados."

[47] "Pas besoin de gril, l'enfer c'est les Autres." Sartre.

[48] "Je demeure convaincu que c'est seulement par rapport à la grâce que la liberté humaine peut être définie en profondeur." Marcel, *L'homme problématique*, Paris, 1955, p. 71.

Or, is perhaps even something of this "yes" also given to me?

Love's Clear-sightedness. In concluding this section, let us return briefly to its starting point—namely, the clear-sightedness of love. The "you-for-whom-I-care," as present to me, is accessible to me, on condition that I love the other. Neither the physical sciences nor positivistic psychology or sociology are capable of "observing" this "you." Only love "sees," and what I see is no longer disputable. The indisputably real character of this "you" is at least to some extent intelligible now that we have become aware of love's creativity. For through love I "create" that which I see. I "make" the other "be" what I see. Therefore, there is no possibility that one who does not love will see what I see. At the same time I remain in-

different to his denial of what I see, for I know that he is denying something else than what I see. Hence I will not even try to prove that I am not mistaken, for, as Husserl says, "it is impossible to come to an understanding with one who does not want or is unable to see."

Bibliography

Texts

Existential Phenomenology. Pittsburgh: Duquesne University Press, 1960, rev. ed., 1969.

Phenomenology and Atheism. Pittsburgh: Duquesne University Press, 1965.

Phenomenology and Metaphysics. Pittsburgh: Duquesne University Press, 1965.

Phenomenology of Natural Law. Pittsburgh: Duquesne University Press, 1967.

32

Introduction

Maurice Nédoncelle was born at Roubaix in France in 1905. He entered the seminary and studied for the priesthood, attending St. Sulpice in Paris and working on his *license* in philosophy at the Sorbonne. After ordination and while teaching at various schools he continued working toward his doctorate in philosophy and received his Doctorat-ès-lettres from the Sorbonne in 1943. His dissertation was *La réciprocité des consciences* ("The Reciprocity of Consciousnesses," or "of Centers of Consciousness," as the translator of our selection renders it). This still untranslated work, subtitled "An Essay on the Nature of the Person," established him as one of the foremost living personalists in Europe. More recent than Max Scheler, Martin Buber, and Gabriel Marcel, personalists of the first order on whom he drew generously and gratefully and without whom his very carefully reasoned work could never have been written, Nédoncelle joined the ranks of French reflexive philosophy of the person, associated with the names of Gabriel Madinier (*Conscience et amour: Essai sur le Nous*) and Jean Lacroix (*Personne et amour*), to name only a couple. Thus he entered the speculative tradition rather than become a personalist of the sociopolitical orientation, Emmanuel Mounier being the best-known French exponent.

Nédoncelle's second major philosophical work, *La personne humaine et la nature* (first published in 1943 and then redone with an important preface in 1963 as *Personne humaine et nature*), was both a sequel to or continuation of his first work and a separate publication of a part left

out of that first work. The two taken together form his major statement on the "collegial" or interpersonal nature of man, on man as fully coming to himself only in the enactment of the We of community.

In 1945 Nédoncelle became professor of theology at the University of Strasbourg (he also has a doctorate in theology). From 1956 to 1965 he was dean of the faculty (i.e., department) of Catholic theology at the university, where he is still a professor.

In 1957 he published *Vers une philosophie de l'amour et de la personne*, the work translated as *Love and the Person* and from which our selections are taken. In them we note several important themes relevant to an understanding of man's personization, that is, his becoming a person. For Nédoncelle, the purpose of love is personization: in loving one becomes a person. It is an act that wills not only the existence of the other but his or her full becoming. The other is not created as a person but is met as a potentiality to be actualized. To will that this potential person become actual is to love that other for the other's own good. In the other's act of becoming a person is implied his own will to promotion, so that through that other my desire to be loved can be met, and thus a reciprocity or mutuality of acts of consciousness and of acts of will enact a communion of I and Thou into We. Communion is enacted when two persons who say Thou *to* one another begin to say We *with* one another. And communion becomes community when the *actus* of communion becomes the *habitus* of communion, that is, when fidelity extends into the space and time of community the here and now of communion.

LOVE AND THE PERSON *

To know the strange diversity of human relations one has only to watch briefly the passersby on a busy street. One person avoids men and remains a stranger to his fellows. Another challenges them and delights in the strategies of competition and conflict. Still another loves them and advances eagerly to an encounter with friends. . . .

Each time a person consciously relates to another, a complete system is formed, having its own end and means. It is like a world within the world, a sphere of countless attitudes that, for all its originality, can communicate with other conscious spheres. In the presence of others we pass at each moment from one of these worlds to another; we create or repeat a variation of relationship that immediately rearranges the whole chain of our personal associations. Every glance has the power to transform our outlook; with each new encounter the network of interdependent minds, cast together in the adventure of existence, is unraveled and woven together again into a new design. We shape our own destinies in the progressive, radiating moments of time; we change ourselves with our changing social vision; and society itself changes in the play of interpersonal glances.

Let us examine love, one of these spheres of personal encounter. We soon discover that it contains a thousand kingdoms that at first overwhelm us by their variety and number. Here is a couple walking arm in arm in ecstasy; this, certainly, is the way of lovers and, presumably, a loving state of soul. But here is a mother cradling her child and this, too, is love. And there is a youth leading his little brother by the hand, ready to defend him from a bully's brutality; and this, too, is love. The handclasp I exchange with my friend, the coin I drop in the blind man's cup, the bittersweet generosity of

* From Maurice Nédoncelle, *Love and the Person.* Sheed & Ward, Inc., New York, 1966. Translated by Ruth Adelaide. Reprinted by permission of the publisher.

hidden self-sacrifice . . . what a multitude of forms love takes! Protective strength and timid sensitivity, the frank exchange of a common gift, the tears that beg pardon and the ones that forgive, the visit to the sick man, Hermione's wrath and Abraham's poised blade—one thing only is common to them all: the love that evoked them.

Because the philosopher must first determine the psychologic essence of love, we shall begin by trying to isolate that unique element that is at once diffused and hidden in the species and occasionally bestirs itself to produce strange and agonizing metamorphoses. What is the nature of the love at the heart of all loves?

The Essence of Love
A Will to Promotion

Among all the concepts attached to a given word we should choose the most authentic one, the one that can help us understand even the anomalies, twists and distortions to which the word is liable. Now, the concept that satisfies these requirements and that should enter into the definition we are looking for is the following: love is a will to promotion. The *I* that loves is willing above all the existence of the *thou;* it subsequently wills the autonomous development of the *thou;* and finally wills that this autonomous development be, if possible, in harmony with the value the *I* anticipates for the *thou.* Any other desire would be either a timid hesitation on the threshold of the temple or egoistic delight in a mirrored reflection. There is no love properly so-called unless there are two, and unless the *I* undertakes to go out to the *thou* in order to regard him in the truest possible sense, not as an object of curiosity, but as an interior existence having perfect subjectivity.

Max Scheler defined love in a way that coincides partly with our proposal but ultimately differs from it. According to him, love is an intentional movement causing a superior value to appear in a concrete being. It is never motivated by the knowledge of a value that that being may have already acquired in its empiric existence. Thus one can love a criminal as well as a saint: in both cases the lover rises toward an excellence inherent in the one of whom he is enamored; and this excellence subsists in the realm of value no matter what may have been the conduct of the loved one up to this time. But what is the object of love? It may be three-fold: I can become attached to the vital being of the other, and the highest value I see in him——the exaltation of sexuality for example——becomes the nobility of his being. I can place myself on a higher level and love the psychic reality of the other; this new orientation will lead me to values of culture and truth. Finally, at the highest level, it is his spiritual nature that enthralls me, and the value I then perceive is the very person of the other. Only personal love is moral; here the good is not extrinsic to the *thou*, it is the *thou* itself.[1]

There is much to be retained from this analysis. But Scheler adds certain refinements to his thesis that make it very debatable. In love, as he sees it, there is never anything to be accomplished. "What," he asks, "can a mother really will as she lovingly contemplates her sleeping child?" Certainly, the active, educative attitude may be a consequence of love, but it would not be essential to love itself. It is, in effect, impossible for Scheler to insert the will into love, for according to him, the will is purely executive in character; it is devoid of any intentionality or direction of its own.

[1] We should remember that for Scheler the person is ruthlessly separated from psychic self-awareness. It is a supra-conscious center of heterogeneous intentional acts (for example, sentiments and representations). It follows that certain social realities—nations for instance—can be persons. I would have numerous reserves to make about this divorce and this corollary. Of course the person does not seem to me to be identical with what is ordinarily called psychic awareness, but it does involve a certain kind of awareness: the kind inherent in an *I* and diffusing the *I* in the form of the *self*. But it is only in metaphor that one can speak of a subjectivity of this kind with reference to social groups.

I fear that his decision to limit love to an emotional contemplation is a grave error. If we separate sentiment and self-sacrifice at the base of love, love itself is destroyed. The primordial drive of the self is not only an impulse toward the other and toward the inner value of the other, as Scheler so admirably showed; it is also an efficient energy that wants to contribute to the existence and development of the other. Thus it is not a question of directing him toward some extrinsic end nor of using him as a means for the triumph of a value foreign to his unique vocation. It is a question of giving him the solidity and perfection of his singular personality and striving for the boundless liberty of his unfettered being. Love is not a lazy repose in the beauty of an image, but a vital involvement, a vigorous commitment, a straining toward the fulfillment of the *thou*. Even in contemplation there should be an active desire.[2]

Does this mean that the will to advancement is a will to creation? Perhaps. In principle, the lover longs to engender wholly the being of the beloved. However, a human person cannot, in fact, pretend to such a thing. We try to consolidate the existence of the *thou* or contribute to his growth. But we always fall short at some point. Often our control goes no farther than our imagination, as in the case of the novelist who brings his characters to life on paper; sometimes he manages to stammer out a new essence but his phantoms evolve in a misty existence, powerless to come fully alive. We give a child bread to help his physical growth; we may come to the assistance of a friend, influence a mind and modify its qualities. But man does not create man.

[2] I have made use of Scheler's most important work on the subject, *Nature et formes de la sympathie* (Paris, 1928). However he seems to have broadened his views in certain respects when, in other works, he opposes the creative love of Christians to the preservative love of the Greeks. See *Le Sens de la souffrance* (Paris, 1936), pp. 154–5 and *passim*. (Translator's note: *Nature et formes de la sympathie* is available in English translation under the title *The Nature of Sympathy*, translated from the original German by Peter Heath (New Haven, Yale U. Press, 1954).

Someone will object, saying that he procreates him. Is this truly an objection? On this point I find myself again in agreement with Scheler: procreation is not a relation of spiritual causality. There is no direct continuity between the parents and the soul of their child. The *ingenium* of the son descends from heaven to earth. To the degree that the son is himself he is not hereditary; he is not proportionate to the paternal *ingenium*. His arrival is basically independent of the designs of the parents. The sex act is subjectively the expression of conjugal affection and implies in itself nothing more in this respect. The fact that conception may take place without any thought being directed to the possibility of offspring should suffice to show up the weakness of the alleged creative powers of the procreators. Conjugal love may indeed include the desire for the child and penetrate the sex act with an intention it did not originally have. The moralist will be generous with good advice on this subject. But the fact remains that the arrival of the child is always a gift and a surprise. What is hereditary is not owing to the will of the parents; it is only the resemblances of repetitious qualities that are transmitted from one generation to the next.

Now, a child is something other than a mass of qualities, he is a new germ of personality who will have to make his own choice from among the totality of traits to which he is liable and integrate them little by little according to an unforeseeable design. Strictly from the viewpoint of causality, which supposes a conscious will to advancement, influence cannot begin unless the child is already there. We never create another personality, we discover it. Between it and us there is an initial gulf that cannot be crossed. In the geometry of souls the lines are at first parallel; only later do destinies. touch and intersect.

Wise old Plato was right on this point. He maintained that in our human experience love originates in the loveableness of the beloved. We receive the beloved, we discover in him reasons for cherishing him even if he be vile or vilified. The stream of love then flows from the beloved to the lover and back again, enriched in its content and intensified in its movement. But Plato, I will admit, does not take into sufficient account the gratuitous initiative of the lover— an initiative proportionate to the nobility of his love. Even though love may be rooted in necessity it flowers in freedom; it is perception, but it is also creative imagination; the autonomy love would give, it first acquires itself; and if, to some extent, it always receives what it gives, it is simply to learn to give more and more while receiving less and less. The very act of receiving tends to be the result of a conscious work; the act is experienced in order to be confirmed; and from then on it is willed.

If the lover is not entirely the creator, must we conclude that he means to withdraw for the greater good of the *thou* and that this good is realized only by his retreat? This extreme does not necessarily follow. When it is a question of material goods, sincere love should, it is true, be disposed to share them even at considerable cost to self and one may soon suffer want of support. But however painful the results of his catering to the needs of the beloved, the lover suffers no mutilation or suppression of his fundamental will to advance the beloved. He cannot deny the act that is constitutive of his own being, i.e., willing himself for the sake of the other; and how could the effacement of the self automatically produce positive progress in the other? Recourse to voluntary self-limitation solves nothing.

All this brings us back to our original statement and calls for this additional remark: the self is convinced that in love it can influence another center of consciousness and produce, to a degree, the growth of an interior character that exists for itself in his presence. Every lover has this ambition, and to take it away from him is to take away his love itself. Illusory or not, his intention rests on this fundamental belief in a transitive action of one consciousness on another.

A Will to Mutual Promotion

To love implies the desire to be loved, and in a certain sense, the fact of being loved. I am well aware that this double affirmation will cause some astonishment. Those who disagree with me will cry shame, as though I were introducing egoism into the heart of generosity. They will also accuse me of mistaking chimeras for realities; it is only too evident that affection is not always requited. However, I do not see how I can relinquish my paradoxes.

In my defense I will first expound and evaluate the contrary opinion. It has recently been brilliantly presented by Anders Nygren in *Agape and Eros*.[3] This Lutheran philosopher conceives of two kinds of love. One is *Eros*, the desire for the best: the aristocratic aspiration of the human self that would wish to raise itself to the level of the divine; it cannot be satisfied except by taking God Himself for its object. It is motivated by the perception of the beauty residing in this supreme object.

The other type of love is *Agape:* it is the gift and sacrifice of self for the loved one; it creates the value of its object; it is spontaneous and kind; it is not in the least motivated by the excellence of the beloved. Eros is centripetal; agape is centrifugal. They are two spiritual movements that have nothing in common.

This psychological opposition, continues the author, is rooted in history. The Greek philosophers knew eros; it was Christianity that revealed agape. Within the Greek perspective, love expresses man's nature and responds to his tendency toward perfection. We must not confuse the popular Venus with the celestial Venus: eros is, of course, noble. But it is a superior egoism, none the less. It postulates a human soul with a divine value buried in its depths; its goal is the divinization of the self. Through love, the soul is awakened to the desire to arrive at the absolute perfection from which it is exiled here below and for which it has an

indestructible nostalgia. The lover is enamored of himself and therefore seeks to possess God in order to become divine. As for the love of other human beings, it can be, under these conditions, only an instrument for going toward self and toward God. The neighbor is a step on the ladder to the divine and we can appreciate our fellow men only insofar as they serve as means to our ascension: we love them *propter Deum*.

On the other hand, agape is the supernatural love emanating from God himself and subsisting in Him alone; it is bestowed on us gratuitously as a consequence of a sacrifice of the Most High. We who are the object of this love and receive it, are nothing but miserable creatures; our self has nothing lovable in itself, no rights, no intrinsic value. If we love our neighbor it is because the divine agape in us, by passing through us as an efficient and not as a final cause, impels us to act thus. In the true Christian tradition the other need not fear he will be treated as a simple means *propter Deum*. . . . Man is loved by man because the gift which comes from God demands it, and this gift is entirely disinterested: it is free of any egoistic infiltration. Agape alone respects and establishes true "philanthropy." This is strikingly evident in the evangelical precept to love one's enemies. Such an attitude is inconceivable to pagan philosophers, totally concerned as they are with allowing the delectable riches of the Good-in-itself to flow into them.

Nygren thinks that any synthesis of these two historic forms of love is impossible. St. Augustine forged a hybrid notion, *Caritas*, which mixes the Greek eros with the New Testament agape. Theologians of the Middle Ages often prolonged this error or erected it into a system; but the cement has never held. Their compromise raised insoluble difficulties and engendered repeated crises in the speculative order. However, these attempts have been useful, for their failure has helped place the exact notion of agape in bolder relief. Through successive "reforms" the Christian conscience has stood out with greater clarity, it has understood

[3] Trans. Philip S. Watson (2 vols., Philadelphia, Westminister, 1953).

its own originality and supernatural character. The salvation of love is not from man, whose nature is all desire; salvation comes from heaven; it overcomes and transcends desire, for it is gift.

Such is Nygren's thesis: neat, elegant, and basically dualist. Here and there it lends itself to admirable developments. But I must admit that on the whole I cannot subscribe to it. My first objection is that it reduces man's role to nothing and makes impossible any dialogue between the creature and the Creator, or even between the beloved and the lover. It suppresses the very notion of a return of love. All it leaves is the divine solitude. Indeed, to what could our response to the Lord be reduced? An acceptance of grace? Submission? But is that love? If so it would be either eros or agape: if eros, the attitude of the beloved is egoistic and to be condemned. If agape, it ought to be in a form that can flow from the creature. Now, it seems to me that this is not a love that descends from God and has not yet met our being, but a love that is implanted in us to be reborn and rise again in newness toward God. Thus we are brought back either to the notion of a good eros excluded by Nygren or else to that kind of created grace that duplicates agape and makes us imitators of God by elevating our nature to a supernatural state without destroying its personal spontaneity. In its communion with God the self is saved from its supposed fundamental perversion; personality responds freely to Him who calls it; it is not a stranger to transcendence but blossoms forth in it. But at this point we do not understand in the same way as Nygren the vicissitudes of a divine love loving itself in us. So we abandon his thesis to save the possibility of a loving exchange.

There is a final hypothesis possible: that obedience to grace would be neither eros nor agape. But by definition it would no longer be love, since love, it is maintained, can take only these two forms. We must conclude, then, that for Nygren the creature loved by God is itself incapable of love. If God expects something from us it can be only the docility of the slave. Under these circumstances should the divine liberality be called a work of love? It is the omnipotence of an artist who brings passivities to light; it is not the gift of a goodness that causes personalities to unfold.

No doubt one could answer that the attitude of the soul submissive to God has a name, and that that name is faith. However, the difficulty still remains. Either faith has, indeed, been aroused in us by divine charity without ever being called to consummation in an act of love (but this affirmation, hardening as it does the theological distinction between faith and charity, would have the paradoxical result of making Nygren more Catholic than the Catholics themselves: under pretext of respecting the originality of faith, the whole religious life of man would be impervious to love). Or else, on the contrary, in keeping with the tradition of the Reformation, faith is formed by charity, and that formula would have to be interpreted in this instance as the affirmation of a loving response by man to God (but then we find again in our supernatural state and, under cover of faith, the difficulties regarding eros and agape I have already pointed out). Thus we shall either have to reject the thesis or deny any particle of generosity in man.

Actually, dialogue is essential to the reciprocity of love, and if there is to be dialogue between the Creator and the creature, the creature must be something other than a necessary reflection or an automatic echo. He must be capable of disinterestedness, and that by free choice. This living response supposes that the loved one desires to share in the perfection of the supreme lover in order to offer him an autonomous image of it. In a word, the love of God urges us and compels us, not in order to constrain us as things, but to oblige us to be free.

Let us suppose that we have this liberty and that Nygren accepts it. His doctrine would not be any more satisfactory; it would lead straight to a new impasse and strip human beings of the dignity proper to them: the power to delight and to grieve their Creator. It makes any disappointment of the divine Lover impossible. If the gift alone counts, if true love is centrifugal, the attitude and response of the beloved matters little; the lover can only cease being interested in the use the beloved will make of his freedom.

By an odd coincidence we come upon that unforgettable passage in which Goethe exclaims: "If I love you, what is that to you?" No doubt this proud cry represents a lofty state of soul; between unilateral love and spiritual beggary Goethe chooses unilateral love, and rightly so. Reciprocity is elusive; he fails to achieve it and resigns himself to choose the lesser of two evils. This designates a makeshift and not the perfection of love. The inevitable consequence of his protestation is the challenge: "If you don't love me, what is that to me?"

All these haughty questions are dangerous. There are two ways of being disappointed: one is to feel oneself thwarted, the other is to discover the moral mediocrity of the one loved. Now these two ways merge into one for the perfectly loving soul; for, unresigned to evil, it says: "My satisfaction is your value; my sorrow is your refusal to fulfill the value that was in you and that my love wants to help you to realize to the fullest."

Finally, just as the gift of the Creator includes the desire to elevate the beloved toward the harmony He offers, so also the mounting desire that moves the beloved, leads him to seek supreme perfection and admit that it consists in generously giving oneself. There is an eros of the agape, a need to possess the spirit of dis-possession, a desire to find one's soul in losing it. Why should eros be only a will to monopolize and use? It is the desire of the best, and as such is destined not to use everything but to learn that it ought to serve the spirit of generosity. The contrast proposed by Nygren is a psychological error. He condemns eros, whereas it is only the limits imposed on eros that are condemnable, limits which a sincere eros itself condemns, since it discovers that its vocation is to be converted to generosity.

Setting aside these theological discus-

sions, let us turn to the direct and more modest analysis of the reciprocity of centers of consciousness—it will lead to analogous conclusions. Above all, it leads us to believe that every lover wants to be loved and all love finds at least a minimum of reward.

1) There is a *minimum of reciprocity* in the fact that love originates in the perception of the lovableness of the beloved. If it is truly another that I love and not an impersonal quality pinned on him, it is he who, in a sense, has begun to love me. He has advanced me and enriched me simply by his very presence open to my perception. My love for him ought to begin in a kind of thanks, and I can tell him with the poet: *"C'est moi qui te dois tout, puisque c'est moi qui t'aime."* ("It is I who owe you everything since it is I who love you.")

It will be objected that this person does not even know that virtue has gone out of him, and he may be unaware of my existence. How can you say he is my benefactor? I answer: he has not willed me by name, he has not turned toward me as a result of a special decision, but he has given himself to the world, he has willed this in willing to display his activity and allow his personality to be glimpsed there. Thus is it that he has caused his being to shine in my own.

Nietzsche speaks of an enriching virtue— *schenkende Tugend*—emanating from certain personalities. This radiance is not the prerogative of a Socrates or a St. Francis of Assisi; it is inseparable from all personal existence. To be in the world is to be a minimum of goodness publicly exposed. Human centers of consciousness are hidden in many respects by the cosmic masquerade; but there is one aspect under which they cannot do otherwise than show themselves and communicate their share of excellence to those who contemplate them. There are so many tragic and absurd angles to the human condition that we can only rejoice to discover this happy feature of our destiny. To be in the world is *to be able* to dissimulate and to wreak havoc, that is true; but first of all, before ugliness sets in, it is to open one's soul to other souls and bring them an initial presence which is itself a gift. A countenance that appears is a reality surrendered, a secret cautiously unveiled, a value poured out and not taken back. Everyone knows there is a play of light behind the lattice wall, and in the weakest or most retiring mind there is a fundamental will that continues to sing the joy of this necessary and innocent gift. The person is an expression and a role: he soon learns to calculate his effects or to poison the atmosphere. But in the beginning he is unaware of his grimaces and is all freshness and trust. Love is always watching for this initial moment, and that is why it is born in mutuality even though it must often sink into solitude.

2) But love does not have a hermit's vocation; it always seeks a *maximum of reciprocity.*

The response that a person to whom I am attached can give me may exhibit four successive degrees:

At the lowest, the other responds to my will to promotion by the *simple fact of his existence and growth.* The little child or the unconscious patient may never be aware of the care I lavish on them. My reward is that they live; their very existence is a recompense.

Then there is the reciprocity that is already psychological if *the other is aware of my project,* even though he rejects it or, while being aware of it, does not know its author. I provide him with a new theme. I plant in his being a virtual personality. Whatever variations he may weave on the theme or whatever may be his ignorance of the fact that he received it from me, he has truly received it and the theme is truly in him. My loving intention remains in his presence, at least under the form of an anonymous ideal of his self. It is a path that may be barred or that he may choose not to take; but something of my will is, as it were, really knit into his substance. Newman wrote in this fashion on the subject of the kind of presence that faithful Christians can have even in their persecutors: "They have a friend of their own in each man's bosom,

witnessing for them; even in those who treat them ill." [4] This statement is rich in meaning and expresses in a particular instance the larger truth I am trying to define.

3) At the third level of reciprocity the *thou ratifies the loving design of the I for the thou.* He has accepted the theme offered him, and the variations he composes are in harmony with it. It is thus that the disciple repays the master and the child honors the education he has received. It is not a question of copying an effect or slavishly aping a model but of adopting a spiritual orientation and freely responding to a source of inspiration.

4) Lastly, reciprocity is complete when *the beloved in turn wills the advancement of the lover* and turns back to him with the same intentness that had turned the lover toward him, choosing the lover's personal development as the goal of his activity. At this moment the circuit of love is complete.

If we now analyze the gift of self that characterized the impulse of the loving person, we see that that person implicitly wants the four degrees of reciprocity whose progression we have just noted. By the very fact that he wants to help another be himself, the lover seeks to obtain, insofar as circumstances and the attitude of the loved one permit, the perfect constitution of the full circuit of love. This is equivalent to saying that by loving he aims somehow to be loved: the two movements inevitably converge.

What does it mean to *give oneself to another?* It is to commit oneself to be concerned about him, to make him exist more fully. But the lover would deny the worth of his love did he not desire the beloved to share it and be loving in his turn. To will that the other be loving is to will that he love in me what makes me able and willing to love him; it is to will that he love me. "I belong to you" means: depend on me for yourself, I dedicate myself to you. But the expression is equivocal and it is logical

4 John Henry Newman, *Selection. Parochial and Plain Sermons* (London, 1900), p. 404.

that it be so. It also means: I depend on something in you to help me so that I can be worthy of you and useful to you. Help me to help you. I want you to be such that I, in my turn, can place myself in your hands and receive a greater value from you. By the fact that I attach myself to you, I make it possible for you to transform me for yourself. In one and the same act I believe in you and in myself; I hope in you and in myself; my love is an invocation that I address simultaneously to you and to me.

Doubtless, when I love you I first will that you be love-worthy and, perhaps, even that your generosity turn away from me, in order to turn toward the world and give it a greater value. It is thus in conjugal love and friendship: I want the other to be able to forget me temporarily, should that be necessary for him to better fulfill his duty; I wish, in certain circumstances, that he go to those who need him before he concerns himself with me who can do without his help; I wish, in a word, to be able to esteem him. This is particularly so in parental love: a popular saying has it that parents do not rear their children for themselves, and that love descends from the older to the younger generation instead of rising from the younger to the older. These aphorisms not only express a fact of nature, they indicate an order of duty. But by consenting to my request that he leave me, the beloved richly rewards me at the very moment he seems to ignore me. And at the end of his charitable action, will he not meet me again? As the object of his act will I ever be absent from his horizon? It is only from his work, and in appearance, that he had to exclude me. I am not excluded from the deeper impulse that inspired his work. It was from me he drew the noblest reason for his withdrawal, since it was I who said: "If you love me, leave me."

Neither sacrifices nor delays can shut me out from the circuit that would draw my beloved toward me—it would be contradictory if they could. The journey of the beloved will be complete only if it comes to an end in me after having encompassed, in a way, a universe of other selves. Even in the cases in which a physical distance is morally indispensable to the work of love, the lover wishes implicitly that the beloved, while setting forth from him, should come back to him in the end. The four degrees of reciprocity indicated above are in the will of the lover from the beginning; but he cannot fully live them except by stages, and he would destroy the purity of his intention if he omitted the intermediate steps through pride or impatience.

Thus, in the gift of self the *I* enhances the *thou* and this constitutes an agape; and the *I* is enhanced by the *thou*, which constitutes an eros. This circle is inevitable. What is willed is a manner of being of the *thou* and the *I* which derives directly from the loving will and has its origin in it. A sincere eros leads to agape; a sincere agape brings us back to eros; each leads to the other while remaining present in the other, once it has led there. The lover who has understood the implications of eros does not desire the other as an instrument to be subordinated to his use, but as an end that is equal or perhaps superior to himself. An analogous statement is true for the lover inspired by agape. If we raise these statements to the level of the principle that sustains them, we discover their transcendent unity: Plotinus taught that God is eros itself; his definition, properly understood, is meant to be illuminated and completed by the Johannine word: "God is agape."

The love of self, therefore, is not necessarily a form of egoism. It should culminate in self-sacrifice and is indeed implied by it. The two ways, while apparently opposed to each other, are really complementary. In principle they are inseparable. But whence comes *the inveterate distrust of moralists with regard to one of these two?* These men are severe toward eros and well disposed toward agape. The reasons for their attitude are mysterious and more difficult to explain than one would think. The facts are clear and no educator can doubt them. To suggest to a child that he take as his ideal the fullest development of his personality is to risk making a hard-hearted person of him, unsympathetic and unfeeling. He may become an "angelic epicurean" but he will still be an egoist. On the other hand, to exhort him to self-sacrifice and renunciation is to point out a short cut to perfection and propose a healthier and safer method of education.

The facts are clear . . . it is the reason for them that is obscure, and we cannot be satisfied with an argument *in terrorem*, or a pious sermon by way of explanation. Why, then, is the cult of self so equivocal and so apt to turn us away from the fullness of love instead of leading us to it?

A first reply would be as follows: the love of self is a spontaneous, constant and incoercible tendency. The gift of self, on the other hand, is fragile; it demands effort, which alone is meritorious. —That reply is, basically, quite insufficient. Let us rid ourselves of our prejudices and look at things impartially. What do we observe? On the one hand, in order to reach its goal, the desire for the best demands a host of sacrifices and heroic decisions. The lower self must be constantly immolated to the higher. In Plato's temple of wisdom there is an altar for holocausts; and even Nietzsche, who downgrades the will-to-good in favor of the will-to-power, is not a gentle master in this respect: in order to fulfill himself he tears himself like a corybant. —On the other hand, is it true that self-sacrifice for the sake of others is a disposition that is parsimoniously distributed among mankind and always hard to cultivate? I would be tempted to believe the contrary. Altruistic tendencies are as spontaneous as the others. There is a prodigal sacrifice of self all around us. But how many of these sacrifices are blind or stupid! . . . Many people will deprive themselves of necessities and spend themselves recklessly for a dog or a parrot. There are some who, in times of disaster, would rather lose their lives than be separated from a favorite house plant. Agape, too, has its excesses, its mistakes in perspective, and its perversions,

sometimes touching, sometimes scandalous. The solution must be sought elsewhere.

A second reply is more satisfactory. It would have us note the ease with which love, whether it be selfish desire or self-sacrifice, ceases to be directed toward a *thou* properly so-called, and turns to impersonal objects. Thus it is that we become attached to things or institutions without making of that attachment a means for advancing personal subjects but rather a frontier that limits and satisfies us. But if it is an impersonal being we love it is impossible to give it true autonomy. A plant, a dog, or even a social form, such as the fatherland or humanity, are not subjects endowed with a free inner life. They are not universal perspectives like you and me. It follows that the loved one is, in this case, unequal to the lover; and even if the lover were to immolate himself for an object of this kind, he would be using it much more than he would be serving it. The will to possess necessarily gets the better of the will to give. If I realize that my dog is a dog, I shall never be able to love him for himself as much as, or in the same way that, I love him for myself. A kind of generosity and even reciprocity may unite us, but they are not of the same species as when the *thou* is a person. There will be a difference of level between an eros that is personal and an agape that cannot be so. True, I can forget that my dog is a dog and naively treat him as a friend and equal. But this naivete is suspect: I pretend to be unaware that the dog is not a personal self because in that way I can imagine that I am dominating a free being. The love of animals, and of children, too, affords us, at little cost, what we obtain only with great difficulty in the love of adults: security.

Besides, this illusion will not restore the balance between the two aspects of love, self-centeredness and self-sacrifice, for the failure of a frank and total reciprocity between the loved one and myself maintains a difference of nature between my desire turned toward my subjectivity and my devotion turned toward the weak form of consciousness that is my dog's. Willy-nilly the reach of my devotion will be shortened and the level of my objective will be lowered; the love I have for myself will direct and utilize my devotion in a tyrannical fashion. And this is normal.

But the psychological habit we contract in our relations with natural creatures or social institutions is apt to contaminate our relations with personal beings. We are tempted to transpose into inter-human love a behavior that is unjustifiable, since it makes us regard the other as a thing or an idea, and leaves us on the periphery of his subjectivity. At last we understand why moralists distrust the ways of eros and warn against its dangers. We understand it all the better when we see how facts confirm their fears. The attitude proper to the pseudo-love that persons bear toward things often invades the mind and spoils the love one bears toward other persons.

This explanation is interesting; but it calls for additional comment. The great mystery is the malady that impels eros and agape to stop short in their elementary stages and lazily rest there. We lack ambition for ourselves and others. But to this weakness it shares with agape, eros adds another of its own. Love of self is more quickly and thoroughly corrupted than devotedness. Whenever there is gift there is inevitably self-desire, too: we love ourselves as being able to help the *thou* we have chosen. On the other hand, where there is love of self there is not necessarily gift also; I can love myself in such a manner as to rid myself of all devotedness to others. In this sense, any gift, mediocre though it be, involves a certain attention to the interests of the self, it considers them and respects them; while the love of self, if it is mediocre, can wrap itself up in a strictly private pleasure and preclude any turning toward others. It is greedy and in too great a hurry. Thus the spell of evil paralyzes eros more completely than it does agape.

Nevertheless, evil does profit from the growing pains that hamper agape. If I renounce the noble love of self, it is because

of deep-seated inertia. If, on the contrary, I get discouraged in my generosity toward others, it is not only from a lack of energy that has its source in me (and for which I am to blame), it is also occasioned by the ingratitude I experience on the part of others or their refusal of the value I wish to offer them. The inclination to give oneself meets with obstacles from within and without; the love of self finds them only within; its value and success depend, ultimately, on the self alone. In both cases, the soul suffers defeat; but morality, which is concerned only with what depends on us, will insist on the duty to fight against egoism and profess an *a priori* mistrust of the search for self. Renunciation and devotedness will be, in its eyes, the sole way of access to virtue.

Abandoning these subtle, irritating discussions, we shall next consider the most frequent symptoms of the disease that strikes love. The first is bitter jealousy. The self strictly limits the scope of its generosity, it goes out to the *thou* to the exclusion of others or against them. The second symptom is a slowing down in the soul's ascent toward value, or a descent into the cheap marketable values of sensuality; it is a sealing off of approaches from above, a kind of monstrous insensibility to spiritual perfection. In jealousy and sloth are summed up the majority of love's tragedies. On the one hand there is belligerent tension and bitterness; on the other, the "vertiginous sweetness" of the rests or *decrescendos* that used to disturb Baudelaire.

To be cured, one has to go to the moralists. And the reform they propose will be first to stop loving one being at the expense of another. The avid and exclusive soul is already half converted when he can get along without rivals. Many couples feel the need of eliminating a third party and making him suffer in order to taste the happiness of their union. Their intimacy is heightened by these battles. This smiling sadism that persecutes everyone else in order to realize a sweeter life for two alone, has been little studied. It is, however, as mysterious as, and more frequent than, the frowning kind! Charles Lamb alludes to it humorously in his "A Bachelor's Complaint About the Behavior of Married People": "What I am complaining about," he says, "is that you can't be in their company a moment without being made to feel, by some indirect hint or open avowal, that *you* are not the object of their preference."

Conversion is complete when it is realized that to truly love a person one must wish to make him infinitely lovable, for in this radical wish the need for all the values stands out. My partner will not be infinitely lovable unless he infinitely loves the universe of persons and makes himself worthy to be loved by them. I wish to raise him to a point where my jealousy is wiped out once and for all and where all the doors of the world are wide open to him. The will to advance the beloved is demanding: it tolerates neither pettiness nor laziness; it leads us much farther and higher than we had suspected at first; it implies, in effect, an unlimited development of the *I* and *thou*; and in the personal identity it pledges to confer on the lovers, it is the identity and development of all conscious beings that it is logically committed to promote, step by step, to the point where there is a mutual interpenetration of all by God and God by all.

Love Links Persons into a Spiritual Community

The reciprocity we have just analyzed is a journey of the *I* toward the *thou* and the *thou* toward the *I*. From the outset there is a vague perception of the bond that unites two centers of consciousness and all others in them. In a word, the relationship now takes the form of a *we*. But there are many forms of the *we*. F. Perroux distinguished the *we* of similitude (*I* as *thou*), the *we* of association (*I* with *thee*), the *we* of dilution (*I* in *thou*), and the *we* of love (*I* for *thee*). Though the list is incomplete and tentative,[5]

[5] F. Perroux and R. Prieur, *Communauté et société* (Paris, 1941), p. 12. See ch. 7, for an attempt at a more detailed classification of the varieties of collective consciousness.

it suffices to introduce the problem of the nature of the *we* of love and how it is distinguished from the others.

1) To understand its special character, let us take as an example an old man who loves the charm of a child. Shall we say that he seeks to acquire the child's charm and share it with him? Evidently not. It is not a question of fusing or confusing their respective domains. The old man wants the child to have its own charm and to keep it in the measure that it is a gift having its own nuances proper to the development of the little one. The child, who is attached to the old man, in his turn ratifies and advances, after a fashion, the wisdom or goodness of the old man. Each is happy to improve a wealth he does not possess in himself. Each has an asset in the other: it is a centrifugal possession. What is more, it is an existence of each self in the other, for it is their very being that grows and lives on in another being. Their inner will establishes itself in an outer world, and what is most intimate to it lodges in a stream of life different from their own. Thus it is in every personal love. It is hard for us to translate this situation into metaphorical language because it cannot be conceived as a community of bodily qualities or as a natural possession. We imagine presence in another as a good separate from the gift: thus we see the old man as possessing the loveliness of the child in the same way a wealthy man has his fortune at the bank. Matters of love are more subtle. The qualities which express each self do so only by being born in the other self and in developing for his sake. It is through him that they come back to the lover in an atmosphere which is an offering in return.

The *we* of love is the very meeting of these two subjects whose having is in the other, and it is the awareness of this double, generous transposition that is its very being. More vital or more actual according to the degree of reciprocity attained, this is what characterizes all love. The communion of the subjects is but the coexistence of these two out-of-center series in which individual qualities can finally circulate in the continuity of persons. No other experience enables us to understand so clearly the reconciliation of the one and the many in the life of the spirit. *Aut duo, aut nemo.*

2) It follows that the *we* of love is a *heterogeneous* identity of the *I* and *thou*. It is the community of two subjects as subjects. Too often in the past philosophers have maintained that every identity is homogeneous. They regard as identical any two elements that we are unable to distinguish upon the most methodical examination. But while reason wishes to identify everything, reality opposes this reduction. The notion of an absolute identity may even be contradictory. This is what Plato was forced to conclude in his metaphysical dialogues on the same and the other. Closer to our own time, Bradley rejects identity as well as diversity in the world of appearances. And Meyerson admits that identity breaks down unless there is irrational diversity subsisting in contrast with it.

We should be spared many a philosophical dilemma if we admitted that identity is heterogeneous and does not concern objects but subjects. Just as Bergson abandoned the false continuity of homogeneity and introduced the idea of a profound continuity with irreducible aspects, it seems we must realize that true identity is heterogeneous and supposes the diversity of subjects and their irreplaceable character. Far from causing confusion, this identity, which is the identity of love, abolishes errors. It disengages and dissolves the inferior, woolly form of identity; it forces us to sacrifice what obstructs the originality of personal subjects and prevents them from being themselves. It does not rest on the similarity between its participants but on their harmonious originality. Certainly it leads us to state, without fear of presumption, that the *I is the thou,* but only in the perspective in which it *causes the thou to be,* and is itself willed by the *thou.* By this will, the subjects identify with each other, and do so only in the measure in which they become different.

3) On the other hand, the *we* of love is inactive in the sense that it does not create the *I* and *thou* but simply expresses their mutuality. Friendship is not something added to two friends like a third individual, or even like a third force separable from their two wills. It does not establish them in their love by a kind of feedback; it simply accompanies them; it is the spiritual nature of their persons.[6] We are tempted to believe the contrary because we thoughtlessly assimilate the community of minds with the community that results from a juridical contract sanctioning social engagements. It is quite true that the contract is separate from the contracting parties and subsequently binds them before the law no matter what changes may have occurred in their inner disposition. But though the loving exchange does constitute a new situation, it does not create it in the same way a contract would. It is in the very tissue of the subjects who make the agreement, and if they separate, it is torn apart. It leaves them as the sparkling of the sea flees with the setting sun.

If the exchange is active, it is through the weight of the past that has been inscribed in a common biography and which, in this regard, is indestructible and active even in the separate biographies. The *we* is dynamic from another point of view: it is a broadened, stimulating awareness that urges its participants to further progress, with due regard for their free decision. It is not a prop that forces us to grow just so, nor a technique for retraining ourselves. It is an energy and an attraction inviting us to make a common effort toward the highest values. Its own impulse—if it can be said to have one of its own—is to perceive vaguely a superior power of identity, more cohesive than the one previously experienced. The *we* is more or less closely knit: each degree of union it expresses awakens the dread of disunion and impels us to seek an ever closer reciprocal belonging.

4) Finally, even though the subjective *we*

---

[6] All proportion guarded, the *we* is here an image of what theologians call the nature of God in the Trinity.

may be indifferent, in principle, to the number of its associates and capable of an indefinite extension without its form undergoing any radical change, in the human condition the *we* seems to be limited to a dyad: subjective awareness does not achieve real reciprocity except between two personal beings. Such is our situation. The biblical notion of Adam and Eve is to be taken seriously. Even the dyad itself is weak, intermittent, and maintained in fragmentary fashion. *Nec sine te, nec tecum.* How often trajectories cross only to move apart from each other! Even the fairest climates have their fogs and tempests.

Naturally, there are many possible dyads (Eve and Abel, Abel and Cain, etc.). But the existence of a triad or a quadrad is rather problematical: I mean a community in which three or four individuals are simultaneously translucent to each other in such a way that each turns lovingly to the others as if they were but one and receives from them simultaneous and equal attention. The triad has the formula: a–b, a–c, b–c. The family group would seem to furnish its elementary type; but who will maintain that father, mother, and child are each able to think of the other two at the same time without some faltering on the part of one of the three? Two beings can unite personally in the devotion they have for a third person: the dyad accompanied by a "for him" is frequent. But does the third party then turn to the other two with the same refinement of perception and without any loss of contact?

This distribution, if it occurs at all, and if it truly concerns the will to mutual advancement, is certainly very unstable. Either there is a swift passage from one dyad to another, or the triad descends below the personal level we are presently considering and sinks into a confused impression of community, as in a team or a group. In that case it is the idea of a common task and not their individual selves that unites the members of the group. In place of the subjective *we* there is substituted, in a sense, the image of the other or others, i.e., an objective *us*. It is by the mediation of an objective *us*

and the shift from one dyad to another that love maintains its power to unite morally all men, in spite of their discontinuity, and according to the demands already implicit in the sincere relationship between two lovers. But these vast horizons are always enclosed in a more humble form; they are reflected obliquely in the narrow mirror of the dyad.

What Does Love Seek?

The inner logic of love impels it to develop until it has achieved the total fulfillment of its potentialities. It is not inevitable that it reach its utmost limits, for every human being is free up to a certain point to oppose it or respect it or, more exactly, to sink or rise in the current of love that bears him along. But each time we correspond to the essential demands of that impulse we are aware of implicitly willing the infinite perfection of the beloved and, indirectly, of ourself as loving. We commit ourself to make the other and ourself utterly lovable and loving. But for a consciousness to be so it must embrace the whole universe and strive for the promotion of all other centers of consciousness according to the same value system. The human love of one person leads to the love of all persons. First of all, it wishes their existence and makes it an initial value. Next, it desires that their perfection or eternal essence be revealed, for it is through this eternal essence that the successive images of the ideal it has of itself are manifested to the discriminating conscience. Finally, love desires the autonomous development of individuals in time to be in as harmonious accord as possible with that ideal, which is their call to perfection. Briefly, the sincere lover wills the total order of persons and strives to encourage, insofar as he can, the growing identity of each self in its vocation to value. *Aut omnes, aut nemo.*

In order to clarify these ideas it may be useful to define more accurately the word that the problem of love obliges us to repeat over and over: "person." For the sake of simplicity we will abstract from the nuances that could be established between person and personality [7] and simply say: *personality is the condition of the self* [8] *that obliges it to seek its progressive fulfillment by itself, according to a perspective at once unique and universal.* This definition implies the notion of irreversible duration: each person is an historical development; at least we have no experience of a form of personality other than this. It supposes, besides, a self-creating continuity, that is, the presence of free causality in the self. And finally, it establishes the self in a vocation to totality; it recognizes in the self, by that very fact, the highest form of finality and value. The person must reach out to everything without consenting to dissipate itself in triviality or enclose itself in egoism; it is called to possess itself in order to give itself and, by this double movement, fulfills itself in an equilibrium at once mobile and continuous. In appearance a human being is only a tiny drop of psychic awareness; in reality it is a crucible wherein the spiritual universe seeks to give and receive all its energy in an irreplaceable individuality.

The real difficulty with the notion of person is that it has to be defined as a universal perspective, i.e., by the juxtaposition of two seemingly incompatible terms. How can a perspective, or individual consciousness, be total without losing its very individuality? This cannot be seen at first glance. Thus the ordinary tendency of philosophers is to classify person with bio-social individuality and regard the life of the mind as impersonal. This was, as is well known, the policy adopted by M. Brunschvicg. He used to tell me: "The farther I go, the more impersonalist I become." He would add that in formulating the *cogito* Descartes certainly

had no intention of proclaiming *ego sum Curtesius.*[9]

But such a position, no matter how noble the motives, is unsatisfactory. In the first place, it conflicts with the fact that the representation of the impersonal is an eminently personal act; this representation does not make the self disappear, it purifies it by contact with objectivity and the intellectual exercise of anonymity, which is not the same thing as mere impersonality. Is it not remarkable that the strongest personalities, those whose unique character is revealed in genius, should be precisely the ones who are the least embarrassed by the conscious awareness of their best and deepest self, or by their immersion in the absolute of the spiritual life? We may find it difficult to imagine the survival of a weak individuality in the ocean of infinite truth, beauty, and goodness where it would be rudely thrown and obliged to grow; but it was in a divine milieu that Aristotle, Beethoven, and Shakespeare accentuated the traits of their original consciousness, instead of allowing them to fade away there. The imprint of their personality is deeper in proportion as their elevation is greater. The higher they are the more readily they can be discerned. If there is any conclusion to be

[7] In *La Réciprocité des consciences. Essai sur la nature de la personne* (Paris: Aubier, 1942), I limit the word "person" to the spirit that animates and stirs all personalities into being; in other words, for the moment I shall ignore this distinction and speak only of human subjects.

[8] A more explicit analysis would also require a further definition of "self," "I," and "subject."

[9] R. Lenoble has taken up the challenge and proposed a personalist exegesis of Cartesianism that sacrifices none of the prerogatives of the mind. See his book on the *Notion d'expérience* (Paris, 1942); also G. Lewis' work: *L'Individualité selon Descartes* (Paris, 1950).

One day, as I was arguing the point with M. Brunschvicg, I asked him: "Don't you see any way to save the person? According to your view can't it escape from the shipwreck of the substance of the realist?" He answered by expounding a theory on the function of personalization that I found very simply and clearly stated again in his posthumous work, *Héritage de mots, héritage d'idées* (Paris, 1945, p. 71): "Man will have access to his soul only by the exercise of a personalizing function which of itself is in no way limited to the horizon of his individuality . . . but is capable of making one's self and that of the other communicate interiorly, or better still, which substitutes the limitless comprehension and generous expansion of the Cartesian *cogito* in us for the realist's impenetrable self."

The concession should not be overlooked; but it does not in any way constitute a retraction, and I should not wish to take unfair advantage of it.

drawn, it is that the growth of inwardness and personality, far from conflicting with each other, run a parallel course.

Finally, and above all, the reconciliation of the self and the spirit is evident as soon as one analyzes the fact of love: in it, and in it alone, we understand that the self can keep and increase its singular self-awareness by becoming universal; for the self, by loving, wills to promote other selves and reach the entire universe of the spirit through them, step by step. The very act by which the individual consciousness is determined, leads it to all things and bids it develop them, i.e., understand them and help them to understand themselves and to be. In this way the route by which we were seeking to unite the subject and the absolute, the one and the many, the individual perspective and the universe, is opened wide to us. Thus, just as the person is basically committed to love, the purpose of love is to constitute persons. . . .

COMMUNITY AND THE FORMS OF THE WE

Collective consciousness is the consciousness of the *we*. But it is far from being homogeneous. It always includes at least an embryonic sense of an *I* and *thou;* however this often occurs without the deep personalization of the *I* and *thou*. Therefore we must distinguish a host of forms and degrees in collective consciousness. The following schema is a tentative classification.[10]

Undifferentiated "We"

This is an extremely weak consciousness that would, in the extreme, be equivalent to a kind of vegetative sense, anterior to any reflection and even to any particular repre-

[10] For those who wish to study the problem, I recommend: G. Gurvitch, *Essais de sociologie* (Paris, 1939), pp. 9–112; W. McDougall, *The Group Mind* (Cambridge, 1920); the indispensable *Handwörterbuch der Soziologie*, edited by Vierkandt; and the fourth Semaine Internationale de Synthèse, devoted to *La Foule* (The Crowd), Paris, 1934.

sentation. Neither the subject that senses it nor the *thou* it joins are discernible from the background of community solidarity. Likewise, this group is indistinguishable from other groups: its boundaries and content are equally vague. To adopt F. Perroux's expression, it is a *we* of indistinction. Undetermined though it be, it is, however, likely to have varying intensities. It is all the more intense as the beings it gathers together are:

1) Qualitatively More Alike. For example, we doubtless have the vague impression of being one with the cosmos, a landscape, or material objects; or again with the vital force that animates the plants, animals, and people around us. But the feeling is weak and unperceived in this case. On the contrary, without being more distinct, it becomes stronger when we sense it with regard to human beings and, especially, with regard to our compatriots, our family, individuals of our own generation, etc. In any crowd the consciousness that "de-partitions" individuals and welds them into one is all the more lively as these are stripped of all their differences and their psychic character is reduced to a single quality (fear, admiration, anger, etc.)

2) Quantitatively More Numerous. Crowd psychology shows this again, and also the psychology of all kinds of mass consciousness.

3) Closer in Space and Time. This is why the common feeling of the masses is less strong than the self-awareness of a crowd. It is true that centers of attention help the masses to effect their rapprochement. This is the purpose served by posters and newspapers, for example. In the crowd itself the leader's slogans, gestures, and facial expressions are mirrors that prevent the spatial separation of the individuals. A crowd directed by a strong agitator is not strictly speaking a differentiated crowd; the presence of the demagogue is only a pseudo-differentiation; he helps the crowd be more purely a crowd, i.e., a collection of "de-cerebrated" individuals. It may happen that he is directing the crowd according to an intelligent plan, but this is beside the point. In the measure that he participates in the common consciousness, the same current flows through him as through the others; his sole function is to be passively the lens that catches the rays of light and magnifies them to the burning point.

The intensity of the *we* does not mean that it is mentally active. Though it moves muscles it does not renew minds; it is simply a spontaneous and compelling sentiment that is born when individuality abdicates.

Differentiated "We's"

Unlike the simply lived *we* just alluded to, the forms of collective consciousness we are going to consider suppose distinct representations of the whole and the parts. We will examine the situational *we*, the functional *we*, the interpersonal *we*, and the *we* of theandric relation.

The Situational "We". This is the name I give collective consciousness accompanied by a representation of the multiplicity of its members; but each individuality is simply lodged there in a portion of space and time, and its psychic originality is still scarcely considered. This is the application to the *we*, of a system of geometrc, geographic, or historic indicators. The locations of the component points are established: such an element is next to such another, or in front of it, or behind it. The community and its members are seen in the spectacle and are thus passive, but our knowledge of it is objective; it is no longer the foggy sense of the undifferentiated *we*. We imagine a field of forces constituted by a gathering together of animated bodies; we are not interested in the inner life of the participants; they are mere numbers as far as we are concerned; but at least we distinguish them from each other and situate them in the whole by the determination of their place. We could still say it is a question of a localized *we*.

It is apposite, therefore, to show the distinction between masses at a distance ("we businessmen," "we soldiers". . .) and masses nearby (the consciousness of pupils in a classroom, of travelers in a bus . . .) and also of aggregates or groups (passersby on the street, witnesses to an accident . . .). In contrast with a system of localized selves, collective consciousness can thence represent to itself other systems of distribution. It can class the inhabitants of a village in a number of ways (communities of men, women, farmers, craftsmen, etc.), and a single individual can be a member of an unlimited number of distinct systems to which it belongs by different titles. In any case, the *we* that I am examining disregards the nature of the roles; it is only a series of distributions. It is collective consciousness *sub specie quantitatis*. In the undifferentiated *we* these quantitative relations affected collective consciousness without its being aware of it; in the present instance the *we* grasps itself intellectually in its quantitative and especially its geographic structure.

The Functional "We". This is the most important form of objective group consciousness. Here we imagine not only positions but functions. The main ideas inherent in it can readily be enumerated as follows:

1
Individual qualities are ascribed to members of the group: each is distinguished from the others by something other than his place.

2
Each one has a role to play in the whole; he serves the group either passively or actively.

3
The group itself has its own function which results from its components but which is also expressed in them and can go beyond them. It is not a simple addition but a synthesis.

4
The group, while having its originality and specific functional character, also has a history; it evolves or can evolve.

5
The consciousness of being part of a group is accompanied by the consciousness of being able to form subgroups (for example, the relation of comradeship between two members of a team), or enlarge or enrich the *we* of the group itself (other members can be added to the group).

6
Qualities can be communicated among the members of the group or between the group and its members.

7
The group and its action can be in contact with other groups and actions situated outside the circle of the functional *we*.

8
The group is not only in contact with its members within itself and with other groups nearby but also with a value and an idea incarnated in it. Thus the idea of the family is manifested in the institutional structure revealed in history, and its value is expressed by the place it occupies in the hierarchy of social ends offered to the moral perceptions of persons.

In this kind of collective consciousness there is a whole set of very complex reciprocities. Each one knows not only that he possesses and uses the others but that he belongs to them and serves them. Moreover, it is essential to community consciousness that each one recognize the presence in the others of an intellectual awareness similar to his own. Of course, communion in the same objective representation cannot be absolute, and each sees the whole according to a perspective adjusted to that of the others more readily than it identifies itself with it perfectly. But the objective *we* supposes faith, at least in this correspondence.

The structure of the functional *we* comprises three principal elements:

An idea and a value of which the group is the vehicle or witness and which can be of a vital, psychic, spiritual, or other kind of order;

The collective feeling itself and the representations or tendencies related to it. We discern that the community to which we belong is different according as it is:

a
Qualitatively composed of a common sharing of will, memory, sentiments, etc.;

b
More or less broad or voluminous;

c
More static or more dynamic;

d
More convergent or more divided;[11]

e
More or less autonomous (really, on this plane no collective consciousness goes so far as to feel self-sufficient; the consciousness of being a citizen of the world is as threatened and dependent, if not more so, than that of being a villager; it depends on values that are not the very conscience of the group; besides, every functional group supposes the thought of other groups, be they rivals or friends);

The representation of individuals and their reciprocal functions. The inventory of these relations can be attempted in several ways; let us point out at least:

—The hostility of the members: this is the *we* of war (my adversary and myself);

—Domination by one or several members and subjection of the others (the feudal *we*);

—Egalitarian collaboration by an identical attitude on the part of each, by the complementarity of diverse functions (this is the distinction that Durkheim makes between mechanical and organic society), or by substitution and alternance (*we* playing see-saw).

---

[11] Convergence or condensation of the group must not be bound to differentiation of the members of the group. A clan is convergent, but its members are not differentiated; a commercial enterprise has differentiated members, but can itself be more or less convergent.

It would be interesting to try to deduce some laws related to the consciousness of the functional community according as one or the other element of its structure predominates in the representation. Here, by the way of example, are some possible notations in this direction:

1) The predominance of *value* in the conscious representation will tend to erase, by definition, the group feeling and the feeling for individuals in the functional *we;* but it will accelerate the historical development of the idea in the group in which it is embodied. In this case value is comparable to the sun; and the idea it embodies in the group is comparable to the plant the sun makes grow. This growth will be accelerated because the value and the idea, instead of acting only as efficient causes, will now further act as final causes sought for themselves (e.g., the exaltation of the values of courage, work, power, etc., will hasten the development of the "national idea" in history; a country that is aroused by these goals takes on the awareness its citizens have of a new form and more quickly realizes the potentialities of its destiny).

2) The predominance of the *collective sense* itself threatens to make the *we* more egotistical, more vague (especially if this *we* is broad or voluminous: no distinct representation of its members is possible in this case, even with good will, as can be seen in the feeling of large communities such as a city or a country; this will be all the more true when one tries systematically to separate the representation of the participants from the consciousness of the whole). But on the other hand, the exaltation of the sense of a pure community will tend to make the functional *we* more intense and durable. This is doubtless why party or patriotic propaganda does not hesitate to make use of it. The fact that the community here takes itself as its object prevents it from falling back into an undifferentiated *we* like that of the crowd which, deprived of this representation of itself, is doubtless an intense consciousness but also an unstable one.

3) The predominance of the *representation of the members* and their mutual functions in the whole, will threaten the permanence of the original *we* and easily lead to the rise of persons. The latter are always born in a social group and their destiny is to detach themselves from it in order to be faithful to their own vocation; for they do not have to be instruments or expressions of a natural society but the free agents of a spiritual realm. Directly threatened by the claim of the participants, the functional community can, however, benefit from it in certain respects; in fact, it is the consideration of individuals that obliges society to reform itself and be impregnated little by little with personal works, which is what civilization is. The functional *we* thus becomes more discerning, more careful about justice in the laws it formulates.

In short, the predominance of values in the *we* under examination ends in a *flowering of institutions;* the predominance of the pure sense of community leads to blind habits or *traditions;* the predominance of individual particularities, despite its ferments of crises or anarchy, brings about the birth of *progress,* not only because it constrains the group conscience to reform but because it permits the *we* of psychology to emerge from the *we* of sociology.

The Personal "We," or "We" of Love.   The personal *we* is realized only by love because with love alone is the complete communion of persons possible. What characterizes this form of communal consciousness is actually the will to promote a *thou* and be promoted by him. There follows a heterogeneous continuity of centers of consciousness and a double centrifugal possession in the other that we analyzed earlier. While everything remains subordinated to an objective task or proceeds from it in the bio-social, functional *we,* it is the development of the persons themselves that love wills; and consequently the essential aim is no longer that of the object but of the subject. Specifically, it is not the aim of a limited subject but of an *I* and a *thou* who are universal perspectives beyond all the social communities nature offers us.

That it is very difficult to live this subjective *we* without mixing a natural representation in it and degrading it into an objective *us*, has already been frankly conceded in the course of this study. Only the dyad allows a direct communion of persons; even then it is intermittent. Beyond it, the *we* almost certainly loses its personal distinctness and sinks into the larger but inferior forms enumerated in the preceding paragraphs.

The "We" of Theandric Relation. This is what unites the personal consciousness to the divine Absolute; it is by a creative will of God that it can really explain its origin and the identity of its essential ideal, thanks to which it subsists and is unified independently even of its earthly encounters.

Bibliography

Texts

Love and the Person. New York: Sheed & Ward, Inc., 1966.

Is There a Christian Philosophy? New York: Hawthorn Books, Inc., 1960.

God's Encounter with Man. New York: Sheed & Ward, Inc., 1964.

Réciprocité des consciences: Essai sur la nature de la personne. Paris: Aubier, 1942.

Personne humaine et nature. Paris: Aubier, 1963 (2d ed.).

Conscience et logos. Paris: Aubier Épi, 1961.

De la fidelité. Paris: Aubier, 1953.

Study

Liddle, V., "The Personalism of Maurice Nédoncelle," *Philosophical Studies* XV (1966), 112–130.

NAME INDEX

Abbott, T. K., 79
Albert, Saint, 32, 219
Alcibiades, 106
Allen, E., 172
Ambrose, Saint, 24
Andison, M. L., 48
Anschutz, R. P., 106
Anselm, Saint, 219
Anstruther, G., 41
Aquinas, St. Thomas, 32–41, 155, 156, 159,
    214–223, 235n., 247, 252n., 253, 254, 277n.
Aristotle, 1, 9–24, 32–35, 37, 40, 101, 130,
    133n., 159, 173, 217–219, 277n., 249n., 328
Augustine, Saint, 24–35, 91n., 129, 131, 132,
    217, 218, 312n., 318
Averroës, 32, 33

Bacon, F., 49
Baillie, J., 89
Baker, K., 223
Ballard, E. G., 197
Bardy, G., 31
Barendse, C., 279n.
Barnes, H., 290n.
Barral, M., 268
Barth, K., 125n.
Baudelaire, C., 324
Bax, E. B., 96
Beck, L. W., 83
Becker, H., 135
Beek, M. A., 145
Beethoven, L. van, 328
Bentham, J., 101
Berdyaev, N., 120–128
Bergson, H., 155, 159, 198, 256, 262n.,
    326
Berkeley, G., 54 60
Bérulle, P. de, 42
Binswanger, L., 129, 296, 308n.
Boethius, 32
Bonaparte, N., 84, 125
Bonaventure, Saint, 217, 219
Boule, M., 146
Bourke, J. J., 31
Bradley, F. H., 289, 326
Brentano, F., 136, 173
Bretall, R., 113
Broad, C. D., 60
Brock, W., 187
Brunner, A., 275n.
Brunschvicg, L., 328
Buber, M., 129, 135–144, 160, 314
Buber, S., 136
Buddha, 90
Burnet, J., 8
Buytendijk, F. J. J., 294, 295, 310n.

Caesar, 125
Caird, B., 89
Cairnes, D., 198
Calvin, J., 105, 106
Camus, A., 153

Carr, D., 268
Carrel, A., 245n.
Cassirer, H. W., 83
Christ, Jesus, 24, 25, 33, 42, 98–101, 106, 107,
    111, 114, 122, 127, 134, 153
Churchill, J. S., 174
Cicero, 24
Clark, O. F., 128
Collins, J., 113, 172, 187, 197, 232
Comte, A., 101, 289
Copelston, F. C., 96, 119
Crauford, E., 287n.
Cronin, J. F., 100

Dahlke, H. O., 135
Dante Alighieri, 127
Darwin, C., 131
Democritus, 34
Desan, W., 232
Descartes, R., 42–49, 54, 245, 257, 261, 286,
    290, 291, 298, 300, 328
Dilthey, W., 136, 198
Dondeyne, A., 253n., 307
Dufrenne, M., 285
Durkheim, E., 331

Epicurus, 132
Erasmus, 49
Eucken, R., 129
Evans, J., 159

Farber, M., 198
Fauré, G. U., 189
Fecher, C., 159
Fichte, J. G., 84, 122
Francoeur, R., 154
Frankl, L. A., 250
Fraser, A. C., 49, 54
Frechtman, B., 229
Freud, S., 126, 136
Friedman, M., 145
Frings, M., 135, 187

Gallagher, K., 197
Gassendi, P., 49
Geiger, M., 129
Gibson, J., 53
Gilson, E., 256
God, 9, 24–27, 36, 42–48, 68, 69, 71, 85, 105,
    107, 109, 112, 120–123, 131–133, 135, 157,
    174, 176, 223, 250n., 318–320, 322, 326,
    333
Goethe, J. W. von, 312n., 320
Gough, J. W., 53
Grabau, R. F., 172
Greef, E. de, 310n.
Green, T. H., 67
Grosse, T. H., 67
Guardini, R., 213
Gurvitch, A., 198, 232

335

SUBJECT INDEX

Abstraction:
  and intellectual knowledge, 37–39
  and sensation, 55, 56
Actuality as content of philosophy, 88
Actuation:
  and I-Thou relation, 136–144
  of person through relation, 136–144, 160,
    315–327
Anthropology, philosophical, as science of man,
  174–178
Appetite, function of soul, 22, 23
Assent, notional and real, 97–100
Availability as human existential, 189–197

Beauty, nature of, 6, 7
Being, pure, and pure thought, 222–223
Belief as real assent, 97–100
Body:
  in encounter, 295–301
  and imagination, 15, 16, 20, 21
  as intermediary, 297–301
  as machine, 46, 47
  "my" body, not "a" body, 298, 299
    not isolated from me, 299
    not a mere instrument, 299
    not an object of "having," 299
  and soul, 11

Care as human existential, 181, 182
Cartesian cogito, 42, 43, 286, 301
Causation, knowledge of, 61–67
Coexistence as human existential, 297, 298,
  300–303, 310
Cogito, Cartesian, 42, 43, 286, 301
Communication, 273–275
Community:
  and communion, 314
  and human unanimisation, 150–154
  nature of, 129–133
  and person, 158, 159
    (See also Person; Personization)
  and spatio-temporal proximity, 168, 169
  and the We, 329–333
Concern as human existential, 181, 182
Conscience and the sovereign, responsible
  individual, 115–119

Doubt, methodical, 42, 43

Embodiment, 246–249
  phenomenology of, 258–265
Encounter:
  and the creativity of love, 299, 300
  phenomenology of, 295–303
  role of the body in, 295–303
Engagement (commitment) as human
  existential, 189–197
Evil, freedom and the origin of, 25, 26
Existence and the individual, 108–113
Existential, human: availability as, 189–197
  care as, 181, 182

Existential, human: coexistence as, 296, 297,
  300–303, 310
  concern as, 181, 182
  engagement (commitment) as, 189–197
  solicitude as, 181, 182
  togetherness as, personal and impersonal,
    178–187

Faith, 275
Freedom:
  as affirmation, 285
  concept of, 79, 80
  and individuality, 102–106
  nature of, 266–268
  and the origin of evil, 25, 26
  and prereflexive self-imputation, 287
  as project and self-relation, 288, 289
  and responsibility, 225–232, 286, 287
  as self-appropriation, 285
  and self-consciousness, 289
  as self-constitution, 291, 292
  as self-determination, 285–292
  as self-enactment, 285–292
    in commitment, 290
    of self-potential, 291
  as self-referential judgment, 286, 287
  will and categorical imperative, 80–83

God:
  existence of, 43–46
  love of, 26
  nature of, 43–46

"Having," "being," and the concept of the
  soul, 233–236

I-Thou relation, 136–144
  and the We, 329–333
Idealism, 54–60
Ideas, complex, of substances, spiritual and
  corporeal, 49–53
Immortality, 5–8
Imperative, categorical, 80–83
Impersonal, phenomenology of the, 206–212
Individual, the:
  and conscience, 115–119
  and existence, 108–113
  and freedom, 102–106
  and the person, 156–158
  and responsibility, 115–119
Intellect:
  agent, nature of, 217–222
  different from will, 90–96
Interpersonal, phenomenology of the, 199–206
    (See also Community; Person;
      Personization)
Intersubjectivity, phenomenology of, 295–313

Judgment(s):
  analytical, 72–75